GLOBAL ART CINEMA

GLOBAL ART CINEMA

NEW THEORIES AND HISTORIES

Edited by

Rosalind Galt
Karl Schoonover

OXFORD

UNIVERSITY PRESS

2010

OXFORD
UNIVERSITY PRESS

Oxford University Press, Inc., publishes works that further
Oxford University's objective of excellence
in research, scholarship, and education.

Oxford   New York
Auckland   Cape Town   Dar es Salaam   Hong Kong   Karachi
Kuala Lumpur   Madrid   Melbourne   Mexico City   Nairobi
New Delhi   Shanghai   Taipei   Toronto

With offices in
Argentina   Austria   Brazil   Chile   Czech Republic   France   Greece
Guatemala   Hungary   Italy   Japan   Poland   Portugal   Singapore
South Korea   Switzerland   Thailand   Turkey   Ukraine   Vietnam

Published by Oxford University Press, Inc.
198 Madison Avenue, New York, New York 10016

www.oup.com

Oxford is a registered trademark of Oxford University Press

Library of Congress Cataloging-in-Publication Data

Global art cinema : new theories and histories/
edited by Rosalind Galt and Karl Schoonover.
p. cm.
Includes bibliographical references and index.
ISBN 978-0-19-538562-5; 978-0-19-538563-2 (pbk.)
1. Motion pictures—Aesthetics. 2. Independent filmmakers.
I. Galt, Rosalind. II. Schoonover, Karl.
PN1995.G543 2010
791.4301—dc22   2009026100

2 4 6 8 9 7 5 3 1

Printed in the United States of America
on acid-free paper

FOREWORD

Dudley Andrew

I never apologize for combining the word "art" with the word "cinema." You would need a nineteenth-century conception of art—a cliché even then—to cast it as effete. After Freud, Trotsky, Benjamin, and Adorno, after futurism, constructivism, dada, surrealism, and the explosion of pop, it seems hard to remember that art—and the art film—was once considered the spiritual playground or retreat of a bourgeois elite. True, there had been "Film d'Art" around 1910, best remembered for the black-tie audience assembled for the premiere of *L'Assassinat du duc de Guise* at the Paris Opéra with music composed by Saint-Saens. And in the 1920s certain patrons of "The Seventh Art" treated cinema as though it were a debutante being introduced into high society. In *Film as Art* (*Film als Kunst*, 1932) Rudolf Arnheim consolidated the aesthetic principles achieved toward the end of the silent era, principles based on classical painting (balance, emphasis, discretion, and so forth). But Duchamp, Leger, and Buñuel had already blustered in to spoil the ball.

When cinema next attached itself to art, after the Second World War, it was not to emulate the forms and functions of painting or drama, but to adopt the intensity of their creation and experience. For even when it is seemingly "ready-made," "trouvé," "informe," or "absurd," art is exigent in the demands it makes on makers and viewers. Art cinema is "ambitious," the word with which François Truffaut characterized the filmmakers he championed, the film-maker he wanted to become. If cineastes are artists, it is because they partake of the ambition of genuine novelists, painters, and sculptors to supersede the norm, each in his own domain.

In 1972 Victor Perkins answered *Film as Art* with his own *Film as Film*. We loved this title. It demonstrated that cinema had arrived, had come into its own and no longer needed the corroboration of established aesthetics to be taken seriously. A terrific book, it pointed to the most telling and complex moments within a spectrum of films from Hollywood genre pieces to silent classics. As his title announced, Perkins oriented us to experience and to explore films on their own terms. He adjusted his rhetoric so as to enter not so much the *discourse* as the *world* projected before him. You can argue that art cinema, like art in general, serves contradictory functions (as cultural capital—indeed as actual capital—as propaganda or critique of ideology, as mass entertainment, etc); but those who live their lives in tandem with cinema care precisely about the function of film as film, even while understanding it to be congenitally impure—as Bazin insisted—and enmeshed in the terrestrial and the social.

Global Art Cinema: the first adjective of this title binds what it modifies to a mesh of relations that keep the whole thing from floating up and away like a balloon. At the same time "Art Cinema" is by definition pan-national, following the urge of every ambitious film to take off from its point of release, so as to encounter other viewers, and other movies, elsewhere and later. The title in fact begs a question debated in comparative literature over the vexed term, dating from Goethe, of *Weltliteratur*. For David Damrosch, a text joins the community of world literature when it finds sustained reception beyond the borders of the specific community out of which it arose. World literature comprises not just a huge bibliography of works, but more pertinently the complex interactions among these works, as they form the mixed traditions absorbed by later writers, as they are consumed by various communities of readers, and as they are tracked and interpreted by scholars and academics. Perched on the promontories of their carefully erected theories, scholars have been tempted to sense intelligent design in the evolution of world literature. On behalf of literature they take note of contributions that come from unlikely quarters where new topics, new techniques, and new generic hybrids stretch language across more and more realms and types of experience. As for the rest of writing (all those newspaper essays and serial stories that are thrown away, those folktales never leaving the local language, that doggerel whose echoes remain in homes and cafés), is this not material for the anthropologist more than the literary scholar? Such materials give insights into what is valued by individuals and groups, but, if never translated, these texts interact not at all with readers outside the community. Goethe and Damrosch would leave them alone, and so does global art cinema.

No one would dispute the value of the visual culture of any given time or place, or even the beauty of some of its expressions; no one would doubt the artistry, intelligence, and wit that has gone into innumerable state-commissioned documentaries, popular television shows, advertisements, home movies, and episodes of local film series. But insofar as these remain within the culture, discovered perhaps by scholars interested in those cultures, they do not participate in the cultural economy of world film and certainly do not belong to anything one would label global art cinema.

The latter might best be thought of as festival fare, since today every film programmed by an international festival becomes de facto visible to spectators anywhere on the globe who seek out distinctive movies. In the early days of festivals, titles were selected by national commissions to go abroad, whereas today festivals select what they show, sometimes even commissioning work by artists they deem talented. This does not upset the rapport of national culture to the culture of the cinephile, but it accelerates its movement. For example, of the hundred films made each year in the Philippines this past decade, only fifteen or so can be identified as part of the Philippine art cinema, specifically those that have been selected to be screened abroad. Whereas it took the Taiwanese new wave several years to penetrate the international market, the Philippine titles in today's global network have instantly left their imprint, altering the profile of Asian cinema in toto. So there would seem to be two distinct Philippine cinemas, one belonging to a specific culture bound principally by the Tagalog language, and the other taken up by a polyglot international audience who can access these films at festivals or download them on their computers.

To take an even clearer example, every other year FESPACO (Festival du Cinéma Panafricain) screens about 100 films from Francophone African countries, both sub-Saharan and Maghrebian, as well as an increasing number of titles from South Africa and Zimbabwe. My students learn the names of cineastes from Senegal, Mali, and Burkina Faso whose work is funded in Europe and who expect to be screened on several continents, then distributed on DVD through the Parisian outlet Cine3mondes. Only one Nigerian film, however, has ever been showcased at FESPACO or been treated to the chance at wide reception, despite the fact that Nigeria produces an estimated 1,500 videofilms annually. *Ezra*, which took top prize at that festival in 2007, was, you might suspect, an exception to Nollywood, financed as it was mainly outside Nigeria (by ARTE), with screenings in Paris and a brief run in New York. Otherwise Nollywood has been an antiglobal phenomenon of stupendous proportions, worth a place in a course on world cinema, but a place apart. Whereas FESPACO titles attract local and "tourist" audiences, exhibiting a dialectic central to my course's conception of world cinema, Nollywood doesn't look out for us, and hasn't been concerned about our reaction. Hence it gets treated, if at all, as rich anthropological material, a vibrant folk expression, grassroots graffiti, not meant for viewers outside the community. Of course these videofilms now crop up in London, New York, Toronto, and New Haven, wherever the diasporic community thrives. And some titles may well drift beyond these communities to be discovered by a broader audience, in the manner of certain Bollywood films recently. This could include some "classic title" that was made in the early years of this folk phenomenon, now rediscovered and singled out for a festival showing or DVD release because a cultural entrepreneur thought it had something to show (or say) to seasoned film viewers. The distinction between local and international is thus not about value, but about address. What "global" adds to all this is simultaneity. We used to discover local films belatedly and gradually. Look at the example of Mizoguchi or of the Yugoslavian "black wave" of the 1960s and 1970s. Today, however, an art film made in Tajikistan may well be seen in Japan before it screens at home.

As for the designation "art" within global art cinema, the local plays a key role. I have always credited art, and particularly film art, with exposing or figuring phenomena previously unrepresented. I rely for this on Bazin's incomparably crucial distinction between realism as a set of conventions and neorealism as a moral attitude toward the alterity of what is nearby. In his day, *La terra trema* allowed all of Italy, and then the world at large, to hear for the first time the sounds (the poetry) of Sicilian dialect, and to sense the complex economy linking extended families to larger social groups, and those groups to both an exploitative economy that went beyond the visible and the fishing fields themselves, including the boats and nets and human beings that make it into an industry. As Giorgio De Vincenti understood, perhaps before anyone else, modernist cinema arose when new realities such as this one in postwar Italy forced filmmakers into concocting ingenious narrative and stylistic strategies to bring them onto the plane of expression.

From neorealism flowed the various new waves of the 1960s and of the 1980s, the core of what has become global art cinema. Take Taiwan in 1983. Hou Hsiao-hsien had little schooling in world cinema; effectively a cog in the Taiwanese genre system of the 1970s, Hong Kong films comprised most of what he took to be foreign fare. Yet, when given a chance, he came up with his distinctive style in response to a need to represent the invisible peoples of Taiwan and their unheard voices. A literary neorealism preceded him there, it must be said, just as Elio Vittorini preceded Visconti in giving voice to Sicilian language and concerns. The style Hou Hsiao-hsien perfected during the 1980s, leading to his triumph at Venice with *City of Sadness*, did not involve studying global cinema or international modernism; it came about as he worked out solutions to problems in representation posed by the local (historical) situation he was determined to do justice to.

Might we expect another such talent, nearly autodidact, to arise somewhere else? Should we be looking near and far? Probably not. Since the 1980s, VHS tapes and then DVDs have made every ambitious filmmaker perforce a global artist. True, festivals reward novelty. They seek it out and they provoke it. They tempt filmmakers into stylistic postures that are calculated to sit attractively and prominently within a spectrum of other styles that the filmmaker has undoubtedly already examined. More often, the novelty needed to keep the economy of film art moving ahead is produced through generic hybrids. Festivals are hothouses where such hybrids are concocted, take root, and eventually flower; this is where a European cameraperson can meet a Chinese designer at dinner with a Japanese producer interested in exploiting a variant of the ghost-melodrama or horror-comedy. I don't mean to sound cynical. Such hothouses "force" the flowering of films that are often wonderful to see. But we should be alert to disingenuous hyping, whether of supposedly innocent auteurs or of brand-new new waves. The very idea of "independent cinema" has been altered by what is now a fully global network that makes every film quite "dependent."

Yet these new conditions have not fundamentally altered conditions that have been with cinema for most of its existence. Distributors, exhibitors, and, above all, critics, have always identified notable titles, trying to amplify them so they could be recognized above the hum of standard industrial fare. Even before festivals began collecting each year's most talented cinematic voices, distinctions were made. Whether or not "art cinema" named such distinctions, exporters aimed to sell what films they could abroad. In the period I know best, France in the 1930s, out of about 130 films made each year, a score found themselves shipped out of the country, where they interacted with other export films in an unofficial competition. Poetic realist titles by Carné, Duvivier, Feyder, Renoir, and Grémillon were viewed throughout Europe, and then were acclaimed in Japan, and played well in Latin America. They were treated as sophisticated and "artistic," first in comparison with other internationally distributed films, and then in relation to standard fare wherever they played. Standard fare, including the more than one hundred French films that never left the country, kept the national system afloat and arguably better defined the national community and its values than did those early avatars of global art cinema.

To distinguish not just particular styles in the 1930s, but larger contexts affecting production, reception, and film culture (criticism, government support or regulation, advertising and exhibition strategies), I came up with the neologism *optique*. In the context of this anthology, I would distinguish three *optiques* that have been operative for a long time, even while technological and social developments have caused them to vary: (1) national folk films, (2) global entertainment movies, and (3) international art cinema. The first category covers Nollywood, as we have seen, nearly invisible outside the Nigerian community, but also those massively popular genres scarcely comprehensible outside the community that they address and express (Tagalog comedies, German *heimat* melodramas, etc.). The second category, apparently ascendant in our era, includes blockbusters, to be sure, but most Hollywood films as well, whose income derives more from offshore than domestic performance. Pan-national genre productions, like Asian horror, spaghetti westerns, and Swedish soft-core, show that the global *optique* need not address all spectators everywhere, but can target a subset that globalization allows them to locate. Television series made in Mexico or Korea but viewed in the Middle East, Africa, Russia, and by individuals in the United States have added a new dimension to this global entertainment category.

Festivals and critics work tirelessly to distinguish the third *optique*, lest "art cinema" be taken as merely a niche genre of this second category. Thus no festival that I know of calls itself "global," while many are called "international" or "world" events. Hence the provocation and the challenge of this anthology's title and mission. What used to be treated as a tension between national values and the international market, today takes place across a global network that has absorbed both. The Web is quickly providing new distribution channels, formats, and cultures of reception. Those frightened by such a seemingly unregulated proliferation need only remember recent clashes of national and "art cinema." Such was his pique at the treatment he had been given in Taiwan that Edward Yang could produce an international art-house (and global DVD) hit like *Yi Yi*, yet refuse to let the film play in his native country where it was shot. The struggles filmmakers face at home often generate the heat that forges the strength of their creations. Jia Zhangke charisma derives in large part from the difficulties, even the hostility, with which he has been treated in China. The existence of something like "global art cinema" is, in his case, literally a saving grace. And what he has produced under that mantle graces us all.

By whatever name we call it, may the *optique* that informs ambitious filmmakers continue to galvanize ambitious viewers (let's not call ourselves consumers), so that a vibrant film culture may grow in response to strong films and to the realities they figure.

ACKNOWLEDGMENTS

This book benefited greatly from the critical eyes of our colleagues Jennifer Fay and John David Rhodes, as well as from the feedback of the volume's anonymous readers. It could not have happened without the generosity of many other people as well: Nicole Rizzuto, Jennifer Wild, Corey Creekmur, Chris Cagle, Laura McMullin, Michael Lawrence, Patrick O'Donnell, and especially Lloyd Pratt and Adrian Goycoolea. Elizabeth White, Emilia Cheng, and Hyun-soo Jang provided invaluable help in the final stages of the project. Our students enriched and refined the conception of this project, especially those in Karl's undergraduate seminar "The Geopolitics of Art Cinema," in his graduate course "The World," and in Rosalind's graduate seminar "Rethinking European Cinema." This book also benefited from the enthusiasm and guidance of our colleagues at the University of Iowa, the University of Sussex, and Michigan State University.

The editing and research of this book was a transatlantic venture and would not have been possible without the generous support of Michigan State University. In particular, the project received essential funds from three university sources: the Global Literary and Cultural Studies Research Cluster, the College of Arts and Letters Research Initiation Incentive Grant, and the Department of English. Librarians at the British Library, the British Film Institute library, Anthology Film Archives, and the Billy Rose Theatre Collection in the Dorothy and Lewis B. Cullman Center for Scholars and Writers at the

New York Public Library for the Performing Arts were extremely helpful. We would particularly like to thank the staff at the Cullman Center's copy center, who are, as always, amazing.

Shannon McLachlan at Oxford University Press embraced our conception of what *Global Art Cinema* might look like from the start. Her unwavering commitment has sustained the project, and her enthusiasm for what we were trying to do sustained us. Moreover, her keen sense of exactly what was needed and how to achieve it has shepherded the collection brilliantly. Brendan O'Neill at Oxford has also been a great help and a reassuring presence. Finally, we would like to thank our contributors. Some of you were involved in the project from its inception and have remained faithful over its *longue durée*. Others of you joined us along the way, unflustered by quick turnarounds. All of you surpassed our expectations by bringing nuance and depth to the subject in ways we could never have anticipated.

CONTENTS

PART II. THE ART CINEMA IMAGE

PART III. ART CINEMA HISTORIES

CONTRIBUTORS

THE EDITORS

ROSALIND GALT is a senior lecturer in film studies at the University of Sussex. She is the author of *The New European Cinema: Redrawing the Map* (2006) as well as articles in journals such as *Screen, Camera Obscura, Cinema Journal,* and *Discourse,* and in the collections *European Film Theory* (2008) and *On Michael Haneke* (2010). She is currently completing a book on the aesthetics and politics of the pretty.

KARL SCHOONOVER is an assistant professor of film studies in the Department of English at Michigan State University. His research focuses on realism, classical film theory, international cinema, and theories of the photographic image. He is completing a book that examines how Italian neorealist films shaped U.S. film culture after World War II, refashioning the practice and politics of film-going. He has published essays on spirit photography, U.S. advertisements for foreign films, and the politics of stardom in trash cinema.

THE CONTRIBUTORS

DUDLEY ANDREW, the R. Selden Rose Professor of Film Studies and Comparative Literature at Yale University, began his career as a commentator on film theory, including the biography of André Bazin, while publishing on complex films, especially those by Mizoguchi (*Film in the Aura of Art*, 1984). Then came work on French film and culture, anchored by *Mists of Regret* (1995) and *Popular Front Paris* (2005). Currently he is writing *Approaches to Problems in World Cinema*, as well as contributing a volume on cinema for the Blackwell Manifestos series.

DAVID ANDREWS has taught on four college campuses. Now an independent scholar, he has published articles on art cinema, pornography, and aestheticism in many journals, including the *Journal of Film and Video, Cinema Journal, Velvet Light Trap, Post Script, Film Criticism*, and *Television and New Media*. The Ohio State University Press published his most recent book, *Soft in the Middle: The Contemporary Softcore Feature in Its Contexts* (2006), the first genre survey devoted to soft-core cinema. He is currently finishing his third single-author book, *Theory of Art Cinemas*, which is under contract with the University of Texas Press.

MARK BETZ is a senior lecturer in the Film Studies department at King's College, University of London. He is the author of *Beyond the Subtitle: Remapping European Art Cinema* (2009) and has published essays on art/exploitation cinema marketing, the academicization of film studies via book publishing, and contemporary film modernism. He is currently working on a study of foreign film distribution in America.

TIMOTHY CORRIGAN is a professor of English, cinema studies, and history of art at the University of Pennsylvania. His work in cinema studies has focused on modern American and international cinema, as well as pedagogy. His books include *New German Film: The Displaced Image* (1983, 1994), *The Films of Werner Herzog: Between Mirage and History* (1986), *Writing about Film* (1989, 2009), *A Cinema without Walls: Movies and Culture after Vietnam* (1991), and, co-authored with Patricia White, *The Film Experience* (2004, 2009). He has edited two forthcoming books, *American Cinema 2000–2009* (2010) and, with Patricia White, *Critical Visions: Classical and Contemporary Readings in Film Theory* (2010). He is presently completing a study of the essay film.

ANGELA DALLE VACCHE is a professor of film studies at the Georgia Institute of Technology and the author of *The Body in The Mirror: Shapes of History in Italian Cinema* (1992), *Cinema and Painting* (1996), and *Diva: Defiance and Passion in Early Italian Cinema* (2008). She has also edited *The Visual Turn: Classical Film Theory and Art History* (2002) and, with Brian Price, *Color: The Film Reader* (2006). She has received grants and fellowships from the

Fulbright Program, the Mellon Foundation, the Rockefeller Foundation, and the Leverhulme Trust. She is currently working on a book titled *André Bazin: Film, Art and the Scientific Imagination.*

MANISHITA DASS is an assistant professor at the University of Michigan, Ann Arbor, with a joint appointment in screen arts and cultures and Asian languages and cultures. Her research focuses on the intersection of film, literary, and political cultures in early- to mid-twentieth-century India, colonialism and silent cinema, the geopolitical imaginary of film studies, and the visual and literary worlds of Bengali modernity. She is currently completing a book, *Outside the Lettered City: Cinema, Modernity and Public Culture in Late Colonial India,* and has an article on Indian silent cinema in *Cinema Journal* (Summer 2009).

AZADEH FARAHMAND has a Ph.D. in cinema and media studies from the University of California at Los Angeles. She has worked in the advertising department of nationwide chain Landmark Theatres and managed international marketing and festival placement of films at Peace Arch Entertainment, a Canadian-based international sales agent. She contributed a chapter to *The New Iranian Cinema: Politics, Representation and Identity* (2002), and her writings have appeared in *Film Quarterly, Jusur,* and *Intersections.* She currently conducts marketing research at the motion picture group of OTX, a global research and consulting firm, and teaches in the communication studies department at California State University, Los Angeles.

RACHEL GABARA is associate professor of French at the University of Georgia, where she teaches French and Francophone literature and film. She is the author of *From Split to Screened Selves: French and Francophone Autobiography in the Third Person* (2006), and her articles include "'A Poetics of Refusals': Neorealism from Italy to Africa," in the *Quarterly Review of Film and Video,* and "Mixing Impossible Genres: David Achkar and African AutoBiographical Documentary," in *New Literary History.* She is currently writing a book entitled *Reclaiming Realism: From Colonial to Contemporary Documentary in West and Central Africa.*

RANDALL HALLE is the Klaus W. Jonas Professor of German Film and Cultural Studies at the University of Pittsburgh. His essays have appeared in journals such as *New German Critique, Screen,* and *German Quarterly.* He is the co-editor of *After the Avant-Garde* (2008), *Light Motives: German Popular Film in Perspective* (2003), and a special double issue of *Camera Obscura* on "Marginality and Alterity in Contemporary European Cinema." He is the author of *Queer Social Philosophy: Critical Readings from Kant to Adorno* (2004) and *German*

Film after Germany: Toward a Transnational Aesthetic (2008). He has held fellowships from the National Endowment for the Humanities, Deutscher Akademischer Austausch Dienst (DAAD), the Social Science Research Council, and the Fulbright Program.

DENNIS HANLON, a doctoral candidate in film studies at the University of Iowa, is completing a dissertation on the films and theory of Jorge Sanjinés. His articles have been published or are forthcoming in *Mosaic* and *Film and History*.

SHARON HAYASHI is assistant professor of cinema and media studies in the Department of Film at York University, Toronto. Her current research interests include the uses of new media by new social movements and the architecture of cinema. She has published articles in Japanese and English on new media, Japanese pink cinema, and the travel films of Hiroshi Shimizu, and is currently completing a book on the transition to sound in the Japanese wartime cinema.

E. ANN KAPLAN is Distinguished Professor of English and Comparative Literary and Cultural Studies at Stony Brook University, where she also founded and directs the Humanities Institute. She has written many books and articles on topics in cultural studies, media, and women's studies, from diverse theoretical perspectives, including psychoanalysis, feminism, postmodernism, and postcolonialism. Her pioneering research on women in film has been translated into six languages. Her recent books include *Trauma and Cinema: Cross-Cultural Explorations* (co-edited with Ban Wang, 2004), *Feminism and Film* (2000), and the monograph *Trauma Culture: The Politics of Terror and Loss in Media and Literature* (2005). New projects include *Public Feelings and Affective Difference* and *The Unconscious of Age*.

PATRICK KEATING is an assistant professor in the Department of Communication at Trinity University, where he teaches courses in film and media studies. He is the author of *Hollywood Lighting from the Silent Era to Film Noir* (2009). In addition to his research on the history of cinematography, he has written articles about cinematic realism, the film theory of Pasolini, and the structure of Hollywood narrative.

JIHOON KIM is a doctoral candidate in the Department of Cinema Studies at New York University, where he is currently working on a dissertation entitled "Relational Images: Moving Images in the Age of Media Exchange." His essay "The Post-Medium Condition and the Explosion of Cinema" recently appeared in the fiftieth anniversary issue of *Screen*, and other articles on Stan Douglas and contemporary Korean cinema will be published in *The Place of the Moving Image* (forthcoming) and *Storytelling in World Cinema* (forthcoming).

ADAM LOWENSTEIN is associate professor of English and film studies at the University of Pittsburgh. He is the author of *Shocking Representation: Historical Trauma, National Cinema, and the Modern Horror Film* (2005) as well as essays in *Cinema Journal, Critical Quarterly, Post Script*, and in anthologies such as *Hitchcock: Past and Future* (2004). Among his current projects is a book concerning the intersections between cinematic spectatorship, surrealism, and the age of new media.

JEAN MA is an assistant professor in the Department of Art and Art History at Stanford University, where she teaches in the film and media studies program. She is coeditor of *Still Moving: Between Cinema and Photography* (2008), an anthology that brings together writings by film scholars, art historians, filmmakers, and artists on the intersection and overlap of photography and film. Her work has appeared in *Post Script* and *Grey Room*. She is currently working on a manuscript on contemporary Chinese-language art cinema entitled *Melancholy Drift: Marking Time in Chinese Cinema*.

BRIAN PRICE teaches at Oklahoma State University. He is author of *Neither God nor Master: Robert Bresson and the Modalities of Revolt* (2010) and co-editor of *Color, the Film Reader* (2006) and *On Michael Haneke* (2010), as well as the journal *World Picture*.

ANGELO RESTIVO is associate professor and graduate director in the moving image studies program at Georgia State University. He is the author of *The Cinema of Economic Miracles: Visuality and Modernization in the Italian Art Film* (2002). His current book project explores global cartographies in the art cinema since 1960.

JOHN DAVID RHODES is author of *Stupendous, Miserable City: Pasolini's Rome* (2007), a founding co-editor of the journal *World Picture*, and the co-editor of two forthcoming collections: *On Michael Haneke* (with Brian Price) and *The Place of the Moving Image* (with Elena Gorfinkel). His essays have appeared in *Modernism/Modernity, Log, Framework*, and *Film History*. He teaches at the University of Sussex.

PHILIP ROSEN is Professor of Modern Culture and Media at Brown University. He has published widely on the history and theory of cinema and culture. Among his publications is *Change Mummified: Cinema, Historicity, Theory* (2001).

MARIA SAN FILIPPO is a graduate of UCLA's doctoral program in cinema and media studies and is the Mellon Postdoctoral Fellow in Cinema and Media Studies at Wellesley College, 2008 to 2010. Her articles and reviews have been published in *Cineaste, English Language Notes, Film History, Journal of Bisexuality, Scope, Senses of Cinema,* and *Quarterly Review of Film and Video.* Currently she is completing a book titled *The B Word: Bisexuality in Contemporary Film and Television.*

GLOBAL ART CINEMA

Introduction: The Impurity of Art Cinema

Rosalind Galt and Karl Schoonover

For over fifty years, art cinema has provided an essential model for audiences, film-makers, and critics to imagine cinema outside Hollywood. At various points, it has intersected with popular genres, national cinemas, revolutionary film, and the avant-garde, and has mixed corporate, state, and independent capital. An elastically hybrid category, art cinema has nonetheless sustained an astonishing discursive currency in contemporary film culture. This book uses art cinema's mongrel identity to explore central questions for current film scholarship. Since the term "art cinema" has always simultaneously invoked industrial, generic, and aesthetic categories, a current reckoning of the field exposes otherwise unseen geopolitical fault lines of world cinema. Despite its more conservative connotations, art cinema retains at its core both a comparativist impulse and an internationalist scope that might be productively brought to bear on globalized culture. From our perspective, art cinema has from its beginnings forged a relationship between the aesthetic and the geopolitical or, in other words, between cinema and world. Thus, it is the critical category best placed to engage pressing contemporary questions of globalization, world culture, and how the economics of cinema's transnational flows might intersect with trajectories of film form. Because of its flexibility as a category, the term "art cinema" can be an unreliable label. In fact, it names a dynamic and contested terrain where film histories intersect with the larger theoretical questions of the image and its travels. *Global Art Cinema* outlines new shapes and boundaries for art cinema, rejecting the commercial logic of ever-burgeoning markets, as well as conventional progressive histories of style and the myths of transmission from core to periphery. The collection thinks comparatively on topics often addressed only locally, focusing on intersections in the emergence, reception, and status of international cinema.

How does one approach such a complex category? One possible entry point to the field of global art cinema is *The International Film Guide*, an annual survey of film production, published since 1964, and aimed primarily at distributors, critics, and other film professionals. As an archive of writing on international film, the *Guide* provides detailed evidence of which films, countries, and directors took part in critical debate and industrial exchange, while as a historical document, it powerfully indexes the changing discursive terrain of art cinema. Addressed to those audiences interested in "serious cinema," its inaugural editorial argued for quality films, specialist cinemas, and the need to secure "a wider and more thorough distribution of overseas *films d'art*."[1] Without using the term "art cinema," it clearly outlined the category's institutional terrain: overtly artistic textuality, art-house theater exhibition, and the international circulation of foreign films. In perusing the guide from the 1960s to the present, we can trace the emergence of art cinema as a central term. Moreover, we see vividly mapped art cinema's development as a geographically organized force field, centered around a Euro-American critical and industrial infrastructure. The guide's very first "directors of the year" were Luchino Visconti, Orson Welles, François Truffaut, Andrej Wajda, and Alfred Hitchcock, and subsequent years added a canonical array of mostly West European auteurs (Federico Fellini, Louis Malle, Ingmar Bergman), with a number of East Europeans (Roman Polanski, Miklós Jancsó, Dušan Makavejev), several Americans (John Frankenheimer, Stanley Kubrick), and very few Asians (Satyajit Ray, Akira Kurosawa). This yoking of authorship and nation to globality precisely figures the development of art cinema from Italian neorealism's "discovery" in the United States to a model of international flows that centered on the West Europe–North America axis, including only a few exemplary filmmakers from cinematic cultures beyond that axis.[2]

Demonstrating art cinema's foundational Eurocentrism, the *Guide* goes on to chart the expansion of its global reach from the early tokenistic inclusion of Ray and the Japanese directors to a vision of world cinema in the 1980s and beyond. While occasionally a director from a hitherto unrepresented country appears on the best film list— Dariush Mehrjui's *Postchi / The Postman* in 1973 and Arturo Ripstein's *El castillo de la pureza / Castle of Purity* in 1975, for instance—the conception of what constitutes the international is at first fairly limited. In 1964, the "World Survey" section includes only thirteen countries, but by 1989 almost sixty are included and in 2006 more than one hundred. Indeed, the breadth of the *Guide*'s global reach is a major point of editorial pride in the 2006 issue, with Roya Sadat, the first female director from Afghanistan, and Sharunas Bartas, the first Lithuanian to show at Cannes being highlighted along with new reports from Guatemala and Uganda. In 2008, the *Guide* presented itself not as the champion of serious cinema but as "the definitive annual survey of contemporary global cinema." Here, the global rhetorically implies the serious, while the diversity of locations and types of production supersedes the rejection of commercialism as the key indicator of distinction. This changing construction of art cinema as a global field of industry and aesthetics evokes the ambivalence and complexity that we find in the category: clearly enmeshed in an imperialist and Eurocentric history, art cinema also provides both material for critique and nourishment for a diverse range of cinematic spaces.

The *Guide*'s shift from European *films d'art* to global cinema registers not only a changing discourse in film journalism and distribution patterns, but points also to why we think a collection on global art cinema is needed. Art cinema is resurgent in the new century, with cinemas from South Korea, Denmark, and Israel garnering international acclaim and finding enthusiastic audiences at festivals, in theaters, and on DVD. The term "art cinema" itself has both a historical importance and a contemporary currency. Used in critical histories of postwar European and U.S. cinema to carve out a space of aesthetic and commercial distinction that is neither mainstream nor avant-garde, the term remains an everyday concept for film industries, critics, and audiences. Nonetheless, the sense of art cinema as elitist and conservative remains in such force that many scholars to whom we spoke about this volume responded with perplexity that we would endorse such a retrograde category. This attitude is common in art cinema discourse: both postclassical film theory and the turn to cultural studies deliberately focused intellectual attention away from the previous decades' canon of "serious" films. Little sustained scholarly attention has been paid to refining and updating the parameters of art cinema as a category since the pioneering essays of the 1960s and 1970s. And even the institutions that helped create the category of art cinema often held the term in uncertain esteem. The Museum of Modern Art's comprehensive 1941 index to cinema had no category to distinguish a genre of feature-length films of special artistic interest.[3] Moreover, Joseph Burstyn, perhaps the most influential of distributors of European art films in the United States, early on rejected the term "art cinema."[4] As both a historical problem and a contemporary aporia, art cinema names a field that has not been sufficiently interrogated by film studies.

And yet, while film studies has too often foreclosed on the potential of art cinema as a category, and even as the art-house theater teeters on the brink of extinction in all but the most cosmopolitan of centers, scholars have nonetheless consistently engaged with films that fall under this rubric. Historians have written compellingly on film festivals and national film histories, and theorists continue to find rich material in the work of directors such as Lina Wertmüller and Zhang Yimou. This anthology recognizes not only the growing significance of this scholarship, but also the centrality of art cinema to the larger field of global film studies. Scholars have demonstrated a gathering impulse to teach and rethink cinema as a global phenomenon, and we also find important research on art cinema in recent theorizations of the film image; in revised industrial, legal, and exhibition histories; and as part of renewed debates about national, postcolonial, and regional cinema cultures. The commonly held notion of art cinema as a retrograde category, then, does not actually reflect a lack of interest in the object, but demonstrates a critical reluctance to acknowledge art cinema as a field within which these objects of study circulate. Given the ability of the category to define an area of cultural, economic, and aesthetic meaning, it is perverse, we think, to ignore or deride art cinema. This volume seeks to focus on art cinema as both an active aspect of global film culture and as an indispensable category of its critique.

PROBLEMS OF DEFINITION

Art cinema poses a problem for film scholarship, because while the term is widely used by critics and audiences alike, it has proved very hard to pin down within any of the common rubrics for categorizing types of cinema. Geoffrey Nowell-Smith says that "art cinema has become a portmanteau term, embracing different ideas of what cinema can be like, both inside and outside the mainstream."[5] To combat this looseness, he proposes that we separate art film into two types, with relatively mainstream "quality" films like the British heritage film or Chinese Fifth Generation films on one side, and more radical low-budget independent production like that of Aki Kaurismäki or the original French New Wave on the other. This binary is appealing but hard to sustain in practice. Even these few examples illustrate the vast disparities in form, style, and historical and economic context that make taxonomy so difficult. Moreover, the systems of distinction and evaluation that would label a film more mainstream or more independent are also historically and geographically contingent. The diverse contexts within which art films are made and viewed does make definition challenging, but perhaps instead of trying to enforce a taxonomic principle, we should focus on the nature of art cinema's instability.

Speaking of the interwar modernist films that formed the foundation for the European canon of film art, Martin Stollery points out that their diverse backgrounds include major studio productions, private funding, and advertisements for tea.[6] If the postwar films that are canonically understood as art cinema are not quite so diverse, they certainly inherit the mongrel nature of the art cinema's prehistory.

The first problem for a collection on art cinema, therefore, is to define the term. Is art cinema a genre, in the way that mainstream criticism often uses the term? A mode of film practice, as David Bordwell claims?[7] An institution, as for Steve Neale?[8] A historically unprecedented mode of exhibiting films, in Barbara Wilinsky's terms?[9] Is it, even, as Jeffrey Sconce writes of trash cinema, a language able to disarticulate excess, style, and politics from taste and to map the promiscuous hybridity of cinematic forms?[10] In common usage, "art cinema" describes feature-length narrative films at the margins of mainstream cinema, located somewhere between fully experimental films and overtly commercial products. Typical (but not necessary) features include foreign production, overt engagement of the aesthetic, unrestrained formalism, and a mode of narration that is pleasurable but loosened from classical structures and distanced from its representations. By classical standards, the art film might be seen as too slow or excessive in its visual style, use of color, or characterization. The elasticity of this conventional definition may explain the category's resilience in the public eye but fails to resolve discrepancies among the scholarly interrogations of the term. We contend that the lack of strict parameters for art cinema is not just an ambiguity of its critical history, but a central part of its specificity, a positive way of delineating its discursive space. We propose as a principle that art cinema can be defined by its impurity; a difficulty of categorization that is as productive to film culture as it is frustrating to taxonomy.

To be impure is not the same as to be vague or nebulous. Rather, we contend that art cinema always perverts the standard categories used to divide up institutions, locations, histories, or spectators. Art cinema's impurity can be understood in a variety of ways. First, it is defined by an impure institutional space: neither experimental nor mainstream, art cinema moves uneasily between the commercial world and its artisanal others. As Nowell-Smith points out, at the more mainstream end of the spectrum some contemporary European art films look more like the cinema of quality that the French New Wave rejected than they do the films of Agnès Varda or Jean-Luc Godard. But at the other end, artists like Matthew Barney and filmmakers like Apichatpong Weerasethakul mix theatrical space with gallery space in practices that are as close to the avant-garde as to commercial cinema. Exhibition practices augment this uneasiness of location: for the art house holds a unique place in constituting art cinema as a field. Art cinema is often characterized as an outsider: It has not been assimilated to mainstream tastes, and it lives in a ghetto, albeit often a posh or bourgeois one. This institutional definition is strangely contingent. In many cases, art films are simply those films shown in art-house theaters, or at film festivals, so that their very existence is dependent on certain critics, programmers, or distribution models.

Second, art cinema articulates an ambivalent relationship to location. It is a resolutely international category, often a code for foreign film. While certain kinds of popular films can circulate globally (Hollywood, Hong Kong action films, Hindi films viewed by Indian diasporic audiences), for most countries, art cinema provides the only institutional context in which films can find audiences abroad. Indeed, it has been widely noted that many films that are understood as popular in their domestic market become art films when exhibited abroad. In these cases, it is the fact of traveling internationally that constitutes a film as an example of art cinema. This international identity constructs art cinema as cosmopolitan or, in Mette Hjort's words, "an attempt to resist the dynamics of an intensified localism fuelled by globalism by focusing attention, not on heritage and ethnicity, but on the very definition of cinematic art and on the conditions of that art's production."[11] The sense of internationalism that opens Krzysztof Zanussi's or Lucrecia Martel's films to audiences far from Poland or Argentina opposes the localism of national cinema discourse. Conversely, art films play a major role in creating canonical national cinemas, and representations of locality often ground claims on art film seriousness. In traditional film historiography, art cinema has been a way to organize national cinemas via canons of "great directors," so that the very international reception of art cinema becomes proof of its national importance. While we recognize the past half-century's critical tendency to conflate art cinema with national cinema, we resist repeating this mistake and suggest that art cinema always carries a comparativist impulse and transnational tenor.

Third, art cinema sustains a complexly ambivalent relationship to the critical and industrial categories that sustain film history, such as stardom and authorship. On the one hand, it is constituted for many by a rejection of Hollywood systems and values. On the other, we find director and star systems in art cinema that closely parallel Hollywood's own structures, even where they reject its aesthetic hierarchies. Thus, art cinema has nurtured stars such as Hannah Schygulla, Jeanne Moreau, and Gong Li, but it might define the nature of stardom or the bodily qualities desired in a star differently from Hollywood. Likewise, art cinema contains an auteurist impulse but demands a different version of authorship than the Hollywood auteur. An especially productive question raised here is the political history of the auteur. Janet Staiger has argued that whereas auteur studies have been largely rejected as an inadequate model of meaning production in cinema, authorship matters to those filmmakers in nondominant positions for whom "asserting even a partial agency may seem to be important for day-to-day survival or where locating moments of alternative practice takes away the naturalized privileges of normativity."[12] Jean Ma's essay on Tsai Ming-liang in this volume, for example, speaks eloquently on the politics of auteurism and globalization. Since art cinema authors often speak from outside of Europe or America or locate themselves outside the mainstream of representational practices, it could be argued that authorship takes on a pressing significance for thinking the potential of art cinema as a platform for political agency.

Fourth, and in another major category of film historiography, art cinema troubles notions of genre. As mentioned previously, scholars have drawn upon various elements of genre theory in defining art cinema in terms of narrative, aesthetic modality, and historical development. Despite this influential rubric, it is not at all clear that art cinema can fit into the generic models that have sustained analysis of the musical, the western, or melodrama. Not only are the practices of art cinema radically different across national lines, but its meaning has altered substantially across time. To take just one recent example, the emergence of an "artsier" version of Hollywood film in the 1990s in response to American independent cinema produced a more popular iteration of art cinema that included the narrative products of boutique production divisions in Hollywood studios. Folding "indie" filmmakers like Todd Haynes and Miranda July into a public discourse of art cinema brings together experimental film and major Hollywood stars and infrastructures in ways that thwart conventional descriptions of genre.

Lastly, art cinema constitutes a peculiarly impure spectator, both at the level of textual address and in the history of its audiences. The spectator of Italian neorealism or of a recent film like Fatih Akin's *Auf der anderen Seite / Edge of Heaven* (2007) is asked to be both intellectually engaged and emotionally affected. Aesthetic distance is called for, but the rigor of distanciation is constantly crossed with an emotive bodily response and a virtual engagement with the other. What often reads as a failure of difficulty for critics writing from a modernist Marxist perspective can equally be seen as a way to address a viewer who responds to what Eric Schaefer has called "a confluence of contradictions."[13] The literature on the emergence of art-house audiences meshes with this sense of a hybrid spectator. For example, early art film spectators in the United States were constructed simultaneously as thoughtful and responsible people who wanted to view films about serious subjects and as hungry voyeurs drawn uncontrollably to the salacious imagery allowed for by the new foreign realisms.[14] And while early sociological studies of the art cinema audience suggested that it appealed primarily to men, art cinema has often been represented in the public eye as feminine, effete, or queer.[15] Its openness to aesthetic experience is not unconnected to its openness to minority communities, who have formed a significant part of art cinema's audience as well as its representational politics. Thus, in a minoritizing move, even quite conventional gay and lesbian films are often categorized as art cinema, in the same way that popular foreign films are. But at the same time, this discourse can operate to exclude challenging minority films from the art cinema canon, as happened with the films of Charles Burnett until recently.[16]

We find in these impurities the kernel of art cinema's significance: as a category of cinema, it brings categories into question and holds the potential to open up spaces between and outside of mainstream/avant-garde, local/cosmopolitan, history/theory, and industrial/formal debates in film scholarship. In the sections that follow, we map the discursive fields that shape art cinema.

GEOGRAPHY AND GEOPOLITICS

If the label "art film" frequently signifies simply a foreign film at the box office, then it is clear that we are already speaking not only of geography but of the politics of geographical difference. Foreign to whom? Traveling to and from which cultures and audiences? The geopolitical realm is central to the discursive field of art cinema, but it has been stifled or depoliticized in much existing scholarship. Criticism that focuses on the auteur either personalizes style and mode of production out of all locational context or reifies style in terms of national cultural specificity. Alternatively, more synthetic accounts of European art cinema tend toward a taken-for-granted sense of "European-ness" that connects and nourishes the canonical art cinema directors, usually in opposition to Hollywood as the commercial and stylistic other. Thomas Elsaesser has pointed out the binary logic involved in thus constructing European cinema against Hollywood, and he argues that spectators of the European films that circulate globally as art cinema "have traditionally enjoyed the privilege of feeling 'different' . . . in a historically determined set of relations based on highly unstable acts of self-definition and self-differentiation implied by the use of terms such as 'auteur,' 'art,' 'national cinema,' 'culture,' or 'Europe.'"[17] Thus, in what many audiences think of as its most typical manifestation, the North American exhibition of European art films, art cinema's geography is no more than a mutually beneficial circulation of Western cultural capital.

Because of the Eurocentric structure of this dominant history, art cinema has been commonly linked with a narrow and reactionary version of the international, rather than with more expansive, radical, or controversial frames such as world cinema, postcoloniality, or globalization. But several influential models exist for refuting this binarism. We might turn to the theorists and filmmakers of the New Latin American Cinema, who often opposed art cinema as a bourgeois form, but who also forwarded concepts such as "imperfect cinema" as an alternative to the aesthetic and geopolitical dead end of Europe versus Hollywood. Julio García Espinosa's rejection of Europe's artistic "-isms" linked the European reception of Third Cinema in the art house with the need to imagine other poetics and geographies of cinema.[18] Or, in a quite different register, Miriam Hansen's concept of vernacular modernism can be read as a way of formulating a nonbinary relationship among Hollywood classicism, modernist cinema, and the world. Hansen finds in American cinema "a metaphor of a global sensory vernacular," in which the opposition of (American) classicism to (European) political modernism is revealed as inadequate to the global flows of modernization.[19] (Kathleen Newman and Lúcia Nagib both critique and revise the scope and trajectory of Hansen's globality, and in doing so propose views of history more in keeping with traditions of Third Cinema and postcolonial theory.[20]) We contend that art cinema cannot (and never could) be defined solely by the Europe-Hollywood relationship, that the category demands a more complex vision of the global that is responsive to geographical complexity and, more important, susceptible to geopolitical analysis.

One way of approaching art cinema's geopolitics is its sustaining concept of universal legibility. If art films are to travel to international audiences, they must make the claim that their forms and stories are comprehensible across languages and cultures. Thus, part of art cinema's stake in art is an investment in visual legibility and cross-cultural translation. Unlike popular cinema, it does not claim to express a locally defined culture but an idea of (cinematic) art as such. For this reason, the institutions of art cinema often deploy quite overt ideas of cinema as a universal language. The Landmark Theatres chain in the United States, for example, introduces each program with the phrase "The language of cinema is universal" spoken in several languages. In Europe, theaters associated with the Europa exhibition network show a graphic list of the cities in which it is located. In both cases, these corporate logos hail cinema audiences as an imagined community of international viewers, participating across cultures in a shared form of experience. At the same time, of course, they are universal consumers, able to enjoy films from wherever. Here, cross-cultural cinema is both a corporate marketing technique for the art house and a promise held out of a certain kind of spectatorship. And in mainstream film criticism, films are often lauded as universal stories in order to reduce the threat of unpleasurable difference, to manage the irreconcilable fissures produced by translation, and to construct texts as easily assimilable to Western cultural norms. For these reasons, no doubt, universal legibility is widely critiqued as a Western/patriarchal/neocolonial perspective imposed across the geopolitical field. While we don't dispute the potential for art cinema to take up these conservative versions of universality, we suggest that the problem of universality in art cinema is too complicated to be addressed by a simple dismissal. We feel strongly that a move toward the universal does not always have to be simple or naive. We refuse to underestimate the potential of the international.

Indeed, the relationships among ideas of cinema as a universal language, the uneven international flows of films and audiences, and the changing geopolitics of the twentieth and twenty-first centuries strike us as a uniquely rich intersection for the analysis of cinema, politics, and geography. Where film studies has mostly rejected universality as ideologically tainted, art cinema secretes away a valuation of its powers. (Dudley Andrew articulates this impetus very clearly, and his engagement of art cinema's desire for the universal surely contributes to his centrality in the scholarship of art cinema.[21]) The fantasy of transparent transcultural exchange nourished the impulse in the 1920s to see cinema as a vehicle for international comprehension, and it continues to construct the transnational articulation of art cinema.[22] The criticism is almost too easy to make—of course we cannot have transparent exchange across cultures and transparency is too often a cover for dominant hegemony of late capitalism—but what do we do with filmmakers who reject cynicism and continue to ask foreign audiences to see their films? Art cinema traces a history of attempts at cross-cultural communication even in the face of its impossibility. The films of Ray or Im Kwon-taek persistently engage the concept of universality even in the experience of its inadequacy or lack. In this respect, art cinema mobilizes art's traditional function of giving expression to that which is otherwise inexpressible. The impossibility of transparent cross-cultural legibility is just another way of describing what art (cinema) does.

Another way of thinking this problem is to propose that the international address, circulation, and content of art cinema enables us to think about the global, focusing our attention on issues of world. Art cinema demands that we watch across cultures and see ourselves through foreign eyes, binding spectatorship and pleasure into an experience of geographical difference, or potentially of geopolitical critique. But these productive features of art cinema also work to draw our attention to the perils of thinking the global. As much as art cinema holds out a promise of international community, it stands to be recuperated into dominant circuits of capital, stereotype, and imperialist vision. Therefore, it is imperative to analyze its terms of geographical engagement, thinking closely about the formations and deformations of art cinematic space. These weighted histories and practices of framing demand that we think carefully about terminology. How should we describe art cinema's geopolitics: as "global," "world," or "international"? Clearly, between the Eurocentrism of art cinema's emergence to the global flows of the film festival circuit, the choice of words carries significant baggage.

This book is titled *Global Art Cinema*, and the word "global" perhaps excites more conceptual anxiety than any of the other terms. It speaks to the all-encompassing nature of an art cinema that exists around the globe, but it might also imply an imperialist or globalized contamination of political space. The rhetoric of a global cinema could indicate an economic model and hence a capitalist or Hollywood-centric one. Many critics of globalization reject the term: Gayatri Spivak, for example, counters the digitalization and instrumentalism of globalized thinking with the more collectivist term "planetarity," which she finds more sensitive to the local, the material, and the powerless.[23] To pay proper attention to the terrain of cinema and its pathways of privilege, we might feel similarly reluctant to take on the geopolitical connotations of the global.

However, the alternative words available are hardly less ambivalent. "World" art cinema, like "world cinema," could enable the kind of postcolonial revision of canons sometimes implied by "world literature."[24] Or it could suggest a cosmopolitanism that looks usefully beyond the scope of the nation, or less usefully, erases material and political boundaries.[25] Worse, it might bespeak a fetishistic multiculturalism similar to that often implied by "world music." "World" as a modifier suggests at worst a Putamayo world of commodified and sanitized exoticism, and at best an emerging scholarly discourse of world cinema in which "world" does not mean the whole world but those areas outside of Europe and North America.[26] (Ironically, cinema's supposed universalism has, to some degree, saved film studies from the easy Anglocentrism of literary fields, but films from the global South are still often confined to "world cinema" classes.) As a code for nonwhite or non-Western, "world" can hint at a troublingly unexamined liberalism.

The term "international" opens out onto a different history of canonical exclusion and inclusion. Through much of film history, international film was a limited category, including West European films for the most part, and only recently expanding to encompass African, Latin American, and a wide range of Asian films. "Internationalist," of course, must be seen as a subheading or side note to the international, bringing a useful political demand that these categories not be simply descriptive terms but rather active agents of meaning. Internationalism understands the circulation of films across national borders as a political act, as with the European leftist groups who helped circulate Soviet modernism or the commitment to international cinema in the years following the Cuban revolution. While the Marxist history of internationalism might not always fit snugly with our analysis of global art cinema, its demand for a geopolitics of cinema remains an important spur. Ultimately, none of these words is perfectly and unproblematically adequate to fulfill our needs, although the debates engendered by the terms do delineate sharply the contested terrain of art cinema as a geopolitical term.

Our current historical moment asks more pressingly than ever: How does one think the categories of global culture? If art cinema instantiates an optimism about the possibility of speaking across cultures, the early twenty-first century seems inclined to dash that optimism. Postwar histories of art cinema focus on successive waves of new waves—as if cinema could perform the infinite expansion foundational to capitalist growth. This model is articulated in the cosmopolitan audience who always had more auteurs and national cinemas to discover. Likewise the era of decolonization promised a postcolonial openness to the world, as audiences forged new relationships with film-producing nations. (Of course, it goes without saying that we describe here a set of myths and fantasies as much as any empirical history of movie-going. Nonetheless, it seems clear that art cinema benefited from dominant postwar modes of capitalist expansion and ideologies of cross-cultural openness and cosmopolitanism.) But where does this ethos of art cinematic openness go in the post-9/11 world of anxious globalization, economic recession, and environmental crisis, where cultural transits are something to fear and the doctrine of infinite expansion is finally reaching a breaking point in the economic and environmental spheres? Notions of increased global networking that not long ago sounded utopian now evoke terror, and international travel becomes increasingly policed by race, class, and corporeal and national demarcation. On this emerging world stage, ideas about cultural globality must surely respond, as will the material conditions of cinematic spectatorship.

HISTORICAL AND AHISTORICAL IMPULSES

Art cinema has been an enabling concept for film historiography and has been a particularly forceful concept in the writing of national and auteur-based film histories. In tension or even contradiction with this historicizing tendency, though, the term evokes a certain timelessness that has been equally persistent in both the scholarly discourse and popular usage of art cinema. Ideas of art cinema as a textual practice remain fairly static, from pop cultural clichés of ponderous dialogue to critical regimes of value around what constitutes cinematic "art." This sense of art cinema as unchanging might not be accurate, but it nonetheless operates as a mode of institutional exchange, a way that films can promote themselves as part of an already constituted cultural space. We can illustrate this ambivalence by considering one of the ways in which new art cinema objects enter into the field: the discovery of an emergent national new wave via two or three films in the international festival circuit. Thus, in the 1990s, Iranian cinema became big news with Mohsen Makhmalbaf, Abbas Kiarostami, and Jafar Panahi showing films across the international festival circuit: The new Iranian cinema rapidly entered into the art cinema canon. More recently, the 2000s saw the emergence of a new Romanian realism, with Cristi Puiu's *Moartea domnului Lazarescu / The Death of Mr. Lazarescu* (2005) showing at Cannes and Toronto, and Cristian Mungiu's *4 luni, 3 saptamâni si 2 zile / Four Months, Three Weeks and Two Days* winning the Palme d'Or in 2007. The category of art cinema enables audiences and festival programmers to process these new films, assimilating them to already proven means of engaging unfamiliar texts. Perhaps it is this assimilation process that troubles those scholars who reject the category. After all, it appears to mirror the structures of cosmopolitan consecration associated with the flattening impulses of neocolonialism and westernization in the late twentieth century. Despite, or perhaps because of these politics, films continue to follow this trajectory of "going international." Audiences who might have little specific prior interest in Romanian culture or film history are drawn to the films as the latest must-see festival prizewinners. The experience offered is not located in director, star, or nationality but is constructed as a similar pleasure to that of previous "new" art cinemas. And the thrill of discovery for those audiences eagerly consuming the next big thing repeats a fantasy at the heart of art cinema: that of making the transformative discovery of neorealism. The structure is ahistorical, in the sense that each new cinema is a repetition of the ever-same fantasy, and any new national cinema can become the vehicle for this fantasy. At the same time, the structure is decidedly historical, since Iranian or Romanian cinemas emerge from specific material historical circumstances and cannot be reduced to a critical or distributive cycle. The new Romanian cinema, for example, emerges at the same moment that Romania joins the European Union: The cinematic and geopolitical institutions interconnect in a temporally and materially legible manner. Furthermore, the question of which national cinemas are brought into the art cinema fold and at what historical juncture correlates to structures of uneven development and postcolonial power. Here, history and ahistory are mutually implicated: if the pleasure of art cinema is one of repetition it is also one of difference, and, like genre, the interplay of these elements forms a defining dynamic.

Historicist accounts have formed a central mode of accessing art cinema as a scholarly category. Film histories have traditionally emphasized the development of national cinemas, with art cinema directors and movements forming the backbone of many such narratives. In part, the notional canon of art cinema is created simply by cherry-picking the major names out of national film histories that narrate Youssef Chahine, Andrei Tarkovsky, or Edward Yang as significant directors.[27] And while some of this work might be viewed as mere canon formation, these approaches also enable scholarship that examines the complex transits between film movements and political or economic histories. Historical studies have also made visible transnational trajectories of influence, tracking, for example, Luis Buñuel's movement from European surrealism to the commercial idiom of his Mexican films. Patrick Keating's essay in this collection addresses this question with regard to Mexican cinematography. Or, traveling in the other direction, we might trace the engagement of Glauber Rocha with Catalan filmmakers in the 1960s.[28] Such comparative or relational studies suggest how industrial issues and modes of production intersect with supra- or transnational histories. Thus, postcolonial studies consider how colonial history inflects the influence of Euro-American art film on Indian and sub-Saharan African cinemas and vice versa.[29] And we should not omit the tremendous importance of history as a textual subject of art cinema: Filmmakers such as Ousmane Sembene and Rainer Werner Fassbinder have taken the formal interrogation of their national and colonial histories as a cinematic and historiographic project.

However, while art cinema has been a prominent element in many film histories, the category itself has been inadequately historicized. While the turn to industrial history in film studies led to a rigorous body of scholarship on the inseparability of Hollywood's modes of production and its narrational forms, and to some such work on various national cinemas, art cinema as such has rarely been investigated in this way. Too often, the usage of the term "art cinema" assumes an unchanging and obvious object. As Mark Betz has noted, "While economic and industrial approaches to the history of Hollywood cinema are a matter of course in Anglo-American film studies, such approaches remain rare in the historiography of European art cinema."[30] This lack of historical analysis is an issue that this volume aims to address, but there is something more at stake here than simply a gap in the scholarship. There is a particularity to the way that art cinema has been constituted as a category that prompts audiences and critics to imagine it as ahistorical. Its lure to audiences has changed much less over the postwar era than we might expect with such a large field of production and consumption. Its persistence as a category in general circulation holds open a unique communicative space across historical contexts. While not as formally coherent as classicism, art cinema shares with it a sense of constituting a broad modality of cinema, seemingly always available to filmmakers and audiences alike. Thus, while the value of historical scholarship on art cinema is evident, its ahistorical qualities might be equally productive in defining the flexible appeal of the category. In fact, a refusal of traditional historicism might be a way to avoid replicating the ethnocentric bias embedded in art cinema's unidirectional trajectories or waves. The valuable revisions to the history of cultural transmission mentioned previously offer a hiatus from the larger sweep of the art house-as-assimilator model. This complication of historicism allows us to account for art cinema without reifying west-to-east patterns of "development," endorsing naive fantasies of cultural universalism, or reproducing the cultural hegemony of Western spectator. We find both of these impulses (the historical and the ahistorical) to be integral to art cinema, and, indeed, we think that its specificity lies in its ability to maintain these apparently opposite qualities in a productive tension.

REALIST AND MODERNIST IMPULSES

The quarrel between realism and modernism has been one of the sustaining aesthetic debates of the twentieth century. In cinema, the divide produced many of the key conceptual models of the cinematic image, including André Bazin's realism and *Screen* journal's modernist Marxism. Likewise, in film practice, avowedly realist movements such as poetic realism and neorealism jostled for canonical status with modernist counter-cinemas and new waves. However, in recent years, critical theorists and film historians have increasingly argued for the interconnection of these cinematic modes, sometimes even finding that the two sides of the divide look surprisingly alike. Writing on Italian neorealism, Frederic Jameson exposes the imbrications of realism, modernism, and postmodernism. Miriam Hansen's work, both on Siegfried Kracauer and in her conception of "vernacular modernism," finds the modernist project engrained in realism and classicism.[31] Art cinema plays an important role in this critical history, because, as a category, it has often yoked these otherwise incommensurate traditions together, and in doing so it often negotiated, merged, and complicated these competing impulses for audiences.

On the one hand, art cinema has often been coterminous with specific realist movements. Art cinema's cohesion as a category first emerges with the popularity of Italian neorealism, and it retains a close association with the thematic and aesthetic impulses of that postwar tradition. Even several decades after neorealism, art films continue to grant priority to the downtrodden, the underdog, and the abjected members of human communities. They take as a moral prerogative the representation of the underrepresented; these films embrace the socially excluded, including working-class subjects (Kidlat Tahimik, Ken Loach), national subjects (Hany Abu-Assad, Haile Gerima), and sexual minorities (Gregg Araki, Deepa Mehta). Realism's claim to make visible what otherwise goes unseen meshes with art cinema's attempt to represent the forbidden or unspeakable. Hence the appropriation of realist style by recent Iranian and French cinema (Samira Makhmalbaf, Laurence Cantet) to critique national gender and class economies. Art cinema promotes itself as uncensored, revealing what commercial cinema deems unfit for general consumption. From Roberto Rossellini's *Roma, città aperta / Rome Open City* (1945) to Park Chan-wook's *Oldeuboi / Oldboy* (2003), the industrial history of exploitation and titillation intersects with textual strategies of realism, grounding art cinema's theoretical claims to truth in the revelation of the imperiled or impassioned body.

On the other hand, art cinema has been closely associated with modernism. In delineating art cinema as an institutional practice, Neale argues that if, as conventional perspectives posit, cinema is a novelistic medium—an extension of a particular literary genre—then art films are modernist novels and Hollywood films are popular genres. As with artistic modernism, then art cinema defines itself largely in opposition to dominant re-alisms. What the nineteenth-century novel is to modernist literature, classical Holly-wood is to art cinema. As in theoretical accounts of modernism, art cinema explores subjectivity and temporality in ways that frustrate or attenuate classical Hollywood nar-rative. Art films delight in precisely the things tossed away or willfully ignored by Holly-wood, repurposing the detritus of the industrial model of storytelling's efficiency and tightness. The art film extends its modernist tendencies in its privileging of internal conflicts, self-reflexivity, extradiegetic gestures, and duration over empiricist models of knowledge and pleasure (Michelangelo Antonioni, Tsai Ming-liang, Bergman).

These modernist impulses have led some critics to deem the art film overly for-malist, pretentious, and self-aggrandizing. *L'année dernière à Marienbad* / *Last Year at Marienbad* (Resnais, 1961) is an easy target here. Despite its popularity with art-house audiences in the early 1960s, the film's tone strikes many viewers today as impossibly slow, wastefully loose, and artistically decadent. To many casual viewers, its mixture of pompous affect, labyrinthine uncertainty, and lack of humor feels anachronistic and self-important to the point of silliness. Probably because of the obdurate seriousness of its elaborate and aristocratic formal language, *Marienbad* may be the most difficult major art film of the period to redeem today, a summation of art cinema's modernist misdemeanors. However, when watched in the context of Alain Resnais's more explic-itly political work or of recent films that lay bare the racializing logic of contemporary European history (the Dardenne brothers or Michael Haneke), the film's overwrought tenor trembles with the psychic aftershocks of French political repression at the end of the colonial era. The ambiguities and ambivalences formally indulged by this film reg-ister the violent bifurcation of French national subjectivity during the colonial and neocolonial periods. Films such as *La Noire de . . .* / *Black Girl* (Sembene, 1966) or *Cléo de 5 à 7* / *Cleo from 5 to 7* (Varda, 1962) could be seen to offer alternate accounts of the same subjective instabilities. The highly aestheticized horror of Georges Franju's *Les Yeux sans visage* / *Eyes without a Face* (1960) similarly plays with a postwar French desire to disappear bodies, identities, and the past. As these examples demonstrate, even in its most enigmatic permutations art cinema has formed a space in which to negotiate the historical challenges of realism and modernism, and we contend that it presents an opportunity to interrogate the continued influence and significance of these concepts in film studies.

If it is now no longer necessary to choose sides in the battle between realism and modernism, then art cinema is perhaps one key site where the tension of that binary opposition has slackened. Bordwell's influential essay on art cinema tries to define the category not as an institution or a genre but as an aesthetic practice. He begins his essay with a description of two features that characterize this practice: realism and authorial presence. The first he links with neorealism, while the latter presents itself through a series of modernist tropes. Bordwell then tells us that these two qualities are actually in conflict within the film text. How can a film that turns itself over to the real also be the work of a single self-aware consciousness? To remedy this contradiction, he observes, the art film must introduce a third key quality: ambiguity. What is interesting here is how art cinema is posed as a unique formal practice that can reconcile the long-standing tension between otherwise discrete artistic movements. Art cinema emerges as a hybrid form that allows realism and modernism to co-exist within one text. It is not a practice of the same order as the other two, but more like a composite mode, a rubric that is able to yoke together disparate modes of expression and, hence, may be uniquely equipped to address equally incommensurate modes of experience and engagement. If we are to return to our definitional impurity, we might say that the realism of an art film is never exclusively realist, because film's narration remains always inflected by the admission of a modernist sensibility. At the same time, its modernism can never achieve absolute purity because it remains tinged by realist tendencies. Art cinema draws our attention to the persistent inadequacy of these terms, especially in their constantly melodramatic binary opposition. Not only do we not have to pick sides, but art cinema operates in a dialectical (or at least triangulating) fashion that demands that we overcome the binary debate. Impurity emerges not only as a constitutive element in the history of art cinema's style, but also as a profound statement about the place of art cinema within a larger history of cinema's shifting function and place in the world.

THE ART IN ART CINEMA

Art cinema most often names a postwar object of study, but the term echoes movements, discourses, and constituencies circulating in 1920s and 1930s Europe, Asia, and the Americas. The early twentieth century, for example, saw a proliferation of arguments for the inclusion of cinema as legitimate art, including those of D. W. Griffith, Ricciotto Canudo, Vachel Lindsay, Rudolf Arnheim, Erwin Panofsky, Iris Barry, and the writers associated with *Close-Up*. Early theories of cinematic specificity asked what defined cinema as a unique form of expression. Drawing from works of aesthetic theory such as Gotthold Ephraim Lessing's *Laocoön*, this scholarship defined film as an art, and hence located its study within major pathways of thought in the humanities. These critical assertions of cinema as "The Seventh Art" coincided with the emergence of innovative practices of narrative film. In the years preceding the establishment of synch-sound as an industrial standard, a series of debates erupted about the best language for cinema. While rarely reaching agreement, these formal innovators often aimed for the same goal: a new means of cinematic expression that would allow for both maximum expressivity and universal comprehension. The film as art became a concept important for identifying what Andrew Tudor calls artistically distinctive cinema practices, lending a certain cohesion to a diverse set of films and in turn enabling the international recognition of specific directors (C. Th. Dreyer, Jean Epstein) as well as stylistic movements (German Expressionism, French Impressionism).[32] Unpacking the postwar conception of art cinema, then, presents a historiographic challenge not only because it refers to precursors drawn from various facets of interwar film culture, but also because the term conflates the discourse on cinema as an art with the specific textual practices of artistic film movements. Writers advocating for "The Seventh Art" and interwar filmmakers shared a tendency to collapse theoretical questions of cinema with favored forms and styles. The way in which later concepts of art cinema confuse medium (cinema as art) with film practice (art films) is understandable, because the interwar debates understood these areas as mutually imbricated.

We can find the legacy of this imbrication in the more recent usage of the word. Art cinema emerges as a series of movements and practices, but it can also be seen as a way of thinking about the aesthetics of the image. The first approach enables us to interrogate and integrate important film movements. Here, art cinema stands as an umbrella category able to contain and connect various subsets: a series of new waves, a cohort of national cinemas, a collection of schools or approaches. Perhaps more important, but underemphasized, is the second usage in which art cinema asks us to think about the status of the image in cinema. As Basil Wright's epigraph to Raymond Spottiswoode's technical handbook puts it, "Despite the sound track, [cinema] is an art because it is visual."[33] Barbara Klinger, one of the few recent film scholars to recognize the urgent need for an aesthetic theory of art cinema, argues that the category has always asserted one predominant feature despite its hard-to-pin-down nature: "the spectacular, enigmatic, and captivating image." In other words, Klinger suggests that a characteristically overabundant visuality constitutes the art of art cinema.[34] Like Klinger's own work, the essays in this collection *engage* that image head-on, refusing to dismiss art cinema's formal surpluses as semantically bankrupt, aesthetically decadent, or simply apolitical.

Art cinema has never been simply an empirical label, an arbitrary moniker, or an empty placeholder. Instead, both the term and its referent have grown in the cracks of film history, sprouting up from the fault lines of theoretical writings on film and histories of specific film practices. To understand the term, we must explore the historicity of applying the word "art" to the cinema. Terminologically, the art–cinema couplet continues to express its constitutive confusion—a conflation of *inter*medial claims (cinema's aesthetic affinities to other media or art forms) and *intra*medial claims (how to best develop an aesthetics of cinema). This confusion not only obfuscates the term, but also contributes to its association with elitism, which raises a final concern. Part of art cinema's stigma is its perceived irrelevance: While critics have argued for realism, postcoloniality, or genre as engines of social and cultural change, art cinema has not been mobilized as such a conceptually productive category. Modernism *has* been understood in these terms, but while a director such as Jean-Luc Godard is credited with political and aesthetic radicality, his status as counter-cinematic (part of Peter Wollen's European avant-garde) separates him from the main body of art cinema in terms of his modernist political form. For some Marxist critics art cinema per se is merely reflective of bourgeois values, while for scholars of popular culture it lacks the mass audience appeal that would make it culturally significant. In part, this problem derives from a willingness by previous studies of art cinema to concede that the term "art" speaks mostly of high culture—and thus signals class bias and an exclusionary attitude. Art is too readily banished from discussions of film as popular or mass culture. Indeed, we find the ready acceptance of bourgeois conceptions of autonomous art to be a troubling facet of much discourse on art cinema. In this book, we have tried to remain sensitive to how elitist and ethnocentric impulses may haunt the category of art cinema. Nonetheless, we refuse to accept a narrow definition of art and insist on maintaining art as an experience available to all.[35]

CLAIMS AND CONCLUSIONS

While most previous accounts of art cinema have tended to privilege either extratextual, industrial features or histories of style and form, the approaches in this book represent a move away from purely institutional or formalist definitions. While style and mode of production remain crucial to our contributors, they refuse to regard image, industry, and politics as separate spheres. The crucial influence of Neale's definitional essay can be felt in the various methodologies of this book. Looking back at the shape of this seminal essay, we find that its claims for art cinema as an institution begin by isolating the key aesthetic features of films in this category. One such feature is how the art film goes to great lengths to mark images reflexively *as images*. In the larger sweep of the argument, holding out the image for attention in this way is critical because Neale argues that art films depend on marking themselves as works of art. In other words, only as a vessel of self-expression will the art film be able to achieve differentiation and commercial viability in a market dominated by Hollywood products. The art film requires its images to belie a self-conscious quality, and in this overt self-awareness, the art film links itself to the attitude present in much twentieth-century art. Here we are reminded of Nowell-Smith's caveat that the art referenced by the term "art cinema" carries a distinctly twentieth-century understanding of the artistic. In fact, we can further specify this historical reminder. If we are to introduce a wider historical perspective to Neale's model, it becomes clear that the art film's long-term differentiation depends on its ability continually to transform the means of demarcation, shifting them to compensate for stylistic cooptation, technological innovation, shifts in access, and ever-morphing tastes and fashions.

For example, during the 1960s and 1970s, the zoom might constitute one legible and circulable sign of the art film. While it is true that the zoom was used widely by other genres, including mainstream popular cinema, kung-fu movies, and the avant-garde, it served as a widely recognizable marker of the art cinema's identity. Sembene and Visconti use the zoom frequently to draw spectatorial awareness to image, and thus to figure the image's rich conceptual productivity. In the work of these directors, the zoom might indulge the excesses of the mise-en-scène, allow the most agile apprehension of movement, reorganize the spatialization of history in the image, and/or denaturalize the knowledge provided in looking. In Bordwell and Kristin Thompson's general primer on cinematic form, *Film Art*, the authors discuss how certain special techniques are associated with particular types of cinema. For them, the zoom or telephoto effects were originally thought to be part of the syntax of sports and news films but quickly became associated with art films. The zoom "flatten[ed the image] in blocks like a painting."[36] If we carry the analysis further, the zoom reveals a fascinating history of aesthetics and politics. Although the technology of the zoom has been available since the 1920s, Paul Willemen writes that it was not until after the Second World War and the zoom's extensive use in aerial surveillance that it began to infiltrate the space of fiction film in the mid-1950s, and thus to coincide with the postwar rise of art cinema. In fact, Willemen goes so far as to claim that the zoom "re-activates the question of the public sphere and its re-configuration consequent to the triumph of capitalism in the second half of the twentieth century . . . as well as raising the question of what happens to modes of discourse in the process of modernisation itself."[37] Imbedded in this one technique, then, we find a complex interaction of art, cinema, technology, and global politics. How could we understand Pier Paolo Pasolini's use of the zoom in *Il fiore delle mille e una notte / Arabian Nights* (1974) without engaging the histories of postcoloniality, the flatness of baroque painting, the gaze of anthropology, lightweight/low-budget camera technology, and the realist poetics of art cinema?

The category of art cinema demands more than merely inflecting industrial history with a light dusting of theoretical concerns. We propose that the category of art cinema can only be mapped with an approach that intersects industry, history, and textuality. Furthermore, we believe that art cinema's specificity emerges in a relationship between *art* and *global*. Hence, the title of this volume is not merely descriptive but definitional, even polemical. "Global" is not a subset of art cinema but an inherent element, alongside and interpenetrating "art" and "cinema." To understand the category, we must interrogate each of these terms as mutually dependent. The term "global" speaks to the international address, distribution, audience, and aesthetic language of the art cinema. This globality is, however, enabled by the term "art," which connects ideas about the status of the image to international aesthetic, critical, and industrial institutions. This connection is not univocally positive: art cinema might refer to an imperialist flattening out of differences as easily as it identifies sites of resistance. Indeed, the push and pull between these tendencies is another way to name the dynamism of the field.

However, we make two further claims on the political significance of our definition. First, while art cinema traverses the political spectrum, our definition of how aesthetics and geopolitics work together in its construction allows for new and more nuanced analyses to be made. The commonplace dismissal of art film as wholly conservative is thus inadequate, and we seek to overthrow it. If we settle for the reductive version of art cinema as an always already compromised or disappointing practice, then we risk missing significant arrangements of aesthetics and geopolitics that underlie—and perhaps can be diagnosed exclusively through—even the most reactionary of art films. Second, we believe that art cinema has been underestimated as a site for political and theoretical work. Given that contemporary film studies remains deeply concerned by both the nature of the film image and the global geopolitics of cinema, it is odd that the discipline has largely ignored art cinema as a nexus for critical engagement with cinematic globality. While it may be tempting to regard art cinema's emphasis on the aesthetic as apolitical, we argue that by connecting the cinematic image to international spaces, it inherently makes a political claim. Art cinema is both an aesthetic category—involved in broadly constituted debates on realism, modernism, the image, and its implications—and a geopolitical category, bound up in modernity and the traumas of twentieth-century history. We feel strongly that the category's enduring relevance derives from this combination of elements and their persistent remixing. Moreover, we propose that the study of art cinema provides an important lens through which to interrogate the consequences of globalization, whether this means programmatic ideologies or the experience of living in a world community.

SECTIONS OF THE BOOK

From its earliest conceptions, the goal of this anthology was to approach art cinema's geography from a variety of critical methodologies. Since the category has been so undertheorized, it seems crucial to revitalize the field by placing contestatory modes of analysis into productive relation. By bringing these approaches together in one volume, we aim to provoke a conversation of ideas on art cinema, as well as find unexpected connections and nourish lively debate. Each of the authors takes on a specific topic in the field of art cinema, from individual films and directors to broad questions of genre or nation. At the same time, however, we believe that the essays all make significant contributions to larger contemporary debates in film theory and historiography about the global character of cinema.

The essays in the first section of the book tackle the demarcation of art cinema's categorical terrain. For over fifty years, art cinema has defined how many audiences encounter commercial films produced outside Hollywood (as well as Bollywood and Hong Kong). The essays in this section propose different ways of understanding art cinema's unique position in the market. They attempt to specify art cinema by thinking about how it challenges contemporary scholarly rubrics of film cultures, genres, and modes of audience engagement. This section outlines new shapes and boundaries for art cinema, rejecting any wholesale adoption of the commercial logic of ever-burgeoning markets or of the conventional progressive narratives of style while never neglecting the influence of those ideologies. Several of these essays are less concerned with establishing art cinema's definitional center than they are with locating art cinematic practice at the borders between divergent practices of cinema.

Mark Betz begins the collection with a reconsideration of David Bordwell's concept of parametric cinema. Isolating the usefulness of the category as a way to engage cinematic style, Betz nonetheless strips out the formalism of Bordwell's definition in order to re-envision the parametric as a historical modality. Seen in the light of art cinema's modernist and postmodern history, the parametric indexes the decline of a Eurocentric arthouse model and the rise of global parametric art cinema. Sharon Hayashi's essay argues that an erotic genre popular in Japan since the 1960s, pink cinema, refracts the definition of art cinema both within Japan and beyond its borders. Pink cinema, the quasi-pornographic feature films short enough to be seen on a lunch break in special sex theaters, was reframed by exhibition in prestigious film festivals. By unpacking the international recognition of these films within the category of art cinema, Hayashi uncovers a rich layer of social commentary and political irony in the violenced and sexed bodies of these films. In another repositioning of the sex film, David Andrews forms a polemic against thinking of art cinema as a distinct genre. Struck by how frequently designations of quality and artfulness stratify films across the cultural spectrum and well beyond the art house, Andrews investigates how "art cinema" carries such terminological utility and what this suggests about its philosophical underpinnings. Maria San Filippo embraces the polymorphous sexualities that appear in art films, arguing that the bisexual recurs not simply as a trope of pseudo-liberal posturing but as a crucial and radical figure in the constitution of the category of art cinema. Writing across a global spectrum of texts, San Filippo links the visual ambivalence of the bisexual to the constitutive ambiguity of the art cinematic image. Adam Lowenstein offers a radical comparison of Buñuel's *Un Chien andalou* and Cronenberg's *eXistenZ* by examining how each film configures interactivity. By juxtaposing two art films made at either end of the twentieth century, Lowenstein not only rethinks the idea of interactivity beyond the clichés that often mire such intermedia studies, but also proposes the art film as one of cinematic modernity's riskiest games.

As mentioned previously, one central defining characteristic of art cinema is its sustained engagement with the idea of cinema as image, and the essays in the second section attend to the variations, specificities, and stakes of that image. From classical film theory forward, critics have sought to identify the essence of cinema through its visuality. Art cinema is the site where this question is now most often staged. Conscious of this tradition, this section's essays propose their own new polemics on where to locate the art in art cinema. The aim here is to demonstrate the range of contemporary approaches to art cinema's visuality, to bring these diverse perspectives into conversation, and to offer emerging global cinema practices as a means of re-grounding theories of the cinematic image. Brian Price examines how the stubborn rootedness of art institutions (museums, gallery spaces, etc.) and the ephemeral placeness of site-specific art practices (Gordon Matta-Clark) not only trouble global capitalism's armchair cosmopolite but ask us to consider what it means to travel to see a film. By careful attention to the experiential nature of post-cinematic artworks by Douglas Gordon and Matthew Barney, Price brings film theory to the white cube exhibition space to reveal the sociogeographic fault lines of contemporary connoisseurship. Jihoon Kim also looks at the intersections between art cinema and time-based gallery installations, focusing on a particularly prominent figure in contemporary Thai cinema, Apichatpong Weerasethakul. Kim traces how Apichatpong's video works and feature films cross-pollinate, particularly in their articulations of space, provoking questions about the idiom of the cinematic in the history of video art. Pier Paolo Pasolini's notoriously opaque but crucial theoretical treatise, "The 'Cinema of Poetry,'" benefits from John David Rhodes's authoritative and lucid rereading. What Rhodes calls "a curious and curiously unassimilable feature of the landscape of film theory," Pasolini's most famous essay emerges from this new analysis as a crucial negotiation of the growing schism between formalist film aesthetics and the political cinema in the mid-1960s. In an equally groundbreaking reassessment of another familiar text, Angelo Restivo locates *Il conformista / The Conformist* at Bertolucci's transitional moment between an art cinema of overt political realism and one of glossy baroque formalism. Restivo is simultaneously committed to theoretical depth and to the film image's surface, and his essay compellingly reorients—and in many ways, rejects—conventional theories of film style. Angela Dalle Vacche also uses an analysis of the image to dethrone engrained histories of art cinema style. Exposing startling concordances between late surrealist artworks and art house's canonical auteurs, Dalle Vacche suggests that the films of Bergman, Godard, and Resnais appropriate not simply surrealism's optical mayhem but the political force of its representational transformation; how they process the brutality of history, she suggests, will come to serve the art-house directors of the 1960s.

The next section addresses the historicity and historiography of art cinema. From several historical perspectives, these essays complicate the conventional trajectory of film historiography that installs postwar European cinema as the predominant aesthetic and industrial basis around which other art cinemas develop. Patrick Keating reassesses the relationship of Mexican cinematographer Gabriel Figueroa to directors Emilio Fernández and Luis Buñuel, arguing that the shift from Figueroa's heroic landscapes to Buñuel's surreal squalor frames not just an aesthetic difference but conditions of possibility for the global visibility of Mexican space. Manishita Dass also finds in the history of one filmmaker a way to reframe the horizons of art cinema: analyzing the neglected Bengali director Ritwik Ghatak, she finds that the particularity of his melodramatic and modernist style (in contrast to Ray's realist humanism), as well as his determined engagement with the consequences of Partition, produce a form of critique that contests expectations of what art cinema could be. Timothy Corrigan takes, perhaps, the opposite approach, returning to the highly canonical moment of the French New Wave in order to excavate the history of the essay film. Locating the nonfiction films of Chris Marker, Jean-Luc Godard, and Agnès Varda firmly within the intellectual and institutional currents of postwar France, Corrigan compellingly proposes the essay film as a parallel development, closely entwined with the emergence of the art cinema. If the essay film draws from the interwar development of local cinematheques and film clubs, then the contemporary art film is largely supported by the international film festival circuit. Philip Rosen also returns to the postwar history of the art film, beginning from the contemporaneity of art cinema's development with anticolonial movements in Africa. While the proponents of Third Cinema rejected art cinema as politically complicit, Rosen finds that in practice, the situation is more complex. Contrasting films' African aesthetics with their international funding and distribution, he powerfully argues that postcolonial African cinema is characterized by its utopian address. Azadeh Farahmand's essay investigates how the festival marketplace has come to genericize national cinemas as art cinema. Contrasting pre- and postrevolutionary Iranian films, she draws together the cultural politics of festival success with the recent political history of Iran. These historiographies expand the object of study, reassessing the terrain of art cinema as a historical object and finding connections where perhaps none had been seen before.

Despite the Eurocentrism of its earlier conceptions, art cinema has always aspired to globality. Contemporary academic, critical, and festival rubrics include a growing range of contemporary film practices under the moniker of art cinema, including the work of Claire Denis, Jia Zhangke, Alfonso Cuarón, Takashi Miike, Wong Kar-wai, and Aleksandr Sokurov. Utilizing various conceptual frames, each of the essays in the book's final section proposes a critical geography of art cinema. Randall Halle investigates the industrial structures of transnational coproduction, in particular European funding of films from North Africa and the Middle East. The essay asks searching questions about who has agency to tell "national" stories in this production scenario, and how these European outreach programs determine the kind of stories that European audiences hear about outsiders. Taking a contrasting approach, E. Ann Kaplan considers the ethical and affective work of European art film in postcolonial encounters. For Kaplan, the emotional valence of films by Werner Herzog, Denis, and the Dardenne brothers promises a transformative spectatorship that can embrace both intense affect and political responsibility toward the Other. Rachel Gabara is also interested in postcolonial encounters, but her analysis of

Abderrahmane Sissako reverses the direction of travel, following the director's journeys from Mauritania to Russia, France, and then back to Africa. Sissako's films reevaluate the position of the African filmmaker vis-à-vis Third Cinema and Second (or art) Cinema, as well as the politics of self-presentation in the global South. Gabara's essay elegantly demonstrates the stakes of these intersections for contemporary African cinema. The final two essays in this section rethink the relationships of non-European cinemas to canonical Euro-art film. Jean Ma asks why critics of Taiwanese films are constantly compelled to compare directors such as Tsai Ming-liang to Antonioni and Fassbinder. She suggests that these comparisons reveal hitherto untheorized tensions between the local and the universal and, moreover, that they demand a reassessment of art cinematic authorship in light of today's global transactions. If Tsai's work is all too often compared to the European tradition, Dennis Hanlon suggests we reconsider a connection that is usually repudiated. Bolivian filmmaker Jorge Sanjinés is usually placed firmly within a political Third Cinema, rejecting art cinematic formalism. Hanlon, however, suggests that Sanjinés's use of the traveling shot, borrowed from Greek director Theodoros Angelopoulos, reflects a dynamic exchange between Latin American and European Marxisms, and moreover opens up an often ignored discourse on aesthetic beauty in New Latin American Cinema.

Together, these essays specify the connections, transits, and fractures that cut across this—real and phantasmatic—global field, highlighting the relationship between cultural specificity and cross-national influence in the development of art cinema. How might art cinema relate to other models of transnational film production such as Third Cinema or European coproductions? What are the political stakes of forging connections (recognizing global transits, encouraging allegiances otherwise unrecognized, overlapping visual styles) or in maintaining differences (keeping distinctions, refusing heritages, rejecting imperialisms)? Should we continue to foster art cinema? Cherish it as a popular institution of cultural exchange? The contributions to this book answer these questions with divergent but equally provocative responses, and in doing so polemicize what it means to think cinema globally. Furthermore, they suggest art cinema as not simply a crucial vehicle of global culture—such as cultural specificity, cross-national influence, diasporic subjectivity, neocolonialism—but as a category that allows for and produces these modes of engagement and imaging.

Notes

1. Introduction to *The International Film Guide* (London: Tantivy, 1964), 7. The *Guide*, along with many postwar publications, uses the term *film d'art* to refer to what we would now call art cinema (or, in French, *film d'art et essai*). We follow this usage when we are discussing the prehistory of art cinema or indicating how film criticism conceived the category before the term "art cinema" came into general use. It should not be confused with the specific historical use of *film d'art* to refer to French theatrical films made by Pathé in the early years of the twentieth century.

2. The tokenistic inclusion of directors like Ray or Kurosawa may also reflect a larger ideological logic in which Western versions of aestheticism are read onto Asian art. Clearly, certain Asian directors confirmed Euro-American definitions of the

modernist text, and the *Guide*'s inclusion of Ray and Kurosawa may reflect this narcissistic identification more than any desire to see other regions of the world represented. It is important to consider how much a specifically Euro-American definition of "art" (particularly the idea that art must involve a modernist impulse and result in aesthetically complex work) facilitated the yoking of diverse films together during this period.

3. Compiled by the Worker's Project Administration, the MoMA's encyclopedic survey of cinema begins with a volume called "Film as Art." To organize a list of thousands of films, the writers devised an extensive series of more than sixty "types." The breadth of these categories is quite wide, as everything from well-known genres, such as "Romance-Costume" and "Westerns," to more esoteric or quotidian groupings, such as "Social Films" or "Fight and Wrestling Films," is included. It should be pointed out here that this list functions in concert with *The Film Index*'s and the MoMA's larger project: to demonstrate that a wide variety of films should be considered art. Nonetheless, the category of art cinema feels oddly absent from our historical perspective. Films like *Manhatta* and *Le Sang d'un poète* are fit into the category "Experimental Films." Meanwhile, films like *The Golem* and *The Cabinet of Dr. Caligari* fall under the category of "Fantasy and Trick Films" alongside *King Kong* and *The Invisible Man*. Writers' Program (Work Projects Administration, New York), Harold Leonard, and Museum of Modern Art, *The Film Index, a Bibliography* (New York: Museum of Modern Art Film Library and the H. W. Wilson Company, 1941).

4. Herbert Mitgang, "Transatlantic 'Miracle' Man," *Park East*, August 1952, 36.

5. Geoffrey Nowell-Smith, *The Oxford History of World Cinema* (New York: Oxford University Press, 1996).

6. Martin Stollery, *Alternative Empires: European Modernist Cinemas and Cultures of Imperialism* (Exeter: University of Exeter Press, 2000), 17. Stollery is referring to *Metropolis* (Lang, 1926), *Un Chien andalou* (Buñuel, 1928), and *Song of Ceylon* (Wright, 1934).

7. David Bordwell, "Art Cinema as a Mode of Film Practice," *Film Criticism* 4 (1979): 56–64.

8. Steve Neale, "Art Cinema as Institution," *Screen* 22, no. 1 (1981): 11–39.

9. Barbara Wilinsky, *Sure Seaters: The Emergence of Art House Cinema* (Minneapolis: University of Minnesota Press, 2001).

10. Jeffrey Sconce. "'Trashing' the Academy: Taste, Excess, and an Emerging Politics of Cinematic Style," *Screen* 36, no. 4 (Winter 1995): 371–393.

11. Mette Hjort, "Dogma 95: A Small Nation's Response to Globalization," in *Purity and Provocation: Dogma 95*, ed. Hjort and Scott MacKenzie (London: BFI, 2003), 38.

12. Janet Staiger, "Authorship Approaches," in *Authorship and Film*, ed. Staiger and David A. Gerstner (New York: Routledge, 2003), 27.

13. Eric Schaefer, *Bold! Daring! Shocking! True! A History of Exploitation Films 1919–1959* (Durham, N.C.: Duke University Press, 1999), 333.

14. For more on how this postwar American art-house spectator has been theorized in relation to corporeal spectacle and world politics, see two essays by Karl Schoonover: "Neorealism at a Distance," in *European Film Theory*, ed. Temenuga Trifonova (New York: Routledge, 2009), 301–18, and "The Comfort of Carnage: Neorealism and America's World," in *Convergence Media History*, ed. Janet Staiger and Sabine Hake (New York: Routledge, 2009).

15. See Wilinsky, *Sure Seaters*.

16. Berenice Reynaud, "An Interview with Charles Burnett," *Black American Literature Forum* 25, no. 2 (Summer 1991): 28, 29, 334. See also Anne Thompson, "*Anger* Strikes Back: The Non-marketing of Charles Burnett," *L.A. Weekly*, November 16–22, 1990, 57.

17. Thomas Elsaesser, *European Cinema: Face to Face with Hollywood* (Amsterdam: Amsterdam University Press, 2005), 21.

18. Julio García Espinosa, "For an Imperfect Cinema," in *Twenty-five Years of the New Latin American Cinema*, ed. Michael Chanan (London: BFI, 1983), 28–33, and "Meditations on Imperfect Cinema . . . Fifteen Years Later," in *New Latin American Cinema*, ed. Michael T. Martin (Detroit: Wayne State University Press, 1997), 83–85.

19. Miriam Bratu Hansen, "The Mass Production of the Senses: Classical Cinema as Vernacular Modernism," *Modernism/Modernity* 6, no. 2 (1999): 59–77.

20. Lúcia Nagib, "Towards a Positive Definition of World Cinema," in *Remapping World Cinema: Identity, Culture and Politics in Film*, ed. Stephanie Dennison and Song Hwee Lim (London: Wallflower, 2006): 19–37; Kathleen Newman, "Transnational Exchanges vs. International Circulating: Shifting Categories in Film History," Media History Conference, October 13, 2007, University of Texas at Austin. For a broad debate on these issues, see also Nataša Ďurovičová and Newman, eds., *World Cinemas, Transnational Perspectives* (New York: Routledge, 2009).

21. Dudley Andrew, "An Atlas of World Cinema," *Framework*, October 2004, 9–23.

22. Atom Egoyan and Ian Balfour, eds., *Subtitles: On the Foreignness of Film* (Boston: MIT Press, 2004), and Abé Mark Nornes, *Cinema Babel: Translating Global Cinema* (Minneapolis: University of Minnesota Press, 2007).

23. Gayatri Chakravorty Spivak, *Death of a Discipline* (New York: Columbia University Press, 2003), 71–102.

24. See, for example, David Damrosch's *What Is World Literature?* (Princeton, N.J.: Princeton University Press, 2003), and Christopher Prendergast and Benedict Anderson, eds., *Debating World Literature* (New York: Verso, 2004).

25. See, for example, Pheng Cheah and Bruce Robbins, eds., *Cosmopolitics: Thinking and Feeling beyond the Nation* (Minneapolis: University of Minnesota Press, 1998).

26. See Rey Chow, *The Age of the World Target: Self-Referentiality in War, Theory and Comparative Work* (Durham, N.C.: Duke University Press, 2006).

27. See, for example, M. Khan, *Introduction to the Egyptian Cinema* (London: Informatics, 1969), or Jay Leyda, *Kino: A History of the Russian and Soviet Film* (Princeton, N.J.: Princeton University Press, 1983).

28. Rosalind Galt, "Mapping Catalonia in 1967: The Barcelona School in Global Context," *Senses of Cinema* 41 (2006), available at http://archive.sensesofcinema.com/contents/06/41/barcelona-school.html (accessed October 7, 2009).

29. See Priya Jaikumar, *Cinema at the End of Empire: A Politics of Transition in Britain and India* (Durham, N.C.: Duke University Press, 2006); Rachel Gabara, *From Split to Screened Selves: French and Francophone Autobiography in the Third Person* (Stanford, Calif.: Stanford University Press, 2006); Laleen Jayamanne, *Toward Cinema and Its Double: Cross-Cultural Mimesis* (Bloomington: Indiana University Press, 2001); and Raúl Ruiz, *Poetics of Cinema 1* (Paris: Dis Voir, 1996).

30. Mark Betz, "The Name above the (Sub)Title: Internationalism, Coproduction, and the Polyglot European Art Cinema," *Camera Obscura* 46 (2001): 1–45, 7.

31. Fredric Jameson, "The Existence of Italy," in *Signatures of the Visible* (New York: Routledge, 1990), 155–229; Hansen, "The Mass Production of the Senses" and "Introduction," to Siegfried Kracauer's *Theory of Film: The Redemption of Physical Reality* (Princeton, N.J.: Princeton University Press, 1997).

32. Andrew Tudor, "The Rise and Fall of the Art (House) Movie," in *The Sociology of Art: Ways of Seeing*, ed. David Inglis and John Hughson (New York: Palgrave Macmillan, 2005).

33. Raymond Spottiswoode, *Film and Its Techniques* (Berkeley: University of California Press, 1951), vii.

34. Barbara Klinger, "The Art Film, Affect and the Female Viewer: *The Piano* Revisited," *Screen* 47, no. 1 (2006): 20.

35. Our thinking here is inspired in part by the two essays by García Espinosa mentioned previously that offer a radical stance on the role of art in life.

36. David Bordwell and Kristin Thompson, *Film Art: An Introduction*, 8th ed. (Boston: McGraw-Hill, 2008), 170.

37. Paul Willemen, "The Zoom in Popular Cinema: A Question of Performance," *Rouge* 3 (2003), available at http://www.rouge.com.au/1/zoom.html (accessed October 7, 2009).

I

DELIMITING THE FIELD

1

Beyond Europe: On Parametric Transcendence

Mark Betz

"Art cinema" is no longer a phrase with the same institutional currency that it once enjoyed some twenty years ago, when it served to demarcate a coherent body of contemporary film practice. "World cinema" is now a moniker of choice, albeit one with a more encompassing range of stylistic possibilities. And while art cinema, too, can refer to many types of films and film aesthetics, the high-water mark of its most "difficult" and ambitious formal guise is arguably parametric narration, David Bordwell's term to describe a mode of filmmaking that foregrounds style as an organizing principle. Whether aligned with the transcendental (Yasujiro Ozu, Carl Theodor Dreyer, Robert Bresson), serialism (Alain Resnais, Bresson again, Jean-Luc Godard on occasion, Chantal Akerman), or long takes, often combined with camera movement (Kenji Mizoguchi, Miklós Jancsó, Michelangelo Antonioni, Andrei Tarkovsky, Theodoros Angelopoulos), a special place has been reserved for parametric filmmaking from the 1950s through 1970s among art film cognoscenti.

In the nearly quarter-century since Bordwell's delineation of this style, an identifiably contemporary parametric film practice has gained prominence increasingly and crucially situated outside of Western Europe, its erstwhile home. Challenging films that employ modernist aesthetic strategies continue to be made and celebrated on the international stage, particularly through film festival premieres, screenings, and awards, from which follows international theatrical distribution for the cinematheque and specialty theater circuits as well as home viewing on DVD or via niche televisual broadcasting. But the ways in which this cinema has been considered in film scholarship tend to mark it not as a continuing manifestation of modernist art cinema, as I understand it to be, but instead as something different: a particular kind of world cinema tied ineluctably, and often to its critical detriment, to a film festival culture that privileges and honors the style. Indeed, one must acknowledge the international networks of exchange within which many of these practitioners are working, in terms of not only their geographic range but also the transnational provenance of the films' production (many by European finance), reception, and dissemination, frequently by major European film festivals. Increasingly, festivals are themselves commissioning and producing the work of these filmmakers, potentially binding them to a marketplace that cannot but have an effect on the stylistic choices that they make. Jason McGrath, for example, considers Jia Zhangke's *Platform* (2000) as marking a shift in the director's work "away from the documentary or on-the-spot realism movement in China" of his previous films toward a transnational "style of aestheticized realism, with its durations and ellipses," that was "a favorite of the international art cinema and film festival circuit during the 1990s" and as such "unavoidably itself a commodity within the specialized market that supports it."[1] And Azadeh Farahmand addresses how foreign (especially French) investment in Iranian film production was in the same decade tied to the festival economy: "Thus, while European festival programmers and film distributors can pride themselves on the discovery of other cinemas, they have also benefited from the cultural and economic returns of the films they promote. This point demystifies film festivals as the profit motive driving them is brought to the foreground."[2]

To a certain degree, then, this is an international style authorized and promoted via the global film festival circuit—less visibly and concretely articulated than Dogme95, for example, but perhaps equally programmatically. From an aesthetic standpoint, however, I struggle to see any acquiescence in this cinema to formal preferences more easily assimilable to prevailing industry standards, even within this niche market—a propensity for what Thomas Elsaesser notes as a trend in world cinema for "art cinema 'light'"[3]—but instead the opposite: deferred or absent reverse shots, minimalism, serialism, ellipses, long takes. They are still, then, "difficult" films, even when they are tied so closely to the festival economy: two recent examples would be Tsai Ming-liang's *I Don't Want to Sleep Alone* and Apichatpong Weerasethakul's *Syndromes and a Century*, both commissioned by and premiering at the New Crowned Hope Festival in Vienna in 2006. Recognizing and attending to the highly formalized codes of these films on their own terms is as exciting, for me at least, as anything their stories or meticulous mise-en-scènes have to offer. But such excitement is at the same time tempered by a sense of their ineluctable foreignness as manifested in, rather than accommodated by, their measured paces and formal rigor.[4] When I watch a film like *Syndromes and a Century*, for example, I am confronted with an array of spaces, architectures, character types and relations, interpersonal cadences—in short, cultural or local references for which I have little grounding, and ones that draw attention to themselves *through* the parametric stylistics of the film itself, especially the moving camera and long takes: the more I see in the shots, the more in fact I am *shown*, the more I am made aware of my bounded competency to understand (as opposed to simply experience) how the film's form is functioning in concert with its story, which also remains largely inscrutable.

This is, I would argue, a productive *frisson*, as it raises important questions regarding the relation of the global to the local in this style. It throws into relief the ways in which local knowledges are inflected, indeed even explicitly foregrounded as such, by parametric form, knowledges that insist on being heeded (even as unknowns) through that form. As such I see these films as sharing aesthetic features that attest to the persistence of cinematic modernism, *with a difference*, in the so-called postmodern era of globalization—an issue Bordwell himself largely avoids by labeling such films as "parametric" rather than modernist in the first place. But there is also, I think, something to be gained in reclaiming his term and the interpretive practices it engenders, in analyzing the formal codes of such films as a means to understand their operations and procedures for creating meanings, and with an eye toward how such meanings cannot be made complete or fully known, how they remain, on some levels, transcendent.

In this essay I am thus positing a parametric "tradition" that constitutes one strand of an "international style" for contemporary world cinema, indeed contemporary *art* cinema, and that has since the late 1980s continued in Western Europe but has also proceeded in parallel in Eastern Central Europe, sub-Saharan Africa, and especially East Asia. In so doing I hope to highlight some of the issues and implications of the "world cinema" designation used for these films, as well as to advocate for a return to "modernist" and "parametric" as preferred terms that can better address the complex circulations of global art cinema in the twenty-first century, in both its mechanisms and its effects. I believe that we must, if we are to become truly attentive global spectators, acknowledge our position in circuits of contemporary cinematic exchange, a position that is not always or simply one of power and knowledge. We must be prepared to be challenged by what the current manifestations of the parametric tradition can show us and potentially teach us. And we must rise to this challenge by taking seriously their own serious rearticulations of cinematic modernism, and in so doing reconsider received wisdom about what this was through what it now is.

In his 1985 book *Narration in the Fiction Film*, David Bordwell categorizes and amplifies five forms of narration that he finds more or less in accord with certain epochs in the history of fiction filmmaking: classical, historical-materialist, art cinema, parametric, and palimpsestic.[5] The first three of these have, he argues, reasonably clear ties to historical developments of narration—the classical with the "invisible style" of Hollywood cinema from the interwar period through to the 1960s; the historical-materialist with the theoretically tied Marxist forms of the Soviet montage school; and art cinema with the innovations of Italian neorealism extending through the various new waves in Europe, reaching an apogee in terms of both quantity and influence in the 1960s. The other two, however, do not for Bordwell coalesce around an identifiably articulable period, though for different reasons: Palimpsestic narration is considered a particular manifestation limited largely (though not wholly) to the work of Jean-Luc Godard; and parametric narration, he avers, "is not linked to a single national school, period, or genre of filmmaking. Its norms seem to lack the historical concreteness of the three modes I have considered so far. In many ways, the pertinent historical context is less that of filmmaking than that of film theory and criticism. To some extent, then, this mode of narration applies to isolated filmmakers and fugitive films."[6] As the adjectives imply, the examples are comparatively few: only five filmmakers—Ozu, Dreyer, Bresson, Mizoguchi, and Jacques Tati—and seven films: *M* (1931), *Ivan the*

Terrible (1945), *Last Year at Marienbad* (1961), *Vivre sa vie* (1962), *Méditerranée* (1963), *Katzelmacher* (1969), and *L'Eden et après* (1970).

How is it that Bordwell is able to isolate these films and filmmakers from the sea of others? By the particular vagaries of their mode of narration, which he characterizes as "one in which the film's stylistic system creates patterns *distinct from the demands of the syuzhet system.*"[7] The term that he uses to categorize this mode, parametric narration, is one that has not been taken up in the field with much consistency or warmth in the years since the book's publication, and the same holds true for his use of Russian formalist terminology combined with cognitive theory to define the differing systems at work in a given film. I must therefore take a moment to unpack this terminology so that we can all be reminded what is meant by these words, and why they are important.

The first of these is *fabula*, which refers to the "imaginary construct" created "progressively and retroactively" by the spectator of a film.[8] It is, more simply put, the *story* of the film—the chronological order of events that take place in the fictional world played out on-screen, some of which may precede the time of the film itself (i.e., backstory). In contrast, Bordwell uses the term *syuzhet* to refer to what is "phenomenally present," the "actual arrangement and presentation of the *fabula* in the film,"[9] the ordering of the events, actions, and so on—what he and Kristin Thompson refer to elsewhere as the *plot*. The story could be what we remember most of a narrative film; that said, it is not actually present in the film, or rather is only present insofar as it is built out of the plot, the particular ordering and presentation of story details.

Narration consists of the interaction of the plot with story via *style*, a film's systematic use of cinematic devices. In the case of classical narration, "stylistic patterns tend to be vehicles for" the plot's "process of cueing us to construct" the story.[10] In other words, style is subordinated to plot, which itself is subordinated to the needs of the story—the "invisible style" of classical Hollywood cinema being the most notable example. Art-cinema and historical-materialist narration position style more prominently as an overall feature; but even in these cases, "the film's unique deployment of stylistic features nonetheless remains subordinate" to plot-defined functions.[11] What is unique about parametric narration, then, is that only in this mode is style promoted to the level of a shaping force in the film. Plot and style thus do not necessarily have a fixed relation to one another, something foregrounded in parametric narration. They vary in importance and may demonstrate differing levels of arbitrariness, such that some stylistic choices seem not to be motivated by the concerns of the plot but assume an importance in their own right, and at their most extreme entirely for themselves. Following on from Noël Burch's *Theory of Film Practice* (1973), then, Bordwell takes both his term "parameters, or stylistic procedures" and his suggestion that these "are as functionally important to the film's overall form as are narrative ones" as starting points for his positing of parametric narration.[12] The result is a "style-centered" narration, a mode rarer (at least from a 1970s standpoint) than any of the others and as such more difficult to establish clear guidelines for identifying and analyzing.

Bordwell is nonetheless meticulous in his efforts to do so. An initial means is to link parametric narration with two relatively contemporaneous developments in other arts: the "total serialism" of European music of the 1950s (Pierre Boulez, Karlheinz

Stockhausen, etc.); and the structuralism of the same period in the *nouveau roman* and the *Tel Quel* group in France.[13] Characteristically, Bordwell does not push these contextual developments, but instead derives from them formal qualities applicable to his own formalist project: "Both serialism and structuralism held that textual components form an order that coheres according to intrinsic principles. . . . This line of thought suggests that style . . . may form an independent structure in the text. Style need be governed only by internal coherence, not by representational function."[14] Using the example of a graphic match from the Ozu film *What Did the Lady Forget?* (1937), Bordwell draws a distinction between *style* and *flourish*: "Any film might contain an aesthetically motivated flourish—a gratuitous camera movement, an unexpected and unjustified color shift or sound bridge. In the visual arts, a flourish is an embellishment . . . [that] exhibits aesthetic motivation" on the part of a creator. "Ozu's graphic match, however, is not a flourish; the device recurs frequently and systematically. . . . In parametric narration, style is organized *across the film* according to distinct principles."[15] Stylistic devices thus, through frequency and repetition, exhibit in a film constituted by parametric narration a serial or structural prominence that is more than just decorative or ornamental.

In order for style to come forward across a whole film, it must for Bordwell possess an "internal coherence" that "depends on establishing a distinctive, often unique intrinsic stylistic norm. We can distinguish between two broad strategies. One is the 'ascetic' or 'sparse' option, in which the film limits its norm to a narrower range of procedures than are codified in other extrinsic norms. . . . Once the intrinsic stylistic norm is in place, it must be developed," not simply repeated.[16] But this does not mean that its development is teleological in a way that binds it to plot or story. Rather, its development is for its own sake. In contrast is what Bordwell identifies as "a more 'replete' intrinsic norm" that presents "an inventory or a range of paradigmatic options"—his example is Godard's *Vivre sa vie*, which does not conclude but more simply ends once it has covered all of the possible variants of its intrinsic norm: "how to shoot and cut character interaction." In both the "sparse" and the "replete" types, "the film will have a strong inner unity: a prominent intrinsic norm and patterned reiterations of that." But while the plot construction and narration "may possess a cumulative overall shape, often of great structural symmetry," in parametric cinema "the stylistic patterning tends to be additive and open-ended, with no predictable point of termination."[17]

Here is where things start to get messy. The overall effect of such a film on a viewer, even one who has been trained over time to apprehend what Bordwell earlier calls "the schemata for the 1960s 'art film,'" can be not entirely pleasurable, as "it thwarts the chief method of managing viewing time—constructing a linear" story. Burch was unconcerned about this, or rather viewed it as a necessary development for film to achieve formal maturity and autonomy.[18] It is for Bordwell, too, a positive feature of the parametric mode that it "strains so vigorously against habitual capacities that it risks boring or baffling the spectator," as in doing so it "points up the limits upon the art film's extrinsic norms . . . and lets us acknowledge a richness of texture that resists interpretation."[19] This is very similar to a position Susan Sontag had articulated in her essay "Against Interpretation" twenty years earlier, in 1965, which would have been measured at Bordwell's time of writing as the height of both parametric and art cinema. The comparison is suggestive, as Sontag in her book of the same title devoted long essays to both Bresson and Godard's *Vivre sa vie*, as Bordwell does here.[20] Viewers unwilling or unable to take up such a challenge, that is, those in thrall to art cinema's less rigorous and therefore more digestible stylistic norms, will note that parametric films are organized by striking stylistic patterns but misrecognize their singularity, will "seek to insert parametric narration into the art-cinema mode" and, in so doing, actually "neglect the workings of style." Rather than analyze parametric films closely and in purely formal terms, such a viewer becomes for Bordwell an interpretive critic who "is tempted to 'read'" stylistic patterns, "to assign them thematic meanings." It is thus significant that "the most celebrated exponents of the sparse parametric strategy—Dreyer, Ozu, Mizoguchi, and Bresson—are often seen as creating mysterious and mystical films. . . . Noncinematic schemata, often religious ones, may thus be brought in to motivate the workings of style."[21] For Bordwell, reading "stylistic effects in this way" is indicative of a broader tendency, "that of assuming that everything in any film (or any good film) must be interpretable thematically. . . . The critic assumes that everything in the film should contribute to meaning. If style is not decoration, it must be motivated compositionally or realistically or, best of all, as narrational commentary."[22] In other words, a kind of connotative interpretation *is* available for these films, either in the form of thematic or auteurist interpretation, but misattends to the specifically formal play at work in them.

What Bordwell is advocating here is not interpretation, then, but *analysis*, and analysis of a specific sort: one that reveals the exclusively "formal causes" that explain "that aura of mystery and transcendence" that many attribute to parametric films. The implicit yet clear reference for this tendency is Paul Schrader, whose book *Transcendental Style in Film: Ozu, Bresson, Dreyer* (1972) concerns itself with three sparse parametric filmmakers who in his estimation have "forged a remarkably common film form" to "express the Holy."[23] But Dudley Andrew's estimable *Film in the Aura of Art*, which was published the year before *Narration in the Fiction Film* appeared, would not make the grade here either. His book in some ways bears the hallmarks of a parametric study, not the least in his justification for the films he has selected (including Bresson's and Mizoguchi's), films that "demand a type of critical activity not required of more standard cinema. . . . Purportedly outside the system, they teach us how to deal with them. This they do in the midst of our viewing them, or, more often, as we feel called to re-view them. The effort they demand of spectators to learn a new system, one suitable for a single film, places the film outside standard cinema where it may be either ignored or given special, even lasting, attention."[24] But the "aura" of Andrew's title is a giveaway of the zeal, the passion, he brings to what he is happy to call readings, interpretation, criticism: "Edification should be the result, the kind of edification each film in its singularity can offer, and that other kind of edification . . . [which] strives to bring to light the conditions, and method, by which meaning and significance come to us in our experience of the movies."[25] A Bordwellian parametric study, by contrast, views its object with deliberate dispassion: "In parametric cinema, the [plot] is subordinated to an immanent, *impersonal* stylistic pattern."[26] The analyst's role is to identify and map out this pattern—with rigor and detail, but also with similar impersonality.

Here is where, for me, Bordwellian neoformalism demonstrates a certain poverty of intent—it segments and analyses for the sake of it, determining how a film is structured, but with no "what for?" beyond indicating its degree of cognitive intelligibility—an intelligibility achieved *only* through close analysis. And in doing so reduction rather than inflation occurs, as Daniel Frampton has noted: "By *understanding* the genre of parametric narration Bordwell believes we can better appreciate these kinds of films—but in analysing typical art-cinema or parametric narratives Bordwell only seems to want to *rationalise* them. Radical cinema is reduced to *principles, systems*, all towards trying to bring artistic cinema into the *rational* fold of classic cinema. . . . How low-impact can you get, how . . . boring (in the face of such amazing films . . .)."[27] The parametric film text in such a method is assumed to be, and shown at the end to be, a closed circuit of exchanges with itself, exchanges that need not cohere into a unified meaning of any sort, and that at any rate certainly do not refer outside of itself, stylistically or historically. It simply exists.

Bordwell's neoformalist approach to the study of cinema has, alongside the "Historical Poetics" programmatics of the Madison School of which he played so integral a part, achieved a certain prominence in Anglo-American academic film studies, and he is unquestionably among the most bracingly knowledgeable and widely read figures of his and later generations. But curiously, parametrics—not only as a tag but also as an analytical method—has not been taken up with consistency or rigor by film scholars, Bordwellian or no, in the years since the publication of *Narration in the Fiction Film*.[28] To be sure, it has been glossed occasionally in other studies of cinematic narration. But in my research I have only been able to find three examples—all recent—that take up explicitly the very terms of Bordwell's work. One is a curious, self-published, online "book" (actually an extended essay) by Fatmir Terziu entitled *Parametric Narration in Norman Wisdom's Films*.[29] The second is an essay by Colin Burnett on Hou Hsiao-hsien's *The Flowers of Shanghai* (1998), to which I will return later. And the third offers a sustained engagement that stems directly from Bordwell's other work on art cinema: András Bálint Kovács's 2007 book *Screening Modernism: European Art Cinema, 1950–1980*. In addition to his concerted attention to art cinema's formal properties, Kovács in this study is presenting a historical argument, and one that I would put under some pressure: that while art cinema is alive today and "in Asia is probably more inventive and potent than it is in Europe" (no argument there), "modernist art cinema, as we have known it from the sixties, is gone. Modernism is film history now—and not because its inception dates back decades but primarily because today's art films are considerably different from those of the 1960s. . . . [L]ate modernism in the cinema was a universal aesthetic phenomenon but prevailed only in some films and only during a limited period of time."[30]

Bordwell was adamant not to call parametric cinema modernist, to the degree that he ends his chapter with a short section called "The Problem of Modernism"—the problem being that "we cannot posit any influence of" modernist movements in the other arts "upon all parametric films."[31] This strikes me as odd, insofar as he is here turning to extratextual predeterminants or influence as necessary for the ascription of the term "modernist" to the objects of study he has himself selected, "isolated filmmakers and fugitive films"—that is, privileged cases. Parametric narration for Bordwell thus exceeds modernism's grasp, and in any case modernism does not even sufficiently account for art cinema, so it is effectively evacuated from the book entirely. Kovács rightly identifies here "an ambiguity in Bordwell's system. . . . [it] is midway between technicality and historicity. It is historical because it not [*sic*] derived from an abstract categorical system that allows only a set number of cases. In other words, it is a historical taxonomy. But it is technical in the sense that Bordwell does not link any of his categories to historical contexts, and he leaves open the possibility for anyone to discover them in any period of film history." Kovács puts this ambiguity down to the fact that European modernism, at the time of *Narration in the Fiction Film*'s writing, was only just "fading away, and nothing was sure about its trajectory. Twenty years later the picture is clearer: modernism is over, and now we may assert with certainty that Bordwell's nonclassical narrative modes are all specific variations of what we can call modern narration, not one or the other but all of them together."[32]

On the one hand I consider Kovács's work as an advance: It opens up the possibility for a more widespread engagement with parametric narration than does Bordwell's, situating it under a term—modernism—that continues to have critical currency and does not jettison it from historical context. So to Bordwell's list can be added many films by directors that fall under a modernist purview, such as Antonioni, Jancsó, Tarkovsky, Akerman, and Angelopoulos—all exponents of a long-take aesthetic that could collectively be seen as a group (rather than unique) "norm," and one that in fact Kovács calls "analytical modernism." The benefit here is that such a widening of potential objects for study might disengage analysis of parametric narration from individual films and open it out to a consideration of a parametric cinema as a properly *historical* phenomenon, one embedded within (as opposed to distinct from) the extratextual. But on the other hand, Kovács's insistence on historicizing modernism as "over," and his situating its history solely within a European sphere of influence, is something I find highly arguable—indeed counterintuitive on the basis of what I am seeing with my eyes and hearing with my ears in much of contemporary art cinema. On this score Kovács needs to be quoted at some length:

> The question concerning the finished or unfinished character of modern cinema, in the final analysis, should be seen in the broader context of the modern and the postmodern. . . . [O]ne cannot disregard the historical moment when forms hitherto considered as mainstream, productive, rich, sustainable, or simply fashionable all of a sudden become obsolete, empty, and marginal in the eyes of the audience and the artists. . . . Even if many important films of the 1980s and 1990s have continued to use the stylistic and narrative solutions that modernism invented . . . during this period we encounter important aesthetic phenomena in mainstream filmmaking that are essentially uncommon to modernism. To mention but a few, I can point to the emphasis on the nonreal character of the

narrative (whereas one of modernism's main goals was the demystification of narrative fiction), narrative and stylistic heterogeneity (which is contrary to the purity of modernism), and intensification of emotional effects (as opposed to modernism's intellectual puritanism).[33]

Elsewhere in his book Kovács draws further distinctions between modernist and postmodernist cinema. But I cannot square up the latter, at least as it is characterized here, with a prominent sector of contemporary film festival–feted cinematic production that must be recognized as alternately "mainstream, productive, rich, sustainable, or simply fashionable" rather than "obsolete, empty, and marginal"—with, in fact, a modernism that seems quite healthy and hale.

The films and filmmakers practicing such modernism are not by any means all "beyond Europe," as noted in this essay's title. Award-winning and celebrated films of the last twenty years by Michael Haneke, Philippe Garrel, Bruno Dumont, Claire Denis, Jean-Pierre and Luc Dardenne, Pedro Costa, and Ulrich Seidl certainly display modernist styles and narration, and rarely if at all combine them with attendant postmodern features such as "nonreal character of the narrative," "narrative and stylistic heterogeneity," or "intensification of emotional effects." Indeed, many of these films display the elements necessary for Bordwell's more stringent categorization of parametric cinema, particularly the "sparse" approach. This is even more consistently the case for the Eastern Central European filmmakers Aleksandr Sokurov and Béla Tarr, the latter of whose *Sátántangó* (1994) and *Werckmeister Harmonies* (2000) are without question as difficult, as rigorous—and, I dare say, as transcendent—as anything Bresson or Dreyer rustled up for their audiences in the 1960s.[34] Confining myself only to European cinematic production of the past decade, I could easily triple Bordwell's shortlist of five "isolated" filmmakers and seven "fugitive" films, and herein lies a significant point: that three of the limitations he claims are inherent to the parametric mode no longer seem to apply, if indeed they ever did: that such narration is not a widespread filmmaking strategy; that its principles do not constitute a widespread viewing norm; and that the development of the "intrinsic stylistic norm" of a parametric film is unlikely to be perceivable in one cognitive sitting. In short, one cannot dismiss so easily the possibility that parametric narration has in fact settled in, and cinematic modernism extended over, the past two decades in such a way as to become not only widespread and perceivable, but also more recognizable, watchable, and marketable, than Bordwell in his formalism and Kovács his historicism would allow.

My move, then, "beyond Europe" is one that I must flag as being driven by an overriding interest not only in the preponderance of films and filmmakers that (not unproblematically) might be considered as engaging in their practices "elsewhere," but also in coming to terms with the *terms themselves* to be used to describe these practices in a *useful* (extrinsic) rather than merely categorical (intrinsic) way. In earlier work I considered the Malaysian-born, Taiwan-based filmmaker Tsai Ming-liang as a contemporary example and proponent of modernist aesthetics and was even then aware of how doing so could invoke a geo-aesthetic mapping like that undertaken by Fredric Jameson, whose characterization of a "belated emergence of modernism in the modernizing Third World, at a moment when the so-called advanced countries are themselves sinking into full postmodernity," persists as a danger.[35] I would insist that engaging with and characterizing a mode of contemporary cinematic production beyond Europe as modernist should not perforce bind it to the strictures of a historical or geographic stagism, but instead emphasize the degree to which *historical time* is *palimpsestic* and *dispersive* in all cultures, how aesthetic forms may be translated across cultures in multiple circuits of exchange and appropriation. I am not alone here: Janet Harbord and John Orr, among others, have argued for the continuing coexistence of modernist principles and production and postmodern cinematic culture, or for a "chronological inversion" of the very terms themselves, respectively.[36] I am therefore pressing for an investigation of a wide range of filmmakers and films circulating within the same orbit as Tsai, not simply aesthetically (or, in some cases, geographically), but also institutionally, within global art film culture and academic film studies.

The following have directed, some on occasion and others consistently over the past twenty years, films that constitute what I am calling a parametric tradition:

Lisandro Alonso (Argentina)
Idrissa Ouedraogo (Burkina Faso)
Wong Kar-wai (Hong Kong)
Abbas Kiarostami, Jafar Panahi, Samira Makhmalbaf (Iran)
Hirokazu Kore-eda, Aoyama Shinji (Japan)
Carlos Reygadas (Mexico)
Abderrahmane Sissako (Mauritania)
Chen Kaige, Tian Zhuangzhuang, Jia Zhangke (PRC)
Kim Ki-duk, Hong Sang-soo (South Korea)
Hou Hsiao-hsien, Tsai Ming-liang (Taiwan)
Apichatpong Weerasethakul (Thailand)
Nuri Bilge Ceylan (Turkey)

One way into such a list could be to consider in detail the acknowledged influence on the Asian filmmakers especially of Hou Hsiao-hsien, the only director to have been the subject of a properly parametric analysis. The impetus to think Hou's work as parametric derives in some part from the frequent comparisons between his filmmaking practice and that of Ozu, a comparison he initially underplayed and later embraced—his film *Café Lumière* (2003) being an explicit homage.[37] Odd, then, that Colin Burnett in his article "Parametric Narration and Optical Transition Devices: Hou Hsiao-hsien and Robert Bresson in Comparison" opts for Bresson as a precursor instead of Ozu—though on closer inspection not so strange, as Burnett uses Bordwell's extended analysis in *Narration in the Fiction Film* of Bresson's *Pickpocket* (1960) in order to elucidate the specificities of Hou's parametric style in *Flowers of Shanghai*, a film that "virtually imprisons its narrative in ascetic stylistic paradigms."[38] This article demonstrates without a doubt that the film is parametric, and as such goes some way toward puncturing the bubble that would limit such a practice to late modernism as a period and Europe as a geographic locus. But the terms of its analysis are Bordwellian to the letter, purely formal in scope, and as such evince a potential limitation of close analyses of individual films, if not my conception of a parametric tradition as a whole: inattention to geocultural context. This inattention, it must be emphasized, is not on the part of the film itself but, rather, the analysis.

Why must such attention be present, even in an analysis of a film's formal properties and strategies—for surely, other scholarly work on this and other films by the same director can or will perform this critical function? Because to isolate the formal as purely so, without taking thoughtful account of the generative mechanisms for it (and not simply, as in *Flowers of Shanghai*, the stylistic influence of Ozu), is to provide only a partial picture of not only *how* such formal operations work but also how for certain, and potentially different, *audiences*. In other words, the cognitive perceptions of these operations are not separable from the cultural codes available to the spectator— and it is here that the question of global versus local knowledges and histories comes to the fore. In the case of the Ozu/Hou comparison, Abe Mark Nornes and Yeh Yueh-yu proffer how easy it is "to cite a few general areas of overlap: minimalism, a predilection for unusual self-restraint and systematization, as well as a fascination for the graphic qualities of the image."[39] But if the basis for these shared similarities cannot be simply a shared formal paradigm that spans time and national culture, neither can it be characterized (and in some cases dismissed) as "pan-Asianism" or "Asian minimalism."[40] Given the range of filmmakers I have put forward as constituting this parametric tradition, to place this body of work under the lens of close textual analysis of either a purely formal or a slightly expanded auteurist or even national film cultural sort is not enough. But how to provide, to take account of and to analyze, the complex transnational negotiations that this tradition is engaged in its most salient contemporary form, in this sector of film production and reception?

Seeing these films as parametric, and undertaking close formal analyses of them, cannot accomplish this in itself—but it can uncover moments when such negotiations are taking place, a *situatedness* for cinematic modernism that can provide fresh fields to cultivate in our understanding of its history as well as of its abiding presence in contemporary art cinema. And this is why reclaiming parametrics is for me valuable, and for restoring to it something Burch noted in his initial proposal for it: "giving as important a place to the viewer's disorientation as to his orientation. And these are but two of the possible multiple dialectics that will form the very *substance* of the cinema of the future."[41] Having watched (and in many cases rewatched) these films for some time now, I am able to "crack" the parametric codes of them, formally speaking, with some facility and speed, and must honestly attest to the pleasures of such an activity. Wong Kar-wai's *In the Mood for Love* (2000), a well-known example, is built on a developing system of motifs, both aural and visual, that take male/female oppositions as structuring conceits:

She (Mrs. Chan)	*He (Mr. Chow)*
travel agency (transient, future)	journalist (fixed, present)

[similar instruments—typewriter/setter, phones—but hers are more modern]

movies (images, popular)	newspaper serials (words, literary)
cheongsam (China, nostalgia)	suits (the West, modernity)
handbags [fashion—bought by spouses]	ties
screen Left (her position, her flat)	screen Right (his position, his flat)
pans/dollies L–R (seated, noodle shop/diner)	pans/dollies R–L (seated, noodle shop/diner)
Mrs. Suen, L building	[landlords]Mr. Koo, R building

The L–R system marking screen space and camera movements for these two main characters visually breaks down when their roles as dutiful wife and husband to their respective spouses are thrown into question by their ineffable, inevitable slide into affection and desire—the code here being one of a notable, repeated, developed style, of course, but also one of social constraints subtending public displays of intimacy and decorum tied to the historical time and cultural place of their encounter. These breaks are accomplished in circumscribed ways. In their second diner scene one-third of the way into the film, the screen locations are at first as they "should be," inaugurated by an initial L–R dolly shot from behind and over the booth favoring her on-screen left and then a standard OTS shot favoring him on the right. But when she instructs him to order her meal for her, and they for the first time pretend to be a married couple according to this social contract, the camera setup shifts via a cut to a frontal mid-shot revealing their switched positions in the booth, or rather the ones they were already occupying but from another perspective—positions countering a heretofore accepted state of things between them now undergoing, and forestalled slightly by the camera's uncharacteristic delaying of the frontal staging of their relation, complication and development.

A stylistic pas de deux ensues from this point forward, with the code alternately breaking as the two continue to playact or otherwise depart from their socially sanctioned roles and duties, then reinstating itself as they reassume them. A climax (of sorts) is reached when, in a remarkable jump cut, Mrs. Chan relocates from screen left to right in the rear of a taxi en route to a rendezvous with Mr. Chow in hotel room 2046, the anticipation of their long-delayed romantic liaison visualized through an unprecedented break in the visual field.

Her subsequent way into and exit from the hotel, via a riot of jump cuts and hesitant *longeurs*, underscores the emotional turmoil, the societal weight, and the indeterminate outcome of this moment in their relationship. Importantly, what transpires in room 2046 on this night is never, stylistically or narratively—an admittedly false counterposition, given the present discussion, but one nonetheless tantalizingly suggested by the film—resolved. That this event (if it can be characterized as such) inaugurates the third act of the film is thus telling, from a structural point of view. For it provides an unsaid mystery

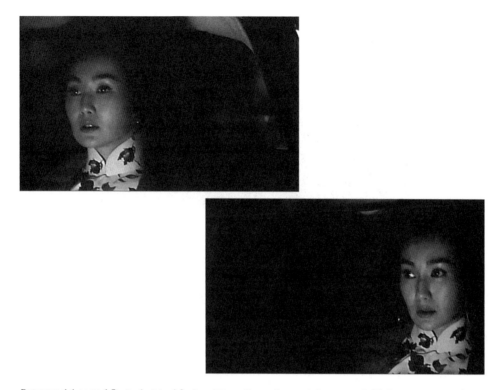

FIGURES 1.1 AND 1.2. *In the Mood for Love* (Wong Kar-wai, 2000). In a remarkable jump cut, Mrs. Chan (Maggie Cheung) relocates from screen left to right in the rear of a taxi.

that motivates *In the Mood for Love*'s finale. Set some years hence at the temple of Angkor Wat in Cambodia, the final sequence of the film witnesses Mr. Chow whispering his (and her?) secrets into a cavity in a wall that is then plugged with turf, so as to seal them for eternity. The unmotivated tracking shots of this concluding sequence are for me among the most resonant and affecting in contemporary cinema, particularly the final exterior shot as dusk falls on the temple, which tracks slowly from left to right. It is "her" shot: not only he but the film itself is maintaining, over and against their clear passion, a respectful distance and propriety regarding the question of their marital fidelity, achieved at the level of film style that, through its own logic, will not, cannot, declare their desire's memory.

The stately low-angle reverse tracking shots through the temple that precede this final one, taking in the worn bas-reliefs and details of the warm sandstone comprising the temple's interior and exterior architecture, recall the famous forward tracking shots that commence *Last Year at Marienbad*, moving across the vaulted ceilings, past the soaring pillars, through the grand entrances, and along the walls of mirrors of a European palace by turns baroque, rococo, and neoclassical in design and decoration. The wordlessness of *In the Mood for Love*'s closing is a tactful inversion of the incantatory, whisperingly relentless voiceover of *Last Year at Marienbad*'s opening, which describes "this structure of another century, this enormous, luxurious, baroque, lugubrious hotel, where corridors succeed endless corridors—silent deserted corridors overloaded with a dim, cold ornamentation of woodwork, stucco, moldings, marble, black mirrors, dark paintings, columns, heavy hangings, sculptured door frames, series of doorways,

FIGURE 1.3. The interior of Angkor Wat at the end of *In the Mood for Love*.

galleries, transverse corridors that open in turn on empty salons, rooms overloaded with an ornamentation from another century, silent halls. . . ." Unlike the unmistakable Angkor Wat, which grounds definitively *In the Mood for Love*'s conclusion in a specific place (and time—accomplished by the newsreel footage of French president Charles de Gaulle's 1966 visit that opens the film's finale), the setting of *Last Year at Marienbad* is indeterminate, a disorienting admixture of Nymphenburg Palace and its Amalienburg Hunting Lodge in Munich, Schleißheim Palace in Oberschleißheim, and Oranienburg Palace in the Brandenburg Marches, all of which stand in for a single hotel in a spa town located eighty miles west of Prague. The unity and restrained monumentality of Angkor Wat in *In the Mood for Love* stand in stark contrast to the incongruity and overwrought grandeur of *Marienbad*'s spaces.[42]

This clear referencing of the dispassionately parametric *Last Year at Marienbad*, the key work of postwar European cinematic modernism, invites reflection on not only the continuing influence of this particular film on contemporary art film practice but also how modernism as a whole continues to be inflected, with difference, beyond Europe. The distinct features, architectures, and histories of use of these films' settings and shooting locations—tied to disparate economies and legacies of capital and of spirit—are thrown into relief by the closing of *In the Mood for Love*, which entreats us in its discretion to recognize how our knowledge of aesthetic film history remains still so partial, how we have really only just begun to attend to questions of geography and culture from a more global perspective for our understanding of film style. Just as important, it discloses its foreignness through a parametric form that reserves, in the end, its mystery and transcendence.

NOTES

1. Jason McGrath, "The Independent Cinema of Jia Zhangke: From Postsocialist Realism to a Transnational Aesthetic," in *The Urban Generation: Chinese Cinema and Society at the Turn of the Twenty-First Century*, ed. Zhang Zhen (Durham, N.C.: Duke University Press, 2007), 102–103.

2. Azadeh Farahmand, "Perspectives on Recent (International Acclaim for) Iranian Cinema," in *The New Iranian Cinema: Politics, Representation and Identity*, ed. Richard Tapper (London: I. B. Tauris, 2003), 94.

3. Thomas Elsaesser, "European Cinema as World Cinema: A New Beginning?" in *European Cinema: Face to Face with Hollywood* (Amsterdam: Amsterdam University Press, 2005), 509.

4. I use the word "foreignness" here deliberately to reference a collection that explores the marks of filmic foreignness, the experience of feeling "outside and inside at the same time": *Subtitles: On the Foreignness of Film*, ed. Atom Egoyan and Ian Balfour (Cambridge, Mass.: MIT Press, 2004).

5. David Bordwell, *Narration in the Fiction Film* (Madison: University of Wisconsin Press, 1985).

6. Ibid., 274.

7. Ibid., 275; emphasis in original.

8. Ibid., 49.

9. Ibid., 50.

10. Ibid., 275.

11. Ibid.

12. Ibid., 278. See Noël Burch, *Theory of Film Practice*, trans. Helen R. Lane (Princeton, N.J.: Princeton University Press, 1973).

13. Bordwell reiterates this context in "The Return of Modernism: Noël Burch and the Oppositional Program," in his *On the History of Film Style* (Cambridge, Mass.: Harvard University Press, 1997); see especially 84–87, 90–94.

14. Ibid., 276.

15. Ibid., 281; emphasis in original.

16. Ibid., 285, 286.

17. Ibid.

18. On this point Burch is emphatic: "The contemporary film narrative is gradually liberating itself from the constraints of the literary or pseudo-literary forms that played a large part in bringing about the 'zero point of cinematic style' that reigned supreme during the 1930's and 1940's and still remains in a position of strength today. It is only through systematic and thorough exploration of the *structural* possibilities inherent in the cinematic parameters I have been describing that film will be liberated from the old narrative forms and develop new 'open' forms. . . . Film will attain its formal autonomy only when these new 'open' forms begin to be used organically" (*Theory of Film Practice*, 15).

19. Ibid., 289.

20. See Susan Sontag, *Against Interpretation and Other Essays* (New York: Dell, 1966).

21. Bordwell, *Narration in the Fiction Film*, 282, 289.

22. Ibid., 282–283.

23. Paul Schrader, *Transcendental Style in Film: Ozu, Bresson, Dreyer* (New York: Da Capo, 1972), 3.

24. Dudley Andrew, *Film in the Aura of Art* (Princeton, N.J.: Princeton University Press, 1984), 13, 6.

25. Ibid., 10.

26. Bordwell, *Narration in the Fiction Film*, 305; emphasis added.

27. Daniel Frampton, *Filmosophy* (London: Wallflower, 2006), 104–105; emphases in original.

28. An exception here, of course, is Kristin Thompson, whose book *Breaking the Glass Armor: Neoformalist Film Analysis* (Princeton, N.J.: Princeton University Press, 1988) appeared three years after her partner's and concluded with explicitly parametric

studies of films by Tati, Godard, Bresson, and Ozu. Another is Bordwell himself, whose *Figures Traced in Light: On Cinematic Staging* (Berkeley: University of California Press, 2005) examines in depth the work of four filmmakers—Louis Feuillade, Mizoguchi, Angelopoulos, and Hou Hsiao-hsien—who are understood as working in a "staging-centered tradition" (9); for my purposes here, it is key to recognize how the term "parametric" is nowhere to be found among the analyses.

29. Fatmir Terziu, *Parametric Narration in Norman Wisdom's Films* (2007), available at http://www.lulu.com/content/917359. I have not seen enough of these films to comment definitively, but Wisdom does not strike me as a particularly profitable figure for a parametric study—though physical comedy of this period is not necessarily a de facto exempt object, as the evidence of Tati in Bordwell (and Thompson) attests. Lisa Trahair draws attention to the potential for cinematic comedy to function parametrically in "Short-Circuiting the Dialectic: Narrative and Slapstick in the Cinema of Buster Keaton," *Narrative* 10, no. 3 (2002): 307–325. And I think the films of the American comedian Jerry Lewis could usefully bear scrutiny on this front as well.

30. András Bálint Kovács, *Screening Modernism: European Art Cinema, 1950–1980* (Chicago: University of Chicago Press, 2007), 2–3.

31. Bordwell, *Narration in the Fiction Film*, 310.

32. Kovács, *Screening Modernism*, 58, 59.

33. Ibid., 47–48.

34. Not yet having seen any of the films directed by the Kazakh Darezhan Omirbayev, the Lithuanian Sharunas Bartas, or the Hungarian/German Fred Keleman, I must cite them here as candidates for future research. I note as well that a "deadpan," humor-tinged parametric style is to be divined in the films of Aki Kaurismäki (Finland), Roy Andersson (Sweden), and Kitano Takeshi (Japan), as well as in the work of several American filmmakers drawing from and extending such a line of influence: Jim Jarmusch, David Lynch, Hal Hartley, Harmony Korine, and Gus Van Sant.

35. See my "The Cinema of Tsai Ming-liang: A Modernist Genealogy," in *Reading Chinese Transnationalisms: Society, Literature, Film*, ed. Maria N. Ng and Philip Holden (Hong Kong: University of Hong Kong Press, 2006), 161–172. The Jameson quotation is from *The Geopolitical Aesthetic: Cinema and Space in the World System* (Bloomington: Indiana University Press, 1995), 1. For a recent example of this tendency, see Elsaesser, "European Cinema as World Cinema," 495–499.

36. See Janet Harbord, *Film Cultures* (London: Sage, 2002), 38–58, and John Orr, "New Directions in European Cinema," in *European Cinema*, ed. Elizabeth Ezra (Oxford: Oxford University Press, 2004), 299–317.

37. See for example Gary Needham, "Ozu and the Colonial Encounter in Hou Hsiao-Hsien," in *Asian Cinemas: A Reader and Guide*, ed. Dimitris Eleftheriotis and Gary Needham (Ediburgh: Edinburgh University Press, 2006), 369–383. Abbas Kiarostami's *Five Dedicated to Ozu* (2003) is another, more radical, tribute.

38. Colin Burnett, "Parametric Narration and Optical Transition Devices: Hou Hsiao-hsien and Robert Bresson in Comparison," *Senses of Cinema* 33 (Oct.–Dec. 2004), available at http://archive.sensesofcinema.com/contents/04/33/hou_hsiao_hsien_bresson.html.

39. Abe Mark Nornes and Yeh Yueh-yu, "Ozu & Hou: Introduction" (1998), available at http://cinemaspace.berkeley.edu/Papers/CityOfSadness/ozu.html.

40. On pan-Asianism, see James Udden, "The Future of a Luminescent Cloud: Recent Developments in a Pan-Asian Style, *Synoptique* 10 (1 Aug. 2005), available at http://www.synoptique.ca/core/en/articles/udden_cloud/; on Asian minimalism, see Bordwell, "Hou, or Constraints," in *Figures Traced in Light*, esp. 230–237.

41. Burch, *Theory of Film Practice*, 15; emphasis in original.

42. I am aware that some of the scenes for the 1962 Hong Kong–set portions of *In the Mood for Love* were shot in Bangkok, and as such this film too "floats" geographically, but this is not contrary to my point: that the Angkor Wat coda calls attention to location and locale in such a way as to make us attend to its significance in all that we have witnessed, and thought we had known, prior to it.

2

THE FANTASTIC TRAJECTORY OF PINK ART CINEMA FROM STALIN TO BUSH

Sharon Hayashi

What can two exceptionally wry and oddly political Japanese pink films made forty years apart tell us about how global art cinema is constructed as a category? Both *Kabe no naka no himegoto* / *Secrets behind the Wall* (Koji Wakamatsu, 1965) and *Hanai Sachiko no karei na shogai* / *The Glamorous Life of Sachiko Hanai* (Mitsuru Meike, 2004) were originally distributed as sex films in Japan but crossed over into the global category of art cinema on the international film festival circuit. Through an analysis of these two films and how they have been framed and reframed in global and local contexts, this essay will explore the filmic and critical practices that created a pink art cinema. The first of these films, *Secrets behind the Wall*, crossed genres almost by accident, due to the desires of an international art film circuit eager to read Japanese film in art cinematic terms, and against the protests of an angered Japanese film establishment. Consequently, Japanese producers began the strategic marketing and distribution of some pink films as art cinema. But even these later films, including *The Glamorous Life of Sachiko Hanai*, could be launched into unintended international careers.

The aim of this essay is not to canonize pink cinema as art cinema. These two films are hardly representative of the more than 5,000 pink films produced in Japan since 1962. Rather, my goal is to look at the ways in which pink art cinema poses a problem for accepted film categories. Film genre scholar Alexander Zahlten has persuasively argued that pink films must be understood as a historically evolving genre of a national film industry.[1] In tracing the global trajectory of pink films, this essay will show how geographical displacement can trouble accepted categories of "art film" and "sex film." The happenstance entry of *Secrets behind the Wall* into the foreign context of the Berlin International Film Festival in 1965 changed its genre-bound status and made it into a symbol of national culture, to the chagrin of Japanese authorities and producers. Forty years later, screenings of *The Glamorous Life of Sachiko Hanai* at more than twenty-five international film festivals specializing in art, independent, experimental, and fantasy films, including the Udine Far East Film Festival, the Vienna International Film Festival, the San Francisco International Film Festival, and the Montreal Fantasia Film Festival, signaled the malleability of pink cinema, allowing it to be framed for specific purposes and demographics that no longer fit into earlier models of national mass consumption or international high art.[2] Thus, at the Frankfurt Nippon Connection Festival in 2005 the film was presented in the idiom of a subcultural, pop, and fantastic Japan, but in 2008 it was shown at a festival in Seoul devoted to reclaiming pink film as an erotic cinema for women.

Pink film occupies a marginalized position in the Japanese film industry despite the fact that it accounts for a third of the yearly output of Japanese films and has provided a training ground for many of Japan's most successful directors. Although they have evolved since their inception in 1962, pink films are generally recognized today as erotic films produced by independent production companies for specialized sex film theaters across Japan. They usually contain five to seven sex scenes and clock in at around sixty to seventy minutes long in order to fit into the lunch hour of the mostly male office worker clientele. No comparable sex film industry exists elsewhere.[3] However, the particular model of pink film production is not due to any intrinsically Japanese notion of sexuality but arises out of the specific historical configuration and collapse of the Japanese postwar film industry. When major film studios were no longer able to meet their own production quotas of erotic fare, independent film companies formed to produce erotic films to fill the screens of exhibitors. Pink film production was an early form of outsourcing that provided the soft-core software needed for the hardware of film theaters. The low-budget pink films were produced quickly, to be shown outside of the mainstream venues of exhibition. This provided the opportunity for a few interested filmmakers to use their pink films to make ironic political commentaries on the contemporary social situation.

THE EROTIC IMPERATIVE OF JOSEPH STALIN

Secrets behind the Wall was an *eroduction*—the contemporary term for films that revealed flesh to titillate—that was also a stunningly violent critique of postwar Japan, charting the disillusionment and betrayal of love and ideals after the failure of the Japanese student movement in 1960. The film opens with two lovers from the movement reunited several years later whose political and sexual desires remain fused to an earlier moment of passionate political struggle. In the opening scene of the film, the naked lovers caress in front of a portrait of Stalin in a bleak public housing complex in Tokyo. Stalin's presence in the bedroom underlines the impossibility of delineating a space of intimacy or desire outside the political. Nobuko injects Toshio's scarred shoulder with steroids and passionately cries, "You're the symbol of Japan, the symbol of Hiroshima, the symbol of the anti-war struggle. As long as I love you, I'll never forget the war, I hate war and will fight for peace." This scene foregrounds Toshio's scarred flesh as a complex allegory for Japan.

While another scandalous pink film released the same year, *Kuroi yuki / Black Snow* (Testuji Takechi, 1965), employed a naked woman running alongside the fence of a U.S. military base to symbolize the occupation of Japan by U.S. forces in a more conventionally familiarized way, in *Secrets behind the Wall* the woman does not represent a suffering Japan. Instead, the object of her desire is the symbol of a wounded Japan and Hiroshima. As Nobuko nurses and lovingly caresses Toshio's scarred shoulder, he chastises her for living in the past and being so obsessed by his keloidal skin. Only the past, however, can ignite her pleasure in the present. Living in the cramped confines of a public housing complex with her estranged husband, Nobuko only finds passion when reunited with her old lover from her student days of political activism. "It is the keloid that joins us," she insists to Toshio, signaling how the desire to fight and to love is irrevocably intertwined with his wounded body. The couple declares their love eternal, like the radiation that courses through his body. As she makes love to Toshio, images of the atomic bomb and the explosive protests against the renewal of the U.S.-Japan Security Treaty are superimposed over her face. Hiroshima and the student protests literally explode within Nobuko. Her ecstasy triggers nostalgia for an earlier moment of political conviction.

In 1960 protests against the renewal of the U.S.-Japan Security Treaty brought together student and labor organizations, peace activists, and citizens' groups in the largest political protest movement in Japan's postwar history. More than 16 million people opposed to the remilitarization of Japan and the restrictions on Japanese sovereignty imposed by the security treaty signed petitions, held strikes, and demonstrated in the streets outside of parliament.[4] The student movement coalescing around these protests provided new leadership and direction for the Japanese Left largely replacing the Japan Communist party and Japan Socialist party, whose ideological directives and suppression of alternate views were seen as outdated. Although the Japan Communist party adamantly opposed the possession of nuclear weapons by the Soviet Union and had split with Moscow over Stalin's support of nuclear armament, the suppression of the Hungarian revolution by Soviet troops in 1956 and the revelations that same year of Stalin's Great Purge left many leftists disillusioned with the Soviet Union. Stalin became a symbol of betrayal.

FIGURE 2.1. *Secrets behind the Wall* (Wakamatsu, 1965).

In a flashback to their student years when Toshio and Nobuko first became lovers, Stalin makes a second appearance, but the composition of the scene is reversed. This time it is Toshio who injects Nobuko with steroids, as she lies in bed under the watchful gaze of a portrait of Stalin. In an extreme gesture of devotion to both her lover and the peace movement, Nobuko has just had herself sterilized. She justifies this drastic measure by telling her lover that a child might "interfere" with their struggle for peace and that she had been told that victims of radiation like Toshio should not have children. She is jolted back into the bleak reality of the present when she overhears Toshio's telephone conversation with his stockbroker. In a complete betrayal of the peace movement and their love, Toshio has invested in Japanese industries profiting from the Vietnam War. The transformation of her lover from antiwar symbol to wartime profiteer exposes the fragility of antiwar ideals in a capitalist market propped up by the war industry. Nobuko sacrificed her body for a man, for a cause, and for a nation, only to realize that she had been betrayed by all three.

Echoing social debates of the time, *Secrets behind the Wall* deploys bodies as contested sites of political discourse. One year before *Secrets behind the Wall* was made, the 1964 Tokyo Olympics was seized on as an opportunity to showcase Japan's phenomenal postwar recovery. As the city was razed to create a modern stage for the games, memories of the war were sanitized. To prove Japan's miraculous recovery, an athlete born on August 6, 1945, the day the nuclear bomb was dropped on Hiroshima, was chosen as a torchbearer of the Olympic flame. Although born only seventy miles away from the epicenter of the bomb, Atom Boy—as he was nicknamed—possessed a perfect athletic body that symbolized Japan's miraculous phoenix-like recovery from the devastation of World War II.[5] *Secrets behind the Wall* contests Japan's postwar recovery symbolized by the perfect body of Atom Boy, by presenting damaged bodies written out of this official history. Toshio's scarred flesh acts as a reminder of the continued effects of radiation from the atomic bombs dropped on Hiroshima and Nagasaki in 1945. The film does not fall into a purely heroic narrative of the student movement but outlines a counternarrative marked by serial political and personal disillusionment. Following Stalin's betrayal of the ideals of socialism, Toshio embraces capitalism at the expense of his student movement ideals.

Similarly, Nobuko's sterility is attributed to an overzealous devotion to a political movement. Although the operation is self-imposed, it is suggestive of the gendered sacrifices made for the student movement. On a metaphorical level, Nobuko's sterile body invokes the sanitized space of Tokyo, razed for the 1964 Olympics. Rather than showcasing the public architecture of Olympic stadiums and newly built expressways, *Secrets behind the Wall* exposes alienated life in the cramped quarters of a drab public housing complex. To escape the futility and despair of everyday life, residents turn to suicide or violence. Under the enormous pressure of prepping for competitive university entrance exams, a frustrated high school graduate sexually assaults Nobuko before stabbing her to death at the end of the film. Nobuko is a casualty of Japan's competitive postwar society where sexual violence and political disillusionment collide.

How did such a violent pink film end up representing Japan at an international film festival? A West German distributor who had bought *Secrets behind the Wall* proposed it to the 1965 Berlin International Film Festival when all of the official recommendations by the Japanese Film Producers Association were rejected.[6] Faced with the prospect of not having any Japanese representation, the festival quickly accepted and included the film as the official Japanese competition entry without the knowledge of either the director or producer. The selection of a Japanese pink film to represent the country was met with outrage by the Japanese Film Producers Association, whose control of Japanese film exports and power over determining the meaning of "Japanese film" abroad had been completely undermined. Coming only a year after the carefully managed staging of the spectacle of the 1964 Tokyo Olympics that showcased Japan's progress and modernity, the selection of *Secrets behind the Wall* to represent Japan in the film festival was deemed a "national disgrace." The Japanese General Consul, acting on orders from the Japanese Ministry of Foreign Affairs, denounced the festival's decision to show the film as regrettable, seeing it as an action that could jeopardize Japanese-German relations.

Using detailed research on the reception of the film in both Germany and Japan, film historian Roland Domenig has shown that for both the Japanese Film Producers Association and the Japanese government the trouble with the film was not simply that it was a low-budget eroduction but that it promoted a "false image" of Japan and failed to adopt the official narration of national unity. The film presented a complex critique of postwar Japanese urban modernity and the violence inspired by alienated living conditions in contemporary Japan that was at odds with the Japanese state's narrative of progress and harmony. Unlike the perfectly sculpted body of the dedicated athlete chosen to be the torchbearer for the Olympics and the perfectly staged landscape of Tokyo in 1964, Toshio was both physically scarred and morally flawed. His actions implicated both the rising phoenix of the Japanese economy (built on Japanese aid to U.S. wars in Asia) while simultaneously disallowing Japan the opportunity to play the role of innocent victim, using Hiroshima as a convenient way to forget its own aggression in Asia during World War II. Although the film's "false image" of Japan was a point of concern, it received a muted public rebuttal. Instead, according to Domenig, the film's sexual explicitness was taken as an excuse to write it off and ignore its content.

Hosting the first Olympic games ever held in Asia allowed Japan to imagine itself as the leader of the Asian nations and fulfilled Japan's dream of finally being accepted into an international community of modern Westernized nations.[7] Since the nation's entrance into the arena of international diplomacy in 1868, Japan largely internalized Western values and sought to catch up to the West. To become a modern nation, Japan had to invent traditions that simultaneously played on Western and Japanese fantasies of Japanese practices and aesthetics. In the postwar period Japanese historical dramas that provided the requisite exoticism for foreign film festival audiences often met with festival success. Akira Kurosawa's *Rashomon* (1950) was awarded the Golden Lion at the 1951 Venice Film Festival. Kenji Mizoguchi received two Silver Lions in succeeding years for *Ugetsu Monogatari / Tales of Ugetsu* (1953) and *Sansho Dayu / Sansho the Bailiff* (1954). Realizing the success of these historical dramas, the Japanese Film Producers Association continued to submit works to film festivals that appealed to foreign notions of Japaneseness. In 1963 the Japanese Film Producers Association entered

Tadashi Imai's *Bushido zangoku monogatari / Bushido* (1963) into the Berlin Film Festival, where it won the prestigious Golden Bear. Although Imai's film about samurai loyalty to the master in the tumultuous period of transition from the Edo to the Meiji periods was not necessarily made with the intention of exoticizing Japan, the international title, *Cruel Story of the Samurai's Way*, captures the gist of what attracted many foreign audiences to the film—the fascination with Japanese martial arts and samurai warrior codes.[8] The entry of this historical drama into the festival was not naive. Throughout the twentieth century the Japanese government and artists alike have participated in the construction and presentation of an exotic Japan that appeals to foreign audiences, efforts that work in conjunction with modern nationalist attempts to promote fantasies of Japan's past. Both the Olympic games and international film festivals in the 1960s appealed to universal standards but revealed the contradictions of competing temporal models of national culture.

The Berlin Film Festival's inclusion of *Secrets behind the Wall* was in line with the other contemporary social critiques in the competition that year, including Jean-Luc Godard's *Alphaville* (1965), recipient of the Golden Bear, Roman Polanski's *Repulsion* (1965), and Jean-Marie Straub's *Nicht versöhnt / Not Reconciled* (1964).[9] The director Koji Wakamatsu and his collaborators took advantage of the relative freedom of and available funding for the pink genre to create a devastatingly violent and critical film that engaged with contemporary social issues. The selection of this film, which reflected the anxieties of modern life in Japan, could only have happened when the centralized control of the Japanese Film Producers Association was circumvented. As an organization representing the interests of the five major studios in Japan, the Japanese Film Producers Association would have never considered a low-budget sex film like *Secrets behind the Wall* produced by an independent pink company for entry into an international film festival. While the majority of major studios produced or exhibited erotic fare to keep up attendance figures, pink films were not considered appropriate for international consumption.

Nationalist outrage against pink films being shown at foreign sex film theaters was equally vehement. Producer Nagamasa Kawakita argued that Japanese film would become synonymous with cheap eroductions, making it difficult to distribute "serious" Japanese films abroad. He also warned, somewhat presciently, that once eroductions were exported they would circulate everywhere. The entry of *Secrets behind the Wall* in the Berlin Film Festival initiated the simultaneous distribution of pink films abroad at both film festivals and in sex film theaters. According to the 1969 records of the Japanese Film Producers Association, the export of pink films that began with *Secrets behind the Wall* in 1965 rose to 30–40 eroductions per year. Pink films sent to the United States were shown in Los Angeles, New York, Chicago, and Okinawa, which was still a U.S. territory at the time. Many found their way to places as diverse as Mexico, Venezuela, Columbia, Brazil, Peru, Singapore, Thailand, and Hong Kong.[10] In Europe, pink films were distributed mainly through West Germany and played on the sex film circuit in Holland, Sweden, Denmark, Luxembourg, Switzerland, Spain, and the United Kingdom until 1968, when they were largely replaced by more local and more hard-core West German productions.[11]

THE PINK AKIRA KUROSAWA

Although the screening of *Secrets behind the Wall* at the fifteenth Berlin International Film Festival set off a furor over national representation, the major consequence of the scandal surrounding the screening was not national controversy but an international notoriety that secured popularity at home for director Koji Wakamatsu. Wakamatsu had nothing to do with his film's entry into the festival, but he deftly channeled the infamy produced by the event into the establishment of his own pink production company and capitalized on every succeeding scandal provoked by the company's productions. When *Taiji ga mitsuryo suru toki / The Embryo Hunts in Secret* (Wakamatsu, 1966) was shown at the Brussels Film Festival a year later, in 1966, students from the University of Berlin tried to disrupt the screening to protest its fascist representation of the rape of a woman.[12] When three prints of *The Embryo Hunts in Secret* were released in France in 2007 it again raised censorship issues when the film was banned to audiences age eighteen and under despite not being classified as pornographic or given an X rating.[13] The international reaction to his films has allowed Wakamatsu to position himself as a heroic sexual liberator and critic of Japanese state authority. His role as executive producer of Nagisa Oshima's *Ai no Corrida / In the Realm of the Senses* (1976) cemented his image as a sexual revolutionary. When the film had to be sent to France to be developed and edited in order to circumvent Japanese obscenity laws, it triggered censorship and obscenity debates that the director and producer exploited.

Wakamatsu's collaboration with renowned directors like Oshima points to the overlap between filmmakers in the pink cinema and "art cinema" worlds since the late 1960s. Wakamatsu's production company gathered together talented filmmakers from the erotic film stables of mainstream studios such as the highly artistic Nikkatsu Studio's Roman Porno group and members of the urban intelligentsia. Their stylized films contained exhortations to revolutionary violence, political allegory, and pronouncements of sexual liberation that appealed to students and the urban avant-garde.[14] While Wakamatsu productions were at first funded by distribution to major studios to fill their rosters of erotic cinema programs and then later distributed directly to specialized pink theater chains, the films also found a secondary audience at alternative venues such as the Art Theatre Guild, which helped fund Oshima's first independent film. Wakamatsu carefully cultivated diverse audiences both within Japan and abroad, taking advantage of the geographic and cultural displacement of his globally distributed films. His nickname, the "Pink Akira Kurosawa," attests to his aspirations of being an internationally recognized "auteur" and speaks to the status and authority that he enjoys as a former director of the Japanese Film Directors Association.

Wakamatsu's success at creating the Wakamatsu Production brand has been largely dependent on his ability to control his own narrative, elaborated by his self-celebratory autobiography and the publication of essays from an international conference about Wakamatsu Production.[15] He has shrewdly preserved prints of his films in order to leave a body of work that can be studied. Generally, fewer prints of films are struck in Japan, even for major releases, with the number being even lower for pink films. Most of the 5,000-plus pink films made in Japan are no longer extant or in viewable condition. Although the National Film Center possesses some pink films, they do not make their holdings publicly available, fearing criticism of using taxpayer money to preserve sex films. Wakamatsu also kept the rights to his films, which he has rereleased multiple times on video, through art-house and other labels, and most recently in high-end DVD box sets though the established Kinokuniya bookstore chain. A self-proclaimed hero of revolutionary pink film, Wakamatsu strategically constructed his image through the careful management of films and his audiences. He has also benefited from the desire of European cultural institutions to read Japanese cinema as art cinema. In 2006 Wakamatsu was invited to screen his work at the Cinémathèque Française in Paris, fulfilling his auteurist role as the Pink Akira Kurosawa.

PINK NOUVELLE VAGUE

The same strategy of appealing to diverse audiences was resurrected in the early 1990s by the pink production house Kokuei. Instead of the highly individualistic Pink Akira Kurosawa's "cult of personality" model, however, Kokuei's crossover from pink cinema to the art-house circuit was a movement by four directors that emphasized the artistic rather than political or sexual freedom of the pink film industry. Extremely varied in the style and subject matter of their films, Takahisa Zeze, Hisayasu Sato, Toshiki Sato, and Kazuhiro Sano repeatedly portrayed themselves as "auteurs" working within the constraints of an independent production company rather than the studio system. They replaced Wakamatsu's revolutionary discourse of sexual liberation with an auteurist framework that emphasized artistic freedom despite the generic dictates of pink film such as sex-scene quotas. Sex is by no means normalized or depoliticized in their works, many of which share the dark sexual and political themes of Wakamatsu's earlier productions. Indeed, this impetus led many customers to complain and critics to coin them the "Four Devils." Looking for new venues in which to show their work, with the help of their adventurous and influential producer, Keiko Sato, the directors strategically planned their crossover into the art-house circuit. In 1993 the directors participated in the New Japanese Auteurs Series (*Shin nihon sakkashugi retsuden*) at the Athénée Français in Tokyo. While continuing to make films for pink theaters, the directors also screened their work at the repertory houses and mini-theatres that had begun proliferating in Tokyo in the mid-1980s and whose audiences were composed increasingly of young working women with disposable incomes interested in art cinema.

While they are known even today as the Four Devils, the single monograph in Japanese devoted to the group is entitled *Pink Nouvelle Vague* (*pinku nuberu bagu*), a reference to both the French New Wave (*La Nouvelle Vague*) and the Shochiku New Wave (*Shochiku nuberu bagu*) movements.[16] If the term *Pink Akira Kurosawa* invoked the master director of the Japanese golden age film of the 1950s, the use of *nouvelle vague* to describe the work of the Four Devils plays on the cultural capital of the foreign and attempts to foreground their films not simply as a new wave within the pink film industry but one that reaches beyond the confines of the Japanese film industry and puts their work on par with global film movements.[17]

In 1995 the Four Devils began presenting their films internationally, first in Rotterdam and Vienna. Larger retrospectives of pink films featuring many of their films were held in Rotterdam in 1997, then Hong Kong and Udine, Italy, in 2002. In the mid-1990s the directors framed their work as serious art cinema made in the context of the pink film genre. They often discussed how low-budget pink films provided them a space for experimentation and creativity that had served as a training ground for directors like Kiyoshi Kurosawa and Masayuki Suo. Their films were part of the revitalization of the Japanese cinema in the 1990s led by directors like Takeshi Kitano, Junji Sakamoto and Shinya Tsukamoto, Hirokazu Koreeda, Shinji Aoyama, and Naomi Kawase, whose success at international film festivals provided a model for them to send their films abroad.

Yet the rise of a more conventional independently produced art cinema necessitated a reformulation of pink art cinema. While pink directors continued to frame their work in auteurist terms at mini-theatres and arthouses, they also began to stage pink film events inspired by more popular forms of culture. In 2000, in an ode to the live performances that accompanied screenings of pink films on tour in the 1970s and underground film happenings at the Shinjuku Art Theatre Guild, pink production houses staged the P-1 Grand-Prix. Inspired by professional wrestling matches, the Grand-Prix pitted the films of directors from different generations and different production houses against each other. Judges drawn from the editorial ranks of pink fan magazines, film critics, and even pink film luminaries like Wakamatsu ranked the films. Fights were staged between directors that emphasized their generational and conceptual differences. The raucous early-cinema-like spectacles of these events created a much more participatory viewing space that also brought different film-viewing communities together. With the mix of high and low and the addition of a new generation of pink film directors, the internationalist Pink Nouvelle Vague was now replaced by the much more amorphous term *J-Pink*.[18] Like its counterparts J-pop music, J-League baseball, or J-Lit, the *J* of J-Pink invokes both popular culture made in Japan but without the connotation of nationalism or national boundaries that Japanese suggests. In contrast to the internationalist term Nouvelle Vague, J-Pink doesn't play on the cultural capital of the foreign but suggests how films made in Japan, such as J-Horror, are embedded in the network of a global marketplace that routinely exceeds national audiences.

J-PINK AND NAUGHTY MR. PRESIDENT BUSH

In 2004 it was no longer surprising that a film like Mitsuru Meike's *The Glamorous Life of Sachiko Hanai* would be screened at international festivals and could capture multiple cult followings among widely divergent demographic groups. The film premiered at the Athénée Français in Tokyo in 2004 as part of the New School of Pink Film series before being shown at more than twenty-five international film festivals. It was broadcast on the European channel ARTE, opened at the Cinema Village in New York, and was released on DVD both in Japan and in the United States. *The Glamorous*

FIGURE 2.2. *The Glamorous Life of Sachiko Hanai* (Meike, 2004).

Life of Sachiko Hanai is a ninety-minute director's cut of a film circulated to pink theaters in Japan in 2003 under the title of *Hatsujo kateikyoshi: sensei no aijiru / Horny Home Tutor: Teacher's Love Juice* (Meike, 2003).[19] Originally commissioned to fit the subgenre of home tutor sex films, the final version of the spy thriller script was written during the U.S.-U.K. invasion of Iraq. If *Secrets behind the Wall* used the solemn appearance of Stalin to question official narratives of Japanese postwar recovery, *The Glamorous Life of Sachiko Hanai* (whose title is cribbed from the Sheila E. song "The Glamorous Life") uses ironic humor to chastise former U.S. president George W. Bush's global reach.

Sachiko Hanai is a hostess at a sex club, where she acts out the sexual fantasies of customers in mundane settings. In the opening scene she plays a home tutor whose satisfied customer tells her that if she had been his home tutor when he was in high school, he would have gotten into college. What begins as a mere role-playing fantasy turns into Sachiko's fantastic reality. She unwittingly stumbles upon and disrupts an international conspiracy to destroy the United States by carrying away a lipstick container housing a replica of George Bush's finger. During the melee she is struck in the head by a stray bullet that lodges deeply into her brain and suddenly turns her into a mind-reading, speed-reading genius able to predict the future. The mental overload of genius takes a toll on her tactile senses, however, so that she can no longer enjoy the simultaneity of sensual experiences. She can only taste food after she has finished eating. While having sex with a professor her faculties are so focused on a discussion about Noam Chomsky's worldview that she only feels the physical pleasure of the act hours later. The operating temporality of Sachiko's new state is one of deferral.

When she releases the replica of George Bush's finger from its lipstick case container, it dives between her legs. Operated remotely by a virtual image of its owner on a television monitor, the finger insists, "I'm the champion of justice and truth. I demand to have you inspected. I'm not waiting for the UN's decisions. I've got you, Sachiko. I'm going in deep." Bush's television talking head continues, "Once I'm inside of you, you can never escape from me. This is the Bush technique. I found the G Spot." As Bush's cloned finger explores the inner recesses of Sachiko's body, his voice returns, "The terrorists are hiding in a cave. You are always being watched. God Bless America." Initially the scene suggests a simple comparison of Bush's sexual attack on Sachiko with the U.S.-U.K. invasion of Iraq. Images of newspaper articles announcing the "Large-scale air raid in Iraq" and "Shock and awe! U.S. and U.K. attack Iraq" are followed by the coverage of the toppling of Saddam Hussein's statue and Bush's "mission accomplished" speech aboard an aircraft carrier.

As the images shift to a ghost of a murdered agent and the remote-controlled device that Sachiko will later use to set off American intercontinental ballistic missiles (ICBMs) that will end the world, the sequence breaks out of a simple political allegory of U.S. aggression that equates Iraq with Sachiko. Instead, the images are Sachiko's visions of the future, inspired by George Bush's touch. Rather than the delayed sensations she experiences from sex and eating, George Bush's replicant touch overwhelms her in the present, causing her to imagine the future. The North Korean agent who has been pursuing her throughout the film has an epiphany and decides to cooperate with Sachiko. We are given a glimpse of what their deferred utopia might be like as they imagine themselves sitting on a sandy beach enjoying a beer in a united North and South Korea.

In a parody of American exceptionalism, Bush contends that his "finger determines the world's destiny." Sachiko, however, takes control of Bush's wayward member, puts it back in its lipstick holster, and unsheathes it only when she discovers a Russian-made detonator that can set off ICBMs directed at America. After Sachiko destroys the world, she appears floating in space singing the U.S. national anthem in translation in breathy Japanese à la Marilyn Monroe. She handily puts the Earth into the bullet hole in her forehead, showing George Bush once and for all what global power really means.

Fantasy here operates as liberation from the historical present. Rather than Sachiko's body being the receptacle of historical forces beyond her control (as in the scarred body of Toshio in *Secrets behind the Wall*), her carnal brain determines the future of the world. While *Secrets behind the Wall* uses the universal symbol of Stalin to reflect on the end of utopias and the grim reality of Japan's failed postwar, *The Glamorous Life of Sachiko Hanai* deploys images and replicas of George Bush to suggest a fantastic outcome of the Iraq War.

Forty years after *Secrets behind the Wall* unwittingly found its way to the Berlin Film Festival, *The Glamorous Life of Sachiko Hanai* was first shown overseas in 2005 at the Nippon Connection Festival in Frankfurt, where pink film screenings have been collaboratively orchestrated by festival programmers and the pink film production house Kokuei to appeal to subculture fans.[20] This has taken place through both the selection and renaming of the films for the festival. Pink films circulated domestically in Japan often have three titles—the release title in sex theaters that often suggests the subgenre of film, the title used when the film is recycled as part of a triple bill after its original release, and the director's title, which is used if the film is screened in arthouse venues or released on arty DVD labels. The English titles of pink films shown at the festival have often been crafted with the specific audience of Nippon Connection in mind. Examples such as *Himo no Hiroshi / The Strange Saga of Hiroshi the Freeloading*

Sex Machine (Tajiri, 2005) cultivate a "harmlessly strange, interesting, stimulating and pop-cultural tone" compatible with the festival. Additionally, in order to appeal to the "non-committal, pop-cultural reception context" of the festival, Nippon Connection has strategically shied away from realism and chosen pink films that portray an "obviated fantasy." The fantastic nature of the pink films shown at the festival helps to regulate sex scenes that tend to be more jarring and less pop in more quotidian pink narratives. While the festival still plays on certain fantasies of Japan, it chooses fantastic pink films that suggest a kind of "desexualized sexuality."[21] The thematic color of the festival's graphics is pink. While the term *pink film* was initially coined to distinguish the genre from illicit hard-core "blue films," the "pink" in pink films is now equated with the contemporary pop sensibility of the festival.

In November 2008 *The Glamorous Life of Sachiko Hanai* was shown at the second annual Pink Film Festival in Seoul, the first festival of its kind devoted solely to screening films of the genre. The festival is unique for its focus on a particular genre from one nation but fits squarely into the recent trend of increasing specialization of international film festivals and their marketing to niche demographics. Unlike the selection of pink films that promote a desexualized sexuality by Nippon Connection, the Pink Film Festival's emphasis has been on creating a gendered viewing space for pink films with many women-only screenings and some nights being reserved for couples.[22] While the gender-specific screenings may be a creative marketing device, they also create a safe space for women to watch erotic films and to discuss the representation of women and sexual and emotional relationships. This displacement of the traditionally male audience for pink films by a female audience in Seoul was only made possible by the lifting of Korea's ban on film imports from Japan, the country's former colonial ruler. Begun in 1998, it was not until 2004 that the final lifting of the ban on all Japanese films, including animation and erotic films, was completed. Pink films were first screened in Korea in 2005 under the rubric of "cultural exchange" as part of the annual Seoul Japanese Film Festival sponsored by the Japanese Ministry of Culture.[23] The Pink Film Festival highlights how the categorization of films as sex cinema, art cinema, or Japanese popular culture is dependent on external factors and cannot be explained merely by internal criteria.

In the forty years that separate *Secrets behind the Wall* and *The Glamorous Life of Sachiko Hanai* the convergence of forces spurring the crossover of the Japanese sex film to the global art cinema circuit has transformed. The willingness of an international film festival to consider a Japanese pink film as art cinema in 1965 despite protests by the Japanese government, coupled with Wakamatsu's careful management of the circulation of his films since, created the conditions that led to the recognition of Wakamatsu as a global auteur. While the desire to read Japanese pink film in art cinematic terms with the global auteur as its reference still persists at established film festivals and cinematheques, the orchestrated crossover of *The Glamorous Life of Sachiko Hanai* was a strategic collaboration by the producer, director, and film festival programmers who now repackage pink films to fit the desires of their multiple imagined audiences. The increasing recognition of pink film as a genre has even led to pink films being shown abroad as erotic fare. Although pink films were once labeled a national disgrace, their export now enjoys the support of the Japanese Ministry of Culture in the form of subtitling and other subsidies. Plans for pink co-productions with German and Korean companies suggest that while geographic displacement remains a crucial element in the creation of pink art cinema, models of cultural exchange have been reversed, with pink films enjoying a cultural capital unimaginable forty years ago.

NOTES

1. For an excellent discussion of pink film as an industrial genre that provides a theoretical approach to the history of pink film see Alexander Zahlten, "The Role of Genre in Film from Japan: Transformations 1960s to 2000s" (Ph.D. diss., University of Mainz, 2007).

2. *The Glamorous Life of Sachiko Hanai* played at the following film festivals: In 2005: Nippon Connection Festival (Frankfurt), Nippon Connection on Tour (Leipzig), PIA Film Festival (Tokyo), Real Fantastic Film Festival (Seoul), Scanners: The New York Video Festival (New York City), Raindance Film Festival (London), Louis Vuitton Hawaii International Film Festival (Honolulu), Chicago International Film Festival, Austin Film Festival (Austin, Tex.), Starz Denver International Film Festival (Denver, Colo.); in 2006: Philadelphia Film Festival, Singapore International Film Festival, San Francisco International Film Festival, Far East Film Festival (Udine, Italy), Camera Japan (Amsterdam and Rotterdam, Holland), Neuchâtel International Fantastic Film Festival (Switzerland), Fantasia Festival (Montreal), Brisbane International Film Festival, Helsinki International Film Festival, Calgary Underground Film Festival; in 2007, Santa Barbara Film Festival (Santa Barbara, Calif.), Brussels International Festival of Fantastic Film, Titanic Budapest Film Fest, Vienna International Film Festival, Numero-Projecta Festival (Lisbon); in 2008, Shockproof Film Festival (Prague) and the Pink Film Festival (Seoul).

3. The best concise introduction to the pink film industry in Japan remains Roland Domenig's pioneering catalog article for the 2002 Udine Far East Film Festival, "Vital Flesh: The Mysterious World of Pink Eiga," available at http://web.archive.org/web/20041118094603/http://194.21.179.166/cecudine/fe_2002/eng/PinkEiga2002.htm.

4. The original U.S.-Japan Security Treaty of 1951 ensured continued U.S. military presence in Japan after the end of U.S.-led Allied occupation in 1952 and created armed forces in violation of Japan's progressive postwar constitution that forbade rearmament after World War II. For a fuller discussion of the movement see Wesley Sasaki-Uemura, *Organizing the Spontaneous: Citizen Protest in Postwar Japan* (Honolulu: University of Hawaii Press, 2001).

5. Yoshikuni Igarashi, "From the Anti-Security Treaty Movement to the Tokyo Olympics: Transforming the Body, the Metropolis, and Memory," in *Bodies of Memory: Narratives of War in Postwar Japanese Culture, 1945–1970* (Princeton, N.J.: Princeton University Press, 2000), 131–163.

6. A thorough account of the screening of *Secrets behind the Wall* at the Berlin Film Festival upon which this summary is based can be found in Roland Domenig, "Shikakerareta sukyandaru," in *Wakamatsu Koji: hankenryoku no shozo*, ed. Inuhiko Yomota and Go Hirasawa (Tokyo: Sakuhinsha, 2007), 47–84.

7. The 1940 Tokyo Olympics planned in celebration of the mythical founding of Japan were cancelled due to the war.

8. Tetsuya Shibuya, "Wakamatsu eiga ga berurin eigasai conpe o kazaru imi," in *Wakamatsu Koji*, 90.

9. Ibid., 91.

10. Keizo Yamada, "Kaigai e yushutsu sarete iru to iu ga," in Pinku eiga hakusho, *Bessatsu Kinema Junpo* (Dec. 25, 1969), 196–197.

11. Ibid., 199.

12. Shibuya, "Wakamatsu eiga ga berurin eigasai conpe o kazaru imi," 93.

13. "Les distributeurs inquiets après une nouvelle interdiction aux mineurs," *Le Monde*, October 4, 2007.

14. For an analysis of the pink films featuring the Marquis de Sade that Wakamatsu made with Masao Adachi, see Sharon Hayashi, "Shikyu e no kaiki: rokuju nendai chuki Wakamatsu Puro sakuhin ni okeru seiji to sei," in *Wakamatsu Koji*, 95–111.

15. Wakamatsu Koji, *Jiko nashi* (Tokyo: Wides Shuppan, 2004), and *Wakamatsu Koji*.

16. The naming of the Shochiku New Wave was largely done as a marketing strategy by Shochiku Studios to exploit the edgy moniker of the independent film movement led by Jean-Luc Godard and François Truffaut.

17. Kenji Fukuma, *Pinku nuberu bagu* (Tokyo: Wides Shuppan, 1996), 18.

18. "J-Pink: The New Generation of Pink Directors," *Eiga geijutsu* no. 392 (autumn, 2000).

19. For a fuller discussion of the film's reception in Japan and New York see Jasper Sharp's ambitious and wide-ranging introduction to the history of sex films in Japan: *Behind the Pink Curtain: The Complete History of Japanese Sex Cinema* (London: Fab, 2008), 319–320.

20. At the 2005 Nippon Connection Festival *The Glamorous Life of Sachiko Hanai* was framed as part of the pink film genre. The evening before, a documentary about the history of the pink film industry, *Pinku ribbon / The Pink Ribbon* (Kenjiro Fujii, 2004), which featured scenes from the making of *The Glamorous Life of Sachiko Hanai*, was screened in part to contextualize the film.

21. Interviews with Alexander Zahlten, programmer of the Nippon Connection Festival, October 17, 2008, and November 26, 2008.

22. The publicity poster for the festival plays on the pink pop aspect of the genre much like Nippon Connection, but the cuteness of the manga character is also suggestively erotic. Peaches and flowers decorate the vibrantly pink poster where pink signals both pop and feminine. The cuteness of the illustration of a young woman in a trench coat flashing a lamppost maintains the balance of the erotic and the cute essential to the festival's attempt to create a safe space for women that simultaneously acknowledges their sexuality.

23. The Seoul Japanese Film Festival is programmed by Ken Terawaki, who is both a pink film critic and former minister of culture of Japan.

3

TOWARD AN INCLUSIVE, EXCLUSIVE APPROACH TO ART CINEMA

David Andrews

Lately, theorists have shown a greater interest in the problems surrounding "art cinema" and its terminological offshoots. For example, in a useful article, Andrew Tudor has noted the strangeness of the term "art movie," observing that in "everyday discourse we do not speak of 'art novel,' 'art picture' or 'art music.'"[1] Indeed, Tudor is pointing to something that has long irritated the ex-composition teacher in me: "art cinema" seems redundant, even *needy*. This is a genre of cinema, the term almost shouts, that is also art. Point taken, but what else could movies be?

Non-art, naturally. I imagine that any reader of this anthology will be dissatisfied with this answer; for me, it borders on offensive. Nevertheless, I believe that it is one measure of art cinema's historical success that we feel this way. Though the cinema was, at the start of the twentieth century, a self-conscious medium that had not yet established its legitimacy, that battle has been so clearly won by the medium's status-heavy genres and subgenres that *all* movies—not just those that claim some special exclusiveness—stand revealed at the start of this century as forms of art. And it is not simply film history that has led to this egalitarian conclusion. The "leveling" trend of so much contemporary discourse on art and culture has led to the same idea. Throughout academia, it seems, the term "art" is not the elitist, exclusionary force it once was.

In other words, if "art cinema" seems strange, it is probably because our *broadest* understanding of cinema, and of art as a whole, is egalitarian, value-neutral, culturalist. Such a perspective is implicit in Tudor's observation that we do not speak of "art novels" because we know that it is established that all novels, no matter how lowbrow, are part of literature and therefore of art.[2] This culturalist (or "sociological") attitude conflicts with "art cinema" insofar as the latter seems geared to exclude other cinematic forms from the status of art. Indeed, the term "art cinema" is even more grating if we enthusiastically embrace this culturalist attitude, collapsing notions of intrinsic textual value into notions of extrinsic contextual use. Though "art cinema" seems to claim that the genre it names is internally valuable as a *group* of texts and as *individual* texts, culturalists view this claim with suspicion, seeing it as a smokescreen obscuring the ways in which all those involved with the genre have put the genre to use across its contexts.

Is the term "art cinema," then, based on outmoded ideas or intellectual mistakes? If we accept the conclusion of Tudor's otherwise excellent article, we might be tempted to say yes. In an analysis influenced by Pierre Bourdieu, Tudor sketches "the historic constitution of the field of cinematic art."[3] He indicates that the medium's claims to intrinsic artistic value were rooted in the elevation of art over commerce. Hence he places great weight on the art house and on other spaces devoted to the film-as-art approach, wherein art cinema played a crucial role. At one time, these spaces seemed to create an autonomous preserve in which art cinema "could be defended as relatively immune" from market "pollution and utilized as a basis for establishing distinction and symbolic capital."[4] Given that the past decades have witnessed the decline of the art-house circuit, it is no wonder that he ends his account with the "fall" of the art movie. There is an elegiac tone to this ending, which imagines the new "pluralisation of the field" as a "fragmentation" and a "decline" rather than as an ironic democratization of a highbrow preserve.[5] "Meanwhile, there has been a proliferation of sectarian audiences," Tudor concludes nostalgically. "What was once primarily the domain of the artistic *avant garde* now hosts cult movies, the 'fans' who cluster around, for example, video distributed horror or semi-pornographic material to which they attribute aesthetic, moral, or social radicalism, as well as the kind of independent cinema familiar in earlier periods."[6]

I find this closing problematic because it obscures, and perhaps even colludes with, the art house's own masking of its industrial nature. "Auteurs" aided exhibitors by testifying to their pure-art ethic, which obscured the economics of their own work. Art cinema does not, then, rely on the art house per se. Neither does it depend on a particular subgenre or a specific audience. It relies instead on a definite ideological dynamic steeped in omissions and distortions. As Tudor admits, this dynamic was never successful in erasing art cinema's "ineradicably commercial character."[7] So it is curious that he assumes on scant evidence that the new market tactics and new technologies have *not* aped this dynamic, have *not* reproduced its symbolic capital. After all, as film historians have documented, the art house was never a monolithic repository of "art-house taste." Rather, it was a pluralist bazaar, interchanging sexploitation, horror, and mondo movies with an ad hoc muddle of traditionally highbrow "foreign films." If this exhibition circuit could maintain its sacralizing function in these transparently commercial circumstances, it seems less odd that this function was readily transferred to the fanzines, blogs, and DVD "extras" that now bear the principal duty of anointing auteurs in an age of home consumption. Such procedures may seem transparent by comparison, but this view owes more, I think, to a sanitized memory of the art house than to a fact-based understanding of what is going on today.

We may deduce, then, that art cinema is *still* based on intellectual mistakes, but those mistakes are *not* outmoded anywhere except in academia. Anyone who bothers to look and see will understand at once that the genre is a going concern. Though market pressures have spurred the emergence of new subgenres, technologies, and audiences, art cinema's persistence in the face of these industrial pressures only corroborates the utility of its new tactics at conferring an ideological sense of anticonsumerist "exclusiveness" across a steadily proliferating array of market differences.

Here it is notable that the *newest* art-cinema vehicles, whether they hail from low-budget subgenres or low-budget nations, may be truest to art cinema's initial imperative—to confer legitimacy on an "insecure" art form. Of course, these vehicles have no absolute reason for being insecure about their status as art, to which all movies have equal claim. While these new vehicles don't need to prove themselves as art within scholarly circles, access to the category is not as assured in the mainstream, where defenses of aesthetic purity and intrinsic value remain very marketable. What this essay does, then, is redefine "art cinema" in a contextual, value-neutral way so that it is truly inclusive, capable of covering all permutations, past and present. This revised theory does not dismiss the genre's old myths and ideals, for these mystifications are basic to the genre's commercial perseverance. However dishonest or mistaken, this "art-cinema discourse" is hardly going away—*and producers, distributors, and consumers in untraditional areas have as much right to this elitist discourse as those in traditional ones.* What we need is a fully relative, multigeneric approach that casts a wide net in gathering examples of cinematic exclusiveness.

What We Can Learn from the Philosophy of Art and Other Fields

One model for developing a contextual definition of art cinema that is simultaneously neutral and inclusive is found in what may seem an unlikely place: the philosophy of art. In keeping with larger academic trends, American aesthetics has been developing contextual definitions of "art" since at least 1956. Following Morris Weitz, analytic philosophers had by 1960 arrived at the neo-Wittgensteinian consensus that the term "art" was too variable to be defined through an evaluative idea of form. But later that decade, George Dickie challenged this "open concept" orthodoxy by arguing that art might be defined through its contextual institutions if not its textual forms. These two interventions gave rise to objections, but their neutrality and historicism remain influential. Today, few aestheticians use "art" as an honorific and fewer still define it through particular forms or contents. In the philosophy of art, popular arts like Hollywood movies and science-fiction novels are now enshrined as "art proper." Even Noël Carroll systematically critiques ahistorical ideas of art and identifies all low art, including pornography, as art proper while still distinguishing between high and low forms of art proper.[8]

The philosophy of art is conservative in that it insists on a rigorous but traditional method that prizes clarity and logical rigor over "postmodern" concerns like the position of the subject. However we feel about the politics of this method, though, we can hardly fault its outcomes, which have often been radical. Consider that aesthetics was already distancing itself from aestheticist ideas of art at the same postwar moment that a wide swath of American moviegoers was embracing an aestheticist idea of art cinema for the first time. That is, by the middle of the twentieth century, aesthetics was already giving philosophers the equipment to see through the rhetoric of even the most ideology-heavy genres. It is also notable that this value-neutral approach has led aestheticians, grudgingly or not, to stake increasingly catholic positions and to create theories that can accommodate popular forms of art as readily as elite ones. This last point is crucial in two respects: it helps us to better understand information recently supplied by film historians while helping us to synthesize that knowledge with our new awareness of contemporary art cinema's "fragmented," or multigeneric, character.

The new aestheticism in postwar art cinema was national as well as international, elevating avant-garde or "underground" movies by Americans like Maya Deren and Stan Brakhage even as it elevated theatrical art films by non-Americans like Ingmar Bergman, Jean-Luc Godard, and Michelangelo Antonioni. Any coherent view must accommodate these two global strains, which have implied different modes of production, exhibition, and consumption in different places at different points in time. What the new historians have brought to light is that the production practices, marketing codes, and exhibition sites once exclusively identified with these two prestigious strains of art cinema were often shared by more downscale productions and audiences. Scholars such as Eric Schaefer, Barbara Wilinsky, Haidee Wasson, Mark Betz, Elena Gorfinkel, Michael Zryd, Tino Balio, and Joan Hawkins have offered insight into what determined these class juxtapositions and what their implications were. Along with important older pieces by Steve Neale and Peter Lev, their work indicates why scholars like Betz have expressed such open irritation at traditional approaches to art cinema.[9]

According to Betz, "Art cinema scholarship has been stuck in the same rut for decades" because it has stubbornly framed the conversation in terms of auteurism and national film movements. As a result, this scholarship has repeatedly "represented its object as a heroic, modernist response to Hollywood global domination in economic and/or aesthetic terms."[10] Betz escapes this dead end—the terms of which were set by the art-cinema industry long ago—by employing the historicist methods of scholars such as Schaefer and Hawkins. These methods lead Betz to claim that the "high and low cinemas of the 1960s" offered more than two different alternatives to Hollywood film practice; they also offered "shared discourses and means of address."[11] Because "high" art cinema and "low" cult cinema shared each other's discursive habits, there is nothing like a clear break between them. A related point is discernible in the work of Wilinsky and Wasson, who examine the emergence of the art-house circuit and the institutionalization of the Film Library of the Museum of Modern Art (MoMA), respectively. Both historians verify that these exhibition spaces were more pluralist than the monolith of "art-house taste" might suggest.[12] If, as Lev has asserted, art cinema "is what is shown in art theaters," we might conclude from this work that art cinema has since its inception been tantamount to most every kind of "alternative" or non-Hollywood cinema.[13]

This work represents a shot across the bow of any formalist definition of art cinema. (Now it seems that not even David Bordwell can lull us into thinking that art cinema is little more than form and style.)[14] Any complete history of art cinema and its discursive trappings reveals a genre so eclectic that we might even be tempted to call it an "open" formal category. We should not go that far, though. As I will argue later on, a contextual or "institutional" theory of art cinema can still make good use, though not exclusive use, of traditional understandings of "art-house style." Moreover, calling the genre open only invites the same devastating critiques that calling art an "open concept" once invited in the philosophy of art, for this maneuver leads rather quickly to the inaccurate and wholly impractical view that *everything* is reducible to art cinema.[15]

Rather than embrace this unhelpful reduction, we should move like the philosophy of art toward contextual approaches. Though art cinema cannot be reduced to textual formulae, it can be defined through its consecrating functions, which differentiate high from low in accord with its myriad contextual circumstances. For decades, producers and distributors in almost every industrial sector have found some notion of the high useful, so it is little wonder that the art-cinema impulse has appeared in most cinematic contexts, regardless of commercialism. It is this blend of cultural aspiration and commercial flexibility that has culminated in a genre so multiform that theorists with investments in older, text-based understandings of it can only throw up their hands when searching for a more compelling definition of the genre. As Angela Ndalianis puts it in the 2007 edition of Pam Cook's *The Cinema Book*, "A clear-cut definition of art cinema has always been elusive, increasingly so in recent years. As the boundaries that separate mainstream and art cinema practices become ever more porous, the question 'Is there such a thing as art cinema?' comes to the fore."[16] For the reasons stated previously, I think that the assumptions informing this question and questions like it are understandable but erroneous. Indeed, it is easy enough to find other reasons for rejecting this sort of question if we consider two dynamic areas of research: cult studies and genre studies.

The plaintive note in "Is there such a thing as art cinema?" indicates that at least two potential answers to the question are unwanted. The first is, *Of course there's such a thing as art cinema! In fact, it is almost everywhere.* The reason this answer is unwanted is that it threatens hierarchies, scrambling them to such an extent that it may even seem advisable to situate art cinema as a subset of cult cinema. Consider that art cinema is adapted to some well-established theories of cult cinema. For example, in *Defining Cult Movies* (2003), Mark Jancovich and his coauthors construe cult cinema as an "essentially eclectic" set of procedures informed not by a "single, unifying feature shared by all cult movies" but rather by a "'subcultural ideology' in filmmakers, films, or audiences" that is "seen as existing in opposition to the 'mainstream.'"[17] Moreover, in his seminal *Screen* article, "'Trashing' the Academy" (1995), Jeffrey Sconce argued that cult areas are regulated by a "reverse elitism."[18] Because theorists have argued that art cinema and cult cinema are eclectic areas whose elitisms are rooted in a shared disdain for the mainstream, it is reasonable to position art cinema as a super-privileged cult practice. What renders art cinema distinctive is that it entails a broader cultural value than most cult subgenres even if it does not always entail a broader audience.

Indeed, the subcultural capital of art cinema's "highest" areas is accepted as *cultural capital*, meaning that even viewers who despise it often condone it. Though we may not like to think of a prestigious cultural form as a *cult* form, such bias resembles in some respects the connoisseurship and the outright snobbery that animates so many cult subcultures.[19] These insights are reinforced if we look at the historical record and see that many film vehicles now considered "cult movies" once played on the art-house circuit decades ago.

The second unwanted answer is, *Good grief, of course there's no such thing as art cinema!* An unwillingness to understand this tart response suggests an unwillingness to accommodate basic facts of genre. Though it is often just practical to apply "genre" to a group of movies, we must remember that such groupings are elastic and forever relative to contextual circumstances, with the corollary that no such grouping is strictly "real." Indeed, as genre theorists like Steve Neale and Rick Altman have shown us, no genre has the clear-cut definition of an individual porn video, whose hard-core sexual images give it an enduring ontological reality in a way impossible for a larger body of texts.[20] When genres refer to textual groups, they refer to provisional realities that we call into being as necessary. These categories appear and disappear. Their "discourse of total order," as Stephen Owen calls it, is a necessary fiction, but one resisted by the hybridity of actual texts, which are always messier than the labels suggest.[21] Altman has shown us that a genre classifier does not "fix" the essence of a movie group but instead serves as a flexible, competitive tool for sorting movies. One reviewer might want to call Jane Campion's *In the Cut* (2003) a work of art cinema and apply that term reasonably. Another might prefer to see it as a woman's film or a feminist film—or an erotic thriller or a work of neo-noir or soft-core pornography—and apply those labels reasonably. By the same token, one critic's horror flick might be another's slasher—and a production studio's gonzo video might be a distributor's anal video. The point here is that many classifications remain reasonable so long as no one of them is applied unitarily or exclusively.

The seduction of rigid classification is apparent when we wonder if there is *really* such a thing as art cinema, with the implication that we might be shattered if the genre has lost its former stability. But a genre cannot lose what it never had. This hardly means that the traditional sense of "genre" is unusable. Theorists may grumble that because genres are constructed by contextual means, they are really "systems of orientation" or "industrial strategies" or even "reception apparatuses." But whatever truth these phrases possess, academics and non-academics alike often find it helpful to use "genre" to refer to a group of movies. By retaining this default usage, theorists preserve their ability to discuss genre with those outside their discipline. And there is no reason that theorists cannot retain this usage while still insisting that textual groupings are always contingent on context—so contingent that their reality is provisional.

These "unwanted" answers are pertinent because they reveal how dishonest and ideological it is to suggest that art cinema possesses intrinsic value at the level of its generic "being." The being of a genre is a shifty thing with shifting values that depend on the competitiveness of its changing uses. These values and their uses are external to any group of movies. How, then, can anyone argue that an individual movie achieves art-cinema status by meeting some internal standard fixed by the *genre?* Were this possible, we might build a functionalist criticism à la Monroe Beardsley in which a given movie achieves art-cinema value based on its ability to fulfill base-level generic criteria. Then we might evaluate that movie as a work already qualified as art cinema, finally arriving at more particular estimates of the movie's value within its generic field. But honestly, this is just a weird fairy tale, one that not even a conservative field like the philosophy of art credits any longer. Though art cinema's claims about its own extrinsic cultural distinction are worth considering, its claims to intrinsic value are not.

A First Attempt at Definition

All of these lines of inquiry suggest how unlikely it is that theorists will ever develop a satisfying definition of art cinema that construes the genre in terms of a specific kind of cinematic text. Not only would this formalist approach overlook basic facts of genre, it would overlook developments in fields such as the philosophy of art, which abandoned its attempt to define "art" in evaluative formal terms (i.e., in terms of a preferred set of texts) some decades ago. It seems unlikely that a new theory of art cinema might succeed where aesthetics repeatedly failed. What is more, film historians have demonstrated over recent years that an art-house circuit nominally dedicated to the film-as-art approach habitually screened films that cannot be covered by any film-as-art definition, including Bordwell's. Preferred viewing contexts and preferred technologies are, then, as likely to lead a definition astray as preferred texts and preferred techniques. Such methods render a definition incapable of dealing with the changing nature of a multiform genre. They also render it incapable of handling or even admitting the genre's "promiscuous" areas of overlap with other alternative modes like cult cinema.

Given these concerns, we might wonder whether it even makes sense to refer to art cinema as a form of high art, that is, in a deflated, indefinite sense that strips "high art" of any claim to intrinsic value. Here I would say yes, we *must* refer to it this way, for "art cinema" has little sense apart from this sense of exclusiveness. But to avoid remystifying our subject, we must be careful to qualify what a high art is and how it may come about. For Carroll, "high art" refers to a kind of genre composed of the most revered sectors of the arts. Here high art refers to a broad yet classic group of genres like classical music, ballet, art photography, and art cinema. This usage is okay but timid, and this timidity makes it too easy to slide into ahistorical myths of fineness.

For example, a simplified view of "high art" might assume that the relative cultural valuation of classical music is corroborated by some inner fineness that justifies its status vis-à-vis genres like hip-hop or even jazz. But an enlarged sense of "high art" predicts the truth, namely, that it is manifestly possible to consider areas of every musical genre, from hip-hop to jazz, "high" while considering others "low." Here my own idiosyncratic specialties, soft-core cinema and modernist aestheticism, are to the point. It is no surprise that soft-core producers prefer smooth jazz while modernist poets prefer art jazz. That any jazz is considered "high" might upset the most reductive view of high art, for jazz is a form of art whose folk roots are recent and obvious. But how much more upsetting is it to learn that in the soft-core community there are fairly respected smooth jazz styles as well as fairly disrespected ones? Thus soft-core fans praise Herman Beeftink for productivity while still insisting that true *class* resides in George Clinton's scores for Zalman King. This sociological fact tells us that "high," "middle," and "low" are differential functions even of contexts that may at first seem undifferentiatable.

My proposed approach to art cinema avoids reducing the genre to the theatrical art film, the avant-garde movie, or any other textual area. It also refuses to align the genre with any particular production practice, like the use of film over video or montage over narrative, or any distribution practice, like theatrical distribution over direct-to-video distribution, or any particular exhibition practice, like the use of public screening over home or classroom viewing. Nor does my approach prefer the movies of one nation to those of any other. Instead, this global approach defines art cinema as a multigeneric, differential high art that is as likely to appear in "low" subgenres, disenfranchised national cinemas, and debased exhibition spaces as in more traditional contexts. This inclusive approach recognizes that the genre's anticommercial trappings can easily adapt to the necessities of a changing marketplace, including one that uses DVD extras—critical commentaries, insider interviews, director's cuts, production documentaries, and so on—to replicate the aura of exclusiveness once imparted by wine, cheese, and lectures.

What might this multigeneric approach sound like? In the years leading up to 1960, Hollywood was in decline. As scholars like Schaefer, Balio, Wilinsky, and Wasson have shown, one factor in this eclipse was the dissemination of competitive strategies, tastes, and ideas associated with art-house production and consumption, which together implied that cinema was not only an art but could also be a high art in the old, simplified sense. In the ensuing years, producers and distributors from across cinema, Hollywood included, aspired to art-cinema status, which is to say the status of high art. Any neutral, egalitarian perspective must conclude that the movies of the post-1960 era may be duly classified as art cinema within a textual taxonomy whether they derive from an elite area like the art film or the avant-garde movie, or a relatively elite "art zone" in a relatively debased area, like "art porn" in hard core or "art horror" in horror. Indeed, most industrial contexts contain an art zone that insiders understand as that area's art cinema even if they do not always consider that art zone "art cinema proper." But a value-neutral approach does not need to position these zones beyond some privileged idea of art cinema. Art cinema would then comprise all theatrical art films and all avant-garde movies, plus all the movies that do not derive from either of these two areas but that still function as art cinema in untraditional contexts. By verifying that art cinema's claims to value are ubiquitous and differential, my approach to the genre allows it a diverse exclusiveness.

Here I should provide one striking example of art cinema as it has appeared in an untraditional location, where the consecrating function of art cinema is under the greatest pressure to provide its object with legitimacy. This example is the soft-core art movies of Tony Marsiglia and the art-cinema discourse that has surrounded them. As I have noted in my book on soft-core cinema, Marsiglia works for ei Independent Cinema, an ultra-low-budget studio that operates labels like Seduction Cinema, which is best known for its pornographic spoofs starring Misty Mundae, including *Play-Mate of the Apes* (2002).[22] Marsiglia has fit into this context in two ways: first, he has supplied movies that hew to the company's soft-core sexual vision, thus protecting its bottom line; second, he has supplied movies that have advanced his studio's efforts to expand its distribution and to move into increasingly prestigious low-budget areas. Contrary, then, to the aestheticist rhetoric that fills his interviews, he is an agent of a larger market strategy. Marsiglia's particular role is to make inexpensive soft-core films like *Dr. Jekyll and Mistress Hyde* (2003), *Lust for Dracula* (2004), and *Chantal* (2007), which demonstrate his technical acumen, his allusive knowledge of film history, and his mastery of auteurist codes. These qualities have made it possible for ei Independent Cinema to bundle his movies with DVD extras, Web-based promotions, and print materials that testify to his control of his art and to his "autonomous" aestheticism. Clearly, though, what makes his work and its immediate context an indisputable example of art cinema is not his auteurism per se or anything akin to the autonomous value of his work. Instead, what marks it as art cinema is the fact that the movies and these ideological materials have worked together to place his movies at the "high" end of an industrial context alongside other cult-art movies. It is the relative distinction that these movies enjoy in their particular cult location—which contains, among other things, grungy fetish films and the aforementioned soft-core spoofs, some of which deploy tinfoil props—that positions them as a kind of art cinema. It would be more difficult, albeit not impossible, to understand Marsiglia's movies as an example of art cinema if we were unfamiliar with this context or with the promotional apparatus that has celebrated his work. In other words, it is the movies in their discursive contexts that are properly seen as art cinema, not the movies alone.

Some Notes on Identification

I do not have space to detail all the implications of this multigeneric definition or the space to explain how it approaches art cinema's status as an antigenre genre, a genre that rejects the very idea of genre. What I can say, though, is this antigeneric posture is most vivid when it is conveyed through movies like Marsiglia's, which would seem like nothing more than "genre pics" were it not for their surrounding discourse, which often rejects any category other than Art. And I can say that this antigeneric posture is one reason that we call art cinema *the* art cinema rather than always specifying which particular art cinema we are talking about. Indeed, this posture is one reliable way to identify an art zone in the lowest cinematic areas. This last point is useful in that it touches on an issue that I must detail: identification.

What pushed twentieth-century aestheticians to arrive at new theories of art was the fact that no existing definition could cover all the new forms of art that sprouted up during and after the modernist period. This problem motivated Weitz in 1956 and Dickie in later years. But even after these philosophers supplied aesthetics with approaches that could cover all of art, identification emerged as a newly problematic issue, for their theories were so broad that they could not be used to identify particular forms of art qua art. Partly to remedy this problem, Carroll introduced his historical, "narrative" approach to identifying art, which proposed that even if art was not the kind of thing that could be defined through necessary formal conditions, it was the kind of thing that could be identified through reasonable narratives about one work's historical relations to past works whose status as art had been largely settled.[23] For example, this approach would consider it easy to establish the art status of, say, some oversize replicas of a Mr. Clean bottle produced by an artist in the 1970s if the status of the Brillo boxes produced as Pop Art by Andy Warhol in the 1960s was no longer in doubt.

Carroll's innovation helps identify works of art cinema within my multigeneric scheme. What I like is its potential for inclusiveness. An evaluative idea of exclusiveness has been a component of art cinema since its inception. Naturally, this idea has been both generative and problematic. Ideally, the genre's identifying narrative should relate a work of art cinema to art cinema's distorting traditions of exclusion and value while observing the necessity of neutrality and inclusiveness. Of course, we do not need to deploy quite as much historical information as I have deployed in reference to Marsiglia's work in order to identify a work as a traditional or untraditional example of art cinema. We should *not*, in other words, act as if overinclusiveness holds some threat. This tendency is a remnant of evaluative rubrics that treated untraditional forms as potential barbarians that might not live up to the necessities of true art. But since *all* art is "true"—and since a genre is at best a provisional reality—nothing is threatened if movies are somehow "misclassified." After all, the issue is not quantitative. We never worry that too many paintings are being made, so why should we worry if critics expand art cinema?

What we need to do to verify a movie's capacity for genre membership is identify a value-generating institution within which a given movie or group of movies has operated in a sensible way. The art-house circuit was one crucial value-generating machine, so it would be reasonable to classify a specific work as an example of art cinema if it has had a normalized place within that exhibition context. We might also classify movies as part of art cinema if they have been archived by the MoMA or the British Film Institute, or if they have been praised by the *New York Times* as art cinema, or even if they have been praised as art cinema by a trade forum like *Variety*, *Fangoria*, or *Adult Video News* (AVN), each of which is devoted to an industrial segment. It would also be reasonable to classify a movie as art cinema if a studio in any sector—whether it be a big-budget outfit like Miramax or a low-budget one like Seduction Cinema—has presented that movie as an auteur work rather than as a "genre picture." We might also classify a work as art cinema if it has won an honor attesting to its artistic value at a festival such as Sundance or an awards night such as the AVN Awards. This approach would canonize movies by sexploitation auteurs like Radley Metzger, Doris Wishman, and Joe Sarno as readily as "classic" art films by more traditional auteurs like Federico Fellini, Luchino Visconti, and John Cassavetes. But the fact is that contexts already exist in which movies by Metzger, Wishman, and Sarno qualify as "classic." My approach identifies these disparate art movies inclusively, without bias toward particular production or consumption contexts.

We may even classify a movie as art cinema based on form alone. This strategy is acceptable because form does not exist apart from institutions. The styles once celebrated as "defining" features of art cinema have achieved their cachet by cultural means. Hence, a movie may be classified as art cinema based on its use of these status-heavy forms even if we cannot confirm that it has operated in one of the value-generating contexts named above. But we should use this tactic with care. When we argue that a movie is art cinema based on its manifest aspirations rather than on its cultural achievements, we are in effect saying, *my description of this movie is enough*. We must, then, present our criteria clearly and generally to demonstrate that those criteria have solid institutional precedents in the work of traditional gatekeepers like Bordwell or Andrew Sarris—or, if applicable, in the work of gatekeepers working in untraditional institutions.

For example, in studying soft core, I came across *Anthony's Desire* (Tom Boka, 1993), a low-budget movie running in a late-night slot. I knew little about this movie besides the fact that it was dense with art-cinema motifs and robust in its soft-core vision. Should that lack of "hard facts" have bothered me as a historically minded theorist of art cinema? Only if I could not relate the movie's forms to critical precedents. Such was not the case, for even the film's soft-core structure is traditional to the art film. (Remember that in his pioneering *Screen* article, Neale argued that "from the mid-1960s onward Art Cinema stabilised itself around a new genre: the soft-core Art Film."[24]) Indeed, if the film's structure were, in combination with its low-budget production and its late-night-cable distribution, taken as overt pornography, *Anthony's Desire* would still conform to influential ideas of art cinema circulated by movements like the French New Wave, critics like Sarris, and scholars like Bordwell. Though Sarris would be unlikely to classify *Anthony's Desire* as art cinema, only the most biased, self-indulgent theorist would exclude this aspirational film from the genre after considering its narrative focus on art; its open, ambiguous psychology; its metafictive self-reflexiveness, which foregrounds the film's production; its allusions to Godard; its disinterested sex; its orchestral score; and its use of long takes, long shots, and slow tracking movements.

The formal identification of art cinema is trickier if the criteria employed derive from both traditional and untraditional areas, or if those criteria hail from untraditional areas alone. For example, theorists could reasonably identify the hard-core short *Living Doll* as a work of art cinema even if they did not know that it was part of a larger work, *Hard Edge* (Andrew Blake, 2003), that had won AVN awards and even if they did not know that its director was a reliable winner of such awards. They could do this, first, by discerning the importance of codes of bodily disinterest in traditional areas of art cinema and then by noticing that *Living Doll* attains its aspirational contours by applying this traditional code to conventional pornographic motifs like hard-core facials. Thus, at the end of this short, the camera tightens on its detached heroine and on the ejaculate that covers her unemotive face, stressing silence and stillness—and using an excruciating span of frame time to suggest abstract visual beauty.

But what if a work in a culturally debased, low-budget area aspires to art cinema through untraditional conventions alone? After all, when an expensive "genre picture" heightens generic codes, we often call the result art cinema. Thus Bordwell classifies Douglas Sirk's melodramas and Alfred Hitchcock's thrillers as art cinema.[25] But the cheapest cinemas are trickier. They are so prolific that it can be difficult for anyone to identify what art cinema might mean vis-à-vis their dizzying conventions. Still, this kind of identification is not impossible—for, as noted, art cinema really *is* almost everywhere. Can a soft-core movie aspire to art cinema through self-conscious use of inexplicit sex? Sure. Look at *Word of Mouth* (Tom Lazarus, 1999). Can a hard-core video aspire to art cinema by rigorously excluding any narrative? Yes. Look at *Fem Adagio* (Michael Ninn, 2003). Cult cinema has long pushed the logic of its subgeneric motifs, so it is only natural for insiders to differentiate between high and low moments of this sort of subgeneric excess.

CONCLUSION

This essay represents a first attempt to define "art cinema" in a contextual, value-neutral way such that its concept is as open to the untraditional as the genre itself. This revised idea of art cinema admits the necessity of building the genre's myths of exclusion into itself, but it does so in an egalitarian fashion that recognizes the right of individuals in fairly debased movie contexts to use art-cinema discourse to their own ends. Though traditional scholars should find my approach to art cinema useful, my main goal has been to develop a solid theoretical framework through which untraditional scholars may justify their exploration of cinema's most disenfranchised areas. The concept uniting art cinema is elastic enough to handle all this multiplicity and more.

NOTES

I am grateful to Mark Kermode for inspiring this essay's polemic. I also thank Elena Gorfinkel, Karl Schoonover, and Rosalind Galt for helping me sort through the ideas proposed here. An abbreviated version of this essay was presented in Philadelphia at the Society for Cinema and Media Studies Conference in March 2008.

   1. Andrew Tudor, "The Rise and Fall of the Art (House) Movie," in *The Sociology of Art: Ways of Seeing*, ed. David Inglis and John Hughson (Basingstoke, U.K.: Palgrave Macmillan, 2005), 125.

   2. Thus Tudor notes that "the constituent genres" of other forms "remain terminologically part of the larger field of the relevant art-form." Ibid.

   3. Ibid.

   4. Ibid., 138.

   5. Ibid.

   6. Ibid.

   7. Ibid.

   8. See Morris Weitz, "The Role of Theory in Aesthetics," *Journal of Aesthetics and Art Criticism* 15, no. 1 (September 1956): 27–35; George Dickie, *The Art Circle* (1984; Evanston, Ill.: Chicago Spectrum Press, 1997); and Noël Carroll, *A Philosophy of Mass Art* (Oxford: Oxford University Press, 1998).

9. See Mark Betz, "Art, Exploitation, Underground" in *Defining Cult Movies: The Cultural Politics of Oppositional Taste*, ed. Mark Jancovich et al. (Manchester: Manchester University Press, 2003), 203.

10. Ibid.

11. Ibid., 204.

12. See Barbara Wilinsky, *Sure Seaters: The Emergence of Art House Cinema* (Minneapolis: University of Minnesota Press, 2001), and Haidee Wasson, *Museum Movies: The Museum of Modern Art and the Birth of Art Cinema* (Berkeley: University of California Press, 2005).

13. Peter Lev, *The Euro-American Cinema* (Austin: University of Texas Press, 1993), 4.

14. See David Bordwell, "The Art Cinema as a Mode of Film Practice," *Film Criticism* 4, no. 1 (1979): 56–64.

15. In the philosophy of art, Weitz's neo-Wittgensteinian open-concept approach led quickly to criticisms that the theory was too inclusive, potentially folding all existence into the category of art. On the limits of Wittgenstein's family-resemblance approach as a theory of art, see Noël Carroll, *Philosophy of Art: A Contemporary Introduction* (London: Routledge, 1999), 218–224.

16. Angela Ndalianis, "Art Cinema," in *The Cinema Book*, ed. Pam Cook (1985; London: British Film Institute, 2007), 87.

17. See Mark Jancovich et al., "Introduction," in *Defining Cult Movies*, 1.

18. Jeffrey Sconce, "'Trashing the Academy': Taste, Excess, and an Emerging Politics of Cinematic Style," *Screen* 36, no. 4 (Winter 1995): 382. Incidentally, I do not like the phrase "reverse elitism" because it privileges the elitism of one social group above that of another. While highbrow elitism might have cultural legitimacy, this elitism is no more straightforward—or intellectually honest—than cult elitism.

19. See Nathan Hunt, "The Importance of Trivia: Ownership, Exclusion and Authority in Science Fiction Fandom," in *Defining Cult Movies*, 198.

20. See Steve Neale, *Genre* (London: British Film Institute, 1980), and Rick Altman, *Film/Genre* (London: British Film Institute, 1999).

21. Stephen Owen, "Genres in Motion," *PMLA* 122, no. 5 (Oct. 2007): 1393.

22. See David Andrews, *Soft in the Middle: The Contemporary Softcore Feature in Its Contexts* (Columbus: Ohio State University Press, 2006), 246–249.

23. See Carroll, *Philosophy of Art*, 251–264.

24. Steve Neale, "Art Cinema as Institution," *Screen* 22, no. 1 (1981): 33.

25. Bordwell, "The Art Cinema as a Mode of Film Practice," 63–64.

4

Unthinking Heterocentrism: Bisexual Representability in Art Cinema

Maria San Filippo

American movies are based on the assumption that life presents you with problems, while European films are based on the conviction that life confronts you with dilemmas—and while problems are something you solve, dilemmas cannot be solved, they're merely probed.

Paul Schrader

Though Schrader's remark, clearly designed for provocation, sweepingly consigns popular commercial cinema and art cinema to opposing sides of the Atlantic, it indicates a general distinction between two ideological schemas that holds true overall.[1] For the majority of films classifiable as "mainstream" or "Hollywood" productions (both terms require troubling), it remains anathema to offer downbeat or ambiguous resolutions, longtime staples of art cinema. In the conventional Hollywood conclusion, as Judith Mayne remarks, "heterosexual symmetry is usually restored with a vengeance."[2] Aimed at creating the happy heterosexual (or, occasionally, homosexual) ever after couple, this narrative teleology endorses *compulsory monosexuality* (to adapt Adrienne Rich's concept),[3] in which heterosexuality is the natural order and opposite-sex coupling the ultimate goal, with "homonormative" same-sex coupling increasingly tolerated and made palatable for straight consumption.[4] Characters not conforming to Hollywood's boy-gets-girl dictate are homosocialized (female friends, male buddies) or else fetishized into spectacles either hypersexualized (lesbian vampires) or romanticized (gay cowboys). Even in films proclaiming to portray queerness more "sensitively" or "authentically," bisexual representability is hindered by their feel-good predilection for using lightweight comedy or cloying sentimentality to depict reassuringly assimilatory characters who reliably encourage a "gay people aren't so bad" response among straight audiences. Crowd-pleasers such as *Philadelphia* (Jonathan Demme, 1993), *Xi Yan / The Wedding Banquet* (Ang Lee, 1993), *Kiss Me Guido* (Tony Vitale, 1997), *Imagine Me and You* (Ol Parker, 2005), and most gay and lesbian coming-of-age stories, for all their uncloseted optimism and (occasional) charm, seem decidedly less queer than edgier "indie" films such as *The Living End* (Gregg Araki, 1992), *Go Fish* (Rose Troche, 1994), *Bound* (Andy Wachowski and Larry Wachowski, 1996), or *Boys Don't Cry* (Kimberly Peirce, 1999).[5] Alongside assessing the relative value of "positive images" versus narrative *and* erotic verisimilitude, daring, or complexity, a critical factor in this queer cinema debate should be whether a film allows a space for bisexuality or elects to relegate potentially bisexual characters and desires to fixed positions as *either* heterosexual *or* homosexual by narrative's close.

Contrasting more substantially with popular cinema than this indie fare does, art cinema historically and cumulatively has mounted a considerable critique of compulsory monosexuality. Art cinema's propensity for bisexual representability seems to hinge on three criteria: sexual frankness, associations with decadent (or deviant) cosmopolitanism, and the embrace of narrative ambiguity. Perhaps more pervasively and pronouncedly than any other cinematic category, then, art cinema opens what critical bisexual theorist Clare Hemmings calls "bisexual spaces."[6] As I conceive it, the *bisexual space* of cinema constitutes textual *sites* (spatio-temporal locations) and spectatorial *sights* (ways of seeing) that indicate how sexuality as well as gender are irreducible to and always already in excess of dominant culture's monosexual, heterocentrist paradigm. Activating bisexual space as a site/sight from which to mediate between heteronormative and homonormative strongholds does not refortify but rather destabilizes these poles—revealing their affinities, interdependency, and pliability. With an acknowledgement of bisexual space, Hemmings observes, "heterosexual behavior is forced to expand to contain the 'other' that it excludes to found its sense of self," and, I would add, a similar imperative is enacted upon homosexual behavior.[7] Analogous to other "inbetweener" discourses (genderqueer, transgender, intersex), bisexuality in this nuanced formulation transcends its reductive relegation to temporary place marker between (and, it is alleged, complicit with) gender and sexuality binaries, becoming instead a strategic toehold by which to reconceptualize the logic of desire around factors apart from gendered object choice: sensorial attractions, emotional alliances, and the material circumstances of time, space, and need. To locate bisexuality *between* sexual polarities, then, is actually to indicate a space *beyond* compulsory monosexuality.

Critical bisexual theory thus establishes a productive route for explorations into characters, texts, spectator positions, pleasures, and readings that operate both through and in excess of gender and sexuality orthodoxies. It is nevertheless a route encumbered with inevitable obstacles to bisexual representability. First and foremost, to assign fictional characters sexual identities is admittedly a dubious maneuver. The label "bisexual" is particularly troublesome in seeming to rely on a temporal component for its actualization. That is, at any given moment a bisexually inclined person (or fictional character) might appear heterosexual or homosexual depending on his or her present object choice—a factor that significantly contributes to bisexual invisibility in society as well as in feature-length films, in which narrative circumstances can preclude a character's bisexual potential. The eponymous heroines of *Thelma and Louise* (Ridley Scott, 1991), for example, would presumably have found occasion to explore their burgeoning attraction had they not been on the lam; as it is, they have only enough time for a quick embrace before speeding over the Grand Canyon's rim. In this regard, the serial format of television drama makes it the medium with the most *bi-potential*, in allowing time for bisexuality to develop over (multi-)seasonal arcs.

Still, art cinema's flexible meanings and open-ended resolutions alleviate the typical obligation for bisexuality to name itself through dialogue or prove itself through action, thus encouraging bisexual representability in the way Maria Pramaggiore describes:

> Chronological narrative structures that assign more weight and import to the conclusion—typical of Hollywood film rather than, say, European art cinema— may be less compatible with bisexual reading strategies, which focus on the episodic quality of a non-teleological temporal continuum across which a number of sexual acts, desires, and identities might be expressed.[8]

This is not without its commercial advantages: by encouraging multiple readings, both across diverse audiences and on the part of individual spectators, art cinema can be thought of as the quintessential example and bisexuality as a specifically sexualized component of global contemporary cinema's multivalent text: one that facilitates, invites, and benefits from multiple interpretations and is thus widely dispersible and more likely profitable. The rationale for *specifically* bisexual approaches to filmic analysis thus becomes that much more vital, as Pramaggiore avows,

> If . . . the contemporary film industry, need[s] to "cheat" their representations of homosexualities for mass audience appeal—making them legible to those on both sides of the fence—it may be the case that the ambiguities, doubleness, and "both/and" of bisexual desire are encoded in contemporary films and may, in part, make bisexual reading practices possible and necessary.[9]

Nevertheless, given the challenges to bisexual representability, the relatively unhindered freedom with which contemporary films may explicitly represent alternative sexualities has not resulted in many more crystallized or "confirmable" screen bisexuals. Real-life *and* cinematic bisexuality is challenged further by our social system's ideological, institutionalized privileging of monogamy—though to say so is not to imply that bisexuals are promiscuous or chronically unable to commit. Rather, *compulsory monogamy*, like compulsory monosexuality, discourages bisexuality not so much as a preference than as a viable, visible identity position. Staking a claim for bisexual space within a film is often prompted instead by its resistance to clearly identifying characters or satisfactorily resolving narratives monosexually—that is, *either* straight *or* gay/lesbian in persuasion or perspective. This would seem to distinguish problematically a given film's bisexual/ity by who, or where, it is *not*—again, often unavoidable given the trickiness of "proving" bisexuality. Justifying this maneuver, Michael du Plessis urges, "we may well insist on our visibility by working through the conditions of our invisibility. . . . We can begin naming ourselves and our various bisexual identities by, paradoxically, negation."[10]

Bisexual spaces emerge in texts that remain resistant to monosexuality and heterocentrism or, conversely, in texts that overcompensate by hammering home monosexual assignations and heterocentric values to the point of seeming that they "doth protest too much" (as in many a storybook happy ending). In films such as *Les Biches / The Girlfriends* (Claude Chabrol, 1968) and *Personal Best* (Robert Towne, 1982), the romantic/erotic triangle plot serves as the narrative device that delays (or prevents altogether) the reproduction of the heterosexual couple. As Pramaggiore points out, triangularity serves to "complicate, rather than enable, hetero- and homosexuality," thereby unsettling cultural belief in the natural order of monosexual coupling.[11] In contemporary cinema, the triangle plot regularly dares to produce a same-sex partnership, albeit typically involving a sexually "confused" character who ultimately discovers his or her "true" nature to be homosexual, as in *When Night Is Falling* (Patricia Rozema, 1995), or heterosexual, as in *Kissing Jessica Stein* (Charles Herman-Wurmfeld, 2001). Films that resist compulsory monosexuality past the end credits by avoiding any implication that gendered object choice was the determining factor—such as *The Crying Game* (Neil Jordan, 1992), *Muriel's Wedding* (P. J. Hogan, 1994), and *Wild Side* (Donald Cammell, 1995)—seem therefore more closely aligned with a bisexual orientation. Even more radical, and thus rare, is to leave characters happily *uncoupled* (remaining single, whether by choice or circumstance, is viewed with suspicion or abjection in most mainstream films).

Despite invoking bisexual stereotypes—indecisiveness, wanting to have it all, a phase eventually outgrown—the recurrence of the triangle plot across the history of fiction films and other narrative traditions indicates bisexuality's cultural ubiquity. Even when no one character behaves bisexually—as in *The Children's Hour* (William

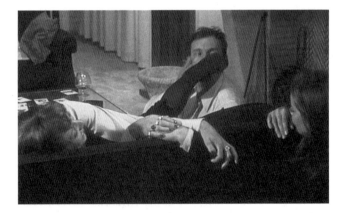

FIGURE 4.1. Bisexual triangle, nontraditional family, or both? Frédérique (Stéphane Audran), Paul (Jean-Louis Trintignant), and Why (Jacqueline Sassard) in Claude Chabrol's *Les Biches* (1968).

Wyler, 1961), *Jules et Jim / Jules and Jim* (François Truffaut, 1962), and *Silkwood* (Mike Nichols, 1983)—the bisexual space that triangularity engenders accommodates bisexual representability in such a way as to circumvent the aforementioned temporal hindrance to "proving" bisexuality. The bi-potential accrues further in films with a romantic/erotic quadrangle, as in Lisa Cholodenko's *High Art* (1998) and *Laurel Canyon* (2002), or in the case of an equal opportunity seducer such as that played by Terence Stamp in Pier Paolo Pasolini's *Teorema* (1968). To read a film *bisexually* or to read a film *as bisexual*, then, is to resist the monosexist assumptions of dominant cultural discourses by recognizing ways in which dialogue, framing, performance, and so on create and sustain the impression of an individual character's bi-potential or of a bond between characters such as Lorelei (Marilyn Monroe) and Dorothy (Jane Russell) in *Gentlemen Prefer Blondes* (Howard Hawks, 1953), which Alexander Doty observes "fosters bisexual spaces and spectator positions."[12] Reading bisexually is therefore an exploratory rather than prescriptive method, intended not to identify a sole or even primary criterion for bisexuality but rather to indicate *bi-suggestive* sites/ sights that, taken cumulatively, work to unthink heterocentrism.

Much as bisexuality is said to occupy a space between (but really beyond) monosexual poles, art cinema occupies an industrial and aesthetic position between popular cinema and the more radical/experimental avant-garde. Art cinema is formally accessible to a broader swath of spectators than the latter, regularly crossing over to a mainstream audience lured by star casts, genre markings, or titillating content. Significantly owing to its willingness (and that of its audience) to explore alternative sexualities at both representational and discursive levels, art cinema metaphorically displays a bisexual disposition of inbetweenness. Despite Paul Schrader's demarcation of American versus European sensibilities, transnational art film co-productions have long troubled the conceptual and industrial borders of national (or continental) cinemas. Moreover, exhibition venues and audience markets for art cinema, concentrated in urban pockets and university towns and increasingly stimulated by the global proliferation of film festivals, comprise an exilic structure insofar as film financing, post-production, and exhibition are frequently dislocated from their home contexts. In certain cases, namely for Iranian and mainland Chinese filmmakers, this exile is politically determined; in others it is more economically driven, as filmmakers such as Michael Haneke, Alejandro González Iñárritu, David Lynch, and Raoul Ruiz seek out more amenable production sources and reception outlets beyond their home markets. These transculturated, hybridized aspects of art cinema mirror the concurrent blurring of boundaries and troubling of binaries that bisexuality (and attendant discourses of queer, trans-, etc.) accomplishes.

"From the mid-1960s onward," Steve Neale observes, "Art Cinema has stabilised itself around a new genre: the soft-core art film."[13] Less constrained by classical-era censorship or contemporary commercial cinema's concerns that "R" (let alone "NC-17") ratings constitute box office poison, art cinema's comparative freedom to openly, unapologetically depict eroticism should make bisexuality visible where it is elsewhere relegated to the connotative closet. As Mark Betz notes, "Virtually all of the scholars who have written on art cinema as a movement or as a field of textuality mention the degree to which sexual frankness and 'adult' displays of sexuality are constituent elements of [its] appeal."[14] True, and yet the vital role played by bisexuality *specifically* goes unnoticed, or unmentioned. As one possible reason, erotic explicitness can undermine a bisexual reading when the desire on display is largely *homo*erotic. Although *hetero*eroticism is often retained in plots and referred to in promotional materials, presumably as a safeguard to reassure spectators hesitant to venture into the "gay ghetto" of films marketed directly at queer audiences, it is specifically the display of same-sex desire that signals a departure from (or flouting of) heterosexist assumption. This alongside the likelihood that such same-sex eroticism will be sensationalized and/ or hypersexualized steers such films toward gay or lesbian (rather than bisexual) readings. Despite these homoerotic scenes having surplus intensity compared to heteroerotic scenes, the bisexual component remains crucial both as an axis on which the film pivots between heterosexual and homosexual alliances, and as a portal for glimpsing an alternative reality beyond monosexuality. That said, for an art film to enact a narrative of resistance does not guarantee its ideological allegiance to social upheaval. Individual texts must be evaluated on a case-by-case basis; even then it is arguable to what degree such films as *The Dreamers* (Bernardo Bertolucci, 2003), *Kinsey* (Bill Condon, 2004), and *Women in Love* (Ken Russell, 1969) are transgressive or exploitative, visionary or reactionary.

Upon the release of *Chun gwong cha sit / Happy Together* (1997), director Wong Kar-wai made equivocating remarks that the film's romantic duo is only incidentally homosexual, in one instance urging that critics "should not view the film from a 'gay film' angle" because it is "a love story between two people [and] love is a word that doesn't differentiate between genders."[15] This universalizing rhetoric pervades the textual, promotional, and critical discourse around art cinema, and in this process, bisexual spaces emerge. As a means to provocatively distinguish and broadly disperse product in a supersaturated global mediascape that holds dire distribution prospects for non-studio films, bi-suggestibility milks the studios' age-old dictum: "appeal to everyone, offend no one." Indeed, bisexuality's universality is precisely the reason for its commercial and ideological import, as Katie King underscores:

> Bisexuality, rather than the identity the bisexual, may be the formation in greatest global circulation today. As one global gay formation, bisexuality has currency in a globalized economy of niche markets where the most circulated objects are those that can be viewed within the greatest range of divergent local markets as "like-us." This doesn't mean that bisexuality is actually "all things to all people," but rather that a highly commodified version of bisexuality can be exploited . . . by a wide range of markets, especially media markets.[16]

Bisexuality, like queerness generally, habitually risks being colonized and commodified by straight *and* gay camps. Aside from keeping a keen eye trained on capital's rarely altruistic cultivation of queer markets and meanings, bisexuality's ubiquity and flexibility require careful monitoring lest they be stretched too thin to be meaningful and effective—as, it has been argued, queerness has. Rather than succumbing to a neutralizing of bisexuality's specificity and a neutering of its potency so as to gain wider acceptance, critical bisexual theory insists rather that heteronormativity and homonormativity remake themselves by making way for bisexuality.

Complicating its male leads' sexual orientation (and audiences' understanding of it), *Brokeback Mountain* (Ang Lee, 2005) constructs bisexual space by reminding us of the complexities, ambiguities, and material realities of sexual experience in a way that incrementally breaks down the rigid demarcation between "normal" and "Other." Yet *Brokeback Mountain*'s progressive use of bisexual space was compromised by the considerable convolutions wrought by its promotional campaign. As I discuss elsewhere, the divergence between remarks made to the mainstream versus the gay press by *Brokeback Mountain*'s cast and crew indicate how, depending on the intended audience, the "love is universal" rhetoric alternated with proclamations that Jack (Jake Gyllenhaal) and Ennis (Heath Ledger) are fundamentally gay.[17] From the opposite direction, bi-suggestibility drives marketing campaigns by teasingly referencing queer desire that never fully materializes or that resolves itself heteronormatively, as in *Le Voyage en douce* (Michel Deville, 1980) or *Y tu mamá también* (Alfonso Cuarón, 2001). As Betz has shown, since the 1960s (if not before) art cinema advertising has taken its lead from exploitation cinema's sensationalist tactics, expanding the "sex sells" axiom to appeal to the broadest possible audience.[18] Yet this propensity for "having it both ways"—to appropriate the allegation made about so-called bisexual privilege—deserves not to be viewed in wholly cynical terms. Rather, by presenting fluid sexualities in ways not ideologically airtight, and that appeal to multivalent spectatorial identifications and desires, bisexual space comes imbued with liberating potential. It stands to note that art cinema contributes substantially to launching these counter-hegemonic images and discourses into worldwide circulation.

Both art cinema and bisexuality share a presumed sensibility of privilege, decadence, cosmopolitanism, and bohemianism, whereby aestheticism *and* fluid desire are perceived as tokens of affluence, elitism, self-indulgence, or countercultural values, often alienating the mainstream "norm" (popular cinema, heterocentrism) while simultaneously being accused of half measures and apolitical frivolity from the "radical" margins (the avant-garde, gays and lesbians). My work on screen representations of bisexuality reveals a number of recurring figures, whose significations I trace through an extensive corpus of films.[19] One of these figures has particular relevance to art cinema: the bohemian, who conjoins bisexuality and art cinema through their shared connotation as an effect of displacement from mainstream values. Typically a white Western figure born of privilege and/or blessed with vocational agency, the bohemian straddles two worlds: the historically dominant Western heteropatriarchy (characterized as stifling and oppressive) and an alternative social sphere shown to be seductive yet potentially dangerous and disturbing. In rejecting social convention in favor of a liminal existence and sexual freedom, the bisexual bohemian becomes susceptible to representation as decadent, deviant, naively idealistic, and destined for redemptive rescue or pessimistic ruin. Like Jack and Ennis, both "normal" and "Other," the bohemian literally inhabits a transcultural site/sight and metaphorically embodies a bisexual site/sight. In so doing, she or he stakes out a space––however utopian––between (beyond) oppositional binaries of race, ethnicity, nationality, gender, and sexuality.

However hypervisible bisexual desire thus becomes, its legibility is suppressed through conflation with the bohemian lifestyle—one that, it is implied, would make anyone and everyone bisexual. While this is not a wholly unappealing notion, it becomes a reductive maneuver within films that claim to represent historical bisexuals, who would presumably protest that their bohemian lifestyle did not determine but simply made it possible to act on their bisexual desire. Two such biopics exoticize bisexuality as one more element of window dressing in the glamorous depiction of bohemian life: recounting the sumptuous adventures of Anaïs Nin (Maria de Medeiros) with her bohemian consorts Henry (Fred Ward) and June Miller (Uma Thurman) in 1930s Paris, *Henry and June* (Philip Kaufman, 1990) glossily aestheticizes rather than more thoughtfully translates Nin's journalistic introspections on eroticism. Similarly, Salma Hayek, playing the eponymous bisexual artist in *Frida* (Julie Taymor, 2002), joins Ashley Judd (as Tina Modotti) to recreate *Il conformista / The Conformist*'s (Bertolucci, 1970) languorously lesboerotic tango, again for the delectation of onlookers both diegetic and non-diegetic. In these cases, an individual film's intricate handling of tone and point of view alongside the spectator's own finessing of modes of identification holds crucial importance. Overall, however, Kahlo's affairs with women and men are given little narrative weight, her bisexual desire subordinated to—and implied as largely symptomatic of—her ongoing struggle to endure husband Diego Rivera's (Alfred Molina) infidelities.

The peak for art cinema's bisexual bohemian fittingly coincides with the late 1960s and early 1970s countercultural moment, when eroticism was given more graphic filmic representation and sexual liberation movements were gaining force. Since this era's "hippies" are often accused of utopian idealism (as are bisexuals), it is unsurprising that most films reflecting on the morning after the revolution regard the bisexual bohemian cynically. In these "hippie hangover films," as I think of them, countercultural ideals are shown to have soured into hedonistic selfishness, which the bisexual character(s) patently serves to personify. Such films soberly survey the excesses and dashed hopes of living according to the hippie creed, in so doing conflating bisexuality with social ills and emotional afflictions.[20]

One of the more harrowing celluloid depictions of the ravages of drug abuse, *More* (Barbet Schroeder, 1969) conjures a utopian social and sexual space only to resolutely dismantle it as wayfaring young couple Stefan (Klaus Grünberg) and Estelle (Mimsy Farmer), reveling in a carefree existence on a Mediterranean island, gradually succumb to erotic betrayal and chemical self-destruction. Estelle's introduction of another woman into their hallowed space is depicted as on par with her heroin peddling, wherein "free love," like narcotics, enticingly promises liberation but eventually destroys their coupled harmony. In Nicolas Roeg and Donald Cammell's *Performance* (1970), Turner (Mick Jagger), Pherber (Anita Pallenberg), and Lucy (Michèle Breton) play house in a shabbily opulent Knightsbridge mansion that initially seems a welcome sanctuary for thug on the run Chas (James Fox). But it is inside this ostensibly utopian space—insulated from the capitalist ills of the music industry and the vice trade that plague Turner and Chas, respectively—that the latter goes mad, provoked by the ceaseless psychosexual games orchestrated by temptress Pherber and narcissist Turner. As in *More*, the hippie ethos of "dropping out" is exposed as an escapist notion inevitably devolving into addiction and social irrelevancy, while the originally alluring wonderland of a nontraditional household dissolves into nightmare.

John Schlesinger's *Sunday Bloody Sunday* (1971) was much lauded for its maturely understated depiction, considered groundbreaking for the time, of a love affair between gay doctor Daniel (Peter Finch) and younger bisexual artist Bob (Murray Head). The film's approach to its concurrent themes—religious conviction, personal loyalty and responsibility, and the difficulty of reconciling free love with emotional needs—is as measured in tone. Yet here again a parallel is drawn between the vagaries wrought by countercultural values and the emotional pain endured by Daniel and Alex (Glenda Jackson) in sharing Bob as a lover. This parallel is articulated in particular by two sequences curiously incongruent with the film's tone and serving no explicit narrative purpose: a surreal episode in a pharmacy littered with addicts, which provides a solemn reminder of the needle and the damage done, and Alex's absurdist discovery while babysitting for her bohemian friends' brood that even the toddlers have parental consent to smoke marijuana. Though Schlesinger's moralizing remains subtle, incorporating such scenes alongside the central tale of a doomed love triangle trains a spotlight on bohemia's dark side. The attribution of blame, albeit also restrained, falls squarely on bisexual Bob—whose stereotypically flighty narcissism is borne out when he leaves Daniel and Alex for greener pastures in America. As in the recent *Kinsey* biopic, *Sunday Bloody Sunday* intently depicts the emotional suffering that can accompany attempts to break out of the monogamous paradigm, without wholly withdrawing endorsement of polyamorous behaviors.

Holy Smoke (Jane Campion, 1999) further confronts these associations of bisexuality and bohemianism with hedonism and idealism, and adds exoticism and exploitative mimicry to the mix. Set in the postcolonial milieus of India and the Australian outback, *Holy Smoke* foregrounds how the bisexual bohemian's shared significations give voice to the colonialist's conflicting anxieties: fantasies and fears of becoming the "Other," enticing and threatening potentials for alternative lifestyles and social reorganization, empowerment for or nonsubordination by oppressed groups, and cross-cultural contamination both social/sexual (miscegenation) and spiritual/ psychological (brainwashing). As an Australian backpacker drawn in by a local spiritual leader while traveling in India, Ruth (Kate Winslet) is implicated in sexual exoticism through both her bisexual desire and a relationship deemed ethically- and age-inappropriate with P. J. (Harvey Keitel), the cult deprogrammer enlisted by Ruth's family to "save" her. Concurrently, Ruth-as-tourist and her subsequent "marriage" to her guru signal cultural exoticism, insofar as postcolonial theory considers that "exoticism itself is deeply rooted in colonialism and tourist experiences of 'exotic' landscapes are a thin parody of the colonial experience."[21] Ruth's bi-potential and sexual/cultural exoticizing are established and linked as early as *Holy Smoke*'s opening sequence, when Ruth is visibly captivated by two young women, one white and the

FIGURE 4.2. The metaphorical conflation of cultural, spiritual, and sexual border crossings in *Holy Smoke* (Campion, 1999).

other ("the Other") Indian, walking past with arms linked and resplendently dressed in saris. Though not necessarily readable as lesbians, their physical intimacy and visible exuberance touches off something in Ruth that sends her seeking similar self-realization in the ashram. This visual instance foregrounds *Holy Smoke*'s central analogy between Ruth's sexual and spiritual awakenings, conflating the two into a single image of Ruth's ideal self: another white woman who appears to have achieved the enlightenment Ruth craves.

A subsequent, similarly entrancing (for all) scene has Ruth languorously embrace, to a seductive nightclub cover of "I Put a Spell on You," a woman wearing the black bob made famous by Louise Brooks—most famous for her own Sapphic dance in *Die Büchse der Pandora / Pandora's Box* (G. W. Pabst, 1929). With this legendary moment of cinematic bisexuality invoked, Ruth flouts both heterosexual convention and the patriarchal authority exerted by older, macho American P. J.'s surveillant gaze. But in the scene immediately following, P. J. is impelled to rescue his charge from a sexual assault by a couple of predatory louts. The abruptness with which Ruth and we the viewers are yanked from *jouissance* to this far more dreadful loss of control links her dance floor transgression to her sexual assault, punctuating the narrative in a startling manner that suggests female transgressors' extreme vulnerability in the face of society's retaliation.[22] Yet Campion's restraint ensures that this scene does not play out as knee-jerk feminism; as Kathleen McHugh notes, Campion "is not interested in the pathos of victimization but in the struggle and consequences of engaged conflict between people with unequal access to established forms of power."[23] In this way, Campion practices a nonprescriptive feminism also seen in the art films of Chantal Akerman, Catherine Breillat, Claire Denis, Lucrecia Martel, Ulrike Ottinger, and Agnès Varda.

More conventionally heteropatriarchal treatment systematically subjects the maligned bisexual bohemian to deprogramming of her cultural and sexual deviancy, decontaminating her of miscegenation with the Other, re-colonizing and domesticating her body, agency, and desire as safely gender conforming and heterosexual, and re-Westernizing her adopted "Eastern-style" exoticism (or re-Americanizing her adopted "European-style" eroticism)—all so as to contain safely her transgression and restore the status quo. *Holy Smoke* derails this heteropatriarchal teleology without acquitting its heroine of her initially self-serving exoticism. The narrative arc focuses instead on Ruth's transformation from touristic passing by (and as) "the Other" into more grounded engagement as a Jaipur social worker. Shedding her stereotype of detached exoticism, Ruth settles into a transcultural, bisexual space beyond borders.

Whereas commercial cinema generally relies on clearly motivated, rational characters and Manichaean divisions between protagonists and antagonists to forge (and force) spectatorial identification, art cinema differs, according to Robert T. Self, in that it

perceives the social subject as a site of contestation and contradiction that is constantly in the process of construction and crisis under pressure from forces in the cultural formation. The subject is a process not yet fixed but open to difference and transformation. . . . The art cinema demands a reading strategy that looks not for resolution but for multiplicity, not for linear causality but for indeterminacy. The art cinema asks to be read in its ambiguity.[24]

By preventing any complete, coherent understanding of character psychology and narrative meaning, art cinema undermines and frustrates the Cartesian ideal of rational self-knowledge, not to mention the Gay Pride ethos of owning one's (mono)sexuality. In art cinema, ambiguity in characters and narrative, as Self observes, is embraced as truthful rather than obfuscating. Notwithstanding the commercial incentive of "having it both ways," in its reluctance to resolve its characters' sexualities along either/or designations, art cinema looks beyond Western modernity's division between heterosexual and homosexual, and between homosexual and homosocial. Art cinema's audiences may respond in kind, adapting their modes of identification to engage with enigmatic characters and to eroticize more freely. As post-Mulveyan theories of looking relations within film spectatorship have established, bisexual desires like transgender identifications are possible (and probable) in nearly any viewing experience—yet the evidence this provides of our collective stance beyond the gender/sexuality binary to which dominant culture still subscribes has gone virtually unnoticed, or unmentioned. Viewers' willingness to experience texts more broadly than their everyday identity positions and behaviors constitutes a way of seeing one could call *bi-spectatorship*, in which the logic of desire is reframed to encompass a greater range of pleasures.

Although art cinema overall has been characterized as resisting simplicity and transparency, a subcategory of art films goes further by embarking upon a justly complex if sometimes confounding exploration of the "dreamworld" of bi-potential that lies beyond heterocentrism. With their unfixed characters, free-floating temporality and spatiality, associative symbolism, and heightened affect, art cinema's *dream narratives* follow a nonlinear, uncanny (il)logic that calls for sensorial response and emotional intuitiveness, redolent of how bisexual desire operates. Dreams and memories, according to Ruth Perlmutter, are explicitly foregrounded in the dream narrative so as

> to express the tension between remembering and repressing an unacceptable past . . . driven by characters with either hysterical transference (such as an exchange of personalities) or a psychological ailment—amnesia, muteness, paralysis. . . . They hide behind these psychic maladies in an effort to seek a new identity or escape into alternate selves (a desire that often gets expressed by serialization—successive what-if scenarios, parallel worlds, multiple outcome narratives).[25]

Though Perlmutter explicitly links these personality shifts to what she terms "gender confusion," she merely hints at the dream narrative's overriding emphasis on erotic fantasy and only faintly acknowledges how substantially alternative desires provoke this will to escape. From *Un Chien andalou* (Luis Buñuel, 1929) to *Swimming Pool* (François Ozon, 2003), these films defamiliarize our naturalized reality by exposing our "fantasies"—both our erotic desires *and* our cultural illusions—to the light of (the every) day. This defamiliarization effect renders reality as perceived from a bisexual sensibility, for which the monosexually ordered world seems decidedly dreamlike, or "familiar yet strange." As in Jean Laplanche and Jean-Bertrand Pontalis's psychoanalytical formulation of fantasy as a staging of desire grounded neither by fixed subjectivity nor by gendered object choice but rather open to shifting identification and encompassing the overall mise-en-scène, our cinematic and erotic imaginary constitutes a consummately bisexual space.[26] The dream world imagined thus conjures the bisexual experience of desire, oriented within a fluid position that resists bounded categories of gender, subjectivity, or desire.

Art cinema so frustrates our ability to identify easily with characters that often we are prevented even from telling characters apart. This trope of multiple personality, "split self," or doubling serves as a conveyance for bisexuality as mimetic desire, even as it carries compound significations relating to anxieties around queer desire: overly close alliances between same-sex individuals, considered suspect, are thereby imagined as a disconcerting likeness. A bisexual's troubling attraction to both men and women is thus imagined as a split self; same-sex desire is thought to be narcissistic or a surrogate for parental love, and so on. In *Persona* (Ingmar Bergman, 1966), young nurse Alma (Bibi Andersson) fantasizes, adopting the identity of successful actress Elisabeth (Liv Ullman), whose ambivalence about her "role" as wife and mother drives her to muteness. Clearly inspired by Bergman, Robert Altman's *3 Women* (1977) features another unhappily married, mute mother-to-be (Janice Rule), who obsessively paints primitive-style murals depicting animalistic males dominating females, symptomatically visualizing the female experience of heteropatriarchy. *3 Women*'s oblique narrative serves as a veritable pastiche of bisexual significations: Twinning, schizophrenia, mother-daughter surrogates, narcissism, and hero(ine) worship are all on display. Furthermore, the post-traumatic amnesia that afflicts Pinky (Sissy Spacek) holds bi-suggestive import: As a "forgetting of oneself," it conjures the stereotype of bisexuals as two-faced and leading double lives, but also affirmatively suggests an escape (however temporary) from our socially constructed selves.

In addition to resisting monosexuality by metaphorically rendering enigmatic characters and employing identity-swapping, dream narratives frequently engender a bi-suggestive *dreamgirl* (for it is nearly always a woman) who reflexively foregrounds the social constructedness of identity by virtue of her diegetic performance as an actor or in another performance role. Examples include stage actress Elisabeth in *Persona*; Anita Pallenberg as the musician's muse in *Performance*; magician/performance artist Céline (Juliet Berto) in *Céline et Julie vont en bateau / Céline and Julie Go Boating* (Jacques Rivette, 1974); ethereal Miranda (Anne Lambert) of *Picnic at Hanging Rock* (Peter Weir, 1975), who leads her schoolmates through "a dream within a dream"; exotic dancer Christina (Mia Kershner) in Atom Egoyan's *Exotica* (1994); and actresses Diane/Betty (Naomi Watts) and Rita/Camilla (Laura Elena Harring) in *Mulholland Drive* (David Lynch, 2001).[27] Again a bisexual stereotype is invoked: the capricious bisexual who flits between heterosexual and homosexual "roles." Yet the dream narrative proves estranging, exposing the performative rather than expressive nature of these roles. In reminding the viewer that subjectivity is not natural but *naturalized*, the bi-suggestive dreamgirl exposes the "role-playing" that constitutes social performances, and herself gradually materializes as a grounded, less fantastical figure of the everyday.

If dominant film narrative traditions often seem guided by a need to resolve queerness or pin down its exact nature, then the fact that the art film's aim is to resist narrative traditions may provide an opportunity for less monosexualized visions of sex and identity to emerge. We can see this clearly across the work of Tsai Ming-liang, where characterization consistently resists traditional psychologization and sexual motivation is never clearly mapped onto a stable identity. While it might be possible to read these refusals as self-conscious responses to stereotypes of Asian people as incomprehensible and unreadable, this reading might overlook how the resistance to positivism around the issue of sexual motivation in his films opens up a space for bisexuality. Tsai populates his films with the disaffected youth of contemporary Taipei for whom it seems sexual relations are but half-hearted attempts at human connection—as indicated by the title of *Hei yan quan / I Don't Want to Sleep Alone* (2006). These characters end up ultimately no more fulfilled than do the ennui-stricken leisure class of Tsai's modernist forebears Michelangelo Antonioni and Bertolucci. Upon introduction to the recurring character Hsiao Kang (Lee Kang-sheng) in *Qing shao nian nuo zha / Rebels of the Neon God* (1992), the first entry in Tsai's early "Taipei Trilogy," we are invited to view the reticent youth as almost pre-sexual, though clearly fixated on an insolent male thug encountered while "cruising" the arcade. By Tsai's second feature, *Ai qing wan sui/ Vive L'Amour* (1994), homoeroticism is allowed greater narrative expression, while actor Lee (whose brooding reticence is redolent of James Dean) is repeatedly displayed in scantily clad poses that established Tsai's muse as a gay icon of global art cinema. It comes as a surprise, then, when the trilogy's final installment, *He liu / The River* (1997), begins with Hsiao Kang's sexual encounter with a female classmate, and more startling still when Hsiao Kang drifts into the gay sauna his father frequents and the two have an (initially) anonymous encounter.

Because Tsai's individual films are not self-contained but tacitly follow a subtle narrative progression from film to film, the temporal component that typically hinders bisexual representability in the feature-length format is allowed to unfold at a pace more akin to that of a television series—or of real life. In his recent films—*Ni na bian ji dian / What Time Is It There?* (2001), *Tian bian yi duo yun / The Wayward Cloud* (2005), and *I Don't Want to Sleep Alone*—Hsiao Kang's and other characters' ongoing opacity calls us to repeatedly reevaluate the nature and context of erotic drives. Because we have been given none of the accompanying signifiers typically employed in mainstream cinema (which identifies nonheterosexual characters primarily by their sexual preference), displays of same-sex desire come as a surprise and force us to reappraise our heterosexist assumptions. For all their outward appearance of taciturn indifference, Tsai's characters shield complex, even tormented, inner lives; in this sense they are not so much depsychologized as kept at a distance, wherein sexual preference (like other conventional markers of background, family, profession, etc.) remains obscured. Denied easy (over)identification with would-be protagonists, we are forced to observe Tsai's characters from the same remove as if meeting them in life. The import this has for bisexual representability is noteworthy: Not only is their erotic potential kept from being immediately definable and self-defining, but these recurring characters and their accumulated episodes across films enable a cumulative appraisal of sexualities in continual flux.

For these reasons, Tsai joins the ranks of other contemporary art cinema auteurs such as Pedro Almodóvar, Araki, Egoyan, and Ozon in presenting queerness unapologetically and matter-of-factly. In so doing, these filmmakers can be said to have initiated a *New* New Queer Cinema, one less overtly politicized than earlier incarnations but arguably more progressive in its movement beyond identity hyperconsciousness and "us versus them" mentality. Those earlier films put queers at the center of the story, but those characters were often reacting against the straights left just offscreen. Immersed in the cinematic worlds of Tsai and Ozon, one gets the impression that not only is queerness the norm, but that we have reached the point once envisaged by Mark Simpson: "The queerest irony of all would be a queer world that had no place for queers."[28] This is not to say that politically we cannot still benefit from identity coalitions, nor that everything, sexually speaking, is hunky-dory in postmillennial queer art cinema. Indeed, the simmering sexual turmoil that Mark Hain notices in Ozon's work pervades the collective consciousness of these new queer auteurs:

Ozon's work explores bourgeois culture as an oppressive and deadening construct, which enforces a stifling repression. This surplus repression, which prevents the subject from realizing the liberating potential of sexual expression, including alternative sexualities derided as "perverse" by the dominant culture, can burst through in horrible ways, including murder, suicide, unhealthy sexual behavior, and insanity.[29]

By drawing narrative attention not only to alternative sexualities but also to the consequences of their repression, these films achieve something more deeply affirmative than their homonormative counterparts' campaigns for "positive images" and visibility. In addition to suggesting *why* we must attend to our culture's "binary trouble," these radically bisexual films and the art cinema legacy that influences them reveals *how* we might undo compulsory monosexuality and unthink heterocentrism. The solution, it seems, lies in the singular distinction between art cinema and conventional Hollywood cinema: as put rather more judiciously by David Bordwell than by Paul Schrader, art cinema's "commitment to both objective and subjective verisimilitude."[30] In showing us what our world and ourselves are *really* like, art cinema reveals the degree to which we all already do experience desire beyond the "straight" and narrow.

NOTES

My title acknowledges my debt to two seminal works: Robert Stam and Ella Shohat's *Unthinking Eurocentrism: Multiculturalism and the Media* (New York: Routledge, 1994) and Patricia White's *Uninvited: Classical Hollywood Cinema and Lesbian Representability* (Bloomington: Indiana University Press, 1999).

1. Quoted in Thomas Elsaesser, *European Cinema: Face to Face with Hollywood* (Amsterdam: Amsterdam University Press, 2005), 44.

2. Judith Mayne, quoted in Frann Michel, "Do Bats Eat Cats? Reading What Bisexuality Does," in *RePresenting Bisexualities: Subjects and Cultures of Fluid Desire*, ed. Donald E. Hall and Maria Pramaggiore (New York: New York University Press, 1996), 65.

3. See Adrienne Rich, "Compulsory Heterosexuality and Lesbian Existence," in *The Lesbian and Gay Studies Reader*, ed. Henry Abelove, Michèle Aina Barale, and David M. Halperin (New York: Routledge, 1993), 3–44.

4. The term "homonormativity" was coined by Lisa Duggan to refer to a sexual (non)politics "that does not contest dominant heteronormative assumptions and institutions but upholds and sustains them while promising the possibility of a demobilized gay constituency and a privatized, depoliticized gay culture anchored in domesticity and consumption." See Duggan, "The New Homonormativity: The Sexual Politics of Neoliberalism," in *Materializing Democracy: Toward a Revitalized Cultural Politics*, ed. Russ Castronovo and Dana D. Nelson (Durham: Duke University Press, 2002), 179.

5. I use the term "indie" primarily in reference to these films' sensibility rather than their production circumstances.

6. See Clare Hemmings, *Bisexual Spaces: A Geography of Sexuality and Gender* (New York: Routledge, 2002).

7. Clare Hemmings, "Resituating the Bisexual Body: From Identity to Difference," in *Activating Theory: Lesbian, Gay, Bisexual Politics*, ed. Joseph Bristow and Angelia R. Wilson (London: Lawrence and Wishart, 1993), 132.

8. Maria Pramaggiore, "Straddling the Screen: Bisexual Spectatorship and Contemporary Narrative Film," in *RePresenting Bisexualities*, 277.

9. Ibid., 275.

10. Michael du Plessis, "Blatantly Bisexual; or, Unthinking Queer Theory," in *RePresenting Bisexualities*, 20–21.

11. Pramaggiore, "Straddling the Screen," 273.

12. Alexander Doty, *Flaming Classics: Queering the Film Canon* (New York: Routledge, 2000), 140.

13. Steve Neale, "Art Cinema as Institution," in *The European Cinema Reader*, ed. Catherine Fowler (New York: Routledge, 2002), 116–117.

14. Mark Betz, "Art, Exploitation, Underground," in *Defining Cult Movies: The Cultural Politics of Oppositional Taste*, ed. Mark Jancovich et al. (Manchester: Manchester University Press, 2003), 204–205.

15. Quoted in Helen Hok-sze Leung, "Queerscapes in Contemporary Hong Kong Cinema," *positions* 9, no. 2 (Fall 2001): 435.

16. Katie King, "There Are No Lesbians Here: Lesbianisms, Feminisms, and Global Gay Formations," in *Queer Globalizations: Citizenship and the Afterlife of Colonialism*, ed. Arnaldo Cruz-Malavé and Martin F. Manalansan IV (New York: New York University Press, 2002), 42–43.

17. See Maria San Filippo, "Having It Both Ways: Bisexualities/Bi-textualities in Contemporary Crossover Cinema" (Ph.D. diss., University of California, Los Angeles, 2007), 336–396. Available online at http://proquest.umi.com.

18. See Betz, "Art, Exploitation, Underground."

19. See San Filippo, "Having It Both Ways."

20. However, this moralistic treatment of the bisexual as scapegoat for a dangerously and destructively lax culture is evident as far back as the silent period in films such as *Die Büchse der Pandora / Pandora's Box* (G. W. Pabst, 1929).

21. Anne-Marie D'Hauteserre, "Postcolonialism, Colonialism, and Tourism," in *A Companion to Tourism*, ed. Alan L. Lew, C. Michael Hall, and Allan M. Williams (Malden, Mass.: Blackwell, 2004), 237.

22. In her compelling reading, Hilary Neroni argues that *Holy Smoke*'s narrative is driven by tension between Ruth's pursuit of and others' resistance to *feminist jouissance*. See Neroni, "Jane Campion's Jouissance: *Holy Smoke* and Feminist Film Theory," in *Lacan and Contemporary Film*, ed. Todd McGowan and Sheila Kunkle (New York: Other, 2004), 209–232.

23. Kathleen McHugh, "'Sounds That Creep Inside You': Female Narration and Voiceover in the Films of Jane Campion," *Style* 35, no. 2 (Summer 2001). Available online at http://findarticles.com/p/articles/mi_m2342/is_2_35/ai_97074180.

24. Robert T. Self, *Robert Altman's Subliminal Reality* (Minneapolis: University of Minnesota Press, 2002), 61, 173.

25. Ruth Perlmutter, "Memories, Dreams, Screens," *Quarterly Review of Film and Video* 22 (2005): 125.

26. See Jean Laplanche and Jean-Bertrand Pontalis, "Fantasy and the Origins of Sexuality," in *Formations of Fantasy*, ed. Victor Burgin, James Donald, and Cora Kaplan (New York: Methuen, 1986), 5–34.

27. Elsewhere I treat *Mulholland Drive*'s dream girls to close scrutiny. See Maria San Filippo, "The 'Other' Dreamgirl: Female Bisexuality as the Dark Secret of David Lynch's *Mulholland Drive* (2001)," *Journal of Bisexuality* 7, no. 1 (Spring 2007): 15–49.

28. Mark Simpson, *It's a Queer World* (New York: Vintage, 1996), 21–22.

29. Mark Hain, "Explicit Ambiguity: Sexual Identity, Hitchcockian Criticism, and the Films of François Ozon," *Quarterly Review of Film and Video* 24 (2007): 278.

30. David Bordwell, "The Art Cinema as a Mode of Film Practice," in *The European Cinema Reader*, 9.

5

Interactive Art Cinema: Between "Old" and "New" Media with *Un Chien Andalou* and *eXistenZ*

Adam Lowenstein

How do we go about mapping the complex network of connections and disconnections between "old" media, such as cinema, and "new" media, such as video games? As increasing numbers of film and media studies scholars turn their attention to this question, the concept of "interactivity," or mutual exchange between text and audience, often defines its parameters.[1] John Belton, for example, claims that the transition from analog to digital cinema in the theatrical context must be characterized as a "false revolution" because digital technologies have been used to simulate analog cinematic experiences, rather than to provide interactive ones.[2] For Peter Lunenfeld, "interactive cinema" can be regarded most accurately as a "myth," a "doomed genre" enslaved to its hopelessly impractical, utopian aspirations.[3] Marsha Kinder attempts to find a middle ground between demonizing interactivity as a "deceptive fiction" and fetishizing interactivity as the "ultimate pleasure" promised by digital technology. With this goal in mind, Kinder turns to Luis Buñuel's films as models for current digital experimentation with "interactive database narratives," which she defines as "narratives whose structure exposes the dual processes that lie at the heart of all stories and are crucial to language: the selection of particular data (characters, images, sounds, events) from a series of databases or paradigms, which are then combined to generate specific tales."[4]

Like Kinder, I believe that Buñuel's films (alongside the surrealist encounter with cinema more generally) provide important touchstones for today's task of charting the relations between old and new media along the axis of interactivity. However, I propose to shift the discussion from an emphasis on narrative to the interrelated subjects of gaming and art cinema. Narrative is certainly important for many forms of new media, but it cannot claim the same kind of centrality for digital culture as gaming can, nor can gaming be reduced wholly to a narrative-oriented phenomenon even if it usually involves some narrative structures. What gets occluded in our understanding of new media when narrative serves as the primary critical point of entry?[5] Art cinema, too, has been defined most influentially by considering narrative form first and foremost. When David Bordwell describes art cinema as a "distinct mode of film practice," his definition leans most heavily on those "loosenings" of classical narrative form that distinguish art cinema from mainstream popular cinema, on the one hand, and from more radically experimental "modernist cinema," on the other.[6] But do these distinctions, however useful for illuminating the particular narrative strategies of art cinema, end up overshadowing other vital aspects of art cinema?

For Bordwell, the "intellectual presence" of art cinema during its heyday in the 1960s "effectively reinforced the old opposition between Hollywood (industry, collective creation, entertainment) and Europe (freedom from commerce, the creative genius, art)."[7] This dichotomy remains with us today at some intuitive level, but as Thomas Elsaesser has argued persuasively, art cinema (particularly after 1989) situates itself toward the coordinates of "Hollywood," "Europe," "popular," and "avant-garde" in ways that the old oppositions fail to capture.[8] In this essay, I hope to contribute toward art cinema's redefinition by juxtaposing two films whose relations to art cinema may at first seem tangential: Buñuel and Salvador Dalí's *Un Chien andalou/An Andalusian Dog* (1929) and David Cronenberg's *eXistenZ* (1999). The former is a famous French film (made by two Spaniards) that is most often discussed as an experimental surrealist film rather than an art film. The latter is a sleeper Canadian film (produced with additional funding from Britain and France) that is most often mentioned as a science fiction film rather than an art film.

Nevertheless, Buñuel's associations with experimental film and popular genres such as melodrama, like Cronenberg's own associations with experimental film and popular genres such as horror and science fiction, have not diminished (and have often enhanced) their status as auteurs whose bodies of work are now read most commonly through the authorship protocols belonging to art cinema.[9] In fact, instructive parallels in the career arcs of these two directors become apparent when Buñuel's beginnings in experimental cinema (*Un Chien andalou*, *L'Âge d'or/The Golden Age* [1930]) are juxtaposed with Cronenberg's (*Stereo* [1969], *Crimes of the Future* [1970]). Both men then endure a period outside major international recognition, only to resurface as an "art cinema director" (with Buñuel's *Los Olvidados/The Forgotten Ones* [1950]) and a "horror film director" (with Cronenberg's *Shivers* [1975]). Later "rebirths" in each of the director's careers, whether Buñuel's from gritty art cinema realist in *Los Olvidados* to flamboyant art cinema surrealist in *Belle de jour* (1967) through *Cet obscur objet du désir/ That Obscure Object of Desire* (1977), or Cronenberg's from the horror provocateur of *Shivers* to the art cinema provocateur of *M. Butterfly* (1993) and *Crash* (1996), highlight the continuity in their authorial signatures across categories of experimental film, genre film, and art film. I will contend that when *Un Chien andalou* and *eXistenZ* are considered together around questions of gaming and interactivity, striking possibilities for understanding art cinema beyond its conventional categorizations emerge. Indeed, what finally binds these two films most powerfully is a shared commitment to a cinematic form perhaps most accurately described as interactive art cinema.

Whether in the form of video games played on home consoles and portable devices or computer games played online with multiple participants, there is no doubt that gaming occupies a dynamic, popular, and lucrative space within the digital culture of new media. Indeed, scholarly studies of these games have begun to emerge as a field of their own, and Alexander R. Galloway's recent book *Gaming: Essays on Algorithmic Culture* represents an important moment in the development of video game studies.[10] Galloway, with a compelling sense of ambition and scope, attempts to address both the unique specificities of video games as well as their shared traits with older media, particularly cinema. He begins by claiming, "If photographs are images, and films are moving images, then *video games are actions*."[11] As this statement suggests, Galloway frames video games within the contexts of earlier visual media, but he tends to highlight how video games depart from their antecedents in the realm of action. He resists the label "interactivity" to describe video games precisely because he feels it is too broad to capture the material specificity of "gamic action." For Galloway, video games constitute an "active medium" due to a materiality that "moves and restructures itself—pixels turning on and off, bits shifting in hardware registers, disks spinning up and spinning down." So for him, "interactivity" risks sliding into more abstract, less materialist notions that could apply just as easily to literature or film as to video games.[12] But what is gained or lost by using "gamic action" to separate one type of interactivity from another? Are video games always actions and never images? Are films always images and never actions?

I wish to reflect on the deployment of "action" to control boundaries between cinema and video games at the level of interactivity. I will argue that cinema, although not interactive in the same way as video games, still offers valuable models for theorizing gaming experiences linked to but not easily explained by narrow definitions of gamic action—models that may help us chart more effectively the kinds of spectator/player experiences that unite and divide "new" and "old" media. Furthermore, art cinema's reliance on particular relays of communication between author and audience lays a foundation for the cinematic interactivity recognizable in both *Un Chien andalou* and *eXistenZ*. By examining *eXistenZ*, a film explicitly engaged with questions of cinema and/as video game, I will show how Cronenberg incorporates certain surrealist notions of gaming to demonstrate how video games and cinema intersect through forms of surrealist interactivity based on associative and embodied stimulation. But first, it is necessary to explore the surrealist commitment to games as central to their theory and practice. This commitment emerges clearly in *Un Chien andalou*, a film often referred to as the birth of cinematic surrealism.[13]

UN CHIEN ANDALOU

Buñuel famously insisted that *Un Chien andalou* must be reckoned with at the level of the "irrational," where the film's images are "as mysterious to the two collaborators as to the spectator" and "NOTHING . . . SYMBOLIZES ANYTHING."[14] In other words, *Un Chien andalou* aims to replicate in the audience's reception certain antirational mechanisms built into the film's production. What Buñuel and Dalí did to uphold the film's commitment to the irrational was what the surrealists often did to preserve the elements of chance and accident in their automatic writing (spontaneous, uncensored free association) and other forms of antirational artistic creation: they played a game. During the writing process, Buñuel and Dalí collaborated by bouncing images off each other, with one man proposing an image (sometimes drawn from dreams) that the other would then question, elaborate, reject, or accept in a continuing conversation designed to screen out everything that seemed tied to the rational and the explainable.[15] This game of images played between Buñuel and Dalí bears strong similarities to automatic writing, but also to surrealist games such as the exquisite corpse, where players would collaborate on a drawing or poem by submitting individual parts toward a collective whole beyond the design of any single participant.[16] One key difference, however, is that the exquisite corpse games rarely took into account an audience outside the immediate circle of collaborators, while Buñuel and Dalí clearly imagined the spectator of their film as a third player in their game of images.[17] For Buñuel, the aim of *Un Chien andalou* is to "provoke in the spectator instinctive reactions of attraction and repulsion." Couldn't these instinctive reactions of attraction and repulsion in the spectator also describe the guidelines for the game of images played by Buñuel and Dalí, especially when their film sets out to be "as mysterious to the two collaborators as to the spectator"?[18] In this sense, *Un Chien andalou* takes shape as a game of images with at least three players and a duration that encompasses both production and reception. At the same time, my description of *Un Chien andalou* as a game of images is intended to blur the boundaries between the film's experimental and popular qualities. After all, surrealist cinema stands apart from other avant-garde film movements, such as Dada, for its investment in "the stories, the stars, the spectacular and the specular" that are more frequently associated (to varying degrees) with art cinema and popular cinema.[19]

Of course, if *Un Chien andalou* functions as a game of images, this does not mean that all players participate in precisely the same way. It's not as if spectators have the privilege of speaking directly to Buñuel and Dalí as the two men did with each other during the writing of the film. But the trails through the film blazed by Buñuel and Dalí are based on a chain of associated images (rather than conventional narrative or causal logic) that invite spectators to find their own associations, to take their own turn in the game of images. Indeed, the film presents a number of tropes familiar from popular romance narratives only to parody or obstruct their usual meanings—a game of critique built into the game of images that extends from narrative structures to social ones.[20] But with regard to narrative, Bordwell's characterization of typical audience engagement with art cinema as "play[ing] games with the narrator" applies remarkably well in this context.[21] For example, the notorious opening sequence of *Un Chien andalou*, where a woman's eye is slit by a razor after a man witnesses a passing cloud "slicing" the moon, certainly includes associations apparent to the filmmakers that would be lost on most spectators: the origin of the film's title in an unpublished book of the same name written by Buñuel in 1927, or Buñuel's casting of himself as the man with the razor whose cigarette produces puffs of smoke graphically similar to the "slicing" clouds in the sky. These associations posit Buñuel as the film's primary author and

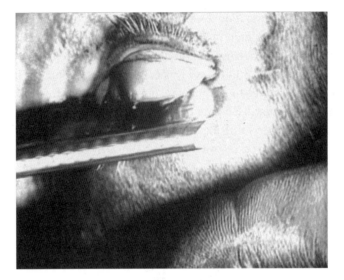

FIGURE 5.1. *Un Chien andalou*: Luis Buñuel as the force that cuts the eyeball on-screen and cuts the film offscreen.

active agent, the force that cuts the eyeball on-screen and cuts the film offscreen.[22] But the graphic associations between the similar shapes and movements of the razor across the man's thumb, the cloud across the moon, and the razor across the eye (along with the multiple verbal associations suggested by these images[23]) may well generate reactions for the spectator beyond the material contributed by Buñuel and Dalí. For the spectator, encouraged additionally by the fantastic opening title "once upon a time . . . ," perhaps this man with the razor is driven to imagine a future crime based on a recent betrayal by a lover. Or this could be the anxious dream of a woman who has left her jealous lover and fears his retribution. Or this could be a film director's fantasy of punishment for an audience that refuses to "see." In other words, the film's form as a chain of associated images solicits images from the spectator in turn, extending the game of the film's construction into the realm of its consumption.

eXistenZ

Such games of association are also woven into the fabric of Cronenberg's *eXistenZ*, where the shuttling between cinema and video game opens a space for the spectator's participation that mirrors the image games of *Un Chien andalou*. For much of *eXistenZ*, Ted Pikul (Jude Law) and Allegra Geller (Jennifer Jason Leigh) are playing game characters within the virtual reality video game designed by Geller called *eXistenZ*. At one point, their characters arrive at a strange Chinese restaurant where they are served a special platter composed of mutant reptiles and amphibians. Although both Pikul and Geller are disgusted by the sight of the platter, Pikul feels compelled to eat it based on what Geller explains is a "game urge," an action Pikul's game character was "born to do." As Pikul eats, he pieces together the discarded bones to assemble a gun that he then points at Geller, proclaiming, "Death to the demoness, Allegra Geller." "That's not funny," Geller replies nervously. After an uncomfortable pause, Pikul apologizes and lowers the weapon.

At the heart of this scene is a series of tensions concerning agency that speaks powerfully to the relations between cinema and gaming. Is Pikul playing the game or is the game playing him when he cannot resist the urge to eat the special platter? Or when he constructs the gun? Or when he points the gun at Geller? The key that unlocks these questions is Pikul's statement, as he nears completion of the gun's assembly, that "this looks awfully familiar." The gun does indeed look familiar, and not just to Pikul. It is a weapon that viewers recognize as a duplicate of the one used earlier in the film during an unsuccessful assassination attempt on Geller. In that earlier sequence, an assassin fires on Geller while issuing the exact same proclamation that Pikul does here, "Death to the demoness, Allegra Geller." The reproduction of the proclamation as well as the gun itself suggests that Pikul is caught inside the game's logic, forced to do what the game insists his character must do. Up until his withdrawal of the gun, it seems that the game controls Pikul's mimicry of the assassin, just as the game controls his desire to eat the special platter.

This transfer of power from player to game simulates a common formal feature of video games called "cut-scenes." Cut-scenes are interludes in the gamic action where the player does not control what occurs on-screen but instead becomes a spectator to what the game itself presents. For Galloway, cut-scenes or "cinematic interludes" constitute a "grotesque fetishization of the game itself as machine" because "the machine is put at the service of cinema." He concludes that cut-scenes are ultimately "nongamic," that they can be explained best as "brought on by a nostalgia for previous media and a fear of the pure uniqueness of video gaming."[24] In Galloway's account, cut-scenes signal a regression from video gaming's most interactive, noncinematic features and a return to cinema's older, more familiar forms of passive spectatorship. But what Cronenberg does by inserting this moment that evokes the player's role during a cut-scene is to invite spectator participation in a game of medium definition that recalls the game of images staged in *Un Chien andalou*. Where Buñuel and Dalí encouraged spectators to contribute their own associations to the series of discontinuous images in their film, Cronenberg asks spectators to associate their experiences of cinema with their experiences of video gaming. To be more specific about the intersections between Buñuel and Dalí's game of image association and Cronenberg's game of medium definition, it is useful to turn to a theorist whose work straddles the realms of surrealism and the sociology of games: Roger Caillois.

ROGER CAILLOIS AND THE LURE OF MIMICRY

Caillois (1913–1978) has yet to receive the kind of scholarly attention accorded to his contemporary and sometime collaborator, Georges Bataille, but his work illuminates the terrain shared by surrealism and gaming in unique and often extraordinary ways. Although Caillois was an official member of the Surrealist Group only between 1932 and 1934, he also participated briefly in or stood nearby the surrealist offshoot collectives

Contre-Attaque (1935–1936) and Acéphale (1936–1937).[25] In addition, he co-founded the famed College of Sociology with surrealist fellow travelers Bataille and Michel Leiris in 1937.[26] Still, Caillois's relation to surrealism was always a tense and difficult one, even if the movement's influence on him was profound and long lasting. As late as 1975, Caillois declared that "I have always been surrealist; what is more, I was surrealist before even becoming one."[27] In fact, the traces of Caillois's most famous essay written during his early years, "Mimicry and Legendary Psychasthenia" (1935), can be detected clearly in the most well-known book from his later period, *Man, Play and Games* (1958). In the space between these two seminal works, Caillois stages the encounter between surrealism and games that will illuminate the exchanges between cinema, gaming, and surrealism present in *Un Chien andalou* and *eXistenZ*.[28]

"Mimicry and Legendary Psychasthenia" studies instances of mimicry in the animal kingdom (particularly among insects) to suggest that it is not, as is often assumed, a primarily defensive phenomenon. For Caillois, imitative acts performed by animals are understood best not as camouflage that protects the organism, but as a desire on the organism's part for self-erasure, for a removal of the distinctions between itself and its surrounding environment. Caillois's mimicry is not an instinct for self-preservation but for self-abandonment, an often dangerous attraction toward "depersonalization through assimilation into space" that resembles the Freudian death drive. These aspects of self-erasure and depersonalization cause Caillois to align mimicry with psychasthenic psychology, or "disorder in the relationship between personality and space." The organism engaged in mimicry is seduced by "a veritable lure of space" where the organism "is no longer located at the origin of the coordinate system but is simply one point among many." In this state, the organism "quite literally no longer knows what to do with itself."[29]

The desire to lose oneself, to become assimilated into the surrounding environment rather than control that environment, connects mimicry to certain aspects of game play. Indeed, Caillois's *Man, Play and Games* returns to "Mimicry and Legendary Psychasthenia" for some of its key theoretical components. Although the critical hindsight granted by more than two decades forces Caillois to distance himself from his earlier claims about mimicry's connections to the death drive and the spatial disorder of psychasthenia, he maintains that mimicry constitutes one of the four major classifications of human game play described in his sociological taxonomy of games.[30] These four types of games are: competition (*agôn*), chance (*alea*), vertigo (*ilinx*), and simulation (*mimicry*). Examples of *agôn* include "football, billiards, or chess"; of *alea*, "roulette or a lottery"; of *ilinx*, "a rapid whirling or falling movement, a state of dizziness and disorder." Games of *mimicry* simulate an imaginary universe, one where the player "forgets, disguises, or temporarily sheds his personality in order to feign another." So examples of *mimicry* include "theatrical presentations and dramatic interpretations" that Caillois labels "cultural forms found at the margins of the social order": carnival, theater, cinema.[31] For Caillois, it is not only the film actor who participates in *mimicry*, but also the film spectator. The actor, of course, pretends to be someone else during his performance. But the spectator is also engaged in acts of imaginative imitation, forgetting herself as she enters the film's world and identifies with the film's characters or stars. Although Caillois considers this sort of identification to be a "degraded and diluted form of *mimicry*," he cannot deny its power to fascinate or its location at the center of modern society, "in a world in which sports and the movies are so dominant."[32] Armed with Caillois's mimicry as a theoretical framework, we are now prepared to return to the games of spectatorship played by *Un Chien andalou* and *eXistenZ*.

MIMICRY AND THE BODY AND THE AUTHOR

Viewers of *eXistenZ* must grapple with the questions of just how gamic can cinema really be, and just how cinematic can video games really be. In one sense, the previously described cut-scene moment in *eXistenZ* breaks the cinematic spell by simulating a video game mechanism and surrendering, at least momentarily, to the video game's rhythms of action. When Pikul eats the special platter or imitates Geller's assassin by repeating his words and gestures, he embodies the lure of mimicry, with its seductive drive toward self-abandonment. Caillois depicts mimicry's self-abandonment as a blurring of distinctions between self and environment, body and space; in *eXistenZ*, Pikul briefly surrenders his own will to the game's logic, releasing control over his own body to the game's commands about what his body should be doing within the space of the game.[33]

Pikul is initially apprehensive about accepting this form of self-abandonment, but Geller encourages him to enjoy it as one of gaming's pleasures—either way, he seems powerless to stop it. "I find this disgusting but I can't help myself," Pikul says as he feasts on the mutant amphibians. He adds, "I'm fighting it, but it isn't doing me any good." Nevertheless, he eats with lip-smacking relish and assembles the gun with eager precision. One of the pleasures provided by this scene is watching Pikul, who has always steadfastly resisted any "invasive" stimulation of his body, submit to an entirely different order of embodied behavior. As if to underline this transformation, Pikul insists that the teeth he removes from his mouth while eating—the gun's "bullets"— must belong to the game's version of his body, not his own "real" body (whose teeth are perfect). Just as Pikul's "game teeth" mimic bullets, so too does his "game body" mimic

FIGURE 5.2. *eXistenZ*: Ted Pikul (Jude Law) submits to a "game urge."

his "real body," thrusting him toward an embodied self-abandonment he has never permitted himself.

True to Caillois's interweaving of progressive, "civilized" mimicry with dangerous, more radically embodied forms of mimicry, *eXistenZ* never allows viewers to draw definitive lines between harmless "game" and threatening "reality," nor between video game characteristics commonly perceived as "interactive" and cinematic characteristics often understood as "passive." Does Pikul's submission to the game reveal the interactive potential of video games or their confinement to the mere shadow of interactivity? Does the viewer's spectatorship of Pikul's submission to the game reveal cinema's capability for delivering "active," embodied experience for audiences or for generating only "passive" forms of experience? And where do the pleasures for the viewer/player emerge in this constellation of links and disjunctions between cinema and video games?

That fact that Cronenberg, as always, channels such questions toward the body—both on-screen and offscreen—means that mimicry's embodied dimensions take center stage in *eXistenZ*. It is crucial that Pikul's disgust while eating is mirrored by the viewer's disgust at the sights and sounds of watching him eat, just as Pikul's self-abandoning pleasure while eating echoes the viewer's enjoyment of surrender to this spectacle ("I find this disgusting but I can't help myself"). Geller's reactions to Pikul also suggest a series of possible models for the viewer's own reactions: she cringes with visceral distaste as Pikul eats, smiles as he submits to the "game urge," reassures him that his responses are normal, and finally shrinks from him as he menaces her with the gun. Positing Pikul and Geller as the primary points of identification for viewer mimicry would support Caillois's later claims about the attachments viewers express toward film characters or stars, but focusing solely on this sort of identification may minimize Caillois's earlier arguments about mimicry as the lure of space. Isn't it possible that viewers mimic not only Pikul and Geller, but also the setting of the game itself? That viewers desire to get lost in the world of the game (or the film) in ways beside or beyond character/star identification? Cronenberg seems quite aware of this possibility—a lurid advertisement for a game glimpsed earlier in the film is called *Chinese Restaurant*, indicating that this scene's setting could be an attraction in itself.

Chinese Restaurant is not the only game on display in the "game emporium" explored by Pikul and Geller in *eXistenZ*. Other titles include *Hit by a Car* and *Viral Ecstasy*. Of course, these two game titles could serve as references to (or adaptations of) the Cronenberg films *Crash* and *Shivers*, respectively, highlighting the opportunities for mimicry of the author presented to the viewer/player of *eXistenZ*. Alongside desires to lose oneself within the film/game's characters or settings comes the desire to lose oneself within the author's imagination, to "play" in the Cronenberg universe. In other words, *eXistenZ* presents its invitation to interactivity through the reading strategies of art cinema, where the "competent viewer" searches the film for the author's "stylistic signatures."[34] Indeed, the proclamation "Death to the demoness, Allegra Geller" recalls a very similar proclamation from Cronenberg's *Videodrome* (1983), when Max Renn (James Woods) declares "Death to Videodrome, long live The New Flesh." "Videodrome" and "The New Flesh," like "Cortical Systematics" and "The Realist Underground" in *eXistenZ*, refer to organizations whose mixtures of corporate, revolutionary, technological, and ideological elements always remain shrouded in ambiguity. Renn, like Pikul, accompanies his statement by wielding a gun that is equal parts animate and inanimate matter. For Caillois, one way of defining mimicry in art is through the melding of the animate and the inanimate.[35] The set of intertextual moves performed in *eXistenZ* joins its networks of mimicry at the levels of story, image, and affect (Pikul imitates Geller's assassin, bodies imitate machines, viewers feel as Pikul/Geller do) to networks of mimicry at the levels of art cinema authorship and spectatorship (Pikul imitates Renn, *eXistenZ* imitates *Videodrome*, viewers "play" across a number of Cronenberg films).

The specific type of play engaged in by viewers of *eXistenZ* will depend partly on their auteurist knowledge of Cronenberg's films, but no previous knowledge at all is required to sense the game of mimicry that occurs between Pikul and the assassin. And it is this mimicking of the assassin by Pikul that foreshadows the revelations of doubled identities that conclude the film, when many of the film's characters are unveiled as players testing a new game called *transCendenZ*; *eXistenZ* is consequently revealed as a gaming experience generated within *transCendenZ*. In one last burst of mimicry, Pikul and Geller then assassinate the game designer of *transCendenZ*, declare "Death to *transCendenZ*!" and finally train their guns on the man who played the waiter they "killed" earlier in the *Chinese Restaurant* of *eXistenZ*. He pleads with them not to shoot him, then asks, "Are we still in the game?" Their silent reply is the final shot of the film: a straight-on, frontal view of Pikul and Geller, guns aimed, fingers on the trigger. Their weapons are pointed directly at this man, but also at us, the audience.

When Buñuel attended the theatrical premiere of *Un Chien andalou*, he carried stones in his pockets to hurl at the audience "in case of disaster." After hearing the applause that greeted the film's conclusion, Buñuel dropped the stones "discreetly, one by one, on the floor behind the screen."[36] But in the end, perhaps Buñuel had not averted disaster. In a prefatory note to accompany the publication of *Un Chien andalou*'s screenplay in a 1929 issue of the journal *La Révolution surréaliste*, Buñuel complains, "*A box-office success*, that's what most people think who have seen the film. But what can I do about . . . this imbecilic crowd that has found *beautiful* or *poetic* that which, at heart, is nothing other than a desperate, impassioned call for murder?"[37] Buñuel's harsh words for his audience must be contextualized with his need to please an extremely demanding surrealist movement that often looked suspiciously on popular success, but still, one wonders whether he ultimately regretted his decision not to throw stones at his viewers. Buñuel echoes André Breton's similarly provocative statement in the "Second Manifesto of Surrealism" (1929), published in the same issue of *La Révolution surréaliste*: "The simplest Surrealist act consists of dashing down into the street, pistol in hand, and firing blindly, as fast as you can pull the trigger, into the crowd. Anyone who, at least once in his life, has not dreamed of thus putting an end to the petty system of debasement and cretinization in effect has a well-defined place in that crowd, with his belly at barrel level."[38] Breton and Buñuel deliberately overstate their cases to achieve a scandalous effect, but one feels clearly their surrealist rage for change in both art and life, as well as how their public audience inspires not only a desire to create, but also fear and contempt. They worry that they will not succeed in communicating their surrealist rage to their audience—they fear, in other words, the failure to accomplish interactivity.

The final shot of *eXistenZ* carries the weight of this same fear, with its realization that the games initiated between author and audience are at once deeply playful and deadly serious. One of the last statements made by Yevgeny Nourish (Don McKellar), the game designer of *transCendenZ*, prior to his assassination is that he was "disturbed" by the anti-game theme that surfaced while playing *eXistenZ*. He comes to the uncomfortable conclusion that since the anti-game theme could not have originated with him, it must have been devised by the players—the interactive audience. The danger posed to the author by the audience runs along both edges of interactivity: failed interactivity diminishes the effect of the artwork, but successful interactivity risks the audience returning to the author with input he cannot process, with desires he cannot fulfill, with interpretations he did not foresee.

Cronenberg speaks about the origins of *eXistenZ* in the lethal fatwa issued when author Salman Rushdie was accused of blasphemy against Islam for his novel *The Satanic Verses* (1988). The spark for the film, according to Cronenberg, grew out of "the question of a writer having to deal with what he has created, that what he creates becomes a living thing out in the world that can come back to haunt you in many ways or stalk you, [as] in the case of Rushdie."[39] This "living thing" that Cronenberg refers to is not a novel or film in isolation, but the interactivity established between author, artwork, and audience. In Rushdie's case, some extremist readers participated in such a fully interactive exchange with his work (or at least an imagined interactive exchange) that they called for the author's murder. The stones in Buñuel's pockets were carried by the director as a defensive measure against an audience the director feared might attack his film, or perhaps even his body during the screening: "I was a nervous wreck. In fact, I hid behind the screen with the record player, alternating Argentinian tangos with *Tristan und Isolde*."[40] So for Buñuel, the film screen is a site for interactivity—it simultaneously exposes him to and hides him from the audience, presenting the author as a silent, unseen presence as well as an active "speaker" through the film's images and the accompanying musical selections. What unites Buñuel, Rushdie, and Cronenberg is a powerful understanding of interactivity's pleasures and dangers, how the desire for an audience to be so deeply affected by your work that they mimic acts of authorship through active responses of their own may become realized as direct or indirect aggression toward the author. And that the author, in turn, may wish to lash back at the audience—witness Buñuel's stones or Cronenberg's final, confrontational shot in *eXistenZ*. "Are we still in the game?" is a question that cannot be answered by anyone within *eXistenZ* because Cronenberg recognizes how it ultimately addresses the audience outside the film, the audience that makes or breaks the interactive loop. It is toward them (us) that the guns are pointed, just as it is they (us) that have the power to hold the author at gunpoint over the work he has created. In this image we can detect signs of art cinema's transformation into interactive art cinema: The viewer's search for the author's "stylistic signatures" has become something simultaneously more of a (risky) game and less of a (innocuous) game. This is precisely the kind of game found within both *eXistenZ* and *Un Chien andalou* in the shape of surrealist interactivity.

NOTES

1. I have begun with this very basic definition of interactivity in order to accommodate the more specific versions of the term developed during the course of this essay. At the same time, the contested status of interactivity's definition when "old" media meet "new" media is an issue too expansive to resolve here fully; I can only hope to offer several additional coordinates with which to continue the debate. To name just two particularly influential contributions to this larger debate whose very different positions help to indicate its outlines, see Lev Manovich, *The Language of New Media* (Cambridge, Mass.: MIT Press, 2001), and Mark B. N. Hansen, *New Philosophy for New Media* (Cambridge, Mass.: MIT Press, 2004).

2. John Belton, "Digital Cinema: A False Revolution," *October* 100 (Spring 2002): 98–114; 104–105.

3. Peter Lunenfeld, "The Myths of Interactive Cinema," in *The New Media Book*, ed. Dan Harries (London: British Film Institute, 2002), 144–154; 154.

4. Marsha Kinder, "Hot Spots, Avatars, and Narrative Fields Forever: Buñuel's Legacy for New Digital Media and Interactive Database Narrative," *Film Quarterly* 55, no. 4 (2002): 2–15; 4, 6.

5. I am responding here to a frequent tendency in scholarship on gaming in new media contexts to turn toward narrative as primary. See, for example, Janet H. Murray, *Hamlet on the Holodeck: The Future of Narrative in Cyberspace* (New York: Free Press, 1997), and Marsha Kinder, "Narrative Equivocations between Movies and Games," in *The New Media Book*, 119–132. Again, I do not wish to discount the importance of narrative to gaming in new media, but I want to seek alternate approaches to this phenomenon that do not necessarily begin or end with narrative.

6. See David Bordwell, "The Art Cinema as a Mode of Film Practice," *Film Criticism* 4, no. 1 (1979): 56–64; rpt. in Leo Braudy and Marshall Cohen, eds., *Film Theory and Criticism: Introductory Readings*, 6th ed. (New York: Oxford University Press, 2004), 774–782, and "Art-Cinema Narration," in *Narration in the Fiction Film* (Madison: University of Wisconsin Press, 1985), 205–233. This is not to say that Bordwell is silent on those historical, economic, and cultural aspects of art cinema that have been pursued in more detail by other scholars. See, for example, Steve Neale, "Art Cinema as Institution," *Screen* 22, no. 1 (1981): 11–39, and Barbara Wilinsky, *Sure Seaters: The Emergence of Art House Cinema* (Minneapolis: University of Minnesota Press, 2001). However, the primacy of narrative in Bordwell's account, coupled with the influential impact of his claims, means that art cinema's place in film studies has tended to be fixed in a particular way for many years.

7. Bordwell, "Art-Cinema Narration," 231.

8. See Thomas Elsaesser, *European Cinema: Face to Face with Hollywood* (Amsterdam: Amsterdam University Press, 2005), esp. 485–513.

9. Bordwell includes Buñuel in his lists of art cinema auteurs (see "The Art Cinema as a Mode of Film Practice," 778, and "Art-Cinema Narration," 232). For a consideration of Cronenberg's relation to art cinema and Canadian national cinema, see my *Shocking Representation: Historical Trauma, National Cinema, and the Modern Horror Film* (New York: Columbia University Press, 2005), 145–175.

10. See Alexander R. Galloway, *Gaming: Essays on Algorithmic Culture* (Minneapolis: University of Minnesota Press, 2006). I have placed Galloway's work

at the center of this essay's discussions of video games because his arguments, to my mind, address my particular concerns with unusual sensitivity. However, this is not to say that Galloway's is the first, last, or only word in video game studies, a field that continues to grow at an impressive pace. See, for example, Espen Aarseth, *Cybertext: Perspectives on Ergodic Literature* (Baltimore, Md.: Johns Hopkins University Press, 1997); Geoff King and Tanya Krzywinska, eds., *ScreenPlay: Cinema/Videogames/ Interfaces* (London: Wallflower, 2002); Mark J. P. Wolf and Bernard Perron, eds., *The Video Game Theory Reader* (London: Routledge, 2003); and the journal *Game Studies*.

11. Galloway, *Gaming*, 2 (emphasis in orginal). I follow Galloway in his use of "video game" as an "umbrella term for all sorts of . . . electronic games" (127n1).

12. Ibid., 3, 128n4.

13. Although Buñuel had not yet joined the Surrealist Group when he and Dalí made *Un Chien andalou*, he often pointed out the film's fundamental debts to surrealism: "*Un Chien andalou* would not have existed if the movement called surrealist had not existed" (Luis Buñuel, "Notes on the Making of *Un Chien andalou*" [1947], trans. Grace L. McCann Morley, in Joan Mellen, ed., *The World of Luis Buñuel: Essays in Criticism* [New York: Oxford University Press, 1978], 151–153; 151–152); "Even the poems I published in Spain before I'd heard of the surrealist movement were responses to that call which eventually brought all of us together in Paris. While Dalí and I were making *Un Chien andalou* we used a kind of automatic writing. There was indeed something in the air, and my connection with the surrealists in many ways determined the course of my life" (Luis Buñuel, *My Last Breath*, trans. Abigail Israel [1982; London: Vintage, 1994], 105). Buñuel joined the Surrealist Group officially in 1929 and broke with them in 1932. His films and writings, however, right up until his death in 1983, testify to a powerfully sustained investment in surrealism.

14. Buñuel, "Notes on the Making of *Un Chien andalou*," 153.

15. See José de la Colina and Tomás Pérez Turrent, *Objects of Desire: Conversations with Luis Buñuel*, ed. and trans. Paul Lenti (New York: Marsilio, 1992), 15–16.

16. For an overview of surrealist games, see Alastair Brotchie and Mel Gooding, eds., *A Book of Surrealist Games* (Boston: Shambhala Redstone Editions, 1991).

17. Simone Kahn, an associate of the Surrealist Group, recalls the original exquisite corpse games as insular, with the surrealists putting on "a fantastic drama for ourselves." Even when the first selections of results from the games were published in a 1927 issue of *La Révolution surréaliste*, they appeared anonymously. Later examples of the game were signed by the players. See Mary Ann Caws, ed., *Surrealism* (London: Phaidon, 2004), 200, 62.

18. Buñuel, "Notes on the Making of *Un Chien andalou*," 151, 153.

19. See Thomas Elsaesser, "Dada/Cinema?" in *Dada and Surrealist Film*, ed. Rudolf E. Kuenzli (Cambridge, Mass.: MIT Press, 1996), 13–27; 26.

20. In this way, *Un Chien andalou* speaks to Buñuel's sense of surrealism as a movement whose aim "was not to establish a glorious place . . . in the annals of art and literature, but to change the world, to transform life itself." Buñuel concludes that surrealism was thus "successful in its details and a failure in its essentials," even though the movement changed his life. See Buñuel, *My Last Breath*, 123.

21. Bordwell, "The Art Cinema as a Mode of Film Practice," 779.

22. At the same time, it is important not to minimize Dalí's considerable contributions to *Un Chien andalou*. According to Buñuel, it was Dalí who convinced him to use the title *Un Chien andalou* for the film. See Luis Buñuel, "Pessimism" (1980), in *An Unspeakable Betrayal: Selected Writings of Luis Buñuel*, trans. Garrett White (Berkeley: University of California Press, 2002), 258–263; 258. For an

extended discussion of Dalí's part in *Un Chien andalou*, see Haim Finkelstein, "Dalí and *Un Chien andalou*: The Nature of a Collaboration," in *Dada and Surrealist Film*, 128–142.

23. For a fascinating inventory of verbal and visual exchange in *Un Chien andalou*, see Stuart Liebman, "*Un Chien andalou*: The Talking Cure," in *Dada and Surrealist Film*, 143–158. In the present context, Liebman's account is usefully paired with surrealist games that utilize the spoken word in a way that games such as the exquisite corpse focus on written words or visual images, for example, the "game of variants" where one player whispers a sentence in the ear of another and so on until the first and last versions of the sentence are compared. See *Book of Surrealist Games*, 32.

24. Galloway, *Gaming*, 11–12.

25. For an excellent introduction to Roger Caillois's career, see Claudine Frank, "Introduction," in Roger Caillois, *The Edge of Surrealism: A Roger Caillois Reader*, ed. Frank, trans. Frank and Camille Nash (Durham, N.C.: Duke University Press, 2003), 1–53.

26. On the College of Sociology, see Denis Hollier, ed., *The College of Sociology (1937–39)*, trans. Betsy Wing (Minneapolis: University of Minnesota Press, 1988).

27. Roger Caillois, "Surrealism as a World of Signs" (1975), in *The Edge of Surrealism*, 327–334; 334.

28. For a related discussion of the intersections between cinema, surrealism, and new media, see my "The Surrealism of the Photographic Image: Bazin, Barthes, and the Digital *Sweet Hereafter*," *Cinema Journal* 46, no. 3 (Spring 2007): 54–82.

29. Roger Caillois, "Mimicry and Legendary Psychasthenia" (1935), in *The Edge of Surrealism*, 91–103; 99–100.

30. See Roger Caillois, *Man, Play and Games*, trans. Meyer Barash (1958; Urbana: University of Illinois Press, 2001), 177n5.

31. Ibid., 12, 19, 21, 54.

32. Ibid., 120.

33. The fact that Geller later interprets Pikul's actions here as a true desire to assassinate her rather than a simulated one only deepens the problem of agency I have been describing in relation to this scene. The assassination scenario is played out during the film a number of times in a number of different ways, constantly foregrounding questions of who or what is in control of the action (or, to put it in Caillois's terms, what counts as self-abandonment and what counts as self-preservation). When Geller accuses Pikul of being her true assassin near the end of the film, she then kills him and declares triumphantly, "Death to the demon, Ted Pikul!" Afterward, she asks, "Have I won the game?" Of course, there is no answer.

34. Bordwell, "The Art Cinema as a Mode of Film Practice," 778.

35. See Caillois, "Mimicry and Legendary Psychasthenia," 102.

36. Buñuel, *My Last Breath*, 106.

37. Luis Buñuel, "*Un Chien andalou*" (1929), in *An Unspeakable Betrayal*, 162–169; 162 (emphasis in original).

38. André Breton, "Second Manifesto of Surrealism" (1929), in *Manifestoes of Surrealism*, trans. Richard Seaver and Helen R. Lane (Ann Arbor: University of Michigan Press, 1994), 119–187; 125.

39. David Cronenberg, quoted in "An Interview with David Cronenberg," in Sean Scoffield, *David Cronenberg's* eXistenZ: *A Graphic Novel* (Toronto: Key Porter, 1999), 93–107; 93.

40. Buñuel, *My Last Breath*, 106.

II

THE ART CINEMA IMAGE

6

Art/Cinema and Cosmopolitanism Today

Brian Price

In 1975, Gordon Matta-Clark and Bruno Dewitt documented, on 16mm film, one of Matta-Clark's most famous architectural building cuts, *Conical Intersect*. Matta-Clark's building cuts were ephemeral and site specific. He sought buildings recently condemned, abandoned, and slated for destruction and made his own sculptural and architectural interventions, cutting holes in walls to radically recreate a sense of space and depth, as in *Bronx Floors* (1973), or simply cutting a house in two, as in *Splitting* (1974), defamiliarizing at once both the object and its setting. Matta-Clark's artwork often lasted only as long as the process of his intervention. Performed without permission, it would disappear just as soon as it was discovered. All that remains of the art are photographs and the lore of passersby who may have been fortunate enough to encounter it. Or, in this particular case, a 16mm film—a medium whose material is less durable, as it turns out, than the architectural structures featured there.

Conical Intersect, in particular, was Matta-Clark's response to the development of Beaubourg; the destruction of Les Halles and the open market area that had been in steady operation since the Middle Ages, only to be replaced by an underground mall that serves as a major transportation hub linking suburban commuter lines to the center of Paris; and, of course, the Centre Pompidou—a building Jean Baudrillard once angrily described as *"a monument of cultural deterrence."*[1] In 1975, Matta-Clark seized two buildings slated for destruction on either side of the Centre Pompidou, which was itself in the process of construction. The project was inspired by Anthony McCall's *Line Describing a Cone* (1973), wherein McCall very famously elaborated the sculptural quality of the beam of light emanating from a projector, at the worthwhile expense of what that beam itself might very narrowly project on the screen at the other end. As smoke passes through an expanding cone of light, one is made aware of the material density of light and the ever-shifting movement of its particles. As Thomas Crow has written, Matta-Clark took an opposite, but no less ephemeral, tack:

> Whereas McCall made the immaterial cone of vision into something one could seemingly observe and touch from the outside, Matta-Clark enlarged and trans-formed it into an invisible, impalpable projectile capable of eating away at the most solid historical matter. He pitched the spectator back inside the monocular, "cyclopean" projection, there to reveal unexpected patterns—of a virtually cubist complexity—torn from the architectural fabric of the crossover between the rectangular divisions of the two interiors and the passage of the elegantly oval conic sections that laid them bare.[2]

In other words, Matta-Clark cut a spiral into the house that began at the top, back end of the house and moved down through the floors and rooms of the house to street level. As such, and as Crow implies, he recreated the traditional position of the cinematic spectator—the space where one's gaze traces the path of projected light to the image ahead. In this case, however, Matta-Clark's spectators would have seen clear through to the Centre Pompidou, to the object revealed at the other end of this soon-to-be-ephemeral gaze. They would also, presumably, have noticed the beauty of the cuts made, the strange new spatial order inscribed in a building that has been stripped of its original function.

A number of points should be made here. For one, it is conceivable to me that neither Crow's description, nor my attempt to restate and clarify it, will give you a complete sense of what *Conical Intersect* actually looked like. Crow was most likely describing photographs, plans (presuming access to the artist's archive), and the same 16mm film that I saw—none of which is especially easy to understand in terms of depth and spatial continuity. The images are beautiful, to my eye, but not thoroughly instructive. The trajectory of the cuts and the overall spatial design of *Conical Intersect* could not be described by the continuous movement of a 16mm camera, certainly not in the same way that Michael Snow's zoom lens once documented the space of a New York loft in *Wavelength* (1967). Mounting a camera along such a path would have been dangerous, not to mention impossible; the time it would take to mount a camera on either track or wire would far exceed the life span of the building. And the installation of heavy equipment in a building already weakened by Matta-Clark's cuts would have crashed the entire edifice. Documentation, in the end, can only hasten ruin. What we have instead is the record of various views of the object as it was being both constructed and demolished. We see, for instance, the camera as it explores space from within the structure, peering back outside through newly carved and often roughly rendered holes. We see, in turn, a series of shots from outside; the camera, clearly hitched to a car, moves toward the major hole in the wall, searching for a view through to the other side that camera cannot find, even with the aid of the zoom lens. The camera, then, documents a series of acts of labor, and the pleasure of labor itself and a series of

FIGURE 6.1. *Conical Intersect* (Gordon Matta-Clark and Bruno Dewitt, 1975). This is not Oklahoma.

possible points of view. But never do we see, within the film itself, the continuous view through the spiral that ran clear through the Pompidou itself. To do so, I assume, one would have to have been there. And thus, most of the descriptions we have of the work can only be an imperfect inheritance of the photographic and cinematic image; an image, it should be said, that cannot follow the gaze made possible by the building cut and by the very idea of cinema.

It is this imperfect inheritance—a willed ephemerality—that best characterizes a major strain of art cinema today. I do not mean the art cinema of Hou Hsiao-hsien, Claire Denis, and Michael Haneke—as much as I love and admire it—rather, that of Matthew Barney, Douglas Gordon, Steve McQueen, and Stephen G. Rhodes, to name only a few. That is, the work of artists who work in and with cinema, as video and/or film, and who exhibit their work largely in the space of the gallery, or in the case of Barney, who project their work in cinemas but refuse to release the work as mass-manufactured DVDs. Barney is, perhaps, the most instructive example. Over the last fifteen years, he has been creating a series of epic-length films (sometimes shot on film, sometimes on video) under his own "franchise," namely the *Cremaster* series, 1–5. Barney's work is a spectacle of Vaseline and muscularity, an exploration of the line between the organic and the inorganic, of how the body builds only when it breaks down. It is likewise a playful exploration of spaces, whether the Busby Berkeley–like spectacles that imagine something like an avant-garde, audience-less Superbowl in *Cremaster 1*, or the scene in which Barney deftly scales the inside walls of the Guggenheim like a modern Fantomas in *Cremaster 3*. In each case, Barney's "films" emulate the large-scale theatrics of the Hollywood blockbuster, but only in its most avant-garde form.[3] In this sense, Barney is as famous for his budgets as he is for the work itself. As Alexandra Keller and Frazer Ward have pointed out, talk of Barney's excessive budgets always circulates alongside talk of the work itself, much in the way the budgets of the special effects blockbuster accompany the release of the film as a promise of the latter's pleasurable excess.[4] Keller and Ward report, for instance, that *Cremaster 3* was rumored to have cost $8 million to produce; the Barbara Gladstone Gallery, which represents Barney, would not confirm it, they tell us, thus preserving the near-mythic circulation of the rumor itself.[5] Barney emulates the blockbuster, then, but only in its most parodic and ephemeral form. For once Barney's films finish their run, whether in a local art-house cinema or in the space of a museum, they remain out of circulation. In fact, the only way to acquire a copy is to purchase a part of the work, one of the many objects of Barney's mise-en-scène, which would cost tens of thousands of dollars, whereas the new Criterion Collection DVD might only cost $30; *Pineapple Express* (Green, 2008), even less. And even then, one would have only one piece. Despite Barney's traffic in cinema, the work itself remains outside of the norms of mass reproduction. Or to be more precise, the films are produced with the equipment of mass reproduction, but only for the sake of their own intrinsic aesthetic interest. The techniques of mechanical reproduction no longer imply mass dissemination.

A number of problems follow from this practice. The most obvious issue to emerge in the work of these artists has to do with the ways in which the populist appeal of cinema as a medium—its wide availability, its comparatively low price of admission or acquisition—is done away with. Cinema was, of course, validated by the museum as a legitimate art form as early as the 1930s, when Iris Barry began the film collection at the Museum of Modern Art (MoMA) in New York.[6] And the status conferred on the object, I would suggest, was not site-specific; or, it was, but only insofar as it appeared there at least once. From there on, it mattered little whether one saw *Psycho* (Hitchcock, 1960) at the Museum of Modern Art or at home in Corinth, Mississippi. Once *Psycho* passed through the museum, it would always be art, and the originality of the object—as an object—is of no consequence.[7] In this way, one could speak of the democratizing effect brought about by the institutionalization of cinema as art, insofar as it unmoors the experience of art from the capitals of cultural commerce: New York, Paris, Berlin, and so on. This effect is, of course, what the limited access placed on the works by contemporary artists like Barney turns back. If I teach Barney, for instance, I can only do so with a few visual points of reference, with a few scenes from *The Order* (2002), a commercial DVD featuring selections from

Cremaster 3. But to do so is to teach a work in its most diminished form. Worse still, the sense of wholeness I bring to the work will require a leap of faith—for my students—about my own cultural mobility as an academic. They will need to presume that I can fill in the gaps because I was there. To be there—to be the one who was or could be there—is also to establish a hierarchy in the classroom that is based on a logic of visibility and class mobility. To teach *Psycho*, instead, is to be in the place at the moment in which the status of art is conferred on an object in institutional terms (which we can also not prevent, no matter how much we'd like and no matter what we want to say about any given film when it appears in a university classroom). We can be with them, as equals—as presumptive equals, as they may see it—and refer to the same thing. We can see together.

While one might be able to see *Psycho* anywhere (and virtually no one, I suspect, would have any interest, at this point, in deciding whether or not Hitchcock's film constitutes art), the same cannot be said of Douglas Gordon's *24 Hour Psycho* (1993). In *24 Hour Psycho*, Gordon projects Hitchcock's film in its entirety on a two-way screen suspended from the ceiling; only, he plays the film in slow motion, such that it takes twenty-four hours to get from beginning to end. Most obviously, *24 Hour Psycho* is a supreme expression of cinephilia, a return to the poetic strangeness made possible by slow motion, a technique that filmmakers like Jean Epstein and Ricciotto Canudo celebrated in the 1920s with the marvelous phrase "the new *dance of manifestations*."[8] No matter how well you know *Psycho*, you are bound to see something you have never noticed before, to see familiar gestures in a radically different register. In this sense, Gordon seems expressly interested in revivifying the tradition of *photogénie*, a fascination with the moving image as a kind of microscope that flourished in the 1920s. But whereas the experience of *photogénie*—the euphoric response to an image stilled, reversed, magnified, or sped up—is now easily achievable through the standard features of any DVD player, Gordon's work restores to spectatorship the element of chance. Paradoxically, the extended duration of *24 Hour Psycho* does not guarantee that we will see it all, but that we will see more of one section. The working hours of the museum make it impossible to watch the film from end to end. Something, in other words, will always go missing, even while we may see more of something else.

The trouble with *24 Hour Psycho*, and with what I am rather provisionally calling limited-access cinema, is not the experience of wonder and conversation that it provokes, but the sense of privilege that attends the experience. As a resident of Stillwater, Oklahoma, I was able to drive seventy miles to Tulsa to see *24 Hour Psycho* at the Philbrook Museum, where it appeared in a traveling exhibition of video art. But that, I'm sorry to admit, is truly a rare occurrence—as likely an event, in this state, as the election of an avowedly secular senator or the lasting presence of a forward-thinking curator. To see the work of Barney and Gordon one has either to live in a major city, or be able to afford to travel there.[9] In this way, the artists involved in the production of limited-access cinema have introduced aura, to cite Benjamin's most famous term, back into the economy of mechanical reproduction. And in so doing, they have also restored the class character of art.

Benjamin, of course, related the liquidation of aura to the newly acquired mobility of images and the immobile spectator: "By making many reproductions it substitutes a plurality of copies for a unique existence. And in permitting the beholder or listener in his own particular situation, it reactivates the object reproduced."[10] What no longer pertains, in this new context, is the permitting of the beholder in his own situation. *24 Hour Psycho* demands that we travel to it—not it to us. Furthermore, the promise of mechanical reproduction, Benjamin very daringly suggested, lay in its capacity to level cultural distinctions: "To pry an object from its shell, to destroy its aura, is the mark of a perception whose 'sense of the universal equality of things' has increased to such a degree that it extracts it even from a unique object by means of reproduction."[11] It would be all too easy to dismiss the class character of Benjamin's remark, that is, to see it as nothing more than an antidemocratic attack on the universal character of popular culture. What Benjamin points to here, however, is a hasty and troublesome conflation of access and democracy, mechanical reproduction and universal equality. And this, I would argue, is the chief virtue of limited-access cinema, as well. There is no denying the class problems that attend anything that can be described as "limited-access," for the reasons described previously. However, limited-access cinema nevertheless raises important questions about the "universal equality of things" and the ways in which the notion of equality Benjamin once described has been realized not as the achievement of a classless society, but as homogeneity and the globalization of culture, and perhaps more fundamentally, the eradication of difference by means of infinite access. Indeed what Benjamin suggests, in his concern with reproduction, is the unjust character of equality itself. Or as Jacques Derrida would more explicitly state it in *Rogues*, democracy—for most—implies freedom and equality, freedom *as* equality. But, and as Derrida put it, "equality tends to introduce measure and calculation (and thus conditionality) whereas freedom is by essence unconditional, indivisible, heterogeneous to calculation and to measure."[12] And by extension, mass reproduction—as a vehicle of equality at the level of access—implies, most obviously, homogeneity—a homogeneity, moreover, that is predicated on the remove and reduction made possible by mechanical reproduction. By turn, limited-access cinema raises important issues about cosmopolitanism and travel, the easy attainability of global cinema, and the necessity of ephemerality and distance to the experience of cinema as a form of community.

It is for this very reason that I would like to make a distinction between global art cinema and limited-access cinema. By global art cinema, I simply mean forms of international cinematic production—typically narrative, no matter how relaxed—that emerge in the various international film festival circuits and that are distributed internationally in art-house cinemas, wherever they may remain, and by way of DVD. I am especially concerned with the circulation of art cinema in DVD form by way of Web-based commerce. For, while many of us in the United States bemoan the disappearance of art-house cinemas, access to films from around the world has never been easier or more comprehensive. The Internet has provided cinephiles with the kind of universal equality that made Benjamin so nervous.[13] The young cinephile in Rolla, Missouri, now has as good a chance of seeing the latest Tsai Ming-liang film as his Parisian counterpart. This is, on the one hand, a promising development for art cinema worldwide, as it allows for larger audiences and potentially more diverse sources of funding. Of course, this development also seems to imply the end of art-house cinemas as we have known them. We can now see anything, but we are likely to see it alone. It is this condition, in particular, that concerns me. For what might it mean for us now to be able to get films from Senegal, Tokyo, and Berlin and never actually leave home? Obviously, one has never had to go to Senegal to see a Senegalese film (though maybe a particular Senegalese film). However, for those of us who lived outside of New York, London, Paris, and Los Angeles, for instance—and prior to the ubiquity of the DVD market, and its catering to the fragmented marketplace (which perfectly suits the relative eccentricity of cinephiles as a group with partially shared ambitions and objects)—the cinephiliac impulse provoked an awareness of the necessity of travel itself, of moving, if for no other reason than to see something that can't be seen where we currently are. The ubiquity of global art cinema on DVD and the Web, I fear, has made it easier for us to become travelers who never actually leave home. Our curiosity is very easy to satisfy and does not require the difficulty of travel, which can provoke experiences—as those of us who persist, as travelers, in the face of extreme expense and advanced degradation, know—that one cannot predict. To live in a state of unpredictability, or in a situation that is planned, but guarantees, as such, that something else will occur, is quite the opposite of the measured satisfaction of online consumption. Could it be, in other words, that our infinite access to world culture has led us instead to an advanced state of cultural isolationism?

These questions point to an important slippage increasingly common today between the concept of globalization and cosmopolitanism, especially around questions of aesthetic production. Whether we view globalization as a form of cultural contraction, the manifestation of difference, or, more productively, as a tension between these two poles, the concept itself implies a virtual and continuous flow of media across otherwise independent nation-states. It is a decidedly top-down operation, even where the work of media production comes to soothe populations deterritorialized by the shifts and expansions of capital. As Arjun Appadurai noted some time ago, "deterritorialization creates new markets for film companies, art impresarios, and travel agencies, which thrive on the need of the deterritorialized population for contact with the homeland."[14] People migrate, but the production of what Appudurai dubs "mediascapes" ultimately fosters a new immobility, a sedimentary existence that will hold at least as long as the given situation of labor demands. The image, in this context, is both compensatory and prescriptive. Such deterritorialized populations can, of course, mobilize their own revolutionary practices around such images, as his example of the creation of the imagined nation of Khalistan makes clear, a nation that continues to be imagined in cinema and the Internet, uniting across disparate lands Sikhs displaced from India and Pakistan in the anti-Sikh riots of 1984.[15] However, even here, the image comes to contain movement, or to suspend migratory patterns until further notice. The image moves so that we don't have to.

Cosmopolitanism, by contrast, privileges the movement of the body across a wide range of borders. What matters to the cosmopolitan is travel, the ceaseless alteration of one's environment *and* one's consciousness. Perhaps the most lasting image of the cosmopolitan is Charles Baudelaire's Monsieur G., about whom he writes in "The Painter of Modern Life":

> The crowd is his element, as the air is that of birds and water and fishes.
> His passion and his profession are to become one flesh with the crowd. For the perfect *flâneur*, for the passionate spectator, it is an immense joy to set up house in the heart of the multitude, amid the ebb and flow of movement, in the midst of the fugitive and the infinite. To be away from home and yet to feel oneself everywhere at home; to see the world, to be at the centre of the world and yet to remain hidden from the world—such are a few of the slightest pleasures of those independent, passionate, impartial natures which the tongue can but clumsily define.[16]

In Baudelaire's view, the *flâneur* was also a dandy—a citizen of the world, to be sure, but one whose citizenship was predicated on wealth and a refined sense of pleasure that travel makes possible. Where labor leaves the worker in a globalized economy deterritorialized and newly sedimented, however paradoxically, wealth accords the cosmopolitan mobility, a fluid sense of belonging and invisibility. The global subject belongs to a nation; the cosmopolitan belongs everywhere and nowhere—and, as such, cannot be instrumentalized.

Cosmopolitanism is thus beginning to re-emerge, for many, as a corrective to the isolating character of globalization. Kwame Anthony Appiah, for example, has recently argued for cosmopolitanism as a form of ethics, a brand of universalism that enforces no consensus. For Appiah, talk of globalization has led too easily to a kind of cultural isolationism that attends efforts to recast national boundaries, or even disparate communities in a single nation, in order to stem the tide of cultural imperialism. Patrimonial appeals to the local—to one's land and birthright—are the major refrain of what Appiah dubs "the counter-cosmopolitan," which he likewise relates to the rise of fundamentalisms worldwide.[17] By contrast, Appiah writes that the cosmopolitan tends toward a more fallibilist view, to "the sense that our knowledge is imperfect, provisional, subject to revision in the face of new evidence."[18] As cosmopolitans, our fallibilist sensibility is the result of continued cross-cultural exchange, of the attempts to come to an understanding premised neither on identical values nor total disagreement; rather, it comes from tolerance and understanding, and the acceptance of the discordant interaction that cannot be easily decided as welcome or rejection. This leads Appiah to privilege a notion of "cosmopolitan contamination," a celebration of cultural hybridity as the antidote to cultural purity.[19]

And herein lies the problem. For Appiah, as well as many others, cultural hybridity is too often understood as the accumulation of different commodities from different cultures rather than as the suspension of an open and pluralistic system of irresolvable values; or, at the very least, the latter is too strongly derived from the former. Our worldliness is marked by an accumulation of objects; thus, a neoliberal economy becomes conflated with diversity and a pluralistic society.[20] Whence, Appiah can suggest:

> Cultural purity is an oxymoron. The odds are that, culturally speaking, you already live a cosmopolitan life, enriched by literature, art, and film that comes from many places, and that contains influences from many more. And the marks of cosmopolitanism in that Asante village—soccer, Muhammad Ali, hip-hop— entered their lives, as they entered yours, not as work but as pleasure. There are some Western products and vendors that appeal to people in the rest of the world *because* they're seen as Western, as modern: McDonald's, Levis. But even here, cultural significance isn't just something that corporate headquarters get to decree. People wear Levis on every continent. In some places they are informal wear; in others, they're dressy. You can get Coca-Cola on every continent, too. In Kumasi you will get it at funerals. Not, in my experience, in the West of England, where hot milky Indian tea is favored. The point is that people in each place make their own uses even of the most famous global commodities.[21]

The problems here are legion. There is no denying that cultures regularly revise the native and ideological connotations of imported commodities. However, one might begin to wonder just how meaningful those acts of appropriation might be. In Pakistan, dubbing *The Simpsons* on national television will radically alter the American context that fuels its humor and thus make the show more amenable to Pakistani values, but the licensing fees paid out by the Pakistani broadcaster will still travel back to Fox in the United States. Likewise, the Coca-Cola that is ritually consumed at funerals in Kumasi only diversifies Coca-Cola's reach as a corporation. What, after all, do they care about controlling cultural significance? Diversity is lucrative. Perhaps the most bizarre implication of Appiah's scenario rests on his positive proclamation that one can live a cosmopolitan life simply by noticing the commodities one currently possesses from other cultures. Seen as such, cosmopolitanism comes to describe the movement of objects rather than bodies.

That these cosmopolitan objects come to me or anyone else as pleasure solves nothing. What matters is that cosmopolitanism has become but a new way of describing the immobile consumer, the virtual traveler. By remaining in place and purchasing the DVD that will allow us unprecedented access to films from around the world—we become figured as a kind of cosmopolitan consumer by the producers of global culture. This might be, for example, one way of explaining the multinational casting practices of so much recent global art cinema. Consider, for instance, Cédric Klapisch's *L'Auberge espagnole* (2002), a film about a group of young people from England, France, Italy, Germany, Denmark, and Belgium living together in a flat in Barcelona. The kinds of conflicts and alliances that attend cross-cultural exchange and remain a function of cosmopolitan existence are imagined on-screen; that is, in a strictly virtual form, and one that is nothing less than a love letter to the notion of a newly unified Europe.

Moreover, cultural diversity must also be understood as a way of expanding the marketplace. We can participate in world culture by watching, and by watching we can experience a form of cultural diversity without ever leaving home. And as such, our response to transnational conflict remains free of the lived pressures that actually force one to make the necessary and imperfect adjustments that follow from the face-to-face exchange of a lived encounter. Or, at least, one is decidedly less accountable to the other. Subsequently, the experience of cross-cultural conflict in a commodity form cannot mitigate against a retrenchment of nationalist and isolationist sentiments, the partial response to a fiction that can be generalized—from within a unified space—as national pride.

Worse still, assigning objects a cosmopolitan status, as Sean Cubitt has argued, renders the spectator subject to a process of informationalization, where we ourselves become both laborer and commodity. Considering the ways in which the global producer figures his audience as a cosmopolitan consumer, Cubitt argues that:

> The more data fuses with money, the less locality bears on consumption, save only as a numerical parameter of consumption. As space sheds its sensuous particularity—its use value—in exchange for information value, it loses dimensionality to become the entirely communicable object of strategic market planning. To that extent, space ceases to be produced, as it still was when Lefebvre wrote . . . and begins instead to be consumed, not so much by its inhabitants, but by those whose charge it is to extract its surplus value.[22]

As cosmopolitan consumers, we are the ones who extract surplus value. In watching, we become figured as a part of the data set; our pleasure, which is an experience of virtual cosmopolitanism, extends the workday—the key component of surplus value—insofar as we offer our spectatorship as data about our desires, and become ourselves in turn a commodity to be managed. That is, our information can be sold and our pleasure perfected. In watching, we sell *and* we buy. This is the modern predicament Jonathan Beller has come to describe as "the attention economy," where the expansion of viewing opportunities creates the additional time necessary to combat the falling rate of profit that cuts into surplus value, and does so through the creation of global pathways through which images now circulate.[23] Globalization, in this sense, is the expansion of time by the virtualization of space. And all of this is predicated, Cubitt suggests, on what he calls—in a Benjaminian vein—the "democratization of elitism."[24] We can have it all, but only at the price of our isolation and only insofar as we are willing to make ourselves over in the image of the commodity. Equality is nothing less than an experience of domination.

Seen this way, the cost of limited-access cinema is prohibitive, but in a more welcome sense. I cannot afford a piece of Barney's work, but in turn, I cannot be figured by it, either. There is no informational exchange that works to calibrate my pleasure to what I look at, what I look at to what I desire. The experience of defamiliarization and strangeness that regularly emerges in such encounters can happen precisely because the work is made outside of the conditions of statistical research and the calibration of images in relation to a new visual economy. In this sense, the system of patronage, even where the gallery and the dealer have continued it in the twenty-first century, is decidedly less problematic. To be sure, the art market thrives on a form of market research, but it is one—I can only presume—that begins with a consideration of what constitutes art in the moment, even if only by cultivating and assessing a sense of what is popular, and what is next. It has less to do with how its beholder will spend his time, with how looking itself might combat the falling rate of profit, which is a daily chore. The art market caters to the wealthy, and possession is theirs alone. However, possession, as I have suggested, is precisely the problem. They can have it.

Moreover, what limited access restores to cinema is the experience of lived space. It is not that one only sees in the image the very same spaces one is currently inhabiting—though that can happen. Such is the case, actually, with the initial installation of Douglas Gordon's *Play Dead; Real Time* (2003). *Play Dead; Real Time* is video shot by Gordon of a large elephant in the Gagosian Gallery in New York. The work itself was first exhibited in 2003 at the Gagosian Gallery, where one witnessed a large-scale video projection of the elephant sitting, standing, falling, and rolling—playing dead. Among other things, the piece recalls Thomas Edison's *Electrocuting an Elephant* (1903), a nod to the violence of cinematic spectacle already apparent in its nascent state.[25] It also recalls the experience of cinema as a public event, which Gordon is obviously concerned to restore. But it is not the doubling of space—lived and concurrently inhabited—that is important here. If anything, Gordon's *Play Dead; Real Time* is a unique reflection on the significance of the space of exhibition to limited-access cinema, insofar as it reflexively calls our attention to the significance of the space of exhibition itself.

So much of limited access cinema marks its relation to space in similarly interesting ways. In *Dualism #2* (2006), for instance, Stephen G. Rhodes outfits a two-way video screen with a border made of asymmetrical tree branches. On-screen, we see figures in nineteenth-century (I think) clothes drenched in rain and white powder, enacting rituals whose meaning is difficult to discern and yet remain utterly fascinating. Rhodes's figures act out a history that is vital, unfamiliar, and charged with the playfulness of a game with no end. Moreover, Rhodes's quick and angular cutting patterns effect a sense of modernity at odds with the antiquated figures and natural environments we see on-screen. The markers of history are never easily situated. Moreover, the wood frame of the screen forces the image back into nature, into lived space—a gesture that makes us aware of the relation of what we see to the space we are currently inhabiting. When I saw the work, it was appearing in a show called *Art Rock*, where a series of new works were displayed in a temporary gallery installed in front of Rockefeller Center in New York. The galleries themselves were made of shipping containers, the very materials of global export. On the day I viewed the work, it was uncharacteristically cold, dark, and rainy for a New York July. The wind blew the rain into the space of *Dualism #2*, strangely echoing the logic of the frame itself, which extends the image into the realm of the natural—whatever that may be. The rain also made of the space a kind of shelter, creating a community of spectators that had to linger with the work a little longer than a nicer day may have allowed. The specificity of place puts into operation a series of contingencies that will affect—in ways that can be difficult to discern—what we see and how we understand it.

The public character of limited-access cinema thus opens the work to a shifting, communal response. Such, for instance, is the idea that informs Francesco Vezzoli's *Trailer for a Remake of Gore Vidal's Caligula* (2005). Vezzoli's work is a 35 mm trailer for an imagined remake of *Caligula* starring, among many others, Helen Mirren, Karen Black, and Courtney Love, and featuring, in equal measure, images of contemporary celebrities and unsimulated sex. One watches the trailer from within the space of a recreated porn theater, from the dark and shabby seats of a nearly extinct site and practice of exhibition. One of the things that Vezzoli's parody makes clear is that way in which the pornographic image circulates widely, but privately; how the space of the theater as sexual community and the site of the chance encounter has itself become a relic.[26] Infinite access, in this sense, has become another form of censorship.

The film projector itself thus becomes an important component of limited-access cinema. Its appearance onsite is both functional and conceptual. In the case of Vezzoli's *Trailer for a Remake of Gore Vidal's Caligula*, it is needed to project the 35 mm print; but as such, we are reminded of the importance of celluloid as the guarantor of cinema as a communal experience, especially since very few of us can actually afford the kind of home projection system that would include 35 mm film. It is, like limited-access cinema, prohibitively expensive. Such is the meaning, I suppose, of Rodney Graham's *Torqued Chandelier Release*, which features a large 35 mm looped projector that projects in constant succession a five-minute film of a chandelier. We cannot own the work—most of us—but as a consequence we will have to experience it with others; we will have to hear the noise of opinion, which might make us cringe, reply, or spend days trying to figure something out about our encounter there.

The presence of the projector in the space of the exhibition in limited-access cinema likewise signals the importance of ephemerality to the experience of cinema. Over the last few decades, we have become extraordinarily concerned with preservation, certain that with proper care and an indiscriminate view of the objects we might restore, we will see a film as it was meant to be seen, as it actually *was*. "The universal equality of things," to return to Benjamin's phrase, might likewise serve as the guiding principle of the archive. The ubiquity of DVD versions of so many "lost" films (so many, in fact, that the cliché "lost" classics finally sounds as problematic as the notion has always been) too easily assures us that our heritage is secure. And subsequently, we can look back at earlier generations of film writing and correct what others clearly could not see, since private, controlled, and repeated access to film was certainly less possible then. *Then*, of course, is when scholars simply had to describe what they remembered of what they saw, however imperfect that description may be. And as John David Rhodes has suggested in his work on ekphrasis, the descriptions of film we once encountered in writing about film that moved us so often worked to augment our vision of what seemed to have gone missing in the murky bootlegs that fed cinephiles for so long.[27] The writing of film theory and criticism, in other words, was a form of restorative *and* projective seeing; it was, in certain respects, what activated the work as art, even if it did so in a discursive vein.

The question now, of course, is whether one saw correctly, even though it ought to concern whether or not one *can* see correctly. And how, exactly, did seeing get bound up with notions of heritage and cultural preservation? While I confess to not knowing the answer to that particular question, a solution does seem to reside in Matta-Clark's projector and his 16mm film of *Conical Intersect*. What remains of Matta-Clarks's art, as Thomas Crow has shown, are descriptions. The same will be true of any description of Barney's *Drawing Restraint 9* (2005). What kind of writing can this be? For one, we will only ever be able to evoke the fading memory of an intense encounter. Along such lines, it is not terribly surprising that so much of the work that I've tried to talk about in the preceding pages can best be described in terms of nostalgia, or historical events unloosed from a sense of period. Barney's images linger in me very strongly, for instance, but only in the most spectral form. I—along with the others who have seen it—will never be sufficiently able to arrive at a consensus about the work, or something

FIGURE 6.2. *Dualism #2* (Stephen G. Rhodes, 2006). This is not Oklahoma. (Image courtesy of the artist.)

like an intersubjective account of the work's total formal elements, especially considering the fact that the work moves from place to place. My interpretation will only ever be partial and admittedly undecidable; happily so. Whenever we speak of the work we will never be able to move past the limits of our own perceptual activity; we can never say with any certainty that what one or another of us has seen simply *is*. Writing will no longer serve as a transparent vessel to a self-present object. Such has been the promise of both the analytical projector and the DVD, where one can supposedly see all, repeatedly, and thus there is only one way to see.

I am reminded, finally, of that great enemy of consensus, Tristan Tzara. In an early definition of Dada, Tzara declared—in terms we might still do well to consider—that: "It [Dada] is for and against unity and definitely against the future."[28] Along similar lines, I would say that limited-access cinema gathers a community of interested participants that cannot, in the end, be unified or accounted for. Looking in this mode can create only a marginally unified set of perceivers. For one thing, looking itself might also include site-specific impediments—our moods, the weather, the people around us, our predispositions about art we have previously encountered in those same spaces. Of course, such contingencies may also intensify seeing; they may even create possibilities that our sedimentary and closely calculated decisions about what and why we will see rule out in advance. Art, in this sense, bears an interesting and necessarily imperfect relation to ethics. As Maurice Blanchot says in the *The Unavowable Community*, "Love simply puts ethics into question by imitating it."[29] Art, I would add, does the same to our will to consensus. It is both for and against it, and it cannot decide our future; that is, it cannot cast the future in the image of the present. We might be drawn to certain works and likely we will have seen these works in different places and different times. Thus, as viewers, we are an always imperfectly formed community armed with the fading memories of our encounters, drawn into conversations about shared objects that are both intense and necessarily provisional. What matters, in the end, is the conversation as much as the object, the saying over the said. And the same, in the end, should be said of true cosmopolitanism, of the cosmopolitan. The cosmopolitan is a part of an imperfect and always expanding community, a group unified only by its own restless nature and its refusal to remain fastened to a set of provincially prescribed values. The cosmopolitan knows that the city can be as provincial as the country, that we are both unified and unbound by our movements. What is true of our relation to art as cosmopolitans will be true of the world for us, as well: we will see, talk, and revise at will. We will be as disinclined to see the *Mona Lisa* and become the anonymous inheritors of someone else's tradition as we will be to count film- or picture-frames and prove ourselves right. We will return to spaces like Beaubourg on the understanding that they are always in flux, even if we don't always care for what we might see. Of course, the ineffable communities constituted by cosmopolitanism will carry the burden of class privilege that the museum as an authenticating site traditionally has. We can go there and decide on art precisely because we have, in many cases, the institutional mobility to do so. However, the affordability of the cosmopolitan commodity does not, as I hope to have indicated, solve the problem of class more effectively, despite whatever utopian claims we care to make on their behalf. We cannot simply trade one for the other. A more productive experience of cosmopolitanism thus demands an expanded conception of what constitutes place. If we consider cosmopolitanism as a form of collecting, as a series of great cities related on the grounds of their well-established similarities—by the luxurious minimum they all contain—the differences we draw in the moments of our lived encounters of places will be less radical or productive than they might otherwise be.

NOTES

This essay is dedicated to John David Rhodes, whose friendship and cosmopolitan spirit has long compelled me to get out of the house every now and again.

1. Jean Baudrillard, "The Beaubourg-Effect: Implosion and Deterrence," trans. Rosalind Krauss and Annette Michelson, *October* 20 (Spring 1982): 6.

2. Thomas Crow, *Gordon Matta-Clark* (London: Phaidon, 2004), 94.

3. Alexandra Keller and Frazer Ward develop this point more substantially in "Matthew Barney and the Paradox of the Neo-Avant-Garde Blockbuster," *Cinema Journal* 45, no. 2 (2006): 3–16.

4. Ibid., 9.

5. Ibid.

6. For an extensive account of the development of the MoMA film collection and the institutionalization of cinema as an art form see Haidee Wasson, *Museum Movies: The Museum of Modern Art and the Birth of Art Cinema* (Berkeley: University of California Press, 2005).

7. Likewise, the sites of institutional legitimization have expanded rapidly since the 1930s and include the development of the concept of the auteur in France in the 1950s and its exportation in the 1960s to the United States, where it has lived on in the academy. Cinema thus became, as we all know very well, an object not only of artistic merit, but also of scholarly inquiry of all kinds. Consequently, the very act of watching film, or television, within the space of the classroom confers a kind of legitimacy on the object that bears no specific claims about its quality. It is legitimized, one might say, without merit.

8. Ricciotto Canudo, "The Birth of the Sixth Art," in *French Film Theory and Criticism*, Vol. 1, *1907–1929*, ed. Richard Abel (Princeton, N.J.: Princeton University Press, 1988), 59.

9. As Karl Schoonover has rightly suggested to me, there are—of course—barriers to access even for city dwellers—the cost of museums, hours of operation, and so on. This is an important point and well describes the paradox that appears at every turn just as soon as the question of access is raised. It certainly squares with my own experience of being a poor graduate student in New York, living without savings, a decent wage, or trust fund (a phrase that seems just the opposite of what it actually describes). All I can say, in this case, is that to be in a city is to have the potential to see limited access cinema. Like any contingent phenomenon, access in the city is possible, but not guaranteed. But the possibility, though not guaranteed, is much higher.

10. Walter Benjamin, "The Work of Art in the Age of Mechanical Reproduction," in *Illuminations*, ed. Hannah Arendt, trans. Harry Zohn (New York: Schocken, 1968), 221.

11. Ibid., 223.

12. Jacques Derrida, *Rogues: Two Essays on Reason*, trans. Pascale-Anne Brault and Michael Naas (Stanford: Stanford University Press, 2005), 48.

13. In a slightly different register, Jeffrey Sconce has argued that attainability has, in most respects, had an all too sobering effect on the cinephile, who can now easily see again a film he once cherished and overvalued in its absence. The art of art cinema, in other words, depends as much on absence, in Sconce's view, as it does on presence. See Jeffrey Sconce, "The (Depressingly) Attainable Text," *Framework* 45, no. 2 (Fall 2004): 69–75.

14. Arjun Appadurai, "Disjuncture and Difference," in *Planet TV*, ed. Lisa Parks and Shanti Kumar (New York: NYU Press, 2003), 45.

15. Ibid.

16. Charles Baudelaire, "The Painter of Modern Life," in *The Painter of Modern Life and Other Essays*, trans. Jonathan Mayne (London: Paidon, 1965), 9.

17. Kwame Anthony Appiah, *Cosmopolitanism: Ethics in a World of Strangers* (New York: Norton, 2006), 143–147.

18. Ibid., 144.

19. Ibid., 113.

20. I owe this particular insight to Meghan Sutherland, who has developed, at great length, a discussion of the conflation of cultural diversity, aesthetic variety, and neoliberal economics in her book, *The Flip Wilson Show* (Detroit: Wayne State University Press, 2007), and in her dissertation, "The Logic of Variety" (Ph.D. diss., Northwestern University, 2007).

21. Appiah, 113.

22. Sean Cubitt, *The Cinema Effect* (Cambridge, Mass.: MIT Press, 2003): 339–340.

23. Jonathan Beller, *The Cinematic Mode of Production: Attention Economy and the Society of the Spectacle* (Lebanon, N.H.: Darthmouth College Press, 2006).

24. Cubitt, 336.

25. I owe this observation to Michelle Dent.

26. On the social and political implications of the demise of the porn theater, especially as they relate the conflation of urban renewal, discourses of purity, and real estate, see Samuel Delany, *Times Square Red, Times Square Blue* (New York: NYU Press, 1999); see also Elena Gorfinkel, "Wet Dreams: Erotic Film Festivals of the Early 1970s and the Utopian Sexual Public Sphere," *Framework* 47, no. 2 (Fall 2006): 59–86.

27. John David Rhodes, "From Description to Prescription: The Ekphrastic Imperative in Film Theory," unpublished paper given at the Framework Conference on the Future of Film Theory, November 3, 2006, Oklahoma State University.

28. Tristan Tzara, "Manifesto of Mr. Antipyrine," in *The Dada Painters and Poets: An Anthology*, ed. Robert Motherwell (Cambridge, Mass.: Harvard University Press, 1951), 75.

29. Maurice Blanchot, *The Unavowable Community*, trans. Pierre Joris (Barrytown, N.Y.: Station Hill, 1988), 40.

7

BETWEEN AUDITORIUM AND GALLERY: PERCEPTION IN APICHATPONG WEERASETHAKUL'S FILMS AND INSTALLATIONS

Jihoon Kim

Thai filmmaker Apichatpong Weerasethakul has been so acclaimed since the early 2000s that he is now heralded as one of the most renowned and innovative figures in film rather than as a "mysterious object" of discovery. Besides five feature films that were enthusiastically welcomed by international film festival circuits and world cinéphiles, his creative energies have found expression in a variety of media formats, resulting in a multifaceted body of work that includes shorts (both film and video) and single/multichannel video installations. These diverse experimentations reveal him not simply as an idiosyncratic auteur but as a border-crossing maverick who eludes the grasp of simple classification. His feature films can be termed "a cinema of odd conjunctions"[1] insofar as they are mergers of several notable oppositions—primordial/postmodern, indigenous/global, rural/urban, magical/prosaic, corporeal/spiritual, fiction/documentary, Eros/Thanatos, surreal/real, and the like. In terms of his whole universe, they revolve around the mutual proliferation of cinematic and artistic traditions that had been deemed distinct—European modernist film/American avant-garde film, art cinema/video art, and the dark room/white cube. In these senses, it can be construed that his transversal works are emblematic of a notable condition of today's art cinema: It is striving to redefine and transform itself through its negotiation with and the containment of its contiguous media practices and the spatiotemporal aesthetics they articulate.

Apichatpong's interplay between art cinema and video work is closely associated with two interrelated tendencies over the past decade: first, many video artists—Pierre

Huyghe, Douglas Gordon, Mark Lewis, Sam-Taylor Wood, and so forth—have produced film and video installation with a distinctly cinematic feel that is distinct from earlier artistic experiments with film in the theater; and second, there have been a number of filmmakers who have translated their works into installation or conceived new works only accessible in the darkened space of the gallery, while continuing to produce films for traditional theatrical release (including Chantal Akerman, Chris Marker, Harun Farocki, Atom Egoyan, Peter Greenaway, Victor Erice, Raul Ruiz, and, recently, Jean-Luc Godard).[2] These two tendencies are significant for the current state of cinema, what Jacques Rancière once called cinema's "double existence": "There is an 'autonomic' existence which is eventually welcomed for artistic performances but which does not count upon the definition of artistic modernity; and there is another existence, where cinema . . . is inscribed by the redefinition of contemporary art."[3] Here Rancière's observation attests to the fact that cinema and contemporary art commonly enter into a new mutual relationship by which one influences the other: Just as cinema's status as a unique art form continues to be confirmed by the artists and filmmakers' appropriation and investigation of it, so it is ready to be transformed by other artistic media—particularly video and the digital. It is the ontological duality of cinema in relation to contemporary art—that is confirmed and transformed simultaneously—that Apichatpong demonstrates in his attempt to make a dynamic exchange of forms and techniques between cinema and video art.

In this essay, I will argue that his key three feature films—*Sud sanaeha/Blissfully Yours* (2002), *Sud pralad/Tropical Malady* (2004), and *Sang sattawat/Syndromes and a Century* (2006)—are strongly influenced by his video installation works that are in turn grounded in formal and technical aspects of cinema. For this aim, I will pay particular attention to two notable characteristics shared by the three films and examine how both relate to the elements of his "cinematic" video installations: one, the elongated duration of shots, which provides enhanced sensory perception of the space depicted in each of the three films; and, two, a narrative structure marked by a spatial gap between two halves of a story—what I will call "interstice" later, whereby it is hard to explain a temporal relationship between them in the sense of the narrative unfolding of feature film. As discussed later, those two characteristics— "durational space" and "interstice"—form a large part of his cinematic experiment with the spatialization of image and narrative, and are drawn from the formal and technical features of "cinematic" video installations, which his own video works deploy. My investigation into his feature films will be in line with Chris Darke's argument that in "cinematic" video installation, cinema is being "exploded . . . for the radical fracturing of the forms of [its] narrative and experimentation."[4] More important, however, I will claim further that the wavering of cinematic forms between movie theater and gallery, exemplified by Apichatpong's case, forces us to relocate cinematic medium specificity in the field where cinema stretches out to other arts and vice versa.

CINEMATIC REWORKINGS OF VIDEO'S DURATIONAL SPACE

The fact that Apichatpong's practice resides in a position in between theatrical film and video installation reflects his aspiration to amplify sensory perception by projecting onto the screen the depicted space he has experienced. In his feature films, Apichatpong constructs immersive spaces teeming with sensual and affective charges through an array of various cinematic techniques, wherein the viewer is held in fascination and then led astray. The transposition of everyday life into dreamlike, mystical, and infinite landscapes—a dense forest in *Blissfully Yours* and an obscure jungle in *Tropical Malady*—is accentuated by elliptical editing, extremely long takes (with fixed camera or smooth tracking), and the deep ambience of diegetic sound. Near the end of *Syndromes and a Century*, one encounters an eccentric vignette of the interiors of an urban hospital: It consists of a static long shot of a creepy woman walking along the dreary corridor, a track-out of seemingly plaintive Dr. Toey sitting in her office, and a long and slow 360-degree pan of an underground workroom where enigmatic smoke gradually comes out; a mesmerizing soundscape of an electric guitar's intermittent monotone against the backdrop of an electronic synthesizer amplifies the eerie and ethereal effect. Captivating and estranging, these spatial organizations allude to the atmospheric experience of the moving image not necessarily confined to the cinema theater.

Here it is worth noting that Apichatpong studied architecture in Thailand before obtaining an MFA in filmmaking from the School of the Art Institute of Chicago. Based on his earlier training, he connects architecture to film narrative in a manner that illuminates the immersive spatial properties of his work.[5] In this sense, the affinity between cinema and architecture has been underlined by a number of critics or theorists. Cinema has been considered to be a two-dimensional equivalent of three-dimensional experiences of the body in space such as travel and streetwalking, providing the spectator with a "mobilized virtual gaze"[6] constituted by shifting perspectives, a montage of various rhythms, and shots in moving cameras. The viewer's journey through the moving itinerary of the cinematic map corresponds less to appreciating the pictorial representation of spatial imaginary than to being a way of "lived" experiences produced by "a narrativized space that is intersubjective."[7] The overlapping of moving bodies in space and the spectator's corporeal dimensions render cinema not just visual but haptic, involving the tactile sensing of territories and interiors through eyesight. Through the architectonics of storytelling, concretized with the stylistic material, the viewer actually feels the space. From this standpoint, Apichatpong's three aforementioned features—*Blissfully Yours*, *Tropical Malady*, and *Syndromes and a Century*—are paradigmatic cases for the *story about space* and the *story embedded in space*. On the one hand, they bring to the fore a passage from an urban landscape sketched by the quasi-documentary technique to a natural dreamscape disorienting the viewer's (and also characters') multisensory attention (*Blissfully Yours* and *Tropical Malady*), or the migration from the pastoral overtone of a rural hospital to the dry but uncanny undertone of an urban hospital (*Syndromes and a Century*); on the other hand, all the places in these films—forest, jungle, and hospital—carry their own story—for instance, the story of a ghost that incarnated a tiger in *Tropical Malady*. They can be called "a phantom zone [where] the hard, 'real' world . . . cedes dominion to a magical realm of reverie and desire."[8] Nature in Apichatpong's world provides a venue for the three characters' floating passion and the slow streams of sexual ecstasy (*Blissfully Yours*) or the supernatural metamorphosis of two male heroes (a solider who falls in love with a young countryman in the first part of *Tropical Malady*). It appears to entrance all of them and thereby enable crossings over the threshold of consciousness.[9]

In another sense, however, the sensory intensity of space in these three features cannot be wholly reduced to the purely cinematic approximation of architecture or natural environment, for it is activated in a series of shots with extended duration that exceed narrative economy. This dilation of time allows viewers to become engrossed in the spatial properties of the individual shots and consciously aware of screen time. In other words, the spatial continuum of time induces a temporal perception in the viewing present. The passing of space in time, then, overtakes a recorded presentation of past time. The spatial dimension of duration acquires a phenomenological depth and length in which the moment of the viewer's perception and the temporal register in the image are inseparably fused together. The spatial manifestation of duration as such in Apichatpong's filmic corpus, I suggest, is akin to a "cinematic" tendency of recent video art with which he has continually engaged. Unlike the early video installation equipped with the small-scale monitor, the "cinematic" video installation uses the large-scale screen or the plasma screen reminiscent of home viewing. This sort of video installation is also referred to as "cinematic" because it imitates, appropriates, and even manipulates the technical and aesthetic constituents of cinema so pervasively that the boundaries between video art and cinema become more indiscernible. Apichatpong's body of video works, as I shall examine later, has been in line with this aesthetic trend, rendering itself distinct from the institutional context of theatrical films in its exhibition yet aesthetically attuned to them.

Recent scholarship identifies the "cinematic" video installation in terms of the transformation of the apparatus and the moving image it delivers. Chrissie Iles uses the term "cinematic phase" to differentiate it from its previous phases, the "phenomenological phase" and the "sculptural phase."[10] This historiography is predicated upon the demarcated, nearly mutually exclusive, development of film and video as mediatic and artistic practices: while film, as an indexical art, has been primarily authenticated by its inherent quality as a photographic medium inscribing the flow of time that "has passed," video entered into the artistic realm as a medium delivering the flux of time that "is now," a single and simultaneous real-time. The phenomenological and sculptural inquiry into video aimed at intervening in this "real-time," whether delaying it or relaying it to a single monitor or multiple ones in the time of viewing experience. The early video artists assumed that the monitor in the gallery could furnish the viewer with the opportunity to contemplate a perceptual process of domesticated spectatorship triggered by the televisual devices within various physical positions and settings. Here the space of exhibition was turned into the media-space that could evoke the temporality of viewing, what Peter Campus has called "durational space."[11] Situated in an artificially designed environment that opened up the liminal point between monitor world and external space, spectators made a comparison of their embodied time with variable temporal dimensions forged by the deconstruction and reconstruction of the TV or video sets.

The switch to the "cinematic phase" is congruent with a technological development of the projected image in scale and resolution. As Catherine Elwes puts it: "The video monitor . . . with the three-dimensionality of the box was lost and replaced by the spectacular, immersive experience of the cinema, sometimes enhanced by comfortable seating."[12] By way of encouraging numerous artists and filmmakers to liberate themselves from the terrain of the theater and its formal confinements, a darkened room with the diverse formats of screens as well as various means for the transfer and transformation of the moving image have offered them a new institutional and cultural form of cinema: as a newly prosperous art form of the projected image, the "cinematic" video arts (or cinemas of the gallery) have recycled and manipulated the particular fragment of the already existing film, or exploited a panoply of film forms—complex modes of narration, figurations of shots, and miscellaneous editing techniques. In so doing, they are limited to neither radical experimentations with the filmic apparatus and viewing process in the structural/materialist film nor to the deconstructive critique of the television medium in early video art.

Still, what is crucial about the mélange of the video installation and the cinema is the temporal ontology of the video. Whether it is for archiving and analyzing the fragments of found films or for reconfiguring the diegetic world, video has newly opened out from an obstinately present tense to include a past tense. This change has aroused skepticism in those who have great concern about the loss of the video's medium specificity, along with a polemical questioning of whether video's absorption of the cinema constitutes a radical rupture with the modernist formation of projection art in the gallery.[13] For instance, Elwes claims that the association of video with the past "is not yet a feature of video." Championing early video art's modernist deconstruction of television, she goes on to note that the recent cinematic expansion of video installation in the gallery is nothing more than "a re-immersion in the escapist enchantments of a celluloid dreamland."[14] But what underwrites this argument is a common notion of medium specificity grounded in any integral identity or unique substance of an artistic medium. In my view, this notion fails to recognize changes in the relationship of the video image to physical space as well as changes in the image itself.

From my perspective, the convergence of film and video in the contemporary "cinematic" installation is not necessarily a negative development. In form and content as well, this transition signals that film and video belong to a time-based medium that records the trace of light and inscribes temporal duration. As Peter Wollen contends succinctly, "The relationship of film and video . . . involves many different and complex ways of presenting time" and that both mediums can "function in a very similar way."[15] Although there have been some notable technological and artistic differences between film and video in harnessing the problems of temporality, both are subject to a common

denominator, to articulate time in different modalities—past and present simultaneously. Hence the historical duality of film and video in dealing with time is due less
to any mutually irreducible differences of formal or technical dimensions than to
functional or institutional ones subjected to change. The burgeoning of artists' video
installation and the increasing migration of filmmakers into the gallery became possible
because of, and also promoted, the functional change of video from the self-contained
assertion of its formal and technical specificity to the exploration of a common ground
it shares with cinema. In this sense, the recent shift of emphasis in the properties of
video, from the simultaneous transmission of images to the artist's enhanced intimacy
with the techniques associated with the past tense—a foregrounding of recording and
editing—can be seen as playing with the variability of its temporality: that is, video has
not been confined to the present tense but extended into a past that had been primarily
considered as immanent to the filmic medium.

What should be stressed in the "cinematic" video installation is that its
relationship of the video image to physical space points to the different constitution
of temporalities from that of previous video arts, not to the disappearance of
"durational space." In the phenomenological and sculptural video arts, the durational
space of the viewing situation in the present tense meets the present transmission of
audiovisual data through the monitor. Conversely, the projection in the "cinematic"
video installation enables the durational present of viewers to merge with the
recorded—and replayed by the looping projection—duration as the past. The viewers'
work of memory is then induced by the passage of time in the moving image. For
instance, one of Apichatpong's single-channel video installations, *It Is Possible That
Only Your Heart Is Not Enough to Find You a True Love* (2004),[16] was basically made
as a preliminary sketch for his not-yet-realized feature film entitled *The Heartbreak
Pavilion*, based on a monthly pocket-size magazine of the same title widely read by
working-class Thais. It dramatizes the two sequentially linked stories of an anonymous
couple, *True Love in Green* (10 min.) and *True Love in White* (20 min.), both of which
share dialogues and dreams they once held dear. Each story shapes the two gardens
where two souls are entrapped: just as the former shows an exuberant labyrinth of
green trees and fields, so the latter presents an unworldly modern garden. These two
strands of memory are captured by such cinematic devices as landscape-like long
shots, modest handheld camera movement adhering to each character's bodily
movement and breadth, and intimate close-ups of his or her face. All of these
components are also deployed in "A Spirit's Path" of *Tropical Malady*. They invite
viewers to intermingle their own past love with, and to reconstruct it from, what is
shown on the video screen. In the exhibition, the work looks as though it were a
spatial construction of the "pavilion," for the size of the screen fits well into the
meditative viewing with sitting. The cinematic underpinning of this work's visual
language meets the temporal and affective spectatorship of the screen in the gallery.

Iles attributes the viewer's phenomenological modes of experiencing the projected
image—"psychological engagement" and "a profound self-consciousness of one's
physical and emotional reactions"—to the transformation of an architectural space into
a perceptual field in the film and video installation of the 1970s.[17] Yet inasmuch as the

"cinematic" video installation remakes the durational space in conjunction with the image's extended duration, these properties are not wholly unique to that era. Apichatpong's case is in this sense interesting; for he equally introduces the film spectator and the gallery viewer to a realm of perception that evokes a sense of temporal disorientation, in both cases by virtue of exchanging multiple sensory impressions with the audience.

Video is associated with excessive duration in a way that film is not. Apichatpong carries this technical affinity of video into the visionary and tactile long-takes of his feature films accompanying the ambient sounds of diegetic surroundings. It is worth noticing that the scene of nature in *Blissfully Yours* and *Tropical Malady* provides a diegetic soundtrack that continues through the excessive length of peculiar shots, even when a line of action in the scene comes to an end. The credit sequence of *Syndromes and a Century* is a remarkable example (see figure 7.1): a handheld shot follows Dr. Toey and an assistant, Toa, who fetches her to the principal of the hospital; then we hear the dialogue between them with an equal volume even when they disappear into the offscreen space and the camera stays static, showing a shiny grass field around the rural hospital. The soft discrepancy between the visual and the audible interestingly mutually reinforces the qualities of each: the visual track acquires the phenomenological duration of its presence reinforced by the spatial disorientation from the deep diegetic soundscape of the audio track. This strategy does not simply impose on the stream of images a linear sense of time, but it combines the past that is recorded in them with the temporality of their presence, the projection time as the present.[18]

FIGURE 7.1. Dialogue between Dr. Toey (Nantarat Sawaddiukl) and Toa (Nu Nimsomboon) in the opening sequence of *Syndromes and a Century* (Apichatpong, 2006).

Haunted House Project: Thailand (2001), originally made as a sixty-minute video, adapts two episodes about ghosts from a popular Thai soap opera. They are not true to the original drama, but based on memories of villagers who enjoyed it and reenact it, participating in the filmmaking by playing its characters' roles. Actors change as the filming location shifts from one village to another, with the result that all stories are interlaced but contradict one another according to the memories they impersonate. Not only villagers but also their houses as the setting for those stories are treated like another medium that is "haunted" by various images and narratives of the TV drama that shapes each of their memories. Apichatpong varied this work's form and delivery by reconceiving it for different media, including an audio installation for an exhibition in Thailand and a double-screen projection in Belgium. Consequently, his configuration of perception through the close dialogue between cinematic form and video installation responds to the ubiquity of the moving images that are saturated in our environment and affect our senses, as he states:

> The moving images are always there when we grew up, in the bedroom, the living room. I think we are just used to analyze and reflect the idea, the living, through moving images—like a universal language. When something is projected and moves, it still exudes the magic and wonderment. It's erotic to the brain.[19]

THE SPATIALIZATION OF BROKEN NARRATIVE

The most extraordinary and subversive maneuver in Apichatpong's three feature films lies in the double structure of narrative marked by what I will call the "interstice"—an abrupt extradiegetic gap that interrupts the spatiotemporal continuity of a film's narrative in such a way that it is not chronologically or causally justified by its diegetic elements. In *Blissfully Yours*, the slippage from the minute vignettes of the three protagonists' daily lives—consulting the doctor, working in the factory, and the like—to their bucolic and sensuous outing in the forest occurs when within the long traveling shots of a moving car, mainly ones from the view of windshield, the opening credits suddenly appear after more than half an hour of the film's running time. The narrative's bifurcation into two halves is evolved in *Tropical Malady*, where its first part, the matter-of-fact recounting of two men's tender romance, is transformed into a shamanistic fable in the midway point, with about a minute-long black screen and new set of credits, reminiscent of a moment of brief intermission. *Syndromes and a Century* does not have such a mark to break the narrative chain, but its two parts begin with the same scene—Dr. Toey interviews a newcomer, Dr. Nohng, to determine his position in the hospital with a dozen questions, some of which are trivial and playful—in separate settings: the former a rural hospital, the latter an urban one. They are correlated in a structural and compositional symmetry that is as though one could be seen from the point of view of the other (the first part's interview shows Dr. Toey's point-of-view shot to Dr. Nohng; inversely the second one does Dr. Nohng's point of view with the same lines of dialogue).

All of these interstices are constituted by extradiegetic elements that do not serve to unfold their own narrative. The insertion of the opening credits in *Blissfully Yours* and *Tropical Malady* is not content to disrupt narrative causality. More important, the interstices exist for themselves as if to obscure the succession of past events and function as a compositional limit between each film's two subsets. The automated projection of their images is still irreversibly linear, but this fact no longer guarantees the temporal coherence of the fictional world. For the devices that cleave each film in two leave spatial gaps not reducible to the temporal ellipsis in the conventional narrative film. They are all the more spatial and extradiegetic inasmuch as they do not endow the viewer with any cue to channel her into a plausible reconstruction of storyline. The explicit gaps in both films are replaced by the relatively hidden compositional symmetry of the two halves in *Syndromes and a Century*, but their juxtaposition becomes more complex. The spatial disjointedness of the two episodes is so radical that they could be redistributed into two screens played simultaneously: that is, the two temporal events of the film are so fully spatialized that they become apprehended as two self-contained stories within two different locations, although they have some meaningful resonances with each other. Hence their constellation could be articulated as architectural rather than in strictly cinematic terms, as though we enter into two separate rooms for the same characters' flows of life. By examining the degree to which the variations of this double structure secede from the narrational temporality of the art cinema as we can see it in the theater, I will suggest that the spatial gaps expand the temporality of cinematic storytelling so profoundly that they incorporate more intricate forms of simultaneity and parallelism that spread out the confluence of narrative films and gallery ones.

At first sight, all three films share the nonlinear order. Even the loosened sense of temporal succession held out by the halfway car sequence in *Blissfully Yours* is totally abandoned in *Tropical Malady*, unrolling the complication of interpretations about the relationship between its two parts: The first story deals with a romance of prudent courtship (of Keng) and naive bashfulness (of Tong) in the shiny town and countryside; and the second one presents a totally isolated primitive world engulfed in deepest darkness. Therein the pure flow of desire passes through the zone of sensation populated by plants and animals as precursors of violence and apparitions. The relation of the pursuer and the pursued becomes interchangeable and at times even indiscernible in the mutation of spirit into becoming animal. The seemingly most plausible hypothesis is to read the second part as the first's psychoanalytic subtext, as a dream ruled by the logic of lunacy and delirium; or, another hypothesis is that the second part is a Leibnizean "possible world" of the first, inasmuch as the two stories cannot exist simultaneously in a single event but nevertheless have a relationship in a complementary way.[20] In either case, *Tropical Malady* seems to probe the cinematic linkage between two temporal durations in the immanent plane of time. But it does not show any trace of a character's inner state from which we draw personal memory.[21] *Syndromes and a Century* more elaborately flirts with the impersonal orchestration of narrative time. Its first part focuses on Dr. Toey and Toa—the assistant who works at the same hospital and has a crush on her—her past story about an encounter with an orchid grower, and a friendship between a Buddhist monk named Sakda who dreams of being a DJ and a dentist who acts as a pop singer after hours. The main character of the second part is Dr. Nohng, who disappeared in the first part after the interview with Dr. Toey. All the characters of the first part dwell in an urban hospital with other characters not included in it, showing different manners, dialogues, and roles. It is impossible for the viewer to attribute any chronological order or personal focalization to their recurrent splitting. Leading us nowhere in the story and making our temporal consciousness deluded, all that remains is the flow of beautifully composed takes guided by the slow camera, in which space is a vehicle to deliver emotions and memories.

How do the interstices of the three films endow this dechronological and impersonal narration with the ordering of the memories that do not pertain to any of their characters? In several interviews, Apichatpong has highlighted his "burden of memory"[22] in his filmmaking, as he states in a discussion with Tony Rayns about *Syndromes and a Century*.

> It [memory] may well be the only impulse! Everything is stored in our memory, and it's in the nature of film to preserve things. . . . But I've never set out to recreate my memories exactly. The mind doesn't work like a camera. The pleasure for me is not in remembering exactly but in recapturing the feeling of the memory—and in blending that with the present.[23]

Indeed, his strategy of "blending his feeling of the memory with the present" is to encourage spectators to enter into and interact with his memory-world throughout the unfolding of screen time, the only place where the two disjointed halves of his feature films conjoin. He paints his fragments of memory with enhanced audiovisual senses, without ever inserting his self-reflexivity into his characters and ensuring their psychological depth. More significantly, the interstices achieve resonance between two types of durations: two interspersed durations of the director's memory in the diegetic space; and the duration of images on the screen space embodied by the viewer's phenomenological perception and attentiveness. This resonance achieves a reconstruction of narrative space with respect to the presentation of memory, which modern and contemporary cinema has limitedly explored in order to combine disjointed episodes or fragments. Unlike other experimentations with storytelling in the cinema, the interstices in Apichatpong's feature films break with any tradition of channeling the viewer's narrative comprehension into only a linear and irreversible screen time wherein the interweaving of the character's consciousness unfolds. The temporal depth of each film appears only via a strategic spatialization that abandons its narrative streams to a fluid arrangement of relations. This spatialization can be inclusively apprehended by examining narrative experiments in a staple of "gallery films" whose viewing conditions escape the experience of the film theater. The interstice serves to transform the divided parts of Apichatpong's films into "time zones" reminiscent of the two-screen installation inside the gallery wall. As I will discuss later, the multiscreen projection has been introduced in the course of searching for a spatial model that is capable of overcoming and expanding the theatrically-bound cinematic rendering of temporal events,[24] and Apichatpong's inquiries have involved the spectator in the interplay between this model and his feature films.

Many experimental film practitioners and video installation artists have adopted various formats of multiscreen projection for two key reasons: these formats open up more flexible space wherein the artist's audiovisual expressions are intimately interlocked with the spectator's perceptual activity; and they can formally subvert the linearity of screening time that controls the narrative feature film in general—"breaking the frame, invoking the process of making the work, using repetition and looping to avoid the dramatic structure."[25] In this vein, multiple screens organize the spatial arrangement and distribution of various temporal modalities—simultaneity, ellipsis, comparison, leap into the future, the disparity between past and present, contestations between different viewpoints on a single event, and so forth. It is well known that modern cinema, avant-garde feature films, and contemporary "alternative plot" movies have investigated the breakdown of chronological time, but they commonly stick to the restriction imposed by the screen time passing within a single frame. The multiplication of screens asserts the imperative that different temporal parameters can coexist through the dissemination of a single linearity into disparate spaces. Those spaces are then interwoven by such internal logics as comparison, contrast, and association, all provoking the viewer's engagement with the layered durations of time. Catherine Fowler observes that the gallery film facilitates the "vertical investigation" of a narrative event. Originally Maya Deren's term, "vertical investigation" designates the level of "what it feels like or what it means" in contrast to its "horizontal" occurrence rooted in the seamlessness of conventional screen time.[26] If one is to apply Deren's notion to gallery films and video installations, then the multiscreen technique transposes "verticality," hitherto implicated in the "inside" of diegesis through nonlinear editing, onto the viewing interface, the "outside" of the frame. The expansion of verticality also provides the viewer with a vantage point for combining the different in-frame contents of storytelling in her viewing experience. Thereby comes a new mode of narration that enacts the indeterminacy of temporal relationships not necessarily resting on the permeability of the "passing time" and the "virtual past." Apichatpong's feature films spatialize the dimension of verticality through posing the interstices, in tandem with his multichannel screen installations.

First, the interstices render his divided narrative structure as such an equivalent of split-screen formation. This is most salient in the black screen of *Tropical Malady*, where the sequential stream of narrative comes to a halt. This interruption propels the viewer to notice the outside of the frame in terms of space as well as to reorganize the two parts into a new horizon in terms of time. The black screen draws a borderline that separates the continuum of screen time. Here the viewer could integrate the two parts into the plane of remembrance in such a way that she returns to the first part retrospectively while watching the second part. The continual coincidence between the two parts affirms viewing time and cognitive space as the only point of reference for the viewer's potential comprehensions of their relationship. All of those comprehensions are more or less contingent. The first part might be an actual facet of urban life, each moment of which is split by its fantasmatic virtual side (the second part), but is this virtuality past or present? In either case, the temporality of the first story is in turn influenced by this indeterminacy: We might say that the two stories shape two different modalities of a past or present, and that the absence of one would make the other imperfect and meaningless. Like a Leibnizean "monad," each half maintains the spatial distinctiveness and its own duration as much as each screen does in the two-channel video installation, but the temporal relationship between the two halves is interdependent and cross-contaminating. This complimentary and comparative temporality can also be found in *Syndromes and a Century*. Its two stories are the different reincarnations of Apichatpong's parents as much as they are evocative of "larger dualities in mind—such as day/night, masculine/feminine."[27] The temporal relationship between them could be the distribution of two coexistent memories into the present, or the confrontation of the purely "expanded" past (as reminiscent of his childhood, the days of his living in rural hospital environments) with the past that is "contracted" into the present (as the urban world he now lives in). In any case, the two parts are connected as though they would face each other, shaping structural similarities and differences but not being totally commensurable.

Apichatpong has been fascinated with this spatialized structure encompassing the feature film and other media works since his early career, as in *0116643225059* (1994), a five-minute 16mm short later exhibited with the two-screen format: In its original film version, two images—a childhood picture of his mother and his family home in Thailand, and a sketch of his apartment interior in Chicago—alternate while being

FIGURE 7.2. *Masumi Is a PC Operator* and *Fumiyo Is a Designer*, part of an exhibition entitled Narratives (Apichatpong, November 4–6, 2001). Courtesy Intercross Creative Center, Sapporo, Japan.

connected through the telephone call marking "the distance between the two places and the periods of time."[28] This differing conjunction has been varied with such great complexity that it lets the relationship between two separate contents be indiscernible. This is the case with the contiguity of *Masumi Is a PC Operator* (6 min.) and *Fumiyo Is a Designer* (6 min.), part of his exhibition entitled "Narratives" (November 4–6, 2001; Intercross Creative Center, Sapporo, Japan). Both works are the reflection of ordinary lives in contemporary settings, but because they are devoid of sound the viewer is forced to draw his or her own conclusions about the relationship between two female characters and what each feels. It is the viewer's mental synthesis that grants the characters possible temporal dimensions—whether they share the same present or past or reside in different temporal phases.

The interstices also obtain two more formal and functional attributes that are commensurate with those of the video installations: looping, and doubling or mirroring. In the first place, the interstices weaken the sense of linear narrative's beginning and closure, allowing his feature films to retain a cyclical facet evocative of the looping in video art.[29] The halfway point insertion of opening credits in *Blissfully Yours* has the effect of leaving randomized the drift from the first part to the second one. But the more delicate looping-like structure is alerted by the black screen in *Tropical Malady* in parallel with the disturbing opening scene: A group of soldiers (Keng does not appear in it) searching in a field of reeds recovers something and poses with it for a camera in a group picture. The innocent happiness of their smiles is inverted when the shot reveals that what they have recovered is a dead body. After arriving at the second part's climactic moment when Keng's mind succumbs to the tiger and seems to be possessed by it, the viewer could have the impression that the body might be Keng's, and therefore be puzzled as to which part is chronologically anterior to the other. The interstice in this film grants the entanglement between Tong and Keng, or man and beast, the feeling of perpetual transmutation through which the existential distinction between them is dissolved. This circular structuring of time might be compared to a tendency of video installation artists such as Francis Alÿs (Mexico) and Anri Sala (Albania). Conceiving of the complexity of time as belonging to local specificity, both artists foreground "the potential coexistence of temporalities and spatialities within and between place," which questions the unified notion of time in Western modernity as a linear and homogenous succession of discrete moments applicable to any location.[30]

The symmetrical repetition of the interview sequence in *Syndromes and a Century* invites the viewer to a constellation of dualities distributed in its other scenes, while simultaneously inflecting its entire structure with cyclical nuance. Many contemporary video installations have revolved around a mirroring effect to invoke a set of oppositions—self and other, subject and object, good and evil, reality and fiction, and the like—through various combinations of two screen spaces: to split a single screen into two distinct windows, to locate two screens side by side horizontally—*Win, Place, and Show* (Stan Douglas, 1998) and *The Third Memory* (Pierre Huyghe, 1999)—or to install two projections separately in the opposite direction while making them face each other—*Through a Looking Glass* (Douglas Gordon, 1999).[31] This spatialization also complicates the temporal relationship between a pair of screens as it is determined by structural patterns of resemblance and dissimilarity. Besides feature films, Apichatpong has experimented with the juxtaposition of mirror-like dual screens. In *Secret Love Affair (for Tirana)* (2001), he keeps two small monitors apart at the corner on the floor, so that the viewer has to bow her head to watch them standing in line with her. As in other installation works, the viewer should fill the interval between those two monitors because they are not linked by any chronological coherence and spatial continuity. This work shows the looping of a man and woman glancing and smiling at each other while nostalgic and mournful music plays. Thanks to this formal correspondence, it looks to be conjuring up an eternal recurrence of a couple already dead. Meanwhile, another two-channel video installation, *Faith* (2006),[32] charts a variation of *Tropical Malady*: while converging into a lonely space traveler, two screens display different stories—romance and sci-fi—which at once run parallel to and contrast with each other. Sometimes they show great similarity in their reciprocations; but at other times they keep on showing notable polarity and interpenetration as if one line of memoir would efface and replace the other, to the extent that their spatial backgrounds and generic boundaries fade into the loop, underscoring the fleeting present and the perpetual transformation of the past.

Today's video installation, spurred by and capitalizing on film's material assets and formal languages, quintessentially inaugurates the rehabilitation of the cinema as a prominent art for engaging time and space through moving images. In so doing, it in turn encourages one to rethink the medium specificity of film that has been pursued by art cinema and the avant-garde in the age of its unsettledness. Hence the close encounter of the cinema with video in the alliance between auditorium and gallery, or between sedentary viewing and perambulatory watching in the terrain of contemporary arts, does not simply raise the question, "Where is cinema?" Through examining these phenomena, we can witness the ways in which the cinema actually maintains its distinctiveness by running the risk of allowing for hybrid forms and functions as its constitutive parts. More than the "mysterious in-between" of the art cinema and the video art in the gallery, Apichatpong's crossbred body of work, characterized by blending both forms together, is no less difficult to pin down. But a significant consequence of this fact is that he has exemplified two ways that cinema is ontologically changed: It is being mutated through redistributing its properties into other artistic media (the creation of "cinematic" video installation) and appropriating their forms and techniques (the application of video installation to filmmaking) simultaneously. His double movement reminds us of what has been and will be the larger stake in the cinema in relation to other arts. Alain Badiou suggests that cinema as the seventh art has been viable in its essential dependency upon a "general space" in which it manifests its own specificity as a kind of impurity, through its relationship to that which it is not.[33] In this sense, cinema's purity has no less been supplemented by than benefited from other arts. By aligning with this paradox, we are aware of the extent to which Apichatpong's blurring of the boundaries between feature films and video installations has furthered what has been in cinema all along. The deepened durational space and the spatialized form of narrative temporality renew the forms that satisfy our long-standing and ongoing craving for the cinema's own specificity, and thus, these formal strategies represent less an imperative to purify cinema's medium specificity than to invoke its dynamic associations with its neighbors.

NOTES

1. Brett Farmer, "Apichatpong Weerasethakul, Transnational Poet of the New Thai Cinema: *Blissfully Yours*," *Senses of Cinema* 38 (Jan.–Mar. 2006). Available online at http://www.sensesofcinema.com/contents/cteq/06/38/blissfully_yours.html (accessed April 10, 2007).

2. Raymond Bellour once named these two tendencies "*autre cinéma*" (other cinema). See his "Of an Other Cinema," in *Black Box Illuminated*, ed. Sara Arrhenius et al. (Switzerland: JRP Editions, 2003), 39–62.

3. Jacques Rancière, "Le cinema, dans la 'fin'de art," *Cahiers du Cinéma*, October 2000, 51.

4. Chris Darke, "Cinema Exploded: Film, Video and the Gallery," in *Light Readings: Film Criticism and Screen Arts* (London: Wallflower, 2000), 160.

5. See Thunsk Pansittivorakul, "A Conversation with Apichatpong Weerasethakul," *Criticine: Evaluating Discourse on Southeast Asian Cinema*, April 30, 2006. Available online at http://www.criticine.com/interview_article.php?id=24 (accessed April 10, 2007).

6. See Anne Friedberg, *Window Shopping: Cinema and the Postmodern* (Berkeley: University of California Press, 1993), 15–40.

7. Giuliana Bruno, *Atlas of Emotions: Journeys in Art, Architecture, and Film* (New York: Verso, 2002), 65.

8. James Quandt, "Exquisite Corpse," *Artforum* 43, no. 9 (May 2005): 227.

9. It could be for the reason that the tales nature carries entail a nonverbal narration, scribbling handwriting and pictures with minimal dialogues (*Blissfully Yours*) or primordial illustrations with subtitles (*Tropical Malady*).

10. Chrissie Iles, "Video and Film Space," in *Space, Site, Intervention: Situating Installation Art*, ed. Erika Suberburg (Minneapolis: University of Minnesota Press, 2000), 252.

11. Peter Campus, "The Question," quoted in *Space, Site, Intervention*, 255.

12. Catherine Elwes, *Video Art: A Guided Tour* (London: I. B. Tauris, 2005), 151.

13. On the helpful agenda-setting debate about this issue, see Malcolm Turvey et al., "Round Table: The Projected Image in Contemporary Art," *October*, no. 104 (Spring 2003), 71–96.

14. Elwes, *Video Art*, 168, 170.

15. Peter Wollen, "Time in Video and Film Art," in *Making Time: Considering Time as a Material in Contemporary Video and Film*, ed. Amy Cappellazzo (Palm Beach, Fla.: Palm Beach Institute of Contemporary Art, 2000), 12.

16. This work was exhibited at Busan Biennale in 2004 (August 24–October 31, South Korea).

17. Chrissie Iles, "Between Still and Moving Image," in *Into the Light: The Projected Image in American Art, 1964–1977*, ed. Iles (New York: Whitney Museum of American Art, 2001), 33.

18. See Michel Chion, *Audio-Vision: Sound on Screen*, trans. Claudia Gorbman (New York: Columbia University Pres, 1994), 13–16.

19. Gridthiya Gaweewong, "Apichatpong Weerasethakul Talks with Rirkrit Tiravanija on Art, Film & Etc." Available online at http://www.project304.org/beff/beff4talk.htm (accessed April 10, 2007).

20. Hervé Aubron, "Tropical Drive, Mulholland Malady: Trafic d'âmes entre Lynch et Weerasethakul," *Revue Vertigo*, no. 27 (March 2005): 5–6.

21. Here I am referring to Gilles Deleuze's description about the mode of narration in European modern cinema. One of the most profound stakes of his two-volume cinema series, particularly in *Cinema 2: The Time-Image* (Minneapolis: University of Minnesota Press, 1989), is to conceptualize modern cinema as the direct presentation of the mental world governed by de-chronological time wherein causal connection between story events disintegrates into the coalescence of past and present. In Alain Robbe-Grillet and Alain Resnais's films analyzed by Deleuze (for instance, *L'Année dernière à Marienbad/Last Year at Marienbad* [Resnais, 1961] and *L'Homme qui ment/The Man Who Lies* [Robbe-Grillet, 1968]), the cinematic image shapes a mode of narration that makes indeterminable the distinction between the actual present (as the moment of perception) and the virtual past (as the ocean of memory) in their mutual exchange. The actual "passing present" and the virtual past are not totally different temporalities, but rather two modalities of the time as duration that constitutes "the only subjectivity" (*Cinema 2*, 82.).
In a sense, the two-part narrative structure of Apichatpong's feature films shares with the mode of narration in modern cinema an ineluctable difficulty in differentiating that which happened in the past from that which is happening in the present. Nevertheless, it should be noted that there is a crucial difference between the two. The mode of narration in modern cinema depends on certain correspondence of diegetic elements between the actual and the virtual—what Deleuze calls the "crystal image," such as the reciprocity between a character and his or her mirror-reflection (see *Cinema 2*, 83–97). Conversely, Apichatpong's narrative strategies do not rest on diegetic elements, but use the extradiegetic interstices to push the indiscernibility of the actual and the virtual to its limit. In so doing, the two threads of the three films are so totally disjointed that their temporal relationship can be interpreted in multiple ways, not confined to the relationship between present and past: it might be a coexistence of "virtual" events that did not "actually" take place in the past, or a chain of interrelated "virtual" presents that cannot coexist in the horizon of "actual" present.

22. Quandt, "Exquisite Corpse," 230.

23. Tony Rayns, "Memories, Mysteries: From an Interview with Apichatpong Weerasethakul" (Bangkok, July 2006). Available online and updated at http://www.kickthemachine.com/works/Syndromes.html (accessed April 2, 2007).

24. See Daniel Birnbaum, *Chronology* (New York: Lukas and Sternberg, 2005), 68.

25. Catherine Fowler, "Room for Experiments: Gallery Films and Vertical Time from Maya Deren and Eija Liisa Ahtila," *Screen* 45, no. 4 (Winter 2004): 331.

26. Amos Vogel, "Poetry and Film: A Symposium with Maya Deren, Arthur Miller, Dylan Thomas, Parker Tyler. Chairman Willard Maas," in *Film Culture Reader*, ed. P. Adams Sitney (New York: Cooper Square, 2000), 174; see also Fowler, "Room for Experiments," 327–328.

27. Rayns, "Memories, Mysteries."

28. Anchalee Chaiworaporn, "A Perceiver of Senses—Apichatpong Weerasethakul." Available online at http://www.thaicinema.org/Essays_07apichatpong.asp (accessed April 10, 2007).

29. It should be noted that while the looping in video art is actual—the video in the gallery keeps repeating itself so that its beginning and end are sometimes even indistinguishable—Apichatpong's films make it take place in the viewer's mind.

30. Jessica Morgan, "Time after Time," in *Time Zone: Recent Film and Video*, ed. Jessica Morgan and Gregory Muir (London: Tate, 2004), 20.

31. A notable exhibition on this theme is Stan Douglas and Douglas Gordon: Double Vision, held at Dia Center for the Arts, New York, February 11, 1999–June 13, 1999.

32. This work was commissioned by Liverpool Biennale.

33. Alain Badiou, "The False Movements of Cinema," in *Handbook of Inaesthetics*, trans. Alberto Toscano (Stanford: Stanford University Press, 2005), 78–88.

8

PASOLINI'S EXQUISITE FLOWERS: THE "CINEMA OF POETRY" AS A THEORY OF ART CINEMA

John David Rhodes

The labour pains at the birth of new concepts.

Don't for heaven's sake, be afraid of talking nonsense! But you must pay attention to your nonsense.

Ludwig Wittgenstein, Culture and Value

We are in New York in 1966. A half dozen women and men (three of each), caught by the photograph and suspended in time. Their photographic stillness suspends, forever, what was one moment in the welter of the New York Film Festival. One might read some unease in this photography, some level of polite enmity. This photograph is a historic text. It demands close reading. The photograph will instruct us in the contours of an era, that of the independent cinema, sometimes also called the "art cinema," and of the "New American Cinema," also called the American Avant-Garde. This is one seminar attended by the class of 1966.

On the far left of the image sits Pier Paolo Pasolini, the *ragazzo di vita* of international cinema. He is here because his film *Uccellacci e uccellini / The Hawks and the Sparrows* (1966) has been screened at the festival. His right hand is raised, and although his lips are pursed, we assume he is speaking. The heads of the three persons nearest him are pivoted in his direction. Two folding tables drawn together form the literal "panel" at which this colloquy is gathered. It divides the image into upper and lower halves. Beneath the table we can see that Pasolini's legs are crossed, his tightly tailored trouser hems rise above his ankle, revealing dashingly striped socks. Next to Pasolini, leaning in to hear him carefully, is his translator; I do not know her name. Next, third from the left, is the film critic, American "author" of the auteur theory Andrew Sarris. His gaze is also directed toward Pasolini, his eyebrows raised, slightly,

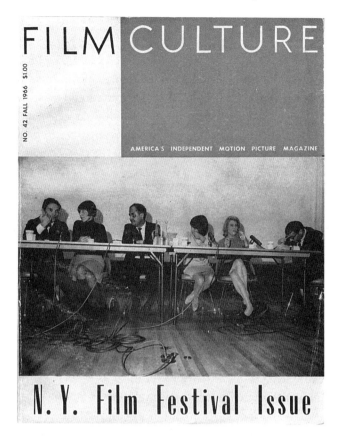

FIGURE 8.1. Fall 1966 cover of *Film Culture* journal.

whether in concentration, attentive sympathy, or mild skepticism, we know not. His legs are not crossed. His socks are dark, matching his dark suit. Our fourth figure also gazes in Pasolini's direction; her head bowed slightly in concentration, she is garbed in what appears to be a white minidress, right ankle tucked behind left ankle, below the table. This is the filmmaker Agnès Varda, whose work precedes, apotheosizes, and flourishes long after the French *nouvelle vague*. Next to Varda, the first of our subjects to look away from the speaking Pasolini, is Annette Michelson, sometime art critic for the *International Herald Tribune*, staff writer, at this moment, for *Artforum*, who was, when this photograph was taken, in the process of instituting herself as chief exegete of avant-garde film practice in the United States. She appears to be in the process of lighting a cigarette. Dressed in a gray sweater and black miniskirt, her right ankle is tucked behind her left, making a chiasmus of sorts with the crossed ankles of Varda. Finally, his head bowed in—concentration? boredom?—is the French film director René Allio, perhaps best known for his adaptation of *Moi, Pierre Rivière, ayant égorgé ma mère, ma soeur et mon frère . . . / I, Pierre Rivière* (1976), but here on this panel on account of having presented his 1965 film *La vieille dame indigne* at the festival.

We should also not forget that this image is presented as the cover of *Film Culture* (copy price $1), the primary organ for the articulation and dissemination of the activities of the New American Cinema during this period. We see at the bottom of this cover that this is the "N.Y. Film Festival Issue." We see beneath the publication's title its declaration that it is "America's Independent Motion Picture Magazine."

I am primarily interested in our first figure, the one sitting on the far left, caught in mid-sentence, toward whom most of the other figures incline their attention (if not their sympathies): Pier Paolo Pasolini. His contribution to this discussion included, among other remarks, major reference to a theoretical concept (or category)—the "cinema of poetry"—that he had first announced a year earlier in a talk entitled "La mimesi dello sguardo" ("The Mimesis of the Gaze") that he gave at another film festival, the Prima Mostra Internazionale del nuovo cinema, held at Pesaro, from May 29 until June 6, 1965. Other speakers at this festival included Geoffrey Nowell-Smith, Lindsay Anderson, Andrew Sarris, Miloš Forman, Mino Argentieri, and the Taviani brothers. In the first half of his talk, Pasolini waded deep into the terminology of scientific linguistics and semiotics in order to theorize cinema's signification. Pasolini's use of semiotic theory in elaborating the "cinema of poetry" has been the object of abuse from film theorists and semioticians ever since Pesaro. However, when this talk was first published as an essay in the Italian film journal *Filmcritica* (nos. 156–157), the essay appeared with the title "Il 'cinema di poesia'" ("The 'Cinema of Poetry'") and in a truncated form, entirely shorn of its first movement, the section that occupies itself with semiotics and linguistics. Instead, the essay opens with this sentence: "The entirety of recent cinema, from Rossellini, regarded as a Socrates, to the 'nouvelle vague,' to the production of the last few years and months tends towards a 'cinema of poetry.'"[1] Lightened of much of its theoretical heavy baggage, the essay, in this, its first published form, appears to be, somewhat straightforwardly, simply an essay on what we commonly call art cinema, and it is precisely as a theorization and a description of art cinema that I want to consider Pasolini's essay in the present chapter. In what follows, I shall be working through a close reading of key passages in the first English-language translation of the full essay. In my reading, I hope to show that Pasolini's essay provides us with a striking—if somewhat torturous—theorization of art cinema. Whereas art cinema has often been dismissed as by turns decadent, apolitical, or middle-brow,[2] Pasolini's theory of the "cinema of poetry" asks us to consider the art cinema as a privileged medium of political filmmaking. His theory, moreover, asks us to think closely about avant-garde aesthetics, the relation of this aesthetics to "art cinema" and its aesthetics, the politics of both modes, and the politics of deciding between them.

"The 'Cinema of Poetry,'" in its original length, begins thus:

I believe that it is no longer possible to begin to discuss cinema as an expressive language without at least taking into consideration the terminology of semiotics. Quite simply, the problem is this: while literary languages base their poetry on the institutionalized premise of usable instrumentalized languages, the common possession of all speakers, cinematographic languages seem to be founded on nothing at all: they do not have as a real premise any communicative language. Literary languages thus have an immediate legitimacy as instruments (pure and simple instruments), which do, in fact, serve to communicate. Cinematographic communication would instead seem too arbitrary and aberrant, without the concrete instrumental precedents which are normally used by all. In other words, people communicate with words, not images; therefore, a specific language of images would seem to be a pure and artificial abstraction.

If this reasoning were correct, as it would appear to be, cinema would simply not exist; or, if it did, it would be a monstrosity, a series of meaningless signs. Instead, cinema does communicate. This means that it, too, is based on a patrimony of common signs.[3]

This opening movement is typical of Pasolini's essay style: It is characterised by the language logic of deductive reasoning, prone to reversals, false dead ends, surprising paths forward that seem to emerge from the thicket of language. The first dead end, the putative nonexistence of cinema, is surpassed no sooner than it is announced. Cinema has "a patrimony of common signs." To prove this assertion, Pasolini argues, just a few short paragraphs later, that "there is a an entire world in man which expresses itself primarily through signifying images . . . . : *this is the world of memory and dreams.*"[4]

This second assertion is the first step of what will become one of the most obsessively returned-to preoccupations of Pasolini's film theory: that the natural world speaks a language of itself, and that cinema is the "written language" of this natural language—the "written language of reality." The title of his essay "Res Sunt Nomina," which, translated, means "things are names," neatly summarizes the basis of Pasolini's belief that the world speaks a language of itself.[5] Pasolini must have known that he would annoy semiotic officialdom with this claim. His unsympathetic critics have been numerous and influential: Christian Metz (a stringent but sympathetic critic), Umberto Eco, Stephen Heath, and Antonio Costa, to name a few. Metz dismissed the distinction between poetry and prose; Eco accused Pasolini of "reduc[ing] cultural facts to natural phenomena"; Heath argued that Pasolini's thought led to a "denial of the cinema as a semiotic system"; and Costa accused Pasolini of occult mystification: "His premise . . . is anti-semiological and anti-analytical."[6] The heresy of *Heretical Empiricism* is largely bound up in Pasolini's self-consciously stubborn insistence on conflating the symbolic (or, more specifically, the linguistic) and the object world (what Pasolini calls "reality").[7] In my own heretical take on Pasolini's heresy, however, I want to sidestep this preoccupation; I want to move, in jump-cut fashion, toward the part of the essay that concerns itself with the "cinema of poetry," a category that can be considered in relative isolation from the claim that cinema is the written language of reality.

I am rather more concerned to entertain the (structural) linguistic dimensions of the essay, insofar as these inform the eventual formulation of the "cinema of poetry." To this end, I am interested in Pasolini's interest in the fact that cinema has no lexicon (much less a "language system").[8] Whereas the writer has at her disposal the words that already exist and are found in a dictionary, the filmmaker, however, is deprived of such a lexicon but is enriched by virtue of this deprivation: "There is no dictionary of images. There is no pigeonholed image, ready to be used. If by any chance we wanted to imagine a dictionary of images, we would have to imagine an infinite dictionary, as infinite as the dictionary of *possible words*."[9] Pasolini goes on to say that "while the activity of the writer is an aesthetic invention, that of the filmmaker is first linguistic and then aesthetic."[10] This would seem to mean that the filmmaker must wrest her "language" from the object world, despite the fact that this object world is already meaningful. It is as if the filmmaker finds ready-made linguistic signs in the world; however, she must first perform the labor of finding them.[11] However, Pasolini goes on, in a crucial passage, to say that "it is true that a kind of dictionary of film, that is a convention, has established itself during the past fifty years of film. This convention is odd for the following reason: it is stylistic before it is grammatical."[12] Style before grammar. The strange priority that Pasolini ascribes to style is, as I shall aruge, one of the chief problematics of the "cinema of poetry." Style, which is often considered nothing more than "excess" or epiphenomena in many accounts of cinema, figures for Pasolini as the primary mode of cinematic articulation. That this is so in his general account of cinematic representation only foreshadows the significance ascribed to style in his account of the "cinema of poetry." As I hope to demonstrate, Pasolini's intense interest in style—an interest that becomes more clearly developed in the essay's later movements—offers a provocative way of conceptualizing the political function of style in cinema.

The filmmaker must thus choose her images (Pasolini calls them "im-segni," or im-signs, short for image-signs) from among the infinite array of possible images provided by reality. Images, according to Pasolini, are "always concrete, never abstract," therefore it follows (logically, for Pasolini, in any case) that given its fabrication out of such concrete images, cinema's "dominant" mode is "artistic," characterized by "expressive violence" and an "oneiric physical quality."[13] This consideration, finally, brings us to the question of poetry:

> All this should, in conclusion, make one think that the language of cinema is fundamentally a "language of poetry." Instead, historically, in practice, after a few attempts which immediately cut short, the cinematographic tradition which has developed seems to be that of a "language of prose," or at least that of a "language of prose narrative."
>
> This is true, but as we shall see, it's a question of a specific and surreptitious prose, because the fundamentally irrational nature of cinema cannot be eliminated.[14]

Although the cinema has been co-opted into the service of "the language of prose communication," "its foundation is the mythical and infantile subtext which, because of the very nature of cinema, runs underneath every commercial film."[15] Although the cinema is primarily constituted by "artistic," "poetic" energies, it has been captured and domesticated by the needs of communication. However, despite its deployment in the service of "prose narrative," cinema retains, always, because of its predication on imaging, some vestige of its original poetic nature.

In other words, cinema is a realm of ambivalence. This ambivalence between poetic "irrational[ity]" and communicative discourse is amplified by another ambivalence. Although cinema allows and invites (demands, even) the free reign of the director's "subjective" volition in choosing, from the "dictionary of possible words," the ones that correspond to her vision, these same choices have, in the brief history of cinema, hardened very quickly into conventions, "syntagmas": what begins as "subjective" "style" quickly accedes to "objective" communicative discourse. Or, as Pasolini says, after so much definition and re-definition: "In short, cinema, or the language of im-signs, has a double nature: it is both extremely subjective and extremely objective."[16] As a particularly tricky example, Pasolini offers a film representative of the "canons" of "pure expressivity," *Un Chien andalou* (Luis Buñuel and Salvador Dalí, 1929)—a film that we might want to construe as exclusively subjective, exempt from the claims of a "double nature." Pasolini suggests that, on the one hand, this film exhibits a kind of absolute "impurity" due to the highly subjective nature of its images. On the other hand, according to Pasolini, the film's "oneiric" qualities return its images back to the brute materiality of things themselves, and of images of things.[17] Even in its most densely irrational, subjective articulations, cinema, because it is cinema—that is, because it presents to us photographic (therefore objective) images of "reality"—will always live out its throbbing existence on the borders of subjectivity and objectivity.

Bearing this "double nature" in mind, we can now turn toward the "cinema of poetry," a term that, it would seem, is finally able to be announced only after this "double nature" has been insisted upon and clarified. Only a mere paragraph following his discussion of *Un Chien andalou*, Pasolini passes rather quickly and unceremoniously from these ontological-linguistic speculations, to the modest terrain of film historical periodization, which is, it seems, central to the "cinema of poetry":

> The entirety of the most recent film production, from Rossellini, elevated to the position of a latter-day Socrates, to the *"nouvelle vague,"* to the production of these months (including, I would imagine, the majority of the films of the first Festival of Pesaro), tends toward a "cinema of poetry."[18]

This cinema, in other words, is one that traces its genealogy back not so much to the cinema of the historic avant-garde (i.e., *Un Chien andalou!*), but only as far back as neorealism. In fact, works that explicitly and self-consciously label themselves as avant-garde do not interest him for the purposes of theorizing the "poetry of cinema." (I will have more to say on the relations between the "cinema of poetry" and the avant-garde later.) This taxonomic and periodizing gesture signals clearly that whatever the "cinema of poetry" is, or will be defined to be, it is not to be confused or identified with the avant-garde. Already, given Pasolini's examples, he has implicitly suggested that the "cinema of poetry" might instead be identical to, or might at least coincide with, "art cinema."

The essay then proceeds to make its next curious turn, this time away from semiotics and toward the language of the theory of literary narration. Immediately following the passage just quoted, Pasolini stages a series of rhetorical questions:

The following question arises: how is the "language of poetry" theoretically explicable and possible in cinema?

I would like to answer this question outside a strictly cinematographic context, that is, by breaking the logjam [*sbloccando la situazione*] and acting with the freedom which is guaranteed by a special and concrete relationship between cinema and literature. Thus I will temporarily transform the question "is a language of poetry possible in cinema?" into the question "is the technique of free indirect discourse possible in cinema?"[19]

The transformation of this question is somewhat staggering. The recourse to literary theory does not surprise us, given Pasolini's long engagement in this field, and although we might wonder if the poetic in cinema *demands* this recourse to *this* literary theoretical concept, we are obliged to follow Pasolini's deployment of it. We may not see the necessity of turning the question of the "cinema of poetry" into a question of "free indirect discourse," but we will see that the necessity abides not in the "poetic" itself but is, rather, integral to Pasolini's desire to steer the question of the "cinema of poetry" into a discussion of the representation of subjectivity and the relation of this representation to cinematic form.[20] Moreover, free indirect discourse is yet another realm of ambivalent fluctuation between objectivity and subjectivity, thus Pasolini's choice of it as a theoretical and critical heuristic allows him to carry this part of his investigation forward.

Pasolini quickly decides quickly that the equivalent of free indirect discourse in cinema is *not* the optical point of view shot, which instead corresponds to direct discourse. The equivalent is, instead, the "free indirect point-of-view shot," which is further not to be confused with an attempt to represent inner speech.[21] The problem with the notion of the "free indirect point-of-view shot" is that, whereas in the realist novel (the humus out of which indirect discourse develops), free indirect discourse is "always linguistically differentiated when compared to the language of the writer," in cinema, because "our eyes are the same the world over," the "free indirect point-of-view shot" cannot exist. (We will notice here, again, the positing of categories, concepts, followed by the positing of their impossibility, followed, in turn, by a way of solving this impossibility; this is the rhythm of Pasolini's thought.) Because cinema has no language, as such, the director cannot merge her vision with that of her character because cinema can only represent the world through images, which is to say, objectively. Pasolini admits that a peasant may see the world differently from a bourgeois, but that the cinema, lacking language, cannot let us see this difference, cannot effect a "naturalistic *mimesis*" of this character's vision. This means, in the end, that the director's *"activity cannot be linguistic; it must, instead, be stylistic."*[22]

This curious proposition, difficult to grasp, is worked out more fully in the paragraph immediately following the last quoted passage, which I will cite in full. This paragraph is, in a sense, the culmination of the theoretical argument:

Moreover, a writer, too, if he were hypothetically to reanimate the speech of a character socially *identical to himself*, can differentiate his psychology from that of his character not by means of a language which is his own language, but by means of a style—that is, in practical terms, through certain characteristic traits of the "language of poetry." Thus, the fundamental characteristic of the "free indirect point-of-view shot" is not linguistic but stylistic. And it can therefore be defined as an interior monologue lacking both the explicit conceptual element and the explicit abstract philosophical element. This, at least in theory, causes the "free indirect point-of-view shot" in cinema to imply the possibility of an extreme stylistic articulation. In fact, it causes it to free the expressive possibilities compressed by the traditional narrative convention through a sort of return to the origins until the original oneiric, barbaric, irregular, aggressive, visionary quality of the cinema is found through its technical devices. In short, it is the "free indirect point-of-view shot" which establishes a possible tradition of the "technical language of poetry" in cinema.[23]

Va bene. Let's try to take this nonsense seriously. In cinema, there can be no real way of "linguistically" producing a differentiated vision of the world: the cinema can only produce images, possible words, but these do not cohere linguistically to allow the filmmaker to construct a specific character's (class-based) differentiated vision of this world. Since the language-system cannot make this specific, class-specific vision of the world appear, then the only thing (process, activity) that can make this appear is *style*. *Style, in other words, comes to stand in for a class-consciousness that cannot otherwise appear in the cinema.*

This theorization of the necessary link between style, subjectivity, and class-consciousness is remarkable and potentially fruitful. It would seem that none of these things can appear in the "cinema of poetry" without the other two. The "cinema of poetry" therefore becomes a privileged, indeed, a seemingly unique vehicle for the representation of class-consciousness in the cinema. The ability to create class-consciousness happens in and through the stylistic expression, and stylistic expression is possible thanks to class-consciousness. Let us see now where Pasolini sees the "cinema of poetry" at work.

When Pasolini finally begins to offer actual examples of what the "cinema of poetry" is, what it looks like, and who makes it, it is clear immediately that he is referring to works of cinema that have been referred to as "art cinema": filmmaking of the postwar years, originating primarily in Italy and France, that extends (as mentioned before) out of the experiments of neorealism. This is the cinema of European independent production, a cinema that has digested the lessons of high modernism, but that is committed to exploring formal experiment in the context (if not exactly the service) of cinematic narration. In pinpointing specific examples of this cinema, Pasolini makes the move from theory to criticism:

As concrete examples of all this, I will drag into my laboratory Antonioni, Bertolucci, and Godard—but I could also add Rocha from Brazil, or Forman from

Czechoslovakia, and naturally many others (presumably, almost all the film-makers of the Festival of Pesaro).[24]

Of Pasolini's discussions of these three filmmakers, I want to concentrate on his treatment of Michelangelo Antonioni. Pasolini mentions, in a rather offhand way, that he will dispense with any discussion of specific sequences from *Il deserto rosso/Red Desert* (1964), the film of Antonioni's that he bears most in mind (and the one that had been most recently released). He says he doesn't want to "linger on those aspects of the film which are universally recognized as 'poetic.'" However, he does list several examples, including, "those two or three out-of-focus violet flowers in the foreground in the shot in which the two protagonists enter the house of the neurotic worker and those same two or three violet flowers which reappear in the background, no longer out of focus, but aggressively in focus, in the shot of the exit."[25] Rather than spend time on such a specific moment (despite the ekphrastic energy expended in calling the above moment to mind), Pasolini speaks globally about the film's style. He argues that "formalism," of which the previously mentioned shots are an example, is "the premise of the film." This formalist premise or, in Pasolini's words, "stylistic operation" has two defining features:

(1) the sequential juxtapositions of two insignificantly different points of view of the same image; that is, the sequence of two shots which frame the same piece of reality, first from nearby, then from *a bit* further; or, first frontally and then *a bit* more obliquely; or, finally, actually on the same axis but with two different lenses. This leads to an insistence that becomes obsessive, as it becomes the myth of the actual, distressing, autonomous beauty of things. (2) The technique of making the characters enter and leave the frame, as a result of which, in an occasionally obsessive manner, the editing comes to consist of a series of "pictures"—which we can call informal—where the characters enter, say or do something, and then go out, leaving the picture once again to its pure, absolute significance as picture.[26]

Antonioni's "obsessive" or excessive formalism represents a "liberated" formalism: in other words, a formalism allowed to develop and expand to an unusual extent. Such a "liberation" has been made possible "by creating the 'stylistic condition' for a 'free indirect point-of-view shot' that coincides with the entire film."[27] Thus, it is not a matter of *Red Desert* exhibiting poetic moments or passages. Rather, the entire film has been swallowed by a formalist (poetic) impulse:

In *Red Desert* Antonioni no longer superimposes his own formalistic vision of the world on a generally committed content (the problem of neuroses caused by alienation), as he had done in his earlier films. . . . Instead he looks at the world by immersing himself in his neurotic protagonist, reanimating the facts through her eyes. . . . By means of this stylistic device, Antonioni has freed his most deeply felt moment: he has finally been able to represent the world seen through his eyes, *because he has substituted in toto for the worldview of a neurotic his own delirious view of aesthetics*, a wholesale substitution which is justified by the possible analogy of the two views.[28]

To achieve a representation of an intensely personal and specific vision of the world, Antonioni had first to establish the "pretext" of Monica Vitti's character, Giulia. This character's class position and her illness justify, in realist terms, the production of unreal (or unusual) images, images that Pasolini finds "delirious" and "intoxicating."[29] In other words, style is paid for in the currency of subjectivity: that of the author and that of the character, whose performance and vision is but the vessel of the former.

This theoretical interpretation of *Red Desert*—and of the "cinema of poetry," the art cinema, of which it is an example—privileges subjectivity and its representation, despite this film's tendency (and that of the "cinema of poetry") toward narrative abstraction and opacity. So far, Pasolini's theorization and description seem to accord neatly with David Bordwell's theorization of art cinema in one of the first and only theoretical treatments of art cinema as a mode: "The art cinema motivates its narratives by two principles: realism and authorial expressivity. . . . [A] commitment to both objective and subjective verisimilitude distinguished art cinema from the classical narrative model."[30] Directors like Antonioni and Jean-Luc Godard hyperbolize techniques inherited from neorealism in order to block our access to the subjective interiority of the character. According to Bordwell, such hyperbolization is a means of "maximizing ambiguity."[31] Whether by the character's muteness (Antonioni), her words being silenced or jammed on the soundtrack (Godard), or the constant pressure of reflexive strategies, much of art cinema would seem to want to make us very unsure about our access to subjectivity. At the same time, however, both Pasolini and Bordwell agree that subjectivity—whether the character's or the director's—remains central to the experience of the "cinema of poetry"/art cinema.[32] (We shall return to Bordwell's theory at the end of this essay in order to understand where he and Pasolini part ways.)

To return our focus to Pasolini's theory, however, we might say that, broadly, the "cinema of poetry" recuperates the subject for modernist experiment.[33] This recuperation is at the heart of the essay's various contortions, its laborious working through of the linguistic or nonlinguistic nature of cinema, the problematic of cinema's objectivity and/or subjectivity, the minting of the notion of the "dictionary of possible words." Pasolini is sympathetic to modernism, to its refashioning of received forms, its deconstruction of   concepts, modes of address, its reflexivity, its commitment to aesthetic autonomy, its restless impatience with the world, and its appetite for critique. However, Pasolini is also deeply, deeply committed to reference, to the relation between the work of art and the world out of which it emerges and back toward which (for Pasolini) it must invariably point. As I have written elsewhere, we can only understand

Pasolini's modernism insofar as we understand his realism, and we can only grasp his realism insofar as we entertain its convergence with modernism; in his films "the material of the real world is never dissolved in formalist complexity, and yet, at the same time, the vision of the world that these films provide" is one in which "the materiality of the medium is always felt."[34] The "cinema of poetry" becomes, therefore, an attempt to theorize a dual allegiance to formal experiment and to social referentiality, or realism. I don't intend that the essay is purely autobiographical, but that it is characterized by one of the chief obsessions of Pasolini's entire corpus, from poetry to fiction to theater and the cinema: the reconciliation of modernism and realism.

This agonistic enterprise informs the essays that accompany "The 'Cinema of Poetry'" in *Heretical Empiricism*, including, most significantly, "What Is Neo-Zhdanovism and What Isn't," "The End of the Avant-Garde," and essentially all of the essays on cinema that together constitute the largest section of the book. I believe the turn to cinema that Pasolini made in the early 1960s was essentially and principally nourished by this desire for reconciliation.[35]

Pasolini's discussion of Godard, seen in this light, is especially curious. Godard presents Pasolini with a problem rather different from Antonioni's "formal classicism":

> He retains nothing of the old sensuality which stagnates in the conservative, marginal area between the Po and Rome, even when it has become very Europe-anized, as it has in Antonioni. Godard has not accepted any moral imperative. He feels neither the obligations of Marxist commitment (old stuff), nor the bad faith of academia (provincial stuff). His vitality is without restraint, modesty, or scruples. It reconstitutes the world within itself. It is also cynical towards itself. The poetics of Godard is ontological—it is called cinema. His formalism is thus a technicality which is intrinsically poetic: everything that is captured in movement by a camera is beautiful. It is the technical, and therefore poetic, restoration of reality.[36]

This is one of the most incisive descriptions of Godard's poetics (particularly in regard to the films that he had produced up until 1965 when Pasolini wrote this essay) that exists. In it, Pasolini accurately captures the flavor of Godard's modernism, a modernism predicated on a radical cathexis of the archive of film history and an unprecedented reflexive engagement with the cinematic apparatus itself: cinephilia times two, in other words. How does this evocation of Godard's cinema, however, square with the "cinema of poetry"? In the paragraph immediately following the passage quoted previously, Pasolini remembers himself, not a moment too late:

> Naturally, Godard also plays the usual game; he too needs a "dominant condi-tion" of the protagonist to guarantee his technical freedom, a neurotic and scandalous dominant condition in the relationship with reality. Thus, Godard's protagonists are also sick; they are exquisite flowers of the bourgeoisie.[37]

This passage convinces me less. Godard does not need the pretext of the sick protagonist. Rather, Pasolini does if he is going to be able to make his theory of the "cinema of poetry" stick to Godard. The sick protagonist is the pretext for the similarly sick director (because bourgeois). Godard, however, out of all of Pasolini's examples, is the least preoccupied by character subjectivity as we experience it in Bertolucci and Antonioni. It is more than telling that Pasolini's trope for these characters, the "exquisite flowers," figures a return to the shots of the (to use Pasolini's language) obsessively reframed violet flowers in *Red Desert*. Despite being able to nail Godard so accurately in the first instance cited previously, Pasolini, in assimilating him to the "cinema of poetry," must assimilate him to Antonioni. The comparison is strained.

I think we sense Pasolini himself sensing this, for the essay then takes another turn, away from specific filmmaking practices, in the last (and immediately subsequent) movement in the essay. Pasolini goes on to suggest that, yes, while the pretext of the "sick, abnormal protagonist" allows the director "great anomalous, and provocative stylistic freedom," at the same time this pretext tends to give itself away as such because "beneath this film runs another film, the one that the filmmaker would have made even without the pretexts of the *visual mimesis* of his protagonist—a film whose character is completely and freely expressive/expressionistic." One wonders if the real pretext here (and perhaps one actually senses Pasolini admitting this himself at this point) is actually the critical category of the "abnormal protagonist" that allows Pasolini to shape the theoretical concept of "cinema of poetry." However, a slightly revised, somewhat more elastic version of the "cinema of poetry" as an emphasis on "language as such," which Pasolini identifies with or as "style," emerges at this point, moving ever so slightly away, for the moment, from Pasolini's "obsessive" rehearsal of the "abnormal" protagonist as pretext for formal and stylistic invention.[38] Pasolini even goes so far as to say, just a few short paragraphs later, that "the first characteristic" of "the cinema of poetry" "consists of the phenomenon that is normally and banally defined by persons in the business as 'allowing the camera to be felt.'" This "felt" presence of the camera contrasts with earlier cinema in which

> language adhered to the meanings, putting itself at their service. It was transparent to perfection; it did not superimpose itself on facts, violating them through the insane semantic deformations that are attributable to its presence as continuous technical/stylistic awareness.[39]

The rhetoric of insanity is forever and obsessively married to the concept of style. What this seems to mean is that style is insane because the subject (the director, whose stand-in is the insane protagonist) who produces it is insane—insane because she is bourgeois. Thus, though this is never explicitly stated as such, style is a mode of making apparent some form or experience of class-consciousness. No style, no "cinema of poetry," no class-consciousness. In other words, Pasolini seems to have managed to create a fantastic (in every sense of that word) method for wriggling free of an injunction against stylistic deformation (modernism) as an obstruction to achieving class-consciousness in art. By conceiving of the surface of the image, and not the character we see, as a medium of subjectivity, Pasolini manages to have formal experiment and political commitment at one and the same time.

The theory of class-consciousness in Marxist thought resonates interestingly with the theoretical role ascribed by Pasolini (according to my reading) to the "cinema of poetry." For Georg Lukács class-consciousness is accorded a dramatic function in the production of social revolution: "The Proletariat cannot liberate itself as a class without simultaneously abolishing class society as such. For that reason its consciousness, the last class-consciousness in the history of mankind, must both lay bare the nature of society and achieve an increasingly inward fusion of theory and practice."[40] While the bourgeoisie possess class-consciousness, this is a "false" consciousness, and yet this false consciousness has the immediate advantage that it is "at least in accord with its class situation."[41] In other words, despite the contradictions inherent in bourgeois class-consciousness, the material conditions of capitalism still support its maintenance as falsehood. Contrarily, the "superiority" of proletarian class-consciousness "lie[s] exclusively in its ability to see society from the centre, as a coherent whole."[42] False (bourgeois) consciousness is, therefore, like a kind of disturbance, distortion, or blind spot in the visual field. Proletarian class-consciousness, however, sees (or will see) things as they are. Following Lukács, then, it seems appropriate to suggest that the visual excess and formal exaggeration—the style—of the "cinema of poetry" is an aesthetic registration of bourgeois class-consciousness.[43]

Of course, this class-consciousness is one belonging to the bourgeois, to the "exquisite flowers," so it never escapes entirely from Pasolini's suspicion. In the last movement of the essay, The "cinema of poetry," despite, or because of the incredible labor that is expended in producing it as a theoretical concept is finally almost brushed aside as so much neo-capitalist epiphenomena: "In short . . . the formation of 'language of poetry of film' may be posited as revealing a strong general renewal of formalism as the average, typical production of the cultural development of neocapitalism."[44] However, the language of this dismissal suggests why the concept may be worth hanging onto: the language of an "average" and "typical" index of a historical moment is, again, the language of Lukács—this time, of his theorization of the realist hero.[45] The style that, in a sense, constitutes the "cinema of poetry," or art cinema, becomes itself a historical protagonist through which one may perhaps grasp, or begin to fumble toward some sense of, the totality of "neocapitalism." This is, it seems to me, despite the baroque convolution of "The 'Cinema of Poetry,'" a striking and original insight, and one that has not been picked up either by commentators (most of them hostile) on the essay, or by sympathetic readers who have wanted to make use of the essay or of the concept of the "cinema of poetry." Style is, in the work of theorists of narrative comprehension, such as Bordwell, usually nothing more than epiphenomena, excess. Because it cannot be described in normative terms—because it resists being "solved"—style hardly bears thinking about. And where style is discussed in the context of the art film, it becomes an object of contempt. Steve Neale laments art cinema's seemingly indelible association with "individual expression" (i.e., style) and "individual names."[46]

Neale equates "individual expression" with "reactionary discourses of high art."[47] This association is enough evidence to banish art cinema from any vision of progressive social productivity. Both the benign neglect of style as a theoretical category and its damning association with high art and bourgeois individualism miss what "The 'Cinema of Poetry'" offers: a theorization of style as the very medium of the appearance of political consciousness in the cinema. In what follows I want to explore the scene of another missed encounter between Pasolini's theory and its critics.

I want to return to the scene of the photograph with which I began this chapter, to return to the New York Film Festival of 1966. In the proceedings of our round table, chaired, we will recall, by Mr. Sarris, Pasolini, René Allio, and Agnès Varda were all asked to respond to a question about their spectatorial predilections, specifically about what distinctions they made between commercial cinema and art cinema (or what Sarris, in his role as moderator, suggested was the difference between "movie going" and "cinema."[48] Allio made a rather stuttering attempt to answer. Varda, for her part, spoke eloquently of cinema being both "a spectacle," or "form of entertainment," and "a form which allows freedom of expression." According to Varda, "There is confusion between the two, and it is a very real problem."[49] Pasolini, we will not be surprised, answers in the following way:

> If I compare a typical Hollywood film with an art film by John Ford, I see that technically they are made in the same way. But if instead I make the comparison between a Hollywood commercial [film] and a film by Godard or *Les creatures* by Varda, I see that there is a technical and linguistic difference. Instead of a distinction between the commercial cinema and the art cinema, I would like to propose a distinction between the cinema of prose and the cinema of poetry. The distinction is not one of value—it is a technical one.[50]

Debate ensues, with audience members asking Pasolini how he would classify Chris Marker, Allio wondering if the "cinema of poetry" is a cinema of aestheticism, Sarris advising that Pasolini's thought is more subtle than it seems (!), and Varda suggesting that the categories of poetry and prose are "really not adequate to explain what cinema is." Varda, does, however suggest that what Pasolini is really concerned with is "style."[51] Pasolini restates the problem and suggests that "the distinction between the linguistics of prose and poetry and prose are [sic] absolutely clear. Each one of us, just by opening a book without even reading it, understands immediately whether the book is poetry or prose." At this point, the typed transcript of the discussion reads:

MICHELSON: Lautréamont?[52]

Michelson's question seems to go, for the moment, unanswered. Pasolini restates his argument, and the discussion spins round for several more minutes. But Michelson returns to her question:

MICHELSON: Mr. Pasolini, have you ever been a teacher?

PASOLINI: Sì.

MICHELSON: I thought so, because it seemed to me that his discussion between poetry and prose, whether in cinema or in any other form, is academic, and, above all, a distinction of a classicist. Mr. Pasolini said before that he considers himself a classicist. There's a clue to this, by the way, in the parenthetical remark that he let drop, that poetry and prose can be even visibly distinguishable, when one picks up the book without even reading it. One is written in rhymes, the other is continuous. At that point I said, "Lautréamont," because Lautréamont represents that point in poetry, in the nineteenth century when the distinction between poetry and prose began to break down. And it seems to me that Mr. Pasolini's attempt to establish these distinctions is interesting but it is not a contemporary kind of distinction that he made.[53]

Pasolini does not take up the challenge, and an audience member asks him about his casting of non-actors. Pasolini responds, "Cinema is reality that represents itself through itself." Responding to another question about distribution in Italy, Pasolini mentions Italian censorship of his films for religious reasons and concludes his answer by saying: "My films aren't so avant-garde."[54]

This curious sequence of exchanges or misfires between Michelson (who was and is, as I have said, the doyenne of the cinematic avant-garde in New York) and Pasolini bears interestingly on the "cinema of poetry" and on discourses on art cinema. Pasolini does himself no favors by presenting his poetry/prose distinction without the complexity of the essay's argument that I have been at such pains to detail. And Michelson, although she can be blamed for being characteristically acerbic (and hilariously pedantic at the very moment she attributes pedantry to Pasolini!), certainly cannot be blamed for objecting to Pasolini's distinction with her example from the archive of French decadent literature. The exchange, however, is emblematic, I think, of a formation that was coalescing at roughly this moment in 1966: This is what I would describe as the condescension of the avant-garde to its nearest cousin, the art cinema, or "cinema of poetry." Such condescension is noticeable across some of the other discussions that were held at the festival and were published in this same issue of *Film Culture*. The most vivid document of this condescension is a diagram by P. Adams Sitney that he distributed to the audience assembled at a panel discussion entitled, "What Are the New Critics Saying?" and also published in the same issue of *Film Culture*.[55] The panel's speakers were Sitney, Parker Tyler, Ken Kelman, Toby Mussman, and Sheldon Renan.

We notice the names that make their way into Sitney's canon: We have the historical avant-garde and Ezra Pound, but as for contemporary cinema, only members of the "New American Cinema": Maya Deren, Stan Brakhage, Peter Kubelka. There is no Jean-Luc Godard, no Pasolini, no Robert Bresson, all of whom screened what were then their new films at the festival.[56] The flavor of this exclusion can be tasted in an essay that Ken Kelman published in *Film Culture* just three years before Sitney distributed his "Secret Diamond" to the audience at the New York Film Festival. This essay is entitled "Film as Poetry," and it begins:

As the lyric poem is the direct manifestation through words of feelings and thoughts, with the expressive possibilities of plot, motion, music, dialogue, and image all muted in themselves, and only serving this pure expression; this is precisely the film lyric's function, through its own available idiom.[57]

The correspondence between the terms of Kelman's essay and Pasolini's "cinema of poetry" is striking. But as Kelman's essay progresses, ranging across, among others, Bergman, Truffaut, Dreyer, Eisenstein, Renoir, and finally (and most significantly) Brakhage, it is clear that "Film as Poetry" is not the same thing as the "cinema of poetry"—is not, in other words, art cinema:

When the film-poem utilizes "real" characters and situations, it must transform them to symbols of the filmmaker's thoughts and feelings. If they retain more than a shadow of their identities, they will live too much on their own, too much as narrative, "realism," etc., and too little as sheer lyric expressions. For this

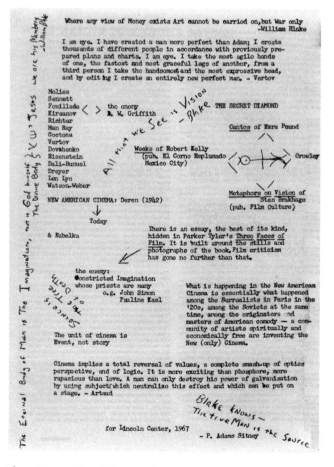

FIGURE 8.2. P. Adams Sitney's "Secret Diamond."

reason. . . . *The Passion of Joan of Arc* and *The 400 Blows* are not film-poetry; nor are they intended as such. A total transformation of forms and materials into mere manifestations of the artist's state of mind is what is required.[58]

Narrative realism, no matter how attenuated or enriched by formal experiment, blocks one's accession to the mysteries of what Kelman calls "film poetry," or Sitney's "Secret Diamond." The best candidate for initiation would seem to be Brakhage, in whose "late work" "we find direct expression of inner, and non-conceptualized states. He has in fact created a filmic equivalent of 'automatic writing.' . . . Out of photographed "reality," in all the fullness of its texture, Brakhage creates his inner world."[59] This "inner world" is quite obviously not the equivalent of our "exquisite flowers" whose class-specific neurosis engender and legitmize the formal experimentation in the "cinema of poetry."

Less articulate *in viva voce* than in print, Kelman, back at our panel discussion at the 1966 New York Film Festival, gropes his way toward an articulation of "film as poetry":

So, um, there's another kind of art, like I was saying, which is, um, well, the high or—or true art, and uh . . . that is, an art which doesn't confirm people in what they already know, um, and it doesn't excite them about anything superficial . . . they arouse a state of ecstasy in those who confront them.[60]

Who can arouse such ecstasy in our critic? Kelman gives some examples: Brakhage, Harry Smith, Kenneth Anger, a little bit of Dreyer, but not much. And definitely *not* Godard: "I don't feel this presence in the work of Godard, intelligent though he is, capable though he is, he is in a limited arena which has to do with psychology and uh and social things, and he does not touch the deep issues of life and death and really, actually, the issue which really matters, which is reality itself."[61] Does Pasolini figure here? Kelman actually is the last critic to comment in the panel discussion: "I thought Pasolini's films—I haven't seen all of them—I missed a couple things—Pasolini's two films were O.K. They weren't bad. They weren't great, they were all right."[62]

My point here is not to defend Pasolini's filmmaking or to express some indignation on Pasolini's behalf. Rather, what Kelman's essay, his stuttering comments in 1966, and Sitney's "Secret Diamond" all amount to is a vernacular expression of an antipathy to art cinema for not being as radical as the avant-garde. This same condescension characterizes Bordwell's aforementioned essay on art cinema and this cinema's production of what Bordwell calls "maximum ambiguity." Such ambiguity is produced by various formal devices (usually the foregrounding of the medium or the process of narration) and demands that the spectator ask herself questions as she watches the film: "Is a character's mental state causing the uncertainty? Is life just leaving loose ends?"; "What is being 'said' here? What significance justifies the violation of the norm?"[63] Toward the end of his essay, Bordwell compares the art cinema to what he calls "modernist" cinema, but which we recognize as the category of the avant-garde, though his canon differs significantly from Kelman's and Sitney's. His examples of such "modernism" include films by Eisenstein, Bresson, Tati, and Ozu. This "modernist cinema is not ambiguous in the sense that the art cinema is; perceptual play, not thematic ambivalence, is the chief viewing strategy."[64] In accounting for these differences, Bordwell concludes that "the art cinema represents the domestication of modernist filmmaking. The art cinema softened modernism's attack on narrative causality by creating mediating structures—'reality,' character subjectivity, authorial vision." For Bordwell, such qualities mean that the art cinema has become "modernist" filmmaking's "adversary."[65] Art cinema, "the cinema of poetry," is, according to critics like Kelman and theorists like Bordwell, a vaguely embarrassing domain of formal nuance, subjectivity, and recidivist realism: modernism, domesticated. It does not provide us with either Bordwell's "perceptual play" or Kelman's ecstasy.[66]

This condescending attitude toward art cinema, I want to propose, is mistaken, and I think the terms of Bordwell's dismissal are actually useful for reclaiming the value of art cinema from such critiques. In Bordwell's account, his art cinema spectator must labor to ask herself questions, to understand what she is watching: she is at work. His account of the "modernist" spectator is one who is at "play"—blissed out, perhaps in something akin to Kelman's ecstatic communion with the eternal realities of life and death. My commitment to the value of art cinema comes from Pasolini, from his agonizing commitment to describing what it is that art cinema, or "the cinema of poetry," is, what it does, what it makes appear. As the meeting ground of a cinema of experiment and a cinema of narration and realist intelligibility, the "cinema of poetry" performs work that is not performed by the films of those working inside the "Secret Diamond." The latter, it would seem, at least according to its exegetes, offers an experience of a perceptual sublime that is far away from the labor of identifying the image as the surface on which an experience of class, of historical reality, is made visible, perceptible, and criticizable. To say this is not to play Bloch or Lukács to Adorno, but is rather to understand and appreciate the different labors performed by different types of filmmaking—both those at play and those at work. There are worse things, certainly, than to follow the example of Bordwell's art cinema spectator, or of Pasolini himself, and ask ourselves, laboriously, question after question after question after question.

NOTES

1. Pier Paolo Pasolini, "Il 'cinema di poesia,'" *Filmcritica* 156–157 (1965): 275. My translation. The full version of the essay, in its original length and under this new title, "Il 'cinema di poesia,'" was collected in Pasolini's *Empirismo eretico* (Milan: Garzanti Editore, 1972). *Empirismo eretico* was translated and published in English as *Heretical Empiricism*, ed. Louise K. Barnett, trans. Ben Lawton and Barnett (Bloomington: Indiana University Press, 1988); the essay appears on the title "The 'Cinema of Poetry.'" Hereafter I shall refer to "The 'Cinema of Poetry'" as CP and *Heretical Empiricism* as *HE*.

2. I will explore such unflattering characterizations of art cinema later in this chapter.

3. CP, 167.

4. CP, 168.

5. Cf. "The Written Language of Reality," *HE*, 197–122; "Res Sunt Nomina," *HE*, 255–260. Other essays in *HE* that are largely occupied by this conception of the language of things and cinema as this language's second articulation include: "Quips on the Cinema," "Observations on the Sequence Shot," "Is Being Natural?" and "The Fear of Naturalism."

6. Christian Metz, *Film Language: A Semiotics of the Cinema*, trans. Michael Taylor (Chicago: University of Chicago Press, 1991), 204–208; Umberto Eco, quoted in Antonio Costa, "The Semiological Heresy of Pier Paolo Pasolini," in *Pier Paolo Pasolini*, ed. Paul Willemen (London: BFI, 1977), 39; Stephen Heath, "Film/Cinetext/Text," *Screen* 14, nos. 1–2 (Spring–Summer 1973): 109; Costa, "The Semiological Heresy of Pier Paolo Pasolini," 41. The essay has also had its admirers, notably Teresa De Lauretis and Gilles Deleuze. Cf. De Lauretis, *Alice Doesn't: Feminism, Semiotics, Cinema* (Bloomington: Indiana University Press, 1984), and Deleuze, *Cinema 1: The Movement-Image*, trans. Hugh Tomlinson and Barbara Habberjam (Minneapolis: University of Minnesota Press, 1991), and *Cinema 2: The Time-Image*, trans. Hugh Tomlinson and Barbara Habberjam (London: Athlone, 2000). Given the notoriety of Deleuze's interest in Pasolini's essay, readers may be surprised that I do not pursue a line of inquiry in this direction. I hope the logic (if not the wisdom) of my decision not to engage Deleuze will become apparent.

7. For this use of the term "reality," cf. the essays mentioned in note 5. In "The Written Language of Reality," Pasolini makes the startling claim that "reality is nothing more than cinema in nature" (*HE*, 198).

8. The term, in relation to cinema, is Christian Metz's. Cf. "The Cinema: Language or Language System," *Film Language: A Semiotics of the Cinema*, trans. Michael Taylor (Chicago: University of Chicago Press, 1991), 31–91. Pasolini was familiar with Metz's work.

9. CP, 169.

10. CP, 170.

11. In fact, Pasolini goes on to describe the filmmaker's "fundamental and preliminary activity" as a "search for a dictionary" (171).

12. Ibid.

13. CP, 172.

14. Ibid.

15. Ibid. This passage in its entirety actually concludes thus, "Its foundation is the mythical and infantile subtext which, because of the very nature of cinema, runs underneath every commercial film which is not unworthy, that is, [which is] fairly adult aesthetically and socially." I think the last qualifying clause is obfuscatory and does not theoretically add anything of interest to Pasolini's central point. The clause is typical of the restlessness of his essay style, which seems never to want to leave anything out.

16. CP, 173.

17. CP, 174. Here one might object to Pasolini's representation of *Un Chien andalou* (and Surrealism, more widely) as "expressive" or even as "oneiric," but such objections are not germane to my concerns here.

18. CP, 175.

19. CP, 175.

20. It may seem odd that a theory of the poetic borrows its terms from narratology. Indirect discourse is associated with Soviet-era, Marxist literary theory. Cf. V.N.

Vološinov, *Marxism and the Philosophy of Language*, trans. Ladislav Matejka and I. R. Titunik (Cambridge, MA: Harvard University Press, 1973 [1929]).

21. CP, 176–177.

22. CP, 177–178. Here and elsewhere, the abundance of italics is found in Pasolini's text.

23. CP, 178.

24. CP, 178.

25. Ibid. Two of the three examples Pasolini gives of "poetic" sequences in the film, including this one, feature a thematic element of a meeting of a worker and a bourgeois.

26. CP, 179. "Informal" art (*informale* in Italian) is what Anglo-American art history and criticism refer to as "abstract" art. Representative "informal" painters in postwar Italy include Alberto Burri, Giuseppe Capogrossi, and Lucio Fontana.

27. Ibid.

28. CP, 179–180.

29. CP, 180.

30. David Bordwell, "The Art Cinema as a Mode of Film Practice," *Film Criticism* 4, no. 1 (1979): 57–59.

31. Bordwell, "The Art Cinema as a Mode of Film Practice," 60. It is important to note that *Red Desert* is one of Bordwell's chief examples of the "ambiguity" of art cinema.

32. Bordwell argues that the author is foregrounded in art cinema and "becomes a formal component, the overriding intelligence organizing the film for our comprehension" (59). This proposition also resonates strongly with Pasolini's emphasis on the motivating link between protagonist and author. Readers of Bordwell, however, will not be surprised by his emphasis on "comprehension." Bordwell contends that whenever viewers are confronted with a "problem" "we first seek realistic motivation" (in character subjectivity), and if that does not solve the "problem," "we next seek authorial motivation" (60). In Bordwell's terms art cinema begins to sound like narrative sudoku.

33. As we shall see later, Bordwell insulates what he calls modernism from art cinema.

34. John David Rhodes, *Stupendous, Miserable City: Pasolini's Rome* (Minneapolis: University of Minnesota Press, 2007), 55. See also a discussion of similar issues on page 133.

35. This is also an argument I make in *Stupendous, Miserable City*.

36. CP, 181. Bertolucci, Pasolini's analysis of whom I do not go into here, was from Parma, in the Po River valley. Pasolini's use of the term the "restoration of reality" makes it sound as though he might be alluding to the work of André Bazin.

37. Ibid. Pasolini's discussion of Bertolucci's *Before the Revolution* (*Prima della rivoluzione*, 1964) also makes much of the "neurotic" nature of the film's protagonist, the character played by Adriana Asti.

38. CP, 182.

39. CP, 183.

40. Georg Lukács, *History and Class Consciousness*, trans. Rodney Livingstone (Cambridge, Mass.: MIT Press, 1971), 70.

41. Ibid, 69.

42. Ibid.

43. Another interesting consonance between Lukács's theory and Pasolini's is that, according to Lukács, class-consciousness is not rooted in individual or even group psychology: "Class consciousness is identical with neither the psychological

consciousness of individual members of the proletariat, nor with the (mass-psychological) consciousness of the proletariat as a whole; but it is, on the contrary, *the sense, become conscious, of the historical role of the class*" (73). The "cinema of poetry" is not important primarily because it gives us access to individual psychology (that of the character or director) or to that of a class (the bourgeoisie, to which character and author belong), but because it puts on view class-consciousness as such, shows it in the process of becoming conscious of itself, through the materiality of aesthetic forms.

44. CP, 185.

45. Writing about the historical novels of Sir Walter Scott, Lukács argues that it is the novelist's task to make the hero's "actions . . . appear the real representative of . . . historical crises. . . . Scott, by first showing the complex and involved character of popular life itself, creates this being which the leading figure then has to generalize and concentrate in an historical deed" (*The Historical Novel*, trans. Hannah Mitchell and Stanley Mitchell [Lincoln: University of Nebraska Press, 1983], 39).

46. Steve Neale, "Art Cinema as Institution," *Screen* 22, no. 1 (1981): 36.

47. Neale, "Art Cinema as Institution," 39.

48. "Pasolini-Varda-Allio-Sarris-Michelson," *Film Culture* 42 (Fall 1966): 96.

49. "Pasolini-Varda-Allio-Sarris-Michelson," 97.

50. Ibid.

51. Ibid.

52. Ibid.

53. "Pasolini-Varda-Allio-Sarris-Michelson," 99–100.

54. "Pasolini-Varda-Allio-Sarris-Michelson," 100.

55. "What Are the New Critics Saying?" (Ken Kelman, P. Adams Sitney, Sheldon Renan, Toby Mussman, Parker Tyler), *Film Culture* 42 (Fall 1966): 76–88. The "Secret Diamond" is first mentioned on page 76 and reproduced on page 78.

56. P. Adams Sitney would eventually publish a book on Italian postwar cinema in which he writes very appreciatively of Pasolini and other Italian art cinema directors. Cf. *Vital Crises in Italian Cinema* (Austin: University of Texas Press, 1995).

57. Ken Kelman, "Film as Poetry," *Film Culture* 29 (Summer 1963): 22. Available through ubuweb at http://www.ubu.com/papers/kelman_ken-film_poetry.html (accessed March 31, 2008). The film and poetry connection in the American Avant-Garde extends at least as far back as the Cinema 16 symposium with Deren, Miller, Thomas, and others.

58. Ibid.

59. Ibid.

60. "What Are the New Critics Saying?" 80.

61. Ibid.

62. "What Are the New Critics Saying?" 88.

63. Bordwell, "The Art Cinema as a Mode of Film Practice," 60.

64. Bordwell, "The Art Cinema as a Mode of Film Practice," 61.

65. Bordwell, "The Art Cinema as a Mode of Film Practice," 62.

66. In "Film and the Radical Aspiration," an address to the 1966 New York Film Festival that was also published in the fall 1966 issue of *Film Culture*, Annette Michelson actually reproaches American avant-garde cinema, whose "aspiration to an innocence and organicity" she finds less persuasive than the "infinitely more radical and powerful" cinema of Resnais and Varda. Her chief example of the American avant-garde is, of course, Brakhage. She observes that the rhetoric of the American cinematic avant-garde "is that of abstract expressionism" and remarks, rather caustically, that "the pages of *Film Culture* represents [sic] in the New York of 1966 the

last precinct of the action painter's active authority." Cf. "Film and the Radical Aspiration," *Film Culture* 42 (Fall 1966): 34–42; 136. (Above quotations from pp. 36, 41, and 42, respectively.) Michelson would, of course, go on to revise her opinion of Brakhage and embrace his cinema much more wholeheartedly. Interestingly, in "Film and the Radical Aspiration," she also regrets that cinema has articulated itself chiefly according to "novelistic forms," especially "in a century which saw a flowering of American poetry" (37). The terms of this observation, at least, show her to be working in discursive proximity to Pasolini. Pasolini, in an essay written after his return from the 1966 New York Film Festival, wrote unflatteringly of Brakhage's work that "transgression against the code is nostalgia for the code." In this sense, he draws very near to a remark Michelson makes at the end of "Film and the Radical Aspiration": "In a country whose power and influence are maintained by the dialectic of a war economy, in a country whose dream of revolution has been sublimated in reformism and frustrated by an equivocal prosperity, cinematic radicalism is condemned to a politics and strategy of social and aesthetic subversion" (42; 136).

9

FROM INDEX TO FIGURE IN THE EUROPEAN ART FILM: THE CASE OF *THE CONFORMIST*

Angelo Restivo

In an interview in *American Cinematographer*, the director of photography of *Flashdance* (Lyne, 1983) Don Peterman, said that he and director Adrian Lyne took as two major influences on the film's visual style Bernardo Bertolucci's *Il Conformista/The Conformist* (1970), and music video.[1] While one could read this as just another anecdote in a long lineage of Hollywood's profound misunderstanding of "art" (even its own)—with the necessary obverse of the equation being Hollywood's reverential piety toward what it deems "artistic"—it would seem more productive to take the phrase as symptomatic of some larger, historical-aesthetic change within the art film itself: a change of which *The Conformist* was a key harbinger. This essay's hypothesis is that this change involved a movement away from the conviction—so central to postwar art cinema—that the photographic image was fundamentally continuous with the world, and toward a view of the image as emblematic, self-referential, and discontinuous with the world. One would then begin by asking, in what ways does a 1970 Italian film whose director is so grounded in the aesthetic innovations of the Italian and French new waves come to resemble—a decade or so later—a popular form in an entirely different medium (music video), with entirely different modes of production, reception, and distribution, not to mention an entirely different audience? An initial answer to this question might simply note formal similarities: one, the ways in which Bertolucci and cinematographer Vittorio Storaro push every image in the film toward the oneiric, overworking the mise-en-scène to the point where the spaces of the film seem "de-realized"; two, Bertolucci's new collaboration with editor Franco Arcalli, who pushed Bertolucci beyond his programmatic aversion to editing by convincing him of its expressive power. Even at the level of truisms about music video—"low-attention-span" editing, images governed by fantasy—formal connections can be made to Bertolucci's film; but I contend the connections go deeper. For Bertolucci edits his narrative in such a way that, despite all the temporal shifts, the story appears to exist in a "perpetual present." This of course is in total keeping with the film's relentless focus on the main character's unconscious (as Freud says, the unconscious does not know time). At the same time, however, the music video, in its very emplacement within televisual flow, enacts the same kind of erasure of history in favor of an "iterative present," if you will. In any case, in *The Conformist*, these formal anticipations of a coming "aesthetics of image" are embedded in a narrative in which Bertolucci stages a decisive break with his own aesthetic "*Bildung*," enacted in the film via a complex series of transference relations—including, but not limited to, a coded "fantasy-murder" of Jean-Luc Godard (represented in the film by Professor Quadri).

Of course, these formal and narrative qualities of the film are well discussed in its critical literature. While the film is set in the 1930s (with a brief coda on July 25, 1943), across the ideological divide of fascism and the popular front, the critical literature quite rightly locates the film's political concerns in those of the European Left in the 1960s. One of the major political projects in those years was to elaborate a theory of cultural production that went beyond the simplistic determinism that turned the artwork into a reflection of an economic "base," one that allowed for some degree of autonomy in the cultural field while at the same time insisting that that field was thoroughly ideological. Thus, suddenly, psychoanalysis took on a new value for the Left, insofar as its notion of an "unconscious" might very well provide the concept needed for a more complex theory of the relation of culture to ideology, or even more broadly, of the individual to the social. This project of bringing together Marx and Freud took on all the allure that a "unified field theory" holds in physics. This is the context in which Bertolucci—not only a member of the PCI (the Italian Communist Party), but also undergoing during these years his own psychoanalysis (which he talked about repeatedly in interviews)—made *The Conformist*.

The film's extreme fragmentation of temporal sequencing (as well as the hallucinatory beauty of the images) makes a plot summary rather complicated. But after a few viewings, the spectator generally understands the following: The film's "present

FIGURE 9.1. The oneiric image in *The Conformist* (Bertolucci, 1970).

tense" (until the coda) represents less than twenty-four hours, as the main character Marcello and his fascist cohort Manganiello drive from Paris to Switzerland in order to intercept the leftist Professor Quadri, whom they have orders to assassinate. This might be described as the film's "frame"—a crucial word we will return to later—with a total running time of perhaps ten minutes of film time. Sandwiched into the frame is a series of nonlinear "flashbacks"—though again, this word needs to be interrogated as we move along, insofar as the flashbacks quickly "take over" the narrative—ranging over Marcello's life, including a dreamlike and strangely Oedipalized homosexual seduction of the schoolboy Marcello by a chauffeur named Pasqualino. After the climactic murder of the professor and his wife, Anna, the narrative jumps to a coda on the night in July 1943 when Mussolini was ousted and the Badoglio government was installed. Marcello walks through the city "to watch a dictatorship fall," and discovers that the chauffeur, whom he thought he had murdered after his seduction as a schoolboy, is alive and well and attempting to pick up a *ragazzo di vita*.

Given that Marcello joins the fascist party as a way to achieve "normality"—not so much as a front for others as a front for himself—the personal and the political become joined in an act of "imaginary misrecognition" in perfect keeping with the theoretical project of the 1960s described previously.[2] In general, taking this as a starting point, readings of the film can be seen as inflected in two distinct ways.[3] The more psychoanalytic readings will note, first, that the flashbacks that take over the film and that are not organized as a "forward movement toward the present" convey that persistence of the past within the present that is a fundamental given of psychoanalytic thinking; the oneiric, intensely worked mise-en-scène must thus be read via the Freudian codes of the dream work, via condensation and displacement. Here a quick example of my own will suffice: When Marcello meets the fascist operative Raoul in Ventimiglia, where he is given a gun and informed that his assignment with the professor has changed to assassination, it slowly dawns on the spectator that Raoul's office is, absurdly, awash in walnuts—disorganized piles of walnuts on the desk, walnuts neatly lined up along the mantle, and so on. Read via the dream work codes, Raoul's office becomes a site of both an excessive overvaluation of masculinity, and its simultaneous undervaluation (in the sense that one can never have too many "nuts"). Within the film as a whole, these charged condensations and displacements begin to resonate transversally across the text, and the film thus connects social/political demystification to a procedure of properly reading the ways in which the ideological is coded within the everyday.

Another line of criticism, one that distances itself more from psychoanalytic reading practice, should be seen more as an addition and complement to the psychoanalytic reading, rather than as a refutation of it. Here, the focus is on the film's foregrounding of the problem of the reliability of vision: while Marcello's best friend in the film is literally blind, Marcello himself is figuratively blind to his own individual and class histories. The metaphor of blindness becomes generalized via the film's great set-piece, which occurs halfway through the film, when Professor Quadri, in his study in Paris, reenacts for Marcello his university lecture on Plato's allegory of the cave, and the film's mise-en-scène turns the study into a dramatic light-and-shadow imagining of the allegory itself. As with the charged objects noted earlier, Bertolucci takes the motif of light/shadow and allows it to resonate transversally across the film, in such a way as to question the extent to which we can ever see "the reality of things," beyond their shadows.

I certainly do not wish to quarrel with what together produces a rich, nuanced, and satisfying understanding of the film. One might note, however, that procedurally, this criticism remains within the established ("modernist") tradition of art-film criticism: one in which meanings are assigned via a certain interpretive protocol connected to the text as a self-contained "system," a system embedded within a certain historical moment that presents the artist with her or his problematic. (There is, to be sure, an acknowledgment via the Quadri/Godard equation that the text's boundaries are not self-contained; I will argue that a more thorough consideration of the transference makes the text's boundaries even more fluid.) But this critical procedure reaches its limit on two key fronts. First, it cannot address the "MTV problem" raised at the outset of the essay; and given that *The Conformist* comes at the end of a decade of politicized cultural production (and in many ways represents its culmination), the forward-looking aesthetic innovations of the film raise critical questions about the "politics of the image" in an increasingly image-dominated culture. Second, it fails to adequately address the question of homosexuality the film poses, a question largely skirted by the critical literature: For this is a film in which homosexuality "blossoms" in an almost Proustian fashion. That is to say: Once homosexuality appears in the film, then it must appear, potentially, *everywhere*. In terms of the film's diegetic world, we could argue that this is in perfect keeping with fascism's heavy investment in "the classical." But to telegraph where my argument will take this idea, queer theory has shown how this phantasmatic of contamination is strictly correlative to a certain kind of crisis of the sign that is induced by the figure of the gay male, especially.

But first, let's simply catalog the ways in which queerness invades this film. We can note first that Marcello's bid for "normality" is also a bid for—no surprise here—the heteronormative: But the film indeed underlines this point, by linking, as Marcello's personal "project," his joining of the fascist party and his planned marriage to the *petite bourgeoise* Giulia ("all kitchen and bedroom"), so that his honeymoon trip becomes the foil for his first fascist "mission." But almost immediately (and with wicked humor), queerness invades this scenario: Giulia confesses on the train that she's not "what he thinks she is," that as a schoolgirl she was seduced while studying Latin by her sixty-year-old "Uncle Prepuzio." "It went on for six years," she confesses casually, as Marcello uses her detailed description of the encounter as a kind of primer for the performance of his nuptial duties.[4] Then the professor's wife, Anna, appears, photographed with all the sexual ambiguity and "deracinated glamour" that Sternberg devoted to his presentation of Marlene Dietrich. Anna, not without some success, attempts to seduce Giulia (while husband Marcello peeks through a doorway); the two couples then begin planning a jaunt "*à quatre*" to the Quadri's house in Switzerland (where fucking causes all the beds to creak loudly); near the film's end, it becomes clear to the spectator that Marcello's best friend ("Italo," no less) is probably gay; a naked *ragazzo* who might have walked out of a Caravaggio painting luxuriates on a mattress at the Teatro Marcello;

FIGURE 9.2. Unkillable homosexuality in *The Conformist*.

while the still-alive chauffeur Pasqualino suggests that homosexuality is unkillable. Given all this, what might seem surprising is that the critical literature tends to treat homosexuality in this film as a kind of "MacGuffin": It's what sets the entire story in motion, is, in fact, the story's "enabling event"; at the same time, it's treated as a kind of "decoy" from which the film can then explore its *real* concerns, as universal as the Universal Plato attempts to construct in the allegory of the cave. But we needn't go back as far as ancient Greek sexual customs to suspect that something might be amiss here: For queer theory has already shown us how this quality of "now you see it/now you don't," of the suggestion that never stops seeking to erase itself, is in fact central to the way that homosexuality has been coded, not only in modern artworks but in the critical reception that seeks to police them.[5]

We might then hypothesize that the crisis of epistemology that is produced by the appearance of homosexuality in the film is strictly correlative to the film's heavy investment in the plastics of the image. For the tradition of the postwar European art film is "grounded" by an epistemological ethics coming out of Italian neorealism and its fundamental conviction that, training the camera on the world, the resulting photographic image registers the world in its inexhaustibility and richness, which then allows us to "open our eyes" to new ways of being in the world. This certainly lay at the heart of André Bazin's, and the French New Wave's, understanding of the centrality of Italian neorealism to "modern" cinema.[6] It was also a key component of Bertolucci's early aesthetic formation (under the tutelage of mentor Pier Paolo Pasolini) and his first features. We could argue that by 1967—with the appearance of Michelangelo Antonioni's *Blow-up* (1966)—this conviction comes to crisis, *Blow-up* being an allegory of the vicissitudes of the photograph in the image-saturated environment of "mod," consumerist London.[7] Here, Antonioni is tracking what we might call the "material conditions" for the crisis in indexicality—namely, the emergence of what Antonio Negri would call "immaterial labor." But in light of the earlier discussion of homosexuality, it is extremely interesting to note how the figure of the male homosexual—this is one of the early arguments of queer theorists[8]—similarly induces a semiotic and epistemological crisis within the text. Insofar as the male homosexual cannot be denoted as such, the relationship of appearance to concept is derailed (is he?

Or isn't he?) so that, whether in language or in the image, the "legalities" of grammar give way to an excess of rhetoricity. In terms of the image, this takes the form of the investment in plasticity, a succession of metamorphoses in the images that then refer only to each other, disconnected from the "indexical" ground that had been the philosophical underpinning of the postwar art film.

The Conformist thus marks not only a crisis in and a breaking away from the aesthetic traditions of the art film, but also an anticipation of a coming aesthetic of the image, one characterized less by a seamless continuum and more by an emblematic or figural quality that pushes the image toward the glossy and the hyperreal. Certainly, a consideration of the image environment of today would easily convince us that this is a development that has only accelerated with the advent of new media: where frames open up within frames, text and image and sound move in and out of synchronicity with one another, and even the elements of a "diegetic world" often seem stitched together by some postmodernized version of the Freudian dreamwork.[9] But for purposes of this argument, the emergence in France in the early 1980s of the *cinéma du look* will suffice to make the case—not an analysis of the films themselves but of the critical discourses surrounding them. For while the early films of this aesthetic trend were not necessarily borrowing from music video, they were certainly connected critically to the advertising image and to the "televisual" more generally.

Since Bertolucci did not break with his aesthetic roots quietly, but rather with much fanfare staged the "murder of the father(s)," it is to the psychoanalytic transference that we will turn first.

ALLEGORIES OF TRANSFERENCE

The question of the relationship of narrative to transference has been on the table at least since Roland Barthes, in *S/Z*, uncovered the pacts, the complicities established between speaker and listener, that marked the exchange of the "story-within-the-story" of Sarrasine's disastrous love affair with La Zambinella. There, we recall, the compact was clear enough: a story exchanged for a night of lovemaking; but the story the narrator tells turns out to so destabilize the sexual binary that the woman who hears it becomes too disturbed to fulfill her part of the bargain. In 1970—the same year that saw the publication in French of *S/Z* (which, Barthes acknowledges, is itself the "trace" of a two-year seminar he conducted at the Ecole pratique des hautes etudes)—the release of *The Conformist* marked Bertolucci's break with the political modernism of Left filmmaking of the late 1960s. We needn't take this coincidence as making a claim of influence—though such an influence is tantalizing to ponder, given that by the mid-1970s we know for certain that Bertolucci was an enthusiastic reader of Barthes. Rather, this coincidence deserves notice because, in breaking with the politically modernist project of "analysis of the code," in breaking his transferential relationship to Jean-Luc Godard, Bertolucci ends up developing an "analytical aesthetic" not that dissimilar from the critical strategy adopted by Barthes. In a way, Bertolucci "reads" Moravia's novel the way Barthes reads Balzac's novella: Both involve a redoubling of the reading process, where each "narrative" is constantly interrupted by the other which is its mirror, each fragment referring itself to some other scene, some other temporal space, in which it might acquire meaning.

This, of course, is one way to define "transference." But it will no doubt be more accessible to begin our analysis of *The Conformist* with the much more obvious transferences that dominate the film, both intratextually and extratextually. Intratextually, *The Conformist* abounds with transferential relationships, certainly the most important of which is Marcello's relationship to his former professor Quadri. Significantly, the reenactment in the professor's study of Plato's allegory of the cave introduces, via ancient philosophy and pedagogy, yet another layer to the entire issue of the transferential relationship. But Bertolucci gives Professor Quadri—as is well known—the Paris address and phone number of Jean-Luc Godard, so that extratextually, the film might be seen as Bertolucci's fantasy murder of his mentor. (We could add here that the professor is murdered in Switzerland, Godard's country of birth.) Besides the well-known, we can however add a number of other transferential relationships to the energy that is driving the author: Bertolucci's relationship to his first mentor, Pasolini (whose homosexuality, preferred cruising locales, and even preferred type of *ragazzo* is alluded to in the film's final sequences); or, Bertolucci's problematic relationship to Hollywood (the bad father); his relationship to the Italian post-neorealist art film tradition (the father fallen into irrelevance?); or even Bertolucci's own conflicted ego-identifications. Does he belong to the provincial intelligentsia of Parma, or the glittering cosmopolitans of Paris and London?[10]

Indeed, one could argue that the dizzyingly complex temporal organization of the film is a direct manifestation of the complex interplay of transferences going on. Peter Brooks, in a superb reading of the centrality of the transference to an understanding of Balzac's *Le Colonel Chabert*, talks about the way transference enacts a "hallucinatory insistence on the denial of time and sequence."[11] As we've already noted, this, along with the ravishing beauty of the images, is typically what one remembers most about *The Conformist*—and it is this that also makes the word "flashback" so inadequate to describe the immediacy of the images that comprise most of the film's running time, but are outside the "present tense" of the film's narrative "drive" (which is literally a "drive," a car ride from the Hotel d'Orsay in Paris to the road in Switzerland where Professor Quadri's car is finally overtaken).

It should already have become clear that transference, conceptually, takes on two closely related valences. On the one hand, it is "interpersonal," as when the student turns the professor into the "subject supposed to know." On the other hand—and here is where it derives all its power in psychoanalysis—this very positioning causes the "action" between the two people to become invariably "refracted" by all sorts of other scenes from the past. The narrative thus produced, while always in the present, is always also in excess of the present. The transference can then be seen as a kind of framing operation: Because the events of the past are reenacted within a different frame, the past itself can be renarrativized. This is precisely how Brooks is deploying the transference in his reading of *Le Colonel Chabert*. Chabert was a colonel who rose to great prosperity under Napoleon and then was presumed to have died in action. It turns out he hadn't died and manages to return to Paris during the Restoration, which provides the "frame" for the narration of his story. In Balzac's novel, the frame functions to supply us with a clearly delineated historical "outside" to the Napoleonic period in which Chabert prospered and then was presumed to have "died"; and what is necessary is that all the events of the now-resurrected Chabert's life be made to resignify in a fundamentally new Symbolic order.

In this regard, what is significant about *The Conformist* is precisely how the narrative frame—the drive combined with the coda—fails to accomplish the work of the transference, that is, fails to resituate the older story from psychic reality to social/historical reality. The boundary between outside and inside becomes blurred, as the frame seems to be enfolded into the narrative. The relationship of the "fold" to the baroque, and thus to an investment in the plastic quality of the image, will be the subject of the final section of this essay. With respect to the transference, however, it would seem more useful to look for the film's conceptual "outside" deep *within* the flashbacks: to, in fact, the professor who is the object of a transference relationship both for Marcello and for Bertolucci; who is outside the fascist Symbolic discourse (he works for the Resistance in Paris)—and whose name, it turns out, is Quadri. In Italian, "quadro" most commonly means "square" or "painting," but it is also used when referring to a "frame of reference" (*quadro di riferimento*), and it is the root of the Italian term for the framing that the motion picture camera performs (*inquadratura*). That the professor is associated with framing is confirmed by his recitation of his university lecture on Plato, whose allegory of the cave dramatizes the movement from appearance (as deception) to concept (as the "eternal") through procedures of framing. The professor's name is, however, plural—suggesting "frames," or "framings," rather than the singular "frame"—thus hinting at the possibility of some fundamental slippage that haunts any discourse of mastery, whether that of Plato, the professor, or the post-1968 filmmakers of the Left.

Plato's allegory constructs a binary opposition between Logos and image, so that the philosophical project becomes one of demystification, of moving away from immanence. In a sense, then, the project of political modernism might be seen as yet another in a long line of updatings of this binary opposition. Bertolucci, while sympathetic to the project of the post-1968 filmmakers of the Left, was unable to conceive of this binary opposition without positing some kind of surplus, or leftover—the surplus produced by the appearance of the plural at the center of the film, at the very point at which "plurality" is supposed to be subsumed by the concept. This investment in plurality opens up to another way of understanding the overcoded quality of Bertolucci's images. This aesthetic contrasts sharply with what we see happening in the images of Godard, for example: As Godard moves toward and into the Dziga Vertov period, his images become more and more schematic (and nowhere more tellingly than in *Le Gai Savoir* [Godard, 1969], which takes the form of a lesson in semiotics and the relationship of signifier to image).

Another way to put this is to say that the project of political modernism was fundamentally linguistic or discursive in relation to the image: What Godard and others want to do is expose the operations of the code, as the first step in a process of ideological demystification. For a time, this was Bertolucci's project as well: in the feature *Partner* (1968), in the post-1968 *"cinema in piazza"* newsreels, and so on. But consider the "venetian blinds" sequence in *The Conformist*, a sequence whose editing blatantly violates the realist code, and thus by all rights should be yet another specimen of the estrangement effects by which progressive filmmaking would bring the spectator to political consciousness. The setting is Giulia's mother's apartment in Rome, where Marcello is paying a prenuptial visit to his intended. The large parlor seems to be illuminated almost entirely by "natural" light flooding in from the windows with venetian blinds, so that the light falls in bands of light and shadow that are echoed in the gown Giulia is wearing, made of a fabric of wider horizontal bands of black and white. (The scene is rightly celebrated for Storaro's bravura cinematography: At one point, the strips of light and shadow cast by the venetian blinds begin to crawl up the wall as Marcello and Giulia are held in a two-shot.) As the scene develops, Marcello and Giulia have a face-to-face conversation about his need to go to confession before the priest will agree to marry them. In this conversation, there are four successive shots—of Marcello and Giulia face-to-face in a two-shot—that violate the 180-degree rule. At every cut, the screen direction completely reverses, so that first Marcello is at screen-left, then suddenly jumps to screen-right, and so forth. Such a destabilization of spectatorial positioning—through the manipulation of the code—might easily be conceived of as an homage to Godard. Instead, though, it is just another nail in the coffin of the assassinated mentor, as the spectator, in sensory overload—the strips of natural light through the venetian blinds gliding up the walls, the light pattern picked up by the black and white stripes on the dress, the muffled sounds of carpet and fabric: in short, the proliferation of *texture* in the image and sound—doesn't even notice the shifts in screen direction!

At this point in the argument, then, we might reformulate the tension driving the film—which earlier we saw as one between concept and image—as a tension between a semiotic project, and the *body* traversed by all sorts of destabilizing pulsions. The advantage to framing the opposition this way is that it allows us to see the connection between Bertolucci's aesthetic strategy and melodrama. Peter Brooks was the first to point out the connection between revolution (the French) and melodrama. For Brooks, the very project of melodrama is to reinscribe the body with meanings, after the traditional meanings attached to the body have been swept away in the construction of the democratic subject. This was the function of the formal device of the tableau, the sudden freezing of the actors' bodies in such a way that a "moral system" can be read from them.[12] More recently, Tom Gunning has attempted to historicize Brooks's work in relation to developments in melodrama that occurred around the time of the emergence of the cinema. For what happens in late-nineteenth-century melodrama is the emergence of what Gunning conceives of as the formal complement to the tableau, namely, the "sensation scene."[13] What is useful from our point of view is the way in which this complementary set of formal devices mirrors the tension produced by *The Conformist*: tableau complements spectacle; eyes-sight-"vision" (which in one way or another is foregrounded by the critical literature on the film) complements "stomach"-sensation-affect (these latter terms coming from a reading of the final scenes of the film, when homosexuality "erupts" in its final, decisive form). To be sure, there is nothing crude about the effects that Bertolucci's images produce; but they nevertheless derail the spectator from his or her analytical distance by allowing us to overidentify with the image, producing an effect not unlike that prized by the cinephile.

Thus, to unlock the mystery of *The Conformist*—as well as to understand its position historically, as an avatar of a new aesthetic of the image soon to emerge—we need to understand fully (and structurally) the nature of this tension underlying the film. Here, the key will lie in the final shots of the film, once we recognize that in these shots, the film is once again reenacting Plato's allegory of the cave, now outside the "frame" of Quadri's study in Paris.

ANTI-LOGOS; OR, THE CINEMA MACHINE

It turns out that also for Colonel Chabert—who, as Peter Brooks points out, suddenly finds himself in an entirely different "frame" than the one in which he had lived the events of his life—the transference is unsuccessful. Chabert refuses to enter into the social world of the Restoration, going even so far as to renounce his given name and to take the name "Hyacinth." His final gesture in the novel is to trace with his cane in the air an "imaginary arabesque"—that is, pure "figure."[14] All of this—the refusal of the paternal name, the identification with the delicate flower, the substitution of gesture for speech, of the arabesque for the line—can be said to announce the ruination of the Logos. In *The Conformist*, the arabesque that is literally "written on the wind" becomes the "Arab boy,"[15] who emerges at film's end in an ironic repetition and deconstruction of the allegory of the cave.

When Marcello leaves the house on the night of Mussolini's fall, he first goes to meet his blind friend Italo at the Ponte Sant'Angelo (the bridge that Pasolini used at the beginning of *Accattone*), as searchlights crisscross the sky and the cityscape, one of which manages to pick out the two of them from the chaotic action on the bridge. On one level, this can be seen as a repetition of a conformist's fundamental terror, the terror of being singled out: the two most notable other instances of this singling out being, one, in the dance hall sequence, when the dancing crowd led by Giulia and Anna encircle Marcello, and, two, the child Marcello's vaguely remembered sexual humiliation by his school classmates, the event that causes him to flag down the limousine driven by Pasqualino. (Of course, the filming of the "pick up" also suggests rather elliptically that "Lino," sensing possible prey, is cruising the boy in his car.) But on another level, the proliferation of the searchlights needs to be interpreted as more than a device for a "character study," insofar as the searchlights impart to the scene—which, we should recall, is no longer Marcello's memory, but his present—the same dreamlike quality that characterizes the entire film. It is, then, yet another example of how the film's frame is folded into the narrative. Continuing the motif of light and shadow that runs through the film and that is anchored in the professor's study in Paris, the proliferation of the searchlights suggests that we are no longer within the totalizing, "solar" optics that are central to the allegory of the cave.

The action suddenly shifts to the Teatro Marcello: the ruins of a Roman theater situated just down the hill from one of Rome's most active gay cruising zones, but also "Marcello's Theater," where Marcello will participate in the final staging of Plato's allegory of the cave. First, however, Marcello and Italo overhear an impeccably dressed dandy attempting to pick up a barefooted, homeless *ragazzo*. As hinted at in the previous discussion of melodrama, the conversation is entirely at the level of the sensual and the tactile: The boy runs his bare foot over the surface of Pasqualino's shoe in order to feel the softness of the leather; when the conversation turns to food, the boy says that rats are a staple of his diet. When the dandy mentions his oriental silk kimono that turns him into a beautiful butterfly, Marcello realizes at once that the man is Pasqualino, as he used the same line when trying to seduce Marcello. (We can note parenthetically that the shortened form of the dandy's name is Lino, which is the Italian word for "linen," and that Lino in the earlier scenes in the film is associated with textiles, and thus with the tactile.) Marcello then publicly denounces both Pasqualino and Italo as fascists, driving them both to run off in the night.

Then, the theater has mysteriously cleared out; the partisan demonstrators and the prostitutes have gone. The Mediterranean *ragazzo* is camped out on a mattress, naked, with a record player. Little bonfires are burning. The *ragazzo* puts a record on the Victrola and cranks it up, so that the sound of the pop song washes over the scene. On the other side of a wrought-iron gate, Marcello moves toward one of the bonfires on the other side (i.e., behind him) and sits with his back to the camera (and in terms of screen space, to the *ragazzo* as well). It is at this point that we understand, through iconography and framing, that the allegory of the cave is being enacted yet again: with the iron bars standing in for the idea of enchainment; the bonfires the light source behind the enchained prisoners; and Marcello at first looking forward, positioned as were the prisoners of the cave to see only the "shadows of things." But then, in the film's final shot, Marcello turns around and looks toward the camera, getting the view that—Plato suggests—would finally perform the demystification, would finally reveal the ghost in the machine that submits us to the symbolic, would finally liberate us from false consciousness. And what is it that stands (or rather, lies languorously, and face down) in the place of the Platonic form? Nothing less than the luxuriating Mediterranean boy, whose most prominent feature in the dark shot are the inviting mounds of his buttocks. The thing, thus, is connected to a site of waste, of transgression, of a *jouissance* beyond the phallus; and so all of the many, repeated variations on the Oedipal scenario throughout the film are nothing more than the defense against this invocation of the hole or void over which both subject and object are constructed. Throughout the film, Marcello keeps pulling his posture to a rigid erectness; against which we can juxtapose the plasticity of the boy, as well as his connection to an expanded sensorium, beyond vision: one that encompasses the tactile, the auditory, even taste (in his earlier discussion with Lino about eating rats). Indeed, the Victrola plays a critical role in these final shots, connecting this scene decisively to the earlier scene in the professor's study, while resituating the Platonic problematic from the dimension of vision to that of sound. For the only other time in the film in which we see a hand cranking anything occurs in a single throwaway shot that is cut into and interrupts the presentation of the allegory in the professor's study. In this shot, Giulia is cranking a mimeograph machine while Anna commands her to go "faster, faster, faster," thus turning into a sexual game the mechanical reproduction of the signifier (and indeed, it is difficult to tell whether anything is actually imprinted on the sheets that are spewing forth from the mimeograph).

In an essay on *The Maltese Falcon* (Huston, 1941), Lee Edelman uncovers in that film a similar destabilization of the Logos: where the veiled, phallic object, the homage to the patriarch/king, turns out to be just another worthless plaster cast, unleashing in both the femme fatale and the non-phallic males a drive that goes beyond the law. Only Sam Spade can right the destabilization that haunts the film, by handing the bird over to the law and then asserting that it is "the stuff that dreams are made of." Thus occluding, in Edelman's words, "the structuring violence through which this Oedipal logic successfully enshrines itself as logic tout court: the violence through which another relation, a non-logic, is denied." Here, too, plasticity threatens to derail Logos; and in his argument, Edelman usefully deploys Paul DeMan's binary opposition between grammar and rhetoric: grammar being that which instates the law, by allowing us to connect subject and object; and rhetoric, that which continually derails, from within the self-enclosure of the signifying system, this connection through its figures and tropes.[16] Within the logic of the Oedipal, or the logic of Platonic philosophy, grammar is productive, while rhetoric is nonproductive expenditure, hindering our search for the thing itself as it revels in sheer appearance, the plasticity of the signifier itself.

TOWARD THE FIGURAL

This disfiguring quality that DeMan connects to rhetoric might be usefully connected to the field of visuality by way of Jean-François Lyotard's notion of "the figural." In *Discours Figure*, Lyotard—not content with what he saw as poststructuralism's textualization of nearly everything—develops the concept of the figural as a way to allow the field of textuality to connect to the field of the sensible world.[17] Significant in relation to *The Conformist*, Lyotard singles out Plato for having first allowed Logos to cast a "penumbra" over the world of sense perception, thus forever tainting that world with "nonbeing," or falsehood. Lyotard's first move, then, is to assert that visuality is connected to the body, and its being-in-the world; the figural then comes to name that sense of "spatiality" that lurks within any linguistic utterance. But Lyotard is not engaging in "phenomenology" here; he is not saying that that sense of spatiality is grounding language in reference, but rather that the figural is that which induces "discord" within the closed system of signification, by way of forces and energies. Here an extended quote is in order:

> We never touch the thing except metaphorically, but this laterality is not, as [Maurice] Merleau-Ponty believed, that of existence, which is much too close to the unity of the subject, as he finally recognized; . . . rather, it is that of the unconscious or of expression, which in one and the same movement opens and reserves all content.[18]

The unconscious and (artistic) expression are the two realms in which the figural "figures."

Both Lyotard and Deleuze see painting—that is to say, the "event" of any particular painting—as constituted by just such a transcription of energies reverberating both within the painting, and from painting to spectator.[19] The image always threatens to fall into cliché (into the familiar, the already seen, or simply the conventions of representational space); the figural is what pushes, as a creative force of deformation, the painting into its originality as event. To be sure, both Lyotard and Deleuze are discussing modern painters (Klee for Lyotard, Bacon for Deleuze, Cézanne for both). But these notions of force and energetics can readily translate to the aesthetic of the baroque; and given that the baroque—especially in French and Italian thought in the 1980s—was widely argued to characterize the aesthetic forms of the postmodern,[20] such a move would allow us to rethink the very way in which the art cinema has re-envisioned its relationship to the image. In the baroque, for example, the elliptical is favored over the linear, the eccentric is favored over symmetry, enfoldings transgress the boundaries between inside and outside: Together, these create energy fields that mark the baroque work with its characteristic fluidity and movement. In Jean Rousset's memorable phrase, the baroque facade is "a Renaissance façade plunged in water; or more precisely, its reflection in agitated water . . . the entire edifice undulating to the rhythm of waves."[21]

We have noted already how *The Conformist* ends by marking the site of the failure of the Logos, in the arabesque of the naked *ragazzo*. We can thus argue that this point of transgression opens up the space of the figural in the film, providing the "logic" for the film's break with an "indexical" tradition in the art film and allowing the images to be organized around a plastics of the baroque. For example, the way the outside folds into the inside of the film; or the ways in which the motifs are organized around series that create resonances (transversally) across the text. This, for example, is how the system of lighting works in the film. The beam of light finds its most coherent expression in the professor's study in Paris, at the center of the film; but both before and after that scene, the coherence of the beam of light is fractured—by the venetian blinds, by the searchlights, by the chiaroscuro of the radio studio, and so forth. A similar principle of seriality and resonance operates with other elements of the mise-en-scène. Throughout the film, we have a series constructed around the associated objects "gun-hat-buttocks": This connection is pinned down in the opening sequence in the hotel room, where Marcello removes the gun from a "purse," then takes his hat, which sits oddly atop the naked buttocks of his sleeping wife. But then, when Raoul gives him the gun in Ventimiglia, Marcello remembers he has "forgotten his hat," while the most charged elements in the scene of Marcello's boyhood seduction are Lino's gun and chauffeur's cap. (The buttocks, significantly, is repressed in these two elements of the series and only emerges in the film's final scene.) Seriality also governs the presentation of the sexes: Dominique Sanda appears two times as a whore before her appearance as the professor's wife. And with the homosexuals, Lino presents us with a series "homosexual-dandy-androgyne-'butterfly'"; while the *ragazzo* at the end exists in a "citation" series: "Pasolini-Caravaggio-ancient Greece-North Africa."

The connection between *The Conformist* and MTV, then, would lie here, in their similar deployments of a neobaroque organization of the image. But if this were the extent of the argument, we would hardly have made the case for the centrality of *The Conformist* to an emergent aesthetic in the art film. But as it happens, during the 1980s—that is, a decade after the release of *The Conformist*—we find that both the glossy, advertising/MTV image and the baroque have become objects of intense discussion in French intellectual life, and in its film culture more generally, and all connected to the emergence of the *cinéma du look*.[22] For a number of critics, a film like *Diva* (Beineix, 1981; arguably the inaugural film of the *cinéma du look*) was troubling in the way that it seemed caught by a fascination for the image itself, without regard for "depth," and a connection was explicitly made between the glossy, clichéd images of advertising and consumer culture and Beineix's seeming recycling of them in the film. Several recent scholars of the *cinéma du look*, however, have begun a reevaluation of the films from the point of view of the baroque[23] (which, as already noted, was itself receiving critical attention in the 1980s—we could even say that certain sections of Deleuze's 1985 *L'Image-temps*, on Welles, the crystal image, and the powers of the false, were at least implicitly about baroque style, while his explicit work on the baroque, *The Fold*, appeared in France three years later). It would be beyond the scope of this essay to do more than nod at these reinterpretations. But, for example, one could argue that the redoubled structure of *Diva* is one of folds and involutions, which—far from being simple decoration—create internal force fields that open up to an invisible, "spiritual" world. Or in Leos Carax, the argument has been made that his wild lines of flight produce the kinds of eccentric effects characteristic of the baroque, but all in the interest of remapping the (now-transformed) spaces of Paris— which of course the New Wave had lovingly done before, but the maps have become out of date.

The Conformist can thus be seen as an allegory in which the relations between image, body, space, and concept are being formally and historically interrogated and reconceptualized. As we have seen, this is all done around the figure of homosexuality, so it is to this last mystery of the film that we must turn. In the brilliant section of *Time-Image* on Joseph L. Mankiewicz and the crystal image, Deleuze notes that in *Suddenly, Last Summer* (1959) homosexuality is *not* the hinge upon which everything devolves (despite it being the "secret revealed" in the film's single flashback). In this film, several temporalities exist at once, in various strata: so that more superficially there is the Oedipal jealousy (i.e., the possessive mother who in postwar America was thought to turn her sons into homosexuals); then there is homosexuality (the mother and Katherine as lures to attract young men); but beneath that are the orgiastic Mediterranean mysteries of dismemberment and cannibalism.[24] Contemporary psychoanalysis would call this last level *jouissance*, or the death drive. But what is important for our argument is that, perhaps surprisingly, here Deleuze seems to anticipate the queer theoretical arguments laid out earlier; namely, that the appearance of homosexuality within the textual system—and in *Suddenly, Last Summer*, this appearance has all the melodrama we'd expect from Tennessee Williams—leads inevitably to the destabilization of forms, as we move into a primal immediacy that precedes Logos.

As we have seen, *The Conformist* ends by bringing us up against the real, in the figure of the Mediterranean *ragazzo*; and here too, there is a stratigraphic layering of time, as the boy indexes a tradition of Mediterranean pederasty that leads back to the Greek *eromenos*. Now, the institution of Greek pederasty was haunted by a problematic curiously similar to the problematic *The Conformist* makes evident at the level of philosophy; that is, the *eromenos* is at one and the same time a representative of the "idea" (of pure beauty) and also a *body*, subject to all the vicissitudes that come with enchainment to the physical world. This contradiction, as Foucault and many others have noted, worked to severely regulate and limit actual sexual practices. Homosexuality was even then connected to a radical alterity, something that threatened to derail the economy of the polis. Homosexuality is thus central to *The Conformist*, but only as an *alterity*, not as an identity—which is why any interpretation that sees Marcello as ultimately "coming to terms" with a "repressed homosexuality" falls so flat. This is a problem that haunts queer theory and queer activism (at least in the West) even today: Is homosexuality a structural, constitutive alterity that haunts any Symbolic regime? Bertolucci's film suggests that it is, just as the film suggests that it is only by way of alterity that the clichéd images that saturate the spaces of late capitalism can be disfigured.

The final question that remains is, what does the case of *The Conformist* have to say about the possibilities of political filmmaking, as we move away from the era of counter-cinema? We might begin by noting that counter-cinema is rooted in a "hermeneutics of suspicion": The spectator must move away from the film's nominal subject (if indeed a subject itself is apparent on the surface) and engage in sophisticated interpretive maneuvers in order to get to that "other scene," which is the film's real concern. *The Conformist*, as we've seen, has one foot firmly planted in this tradition, while at the same time it pushes its psychoanalytical "infrastructure" to the limit. I have borrowed from Lyotard the concept of the figural to name this limit, in which plastic forces push the images toward discord, or multiplicity. The political thus moves away from transcendental critique, and toward the presentation of pure singularities. The extent to which any moving-image work—whether that of MTV or Beineix and Carax—is judged to be political would then depend upon the extent to which the plastics of the image induces the kind of discord that is productive of new thought. This is a new way to understand the politics of the image, and I think it would be safe to call it a politics of the multitude.

NOTES

Earlier drafts of this essay paper were presented at the conference "Italians and Their Others," Institute for Advanced Study, University of Western Australia (Perth 2003); and at "Cinema Europe: Networks in Progress," University of Amsterdam (2005). I'd like to thank the conference organizers at the Institute for Advanced Study for their generous invitation to bring me to the conference, and to Mark Nicholls and Rolando Caputo for helpful comments. Finally, I'd like to thank editors Karl Schoonover and Rosalind Galt for their extremely close reading and suggestions for revision.

1. Robert Veze, "Photography for *Flashdance*," *American Cinematographer*, May 1983, 76.

2. Louis Althusser was one of the early Marxist theorists to turn to psychoanalysis, deploying the Lacanian notion of imaginary misrecognition to reformulate the theory of ideology. See the various essays in his *Lenin and Philosophy*, trans. Ben Brewster (New York: Monthly Review, 1971).

3. Critical commentary on *The Conformist* is rather extensive, and analyses of the film pop up in general books on Italian cinema, as well as in the more expected places (books and essays on Bertolucci's work). Thus, any attempt in a short essay such as this one to synthesize the various interpretations is bound to seem reductive. For the purposes of my argument, I'm focusing on the interpretations of the film by T. Jefferson Kline, in *Bertolucci's Dream Loom* (Amherst: University of Massachusetts Press, 1987), and Robert Kolker, in *Bernardo Bertolucci* (New York: Oxford University Press, 1985). Other notable interpretations of the film are in Yosefa Loshitsky, *The Radical Faces of Godard and Bertolucci* (Detroit: Wayne State University Press, 1995); Angela Dalle Vacche, *The Body in the Mirror: Shapes of History in Italian Cinema* (Princeton, N.J.: Princeton University Press, 1992); and Claretta Tonetti, *Bernardo Bertolucci: The Cinema of Ambiguity* (New York: Twayne, 1995).

4. Heterosexual incest is hardly the most liberatory instance of queerness, and the scene is far too excessive to take seriously as social commentary, but it does pervert heteronormativity quite effectively, as well as remind us of "Totem and Taboo," the dirty secret that must remain disavowed for patriarchy to happen.

5. By now there is a vast amount of literature on this subject. A central work is Lee Edelman, *Homographesis* (New York: Routledge, 1994). Eve Sedgwick's introduction, "Queer and Now," to her *Tendencies* (Durham, N.C.: Duke University Press, 1993), gives a brilliant and hilarious account of how the canon has been policed of queerness; and D. A. Miller's wickedly funny "Anal *Rope*" (*Representations* 32 [1990]: 114–133) shows how both the textual system of Hitchcock's film and the critical discourses surrounding it partake of the same logic of fascination and disavowal.

6. I am deliberately avoiding the use of the word "indexical" here. Recently, two articles have appeared that argue that Bazin's concept of the photographic image cannot be subsumed by Charles S. Pierce's concept of "the index." See Daniel Morgan, "Rethinking Bazin: Ontology and Realist Aesthetics," *Critical Inquiry* 32, no. 3 (2006): 443–482; and Adam Lowenstein, "The Surrealism of the Photographic Image: Bazin, Barthes, and the Digital *Sweet Hereafter*," *Cinema Journal* 46, no. 3 (2007): 54–82. Both of the arguments are compelling. I have in the past used—and continue to use in the title of this essay—the word "index," because I think that it continues to have conceptual validity when thinking about one particular dimension of the Bazinian aesthetic. However, I myself have (admittedly, implicitly) argued that Bazin's notion of the photographic image goes beyond the indexical: It would be impossible to understand, for example, Bazin's essay on Fellini's *Nights of Cabiria* via the concept of the photographic image as indexical. See my discussion of that essay in Angelo Restivo, *The Cinema of Economic Miracles: Visuality and Modernization in the Italian Art Film* (Durham, N.C.: Duke University Press, 2002), 36–39.

7. See my reading of the film in Restivo, *Cinema of Economic Miracles*, 108–115.

8. See note 4 for the principal sources for this argument.

9. For a nice discussion of the banishing of the world by means of the green screen in contemporary film production, see Jean-Pierre Geuens, "The Digital World Picture," *Film Quarterly* 55, no. 4 (2002): 16–27.

10. In a conversation I had with Valentino Orsini in Rome in 1990, he at one point said, "But Bertolucci isn't an *Italian* filmmaker, he's a *European* filmmaker!"

11. Peter Brooks, *Reading for the Plot: Design and Intention in Narrative* (Cambridge, Mass.: Harvard University Press, 1992), 228. The analysis of Chabert in relation to the transference is in chapter 8.

12. Peter Brooks, *The Melodramatic Imagination: Balzac, Henry James, Melodrama, and the Mode of Excess* (New Haven, Conn.: Yale University Press, 1995), chaps. 1–3.

13. Tom Gunning, "The Horror of Opacity: The Melodrama of Sensation in the Plays of André de Lorde," in *Melodrama: Stage Picture Screen*, ed. Christine Gledhill et al. (London: BFI, 1994), 50–61.

14. Brooks, *Reading for the Plot*, 232.

15. While the boy is certainly a "southern" "type," there is no clear evidence that he is North African; I am taking a liberty here for the sake of making a connection.

16. Lee Edelman, "Plasticity, Paternity, Perversity: Freud's Falcon, Huston's Freud," *American Imago* 51 (1994): 69–104.

17. *Discours Figure* (Paris: Klincksieck, 1971) has never appeared in book form in English translation, although five of the chapters appear in translation, scattered in various journals or collections. Recently, the important introductory chapter, "Taking the Side of the Figural," has been translated and appears in *The Lyotard Reader and Guide*, ed. Keith Crome and James Williams (New York: Columbia University Press, 2006), 34–48. This collection also contains the chapter, "The Connivances of Desire with the Figural," which appeared earlier in *Driftworks*. In terms of secondary literature on the figural, David Rodowick has surveyed the implications and developments of the concept in his *Reading the Figural: Philosophy after the New Media* (Durham, N.C.: Duke University Press, 2001). An excellent summary of Lyotard's book in relation to the thought of Deleuze has been done by Ronald Bogue, *Deleuze on Music, Painting, and the Arts* (New York: Routledge, 2003), 112–116.

18. "Taking the Side of the Figural," 42. The "as he finally recognized" no doubt refers to the argument Merleau-Ponty developed in *Le visible et l'invisible*, posthumously published in 1963. Interestingly, this book was the starting point for Lacan's development of the theory of the gaze in Seminar XI, conducted in 1963–1964. While it is certain that Lyotard was attending Lacan's seminars in the mid-1960s, I have not ascertained whether he was present during Seminar XI.

19. For Deleuze's arguments regarding painting and figure, see his *Francis Bacon: Logic of Sensation* (Minneapolis: University of Minnesota Press, 2004).

20. For a short, excellent overview of the interest in the baroque in French thought in the 1980s, see Fergus Daly and Garin Dowd, *Leos Carax* (New York: Manchester University Press, 2003), 42–64. Omar Calabrese's *L'età neobarocca* (Rome: Laterza, 1987) is the classic book-length study of postmodernity as "neobaroque." Translated by Charles Lambert as *Neo-Baroque: A Sign of the Times* (Princeton, N.J.: Princeton University Press, 1992).

21. Quoted in Daly and Dowd, *Leos Carax*, 47.

22. See Daly and Dowd, *Leos Carax*, and also Phil Powrie, *Jean-Jacques Beineix* (Manchester: Manchester University Press, 2001), esp. chap. 2.

23. E.g., Powrie, Daly, Dowd, noted previously.

24. Gilles Deleuze, *Cinema 2: The Time-Image*, trans. H. Tomlinson and R. Galeta (Minneapolis: University of Minnesota Press, 1989), 48–51.

10

SURREALISM IN ART AND FILM: FACE AND TIME

Angela Dalle Vacche

This essay posits a historical continuity between surrealism and art cinema, both in terms of the material histories of French twentieth-century culture and in the development of art cinema's conceptual interest in time and the image. Late surrealism, I will argue, forms a bridge to the postwar development of art cinema in the work of Alain Resnais and Jean-Luc Godard. To understand the techniques of these influential directors more fully, we must return to the histories and aesthetic concerns of the historic avant-garde. A French avant-garde movement founded by André Breton in 1924, surrealism achieved international resonance for years to come across a variety of artistic media in Europe and the United States. In comparison to the much less internationally oriented neoclassical Italian painting or the insular spirituality of Russian Suprematism, the international reach of surrealism was so remarkable that this artistic trend can be said to have been "cosmopolitan" or "nomadic" long before the current phase of globalization. While the egalitarian potential of globalization is unclear, the surrealist impulse was probably able to spread across countries and generations owing to its rebellious stance against social conformism, the assembly line of industrial capitalism, and bourgeois notions of sexuality. To shock, jolt, and twist, in order to disorient, displace, and revitalize, was the core of the surrealist agenda. Notwithstanding a wide range of artistic personalities and cultural backgrounds, this avant-garde movement thrived on the dialectic of word and image, while it also combined a nonlinear definition of temporality with the manipulation of the human face. This double emphasis on history and subjectivity was meaningful inside and outside of France. Both time and face became privileged sites for the exploration of traumas dating back to World War I. For the surrealists, the Great War resonated as a sort of watershed event that imprinted the modern experience with a sense of loss and melancholia, while fostering grotesque combinations of human and nonhuman elements.

Given the international outreach of the movement, I will center my own discussion around Man Ray's ready-made *Indestructible Object* (1923). In order to underline its two tropes of time and the face, I rename this sculpture *The Eye and the Metronome*. As such, this surrealist work will become a returning point of reference for my journeys in France, Belgium, Japan, Sweden, Spain, and Italy and for my investigation of word and image across art and film. At first Man Ray's 1923 *Indestructible Object* showcased the photograph of a single eye. In 1932 the artist replaced this element of surveillance with a photographic cutout of the eye of his former lover, Lee Miller. Thus, Man Ray comments on his lost love for the beautiful American model and photographer.[1] More specifically, the all-knowing gaze implied by the first generic eye was replaced by the facial metonymy of a woman Man Ray had been competing with for professional acclaim. Furthermore, Man Ray acknowledged his own ephemeral level of authorial control by copying his sculpture in an ink drawing and renaming it *Object to Be Destroyed* (1932).

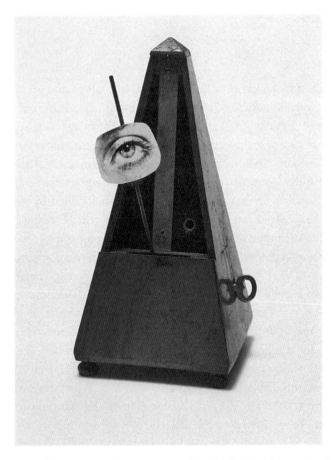

FIGURE 10.1. *Indestructible Object* (or *Object to Be Destroyed*), 1964. Replica of 1923 original. Metronome with cutout photograph of eye on pendulum, 8 7/8 x 4 3/8 x 4 5/8 in. James Thrall Soby Fund. (248.1966.a–e) The Museum of Modern Art, New York, NY, U.S.A. ©2010 Man Ray Trust/Artists Rights Society (ARS), New York/ADAGP, Paris Digital Image © The Museum of Modern Art/Licensed by SCALA/Art Resource, NY.

To be sure, these very same themes of power and desire shape the erratic narratives of post–World War II art cinema, whose strong links to surrealism, to this day, remain little understood. A work originally produced in 1923 may seem remote from the films of Jean-Luc Godard and Alain Resnais. However, Man Ray's call for destruction was fulfilled by a group of students attending the 1957 Dada exhibition in Paris. Always playful and one step ahead of the game, Man Ray had protected his 1923/1932 piece with an insurance policy, so that he was able to change the sculpture's title back again from *Object to Be Destroyed* to *Indestructible Object* in 1958.[2] Such a date marks the birth of the European art film, especially in terms of the French Nouvelle Vague, which coincided with the death of the founder of *Cahiers du Cinéma*, André Bazin, and the subsequent release of François Truffaut's *Les Quatre cents coups* / *The 400 Blows* (1959) and Godard's *À Bout de souffle* / *Breathless* (1960).[3]

Man Ray's sculpture about public surveillance and romantic heartbreak has an undeniable conceptual stance, for it combines the two major enemies of the surrealist manifesto: the metronome's constant time and a single eye whose stare oscillates back and forth. The metronome is a measuring tool used by musicians to maintain the regular "tempo," and Man Ray's sculpture embraces a repetitive view of time. In other words, he attached to his metronome's steady pendulum the all-seeing eye of a punitive entity that demands corporeal absence, facial disfiguration, and visual surveillance at all costs. This kind of disembodied, but intensely ocular subjectivity matches, of course, the Cartesian *cogito ergo sum* from René Descartes' *Principles of Philosophy* (1644).[4] Man Ray's mixing of his own sentimental vicissitudes with a Cartesian reference is in line with the surrealist paradigm for international export based on the celebration of displacement and unexpected analogies. Regardless of its nomadic implantation in different countries, the surrealist paradigm is relevant to at least two more levels of illusionism—the imaginary and the *trompe l'oeil* (trick the eye).[5]

Whereas in surrealism the face is never whole, the imaginary thrives on the privileged status of the maternal face on the cinematic screen and iconicity in classical portraiture. In contrast to other parts of the body and before the acquisition of language, the mother's face for the child represents a whole world in which to lose oneself. It also stands for a landscape of otherness where the adult can project fantasies—ranging from the cosmopolitan to the Orientalist—in search of interface, outreach, and transgression with an unknown culture or even a historical enemy.

Notorious for its three-dimensional relief or photographic realism, the *trompe l'oeil* dates back to the Renaissance, while this trick of the eye briefly invokes tactility. This extreme level of illusionism is also the most surreal way to mimic an imaginary ideal of wholeness. The latter starts with the face and would like to combine itself with touch. While the imaginary image is a sort of myth of origin, the *trompe l'oeil* lasts as long as it constructs a façade. Its components fit together so well that the flat trick looks for a moment three-dimensional and touchable. On the other hand, as a nonquantifiable yet highly expressive entity, the face remains as mysterious as the alchemy of love itself. To "tromp" the face is, therefore, the most difficult of *trompe l'oeil*. As strategies of illusion bordering surrealism, the imaginary and the *trompe l'oeil* claim to arrest the motion-bound features of the human face, even if they respectively offer either an

FIGURE 10.2. Salvador Dalí, *Mae West's Face Which May Be Used as a Surrealist Apartment,* 1934/1935. Gouache, with graphite, on commercially printed magazine page, 283 x 178 mm (sight), gift of Mrs. Charles B. Goodspeed, 1949.517. Reproduction, The Art Institute of Chicago. ©2010 Salvador Dalí, Gala-Salvador Dalí Foundation/Artists Rights Society (ARS), New York.

impossible ideal or a carefully constructed trick. In surrealism, in fact, the faces of René Magritte and Salvador Dalí, to name only a few possible artists, are usually turned away, effaced, cracked, distorted, or they become *trompe l'oeil* that ridicule the trick itself.

Outside of surrealist experimentation, however, the imaginary and the *trompe l'oeil* entertain a special kinship with the human face. As limit-points, the imaginary and the *trompe l'oeil* mark where surrealism may begin and where surrealism must stop to either dismember or reject the face altogether. Finally, in contrast to the respectively holistic and manipulative orientations of the imaginary and of the *trompe l'oeil*, the surreal thrives on producing ruptures and cracks, and on showing discontinuities and deformations. This is why surrealism has embraced metaphor, ambiguity, collage, and photomontage to celebrate, on one hand, impurities and clashes, while, on the other, to embrace the poetry and the imagination that these ruptures and revelations offer against our metronome-like routines.

The opening sequence of Ingmar Bergman's *Persona* (1966) provides the best illustration of an imaginary scenario of lost maternal nurturing. It may seem odd to refer to the illustrious Swedish filmmaker during a discussion of French surrealism. But the fact is that *Persona* is a film essay about the exchangeability of face, screen, and otherness, while surrealism itself has a long history of engagement with the screen as a fourth wall or mirror to be crossed in order to explore the unconscious. The latter, in turn, stands for the other in relation to the self. After a montage sequence whose fundamental topic is death, Bergman's camera dwells on a medium shot of a young boy lying on a cot inside a morgue-like space. The boy tries to touch a gigantic close-up of a woman's face projected on the wall. This image is an optical absent presence and is comparable to the *trompe l'oeil*. Most significantly, Bergman's character is reading a book before he becomes engrossed by a projected image. This tension between word and image in *Persona*'s opening sequence can be said to function as a dialectical trope that runs from surrealism in the 1920s and the 1930s into the French Nouvelle Vague of the 1960s.

COLLAGE AND PHOTOMONTAGE: AMOUR FOU OF WORD AND IMAGE

The history of the "imaginary" as a filmic concept intertwines itself with the surrealist movement through the work of psychoanalyst Jacques Lacan, namely his theorization of the mirror phase in 1936. Lacan knew Dalí quite well,[6] while he was also aware of Roger Caillois, a social scientist interested in the loss of self in animal mimicry and ritual practices. With Georges Bataille, the latter started a surrealist discussion group in Paris on art and science.[7] While the influence of Jean-Paul Sartre's notion of the imaginary on Lacan outgrows the boundaries of this essay, the French psychoanalyst promoted the idea that the constitution of subjectivity stems from a double-process of self-mirroring and self-alienation during infancy. Although rooted in the Lacanian analogy between mirror as screen and screen as face, the tension between recognition and otherness can also translate itself into the techniques of surrealist collage and photomontage.[8] These two approaches are typical of the Modernist avant-garde in general: in fact, they characterize not only surrealism, but also other art movements such as futurism and Dada. One wonders whether these shared practices can be said to have facilitated the international diffusion of surrealist imagery as well.

It is well known that, in collage, the fragments of the world deposit themselves on one single surface, with a special emphasis on the role of chance to bring them together in a state of disarray. Such an allegedly random gathering of debris from daily life coalesces into a new artistic whole, thanks to the victory of parataxis over causality—namely, combinatorial paradigms instead of chain-like developments. Instead of a linear trajectory based on progressive stages within the same theme, parataxis

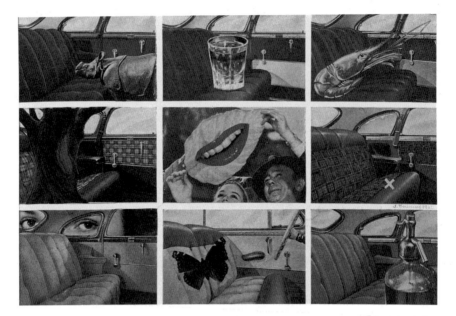

FIGURE 10.3. Jacques Brunius, *Collage in Nine Episodes* (1942). Isidore Ducasse Fine Arts. Photo courtesy Solomon R. Guggenheim Museum, New York.

is about the repetition of comparable elements within different contexts. Collage goes from the dimension of a chaotic plural to one of an unstable singular. Such a balancing act typical of collage can be found in French artist Jacques Brunius's *Collage in Nine Episodes* (1942).[9] After introducing an oversized iconography with a wounded tree, an anthropomorphic leaf, and a black butterfly, the artist suggests that the interior of a car is comparable to a female womb spewing out a strange narrative grafted onto a grid. Here, the return of the repressed goes hand in hand with the invasion of the family space. In fact, Brunius's multisegmented piece stages the sudden emergence of bestiality in the middle of luxury upholstery.

In her book *Surrealist Collage in Text and Image*,[10] Elza Adamowicz points out that Brunius was also an actor, a writer, and a filmmaker for whom collage and montage were comparable to each other. But which kind of montage does Brunius set up? At first sight, Brunius's grid with nine separate, identical squares may look antithetical to the random look cultivated by collage. Were we to consider each square to be the equivalent of a separate shot, we would have to conclude that Brunius offers us nine separate yet interrelated collages through one montage. Taken together, these collages or episodes flaunt their bizarre metaphors. Yet the real shock occurs when we realize that the car upholstery, in each shot-like square, changes according to the invasion of an alien entity. But there is more: Each square of the grid is comparable to one scansion in Man Ray's metronome, while Brunius's repeated inclusion of the car window inside each frame expands on Man Ray's theme of surveillance, by introducing the theme of voyeurism. With Brunius, not only is the metaphorical replacement internal to each shot, but so is the overall and unmistakably surreal metamorphosis, well beyond the subtle changes at the level of the car upholstery. Despite its metronome-like steady routine, the world has gone crazy, even though the oddest mutations remain inside each square. By using the family car as a gigantic box or container, Brunius mocks the order, propriety, and organization meant to guarantee family happiness.

Such a model of montage embraces boundaries and linearity only to show that they are entirely ineffective. It is not difficult to understand why, at the very center of the whole montage, one square shows a father and a son holding a giant leaf with a pair of red female lips inscribed in the very middle of this strange, flag-like object. This mirroring of one center for the whole composition with the middle of its focalizing unit suggests an abyss-like structure, or a temporal vertigo. Furthermore, these two males are the only characters who seem to stand outdoors and who seem to have been able to bring out of the car its deepest fantasy. The sexual, oedipal, and patriarchal connotations of this iconography are, to say the least, trite. Brunius's use of space, however, is innovative, because he turns his metronome-like squares into wild possibilities.

Whereas Brunius's *Collage in Nine Episodes* releases a kaleidoscopic survey, photomontage is about the effort to distance the photographic image from its source or referent. From the 1920s to the 1930s, artists' investment in the indexical link between the photograph and the world had become much more elastic, so that photomontage could go from a destabilized singular to a creative plural. An example of overexposed photomontage or *brulage*, namely several photographs with a tampered emulsion, *The Battle of the Amazons* (1939), by the Belgian Raoul Ubac, handles a group of mutilated, skeleton-like women as mere shells or struggling surfaces. Their fossil-like traces of flesh and incinerated bones and skeletons could be at war with each other

FIGURE 10.4. Raoul Ubac, *Untitled. Attributed title: From the series "The Battle of the Amazons,"* 1938. Solarized photomontage, 26.5 x 39.6 cm. Photo: Jacques Faujour. Musée National d'Art Moderne, Centre Georges Pompidou, Paris, France. © 2010 Artists Rights Society (ARS), New York/ADAGP, Paris. Photo Credit : CNAC/MNAM/Dist. Réunion des Musées Nationaux/Art Resource, NY.

or battling together against a holocaust. An artist involved in the existentialist circles surrounding Jean-Paul Sartre, Ubac was not only a historical member of the surrealist movement in the 1930s, but he also continued his engagement with questions of representation and death in the context of postwar Paris, where he was in touch with debates on humanism and terror after the Holocaust and Hiroshima.[11]

By alternating elongated shapes that are bigger than the nearby horizontal clusters, the composition is emphatically vertical so that it suggests an indelible rupture in time comparable to an abyss leading to extinction. The ripples and undulations in the image are dance-like and convulsive enough that they outline a choreography within a monochrome, silvery surface of living and dead layers. The *brulage* or burning technique looks painful because organic matter floats on a plane of ashes and dust. It is as if Ubac were using photography in an unorthodox way to reach down to an encounter with some unthinkable and unrepresentable "real" through history and death. Needless to say, Ubac's scattering of female limbs and deformation of figures into filaments, scars, and incinerated areas confirm the surrealists' fascination with breaks in time. Even more to the point, this quasi-abstract gathering of photochemical remains includes the last glimpse of erotic nudity, while it anticipates the morbid promiscuity of a postnuclear world.

As a form of collage-in-reverse, photomontage well underlines Ubac's single-handed authorship, for it stages an internal slip, a premeditated wedge, a manual intervention into the otherwise automatically produced photographic image. The camera's click is no longer about life caught in the moment. Instead of functioning like an indifferent cold eye, photography itself has embraced a destructive agenda by flaring up like a bomb out of control. Ubac's emphasis on the chromatic and plastic values of his image—a study in grays and whites—makes a painting out of a photograph.

One could say that Brunius's collage is a timing of space based on his grid's equal and measurable time units eager to burst. On the contrary, Ubac's photomontage is a spacing of time, where the traces left from the burning process convey the lingering of physical and mental pain. By lining up equivalent yet unstable narrative slots through collage and underlining the destructive power of light within photomontage, these two techniques do not produce moving images, but go as far as they can to rely on the weaving of space and time. It is this nexus that art historian Erwin Panofsky associates with cinematic movement.[12] No wonder, therefore, that these two surrealist works are, respectively, both compatible and comparable in terms of technique and theme to two films, Godard's *Pierrot le fou* (1965) and Resnais's *Hiroshima mon amour* (1959).

A work praised by the surrealist poet Louis Aragon, *Pierrot le fou* is the story of Pierrot/Ferdinand (Jean-Paul Belmondo) and Marianne (Anna Karina), who run away from bourgeois life in Paris to the Mediterranean island of Porquerolles. Perhaps because the destruction of cars looms large all throughout the couple's journey, their escape is nonlinear and punctuated by the repetition of long takes to underline uncanny approximations next to disruptive jump-cuts. Godard's method of mixing uninterrupted, quasi-hypnotic camera movement with disorienting combinations of briefer shots is meant to recharge his viewers' imaginative and mnemonic reserves in such a way as to imbue the film with an invisible stream of consciousness open to poetic analogies.

Fraught with dreamlike sequences, ready-made sentences, and staged interviews, the lovers' escape fails to generate a clean slate for the sake of creativity. In fact, they attempt to reinvent love, language, and themselves. But such an ambitious plan ends with death. Meanwhile, this unraveling of romance into destruction taps into the romantic roots of surrealism itself.[13] After feeling betrayed by Marianne, Pierrot kills her, only to blow himself up later on in a sort of semiaccidental fashion. In Godard's film, the failure of reinvention implies a sense of fatality that the characters inherit from their personal past, but also from their rejection of a linear model of temporality. Unable to find a respectable job, despite his wealthy Italian wife's connections, Pierrot leads the life of a loafer. As she is incapable of elevating herself beyond the profession of babysitter, Marianne's talent as a performer finds an outlet only in the woods of Porquerolles or along a shoreline where she joins an armed group of dancers. Despite the machine guns and the aggressive gear worn by these performers, Marianne transforms the straight line of Cartesian rationality into the decorative and freewheeling undulations of Henri Matisse's famous *Dance* (1909).

Pierrot le fou begins with a tennis game. This sequence, shot with hardly any cuts, imitates the metronome's regular tempo, while it is staged like a mirror-structure of two women playing mostly in long shot. The ball between them is never lost, while Belmondo's voice-over reads a passage on Velasquez from the pocketbook history of art written by French art historian Élie Faure.[14] Mesmerized by the continuous traveling of the tennis ball, we listen to Faure on Velásquez's interest in interstitial spaces. We are lulled into the Spanish painter's fascination with colors, whenever they connote the state of being-in-between humans and things. The rhyming hits and the visual trajectory of the tennis ball link the two women, as if the ball were an invisible pendulum inside a metronome. All of a sudden, it becomes possible to believe that not only in Velásquez's art but also in our prosaic daily life separations and differences might be magically overcome with colors radiating and resonating beyond the boundaries of bodies and the contour of objects.

In ways similar to Brunius's taste for odd replacements, *Pierrot*'s narrative is comparable to a game of permutations across verbal and visual signs. In line with the random montages of collage, the filmmaker jump-cuts from the sequence with the female players' beautiful bodies to a shot of Belmondo browsing in a bookstore. As a result of this forceful editing choice, the book, so to speak, replaces the body, while the male voice-over prevails over two speechless women playing tennis. Well aware of Sergei Eisenstein's taste for metaphors of power and collapse, Godard's jump-cut signals a revisitation of the combinatorial, but also disjunctive style of the Soviet director. Yet Godard cites Eisenstein's jump-cut more for the sake of surrealist poetry rather than of Marxist dialectics.

By virtue of its power to bring together two elements that do not belong to the same space, the jump-cut simultaneously hides and underlines distance. Two former lovers who meet again after a long separation, Pierrot and Marianne confuse distance with desire. Later, it becomes apparent that a jump-cut's on-screen magic does not necessarily apply to real life. In contrast to an array of visual, acoustic, graphic, and chromatic permutations within a feast of analogical thought, the distance between

Pierrot and Marianne becomes lack of trust and loss of loyalty. Conversely, in opposition to the unforgiving stare of Man Ray's metronome with its single, beautiful female eye, Godard's opening sequence in *Pierrot le fou* embraces a dream away from measuring or marking time. The darkness of the harbor lit from afar is either the beginning of a new kind of love beyond all rules or the last flickering of color before blindness. In a way, Godard abandons Man Ray's metronome by dropping the two female players out of the narrative. This is why the tennis game is nothing but a dangling prologue. Furthermore, Man Ray's emphasis on Lee Miller's single eye hardly matches Godard's sense that love exists beyond the boundaries of what is visible. In true surrealist fashion, love can be blind, or *fou*, to the point of occupying a realm outside of space and time, beyond the horizon of the sea and the last word of death.

Whereas Godard replaces the corporeal element with spoken text, Resnais turns the body into an audible conversation between two faceless lovers. In *Hiroshima*'s opening sequence, the extreme close-ups make it difficult to distinguish the gender of two intertwined male and female bodies. On closer scrutiny, we realize that, over and over again, a female hand will punctuate different segments of her statements about visiting Hiroshima fourteen years after the dropping of the atomic bomb. The lovers' skin opens to the erotic ambiguity of eros and death, with drops of sweat present due to either passion or agony.

But can the tragedy of "Hiroshima" exist next to "mon amour"? Resnais's extreme attention to the photographic surface turns both human skin and film celluloid into malleable objects. The story of an affair between a French actress (Emmanuelle Riva) and a Japanese architect (Eiji Okada), *Hiroshima mon amour* is much more about her and the West than it is about him and Hiroshima. In response to his declaration that she will never be able to understand what happened, she claims having seen everything about Hiroshima. Later on, intrigued as he is by her overreaction to someone else's trauma, the architect encourages the actress to disclose her painful past: that she was involved with a German soldier during the Nazi occupation. Outcast by her fellow citizens, she was subjected to all sorts of humiliations, all the more difficult to endure in the wake of her lover's death.

Hiroshima mon amour, however, is more than just a film about the atomic bomb, because it relies on the power of first love to grapple with the subtext of French collaboration with the German occupier during World War II. Although Riva's character is punished by her own community, one can sense that a certain kind of guilt haunts the victim as well. During her confinement inside a cellar, the punished woman looks at and interrogates her own hands, as if the burden of collective guilt was impossible to lift.[15] Furthermore, *Hiroshima*'s portions set in Nevers become an interrogation of what the French actress's hands might have done to others and to themselves as body parts. In fact, these hands, in the cellar, take on a life of their own, while they are repeatedly scratched, hurt, and abused against a rough wall, as if some kind of self-flagellation was appropriate. This is also why the image of the crowd casting out the young woman, in the same way French Jewish citizens were denounced, is, perhaps, Resnais's way of coming to terms with the historical stain of French collaboration.

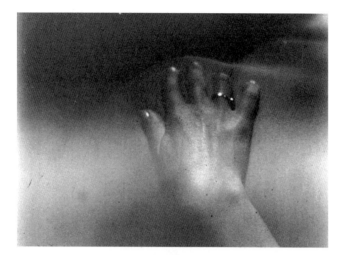

FIGURE 10.5. *Hiroshima mon amour* (Resnais, 1959). Zenith International/Photofest. © Zenith International.

In the guise of an extremely fluid and linear subjective tracking shot penetrating the space toward the vanishing point, Riva's stream of memories about hospital corridors and victims' faces rejecting her look breaks down in favor of a binary montage between street signs from Nevers and the neon lights of Hiroshima. Thus, her stubborn wish to understand the history of her Japanese lover accommodates both her own inner dialogue and a two-person conversation about the dilemmas of remembering too much or forgetting too quickly.

Instead of asking only questions about perception and illusionism, surrealism here raises the problems of value and perspective on the past. Resnais's film explores how geographical displacement can lead to a reassessment of personal memory in light of an even bigger tragedy. Just as in Brunius's open-ended epiphanies for his collages, Resnais's "mon amour," in the title, ambiguously refers to both the young German lover and the handsome Japanese architect. Is this the story of a girl's first love? And is it as banal as a dime novel, or as subjectively traumatic as the bombing of Hiroshima for the architect? In line with the anti-referential thrust of Ubac's photomontage, the consequences of the atomic bomb are so extreme that neither photojournalism nor life-size models in the Hiroshima museum can document the horror experienced by the population. Notwithstanding this representational impasse with history, the legacy of surrealist photomontage becomes most apparent in the museum sequence, where we see sets of grotesque legs with no bodies walking underneath huge boards.

Striving for the right distance between past and present is, by definition, an elusive project that involves constant shifts in time and restless wandering from the hotel to the teahouse in Hiroshima, and from the ruins to the stables in Nevers. At the expense of the Japanese architect's opportunities for self-expression, the French actress becomes the emotional center of the film and a figure of mobility. Significantly, she plays a nurse in a film about peace, shot among Japanese survivors. How fair is it to situate a trauma that belongs to the history of Japan onto a French woman's change of space? The actress and the architect are the representatives of two nations formerly at war, while neither one of these two characters gets a name in the film. Without falling into a sentimental universalism, Resnais's lovers exchange something modest yet deep. Her nominal reinvention into "Nevers" and his new name of "Hiroshima" suggest that the processes of filmmaking and film-viewing alleviate the problems of historical and emotional distance, thanks to the development of a temporary intersubjective zone.[16] This dynamic zone is based on how movement in film activates an exchange between space and time, on one hand, and on how love itself models an attraction between audience and screen, on the other. Reaching this weighted moment of exchange, however, does require traveling, or going to the cinema, in such a way of wandering inside oneself and through foreign lands. *Hiroshima mon amour* is a story of surrealist *dépaysement*, the same disorientation Breton and his friends sought by hopping from one movie theater to the next all night long, and by allowing language to surprise them through insomnia during their nocturnal experiments with automatic writing. *Dépaysement* also means the wrenching of an object out of its natural context and its insertion into a new territory. Needless to say, *dépaysement* applies to both collage and photomontage.

In *Pierrot le fou*, fragments from the chaos of life collate, that is, come together to make art; in *Hiroshima mon amour*, levels of experience—Nevers and Japan—compete with each other. Furthermore, Resnais's extreme close-up sequence on the very surface of the skin distances the image from its referent, the way writing does, by requiring an empty space between words. Whether it is collage or photomontage, the key point here is that, from surrealism to the French Nouvelle Vague, a certain dialectic stays on between the verbal and the visual, music and spoken language.

In the French Nouvelle Vague, the surrealist techniques of collage and photomontage presuppose but also undermine the imaginary trajectories of fusion and alienation at the heart of the Lacanian mirror phase. But precisely because the Lacanian model addresses the working of the cinematic apparatus with no specific context, it is only legitimate to wonder about the reasons that the surrealist legacy is so strong that it implants itself in the Nouvelle Vague, and why it insists on transforming the body into text, while turning the word into a corporeal landscape. What is there in the French cultural tradition, and in surrealism in general, that fuels Godard's collages with primary colors and Resnais's close-ups of erotic abstraction?

In his brilliant book *Downcast Eyes*,[17] cultural historian Martin Jay provides a persuasive answer to this question. Without hesitation, Jay takes us to 1921, the year of *Les Champs magnétiques*,[18] a text based on automatic writing by Breton and Philippe Soupault. In clear antithesis to Man Ray's *The Metronome and the Eye*, automatic writing tampers with linear or repetitive time, either by accelerating language or by stretching its duration. The goal is to elicit the flow of mysteriously linked images. Derived from the psychoanalytic technique of free association, automatic writing was a means of reproducing in the verbal medium the processes of the unconscious. It was a makeshift attempt in language to capture what Freud had already described, in *The Interpretation of Dreams*, as the tendency to speak visually, with images prevailing over words. Surrealist automatic writing stemmed from a fascination with whatever was unspeakable or even unthinkable. Among the surrealists, the assumption was that sleepless nights would pave the way into the metaphorical richness of unconscious poetry. The surrealists felt that grammatical prose and conventional literature in general was not enough to bridge the gap between the inner self and the outer world.

In contrast to the surrealists' intense visualizations triggered by the automatic language of the unconscious, the French cultural tradition, especially in the age of Descartes, worshipped the nuances of writing. Language aspired to math-like precision in relation to its referents: the description of the world as well as the introspection of the soul. This Cartesian cultural paradigm is logocentric, because it is based on the belief that rational and grammatical language is a sort of Godlike entity, one powerful enough to guarantee the presence, hence the existence, of the thinking subject to itself. After Descartes, this feeling of self-confidence—summarized in *cogito ergo sum*—degenerated from the power of clear thought into sheer control and sexual domination with the writings of the Marquis de Sade.

One of the Romantic mentors of the surrealist movement was Isidore Ducasse. Better known as "Lautréamont," he was the initiator of the rediscovery of De Sade. In 1869 he wrote *Les Chants de Maldoror*,[19] a project à la Sade in which he used a cold, controlling, scientific prose as precise as the slit cut by Luis Buñuel's razor onto the mysteries of the moon, the soft surface of a woman's eye, in *Un Chien andalou* (1929). Buñuel also dealt with Sade in his 120 days of Sodom episode for the film *L'Age d'or* (1930). But the Spanish filmmaker's embrace of sadistic images was only a means to an end. With surrealist automatism and collage, the Cartesian "I think, therefore I am" became I combine, collate, collide, make collide, and shock. And in French *coller* is a verb with the same root as *collage*. *Coller* means to have a love affair, a sticking together that might describe relations between characters in *Pierrot* and in *Hiroshima*.

With their mixture of love and death, the films of Godard and Resnais are crucial to understanding the French Nouvelle Vague's surrealist ancestry, but this genealogy is by far more complicated than a direct relation from artists in the 1930s to filmmakers in the 1960s. While Cartesian logocentric rationality was Breton's ultimate enemy, the obsession with language stays on among the surrealists themselves, for they turned grammatical sentences into linguistic play. In a similar fashion, French Nouvelle Vague filmmakers attacked the French films preceding them, namely the polished screenplays and literary adaptations of Jean Aurenche and Pierre Bost. In the wake of their surrealist and anticonformist role models, Godard and Truffaut tuned in Miles Davis's jazz trumpet,[20] Jean-Paul Sartre's philosophy, and Juliette Gréco's songs. Besides using natural lighting and grainy footage in homage to Italian neorealism, the French Nouvelle Vague embraced the popular music of jukeboxes and the automatism of pinball machines in search of a faster and lighter filmmaking style.

Notwithstanding their liberation from the constraints of canonical prose, this new generation, however, continued to rely on the evocative power of poetic and novelistic sources. Literature became a cross-cultural, poetic citation from American novels in Godard's *Breathless*. Likewise, *Hiroshima mon amour* was based on a text by experimental writer Marguerite Duras. In the shift from the literary adaptations produced by a French film industry based on the nationalistic *tradition de qualité* to the Nouvelle Vague's fast and cosmopolitan screenplays, one could argue that the tombstone of Cartesian prose became the new manifesto of surrealist poetry or language play.[21] Such a line of thought is in keeping with Jay's overarching argument in *Downcast Eyes*. There, the cultural historian spells out a systematic denigration of the visual register as such, or a turning of the eye away from the body, in order to privilege the word alone. This is why, perhaps, Man Ray's *The Metronome and the Eye* proposes a disembodied, perceptual organ whose only support is a measuring-machine with no feeling. In this sculpture, sight is haunting and temporal information is redundant.

TROMPE L'OEIL: FACE AND TIME

By functioning like an impossible myth of origin for an avant-garde movement based on rebellion against tradition, the imaginary scenario of the Lacanian mirror phase is built all around the reversibility of looking and touching. This is the case because the mother's touch is as reassuring for the child as her loving face. Yet, in the opening of Bergman's *Persona*, the maternal face is reduced to a projected image whose absent presence is an illusion, and, as such, it requires the rejection of touch. But the face, because of its threshold-like location between external physiognomy and nonvisible interiority, is the most difficult and most desirable corporeal trope to achieve with the *trompe l'oeil*. A seventeenth-century Milanese Renaissance painter, Arcimboldo would construct expressive human faces, despite the fact that his materials were nonhuman.[22] His *trompe l'oeil* were so anthropomorphic as to be called "effigies," or faces that stand out. Despite his alchemical proclivities, Arcimboldo was not far from an orderly and classical view of the world where the maximum of difference would be tolerable only inside the same species. How to explain, therefore, the surrealists' fascination with this odd artist committed to making the grotesque out of homogeneous and separate montages of fruit-faces or vegetable-faces named according to the seasons of the year?

Of course, the utter impossibility of the Arcimboldo effect in modernist cinema of surrealist descent is the central issue for Godard and Resnais. *Pierrot le fou* is a collage

FIGURE 10.6. *Pierrot le fou* (Godard, 1965). Pathé Contemporary/Photofest. © Pathé Contemporary Films.

film because it meditates on portraiture as the loss of aura, individuality, and unique-ness. Portraiture is so impossible that dynamite is the only solution. In *Hiroshima mon amour*, the mother's face is unavailable to the Japanese architect because he is moth-ering the French woman with his embrace. As an architect, he can only make facades in the newly built city of Hiroshima, while the actress is somewhat faceless because she wears the masks of changing roles: the lover, the nurse, the outcast, the tourist.

Considering that art-making is about objects and filmic projection deals with per-ception, it is not surprising that the face is handled differently by Man Ray, Jean-Luc Godard, and Alain Resnais. In the comparison between surrealist works and French Nouvelle Vague films about the space-time continuum, we find art insisting on the presence of objects, whereas the cinema thrives on the way in which projected shadows set in motion an unpredictable world. The latter's elements—as patterned as they may be through color, line, corporeal volumes, and graphic signs in black and white—absorb and refract our fantasies, thoughts, and feelings in erratic and layered ways. Despite predetermined narrative trajectories and the metaphorical imprisonment of the viewers in cinema's black box, these kinds of emotional and intellectual responses are more free-flowing than the encounter with one surrealist aesthetic object exhibited by the museum, in a relative degree of isolation. As a result, filmic perception does not match the aesthetic responses sought by the controlled environment of the art gallery's white cube. This is why the category of the abstract, as such, means two completely different things in art and in film: For, in the first case, abstraction is primarily about the rejection of figuration, ordinary objects, and recognizable locations; by contrast, on the screen, cinematic projection is already an abstracting force that thrives on natural location, corporeal movement, and the powerful mysteries in daily life.[23]

NOTES

1. On the surrealist object, see Lino Gabellone, *L'Oggetto Surrealista: Il Testo, La Città* (Turin: Einaudi, 1977); on Lee Miller, see Mark Haworth-Booth, *The Art of Lee Miller* (New Haven, Conn.: Yale University Press, 2007); and on Man Ray, see Jean-Michel Bouhour and Patrick de Haas, eds., *Man Ray: Directeur du Mauvais Movies* (Paris: Centre Georges Pompidou, 1997). On Lee Miller, Man Ray, André Breton, and the surrealists in their historical context, see Ruth Brandon, *Surreal Lives* (London: Macmillan, 1999).

2. For surrealist art and critical theory, I have relied on Rosalind E. Krauss, *The Optical Unconscious* (Cambridge, Mass.: MIT Press, 1994).

3. On the French Nouvelle Vague, see Emma Wilson, *French Cinema since 1950* (London: Duckworth, 1999); on the perception of surrealism in the cinema during the period of the Nouvelle Vague, see "Surréalisme et Cinéma," *Études Cinématographiques*, nos. 38–39 (1965), and also "Surréalisme et Cinéma," nos. 40–42 (1965).

4. A statement about the self-sufficient and abstract powers of the individual mind, the Cartesian *cogito* anticipates the French Revolution and the Enlightenment as the Age of Reason, thus paving the way for the triumph of the secular bourgeois nation and the dethroning of the God-like absolute monarch. On Descartes and the

iconophobic tradition in French thought, see Martin Jay, *Downcast Eyes: The Denigration of Vision in Twentieth-Century French Thought* (Berkeley: University of California Press, 1993), 211–262.

5. On the imaginary in film, see Christian Metz, "The Imaginary Signifier," trans. Ben Brewster, *Screen* 16 (Summer 1975): 14–74. Indispensable books on surrealism and film include Linda Williams, *Figures of Desire: A Theory and Analysis of Surrealist Film* (Berkeley: University of California Press, 1981); Ado Kyrou, *Le Surréalisme au Cinéma* (Paris: Éditions Arcanes, 1953); J. H. Mathews, *Surrealism and Film* (Ann Arbor: University of Michigan Press, 1971); Michael Gould, *Surrealism and the Cinema* (New York: Barnes, 1976); and Willard Bohm, *Surrealist Responses to Film, Art, Poetry and Architecture* (Lewisburg, Penn.: Bucknell University Press, 2005). On *trompe l'oeil*, see Martin Battersby, *Trompe L'Oeil: The Eye Deceived* (New York: Routledge, 1996).

6. Haim Finkelstein, *The Screen in Surrealist Art and Thought* (Aldershot, Hampshire, U.K.: Ashgate, 2007); *Surréalisme et Philosophie* (Paris: Centre Georges Pompidou, 1992).

7. On Salvador Dalí and Jacques Lacan, see Haim Finkelstein, *Salvador Dalí's Art and Writing 1927–1942: The Metamorphoses of Narcissus* (Cambridge: Cambridge University Press, 1996), 5–6. Also on Jean-Paul Sartre and Lacan, see Kaja Silverman, *Thresholds of the Visible World* (New York: Routledge, 1996), 163–167.

8. On collage, see Stephen Bann, "The Poetics of Discontinuity," *Word and Image* 4, no. 1 (1988): 353–363; and Marjorie Perloff, "The Invention of Collage," *New York Literary Forum* 10–11 (1983): 5–47. On photomontage, see Dawn Adams, *Photomontage* (London: Thames and Hudson, 1986).

9. Jacques B. Brunius, *En Marge du Cinéma Français. Couverture de Marcel Duchamp* (Paris: Éditions Arcanes, 1954), and *Idolatry and Confusion* (London: London Gallery Editions, 1944).

10. Elza Adamowicz, *Surrealist Collage in Text and Image: Dissecting the Exquisite Corpse* (Cambridge: Cambridge University Press, 1998), 107.

11. On Raoul Ubac, see Robert Guiette, *Ombres Vives. Couverture de Raoul Ubac* (Bruxelles: De Rache, 1969); Jean-Claude Schneider, *À Travers la Durée: Gravures de Raoul Ubac* (Montpellier: Fata Morgana, 1975); Christian Bouqueret, *Raoul Ubac: Photographie* (Paris: Scheer, 2000). On Raoul Ubac and Hiroshima, see Sarah Wilson, "In Search of the Absolute," in *Paris Post-War: Art and Existentialism 1945–55*, ed. Frances Morris (London: Tate Gallery, 1992), 25–52. For a general and concise introduction to surrealist photography, see Christian Bouqueret, *Surrealist Photography* (London: Thames and Hudson, 2008).

12. Erwin Panofsky, "Style and Medium in the Motion Pictures," in *The Visual Turn: Classical Film Theory and Art History*, ed. Angela Dalle Vacche (New Brunswick, N.J.: Rutgers University Press, 2006), 69–84.

13. For this argument in relation to *Pierrot le fou*, see Angela Dalle Vacche, *Cinema and Painting: How Art Is Used in Film* (Austin: University of Texas Press, 1996), 107–134.

14. Élie Faure, *The Art of Cineplastics* [1922], trans. Walter Pach (Boston: Four Seas Company, 1923).

15. Dudley Andrew, "*L'Age d'or* and the Auto-Eroticism of the Spirit," in *Masterpieces of Modernist Cinema*, ed. Ted Perry (Bloomington: Indiana University Press, 2006), 111–137.

16. For a brief yet antithetical reading of *Hiroshima mon amour*, see also Giuliana Bruno, *Atlas of Emotion: Journeys in Art, Architecture and Film* (New York: Verso, 2002), 39–40.

17. Jay, *Downcast Eyes*, 1–82.

18. André Breton and Philippe Soupault, *Les Champs Magnétiques, Dessins de Francis Picabia* (Paris: Gallimard, 1967).

19. Isidore Lucien Ducasse, *Les Chants de Maldoror, par le Comte de Lautréamont* (Paris: n.p., 1874).

20. On Miles Davis in Paris and his involvement with Juliette Gréco and the existentialist scene, see Miles Davis with Quincy Troupe, *Miles: The Autobiography* (New York: Simon and Schuster, 1989), 218.

21. Alan Williams, *Republic of Images: A History of French Film-Making* (Cambridge, Mass.: Harvard University, 1992), 245–326.

22. On Arcimboldo's *trompe l'oeil*, see Michael O'Pray, "Surrealism, Fantasy, and the Grotesque: The Cinema of Jan Svankmajer," in *Fantasy and the Cinema*, ed. James Donald (London: BFI, 1989), 253–267.

23. André Bazin, in "The Ontology of the Photographic Image," *What Is Cinema?* vol. 1, trans. Hugh Grey (Berkeley: California University Press, 1969), writes: "Hence photography ranks high in the order of surrealist creativity because it produces an image that is a reality of nature, namely, an hallucination that is also a fact" (16).

III

ART CINEMA HISTORIES

11

THE VOLCANO AND THE BARREN HILL: GABRIEL FIGUEROA AND THE SPACE OF ART CINEMA

Patrick Keating

In 1946, the Cannes Film Festival celebrated the end of the war years by awarding its top prize to several films, from a variety of countries all over the world. Among the eleven films receiving this honor was Emilio Fernández's 1944 film *María Candelaria*. The film's cinematographer, Gabriel Figueroa, won the Best Cinematography prize for his carefully composed images of heroic peasants standing against dynamic skies. Over the next few years, Fernández and Figueroa enjoyed continued success on the European festival circuit, winning awards at venues like Venice, Locarno, Brussels, Madrid, and Karlovy Vary.[1] French film publications like *La Revue du cinéma* began to run articles analyzing their work. For the emerging institutions of art cinema, Mexican film was nearly synonymous with the phrase "Fernández-Figueroa." Fernández's international success was not to last, as his festival appearances declined during the 1950s. Meanwhile, the Spanish-born Luis Buñuel, now a Mexican citizen, won several prizes while sending seven films to Cannes in the period from 1951 to 1962. *Cahiers du cinéma* produced several articles on Buñuel, with barely a mention of Fernández. Put simply, Buñuel had replaced Fernández as Mexico's leading practitioner of art cinema.

At first glance, the shift from Fernández to Buñuel seems like a 180-degree switch, from utopian nationalism to pessimistic surrealism. Making the shift even more striking is the fact that Buñuel used Fernández's own cinematographer. Forsaking his gift for heroic imagery, Figueroa supplied Buñuel with shocking pictures of wretched squalor. Many critics summarize this switch by referring to an amusing (and probably apocryphal) story. Carlos Fuentes tells the story this way:

> While *Nazarín* was being filmed on location near Cuautla—or so the story
> goes—Gabriel Figueroa prepared an outdoor scene for the director, Luis Buñuel.

Figueroa set up the camera with the snow-capped volcano Popocatépetl in the background, a cactus at the right angle of the composition, a circle of clouds crowning its peak and the open furrows of the valley in the foreground. Looking at the composition, Buñuel said: "Fine, now let's turn the camera so that we can get those four goats and two crags on that barren hill."[2]

Though it is most likely fictional, this little narrative makes a powerful point about the changing style of the Mexican cinema. In his work for Fernández, Figueroa had constructed a new national identity by associating the Mexican people with the grandeur of the Mexican landscape. Buñuel's perverse way of using Figueroa's talents was the ultimate rejection of the classical Mexican style.

While it is useful to think of Fernández and Buñuel in oppositional terms, in this essay I hope to add nuance to this account by looking for continuities in Figueroa's work for the two directors, while finding contrasts at new, unexpected levels. The culture of the international art cinema had developed its own norms of interpretation, and both Fernández and Buñuel took advantage of Figueroa's compositional skills to appeal to those emerging norms. In making this argument, my goal is not simply to add a footnote to the existing literature on Figueroa. Rather, I will argue that a close analysis of Figueroa's style can teach us a great deal about the space of the global art cinema.

Here, I am using the word "space" in three different ways. First, we can think of the space of art cinema in stylistic terms. Figueroa organized space in a meaningful way, using carefully composed foregrounds and precisely chosen backgrounds to enrich the films' themes. This made Figueroa an ideal cinematographer for postwar art cinema—a style of cinema that solicits the interpretation of visual style in spatial terms. For all their differences, both Fernández and Buñuel had an eye on the international art cinema market, and both filmmakers appealed to that market with the help of the Figueroa style.

The second sense of space is more abstract, referring to the principles of inclusion and exclusion that a festival or journal might use in constructing the category of art cinema. The institutions of art cinema, typically based in Europe, worked to construct a global cinematic culture by selecting films from all over the world. However, that global reach had its limits. In the case of Mexico, the institutions of art cinema seemed to make room for one major director at a time, showing a temporary interest in Fernández before settling on Buñuel as the premier representative of Mexican cinema.[3] By comparing and contrasting the films of Fernández and Buñuel, we can better understand the principles of inclusion and exclusion that defined the apparently global space of art cinema.

The third sense of space can help us connect the first two. On one side, we have a set of films that are designed to be interpreted in spatial terms. On the other side, we have a set of institutions (such as film journals and festivals) dedicated to the practice of identifying a set of films that can be interpreted in a rewarding fashion. This would seem to be a perfect match, but a film can never fully determine the interpretations that an institution will produce. The relationship between the films and the institutions interpreting them is mediated by a set of historically specific interpretive frameworks—frameworks that are themselves shaped by spatial concepts.

On this point, my argument is influenced by Benjamin Harshav's concept of the "frame of reference." Harshav is a scholar of literature and art who bases his theory on a variety of models, including German phenomenology and Czech Structuralism. For Harshav, the process of interpreting a text involves the integration of meaningful elements through the construction of various frames of reference. (To take a simple example, a sentence about a door and a sentence about a window can be integrated by supposing that they both refer to the same frame of reference: a house.) On the textual side, we can analyze the ways that texts are designed to encourage the construction of certain frames. On the reception side, we can study how institutions limit the range of interpretations by encouraging readers to employ a particular set of accepted frames.[4] Although Harshav's theory is designed to account for literature, his concept of the "frame of reference" theorizes the process of interpretation in remarkably spatial terms, with the reader constructing the "world" of the story by finding connections between various frames of reference. For this reason, I have always believed that Harshav's theory could be applied productively to the cinema.[5] Here, I want to draw on his ideas to demonstrate the ways that the Figueroa style appealed to a certain frame of reference—namely, a historically specific construction of the Mexican nation. Meanwhile, the institutions of art cinema encouraged European critics to use somewhat different frames to interpret the films of Fernández and Buñuel. Those interpretive frames were often structured by spatial concepts, which shaped the ways that they interpreted the stylistic spaces of the films. As we will see, those spatial concepts included aesthetic ideals like unity and fragmentation, geographical notions like center and periphery, and political discourses like nationalism and universalism. By examining these interpretive spaces, we can better understand why the institutions of art cinema made the interpretations they did—interpretations that would play a decisive role in situating the Mexican cinema within the larger field of the international art cinema.

Broadly speaking, the Mexican film industry did not conceive of the art film and the popular film as mutually exclusive categories. Significantly, Figueroa won his first Best Cinematography award at Venice in 1938, for his work on *Allá en el Rancho Grande/ Out on the Big Ranch* (Fernando del Fuentes, 1936). Far from being a rarefied art film, *Rancho* was one of Mexico's greatest financial successes—the film that popularized the *ranchera* genre. Most Mexican festival films had a similar obligation to appeal to popular audiences. In the postwar period, those popular audiences could be found in several different markets. The first audience was in Mexico itself. Here, as in most countries, local filmmakers had to compete with successful Hollywood imports for screen time. The second audience was in the United States, where Mexican films found enthusiastic support in Spanish-speaking communities.[6] Third, the Mexican industry imported popular films to other Latin American countries, such as Cuba and Venezuela. Here again, the industry faced tough competition from Hollywood, along with milder competition from other Latin American industries, such as the industry of Argentina. Spain was a fourth possible market. To reach these first four markets, the Mexican cinema adopted all the conventions of a popular cinema, putting attractive stars in emotionally engaging genres, while working with the techniques of continuity filmmaking. Festival films might feature other qualities, like eye-catching pictorial beauty, but they usually had to meet these popular requirements first. The somber *María Candelaria* may be the most famous Fernández film, but *Enamorada* (1946) is just as typical: an exciting and funny romantic melodrama, with the internationally recognized Mexican star María Félix.

Because these films were usually successful at home, the primary purpose of sending Mexican films to international film festivals was not financial, though a festival victory would occasionally improve a film's chances with local audiences (as happened with *María Candelaria*). Instead, the government-sponsored Mexican film industry saw festivals as a way of improving the entire country's international reputation. Sending films to Europe was a way to advertise the government's achievements. As stated in an editorial in *Cinevoz*, the industry's trade magazine, "María Félix has produced more thinking and talking about Mexico than all of its best export products or its most famous intellectuals."[7] To keep track of all that thinking and talking, *Cinevoz* would routinely reprint articles from foreign publications that commented on Mexican films.[8] In short, the Mexican film industry (and the government that supported it) cared deeply about international opinion. Sending a quality film to a European festival was one way of shaping that opinion.

Much of the best work in Mexican cinema studies analyzes the complex interaction between the national and the transnational that defined the industry and its films. For instance, Ana M. López has considered the implications of Mexico's success in the Latin American market. On the one hand, Mexico's dominance of those markets was simply duplicating Hollywood's control over Mexico's own market. On the other hand, the Mexican cinema was widely admired for offering a cultural alternative to Hollywood hegemony.[9] Seth Fein has approached the relationship between the United States and Mexico from a different perspective, studying the ways that the U.S. government worked with Hollywood to promote the Mexican industry during World War II, only to adopt a more aggressive stance in the postwar years. Both of these examples are industry-oriented studies, but stylistic studies have also emphasized the interaction between the national and transnational.[10] A case in point is Charles Ramirez-Berg's analysis of the Fernández-Figueroa style. That style may have been an expression of Mexican nationalism, but it was also a synthesis of many different influences, including the Mexican muralists, the Soviet director Sergei Eisenstein, and Hollywood's master of deep-focus cinematography, Gregg Toland.[11] By drawing on this rich tradition of scholarship, I hope to extend Ramirez-Berg's stylistic analysis to consider how Figueroa's seemingly nationalistic style was shaped by international institutional contexts—in this case, the institutional context of postwar art cinema.

The culture of art cinema was partly a culture of interpretation, finding significance in the new visual styles being developed by filmmakers around the world. Figueroa quickly became a recognizable brand name on the art cinema circuit because he had developed a set of strategies that lent themselves to this culture of interpretation. I will consider three of those strategies here: the visual analogy, the composition-in-depth, and the dynamic motif. Understanding the spatial organization of Figueroa's images will prepare us to see how those spaces were interpreted, in different ways, by the institutions of European art cinema.

As an example of the visual analogy, consider figure 11.1, from Fernández's film *La Perla/The Pearl* (1947). The film was produced by RKO, as part of its failed effort to dominate the Mexican market. This thoroughly transnational film still managed to articulate some nationally specific themes. Fernández, nicknamed "El Indio," made films that examined the Indian basis of Mexican identity. According to Julia Tuñón:

> For Emilio Fernández, the indigenous man, in spite of his marginalization, is the essential subject of this confounding country, that which best represents it. [. . .] Although it may seem contradictory that a group of society's marginalized represents the nation in its totality, in Emilio Fernández's mythology it is precisely this marginalization which grants them a privileged place, one which history did not give them.[12]

Fernández suggests that the Indian is the true representative of Mexican identity by associating the Indian with the distinctive features of the Mexican landscape. In figure 11.1, Pedro Armendáriz, as the poor fisherman Quino, momentarily bends his body to mimic the shape of the tree. This visual analogy suggests a spiritual analogy: Both Quino and the tree have emerged, in an autochthonous way, from the harsh yet beautiful soil.

Many critics, including Tuñón, are skeptical of the political purposes guiding Fernández's project. The spiritual analogy between the Indian and the soil constructs a strongly racialized definition of national identity as a natural essence emerging from the land itself—a definition that would be questionable in any context, let alone the context of Mexico, with its complex history of intercultural conflict and convergence.

FIGURE 11.1. Body and landscape in *The Pearl* (Fernández, 1947).

Even worse, this celebration of the Indian essence was being produced by the state-sponsored industry at a time when the Mexican state was distancing itself from the pro-Indian rhetoric of the Revolution, and turning its attention to the needs of big businesses, both Mexican and North American.

The relationship between the rural Indian and the state becomes an explicit theme in another Fernández-Figueroa collaboration, *Río Escondido / Hidden River* (1948). In this film, María Félix plays Rosaura, an idealistic woman from Mexico City who becomes a schoolteacher in a poor rural village. Rosaura acts as a representative of the state—she even receives her job directly from President Miguel Alemán, who plays a cameo at the beginning of the film. In figure 11.2, Fernández and Figueroa use the technique of the visual analogy to reinforce the thematic link between the state and the people. The image shows Rosaura, at the top, looking identical to the other women in the village. The visual affinities suggest that the characters' identities have begun to merge, and not in the direction one might expect. Rosaura came to this peripheral village to change the Indians' sense of identity, encouraging them to think of themselves as Mexicans—that is, as citizens of the state. Instead, this image suggests that Rosaura's sense of identity is the one that has changed, as the film represents her with gendered and racialized iconography. Fulfilling her duty to the government has brought out the Indian aspects of her Mexican identity. It should be noted that this visual attempt to erase the boundary between the state and the Indian population is not entirely successful. The placement of Félix at the top of the frame hints at a hierarchy that continues to divide the city woman from the rural Indians she has come to serve—a hierarchy that the visual analogy has attempted to erase.[13]

Although representing a confined space, Fernández and Figueroa compose the image in depth, with the two women in the foreground, and Félix in the background. Figueroa was a master of this technique, the composition-in-depth.[14] Composition-in-depth is not the same thing as deep-focus, though they are often combined. Like two of

FIGURE 11.2. Visual analogies reinforce the link between the state and the people in *Río Escondido* (Fernández, 1948).

his major influences, Toland and Eduard Tissé, Figueroa usually keeps multiple planes in focus. Toland argued (perhaps implausibly) that deep-focus cinematography approximates human perception more closely. That does not appear to be the primary goal for Figueroa. Instead, Figueroa uses the deep-focus, deep-space composition to encourage the spectator to look for contrasts and analogies between the foreground and background areas of his shots. This strategy draws on the "mise-en-shot" principles that Eisenstein and Tissé had employed in *Que Viva Mexico!* (1932, unfinished). According to Eisenstein's theory, the collisions that would normally be produced by montage could be produced within the context of a single shot.[15] Eisenstein and Tissé usually produced images with strong oppositions between foreground and background, producing a dialectic within the shot. Figueroa would sometimes follow this example, but here the composition-in-depth strategy works hand-in-hand with the visual analogy strategy. There are certainly a number of contrasts between foreground and background—low versus high, two versus one, rural Indian versus city woman, extra versus star—but the visual affinities between foreground and background encourage the spectator to find a higher frame of reference that unifies the image. That frame of reference is Mexican identity—or, at least, Mexican identity in the carefully limited, racially specific way that Fernández conceives it.

Harshav would call this interpretive process "integration." The film solicits an act of interpretation that situates disparate elements within a frame of reference. Another example of this process can be found at the end of *Enamorada*, Fernández's romantic drama set in the Mexican Revolution. According to the political rhetoric of the Revolution, the Revolution was both a racial struggle and a class struggle, with poor Indians and mestizos taking power away from wealthier mestizos and people of Spanish descent. Of course, the reality of the Revolution was much more complicated than this rhetoric can suggest, but the rhetoric served as a frame of reference for many films. In *Enamorada*, María Félix plays a privileged woman (Beatriz) who falls in love with a revolutionary general, played by Pedro Armendáriz. The political meaning is clear: Beatrice rejects her upper-class identity—an identity linked to the Spanish past—and embraces a new, Mexican identity. For most of the film, the dominant visual motif is the church of Cholula, a beautiful example of Spanish colonial architecture. At the end of the film, we see Beatrice walking alongside the general, whose dominance is suggested by the fact that he is riding on horseback. This is the ultimate Mexican couple, and Figueroa frames them against the background of the ultimate symbol of the Mexican landscape: Popocatépetl. By framing the couple against the famous volcano (named after a mythological warrior), Fernández and Figueroa create several oppositions—moving versus static, human versus natural—but the image encourages spectators to integrate these elements within a unified frame of reference: a naturalized, pre-Spanish conception of Mexicanness. Mexican identity emerges from the landscape of the Mexican nation—a landscape charged with connotations of masculine power. Here, the film's attempt to alter a racial imbalance involves the reassertion of a gendered hierarchy, with Beatriz, walking, accompanying the general on horseback.

Following Eisenstein, Fernández and Figueroa also develop meaningful relationships between shots. In figure 11.3, from *María Candelaria*, the filmmakers create an analogy

FIGURE 11.3. The motif of verticality in *María Candelaria* (Fernández, 1944).

between the vertical lines of the trees and the vertical posture of the protagonists. The effect is similar to that of figure 11.1, though here the verticality places the emphasis on heroic grandeur, rather than epic suffering. This vertical motif appears in several other images from the film, but the meaning is constantly shifting. In some shots, the vertical motif is associated with the oars of the Indians who are attempting to deny María the right to enter the community. At the end of the film, the connotations become even more threatening, as the Indians use vertical torches to hunt for María, the innocent victim. These images demonstrate the development of a dynamic motif. The film offers a multilayered exploration of Indian identity, exploring both positive and negative aspects. Similarly, the vertical line motif goes through various transformations, from oars to trees to torches. This dynamic motif is more complicated than the visual analogy, but the goal is similar, encouraging spectators to unify apparently dissimilar elements within a specific frame of reference. It is not simply that we are supposed to notice similarities between various vertical images. It is that we are supposed to see those similarities as meaningful. As in the previous examples, the frame of reference is Fernández's historically specific construction of Mexican identity.

We have already seen that many critics are skeptical of Fernández's nationalistic themes—with good reason. Not only does Fernández use a racial category to homogenize the complexities of Mexican identity; his pro-Indian themes may have inadvertently provided some political cover for a government that was turning away from its previous association with pro-Indian policies. The story of the volcano and the barren hill suggests that we can add Luis Buñuel to Fernández's list of critics. Buñuel refused to create a heroic image of Mexico. Instead, he used his Mexican films to explore his long-standing interest in the themes of violence and desire. This is why the volcano story is so memorable: It captures a very real contrast between two different styles of filmmaking.

However, it is too easy to say that the contrast was absolute. On the most basic level, we can note that Buñuel uses some of the same visual strategies as Fernández.

FIGURE 11.4. In *Los Olvidados* (1950), Buñuel rejects Fernández's idealized analogies.

Figure 11.4, from *Los Olvidados* (1950), is so similar to figure 11.3 that it seems like a conscious (and ironic) citation. In both images, the vertical objects in the composition echo the vertical human figures. In *María Candelaria*, the visual analogy lends grandeur to the characters, naturalizing their identities by associating them with the graceful trees. In *Los Olvidados*, the tree analogy has been replaced by a new analogy, as the bent posture of Jaibo echoes the bent metal forms in the background and right foreground. Far from idealizing the characters, this new visual analogy encourages us to view them as warped and incomplete. The themes may have changed, but the strategy of using the composition-in-depth to produce a visual analogy has remained the same. Similarly, in *Nazarín* (1959), Buñuel stages his scenes of everyday cruelty against dull backgrounds of stone, dirt, and cloudless sky. Wretched imagery expresses wretched themes.

Buñuel and Fernández also share the strategy of the dynamic motif. *Los Olvidados* provides a famous example: the bird motif. This motif changes over the course of the film, sometimes carrying sexual connotations (as when a dove is rubbed over a woman's back), sometimes carrying connotations of love (as when the protagonist cares for his chickens), sometimes carrying connotations of uncontrollable violence (as when eggs are thrown at the camera). For both directors, one of Figueroa's primary tasks was the orchestration of visual motifs.

This does not mean that Buñuel simply continued the classical tradition of the Fernández-Figueroa style. Rather, it suggests that we can look for differences at a different level. Consider their use of the dynamic motif. On the one hand, the strategies are similar: They both require the spectator to track the transformations of a motif over the course of a film. On the other hand, the strategies are different. We might describe this difference by saying that Fernández's motifs are closed, while Buñuel's motifs are open. To borrow the language of Harshav, we can say that there is a relatively coherent frame of reference that integrates the motifs of Fernández. That frame of reference is his recurring theme of a unified Mexican/Indian identity. By contrast, Buñuel's motifs create a network of associations across his films, but their ultimate meaning is never settled. There is no single frame of reference that can integrate all of the appearances of the motif. Indeed, the bird motif carries connotations of incomprehensibility from the very beginning: It first appears when we see a blind man staring into the face of a chicken.

Here, we must take different reading strategies into account. It is not the case that Buñuel's films require interpretation, while Fernández's films do not. Both films require interpretation, since both films require spectators to construct frames of reference to make sense of their imagery. (Indeed, it could be argued that all films require some such interpretive activity, since all films contain gaps and indeterminacies.) Instead, we might describe the difference in the following way. For Mexican spectators familiar with *indigenismo*, a widespread cultural discussion concerning the authenticity and political significance of Mexican/Indian identity, the films of Fernández appealed to a widely available frame of reference. European art cinema spectators could appeal to a similar frame of reference, either by drawing on their knowledge of "El Indio" Fernández's auteur persona, or by relying on their understanding of the films as an expression of Mexican nationalism. By contrast, Buñuel's films were designed to frustrate the attempt to interpret certain images according to a readily available frame of reference. His reputation as a surrealist encouraged a particular viewing strategy, looking for dream-like motifs that would transform over the course of the film in unexpected ways. This quality of open-endedness made the films more suitable for the culture of art cinema, a culture that places a high level of value on creative, elaborate acts of interpretation. Buñuel's films solicited extended—perhaps endless—acts of interpretation precisely because they were difficult to read.

To put this in spatial terms, Fernández and Buñuel had created two different kinds of space. To be more accurate, we could say that their films encouraged spectators to construct different kinds of interpretive space. The space of Fernández was an integrated space, organizing seemingly disparate visual elements around the unifying theme of Mexican identity. The space of Buñuel was an incoherent space, a space that could not be unified. We can see this process at work even in individual shots that rely on Figueroa's most characteristic compositional strategy: the composition-in-depth. In figure 11.5, from *Los Olvidados*, Figueroa composed a shot with three layers of depth, all in sharp focus: a cactus in the foreground, the brutal Jaibo in the middle ground, and a train in the background. In a Fernández film, the cactus would be an unambiguous symbol of Mexican identity, an identity forged by the land itself. We could find an analogy between the cactus and the human figure. In Buñuel's film, Mexican identity is founded on a contradiction between the land and modernity, as symbolized by the irreconcilable images of the cactus and the train.

Perhaps this interpretation seems rather neat, proposing "contradiction" as the frame of reference that integrates the image. However, this interpretive move does not mean that the significance of the image is closed, for the cause of Jaibo's brutality is left open. Should we interpret Jaibo's capacity for violence as something natural, like the thorns of the cactus? Or should we interpret Jaibo as a character shaped by the destructive forces of modernity? The film leaves us searching for a frame of reference that will explain Jaibo's incomprehensible brutality.

FIGURE 11.5. An incongruous image of nature and modernity in *Los Olvidados*.

We can find the same tension in the murder scene from *Los Olvidados*. In the foreground, Jaibo commits a pointless murder. In the background, we see the grid-like structure of an incomplete building. It is possible to interpret this image as an ironic contrast, dryly noting the continued presence of violence within the context of the forward-looking city. It is equally plausible to say that the image proposes a causal connection: Perhaps the grid-like rationality of the modern world increases the likelihood of violent ruptures. If Buñuel himself is to be believed, this scene was supposed to look even more incoherent than it already does. In an interview, Buñuel once claimed:

I wanted to introduce crazy, completely mad elements into the most realistic scenes; for instance, when Jaibo goes to beat up and kill the other boy, the camera pans across a huge eleven-story building in [the] process of construction in the background; and I would have liked to put a hundred-piece orchestra in it. It would have only been glimpsed, vaguely and fleetingly.[16]

This would have made the image almost impossible to integrate into a coherent frame of reference. Even without the orchestra, the image works to encourage an extended act of interpretation, precisely by making interpretation difficult. Like Fernández, Buñuel relies on composition-in-depth to spread layers of meaning across cinematic space. While Fernández uses those layers to reinforce each other, Buñuel's layers of space are often in conflict.

It is significant that Buñuel mentions the orchestra example in an interview with *Cahiers du cinéma*. This journal was one of the major institutions of the European art cinema, and it had helped Buñuel find a place within that institutional field. In this passage, Buñuel attempts to secure his position by telling an anecdote about his stylistic use of space. In other words, this interview highlights the link between two different senses of space: the stylistic space of Buñuel's films, and the institutional space of the European art cinema, a space defined by its boundaries of inclusion and exclusion. Helping to connect these spaces are the "interpretive spaces" produced by spectators and critics attempting to make sense of the films. As we have seen, a film can be designed in such a way that it will encourage the construction of certain frames. However, this process is never final. On the reception side, an institution can encourage the spectator to construct those frames in a particular way, according to culturally determined geographies and hierarchies.

Because those interpretive spaces play such an important role, I would like to conclude this analysis by looking outside the film-texts, considering the ways that European critics responded to the films of Fernández and Buñuel. By examining the frames of reference that they used to make sense of the films, we can gain a better understanding of the principles that defined the boundaries of art cinema's apparently inclusive space.

In the late 1940s, *La Revue du cinéma* ran reviews of several Fernández films: *María Candelaria*, *Enamorada*, and the Ford-Fernández-Figueroa collaboration *The Fugitive* (1947). In his review of *María Candelaria*, Éduoard Klein opens his review in an unusual way—by asking how he should talk about a film that is so different from everything he is used to seeing. We might say that he is searching for a frame of reference. Drawing on some obvious stereotypes, he goes on to suggest that the slowness and simplicity of the film are expressions of the film's Indian-centered themes, explicitly contrasting the "slowness" of Indian life with the speed of the Western world. Significantly, Klein supports his analysis by emphasizing the coherence of the visual design. He writes, "This vegetation is like an extension, or better, an exteriorization of the dramatic action in perfect concordance with the highly particular characters of these Indians."[17] On the one hand, we might say that Klein is simply doing what the film itself seems to mandate; he is interpreting the stylistic space by using Indian identity as the frame of reference. However, Klein's frame of reference has a particular geography, with race and culture marking the boundaries: Indian identity is located outside of Western culture, in another space (and time) entirely. Given the transnational basis of the Mexican cinema, we should remember that Klein could just as easily have appealed to many other frames of reference. For instance, he might have noted that the film's technical polish served to level a hierarchy in which Hollywood had previously assumed a dominant position. Instead, Klein approaches the film by situating it within a category of racial and cultural difference.

Some of the other reviews are more sensitive to the transnational origins of Mexican cinema, noting the influences of Eisenstein, or the investments of RKO. However, the dominant trends remain the same. The July 1948 issue of *La Revue du cinéma* features a lengthy article by André Camp, "Aperçus sur le cinéma mexicain." Camp argues that the Mexican cinema has recently become national—specifically, Indian. He notes the simplicity and slowness of the films, and suggests that Fernández may be using these strategies to reach a Mexican audience, rather than an international one. Camp closes his article with the thought that Mexican cinema has everything to gain from increased international exchange, because internationalization will allow the Mexican cinema to escape its sterile particularism.[18] In other words, Camp employs a frame of reference with a particular geography—a geography of the national and the universal. He recognizes that Fernández is attempting to articulate a culturally and racially specific national identity, but he suggests that this trait, while fascinating at first glance, is ultimately a weakness in the films. If Fernández's films are to have continued success on the international market, he will need to explore more universal themes.

We can contrast this response with the response given to Buñuel's films, starting with *Los Olvidados*. In his book *Buñuel and Mexico*, Ernesto R. Acevedo-Muñoz argues that critics have consistently de-emphasized the Mexican aspects of Buñuel's Mexican films.[19] André Bazin is a case in point. Bazin situates Buñuel within the context of surrealism, drawing direct links between *Los Olvidados* and surrealist classics like *L'Age d'or* (1930).[20] Many of the critics at *Cahiers du cinéma* and *Positif* did the same.[21] Meanwhile, *Cahiers* ignores the recent works of Fernández. In one essay, Bazin states explicitly that Buñuel has replaced Fernández as the most interesting filmmaker in Mexico.[22]

The reference to surrealism is significant, for two reasons. First, it helps us understand how the institutions of art cinema used an interpretive frame of reference as a principle of inclusion. The culture of art cinema had become a culture of interpretation.[23] Within that culture, the apparent "simplicity" of Fernández's films was a disadvantage, because they seemed to lack the uncertainty that encourages extensive interpretation. Figueroa's visual analogies did require a certain level of interpretation, but Fernández's auteur persona encouraged critics to appeal to the same frame of reference over and over again. On one level, Buñuel's auteur persona was similarly constricting: Surrealism was always readily available as the default frame of reference. However, that frame of reference functioned in a particular way, encouraging critics to look for contradiction, rather than integration.[24] The result was a series of articles debating the meaning of Buñuel's difficult works.

Second, by classifying Buñuel as a surrealist, critics were, to some extent, removing him from the Mexican context.[25] This is important, because, as we have seen, Fernández was criticized for being too particular. Here, we should recall that the rhetoric of liberal humanism was an important part of international art cinema during the late 1940s and early 1950s. The institutions of art cinema made an effort to include films from all over the world, as a way of demonstrating that the cinema is a part of an internationally shared human culture. However, that discourse of inclusion had its limits. One way of understanding the success and eventual failure of Fernández's films is by noticing that they had a problematic relationship with the ideals of liberal humanism. On the one hand, they appealed to liberal humanism's desire to include the previously excluded. On the other hand, their insistence on racial and cultural specificity seemed to deny the principle of universal human nature that was motivating the principle of inclusion in the first place. Meanwhile, European critics were only too willing to classify the films as simple expressions of nationalist sentiment, rather than the complex products of a transnational industry that they really were. It may seem odd to suggest that Buñuel's radical surrealism was in any way compatible with the comfortable platitudes of liberal humanism, but the idea that Buñuel was unlocking the shared secrets of the unconscious mind may have given his films a seemingly "universal" appeal that was lacking in the self-consciously Mexican films of "El Indio" Fernández.

Even critics who de-emphasized the surrealist connection located Buñuel within a universal frame of reference. For instance, *Positif*'s Bernard Chardère interprets Buñuel as an unflinching realist. He writes:

> Buñuel is a humanist, in the truest sense of the term. [He is] always avoiding a ridiculous optimism regarding the immediate practical possibilities. (Because he is realist and observational. What can we actually do in our society to stamp out these conditions? Very little. He notes the failure of the houses of re-education and marks his confidence in the "forces of progress"). He has understood and affirmed that there is no Destiny, but a human condition.[26]

At first glance, this approach seems to defy the norm of interpreting Buñuel through the frame of reference of surrealism. However, both frames of reference—the surrealist and the realist—employ a similar geography, removing Buñuel from the Mexican context and placing him in the context of a (supposedly) more universal tradition.

Liberal humanism is often criticized for failing to acknowledge that its ostensibly universal outlook masks a tendency to privilege European ideals. It promised to include the margins, but the center was still located in Europe. We can see this process at work here. Just as the surrealist interpretation of Buñuel emphasized the precedent of *Un Chien andalou*, the realist interpretation of Buñuel emphasized the precedent of *Las Hurdes*. Either way, critics were finding European models for Buñuel's Mexican work. It seems plausible to suppose that this helped ensure his inclusion in the apparently universal but ultimately Eurocentric institutional space of postwar art cinema. While European critics interpreted the work of Fernández with racially specific and often racist frames of reference that categorized his work as primitive and strange, they typically interpreted the work of Buñuel with frames of reference that categorized his work as part of a difficult but familiar European tradition. Buñuel was brought closer to the center, while Fernández was pushed to the periphery.

This brings us to an intriguing paradox. On the one hand, the institutions of art cinema had declared that Fernández was too simple, while the surrealist Buñuel offered more of a challenge. This was a plausible reading, given Fernández's taste for integrated imagery, and Buñuel's taste for contradiction. However, in the spirit of dialectical inquiry, it is possible to turn this contrast on its head. Buñuel's contradictions were, in a sense, easy to read, because critics could appeal to European models (like "surrealism") to supply the appropriate frames of reference. By contrast, Fernández forced critics to employ very different frames of reference, explaining the beauty and slowness of the films by invoking the frames of cultural and racial difference. These themes did not fit within the art cinema's preferred discourse of liberal humanism, which ultimately left Fernández excluded from the art cinema's purportedly inclusive space.

In conclusion, I have tried to use the example of Gabriel Figueroa to show that the different spaces of the art cinema are connected. On one side, we have the stylistic space of the films. Whether he was working for Fernández or Buñuel, Figueroa used a variety of techniques to create images that were dense with meaning—techniques such as the visual analogy, the composition-in-depth, and the dynamic motif. On the other side, we have the institutional space of art cinema, with its own principles of inclusion and exclusion. To connect these two spaces, we must consider a third space, examining how the culture of art cinema would use specific spatial concepts to make sense of a film. This is where Harshav's notion of the "frame of reference" becomes so useful, encouraging us to examine the different spatial concepts that a critical culture might use when interpreting a film. Figueroa's densely layered images were designed to be interpreted, but European critics interpreted the films of Fernández and Buñuel in different ways, in part because they were employing such different frames of reference. These frames of reference had their own spatial structures, shaped by concepts like the unified and the fragmentary, the foreign and the familiar, and the national and the universal. Art cinema critics used these frames to make sense of Figueroa's stylistic space, thereby justifying their decisions about the acceptable boundaries of the international art cinema. In the 1940s, Fernández enjoyed remarkable success, but it was not to last. By the 1950s, the critics' historically specific frames of reference had worked to put the nationalistic Fernández at the margins of the art cinema, while the disturbing but oddly familiar Buñuel soon found himself working at the center.

NOTES

The author would like to thank Lisa Jasinski, Karl Schoonover, and Rosalind Galt for their help with this essay.

1. The list includes awards for *María Candelaria* (Locarno, 1947), *La Perla / The Pearl* (Venice, 1947, and Madrid, 1949), *Enamorada* (Brussels, 1947), *Salón México* (Brussels, 1948), *Río Escondido / Hidden River* (Karlovy-Vary, 1948), *La Malquerida* (Venice, 1949), *Maclovia* (Karlovy-Vary, 1949), and *Pueblerina* (Madrid, 1950). For a detailed list, see Ernesto Román and MariCarmen Figueroa Perea, *Premios y distinciones otorgados al cine mexicano: Festivales internacionales, 1938–1984* (Mexico City: Cineteca Nacional, 1986).

2. Carlos Fuentes, "A Carnivorous Flower," *Artes de México* 2 (Winter 1988): 86.

3. Of course, Fernández and Buñuel were not the only Mexican directors to make festival films. Directors like Roberto Gavaldón and Julio Bracho also found some success on the festival circuit. However, their success was very limited in comparison to that of Fernández and Buñuel.

4. Harshav's essays from the 1970s and 1980s have recently been collected in a single volume. See Benjamin Harshav, *Explorations in Poetics* (Stanford: Stanford University Press, 2007). The essay with the most comprehensive description of the theory is "An Outline of Integrational Semantics: An Understander's Theory of Meaning in Context," 76–112.

5. For an earlier attempt to apply Harshav's ideas to the cinema, see my essay "The Fictional Worlds of Neorealism," *Criticism* 45, no. 1 (Winter 2003): 11–30.

6. See Rogelio Agrasánchez, Jr., *Mexican Movies in the United States: A History of the Films, Theaters, and Audiences, 1920–1960* (Jefferson, N.C.: McFarland, 2006).

7. Anonymous, "Realizaciones y Esperanzas," *Cinevoz* 1, no. 23 (January 2, 1949): 2. My translation.

8. See, for instance, Anonymous, "'Río Escondido' en Checoslovaquia," *Cinevoz* 1, no. 22 (December 26, 1948): 6–7, and Anonymous, "'María Candelaria' en Dinamarca," *Cinevoz* 2, no. 49 (June 16, 1949): 4–6.

9. Ana M. López, "A Cinema for the Continent," in *The Mexican Cinema Project*, ed. Chon Noriega and Steven Ricci (Los Angeles: UCLA Film Archive, 1994), 7–12.

10. Seth Fein, "From Collaboration to Containment: Hollywood and the International Political Economy of Mexican Cinema after the Second World War," in *Mexico's Cinema: A Century of Films and Filmmakers*, ed. Joanne Hershfield and David R. Maciel (Wilmington, Del.: Scholarly Resources, 1999), 123–163.

11. Charles Ramirez-Berg, "Figueroa's Skies and Oblique Perspective: Notes on the Development of the Classical Mexican Cinematographic Style," *Spectator* 13, no. 1 (Fall 1992): 24–41.

12. Julia Tuñón, "Between the Nation and Utopia: The Image of Mexico in the Films of Emilio 'Indio' Fernández," *Studies in Latin American Popular Culture* 12 (1993): 159–174. See also Julia Tuñón, "Emilio Fernández: A Look behind the Bars," in *Mexican Cinema*, ed. Paulo Antonio Paranaguá, trans. Ana M. López (London: British Film Institute, 1995), 179–192.

13. For another analysis of *Río Escondido*, see Fein, "From Collaboration to Containment," 124–129. See also Joanne Hershfield, *Mexican Cinema/Mexican Woman, 1940–1950* (Tucson: University of Arizona Press, 1996).

14. We can trace this skill back to his apprenticeship with Gregg Toland, who employed in-depth compositions in films for Orson Welles, William Wyler, and John Ford. Working with Fernández reinforced this connection, since Fernández himself acknowledged Ford as a major influence. In 1947, Fernández, Figueroa, and Ford all worked together on the RKO production *The Fugitive*, directed by Ford, with Fernández working as the assistant director.

15. See Vladimir Nizhny, *Lessons with Eisenstein*, trans. and ed. Ivor Montagu and Jay Leyda (New York: Hill and Wang, 2000), and David Bordwell, *The Cinema of Eisenstein* (Cambridge, Mass.: Harvard University Press, 1993).

16. Francisco Aranda, *Luis Buñuel: A Critical Biography*, trans. and ed. David Robinson (New York: Da Capo, 1976), 137. Aranda is quoting one of Buñuel's interviews with *Cahiers du cinéma*.

17. Éduoard Klein, "Une tragédie rustique," *La Revue du cinéma* 5 (February 1947): 74. Translation mine.

18. André Camp, "Aperçus sur le cinéma mexicain," *La Revue du cinéma* 15 (July 1948): 33–43.

19. Ernesto R. Acevedo-Muñoz, *Buñuel and Mexico: The Crisis of National Cinema* (Berkeley: University of California Press, 2003).

20. André Bazin, "Cruelty and Love in Los Olvidados," in *The Cinema of Cruelty: from Buñuel to Hitchcock*, ed. François Truffaut, trans. Sabine d'Estrée, with Tiffany Fliss (New York: Seaver, 1982), 51–58.

21. See, for instance, Jacques Doniol-Valcroze, "Par delà la victime," *Cahiers du cinéma* 7 (December 1951): 52–54. See also the August 1954 edition of *Positif* 2, no. 10. This edition was ostensibly dedicated to the subject of Mexican cinema, but a surprising number of articles pay a great deal of attention to *Un Chien andalou* (Buñuel and Dalí, 1929).

22. Bazin, "Subida al cielo," in *Cinema of Cruelty*, 59–64. Acevedo-Muñoz quotes this essay in *Buñuel and Mexico*, 75.

23. Here, my understanding of the postwar art cinema as a culture of interpretation is influenced by David Bordwell's argument that the art cinema encourages the search for ambiguity. See his well-known essay "The Art Cinema as a Mode of Film Practice," *Film Criticism* 4, no. 1 (Fall 1979): 1–8.

24. For instance, Jacques Doniol-Valcroze emphasizes Buñuel's shocking juxtapositions, such as "corpse of a child-pile of trash." See "Par delà la victime," 54.

25. Acevedo-Muñuz has skillfully demonstrated that such a reading of Buñuel's films overlooks the fact that they often contain sharp commentary on Mexican politics and culture.

26. Bernard Chardère, "De l'honnêté: Los Olvidados de Luis Buñuel," *Positif* 1 (May 1952): 15. My translation.

12

THE ESSAY FILM AS A CINEMA OF IDEAS
Timothy Corrigan

Chris Marker's 1958 *Lettre de Sibérie | Letter from Siberia* and André Bazin's immediate and prescient characterization of it as an "essay film" are, for many, key historical markers in the emergence of the essay film from its literary and photographic heritage. In Bazin's words: *Letter from Siberia* is "an essay on the reality of Siberia past and present in the form of a filmed report. Or, perhaps, to borrow Jean Vigo's formulation of *A propos de Nice* ('a documentary point of view'), I would say an essay documented by film. The important word is 'essay,' understood in the same sense that it has in literature—an essay at once historical and political, written by a poet as well. . . . I would say that the primary material is intelligence, that its immediate means of expression is language, and that the image only intervenes in the third position, in reference to this verbal intelligence. . . . There is only one common denominator in this firework display of technique: intelligence."[1]

Despite the historical and mythic importance of this 1958 moment, there is a specifically cinematic history that precedes it, embedded in the evolution of documentary and avant-garde cinemas during the first half of the twentieth century. Both the subject matter and the formal innovations of these earlier traditions, set against the dominance of narrative film, partially anticipate the more pronounced structural innovations of essay films, but just as important are the social and institutional activities that create new frameworks for a critical reception and intellectual interactivity that would help distinguish the essay film and its address in the second half of the twentieth century. By the 1940s, a dynamics of interactive reception associated with the documentary and avant-garde films of earlier decades would dovetail with numerous other sea changes in film aesthetics and technology, as well as with larger shifts in post-World War II culture and epistemology, to introduce, most visibly and pervasively in France, the

FIGURE 12.1. Varda, the auteur of personal expression, remakes herself as Varda, the gleaner of the images of others.

practice of the essay film that has continued to evolve into the present day, where it assumes an increasingly important place in global film culture.

As it develops in and out of those documentary and avant-garde traditions, the history of the essay film underlines a central critical point: that the essayistic should not necessarily be seen simply as an alternative to either of these practices (or to narrative cinema); rather it rhymes and retimes them as a counterpoint within and to them. Situated between the categories of realism and formal expressivity and geared to the possibilities of "public expression," the essay film suggests an appropriation of certain avant-garde and documentary practices in a way very different from the early historical practices of both, just as it tends to invert and restructure the relations between the essayistic and narrative to subsume narrative within that public expression. The essayistic play between fact and fiction, between documentary and fiction, or between experimentation and classical narrative becomes a place where the essay film *inhabits* other forms and practices, in the way Trinh T. Minh-ha has suggested when she notes that the facts contained in her essay film *Surname Viet Given Name Nam* (1989) are the fictions of its stories. Or, to adopt Roland Barthes's phrasing about his own essayistic writing, the essay film *stages* film forms, from narrative to documentary, as a way of feeding knowledge "into the machinery of infinite reflexivity."[2] The essay and essay film do not create new forms of subjectivity, realism, or narrative; they rethink existing ones as a dialogue of ideas.

Two well-known films that might be considered a rhyming frame within the history of the essay film are Dziga Vertov's *Man with a Movie Camera* (1929) and Jean-Luc Godard's *2 or 3 Things I Know about Her* (1967). If the first is a canonical and the second an iconoclastic version of "city symphony" films, Vertov's film is an early documentary anticipation of the essay film and Godard's a confirmation of the historical centrality of essay film on the edges of modern European art cinema. For many, the essayistic connection in Vertov's film is evident in the film's opening announcement that it is "an excerpt from the diary of a cameraman" and in Vertov's description of his role in the film as a "supervisor of the experiment," creating a cinematic language that would express the energy and social dynamics of the modern city. In part, the film is a documentary of a composite city in Russia (with footage from Moscow, Kiev, Odessa), and in part it is a reflexive celebration of the power of cinematic vision.

Integrating these two movements, *Man with a Movie Camera* begins with the awakening of a cinema theater as seats magically open to welcome spectators and the awakening of the city as a woman's eyes open and the cameraman begins his dawn-to-dusk drive around town filming immense activity, filled with the movement of automobiles and trams, workers and athletes, factories and shops. The reflexivity that links the mechanistic energy of the cameraman and the documentary reality of the city is what of course associates the film, for many viewers, with essay films. This is the activity of a constructivist vision, made especially apparent in the celebrated sequence that links shots of a seamstress at work and the film's editor, Elizaveta Svilova, at her editing table, where she examines several images of faces and selects certain ones to insert into a crowd sequence: Here film mimics daily life, and both film and human activity have the capacity to actively affect life through their work. Through this shared activity, the aim and power of *Man with a Movie Camera* becomes the transformation of the multiplicity of different individuals and social functions into a harmonized whole that transcends those vibrant differences. Graphically dramatized by the different shots that superimpose a human eye and the camera lens, Vertov's "cinema eye" (*Kino-Glaz*) overcomes the limitation of subjective human visions by integrating them within the larger objective truths of life (*Kino-Pravda*).

Between 1968 and 1972 Godard and Jean-Pierre Gorin would reestablish the historical connection with Vertov when they formed the Dziga Vertov Group, a collective that aimed to reanimate some of Vertov's political and aesthetic goals. This connection occurs, appropriately, just after the period when Godard begins consistently to describe himself as a film essayist. *2 or 3 Things I Know about Her* thus suggests links and differences across the large historical divide between the 1920s and 1960s, specifically as this film inherits, inhabits, and adjusts the experimental and documentary strategies of *Man with a Movie Camera* into more contemporary essayistic perspectives.

In Godard's fictional documentary as city symphony, the Paris of *2 or 3 Things I Know about Her* becomes the doubled "her" of the city and the character Juliette Janson and then doubled again when she is also identified as the actress Marina Vlady. Superimposed public and personal realms, Paris and Juliette intermingle and continually define and redefine each other as subject and object, while the character Juliette and the actress Vlady open a pronounced gap within the primary subjective identity within the film. In this Paris, commercialism, imperialism, and materialism are the cultural dominants that twist relationships to the point that prostitution becomes a viable employment option for Juliette, whose other self works as a conventional high-rise housewife. Just as Juliette's private and public experiences are stunningly divided, the private and public spaces of Paris (bedrooms, cafés, streets) likewise become separate zones, which, unlike Vertov's city spaces, never geometrically fit together, visualized by the film not as a musical montage but as graphically demarcated mise-en-scènes.

As the title indicates, the film is an epistemological project about ideas and knowing, but embedded within that suggestion is the somewhat ironic awareness that modern knowledge is shaped and frustrated by fragmented and reified subjects within a landscape of acquisition, enumeration, and accumulation. While Vertov's film could be described as a mesmerizing and harmonizing integration of social subjects and public life, Godard's film becomes explicitly about the difficulty of trying to express oneself and to think through this modern, always mediated, world. As one character remarks, "We often try to analyze the meaning of words but are led astray. One must admit that there's nothing simpler than taking things for granted." As a project that attempts to think and know modern life, a politics of semiotics pervades the film, mapping how the world of the city and the self of Juliette become products of signs and symbols that need constant interpretation if language has any promise of mediating and humanizing the divide. Yet, ubiquitous ads and slogans abound as the pervasive filter that continually short-circuits or detours this possibility of a humanizing bond or link with the city and other people, so that expression itself becomes absorbed by the public places that surround it. Indeed, just as Juliette continually engages in a semiotics of naming objects around her, the voice-over commentator (Godard) names and describes Juliette in terms of the framing ("she moves left") that addresses the viewer and her conscious and unconscious entrapment in a semiotic field of space and language. Juliette famously quotes, "Language is the house where man lives," and in the often cited meditative coffee cup sequence, a camera focuses and refocuses in close up on a cup of coffee, swirling with cream, while Godard's voice-over commentary reflects, "Maybe an object is what permits us to link, to pass from one subject to the other, therefore to live in society." Or maybe not.

While the use of montage in *2 or 3 Things I Know about Her* recalls Vertov's film, the sharp juxtapositions of urban scenes of construction and deconstruction and private lives encapsulated in close-ups in Godard's film recreate multiple levels of interaction in the city but without an overarching experiential harmony of *Man with a Movie Camera*. Self and other become reduced in their mutual isolation and objectification, while this postwar man with the movie camera constantly signals his awareness of his own position within the industrial language he exposes. Wryly articulated with essayistic intertitles (taken from titles of actual essays published by Gallimard in a collection called *Ideas*) such as "Eighteen Lessons on Industrial Society," Godard's encounter with this new city can only claim a tentative and temporary position: "Since I cannot tear myself from the objectivity that crushes me nor from the subjectivity that exiles me, since I am permitted neither to lift myself to being nor fall into nothingness, I must listen, I must look around me more than ever at the world, my likeness, my brother." While Vertov celebrates the possibility of a new documentary truth through the cinema, Godard's film inhabits that utopia as a significantly more essayistic staging of documentary desire: skeptical, provisional, self-critical, a cinema that happily accepts its continually frustrated struggle to think the world through language.

Essays describe and provoke an activity of public thought, and the public nature of that subjective experience highlights and even exaggerates the participations of their audience, readers, and viewers in a dialogue of ideas. More than other literary or representational practices, even the most personal of essays speak to a listener who will validate or trouble that personal essayistic voice, and the more immersed that voice is in its exterior world the more urgent the essay becomes in embedding and dispersing itself within the public experience and activity it desires. From Montaigne's implied epistolary address to his lost friend and interlocutor Etienne de la Boétie to Jacob Riis's hortatory public lectures on and photographs of the New York tenements for philanthropic audiences, the essay presses itself as a dialogic and reflective communal experience. In this sense, one of the chief defining features of the essay film and its history becomes an active intellectual response to the questions and provocations that an unsettled subjectivity directs at its public.

As part of what I'll call a precursive history of the essay film, early film reception regularly elicited not only a dynamic audience interactivity but one frequently based in the kind of pedagogical response associated with essays, reformulated cinematically as scientific lectures or travelogues.[3] Even after narrative cinema began to take shape and dominate film culture in the first decade of the twentieth century, many films continued to insist on the capacity of movies to address audiences with intellectual and social imperatives associated with lectures, social pamphlets, and other essayistic formats. A 1909 review of D. W. Griffith's *A Corner of Wheat* (1909), for instance, aligns it explicitly with an intervention in the public domain associated with editorials and essays: "The picture . . . is an argument, an editorial, an essay on a vital subject of deep interest to all. . . . [yet] No orator, no editorial writer, no essayist, could so strongly and effectively present the thoughts that are conveyed in this picture. It is another demonstration of the force and power of motion pictures as a means of conveying ideas."[4]

By the 1920s, the possibilities of an essayistic cinema become articulated most clearly in the work of Sergei Eisenstein and other filmmakers in the Soviet cinema, while certain avant-garde films also experiment with the blending of formalist and documentary aesthetics in ways that foreshadow the essay film. Film historian Roman Gubern claims that in 1922 Benjamin Christiansen "inaugurated the formula for the essay film with his admirable *Häxan: Witchcraft through the Ages*," in its combination of documentary and fiction, realism and fantasy.[5] More often noted, however, are Eisenstein's early references to the essay film and his desire to make Marx's *Capital* as a political and social science argument on film. In April 1928, he writes: "The content of CAPITAL (its aim) is now formulated: to teach the worker to think dialectically."[6] By the late 1920s and early 1930s, documentary films, often intersecting with avant-garde traditions in films such as Alberto Calvalcanti's *Rien que les heures* (1926), Vertov's *Man* with a Movie Camera, and Jean Vigo's *A propos de Nice* (1929), likewise anticipate and adumbrate the structures and terms of the essay film that would make its decisive appearance in the 1950s.

The advent of synchronized film sound in the late 1920s and early 1930s had, as many historians point out, a massive impact on documentary film and, less obviously, on the key formation of a contrapuntal voice that would inform the gradual formation of a particular essayistic address in the cinema as a modulating inquiring into the reality of images. Recognizing this mobility in the documentary voice even at this early stage, Stella Bruzzi countered tendencies to homogenize and standardize the range and movement of these voices in *Land without Bread* (1933), *The Battle of San Pietro* (1945), and numerous other documentaries. As Bruzzi points out, "The reductionism that has plagued discussions of documentary's implementation of voice-over lies in the persistent refusal to either acknowledge any differences between *actual* voices or to distinguish between very different uses of the voice within the documentary context."[7]

Looking forward to the postwar essay films, this gradual mobilizing and concretizing of the documentary voice foreshadows the more definitive play with a more mobile and self-reflexive linguistics and a more mobile documentary voice as a drama of subjectivity enmeshed in the world. As the essay film comes more clearly into historical view, one of its most distinguishing features is its foregrounding of its literary heritage in the material performance of language as part of its encounter with the dominance of a public culture of visual technology, significantly (and frequently overlooked) replacing the voice of a narrator with the very different voice of the essayist.

Besides the formal experimentations that overlapped documentary and experimental practice, as important in these precursive years are the institutional and social contexts that begin to locate a place for film that draws out the public and dialogic potential of these films, most prominently seen in the ciné-clubs that begin to spring up around the world and especially in France in the 1920s and 1930s.[8] Throughout its literary history and thereafter, the dynamics of reception have been a distinctive dimension of the essay and its dialogic intervention in a public sphere, and the historical evolution of a specific kind of audience is crucial to its filmic practice, anticipating what Laura Rascaroli has noted as central to a definition of the essay film: a "constant interpellation" whereby "each spectator, as an individual and not a member of an anonymous, collective audience, is called upon to engage in a dialogic relationship with the enunciator, to become active, intellectually and emotionally, and interact with the text."[9] In the 1920s, the ciné-clubs became central vehicles in the formation of this dynamic and of an audience for whom film was less about entertainment than a forum for debating aesthetic and social issues and experiences, specialized gathering places for artists and intellectuals, and forums for movies about ideas, ideas about film, ideas about the social and expressive powers of the movies. At the beginning of this cultural and institutional shift, Jean Epstein's 1921 commentary "Bonjour Cinéma" rather excessively insists on the distinguishing possibility of a cinematic "photogénie" to create and think ideas in a new way. The cinema, he says, is "a product twice distilled. My eye presents me with an idea of a form;

the film stock also contains an idea of a form, an idea established independently of my awareness, a latent, secret but marvelous idea; and from the screen I get an idea of an idea."[10] Paralleling the cultural, social, and intellectual activity of the French cine-clubs, British writers and filmmakers embrace a similar refashioning of film reception. The founding editor of *Close-Up*, known as Bryher, claims in "How I Would Start a Film Club" that the primary the goal of these clubs is "to build up an audience of intelligent spectators."[11] Or, as Harry Potamkin puts it in 1933, "The film club is to the audience generally what the critic is to the spectator; that is, the film club provides the critical audience," which for Potamkin has both an aesthetic and social dimension, with the latter the most important.[12] By the 1950s, the Cinémathèque Française, founded by Henri Langlois in 1936 with filmmaker Georges Franju, became the most important product of the ciné-club tradition (specifically the Cercle du Cinéma) and ushered in changes and new directions in the spectatorial dynamics of the cine-clubs, changes that would provide the defining structure of essayistic cinema. In 1947 the International Federation of Ciné-Clubs was established, and by 1955 a European confederation of Cinéma d'Art et d'Essai helped to shape the "advanced European art cinema" theaters that programmed more innovative and experimental films, often aided by tax rebates. Kelly Conway recently summed up how these reshaped ciné-club forms in the 1950s promoted their own specific form of essayistic dialogue: "The ciné-club attempted to form spectators in very specific ways: through its diverse programming, through film education internships, and, above all, through the *débat*, the post-screening discussion. . . . The ciné-club did not aspire to replace the commercial cinema in its members' lives or to promote a renaissance in experimental filmmaking, as had the 1920s ciné-clubs. Instead, the post-war ciné-club invested in the forma tion of an active, educated viewer."[13] That is, as signs of larger institutional and aesthetic changes, the ciné-clubs would stage and inhabit the possibility to rethink films according in the formation of the unique spectatorial formation that would come to define the essay film.

The films of Humphrey Jennings stand as creative summaries of some of these early moves toward essayistic structures and anticipation of the more definite essay films that would follow the war, balancing documentary representation with a pronounced subjective chord that consistently calls out for dialogic and ideational reflection. Associated both with the surrealist tradition that defined the interior explorations of his early work and later with John Grierson's documentaries for the General Post Office and the Mass Observation project, initiated with Tom Harrison and Charles Madge, Jennings made a series of films through the 1940s that bear the marks of both movements and that concomitantly lean conspicuously into the essayistic forms that are about to enter definitively into film history.

Listen to Britain is a montage of daily experiences in England during the war: a man on his way to work, schoolchildren playing, soldiers waiting for a train, and so on. References to the war are unmistakable but muted: the businessman carries an air-raid helmet, a sign points to a shelter, many concertgoers wear uniforms. Drawing on the ability of sound to permeate spatial divides, the film's emphasis on sound, notably the signature radio announcement, "This Is London Calling," becomes an audial call for community (and possibly U.S. participation in the European war), pinpointed with scenes of entertainers performing, a Royal Air Force band afternoon concert, and a performance of Mozart's Seventeenth Piano Concerto by Myra Hess in the National Gallery. In each case, the film draws attention to the power of sound and music to unite the audience through its expressive qualities. In the extended second sequence especially, the concentration of the interplay between the music, the audience's enraptured attention, and the cut-away to windows being bricked up (presumably in the concert hall) suggests Jennings's slightly surrealistic twist on a war documentary. Here, actual images of war in process give way to the more important identification and solicitation of the responsive undercurrents of community and camaraderie that those events elicit, prominent undercurrents that follow the soundtrack of the concert into the streets of London, armament factories, and then the countryside. This play between expressive sound and a collage of public images anticipates the essayistic both in its restraint and in its dispersion of a communal expressivity into the crisis of public life. For Jennings, music and voice initiate the public dialogue that redeems individual hardship. More important, sound as expression here does not so much support or illuminate the pressures of the war experience but rather remains tautly in tension with them. Far from registering faith in a reality under siege, the fragile sound and music become expressive measures of longing, recollection, irony, and hope.

In his analysis of *Listen to Britain*, Jim Leach identifies the particular "unsettling" effect of this film as it wavers between propaganda and poetry, between a public gaze and a private eye, between personal and impersonal styles, which results in a distinctive "ambiguity" whose "refusal to impose meanings implies both a respect for the personal freedom of the spectator and an awareness that meanings are always complex and plural." Enacting a form of what Bill Nichols has called "social subjectivity," the film creates a montage of fragile connections between individuals, classes, peace and war, and various cultural practices that, while tentatively destabilizing the public myth of "a people's war," also celebrate it. As the film asks the audience "to listen," "the pull between sight and sounds adds to the fragility of the film's discourse" and so elicits an "alertness in the spectator, who is asked to reflect on the experience of unity within difference."[14]

Another film Jennings made during World War II, *A Diary for Timothy* (1943), continues this early exploration of the essayistic but with considerably more emphasis on subjectivity, the temporality of a public history, and a resulting skepticism about the voice and mind of the public individual that will emerge in the coming years. With commentary written by E. M. Forster, the story of Timothy Jenkins opens with a BBC broadcast reporting Allied advances in Europe. The film cuts to a row of bassinets and the cries of a newborn baby: "It was on the 3rd of September, 1944, you were born. . . . You're in danger, Tim, for all around you is being fought the worst war ever known." Intercut with shots of mother and newborn and of rumbles and planes flying overhead, this was "total war," involving all of England but here focusing on the child as subject. This film becomes less about wartime crisis than about an impending postwar world where, as the commentator later remarks, it will be "back to everyday life . . . and everyday danger."

With an unusually familiar voice replacing the traditional voice of God of earlier documentary commentary, the film orchestrates movements between the past, the present, and the future, spread across the four different social and subject positions of a miner, a farmer, a railway engineer, and a wounded RAF pilot, but addresses the just-born child: "All these people were fighting for you, although they didn't exactly know it." The fissures between these time periods (as when the farmer shows his family a film from five years ago when they were clearing the fields) and the anxious relation between experience and knowledge become an open question: Over the image of a baby buggy, he remarks about these temporal intensities of the present: "You didn't know, couldn't know, and didn't care."

Here, too, sound in the form the voice-over, radio broadcasts, and musical concerts figures in bridging public events and the individual in the community. Myra Hess's Beethoven's Appassionata Sonata is interwoven with a radio account of soldiers' hardships in Europe and the image of London with bombed buildings being repaired by roofers. Drifting through these sounds and music, the commentator (Michael Redgrave) has little of the clarity or certainty that marks earlier documentaries, as he notes that the newly lit streets had become more cheerful, "unless there were bombers around"; or, over an air-raid siren, he hopes "you'll never have to hear that sound, Tim." Even Christmas is an ironic reminder of "death and darkness, death and fog, death across those few miles of water," characterized by the essayistic conditional that this should be "the day all children ought to get to be happy." A conversation about a V-2 rocket before a blast is heard becomes a prophetic encounter in which the massive anonymity of death after World War II would confront the shaky possibilities of knowledge: Where and when the rocket will hit elicits only "I know not" and "do you know?" against a surrealist pan of mannequin faces topped with hats.

Most significantly, the second-person address of the film stands out here as a dramatic redirection that would inform the address of later essay films, here a combination of warning and hope directed at the child Timothy and the spectator inhabiting that newborn position, proleptic subjects still to be formed and so, with a critical irony, implored to think about the future. The wavering voice-over observes that "it's a chancy world" in which a miner's accident becomes one small indication that a postwar climate will bring new dangers and demands. Yet these new repercussive demands of postwar life in England—unemployment, broken homes, scattered families—will also offer a concomitant opportunity for a new public subjectivity: it will be "even more dangerous than before because now we have the power to choose, the right to criticize and even to grumble." For the new child and spectator, this is indeed "something else for you to think over," and only through a strenuous reflection on the past and present as they are documented in the film and as they reshape the future can the presiding questions of the film be answered by the spectator child: "What are you going to say about it, and what are you going to do? . . . Are you going to make the world a different place?"

While many films before 1940 belong to the heritage of the essay film, my contention is that important historical distinctions must be made in order to demonstrate the significant achievements of this practice as it comes into its own. In this regard, the

1940s are the watershed years for the essay film, a period when many of these forces begin to coalesce, the term and its distinction gained currency, and the films themselves more clearly begin to define themselves and their address according to my tripartite structure of a mobile subjectivity, dispersed through public experience, as a forum for thinking ideas. From 1940 to 1945, in short, the essay film definitively reconfigures notions of realism (and documentary representation) outside a narrative tradition and asserts the intellectual and conceptual mobility central to an essayistic tradition. Alongside a confluence of historical forces and shifts, the French "filmology" movement associated with Gilbert Cohen-Seat appears in the 1940s, claiming the cinema as the singular most prominent social force in postwar society and thus requiring serious academic study of, especially, how spectators understand and think through movies.[15] Also in the early 1940s, André Malraux delivers his lecture "Esquisse d'une psychologie du cinéma," arguing "the possibility of expression in the cinema."[16] And, in 1940, artist and filmmaker Hans Richter writes a prescient essay titled "The Film Essay," in which he attempts to describe a new practice evolving out of the documentary tradition, but instead of presenting what he calls "beautiful vistas," it would aim "to find a representation for intellectual content," "to find images for mental concepts," "striv[e] to make visible the invisible world of concepts, thoughts, and ideas," so that viewers would become "involved intellectually and emotionally."[17] Together these three moments announce and identify an increasingly consistent new direction in film practice that would embrace and transform the literary heritage of the essay as a way to create films about rethinking the self as a function of a destabilized public sphere.

Most pervasively, the 1940s represented an epistemological foundation of the essay film for reasons that stretch beyond the cinematic. As Paul Arthur has noted, it was only "after the Holocaust—our era's litmus test for the role of individual testimony in collective trauma—that essay films acquire a distinct aesthetic outline and moral purpose."[18] The crisis of World War II, the Holocaust, the trauma that traveled from Hiroshima around the world, and the impending Cold War thus become a social, existential, and representational crisis that will inform and galvanize an essayistic imperative to question and debate not only a new world but the very terms by which we subjectively inhabit, publicly stage, and experientially think that world. No wonder that Alain Resnais's *Night and Fog* (1955) and its eerie encounter with the concentration camps becomes an early and widely recognized example of the essay film. As if it were a documentary unable to adequately document the reality it seeks, it drifts through horizontal tracks, punctuated by archival stills, across the "peaceful landscapes" and "ordinary roads" that surrounded Auschwitz and Bergen Belsen. Despite the "semblance of a real city" constructed as concentration camps, this is "a society developed, shaped by terror." No wonder that in this encounter with history the commentator fumbles and stumbles through a kind of inadequacy structured as a dialogue between Resnais's images and the literary voice-over of Jean Cayrol: "It is impossible for us to capture what remains. . . . The daily activities and signs no description, no shot can retrieve. . . . We can only show you the outside, the husk." As Sandy Flitterman-Lewis so perceptively notes, this film is a "constructive forgetting"; a struggle to express the inexpressible culminates in a coda that crystallizes what I'd call the essayistic address: Here the interlocutory direct address of the I-You voice-over changes dramatically to We and so demands an "active engagement" bonding the filmmaker and viewer in the responsibility to rethink history.[19]

In postwar France, perhaps the best known pronouncement on the cinematic possibilities that would lay the groundwork for the essay film is Alexandre Astruc's "The Birth of the New Avant-Garde: The Caméra-Stylo" (1948). Here, the key terms of the essay film move from the background of earlier film practices to the foreground in a way that definitely emphasizes a new direction that would dramatize cinematic subjectivity as an intellectual enterprise moving beyond narrative and traditional documentary models:

> To come to the point: the cinema is quite simply becoming a means of expres-
> sion, just as all the other arts have been before it. . . . After having been succes-
> sively a fairground attraction, an amusement analogous to boulevard theatre, or
> the means of preserving the images of an era, it is gradually becoming a
> language. By language, I mean a form in which and by which an artist can
> express his thoughts, however abstract they may be, or translate his obsessions
> exactly as he does in the contemporary essay or novel. This is why I would like to
> call this new age of cinema the age of the caméra-stylo (camera pen). This
> metaphor has a very precise sense. By it I mean that the cinema will gradually
> break free from the tyranny of what is visual, from the image for its own sake,
> from the immediate and concrete demands of the narrative, to become a means
> of writing just as flexible and subtle as written language. . . . It can tackle any
> subject, any genre. The most philosophical meditations on human production,
> psychology, ideas, and passions lie within its province. I will even go so far
> as to say that contemporary ideas and philosophies of life are such that only the
> cinema can do justice to them.[20]

These claims for personal expression on film would immediately become technologically viable with the arrival of portable lightweight camera technology, introduced as the Arriflex system in Germany in 1936 and as the Éclair 35mm Cameflex in France in 1947. Appropriately, these different "caméra-stylos" would also feature reflex viewing systems linking the pragmatics of filmmaking with the conceptual reflexivity of the emerging essay film and its "idea of the cinema expressing ideas" ("The Caméra-Stylo," 159).

This relation between mobile technology, economics, and the essayistic underlines the distinct historical forces that come into play during these formative years and suggests a larger point that remains an undercurrent throughout the longer future of the essay film: that the power of essay may be significantly tied to a representational agency that emphasizes its ephemerality rather than permanency, which in turn may illuminate its notable prominence and success today. As with the early history of the literary essay and its connection with new forms of production and distribution, lightweight technologies of the postwar years through the 1960s—the Portapack and videotape revolution after 1968 (and later the Internet and digital convergences of today)—significantly encourage and underpin the active subjectivity and public mobility of the essay film that begins with the claims and practices of the essayistic in the 1940s. That particularity and paradoxically public intimacy of address and reception has followed the essay through eighteenth-century coffeehouses and pamphlets and nineteenth-century lecture halls and journals to the film festivals and college art cinemas that define the essay film in the postwar years to the specialized television distribution of Germany's ZDF, western Europe's Canal+, Britain's Channel Four, and other cable and television venues. Related are the changing economic demands of documentary filmmaking where particularly in recent years the cost of archival footage, music, and other copyrighted materials has, at least, encouraged more personal perspectives and materials that require considerably less financial resources.

That those cinematic foundations in the 1940s and 1950s are so largely French (just as the theoretical foundations of Walter Benjamin, Theodor Adorno, and others are largely German) should help explain the prominent place of the French New Wave (and later the New German Cinema) in exploring the essay film from 1950 through the 1970s. Within the historical context of postwar French cinema, moreover, several prominent historical and critical touchstones—regarding auteurism, *cinéma vérité*, and the literary heritage of the French New Wave—emerge that not only inform French films of this period but also carry over into the extended global and contemporary practices of the essay film, as well as the global art cinema in general. In addition to Astruc's writings, several specific films, documents, and trends signal and support this relationship and highlight broader practical and conceptual shifts, as this practice evolves through the 1950s into the 1960s, creating a historical and cultural context in which, by the mid-1950s, the term "essai cinématographique" is in frequent use in France.[21] In these defining years, these possibilities become articulated specifically through the potential of the "short film" to provide a freedom from the restriction of the authority invested in the expressivity of auteurism, in the documentary truth of *cinéma vérité*, and in the organizational principles of film narrative, all remade as a conceptual "sketch" capable of releasing a distinctive subjectivity as a public thinking. More exactly, a specific group of films and their contemporaneous or subsequent critical responses to them became flashpoints in the formation and recognition of essayistic practice: Alain Resnais's 1948 short film *Van Gogh*; Jacques Rivette's 1955 "Letter on Rossellini" and its characterization of *Paisà / Paisan* (1946), *Europa '51 / The Greatest Love* (1952), *Germania anno zero / Germany, Year Zero* (1948), and especially the 1953 *Viaggio in Italia / Journey to Italy* as seminal essay films; and Georges Franju's 1948 *Le Sang des bêtes / Blood of the Beasts* and especially his 1951 *Hôtel des Invalides*, as seen by Noël Burch as prototypes for an essay cinema of ideas.

Appearing the same year as Astruc's proclamation of a new kind of expressive filmmaking, Resnais's *Van Gogh* is serendipitously emblematic of a short essayistic portrait, a film less about painting than about the grounds for a cinematic expression that engages, questions, and thinks a painterly style while evading narrative formulas and conventional documentary strategies. Bazin would rightfully insist that this film has little to do with popularizing a painting and a painter but rather it announces a particular "aesthetic biology" that adapts the painting as a cinematic textuality, recreating "not the subject of the painting but the painting itself" as a textual "refraction."[22] Godard would go even farther to claim for it an inventiveness and historical importance that points to a new filmic practice: "If the short film hadn't existed, Alain Resnais surely would have invented it. . . . from the blind, trembling pans of 'Van Gogh' to the majestic traveling shots of 'Styrene' what in effect do we see? A survey of the possibilities of cinematic technique, but such a demanding one, that it finishes by surpassing itself, in such a way that the modern young French cinema could not have existed without it. For Alain Resnais more than anyone else gives the impression that he completely started over at zero."[23] By 1953 this filming degree zero would produce the "Group of Thirty," a body of filmmakers that included Resnais, Marker, Agnès Varda, and Astruc and that revitalized the short film as the grounds for developing essayistic film practices. As François Porcile notes, the short film in this postwar context describes a incipient "hothouse" practice that, instead of suggesting juvenilia, describes an exploratory energy that liberates it as a kind of testing of both expression and address: "Next to the novel and other extensive works, there is the poem, the short story or the essay, which often plays the role of the hothouse; it has the function of revitalizing a field with fresh blood. The short film has the same role."[24] At this point in history, the short film offers especially a form of expression whose concision necessarily places that expression under material pressure as a fragmentary testing and provisional engagement with a subject whose incompleteness insists it is an artistic and intellectual activity in process. The significance of the short also draws attention to what Guy Fihman, in exploring a philosophical and scientific background of the essay that begins with René Descartes, argues is one of the seminal features of the essay and essay film: innovation and experimentation,[25] possibilities that would attract both young and established filmmakers to return to the short film as a break from narrative cinema.

Reconfiguring the implications of the short film in April 1955, Jacques Rivette's "Letter on Rossellini" identifies a trend that also can define longer films as cinematic drafts or sketches. In these films, he argues, "the indefatigable eye of the camera invariably assumes the role of the pencil, a temporal sketch is perpetuated before our eyes," and specifically in Rossellini's *Paisà, Europa '51*, and *Germany, Year Zero*, there is "the common sense of the draft. . . . For there is no doubt that these hurried films, improvised out of very slender means and filmed in a turmoil that is often apparent from the images, contain the only real portrait of our times; and these times are a draft too. How could one fail suddenly to recognize, quintessentially sketched, ill-composed, incomplete, the semblance of our daily existence?" For these films, and most recognizably for Rivette, *Viaggio in Italia*, the model "is the essays of Montaigne," and "*Viaggio in Italia* . . . , with absolute lucidity, at least offers the cinema, hitherto condemned to narrative the possibility of the essay." "For over fifty years now, the essay has been the very language of modern art; it is freedom, concern, exploration, spontaneity," creating "the sense of pursuit and proximity." For Rivette, in these films "a film-maker dares to talk about himself without restraint" so that "Rossellini's films have more and more obviously become *amateur* films; home movies."[26] Here "home movie," "amateur," "pursuit," and "proximity" assume, I'd argue, particularly positive values associated with an essayistic foregrounding and dramatization of the personal, a transitional, barely authorized, and relatively formless shape of the personal subjectivity, the replacement of a teleological organization with an activity defined by the object itself, and a productively distorting overlapping of subject and object.

The "sketch" as a historical prototype and marker of the essayistic thus becomes the vehicle for a public subjectivity in the process of thinking or what Noël Burch would later describe as the intelligent mediation of conflicting ideas. In his *Theory of Film Practice* and its concluding discussion of nonfictional filmmaking, Burch describes two contemporary models as the film essay and the ritual film, the former identified specifically with Franju's *Blood of the Beasts* and especially his *Hôtel des Invalides* as breakthrough films. These "active" documentaries "are no longer documentaries in [an] objective sense, their entire purpose being to set forth thesis and antithesis through the very texture of the film. These two films of Franju are *meditations*, and their subjects a *conflict of ideas*. . . . Therein lies the tremendous originality of these two films, which were to cause nonfiction film production to take an entirely new direction." For Burch in the late 1960s, Franju becomes "the only cinematographer to have successfully created from pre-existing material films that are truly essays," and his heritage becomes especially visible in Godard's essay films of that period, such as *Vivre sa vie / My Life to Live* (1962) and *Masculin féminine: 15 faits précis / Masculine-féminine* (1966), where an "element of intellectual spectacle" announces this a distinctive "cinema of ideas," long ago dreamt of by such dissimilar filmmakers as Jacques Feyder and Eisenstein.[27]

While the prominent French currents leading from Epstein through Marker, Bazin, and Godard describe a central path in the history of the essay film, that history also insists that the foundations of essay film have been pervasively global, extending from Griffith and Eisenstein through Richter and Jennings, from the Denmark of Benjamin Christensen to the Iran of Abbas Kiarostami. Since the 1970s, the essay film has built on those transnational foundations and has proliferated across many international new wave cinemas and various film cultures around the world, including filmmakers like Glauber Rocha, Wim Wenders, Chantal Akerman, Nanni Moretti, Johannes van der Keuken, Peter Greenaway, Patrick Keiller, Su Friedrich, Apichatpong Weerasethakul, and many others. If these filmmakers and their films have commonly recalled auteurist notions of coherent expressivity associated with narrative art film, they have often returned to short films (well after their years as apprentices) to test that auteurist stability and have often described their longer work as essayistic encounters with rapidly changing public spheres. For these global gleaners of ideas and experiences outside traditional narrative, documentary, and experimental logics, auteurist authority frequently gives way to a public dialogue that explores the fissures where subjectivity engages the world as a movement of thought.

The films of Agnès Varda provide an unusually responsive sounding board for the historical movement of the essay film from its association with French cinema of the 1950s through its continued growth and expansion into the digital present. Since her 1958 *L'Opéra mouffe*, a sketch of Rue Mouffetard seen through the eyes of a pregnant woman, and the 1962 *Cléo from 5 to 7*, her fictional sketch of a singer wandering Paris for roughly two hours of real time and film time, Varda has worked the terrain of the essay films across numerous projects, including a portrait of her filmmaker partner, *Jacquot de Nantes* (1991) and the remarkable *The Gleaners and I* (2000). As a most appropriate recollection of the heritage and investment of the essay film in the ciné-club tradition, Varda follows *The Gleaners and I* with another film, *Two Years Later* (2002), which solicits and incorporates viewers and participants in the first film as part of a dialogic rethinking of that first essay film.

The Gleaners and I is a series of sketches, a collage of short takes on different subjects and experiences constructed, first, as a meditation on gleaning. Describing the activity of collecting the surplus left after fields have been harvested, the idea of gleaning expands and contracts through the film, as it triggers other associations, concepts, and debates. In the heritage of its literary and cinematic predecessors, the film proceeds digressively, spinning and turning the experience of gleaning as an idea that moves from the agricultural to the social and the psychoanalytic to the aesthetic and political. Topics such as "The Origins of Gleaners" and "Gleaners Today" guide the course of the film as it wanders the fields and cities of France and its history, and moves according to the seemingly haphazard and associative ways of many essays, between specific experiences and general observations, between similarities and dramatic differences: about the politics of waste and hunger in regulating the modern gleaners, about urban gleaners and supermarket garbage, about gleaning as an art and about the art of gleaning. Gleaning becomes in fact a crystallization of experience as a seemingly endless source of expression: There is "The Gleaning Chef," Edouard Loubet, "the youngest chef to have earned 2 stars in the Michelin Guide," in a kitchen where gourmet food is prepared and little is wasted, and an educational workshop on junk and recyclables becomes a disquisition on "Art from Trash" and "Where does play end and art start?"

Ultimately gleaning becomes defined here as a shifting identity dependent on and defined by the surplus and waste of the world, an identity that creates unique social bonds drifting through the flux of public life rather than inhabiting a position within that life, an identity built of fragments and transience. Abandoned furniture and other objects become homes like "the Ideal Palace of Bodan Litnanski" constructed of old broken dolls and other found objects, and lost souls (alcoholics, the jobless, and dispossessed) find food and friendship by drifting through streets and fields. The relationship, between M. Plusquellecs and his homeless friend Salomon, becomes a gleaned friendship, a bond tentatively made like the gourmet meals they fashion from the chicken and rabbit they pick from the trash, and Alain the dietician of refuse devotes himself to teaching the immigrant refuse of France. Quite appropriately in the midst of her travels, Varda stumbles unwittingly on the renowned Jean Laplanche, psychoanalytic theoretician and wine master of a vineyard, who suggests, in a reflection on reaping and death, time and age, fruition and meaning, the connection between gleaning and subjectivity as an attempt "to integrate the Other above the ego . . . an anti-ego philosophy to show how man first originates in the Other." Here gleaning, like the essayistic identity, is a parasitically productive activity, a subversion or rejection of the authority and primacy of subjectivity and selfhood, as it is enunciated in a language that fails to offer any stable place or meaning.

If gleaning is an essayistic activity, essayistic art and filmmaking become kinds of representational gleanings. Throughout the film, numerous paintings and painters crystallize this particular postmodern art, like Louis Pons, who appears flipping through a book of his paintings whose compositional "junk" becomes a "cluster of possibilities . . . each object gives a direction, each is a line." But the primary subject of this metaphoric shift is Varda herself: Posed beside Jules Breton's painting *The Woman Gleaning*, Varda notes of this famous image of a woman in a field of wheat that "there's another woman gleaning in this film, that's me," happy as she says at another point, "to drop the wheat, and pick up my camera," a small digital caméra-stylo that intensifies the subjective fragments of this contemporary woman with a movie camera in a fleeting world. For Varda and this essay film, representational gleaning moves across the cinematic image, and specifically her digital camera, allowing a continual sketching of the self as it dissolves in the world and specifically as a mounting meditation on the drafting of self against the vanishings of time. In one sequence, one of Varda's hands films the other hand as trucks pass in the background, allowing her "to retain things passing." In another, Varda's reflection in the car mirror precedes a series of shots of that hand opening and closing like a lens on images of different trucks speeding by on the road. "This is my project: to film with one hand my other hand," she remarks. For in this fragmentation of the self in a passing world, the film sketches the passing and loss of self through the world: "To enter into the horror of it. I find it extraordinary. I feel as if I am an animal. Worse yet, an animal I don't know."

The Gleaners and I is not, then, simply an essay film about a community of individuals who live off the refuse and leavings of society; rather it quickly becomes also a subtle, sophisticated self-reflexive meditation on the terms of the essayistic and its film practice—in this case about the struggles to think the self within a field of death and passing, where images of self become redeemed only as a gleaned excess from the world. Over close ups of garbage, Varda says, "I like filming rot, leftovers, waste, mold, and trash," and, appropriately, she visits a mini-museum in the vineyard consecrated to its former owner, Jules Etienne Marey, inventor of chronophotography, the "ancestor of all movie makers," and a pioneer in the study of temporality and change in animal motion. Like the horror of seeing a self as an animalistic other in the world outside, Marey's imagistic time studies oddly anticipate Varda's own digital images whose "stroboscopic" effects fragment the self and that later in the film capture close-up fragments of Varda's eye while her hand holds a small mirror, creating a montage of pieces within the image. Scanning across the pages of a technical handbook for her digital camera, the film returns to a medium close-up of Varda, who places her hand over the lens of the camera recording her. There follows a series of superimposed close-ups and a decentered close-up of her combing her hair and then her hand. "And for forgetful me," she says, "it's what I've gleaned that tells where I've been." As these concluding sequences make clear, *The Gleaners and I* is ultimately a moving sketch that gathers souvenirs of a self, extended through a disembodied hand, fractured through rapidly passing and dying images, and left to drift into the world of others.

Two Years Later becomes then an ingenious recollection and technological rehabilitation of the ciné-club tradition that fostered Varda's work in the 1950s and early 1960s, as it engages in a dialogue with individuals filmed in *The Gleaners* and others who responded to its reception.[28] In a sense, *The Gleaners* becomes a public souvenir that inspires and generates more souvenirs as expanding arguments, reflections, representations, and ideas, becoming a cinematic forum for the dialogic debates, discussions, and differences that the essayistic invites and opens. Equipped again with her digital caméra-stylo in this sequel, Varda recreates the dialogic dynamic that the essay film inherited from the ciné-club format, now incorporating responses that in a sense rethink and remake the first film through the comments and criticism of its audiences. It begins with a screen of thumbnails of images from *The Gleaners and I*, and propels itself through the questions "What effect does a film have? What reaches the filmgoer?" Responding to one curious fan letter (made from an airline ticket jacket), Varda visits Delphine and Philippe in Trentemoult who "transform everyday life" by salvaging objects from the markets and streets. For them, "Seeing this film was like a rebirth . . . We had come from the death of a friend, and this film put us back in touch with ourselves, with life. . . . that's what life's about, learning to adapt."

Particularly inventive in this second film is Varda's return to subjects and people from earlier films. As an ironic reversal of the pathway whereby the *Cahiers du Cinéma* critics turned filmmakers, now those filmed subjects become the critics of the film. Indeed what may be most essayistic about this second film is how it expands outward the questions and issues of the first film to larger or different terms: The film distinctly shifts from commentary about the first film to social and political issues and relationships between people, so that the regeneration of those active subjects within the world maps the centrifugal spin of the essay toward social and public life. Typical of but more extensive than many of the returns in this film, Varda revisits "Alain F., market gleaner, newspaper seller, teacher" who has followed the impact of *The Gleaners* and has become part of a public discussion of the film, one in which he is unabashedly critical (and conventionally mistaken, I'd say) in his response to Varda's "self-portrait": "I think the film is well-done," he comments; "it has reached a lot of people," but "I think your self-portrait is not well-done. . . . unnecessary." Just as a large section of this second film follows Alain into the streets of Paris to run a marathon, the movement of the film is into the public area where Varda casually and quietly sketches the passing public, derouting the camera's point of view in order to capture fragmentary voices: "I walk slowly but often, sometimes with the camera pointing down to record the voices of people who don't want to be filmed."

The response of the film and the responses in the film become, I'd argue, variations on essayistic knowledge. Serendipitously for my purpose, the film contains a card from Chris Marker with a drawing of a famous cat Guillaume and a memory of his CD-rom *Immemory* in which there is a painting of gleaners following a tank and picking through blood. Images of gleaners then proliferate: Lubtchansky's "chromo-gleaners," embroidered gleaners, advertisement gleaners, stamp gleaners, "gleaners of stardust," and on and on through a representational catalog of seekers after knowledge and meaning in the wake of the world's destruction, loss, and passing. Even Laplanche returns to pinpoint the most

FIGURE 12.2. *Two Years Later* (Varda, 2002) retrieves the essayistic fragments of *The Gleaners and I* as part of an expanding dialogue and reflection.

fundamental quest for knowledge through subjectivity as "psychoanalysis is gleaning": "We pay attention to things that no one else does—what falls from speech," he notes, for the "analyst is also in a state of poverty. . . . poor in knowledge," he seeks to discover, to remake, and to disseminate. Toward the conclusion of the film, the many fragmentary close-ups of hands and other body parts remind Varda of her film *Jacquot de Nantes*, an essay portrait of her dead filmmaker-partner. Here "I refilmed on myself what I had filmed of Jacque Demy. . . . how we work without knowing." In the end, it is precisely this essayistic work without knowing that produces the imperative to know and to think that propels these films and the responses they require. As *Two Years Later* dramatizes so powerfully, essayistic ideas about self and others return, remade, as a dialogic knowledge that continually comes back from other views and viewers.

NOTES

1. André Bazin, "Bazin on Marker," *Film Comment* 39, no. 4 (2003): 44. I focused on this particular moment in the history of the essay film in "'The Forgotten Image between Two Shots': Photos, Photograms, and the Essayistic," in *Still Moving: Between Cinema and Photography*, ed. Karen Beckman and Jean Ma (Durham, N.C.: Duke University Press, 2008) 41–61.

2. Roland Barthes, "Inaugural Lecture, College de France," in *A Barthes Reader*, ed. Susan Sontag (New York: Hill and Wang, 1982), 463–474.

3. See the special issue on "The Moving Picture Lecturer" of *IRIS: A Journal of Theory on Image and Sound*, no. 22 (1996), ed. André Gaudreault and Germain Lacasse. See also Rick Altman, "From Lecturer's Prop to Industrial Product: The Early History of Travel Films," *Virtual Voyages: Cinema and Travel* (Durham, N.C.: Duke University Press, 2006), 61–76.

4. Quoted in Tom Gunning, "*A Corner of Wheat*," *The Griffith Project*, vol. 3, ed. Paolo Cherchi Usai (London: British Film Institute, 1999), 135. Of the increasing amount of scholarly material on the essay film, *Der Weg der Termiten: Beispiele eines Essayistichen Kinos 1909–2004* (Wien: Im Vertrieb des Schuren, 2007) is a useful survey of films that are forerunners or classic examples of the practice from around the globe.

5. Roman Gubern, "Cent ans de cinéma," *Historia general del cinema*, vol. 13, *el cine en la era del audiovisual* (Madrid: Catedra, 1995), 278

6. Sergei Eisenstein, "Notes for a Film of 'Capital,'" trans. Maciej Sliwowski, Jay Leuda, and Annette Michelson, *October* 2 (1976): 10.

7. Stella Bruzzi, *New Documentary: A Critical Introduction*, 2d ed. (London: Routledge, 2006), 58.

8. At the center of precursive essay films are larger debates about the mass cultural status of the movies and its social and intellectual potential is the representational confrontation between the technological image and language as expression. If film form has always reflected modernist concerns with spatial fragmentation and temporal motions, early association with mass culture tended to undermine film's radical potentials for subjective expression and interpretation and reshape them as realist transparencies or later versions of propaganda films.

9. Laura Rascaroli, "The Essay Film: Problems, Definitions, Textual Commitments," *Framework* 49, no. 2 (2008): 36.

10. Jean Epstein, "The Senses I," *French Film Theory and Criticism*, vol. 1, *1907–1929*, ed. Richard Abel (Princeton, N.J.: Princeton University Press, 1988), 244.

11. James Donald et al., eds., *Close-Up, 1927–1933: Cinema and Modernism* (Princeton, N.J.: Princeton University Press, 1998), 292. See also Vincent Pinel, *Introduction au Ciné-club: histoire, théorie, pratique du Ciné-club en France* (Paris: Editions Ouvrieres, 1964).

12. Alan Potamkin, "The Ritual of the Movies," in *The Compound Cinema: The Film Writings of Harry Alan Potamkin*, ed. Lewis Jacobs (New York: Teachers College Press, 1977), 220.

13. Kelly Conway, "'A New Wave of Spectators': Contemporary Responses to *Cleo from 5 to 7*," *Film Quarterly* 61, no. 1 (2007): 38, 41.

14. Jim Leach, "The Poetics of Propaganda: Humphrey Jennings and *Listen to Britain*," in *Documenting the Documentary: Close Readings of Documentary Film and Video*, ed. Barry Keith Grant and Jeannette Sloniowski (Detroit, Mich.: Wayne State University Press, 1980), 157, 159, 164.

15. See Edward Lowry, *The Filmology Movement and Film Study in France* (Ann Arbor, Mich.: UMI, 1985).

16. André Malraux, *Esquisse d'une psychologie du cinéma* (Paris: Gallimard, 1946), 14.

17. Hans Richter, "Der Film Essay: Eine neue Form des Dokumentarfilms," *Nationalzeitung*, supplement, May 25, 1940. Reprinted in *Schreiben Bilder Sperechen*, ed. Christa Blumlinger and Constantin Wulff (Vienna: Sonderzahl, 1992), 195.

18. Paul Arthur, "Essay Questions," *Film Comment* 39, no. 1 (2003): 62.

19. Sandy Flitterman-Lewis, "Documenting the Ineffable: Terror and Memory in Alain Resnais's *Night and Fog*," in *Documenting the Documentary: Close Readings of*

Documentary Film and Video, ed. Barry Keith Grant and Jeannette Sloniowski (Detroit, Mich.: Wayne State University Press, 1998), 215.

20. Alexandre Astruc, "The Birth of the New Avant-Garde: The Caméra-Stylo," in *Film and Literature: An Introduction and Reader*, ed. Timothy Corrigan (Upper Saddle River, N.J.: Prentice-Hall, 1999), 159.

21. It is worth noting that the so-called Left Bank of the French New Wave (Marker, Resnais, Varda, and others) figure more naturally in the formation of the essay film because of their consistent interest in film's interdisciplinary connections with literature and the other arts, yet a wide range of other filmmakers, inside and outside France, respond to the possibilities of the essay films.

22. André Bazin, *What Is Cinema?* vol. 1 (Berkeley: University of California Press, 1967), 142.

23. Tom Milne, ed., *Godard on Godard* (New York: Viking, 1972), 115. Always the contrarian, at another point Godard denounces the short films for reasons that, I'd argue, make the relation of the short film and the essayistic so important: "A short film does not have the time to *think*" (110).

24. François Porcile, *Défense du court métrage français* (Paris: Les Editions du Cerf, 1965), 19. The potential and importance of the short film in turn anticipate one of the most fertile and productive forums for the essayistic and its relation to the sketch: anthology or compilation films, such as *Loin du Vietnam* / *Far from Vietnam* (1967), *Deutschland im Herbst* / *Germany in Autumn* (1978), and *Lumière et compagnie* / *Lumière and Company* (1995).

25. Guy Fihman, "L'Essai cinématographique et ses transformations expérimentales," *L'Essai et le cinéma*, ed. Suzanne Liandrat-Guigues and Murielle Gagnebin (Paris: Champs Vallon, 2004), 44–46. Indeed, these two dimensions align the essay film with that important other precedent, the British essayist Francis Bacon, whose pithy essays counterpoint Montaigne at about the same point in history but pursue a more scientific inquiry into the ethics of living.

26. Jacques Rivette, "Letter on Rossellini," in *Cahiers du Cinéma, the 1950s: Neo-Realism, Hollywood, New Wave*, ed. Jim Hillier (Cambridge, Mass.: Harvard University Press, 1985), 194–199.

27. See Conway, "'A New Wave of Spectators.'"

28. Noël Burch, *Theory of Film Practice* (Princeton, N.J.: Princeton University Press, 1981), 159–162.

13

THE CLOUD-CAPPED STAR: RITWIK GHATAK ON THE HORIZON OF GLOBAL ART CINEMA

Manishita Dass

"It wouldn't be an exaggeration to call the maverick Bengali filmmaker Ritwik Ghatak (1925–1976) one of the most neglected major filmmakers in the world," film critic Jonathan Rosenbaum wrote in November 2008.[1] Twelve years earlier, announcing the first ever major retrospective of Ghatak's films in the United States (organized under the aegis of the New York Film Festival in 1996) in a brief write-up in the *Village Voice*, J. Hoberman lamented Ghatak's "scandalously obscure" status.[2] In a *Sight and Sound* article published in 1982, fourteen years before Hoberman's lament and the New York retrospective, the British critic Derek Malcolm described the thrill experienced by Western critics on discovering a major unsung talent at a film festival in Madras four years previously, less than two years after Ghatak's untimely death at the age of fifty-one:

> The prints were tattered, the subtitles virtually unreadable when they were there at all, and the projection was below even Indian standards. But the impact of the films on all present was considerable. Here, we all felt, was a passionate and intensely national filmmaker who seemed to have found his way without much access to the work of others but who was most certainly of international calibre.[3]

The history of Ghatak's reception in the West (especially in the United States) is punctuated by such moments of discovery and rediscovery, none of which seem to have succeeded in fully bringing his work out of the shadows of "scandalous" obscurity for good, thereby leaving the door open for the next burst of critical interest and epiphanic illumination. This curious pattern might be attributed, in part, to the rather long shadow cast by the international reputation of Ghatak's contemporary Satyajit Ray, whose films have come to epitomize "Indian art cinema" to the world. Ray's directorial career spanned thirty-six films, a measure of commercial success, and a host of national awards and international accolades including prizes at international film festivals, an Honorary Award from the Academy of Motion Picture Arts and Sciences (popularly known as a lifetime achievement Oscar), and the honor of being voted by members of the British Film Institute as one of the three greatest directors of world cinema. Ghatak, on the other hand, continuously struggled with market forces, institutional indifference, political opposition, and personal demons in order to finance and complete films throughout his filmmaking career of over twenty-five years, and left behind eight feature films and a few documentaries, a slew of unfinished projects, and the public image of a man with a prodigious talent for both filmmaking and self-destruction.

In a 1997 *Film Comment* profile of Ghatak, titled "Subcontinental Divide: The Undiscovered Art of Ritwik Ghatak," Jacob Levich contrasts Ghatak's authorial persona and cinematic oeuvre with Ray's, comparing the erratic brilliance and often perplexing nature of Ghatak's work to the reassuring accessibility and even tenor of Ray's films:

> If Satyajit Ray was the suitable boy of Indian art cinema—unthreatening, career-oriented, reliably tasteful—Ritwik Ghatak, his contemporary and principal rival, was its problem child. Where Ray's films are seamless, exquisitely rendered, conventional narratives that aim for the kind of psychological insights prized by 19th century novelists, Ghatak's are ragged, provisional, intensely personal, yet epic in shape, scope, and aspirations. With Ray, you feel safe in the hands of an omniscient, authoritative master. Viewing Ghatak is an edgy, intimate experience, an engagement with a brilliantly erratic intelligence in an atmosphere of inquiry, experimentation, and disconcerting honesty. The feeling can be invigorating, but never comfortable.[4]

While the terms of this contrast (which resonate with popular perceptions of Ray and Ghatak in India) obscure the common context that Ray and Ghatak shared, they also throw into relief a crucial difference between the two directors—in terms of their transcultural accessibility and emotional impact—that provides a clue as to why Ghatak still languishes in relative obscurity or, to borrow a metaphor from one of his films, continues to be a "cloud-capped star" on the horizon of global art cinema.

As the following statement by Peter Wollen indicates, the first encounter with Ghatak's films can be fairly disconcerting for a viewer not acquainted with the director's specific context or distinctive approach to filmmaking:

> When I first came across Ritwik Ghatak's films about ten years ago, I was puzzled. I was very impressed by them, but I did not know how to approach

them. It was only later that I discovered that Ghatak was not only a director, but also in his own idiosyncratic way, a teacher and a theorist. As I have read his writings, I have not only come to appreciate his films more, but I have also realized that his outlook on filmmaking is one which has begun to affect my own thinking.[5]

Wollen's initial bafflement and the discomfort that Levich identifies as being central to the viewing experience offered by Ghatak's films are generated, in part, by their eclectic mix of neorealist strategies and melodramatic clichés, leftist critique and creative appropriation of Indian folklore/mythology, sentimental excess and avant-garde formalism (e.g., Eisensteinian editing techniques, Brechtian alienation effects, an intricate and often contrapuntal layering of images and sounds), internationalist impulses and local nuances—a blend that cannot be easily accommodated within conventional paradigms of "art cinema."

To the extent that these paradigms filter out lowbrow genre elements on the one hand and avant-garde impulses on the other, or see these as mutually exclusive and rely on a notion of art cinema as an elevated national cinema with international legibility, they cannot come to terms with the unruly energy of Ghatak's films, which are at once intensely personal and deeply political, shaped by a cosmopolitan cinematic and critical sensibility (informed, for instance, by idiosyncratic readings of Marx, Jung, European film theorists, and the films of Sergei Eisenstein and Luis Buñuel) yet steeped in Bengali history, literature, folkways, and culture, and equally indebted to the popular and the experimental. The rhetorical complexity, stylistic hybridity, and cultural density of these films not only resist easy interpretation or categorization but also force us to reevaluate the boundaries of "art cinema" in a global context. While an exhaustive survey of Ghatak's oeuvre is obviously beyond the scope of this essay, I will—through an overview of his filmmaking career and a brief analysis of *Meghe Dhaka Tara / The Cloud-Capped Star* (1960)—outline some of the challenges that his films pose to prevalent understandings of art cinema.

Ritwik Kumar Ghatak was born in 1925 into an upper-middle-class Bengali family in Dhaka in East Bengal (now Bangladesh) and moved to Calcutta as a young student in the early 1940s. There he would witness thousands of refugees from the countryside and especially from East Bengal—uprooted by the manmade famine of 1943, the ravages of World War II, and then by the communal violence preceding the Partition of India in 1947, and the Partition itself—pour into the city, irrevocably changing both the urban landscape and the fabric of Bengali society. The political turmoil of these years radicalized Ghatak, who became a Marxist activist by 1946, gravitating toward the Indian Peoples' Theatre Association (IPTA), the cultural wing of the Communist Party of India (CPI). He worked within IPTA as an actor, playwright, and director until ideological conflicts and his discomfiture with party orthodoxies led him to leave the organization in 1954.

Ghatak's interest in film dates back to the late 1940s, when he started frequenting the now mythic Paradise Café in south Calcutta, where young, leftist Bengali cineastes and aspiring filmmakers, equally impatient with the conventions of mainstream Indian cinemas and oppressive socioeconomic structures, would gather to discuss films from all around the world and books on filmmaking that pointed toward alternative, socially engaged modes of film practice.[6] In subsequent interviews, he credited the incipient film society movement that both fueled and was fueled by such discussions, as well as films such as Eisenstein's *Battleship Potemkin*, Vsevolod Pudovkin's *Mother*, and the Italian neorealist films screened at India's first international film festival in 1952, and the writings of Eisenstein, Pudovkin, Alexander Dovzhenko, Ivor Montagu, and Béla Balázs (among others) with "opening up a completely new world" before his eyes.[7] The emerging alternative film culture of Calcutta in the 1940s and 1950s, shaped by a cosmopolitan outlook and a desire to bring about fundamental changes in Bengali and Indian cinema, provided a common context for Ghatak's as well Ray's initial forays in filmmaking, even though their stylistic paths would soon diverge.

Ghatak's direct involvement with cinema began in 1949–1950, when he assisted director Manoj Bhattacharya on his film *Tathapi* / *Nonetheless* (1950) and acted in and assisted in the making of Nemai Ghosh's *Chinnamul* / *The Uprooted* (1950). The latter film anticipated the neorealist style (before the director and his colleagues encountered the Italian neorealist films) in its depiction of the predicament of a group of displaced peasants adrift in Calcutta and in its use of location shooting and nonprofessional actors. Ghatak's first completed film, *Nagarik* / *The Citizen*, signaled his thematic preoccupation with the Partition's aftermath; shot in 1952–1953 on a shoestring budget, it traced the downwardly mobile trajectory and growing politicization of a lower-middle-class Bengali family uprooted by the Partition and was acclaimed as a bold experiment in social realism by his contemporaries such as Ray. However, *Nagarik* failed to find commercial distribution during Ghatak's lifetime and was released for the first time in 1977, twenty-four years after its completion, and almost two years after Ghatak's death.

In the six years that elapsed before Ghatak made his second film, he worked briefly in the Bombay film industry (the epicenter of Indian commercial cinema) as a scriptwriter and assistant director, even scripting a major box-office hit, *Madhumati* (Roy, 1958). On his return to Calcutta, Ghatak directed *Ajantrik* / *Pathetic Fallacy* (1957), which focused on a cab driver's emotional attachment to his ramshackle old car; *Bari Theke Paliye* (1958), which explores postindependence, post-Partition Calcutta from the perspective of a young runaway; *Meghe Dhaka Tara*, which traces the sacrifices of the eldest daughter of a refugee family from East Bengal; *Komal Gandhar*/*E-Flat* (1961), a quasi-autobiographical, backstage drama about the travails of a leftist theater group that also functions as an allegorical commentary on the division of Bengal; and *Subarnarekha* / *The Golden Line* (completed in 1962, released in 1965), which narrates the story of two siblings whose lives are disrupted by the Partition and warped by a haunting sense of loss, irrational prejudices, and tragic coincidences. All but *Meghe Dhaka Tara* were commercial failures, and their critical reception was mixed, at best. Critics were, for the most part, baffled by Ghatak's cinematic idiom, at once fiercely formalist and excessively melodramatic, conforming neither to the hegemonic styles of Bombay cinema and mainstream Bengali cinema nor to the emerging modernist-realist aesthetic of restraint pioneered by Ray that was setting the parameters of art cinema in India. Alcoholism and nervous breakdowns also had plagued him since the early 1960s, contributing further to his predicament. As a result, Ghatak found it increasingly difficult to find financing for his projects, or to complete the ones that he had started. He joined the newly established Film and Television Institute of India (India's first state-run film school) in 1964 and during his short stint there (1964–1965), first as a lecturer and then as the assistant director, left a lasting impact on a group of students who would go on to become key figures in the "New Indian Cinema" of the 1970s and the 1980s (e.g., Mani Kaul, John Abraham, Kumar Shahani, et al.). While he made a number of government-funded short and documentary films between 1967 and 1971, he would complete only two more feature-length films: *Titash Ekti Nadir Nam/A River Called Titash* (shot in 1971–1973 in Ghatak's beloved East Bengal, now Bangladesh, released in 1973), a lyrical evocation of the lifestyle and ultimate dissolution of a fishing community in Bangladesh, and the essayistic, explicitly autobiographical *Jukti Takko Gappo / Reason, Debate, and a Story* (shot in 1974, posthumously released in 1977), in which Ghatak casts himself as a frustrated, alcoholic intellectual and tries to articulate his politics of dissent and artistic credo against the volatile political backdrop of Bengal in the early 1970s. *Jukti Takko Gappo* turned out to be Ghatak's last testament to what he often described as his "troubled times." His health ravaged by years of alcoholism, emotional pain, and a bout of tuberculosis, Ghatak died in Calcutta at the age of fifty-one on February 6, 1976, before the film could be released.

True to his ironic predictions, Ghatak's critical reputation has soared in India in the years since his death. While this upward swing has not yet succeeded in dispelling "the threat of oblivion" that still looms over his cinematic legacy or prompted concerted efforts to rescue the master negatives and soundtracks of Ghatak's films from the ravages of time and sustained neglect, Ghatak's shadow now looms large over the landscape of India's alternative film culture.[8] He has become a legendary figure, mythologized as a cinematic prophet and tortured genius, revered among Indian cineastes as one of the few truly radical figures in the history of South Asian cinema for his attempt to reinvent film language from a uniquely Bengali standpoint and embraced as a mascot by a younger generation of leftist and experimental filmmakers and cineastes in their quasi-Oedipal rebellion against Satyajit Ray's aesthetic of restraint, seamless realism, and liberal humanism.

Interestingly enough, especially given his posthumous canonization as a filmmaker's filmmaker, Ghatak consistently denied having any special fondness for cinema and claimed that he had been drawn to the medium as a means of reaching a much wider audience than he could through theater:

> I liked theater because it could create an immediate reaction but soon even that seemed inadequate and limited. When we did street theater, we could reach out to four to five thousand people at most. That's when I thought of cinema and of how it could viscerally affect millions of people at once. That's how I came into films . . . not because I wanted to make films. Tomorrow if I could find a better

medium, I would throw away cinema. I don't love films. . . . I have used the
cinema as a weapon, as a medium to express my views.[9]

Despite his oft-repeated protestations about his immunity from cinephilia, Ghatak's
films and writings on film are animated by a heightened awareness of film form and a
passionate interest in experimenting with it, in "trying to find the limit, the end, the
border, up to which the expression of film can go."[10] His experimental urge was also a
deeply political one, stemming as it did from what he described as his "commitment to
contemporary reality" and his desire to "portray my country and the sorrows and
suffering of my people to the best of my ability."[11] Looking back on his films in 1965,
he described his experiments as "groping to find the most proper expression to the
theme at hand," with varying degrees of success.[12]

Ghatak's cinematic experiments were driven by a thematic obsession with the
Partition of the Indian subcontinent in 1947, which led to the creation of the new
sovereign nation-states of India and Pakistan and was accompanied by widespread
communal violence (resulting in the deaths of approximately 500,000–1 million
people), and one of the largest population transfers in modern history (involving an
estimated 12–15 million people). Like many others of his generation, he was deeply
disturbed by the way in which the Partition seemed to negate or vitiate the promise of
independence and continued to agonize over its far-reaching social, cultural, and
political consequences, especially for the people of Bengal, his home province and one
of the regions hardest hit by the Partition. Undivided Bengal, which occupied a total
area of 78,389 square miles and was perceived in British India as a region where
religious differences (between the Hindu and Muslim segments of the population)
were subsumed within a Bengali cultural and linguistic identity, was carved into two
separate territorial entities in 1947: the Muslim-majority East Bengal, which formed
the eastern wing of Pakistan, and West Bengal, which became a state of the federal
republic of India. Bengal's much-vaunted cultural unity lay in tatters, unraveled by
sectarian sentiments and violence, and overnight Bengalis such as Ghatak, who lived
in or migrated to West Bengal but had deep roots in East Bengal (or vice versa), saw
part of their homeland become a foreign country. While nearly 42 percent of undivided
Bengal's Hindu population remained in East Pakistan at first, continuing communal
tensions led to a steady influx of Hindu refugees into West Bengal from 1948 onward,
creating staggering problems of resettlement by the 1950s and exacerbating the
socioeconomic troubles of an already overcrowded, resource-strapped state. This
process continued throughout the 1960s; in 1981, the number of East Bengal refugees
in the state was estimated to be 8 million, or one-sixth of the population.[13] A large
number of these refugees settled in or around the city of Calcutta, in ramshackle
refugee camps and shantytowns, and struggled to rebuild their lives with little or no
assistance from the state. The government's failure to create an effective refugee
rehabilitation program not only impinged on the everyday lives of millions of displaced
Bengalis but also significantly contributed to West Bengal's economic decline, political
turmoil, and social anomie in the post-1947 period.

The post-independence plight of a "divided, debilitated Bengal" haunted Ghatak; it was a plight made all the more poignant by his memories of the cultural and political vibrancy of Bengal in the 1930s:

> In our boyhood, we have seen a Bengal, whole and glorious. Rabindranath, with his towering genius, was at the height of his literary creativity, while Bengali literature was experiencing a fresh blossoming with the works of the Kallol group, and the national movement had spread wide and deep into schools and colleges and the spirit of youth. Rural Bengal, still reveling in its fairytales, *panchalis*, and its thirteen festivals in twelve months, throbbed with the hope of a new spurt of life. This was the world that was shattered by the War, the Famine, and when the Congress and the Muslim League brought disaster to the country and tore it into two to snatch for it a fragmented independence. Communal riots engulfed the country. . . . Our dreams faded away. We crashed on our faces, clinging to a crumbling Bengal, divested of its glory. What a Bengal remained, with poverty and immorality as our daily companions, with blackmarketeers and dishonest politicians ruling the roost, and men doomed to horror and misery![14]

In almost all of Ghatak's films, and especially in the three films that came to be seen as constituting his Partition trilogy—*Meghe Dhaka Tara*, *Komal Gandhar*, and *Subarnarekha*, the foundational national trauma of the Indian subcontinent is seen through the lens of a specific regional reality: his preoccupation with the corrosive impact of the Partition on the intimate and quotidian aspects of middle-class life in post-independence Bengal. He took it upon himself "to present to the public eye the crumbling appearance of a divided Bengal, to awaken the Bengalis to an awareness of their state and a concern for their past and the future."[15] He was trying, thus, to forge a cinematic idiom capable of not only registering the devastating emotional impact and continuing aftershocks of a historical trauma often assumed to be beyond the scope of conventional codes of representation, but also of jolting Bengali viewers (his primary target audience) into a critical engagement with their contemporary reality. This dual objective partly accounts for the stylistic hybridity and perplexing (at times frustrating) nature of his films, which ultimately veer away from the representational logic of humanist realism on the one hand and the purely affective transactions of melodrama on the other, while drawing on both.

This dynamic oscillation marks the Partition trilogy, in which Ghatak most vehemently articulated his anger and anguish over the disintegration of Bengal. The political critique and emotional charge of these films are refracted through the generic conventions of domestic melodrama and centered around the figure of a young woman— quiet, sensitive, yet strong, resilient, and infinitely patient—who becomes, in these films, a melancholic embodiment of contemporary Bengal and of all that was lost through the Partition. All three films share a somber storyline (*Meghe Dhaka Tara* and *Subarnarekha* more than *Komal Gandhar*, which is probably Ghatak's most optimistic film) and a neorealist concern with evoking the minute, everyday details of displaced lives, but their realist surface is visually and aurally inscribed with a range of regionally specific mythic and cultural references, and repeatedly torn apart by a striking use of melodramatic excess, a modernist aesthetic of fragmentation, and an insistent self-reflexivity.

Meghe Dhaka Tara (arguably the only one of Ghatak's films that enjoyed a modicum of both commercial and critical success during his lifetime), for instance, evokes, in grim and painstaking detail, the day-to-day life of a displaced lower-middle-class family from East Bengal struggling to survive in a refugee settlement on the outskirts of Calcutta in the 1950s. The eldest daughter, Neeta, who is the protagonist of the film, bears the burden of keeping the family financially afloat even though she is still at university herself. Her older brother Shankar, who would normally have assumed the responsibility of supporting the family, spends his days practicing classical Indian music and dreaming of becoming a great singer, with the encouragement of Neeta, who believes him to be a genius. Neeta's mother, a woman embittered and hardened by her experience of drastic downward class mobility and the daily struggle of making ends meet, constantly worries about what would happen to the family if and when Neeta leaves home to marry her longtime suitor, Sanat. He is an ex-student of her father's and a research scientist who describes Neeta as "a cloud-capped star" ["*meghe dhaka tara*"] in one of his letters to her: "I didn't appreciate your worth at first. I thought you were like others. But now I see you in the clouds, perhaps a cloud-capped star veiled by circumstances, your aura dimmed." This romantic metaphor acquires a poignant irony as the film progresses and a chain of events not only reveals the shallowness of Sanat's appreciation of Neeta but also invests this seemingly ordinary young woman with a tragically mythic aura.

Through various twists and turns of the plot (mostly, though not entirely, predictable), Neeta finds herself trapped within her dual role as a provider and a nurturer as her family becomes even more dependent on her earnings. Her father, an eccentric schoolmaster emblematic of a bankrupt Bengali liberal humanism, and her younger brother, a mill-worker representative of the newly déclassé Bengali petit-bourgeoisie, both have debilitating accidents and lose their jobs. Now the family's sole breadwinner, Neeta abandons her studies in order to take up full-time employment and postpones her marriage to Sanat. Tired of waiting for Neeta, who cannot bring herself to forsake her family, Sanat embarks on a clandestine relationship with, and ends up marrying, her younger, coquettish sister, Geeta, with the tacit support and connivance of Neeta's mother, who sees this as a perfect solution to her dilemma. An indignant Shankar leaves home in protest, and Neeta's doting father watches helplessly while Neeta continues to shoulder her burden in stoic silence. The stresses and strains of her life eventually take their toll. When Shankar, the older brother, returns from Bombay after having established his reputation as an accomplished classical singer, he finds Neeta wasting away with tuberculosis, a condition that she has somehow managed to conceal from the rest of the family. He whisks her away to a sanatorium in the hills that she has dreamt of visiting throughout the film, but it is too late to save her.

As even this barebones synopsis makes clear, home in this film—especially for Neeta—is no longer a haven in a heartless world but a site of entrapment, exploitation, and alienation. This is emphasized not only through the twists and turns of the melodramatic plot, which is a staple of popular Bengali fiction and film in the post-independence period, but through repeated shots of Neeta framed against the bars of a window or looking out through the bars at the world outside, or of her face enclosed within a constricting frame. One of the most dramatic instances of this kind of captive framing occurs at the end of a key sequence about midway through the film, when Neeta pays her boyfriend a surprise visit in his new apartment and discovers that he is now involved with another woman, her own sister; a little later, she will come to realize that her mother has been aiding and abetting this secret romance. As she makes a dazed exit from Sanat's apartment and starts going down the staircase, we hear the nondiegetic sounds of a whiplash on the soundtrack and see Neeta at the right edge of the frame, in a shot taken from an extremely low angle. As she slowly, unseeingly descends the stairs, the camera lingers on her upturned face, gently moving to an extreme close-up as she raises her hand to grasp her throat, as if to stifle a cry. This image dissolves into a shot of the Calcutta skyline and of the shadows in the courtyard of Neeta's house, which seem to engulf and obliterate her face as her eyes close.[16] The city itself and the courtyard, traditionally the center of the Bengali household, here become suffocating spaces of enclosure, ones that can, in fact, be seen as microcosmic versions of a dystopic nation-space. The national, however, enters the frame—as always in these films—only obliquely, through regional references, a fact that Derek Malcolm seems to overlook when he describes Ghatak as "an intensely national filmmaker."[17]

This scene is also a striking example of how the film connects Neeta's drama of homelessness at home to a more collective regional (or even national) predicament through an aesthetic of excess often characterized as melodramatic. Ghatak was quite insistent in his characterization of melodrama as "a deliberate refinement of the dramatic," "a birthright," and "a form" that could be effectively deployed to confront audiences with the underlying contradictions of their everyday reality, and to promote an active, interventionist spectatorship. He drew on his experience in leftist street theater, the writings of Brecht and Stanislavski, conventions of Bengali and Hindi melodramatic fiction, theater, and film, and the work of his two cinematic heroes, Eisenstein and Buñuel, to create a style that is simultaneously modernist and melodramatic. Ghatak's stylistic signature is marked by an abundance of extreme camera angles, shifting frames, frequent use of rack focus, unexpected close-ups, and a wide-angle lens, exaggerated chiaroscuro effects, a disorienting blend of naturalistic and expressionistic performance styles, a self-reflexive use of melodramatic clichés like coincidences, the suffering of the virtuous, and acoustic underscoring, and perhaps most strikingly, an intricate layering of images with songs, dialogue, and sound effects. His self-conscious and hyperbolic deployment of the already hyperbolic mode of the melodramatic lays bare its formal operations, arresting the dramatic flow and rending the fabric of realist representation rather than merely facilitating a sentimental identification with an individual's predicament.

In the scene on the stairs described previously, for instance, the extravagance of the nondiegetic acoustics of the whiplash disrupts our illusionistic absorption in Neeta's story and can prompt a viewer familiar with the history of contemporary Bengal to read the betrayal perpetrated by Sanat and Neeta's family in the context of the larger sociopolitical betrayals and injustices that led to the Partition. This is only one in a series of melodramatic jolts that create distance and compel reflection rather than allowing us to drift along with the narrative flow, as in a classic realist film, or a tide of sentimental identification, as in more conventional melodrama. We hear the sound of the whiplash again at the end of the most gut-wrenching sequences in the film, the visceral impact of which, however, relies, in part, on a specific kind of cultural knowledge on the part of the audience. One night shortly before Neeta's sister is about to get married to Sanat, Shankar informs Neeta of his decision to leave the household as a gesture of protest against the family's treatment of her. Instead of responding to his statement, she asks him to teach her a song, as she would be expected to sing at the wedding. A visibly disturbed Shankar lashes out at her for accepting her fate in silence but teaches her a song by Rabindranath Tagore, a writer who had dominated early-twentieth-century Bengali literature and whose songs are an integral part of the everyday lives of middle-class Bengali families: *Je rate more duarguli bhanglo jhare* ("The night the storm tore down my door"), a song about intense suffering and desolation that nonetheless holds out the hope of eventual transcendence through suffering.

As Shankar starts to sing and Neeta joins in, the camera slowly dollies away from them, to a long shot of the pair from across the dimly lit room, and then moves back and forth between the siblings, eventually resting its gaze on Neeta, now seen in isolation against a dark background. The climactic image—a low-angle, medium close-up of Neeta's upturned face—is shimmeringly beautiful in its play of light and shadow and rendered almost ethereal by the soaring yet melancholy strains of the accompanying song. But as the song comes to a close, Neeta clutches her neck with her hands in a now familiar gesture of pain and seems to gasp for air, as if flayed by the sound of a whiplash that again comes up on the soundtrack and grows louder, almost mocking the promise of redemption offered by the Tagore song. For the first time in the film, Neeta breaks down in tears, sobbing uncontrollably, her sobs mingling with the melancholy strains of a *sarod*. Once again, Ghatak's use of the extradiegetic sound of the whiplash manages wordlessly to convey not only Neeta's suffering but also a sense of the lacerating historical and social forces responsible for her individual predicament and the collective wounds that she comes to embody.

Later on in the film, when Neeta's father learns of her terminal illness, he shouts out, "I accuse" (in English), in a patently melodramatic manner, his arm outstretched, finger pointing toward the audience. Neeta's older brother wheels around toward him and asks accusingly, "Whom?" In response, the father only mumbles, "No one," as his lips quiver and his hand comes trembling down. Again, the film uses a melodramatic moment to implicate the audience in Neeta's fate, blaming it not just on the oppressive structures of the family but also on wider networks of exploitation in post-independence, post-Partition Bengal.

The melodramatic note reaches its highest pitch in the penultimate sequence of the film, in which Neeta's brother visits her at the sanatorium in the mountains. While they both know that her tuberculosis is at an advanced stage and possibly incurable, Shankar tries to distract her with cheerful chitchat about the family, especially about the mischievous antics of their nephew—Geeta and Sanat's son, now a toddler. Suddenly, the usually serene and stoic Neeta cries out, "But I did want to live!" and breaks down, clinging to her brother, imploring him to assure her that she will live: "Please tell me that I'll live, just tell me once that I'll live!" Her desperate cry echoes through the landscape, overlaid by the sound of the whiplash and a harsh droning noise, as the camera pans across the surrounding mountains in a dizzying 360-degree turn. Her disembodied voice reverberates in the landscape even after her visual image disappears from the screen, evoking the thwarted desires and shattered dreams of a generation caught in the crossfire of history. Through this hypermelodramatic articulation of Neeta's desire to live, Ghatak not only expresses his personal anguish over the Partition but also registers his protest against what he deemed to be a mockery of independence and the ongoing destruction of a collective way of life. Melodrama thus becomes a formal device for turning his sense of pain and disenchantment into unsettling social critique, and for using an excess of emotional affect to force a close reading of the image and to generate an intellectual awareness of the collective dimensions of Neeta's predicament.

Instead of ending on that high pitch, however, the film follows Shankar back home to the refugee settlement. We see him, alone, in a landscape that we have come to associate with Neeta, and then we follow his gaze to watch an unnamed young woman trudging wearily down a path that Neeta had walked many times in the film, dressed in a manner similar to Neeta's. She pauses for a moment to gaze ruefully at her broken sandal, as Neeta had done in an earlier moment in the film. The camera stays with her for a moment, then returns to Shankar, who covers his face with his hands, as if to block out this poignant visual reminder that Neeta's tragic saga was not an isolated one but reflected the experience of countless other young Bengali women like her and was doomed to repeat itself, time and again, right before our unseeing eyes, hidden in plain sight.

Ghatak's politically motivated use of melodrama is thus marked by a constant negotiation between the clichéd devices of popular melodrama, the critical impulse of the neorealist aesthetic, and the rigors of formal experimentation. The narrative and stylistic regimes of social realism, while painstakingly established, are also repeatedly challenged and fragmented by formal strategies that not only transform the mundane into the mythic but often perform the very limits of representation itself, simultaneously acknowledging the difficulty of representing the historical trauma of the Partition and defiantly asserting the need to keep trying to do so. Ghatak's use of sound is particularly notable in this respect. Repeatedly, the soundtrack serves to destabilize the image by endowing it with the at times unbearable noise/weight of history. In an early sequence in *Meghe Dhaka Tara*, a passing train thunders across the background of a shot as Neeta sits with Sanat by the river, drowning out their conversation entirely with the clatter of its wheels, piercing whistle, and screeching brakes. The noise of the train, unreasonably loud given the distance between the train and the couple, seems to overwhelm the protocols of verisimilitude and surges through the soundtrack with an unstoppable force. It is reminiscent of an emblematic sequence from *Komal Gandhar*, in which the camera hurtles down an abandoned railroad track abruptly truncated at the India-East Pakistan border, as a chorus of women's voices chant "Dohai Ali" (a chant used by boatmen in East Bengal as a ritualized entreaty to gods or to nature to save them from destruction) on the soundtrack. The camera picks up momentum as the chants grow increasingly desperate, and finally flings itself against the buffer at the end of the track, when the chant is drowned out by the sound of an explosion and the scene goes black.

Moments such as these abound in Ghatak's films, when the narrative is wrenched apart from the exigencies of dramatic action, and the continuum of realist time and space is blasted wide open by melodramatic spectacle and/or sound. These extraordinary moments of visual and/or aural rupture combine with the affective charge of melodrama to force a close reading of the image on the screen and of the soundtrack. Ghatak hoped that this process would provoke viewers to interrogate their habitual images of reality and confront them with the need to critically engage with the collective loss of home brought about by the Partition and with a present haunted and rendered unhomely by that devastating loss. Neither the affective responses elicited by his films nor their formal experimentation are ends in themselves but serve as triggers for a critical engagement with both cinematic image and traumatic experience.

Once decried as bizarre, decadent, and self-indulgent, the stylistic mélange that gives Ghatak's films their disruptive force has come to be seen, in the writings of critics such as Kumar Shahani, Ashis Rajadhyakshya, and Geeta Kapur, as the mark of Ghatak's avant-gardist sensibility, and as an inextricable part of his political critique.[18] Such readings, however, have not secured a more prominent place for Ghatak in the canon of global art cinema (at least insofar as it is manifested in the undergraduate or even graduate curriculum in Anglo-American film studies, where Ray still reigns supreme as the primary representative of Indian art cinema) partly because these critics attempt to claim Ghatak for the alternative canon of Third Cinema, constructed in opposition to profit-oriented cinemas on the one hand and auteur-oriented art cinema on the other. Such an approach, however, not only fails to take into account Ghatak's undeniable status as an auteur, the auteurist mythmaking that inflects our reception of his films, the contexts that he shares with Ray, and the ways in which his films are now categorized in India as "art films," but also relies on rather narrow definitions of art cinema and of politics.

What happens if, rather than taking the category of "art cinema" as a given, we use Ghatak's films to prise it open and to question some of the formal and geopolitical assumptions embedded in it, and to explore its historicity (both in the Indian and the international contexts)? If we define art cinema, as the editors of this volume do in their introduction, as a quintessentially impure mode of practice, shaped by an oscillation between realist and modernist tendencies, auteurist impulses and constructions, a plethora of formal surpluses that mark the image as image, and a desire for a hybrid spectator "both intellectually engaged and emotionally affected," Ghatak's films would definitely qualify.[19] However, how does Ghatak's use of emotional excess and the formal and affective elements of a critically denigrated lowbrow genre such as melodrama, conventionally seen as being antithetical to the aesthetic of art cinema, fit into this critical schema? Moreover, what do we do with the fact that much of the emotional affect and intellectual impact of these films depend on very specific cultural knowledge, for instance, knowledge of the specificities of Bengal's regional history, Partition's impact on Bengali society, the Bengali middle-class habitus, the folk music of East Bengal, the songs of Rabindranath Tagore, or the nuances of the Bengali language? Paradoxically enough, many of the leitmotifs and allusions (verbal, visual, historical, mythic, and musical) that make a film such as *Meghe Dhaka Tara* an extremely powerful exploration of displacement, betrayal, social disintegration, and historical trauma, and thus endow it with the potential to resonate across cultural or temporal boundaries, are precisely the elements that can get lost, or at the very least obscured, in translation.

A definition of art cinema predicated on assumptions of international legibility and address thus sits uneasily with films such as Ghatak's. In promoting such a definition, do we run the risk of reinforcing a certain ethnocentric insularity built into conventional understandings of art cinema in the West or of promoting a "sanctioned ignorance" (to borrow an idea from Dipesh Chakrabarty's "Postcoloniality and the Artifice of History") of certain texts, contexts, and histories marked as too "regional" and thus as "peripheral"?[20] Conversely, what do we lose by ignoring the role of regional specificities in the making of films that do travel (such as Satyajit Ray's films, the much-vaunted cosmopolitanism of which is peculiarly Bengali in its provenance) and of the regional roots of national cinemas and global art cinemas? Ghatak's films invite us to reflect on these questions, opening up a space for revising our spectatorial habits and understanding of "global art cinema," and for reconceptualizing the "local" and the "cosmopolitan" as heterogeneous and intertwined, rather than as homogeneous and antithetical, formations.

NOTES

1. Jonathan Rosenbaum, "My Dozen Favorite Non-Region-1 Single-Disc DVDs," available at http://www.dvdbeaver.com/film/articles/dozen_favorite_nonR1_single-disc.htm.

2. J. Hoberman, "Great Leaps Backward," *Village Voice*, September 17, 1996, 37

3. Derek Malcolm, "Tiger: The Films of Ritwik Ghatak," *Sight and Sound* 51, no. 3 (Summer 1982): 184–187.

4. Jacob Levich, "Subcontinental Divide: The Undiscovered Art of Ritwik Ghatak," *Film Comment* 33, no. 2 (March–April 1997): 30–35.

5. Pervaiz Khan, "Ritwik Ghatak and Some Directions for the Future," *Sight and Sound* 1, no. 5 (September 1991): 26.

6. See "Paradise Café" in Mrinal Sen, *Montage: Life, Politics, Cinema* (Calcutta: Seagull, 2002), 105–109.

7. See, for instance, "Interviews," in Ritwik Ghatak, *Rows and Rows of Fences: Ritwik Ghatak on Cinema* (Calcutta: Seagull, 2000), 85.

8. Partha Chatterjee, "Jinxed Legacy," *Frontline*, October 6–29, 2007.

9. Ritwik Ghatak, "Interview," *Chitrabikshan*, August–September 1973, reprinted in *Sakhhat Riwtik*, ed. Shibaditya Dasgupta and Sandeepan Bhattacharya (Calcutta: Deepayan, 2000). My translation.

10. Ghatak, "Experimental Cinema," in *Rows and Rows of Fences*, 30.

11. Ghatak, "Experimental Cinema and I," in ibid., 34.

12. Ghatak, "Film and I," in ibid., 7.

13. Tai Yong Tan and Gyanesh Kudaisya, *The Aftermath of Partition in South Asia* (London: Routledge, 2000), 146

14. Ghatak, "My Films," in *Rows and Rows of Fences*, 49.

15. Ibid., 48.

16. For a detailed and insightful formalist analysis of this scene and other key sequences from *Meghe Dhaka Tara*, see Raymond Bellour, "The Film We Accompany," in *Rouge* 3 (2004). Available at http://www.rouge.com.au/3/film.html (accessed February 1, 2009).

17. Malcolm, "Tiger."

18. See, for instance, Ashish Rajadhyaksha, *Ritwik Ghatak: A Return to the Epic* (Bombay: Screen Unit, 1982); Geeta Kapur, "Articulating the Self into History: Ritwik Ghatak's *Jukti Takko Ar Gappo*," in *When Was Modernism?: Essays in Contemporary Cultural Practice in India* (Delhi: Tulika, 2000); and Kumar Shahani's articles on Ghatak collected in *Ghatak: Arguments/Stories*, ed. Ashish Rajadhyaksha and Amrit Gangar (Bombay: Screen Unit, 1987).

19. See Rosalind Galt and Karl Schoonover's introduction to this volume.

20. Dipesh Chakrabarty, *Provincializing Europe: Postcolonial Thought and Historical Difference* (Princeton, N.J.: Princeton University Press, 2000), 27–46.

14

NOTES ON ART CINEMA AND THE EMERGENCE OF SUB-SAHARAN FILM

Philip Rosen

1

The post–World War II development of art cinema was roughly contemporary with breakthroughs for anticolonial movements in Africa. The end of colonial governance in sub-Saharan Africa is commonly said to have begun with the independence of Ghana from Britain in 1957. Although anticolonial struggles continued in some areas for decades after, by the early 1960s it was clear that something momentous was occurring. In 1960 alone, at least seventeen new states from Africa were admitted to voting membership in the United Nations, most from south of the Sahara. The struggle for political independence and the many victories it now achieved both motivated and enabled the emergence of sub-Saharan cinema.

Thus, if there was an originating heyday of art cinema, when it established itself as a category we now recognize, it certainly included the years during which sub-Saharan African cinema emerged as an identifiable movement. As a matter of film history, art cinema has often been treated as a textual classification, but it is also treated as a rubric for structures of distribution, exhibition, and production. Although there were predecessors, post-World War II art cinema began as a new chapter in the international distribution of narrative films to specialized audiences.[1] In the key market of the United States, for example, its emergence was associated with the success of early Italian neorealism, and it helped give life to smaller cinema houses in a new film-industrial context. At the level of distribution and exhibition, art cinema here appears as something like a branding strategy devised within the difficulties and possibilities of postwar cinema.

But distribution and promotional strategies did also include textual or aesthetic claims: for example, greater realism, breaking cultural or social taboos, and aesthetic innovation in narrative feature filmmaking (see Bordwell's classic accounts of art cinema as a mode of film practice coming into view in the 1950s and 1960s, which in his hands appears as a genre with its own themes and formal tendencies).[2] The institutional and textual levels thus feed off of one another. Developing and exploiting a market for such differentiated films could in turn authorize greater textual flexibility and even experimentation with respect to the norms of narrative fiction filmmaking, as well as the identification of star auteur-artists. Italian neorealism was closely followed by the names that became so familiar in film history textbooks: not only Michelangelo Antonioni and later Federico Fellini, but also by Ingmar Bergman and late Carl Theodor Dreyer, and starting in 1959, the star auteurs of the French New Wave, followed in subsequent decades by other new waves (Brazilian, Australian, Taiwanese, etc.). Audience segments might possess or acquire the cultural capital needed or desired, and this in turn continued to motivate the expansion of exhibition arrangements, as art cinema became a staple not only in specialized theaters in big cities, but also in university classes and theaters near campuses, not to mention a burgeoning film festival circuit. These had predecessors in a range of sites, from prewar cine-clubs to the Venice Film Festival, but became increasingly widespread. Some became relatively permanent modes of cinematic dissemination. Today, for example, there is an abundance of major and minor film festivals that have become part of the global system of film culture and the film business.

Sub-Saharan African cinema was born with decolonization, as the product of distinctive African artists and intellectuals whose ideological and aesthetic predispositions defined it. For many, the processes and promises of independence included a genuinely African culture for a modern age. Indeed, film history up to this moment had coincided with the high tide of colonialism. The worldwide distribution and production oligopoly headquartered since the 1920s in the United States included significant production and distribution strongholds in the major European colonizers of Africa, especially France, Britain, and Germany, and they permitted no effective cinema infrastructure in Africa. For African intellectuals and artists interested in film, it was a given that African life and culture had been distorted by mainstream cinema and popular media, in line with colonialism and racist ideologies, and even affected African audiences. It was also a given that Africans had been excluded from filmmaking for its entire history, except as objects of colonializing and racializing representation. The consequence of these exclusions was not only referential in the sense of incorrect depictions of a real Africa. It was also that screen expressions and constructions by African subjects and informed by African cultural subjectivities were not possible.

With independence, a common response among diverse cultural critics and practitioners across the continent was to envision a cinema whose aesthetic proclivities not only reflected realities of African life, culture, and history, but also drew on African cultural and social practices as opposed to those of the former colonizers. There were of course significant differences among members of the first generation of African cineastes that emerged in the 1960s and early 1970s. The region we identify as sub-Saharan Africa is not only very big, but also its population comprises a large number of ethnicities and languages. The geocultural context is made even more complex by the political boundaries established by the colonizing nations as well their promotion of divisions among the populations. Furthermore, in the absence of a production infrastructure or the long-term commitment of resources to construct one, there were a variety of paths to filmmaking. This can be quickly illustrated by the backgrounds of an arbitrary selection of directors who rose to prominence in the 1960s: Désiré Ecaré (attended the Paris film school IDHEC), Safi Faye (a teacher who worked with Jean Rouch on anthropological films and went on to earn a degree in ethnology), Oumarou Ganda (also worked with Rouch, including acting), Med Hondo (theater), and Ousmane Sembene (an established Francophone novelist, he went to Moscow to study filmmaking).

But it also seemed that these and others who constituted the first generation of African directors had certain things in common, which could lead one to speak of common goals. The way had been prepared by the history of resistance to colonialism, various cultural congresses, and the work of intellectuals around enterprises such as *Présence Africaine*. Furthermore, on a practical level, they all had to negotiate the scarcity of cinematic resources on the continent itself, which was a heritage of colonialism and then exacerbated by neocolonialism. Furthermore, although there was some difference in class and regional or national backgrounds, the filmmakers were generally members of a postcolonial cultural elite, which meant literacy in contrast to the majority of the sub-Saharan population. They might have arrived in this stratum by different routes, but it is probable that almost all of them had some cosmopolitan experiences in the colonial metropole. And then there was the idea of Pan-Africanism, which conceptualized reasons for them to think of themselves as embarked on a common project. This background was especially important for the emergence of sub-Saharan film because the lack of available capital and local or regional distribution-exhibition infrastructure militated toward a cinema of auteurs—writer-directors who spent years getting financing to make a film—rather than any kind of industrial model of production and distribution. But distinctive auteurs were already one of the selling points of art cinema. The art cinema system, which was at its apogee in the 1960s and 1970s, thus offered a venue for films emerging from the contexts of a newly postcolonial Africa.

Ideologically, these filmmakers strongly tended to be aware of at least two overlapping streams of ideas, although in different ways and to different degrees. First, there were national liberation theories and ideologies as well as practices, which conceived of anticolonial and postcolonial political leaders and intellectuals as acting in the interests of "the people," identified with a nation. This suggested a way that cultural producers might understand their own status. The second was the value of specifically African cultural practices, even if modified in a dialectic with non-African or "modernizing" practices that had been denied the people. While there were always local particularities and an idea of the national did not disappear, the interplay of these with Pan-Africanism was a central aspect of African film history, as John Akomfrah has insisted in a remarkable recent article;[3] thus, for example, the cultural dominance of oral narrative was often invoked as a basis for all African narrative cinema, although the films might employ recognizably Senegalese or Malian oral tales, languages, settings, and/or social situations. Such ideas, of course, included some productive logical tensions. On the one hand, for example, national liberation struggle was modernizing, and thus tied to the construction of new cultural practices. On the other hand, it was associated with calls for such cultural practices to be based in practices of the people, which meant deriving them from African traditions. Furthermore, although the call for liberation was grounded in a notion of the nation, it was ultimately part of an international movement, as Frantz Fanon recognized clearly.

Colonialism itself was in effect a global process. (Indeed, several of the theorists of anticolonial national liberation around the world who had a global readership, such as Fanon[4] and Cabral,[5] were African.) So it is not surprising that anticolonial and postcolonial cinemas included a certain transnational consciousness, whatever the specificities within a given colony, nation, or region. Furthermore, the force of cinematic institutions that made it so difficult to make and distribute African films had a global sweep—something especially evident to the filmmakers, faced with the dominance of foreign companies in African distribution sectors. Within international film culture, then, there was mutual awareness among African and non-African "third-world" filmmakers concerned with decolonization, national liberation, and critiques of neocolonialism.

2

For a characterization of art cinema in this kind of global context, one can turn to a famous Latin American manifesto, "Towards a Third Cinema" (1969), by the Argentine filmmakers Fernando Solanas and Ottavio Getino, who were writing as Peronists during a period of political violence.[6] In their conception, first cinema is the global mainstream led and dominated by Hollywood, a consumerist cinema that institutionally and aesthetically displaces genuinely national cinemas. It is naturalized by neocolonial bourgeoisies, who would like to see their own cinemas modeled on it. Third Cinema is the opponent of first cinema. Its leading priority is to produce films according to the needs of the political struggles of the people, or nation, as conceived by national liberation theory. Third cinema is therefore not primarily concerned with aesthetics, but shapes and uses films pragmatically, according to the needs of a specific decolonizing or anti-neocolonial struggle. Since it does not recognize the norms of mainstream film except when they are useful, third cinema may innovate in film language, but only as a byproduct of its first priority. In third cinema, artists and intellectuals—including filmmakers—overcome their social and intellectual separation from the popular strata that are the heart of the nation. This concern with the relation of elite political cadres and cultural producers to the masses along with the foundation of national liberation in the people are Fanonian themes, and there are explicit references to Fanon in "Towards a Third Cinema."

Second Cinema is the equivalent of art cinema; as examples, Solanas and Getino name Brazilian *Cinema Nôvo* and that epitome of a 1960s auteurist art cinema, the French New Wave. Their definitions place it somewhere on a spectrum between first and third cinemas. Solanas and Getino characterize it as a cinema of distinctive auteurs—a cinema progressive only insofar as it enables experiments with "non-standard [film] language." To a limited degree, then, it may contribute to decolonization because it can refuse the naturalization of the norms of first cinema. But it ultimately remains "trapped within the fortress" (this is a citation from Godard). At the infrastructural level, the expenses of making such films mean they require existing marketing networks to recoup costs; hence, they become part of "the System." The consequence for Solanas and Getino is that there are limits to how far any Second Cinema innovations in textual forms and practices can go. Its auteurs and films remain subordinated to the tradition of aesthetics, that is, bourgeois notions such as beauty and universality, rather than functionality in a sociopolitical struggle. The situational functionality of third cinema films abandons such claims to universality, and "the System" cannot digest it.

Given this schema, African cinema should have emerged as a third cinema. This was not just because it came from a decolonized third-world area with a scarcity of filmmaking resources (and as the concept continued to develop, third cinema was not exactly the same thing as a "third world cinema").[7] Nor was it only that some films directly participated in ongoing liberation conflicts, as in the notable example of the newsreels and agitational documentaries of the Mozambique Film Institute, founded in 1976.[8] Interestingly, certain internationally prominent art cinema auteurs, such as Jean-Luc Godard and Ruy Guerra, participated in filmmaking activities and researches of the Mozambique Film Institute. In fact, what became widely known as "African cinema" was often centered on narrative films. However, many of these quickly took on a new critical function still aligned with "the people" of national liberation theory: not only new depictions of African life and histories, but also critiques of the neocolonial social arrangements and neocolonial elites that now governed the new countries. These were often combined with interrogations of internal divisions within African societies and polities, including gender, caste, and class. For example, even what is usually called the first feature fiction film made in an African language, Sembene's *Mandabi* (1968), satirized the greed of the French-speaking Senegalese bureaucracy and middle-level kleptocracy, as well as hierarchies within impoverished African masses, including patriarchal gender relations. But, it should be noted, more somber and respectful depictions of African traditions could still be juxtaposed with contemporary mores, and this in a situation where some intellectuals soon began criticizing a postcolonial governance that some increasingly identified with a neocolonial situation.

Nevertheless, despite this specifically African subject matter, which was sometimes quite rooted in the local, what is now called African cinema survived as something that, infrastructurally at least, looks like Second Cinema, with many globally recognized writer-director auteurs putting together one-off narrative projects, presences at major international film festival circuits, and university tours. Even within sub-Saharan Africa itself there was soon a major film festival of international importance: the historically crucial FESPACO, initiated in Ouagadougou as early as 1969. It represented a specifically Pan-African entry into the global film festival circuit. It was soon supported by the Burkinabe government and has long been a major event.

Yet, the Second Cinema aspects of sub-Saharan Africa also rest on the lack of an African distribution-exhibition network that would feed capital back into local production. This was debilitating. Not only did distribution and exhibition remain dominated by non-African firms and films, but resources necessary for film production were too often available only from the former colonizers. Efforts to establish nationally supported film industries or regional production cooperatives were heroic but achieved only occasional and temporary realization. To this day, there is no broad 35mm feature film industry identified with sub-Saharan Africa. Nevertheless, there are a number of important filmmakers who manage to find financial support for occasional films and generally achieve limited distribution, often in international festivals and specialty exhibition house circuits outside of Africa—in short, in the manner of Second Cinema. For example, in Francophone areas, which quantitatively dominated the first generation of African films, it is well known that many filmmakers received funds from cinema bureaus of the French Ministry of Cooperation, which had its own conditions for financing and even sometimes formal or stylistic parameters.[9] (This funding process, which was probably first motivated in connection with the specifically French notion of a Francophone cultural sphere, lasted in different forms for decades.) The more things changed, the more the structures seemed analogous. By the 1980s, Euro-TV was a major source of funding for African narrative filmmaking. In this situation, to be a recognized auteur is an advantage. But major filmmakers would sometimes have to spend years raising financing before they could make their films, much like diasporic and independent filmmakers.

Despite all this, it is universally recognized by critics, scholars, and, perhaps most importantly, by the filmmakers themselves that there is by now a decades-long lineage of "African cinema." Yet it is a cinema that remained dependent on non-African finance. This splitting has, inevitably, blurred some of the Third Cinema characteristics of sub-Saharan cinema, but not its identification with Africa. It is true that nowadays international financing arrangements for film projects and star auteurs is not that unusual, but it may be a special issue for African cinema, whose colonial and postcolonial lineage centrally involved geopolitical consciousness from its very beginnings. There is no doubt that African cinema has developed its pantheon of auteurs, but the filmmakers' postcolonial concerns meant that they were looking for means to interrogate local and continental political, social, and cultural formations, histories, and subjectivities.

And at the textual level, very distinctive things occurred. This level cannot be explored here, but critics, trying to identify a mode of African cinema, have sometimes perceived a close relation between oral traditions and narrative filmmaking. They have argued that there are distinctive, culturally specific configurations of time, space, and address to the spectator (e.g., see Diawara,[10] Gabriel[11]). On the other hand, as John Akomfrah puts it, "The notion of an African cinema was always premised on the modernist assumption that the films were going to be inventive in some way, that they were going to tackle all kinds of cultural and political questions—in short that they would necessarily, by nature, be avant-garde films."[12] Within this shared set of concerns, however, he suggests a wider range of textual possibilities. For example, he mentions highly influential Senegalese modes of filmmaking starting in the 1960s (undoubtedly meaning Sembene, Mambety, et al.), whose lineage can be traced into Burkinabe cinema of the 1990s.[13] But he differentiates this line from another associated with Ghana and the Ivory Coast, where melodrama and comedy were more welcome. These might be compared to yet other work, such as the elegant *Udju azul di Yonta* (*Blue Eyes of Yonta*, 1992), in which Guinea-Bissau's Flora Gomes—who had worked with Sembene but also studied film in Cuba—narrativizes the remembering of anticolonial struggle. Gomes employed a stylistics attuned to the subjective interiority of individual characters in a way one would never find in Sembene. Gomes's next film—a scandalously unavailable masterpiece, *Po di sangui* (*Tree of Blood*, 1996)—is quite different in its means as well as subject matter (a fictional rural village with a fictional religion is displaced by environmental pillage). These were both inventive festival films yet they were stylistically distinct from one another and demonstrate even within the work of one auteur the textual range of African cinema concerned with African questions and issues.

Yet, as Akomfrah points out, at international film festivals all of these films and many others would be identified as "African cinema." The existence of a recognizable lineage of African cinema makes it appear that art cinema, with its international financing and international market, provided the framework for the emergence and persistence of a cinema that was self-consciously African. This had made it possible to continue to make films developing and extending the types of African subject matter, concerns, forms, and subjectivities that intellectuals and cultural practitioners of the original generation of liberation sought to insert into films. And one of the distinguishing tendencies of this cinema for many years was a concern with the political and social issues of Africa. On the other hand, this was a consequence and contributor to the impossibility of steady financing and establishing a sustained output. There had to be a constant negotiation for every project, with agents ranging from government bureaucrats (most often foreign governments) to representatives of prestigious European television networks. But even if the modernism of the great European auteurs of postwar art cinema was in a different register, the art cinema infrastructure did provide a potential market for aesthetic experimentation and, by some accounts, not only representational and political but formal and even epistemological novelty in African films.

This suggests that part of the distinctiveness of African cinema is that it must construct a double address, and Akomfrah argues that African filmmakers exist in a new kind of Duboisian double consciousness:

> You need to secure a certain degree of international recognition, but you cannot function without the local either, and therein lies a paradox. Francophone African film-makers who have lived in Paris for thirty years are still regarded as African film-makers, even as African film-makers from very specific countries. They are given funds *because* they are from those specific countries, which means they cannot afford to forget, nor to not say they are from there.

It is not just a cynical calculation either. The film-makers genuinely feel they are from those specific places, but they know that the language of nationality does not make sense if divorced from the all-embracing pan-African discourse.[14]

With the emergence of Euro-TV as a funding and distribution source, this double consciousness sometimes seems literalized even in the narrative sources of some films from later decades, something abetted by the cosmopolitan sophistication of so many African filmmakers going back to the origins of this cinema. By the 1990s there had appeared a few major festival films allegorizing African famine and civil war but they were freely adapted from sources that are canonical in Europe. On the face of it, this seems a counterintuitive development, given the anticolonial heritage of African cinema. But it seems to have something to do with the global situatedness of this cinema, including the art cinema context. It may also derive from a local context, namely the devolution of the achievements of independence into civil wars and ethnic division by the 1990s. One of the most prominent examples is *Hyenas* (Mambety, Senegal, 1992), adapted by Mambety from Friedrich Dürrenmatt's play *The Visitor*). Another indicative example is *Genesis* (Sissoko, Mali, 1999), which is an adaptation by a European (Jean-Louis Sagot-Durvaroux) of Jewish Old Testament origin narratives concerned with deadly sibling rivalry (chapters 23–37 of the Book of Genesis.) Yet, it was filmed in Mali utilizing Bambara cultural codes and language. Its cast includes, as the vengeful rejected brother Esau, the albino Afro-pop star Salif Keita, who is said to be a direct descendent of Sundiata Keita, the legendary founder of the Mali Empire. It is as if the very making of the film recapitulates its narrative thematics, which constitute an allegorical critique of identitarian ideologies underlying African civil wars.[15]

There may be another consequence one can speculatively propose about the distinctiveness of a cinema caught in this double (or triple) consciousness, having to do with the absence of an African audience to the filmmakers. Some of the films have intermittently found audiences in some locations within Africa, but the problem of a sustainable, steady African audience has haunted sub-Saharan cinema throughout its history. Generally speaking, many of the most praised films could not be widely seen in Africa, where distribution networks were closed to them and mainstream foreign films remained popular. How could there be a people's cinema if the people did not see the films? From the beginnings of African cinema throughout the rest of the twentieth century, filmmakers struggled with this problem. By the 1990s, when many of the decolonized states were seen as failing their people, some such as Congolese cineaste Mweze Ngangura were arguing that the need was not aesthetically African films, but films that Africans might actually see, even if this meant acceding to mainstream norms.[16] The structure of an auteur cinema that the masses did not see also might tend to reproduce the split between cultural elites and masses that national liberation theory had imagined could be annealed in the political struggle and liberation, and Solanas and Getino thought Third Cinema would overcome.

Whether it was a consequence of the kinds of films made or the structure of distribution, the lack of a dependable African audience was a fundamental problem for this African cinema. In combination with the desire for connection to the people, implanted in African cinema at its emergence, this may suggest something about some of the textual distinctiveness of the films. The filmmakers have had to make films for an international audience in the art cinema tradition, while simultaneously aiming at an African audience. That split means a film would be addressed to a spectator who is not there, but is much desired: an African spectator open to a film's interrogation of African life, history, and subjects, and also to narrative innovations supposedly rooted in African history and culture. These were central to that African cinema which has drawn on the art cinema infrastructure to survive. In that sense, one side of the doubleness of the African cinema best known outside Africa is that it is utopian cinema. It constructs a utopian spectatorship.

3

As a postscript: These notes have emphasized the implantations during the first generation of African cinema. Much has happened since then, and there have been alternatives and dissenters to this line. Today it may be that some of the constraints and related textual practices of African filmmaking are being transformed, though it is not likely the transformation will bring a complete stop to the lineage designated above. For example, the one sub-Saharan state that has had a degree of relatively significant capital for filmmaking is South Africa. South African film institutions are in the process of both establishing mainstream credentials and also of exploring support arrangements with other areas of the continent. This may lead to a greater output and market for sub-Saharan films in general, though it is by no means settled.

The most striking transformation, which has been going on for some years, is the rapid rise of the Nigerian video film, which has spread to other West African countries such as Ghana. These have proven extremely popular at home and also in diaspora markets, with a large output based on a different mode of production. The video film business involves shooting popular narrative forms quickly and directly onto video, rapid production and distribution turnover to get a quick return on exhibition through video parlors and home screenings, and rampant piracy. The video film system thus marks a breakthrough previously inconceivable in sub-Saharan film history. This breakthrough is a profitable popular market. It is fed by rapid, cheap production and turnover enabled by video, bypassing the blockages of distribution and paucity of exhibition resources endemic to the history of African cinema in Africa. By the mid 1990s, more than 250 video films per year were being produced in Nigeria alone, something literally inconceivable just a decade earlier.[17]

There is something like a mass audience here and Ngangura's popular cinema, and thus an address to a spectator conceptualized as actual rather than desired or utopian. So it should not be surprising that video films employ different narrative and visual modes than the kinds of African cinema discussed previously—for example, melodrama, local theatrical and comic modes, address to specific ethnic groups.[18] They may not be what many of the older filmmakers envisaged for African cinema, as they struggled over the decades for means to make films that would be distinctive and novel because they were of, by, and for Africa. These video films usually do not fit well into the protocols of award-winning art cinema. But in the migration of cinema to this kind of production and exhibition structure, there now exist African cinemas that have enough domestic market to be self-sustaining. This does not mean the immediate end of the art cinema/film festival/foreign financing model, and there will undoubtedly be some implicit cross-fertilization, even in personnel as well as textual and aesthetic modes. But there is no doubt that the video film is an alternative structure and a major historical turn in the ongoing history of sub-Saharan cinema.

NOTES

1. On the prehistory of art cinema, see Mike Budd, "The Moments of *Caligari*," in *The Cabinet of Dr. Caligari: Texts, Contexts, Histories*, ed. Mike Budd (New Brunswick, N.J.: Rutgers University Press 1990), 7–119; Barbara Wilinsky, *Sure Seaters: The Emergence of Art House Cinema* (Minneapolis: University of Minnesota Press, 2001).

2. David Bordwell, "The Art Cinema as a Mode of Film Practice," *Film Criticism* 4, no. 1 (Fall 1979): 56–64; Bordwell, *Narration in the Fiction Film* (Madison: University of Wisconsin Press, 1985).

3. John Akomfrah, "On the National in African Cinema/s: A Conversation," in *Theorizing National Cinema*, ed. Valentina Vitali and Paul Willemen (London: British Film Institute, 2006).

4. Frantz Fanon, "On National Culture," in *The Wretched of the Earth*, trans. Constance Farrington (New York: Grove, 1981).

5. Amilcar Cabral, "National Liberation and Culture," in *Return to the Source: Selected Speeches of Amilcar Cabral* (New York: Monthly Review, 1973).

6. Fernando Solanas and Ottavio Getino, "Towards a Third Cinema," in *Reviewing Histories: Selections from New Latin American Cinema*, ed. Coco Fusco (Buffalo, New York: Hallwall's, 1987), 56–81.

7. Teshome H. Gabriel, "Third Cinema as a Guardian of Popular Memory: Towards a Third Aesthetics," in *Questions of Third Cinema*, ed. Jim Pines and Paul Willemen (Bloomington: Indiana University Press, 1989), 53–64.

8. Clyde Taylor, "Interview with Pedro Pimente: Film Reborn in Mozambique," *Jump Cut* 28 (April 1984): 30–31.

9. Claire Andrade-Watkins, "France's Bureau of Cinema—Financial and Technical Assistance 1961–1977: Operations and Implications for African Cinema," in *African Experiences of Cinema*, ed. Imruh Bakari and Mbye Cham (Bloomington: Indiana University Press, 1996), 112–127. See also the account of the evisceration of the Ministry of Cooperation in the late 1990s in Olivier Barlet, *African Cinemas: Decolonizing the Gaze*, trans. Chris Turner (New York: Zed, 2000), 273–275. See Barlet, 242–244, for examples of a few African films that did manage to become local hits.

10. Manthia Diawara, "Oral Literature and African Film: Narratology in *Wend Kuuni*," in *Questions of a Third Cinema*, ed. Jim Pines and Paul Willemen, 199–211.

11. Gabriel, 53–64.

12. Akomfrah, "On the National in African Cinema/s," 281.

13. Ibid., 281.

14. Ibid., 287.

15. I do not mean to argue that the majority of major African films are adaptations of non-African texts, only that this is becoming a standard option. Other examples include a couple of entries in the long history of adaptations of Bizet's *Carmen*: *Karmen Geï* (Ramaka, Senegal, 2001), and *U-Carmen e-Khayelishta* (Dornford-May, South Africa, 2005—unsurprisingly the only one of these Euro-adaptations mentioned here that was funded locally). An Africanist rationale for this development might begin from *Aristotle's Plot* (Bekolo, Cameroon, 1996).

16. Ngangura Mweze, "African Cinema: Militancy or Entertainment?" in *African Experiences of Cinema*, ed. Imruh Bakari and Mbye Cham (Bloomington: Indiana University Press, 1996), 60–64. For a claim that many African films are in fact locally popular when they can obtain screening venues, see Barlet, *African Cinemas*, 242–243.

17. Barlet, *African Cinemas*, 238.

18. See Akomfrah, "On the National in African Cinema/s"; see also Jonathan Haynes, ed., *Nigerian Video Films*, rev. ed. (Athens: Ohio University Press, 2000).

15

DISENTANGLING THE INTERNATIONAL FESTIVAL CIRCUIT: GENRE AND IRANIAN CINEMA

Azadeh Farahmand

During the reign of the Iranian "reformist" president Mohammad Khatami (1997–2005), many Iranian expatriates found it safe enough to travel back to Iran. My turn came in 2001, when I wanted to mix academic research and fieldwork with soul searching and homecoming. I attended the Fajr Film Festival in February and stayed through April to also re-experience the thrill of the ancient tradition of Nourouz (Iranian New Year). One afternoon, I went to a special screening of Amir Naderi's short and memorable movie, *Harmonica / Saz Dahani* (1974). The screening was part of a larger series of film events organized by the Iranian National Film Archive in celebration of the centennial of cinema in Iran. Not surprisingly, the screening had drawn many young Iranian cineastes interested in viewing notable works of the Iranian cinema history on the big screen.

After the film, I started a conversation with a young woman sitting next to me. Once she learned that I resided in the United States and that I was, then, a graduate student in film studies, she asked if there were any film schools in the United States that would teach students to make "art films." I was immediately puzzled by this question. Why did she assume that filmmakers in America were typically not trained in making art films? What were the characteristic qualities of art cinema in her mind, and how did she distinguish between art cinema and American films?

So many assumptions lurked behind this question that I did not even know where to begin to seek clarification. So I just asked, "What do you mean by 'art films'?" Self-assured and without a pause, she replied, "The type that goes to festivals, such as movies of Mr. Kiarostami." I was intrigued by this response. Instead of describing categorical qualities of art cinema, the young woman identified an itinerary (i.e., going to festivals) and a key representative (i.e., Abbas Kiarostami). In other words, by virtue

of the festival acclaim of Kiarostami's films, they generically represented what constituted art cinema.

Kiarostami is one of many Iranian filmmakers who attained international recognition in recent years.[1] Still, the recognition he received via the international festival circuit surpasses that of his cohorts. Yet it is hardly imaginable how Kiarostami would
have attained this iconic status without entering the international festival circuit and
receiving subsequent endorsements via successive festival appearances, awards, critical acclaim, and various forms of media exposure.[2] The international visibility of his
films initiated the process that ultimately led to the articulation and theoretical discussion of a collection of themes and visual styles in his cinematic corpus.[3] These stylistic
and thematic traits qualified his authorship in general *and* reinforced characteristic
qualities of Iranian cinema in particular.

National cinemas and the new waves are often discussed within the general rubric
of global art cinema—as also evidenced by this very anthology that brings together
discussions of locally specific/national cinemas within the general framework of global
(art) cinema. This same critical nexus of global and local frames persists in this essay.
I will address its ambiguities head-on by revisiting the geopolitical fault lines that haunt
generic constructs like art cinema and national cinema. Here, I consider art cinema as
a more generalized class of films that in the context of the international festival circuit
subsumes and adds class value to the generically specific categories of national cinema, film movement, and auteur cinema. As my discussion develops, I hope to illustrate that generic categories overlap not because of essential characteristics they may
have in common, but because of common function and shared exhibition space.

This discussion attempts to show that the exhibition context—in this case, film
festivals—provides films with a set of perceived qualities otherwise unavailable outside
those channels of exhibition. My discussion is also concerned with the process through
which instances of cinematic characteristics mature to form a genre. Traditional genre
criticism in fields of rhetoric and literary theory anchors a genre's definition in characteristics of an exemplary work. This tendency is also prevalent in cinema and media
studies, wherein a single or a number of exemplary works provide the starting point
from which to extrapolate structural or iconographic traits that constitute a genre. In
this essay, I will take an unconventional route to revisit generic categories. Instead of
identifying characteristic qualities of a generic type like national cinema or art cinema,
I will investigate processes through which generic qualities are identified as such. Specifically, I will draw on Rick Altman's genrefication theory and a historical discussion
of the international film festival circuit to account for the emergence and repositioning
of Iranian cinema on the international map.

Genrefication and International Film Festivals

Studies of national cinema, film movements, and auteurs have a central approach in
common: They all aim at deciphering and generalizing common traits across a variety
of different cinematic texts. Like film genres, each of these categories serves a generic

function by evoking a unified range of qualities that typify the films that form the category. Festivals generically exploit film products they showcase in order to reach unique audiences in a competitive global market. However, generic boundaries remain loosely defined and are constantly reorganized. This ensures that festivals can continue to offer fresh products, or at least a new take on the products they showcase. The theoretical framework of genrefication, as originally developed by Altman and briefly sketched later, helps explain how the functional dynamic of the international festival circuit is vital to the genrefication of national cinemas, auteurs, and film movements.

Altman points out that Hollywood studios exploited generic formulas in order to entice audiences into theaters by relying on their expectations of familiar generic characteristics. But a study of the studio publicity records invalidates this assumption. In fact, film publicity materials evoked multiple generic references in order to appeal to wider audiences. It was not so much familiarity but difference and newness that studios employed in order to sell their products.[4] Studios were not interested in creating genres that could be used by other studio rivals; rather, they tended to create film cycles that were not sharable.[5] Successful studio cycles would mature into genres when the features that were once associated with one studio were broadly circulated among other studios and gained an industry-wide adherence.

Altman notes that the transition from cycles to genres depends on "favorable" conditions.[6] While favorable conditions do not guarantee maturation into genres, it seems that they can be retroactively traced and explicated once the genre is formed. In his analysis, Altman does not focus so much on textual characteristics of genres as on the discursive context and uses that the generic terminology ultimately provides. "Once fully formed," Altman says, "genres may continue to play an exhibition or reception role as convenient labels or reading formations."[7] Far from mere inheritors of generic terminology, film critics and scholars solidify genre terms and definitions. They engage in an industry of their own, that of naming, defining, and theorizing. Contrary to studio producers who attempt to ensure the novelty and wide reach of their products, critics need singular, familiar, and reusable terms. Situating himself on the critic's turf, Altman writes:

> We critics are the ones who have a vested interest in reusing generic terminology, which serves to anchor our analyses in universal or culturally sanctioned contexts, thus justifying our all too subjective, tendentious and self-serving positions. We are the ones who see to it that generic vocabulary remains available for use. While producers are actively destroying genres by creating new cycles, some of which will eventually be genrefied, critics are regularly trying to fold the cyclical differences into the genre, thus authorizing continued use of a familiar, broad-based, sanctioned and therefore powerful term.[8]

The festival space brings together and fuses functions akin to that of the studio head and the critic/scholar. Festival programmers emphasize the novelty of their programming choices, while they also position the unique elements within familiar terms. Journalists and film critics carry on the function of deciphering local elements in universal terms; and yet, they often posit or reinforce new directions in cinematic trends. Indeed, many film critics are also festival advisers and have served on festival juries. Plenty of festival directors and art-house programmers have functioned in the capacity of critic, theorist, or historian of films.[9]

In a fascinating discussion of art cinema, Steve Neale calls for replacing aesthetic studies of art cinema with an exploration of its institutional formation. Investigating cases of France, Italy, and Germany, Neale locates art cinema in institutional practices premised on the logic of securing national specificity in contradistinction to Hollywood films. He argues that art cinema has historically come to be more closely linked to national cinema in ways that, say, avant-garde or genre films are not.[10] In this view, art cinema is identified in conceptual opposition to the way in which its "other" (i.e., Hollywood, mainstream, or commercial cinema) is perceived. Accordingly, textual features of art cinema "change in accordance with which features of Hollywood films are perceived or conceived as dominant or as basically characteristic at any point in time."[11] The question posed by the young woman mentioned in this essay's opening also presupposed this categorical opposition. Although she ultimately did not define characteristic qualities of art cinema, her question and elaboration implied a presumed opposition between art cinema and American films.

This conceptual duality is also at work in the ways in which film festivals have historically distinguished themselves, and thereby self-identified as offering a space for discovery, display, and artistic evaluation of films from around the globe.[12] As Neale astutely observes, however, despite its conceptual opposition to Hollywood cinema, art cinema functions within similar parameters that characterize the commerce of Hollywood films.[13] Festivals feed such perceived and yet problematic notions. For example, festival awards would not be useful for distributors if the public were aware of the capital-dependent and politics-driven dynamics of film festivals that could influence the selection of films and allocation of awards. Further, notions of national cinema as generically employed in the festival space are anchored in the assumption that specific films do in fact unravel the true spirit of the nation. In fact, festivals typically pay special attention to films that have escaped local censorship—thereby enhancing the perceived festival image as the forum to display the authentic local reality otherwise filtered by government censorship.

THE GLOBAL FILM CIRCUIT

The metaphor of the "circuit" is crucial in the sense that it posits festivals as nodes interconnected by entities that collectively ensure the livelihood and flow of the circuitry. In addition to festivals of a variety of sizes, functions, and influence, the festival circuit is held together by local components with a stake in the festival (government agencies, tourism industry, corporate sponsors and other advertisers), buyers and sellers (distributors and sales agents), nonfestival sites of exhibition (art houses, museums, universities, and cinematheques), and venues of news dissemination (newspapers, industry trades, and television).[14] The festival circuit propels patterns of replication within and across its constituent networks. Information is disseminated within the circuit by passing through the concentric and conjoined circles of power. For example, people with privileged access to information (such as programmers, producers, or film agents) pass down select news, interpretation, or insights about "foreign" films to the attending viewers and critics, who in turn become the source of knowledge for the general public—hence generating the ripple effect that collectively develops a coherent interpretation and ultimately forms a generic type. But a key extension of Altman's theoretical model is the ways in which the genrefication process interacts with film production and exchange. As I argue later, the festival exposure of Iranian films influences the very processes of production and affects the visual look and narrative tendencies of films—hence reinforcing the generic qualities of the national cinema. The very discovery of "the new" becomes trendsetting. The cycle evolves into a replicable style, and the line between discovery and invention becomes blurred.

In an engaging article on the complex world of film festivals, Mark Peranson offers two models, namely the business festival and the audience festival.[15] The former is the more elaborate type, typically associated with an international competition and an expanding film market.[16] Unlike the audience festival, which caters primarily to the tastes of the local community, the business festival tends to fulfill concerns of distributors, sales agents, and corporate sponsors who feed it with money and prestige. In this overall picture, Peranson argues that business festivals exert the highest degree of influence in the circuit, while they are themselves at the mercy of powerful sales agents. While I find this distinction between the two key models of festivals useful, I disagree with the implication that the bigger, more commercial festivals and ultimately the sales agents are the most powerful and therefore decisive players in setting trends within the global circuit. As my later examination of Iranian cinema in the festival circuit shows, the national genrefication of Iranian cinema came about through favorable conditions that did not initially include the involvement of powerful sales agents or an endorsement by a major international festival. Indeed, cycles begin on a small scale before maturing into genres.

The festival circuit provides a fertile ground for genrefication as festivals increasingly expand into functions such as production, marketing, and distribution of films.[17] The global platform that a festival offers influences the attention a film receives by critics, the public, other festivals, film buyers, investors, and ultimately scholars.[18] Festivals exert a direct or indirect influence on film production because of the role they play in helping a film transition from local economies to the global market. Local producers often internalize and integrate an understanding of festival expectations in the very inception and development of projects. Many festival representatives, programmers, and advisers view films prior to the final festival selection and make narrative and artistic suggestions. Festival prize money or production funds often encourage filmmakers to adhere to the festival taste. As the boundary between film markets and film festivals increasingly blurs, the circuit provides loci of artistic exchange and business collaboration in which films (either at a primitive or finished stage) seek and often find distribution deals.

The competition among the major festivals (and with it the urge to upstage one another) contributes to a circuit that constantly (re)generates cycles and genres. Festivals want to be the "first": the first to premiere a masterpiece, the first to launch the career of a future auteur, and the first to discover a "new" national cinema. The "new" in "national new waves" or "new national cinemas" serves a double function: It both reinstates an already preexisting concept (i.e., a national tradition that the new presupposes and qualifies) and evokes the presence of something different. Nevertheless, festivals benefit from initiating an industrywide trend that in turn validates their function—hence the "ripple effect" of discoveries (cycles) that become trends (genres) adopted by a range of film programmers, critics, and industry professionals.

The theoretical model of genrefication replaces the question of *what* constitutes the characteristic qualities of a genre with *how* generic types are conceived. This shift in perspective does not preclude the possibility of a generic category having exemplary or typical characteristics, but that those characteristics are not essential to the form. For example, what has come to be known as Iranian cinema in recent years is a historically specific construct. The following sections will explore the favorable conditions that contributed to the evolving and historically unique conceptions of Iranian cinema.

Iranian Cinema on the International Festival Circuit

Since the late 1980s and through the 1990s, a select number of films from Iran gained recognition and acclaim in major international festivals. Iranian cinema earned a presence on the global scene that was new and unexpected for a majority of its international viewers until then. By the mid-1990s, hardly any major festival took place without including an Iranian film in the festival lineup, an Iranian filmmaker on the jury, or a special program on "Iranian cinema."[19] In 1997, Kiarostami's *A Taste of Cherry / Taam e Gilas* became the first Iranian entry to win the most prestigious festival award—the Palme d'Or at Cannes. A year later, eighteen-year-old Samira Makhmalbaf became the youngest director to have entered a film in the official selection of Un Certain Regard at Cannes. Many movie critics, festival programmers, and (other) newsmakers referred to this conspicuous presence of Iranian films in the international festival circuit as the New Iranian Cinema, implicating a new wave or a new movement within the national filmmaking scene. Those who reminisced about the brief period of festival glory that films from Iran had attained prior to the 1979 revolution linked the new phenomenon to the previous "Iranian New Wave" of the late 1960s and the 1970s.

In an engaging essay on the geographic nodes of the festival circuit, Julian Stringer observes that the conventional framing of national film industries from the moment of their notice via international film festivals masquerades *"distribution* histories of world cinema . . . as *production* histories."[20] For example, Stringer notes, Kristin Thompson and David Bordwell were prompted by the festival success of the South Korean production *Why Has Bodhi-Dharma Left for the East?* (1989) to assign "a mere sentence to the history of Korean cinema" in their seminal book, *Film History: An Introduction.* Stringer observes, "This example assumes that non-Western cinemas do not count historically until they have been recognized by the apex of the international media power, the center of which is located, by implication, at Western film festivals."[21] The discussion that follows illustrates that the international notice of Iranian films in the 1970s and in the 1990s masquerades a more complex and panoramic picture of the thriving film culture and industry in Iran. I will separately discuss two waves of Iranian cinema's ascent to international notice and will account for different historical circumstances that gave momentum to each wave.

During the two waves of Iranian cinema's international appearance, the local economic and political circumstances encouraged productions that defied the strict confines of mainstream or religious formulas. In each phase, the shift also aligned with specific tastes and expectations of the global festival and art-house community. The following sections examine these and other historical factors that during two periods separated by the 1979 revolution mediated the Iranian films' entry into the network of international film festivals. The very frameworks in which exported Iranian films were viewed via the festival circuit influenced styles and thematic tendencies of Iranian films and the workings of the local industry. In short, the festival conception of Iranian cinema played both a descriptive and prescriptive role.

THE FIRST WAVE

The (former) Iranian New Wave owes much of its discursive formation to the elaborate orchestration of the Tehran International Film Festival (1972–1977). Although numerous local festivals had flourished through the 1970s, the Tehran festival enjoyed an international scope and influence unsurpassed by other contemporaneous local festivals and unmatched by later festivals to this date.[22] By the mid-1970s, the Tehran festival was ranked as the sixth largest and one of the most prestigious competitive international film festivals in the world recognized by the International Federation of Film Producers Associations (FIAPF). During its annual showcase, the festival brought together several hundred prominent filmmakers, actors, festival representatives, journalists, and film critics from around the world to view, debate, and judge notable contemporary film productions from around the world. Its location on the continent of Asia, organization by the prosperous royal establishment, and claim to the historically rich cultural tradition of Persia and the colorful palette of the local landscape gave it a unique—if not mythic—stature, different from and yet comparable in scale to European festivals.

The festival was positioned as a cultural bridge between East and West. In a piece in *American Cinematographer*, the festival's secretary general, Hagir Daryoush, defined "the principal aim of the Tehran Film Festival" as providing "a forum for a confrontation between the developed film industries of the industrialized nations and the emerging national cinemas of the 'Third World.'"[23] The rhetoric generated by the festival's organizers, and further perpetuated by the international participants and journalists, anchored the organization's mission within the context of the country's claim to long traditions of mysticism, philosophy, and indigenous art that included poetry, music, and miniature painting. The welcoming message of the fourth Tehran International Film Festival read as follows:

A millennium before the age of cinema, the Persian poets and philosophers were already thinking four-dimensionally. When they posited "love," they didn't mean a nineteen century romantic notion. They meant the miracle of life captured in the discipline of art. . . . In an age when both poetry and philosophy have been discredited as communications media, the Persians of today are attempting to express the heart, mind, guts, and spirit of life in terms of the new art. . . . The Tehran International Film Festival celebrates the art which captures life through the alchemy of "love."[24]

An unprecedented wave of filmmaking activities in Iran was cultivated through a number of factors that began brewing in the late 1950s. These factors included a thriving local industry that ultimately embraced the untapped market of a relatively young and educated middle class and made room for productions that did not conform to previously successful mainstream formulas. The growing middle class embraced cinema as a medium of intellectual engagement, cultural conversation, and social criticism. Magazines discussing arts and culture proliferated while cinema clubs put together post-screening discussions. Topics such as poverty, corruption, personal revenge, and government bureaucracy were discussed in literature, theater, poetry, and cinema. Emerging social realism in films challenged the older escapist narratives and assembled decor. A number of government agencies and semigovernmental organizations—such as the Ministry of Art and Culture, Iranian National Radio and Television, and the Center for the Intellectual Growth and Development of Children and Young Adults—initiated film funds and instituted training centers that encouraged experimental filmmaking and adaptations from modern literary works.

In the early 1970s, a number of Iranian films caught the attention of international festivals and critics. Daryoush Mehrjui's *Cow / Gaav* (1969) received the International Critic's Award at the 1970 Venice International Film Festival. Mehrjui's later feature film *The Postman / Postchi* (1972) appeared in the parallel section Critic's Week at Cannes in 1972. It won the Interfilm Award at the 1972 Forum of New Cinema at Berlin, and subsequently screened at Rotterdam, Sydney, Melbourne, and London film festivals. In *The Postman*, a meek and good-natured man who works for an animal facility suffers from impotence that has soured his marital life. When he finds that the wealthy and foreign-educated owner of the animal facility has seduced his wife, he loses his cool and murders his wife. The international reaction that *The Postman* received situated the film as a third-world allegory, while the director was positioned as a rising auteur. Surveying the international reaction, Jamal Omid refers to a piece in the French newspaper *Le Figaro* that allegorically reads the film as a narrative of "the poor against forces of imperialism."[25] Omid also quotes a Belgian newspaper that contextualizes *The Postman* as a "political and sociological document that unravels the life of the Third World." The piece refers to Mehrjui as a "new Pasolini."[26]

The Iranian New Wave was ultimately genrefied during the operation of the Tehran festival, at which time the attending foreign journalists began to write about the surge of a distinct group of films that seemed to diverge from past filmmaking traditions in the country.[27] In 1974, the festival put together a special section called the "New Iranian Cinema." It was during this edition of the festival that the phrase "Iranian New Wave" appeared in festival reports. Films that were made prior to 1974 and that were later considered part of the canon of the Iranian New Wave were included in this panorama.

In one of the earliest instances of discussing and delineating the Iranian New Wave, a piece written by a visiting journalist appeared in the daily bulletin of the third festival:

> Those interested in Iranian cinema have yearned for years for just such a retrospective as "Iran's New Filmmakers," to be screened during the festival. . . . [H]ere at last is a chance to grasp the trends of Iranian cinema as a whole, to see some of its most outstanding achievements, and to judge both its recent past and hopes for the future.[28]

This piece sought to carve out a legitimate identity for the featured films by exploring the possibility of defining the "movement" against, and as opposed to, a past national tradition—as other national new waves have been customarily defined:

> There are no real equivalents in Iran to the German Expressionism of the 30's and 40's, the "Classic" French directors of the 40's and 50's. . . . Despite the sporadic ventures from the Qajar period onward . . . no "Bombay talkies" industry took root here. . . . As for the [Iranian] "New Wave," it is just the beginning— one of the major purposes of this retrospective should be to determine whether or not such a movement actually exists, and if so, what it consists of.[29]

American critics Edna Palian and Terry Graham wrote about various industrial and cultural factors that contributed to the growth of a dynamic cinematic movement in Iran with nonmainstream tendencies.[30] In their piece, Palian and Graham specifically posited the new wave as a response to an old mainstream tradition, otherwise generically known as Filmfarsi. The new trend of Iranian films was noted for qualities such as scripts based on contemporary novels, intellectual themes and dialogues, subdued visual backlash against the monarchy, unhappy endings, and the absence of song-and-dance scenes and formulaic narrative lines otherwise exploited in Filmfarsi.

The collective showcasing of these Iranian pictures and the critical notice they received at the high-profile Tehran festival helped define the canon and thus genrefy the "Iranian New Wave." Local critics did not immediately adopt the terminological reference but continued to debate the homegrown film movement. Omid's survey of contemporaneous local reviews of these films shows that Iranian critics used a variety of adjectives such as "art," "alternative," "intellectual," "introspective," and "responsible" cinema to characterize the films.[31] While it is next to impossible to survey the entire corpus of local writings in the 1970s, I suspect that "Iranian New Wave" as an overarching term became fully integrated into the vocabulary of Iranian critics and scholars after the 1979 revolution. In other words, the term emerged in a nostalgic context at a time in which the revolution had already put an abrupt halt to the filmmaking trend. A few years after the revolution, the veteran film critic Jamshid Akrami, who had left Iran in early 1980s and has since resided in the United States, characterized the "Iranian New Wave" as a movement "which produced a body of highly original films that successfully combined an unexpected degree of artistic flair with film craftsmanship and a strong sense of social awareness and political commitment."[32] In this piece, Akrami laments that the movement "did not receive the international attention that it truly deserved" and that it ended with the 1979 revolution.[33]

In is noteworthy that a few Iranian films that had obtained critical acclaim among the growing elite of Iranian intellectuals and that had garnered notice in international festivals in the previous two decades have generally not been considered part of the new wave canon.[34] The canonical texts that have been customarily identified as the inception point of the new wave include Masoud Kimiai's *Caesar / Gheisar* (1969), Mehrjui's *Cow*, and Naser Taghvai's *Tranquility in the Presence of Others / Aaraamesh dar Hozour e Digaraan* (1969/1972). It is no accident that the temporal locution of the Iranian New Wave starting with these three seminal works and ending with the 1979 revolution corresponds roughly to the timeframe of the Tehran festival's operation. The Iranian New Wave would have perhaps not been conceived without the international outreach of the prestigious festival, which invigorated critical debates within a wider international sphere and helped frame the films collectively as Iran's new homegrown cinematic movement.[35]

Nevertheless, the Iranian festival did not provide the only favorable condition for genrefying this cinematic wave. In addition to the local socioindustrial context mentioned previously, non-local factors were also consequential. The international festival community seemed to welcome this new phenomenon as a national film movement that both contained elements of Third Cinema and evoked elements akin to national new waves of the 1960s and 1970s with their auteurist orientation. The reviews previously mentioned capture this dual positioning. The following section highlights the systematic efforts of media players and policymakers in Iran that mediated the recent incarnation of Iranian cinema on the festival circuit. This would not have been possible if the offered products had not ultimately fed expectations of the global festival circuit.

THE SECOND WAVE

After the 1979 revolution and the hostage crisis of the early 1980s, media images of Iran circulating in the Western countries focused primarily on terror and fundamentalism. However, a decade or so after the drastic regime change, Iranian films at international festivals offered a humane view of the people and cultures of Iran that drastically departed from those earlier images. Stories about children, women, and effeminate or gentle men in the exported Iranian films were in stark contrast to the aggressively masculine fervor of the hostage takers, demonstrators, and Ayatollahs seen in newspapers or on the nightly news. Unlike news images of Iran filled with angry, bearded men in dark clothes shouting, "Death to America" or "Death to Israel," Iranian festival films showed people and landscapes filled with life and vibrant colors.

Cinema in Iran became a contested arena throughout the volatile era of the late 1970s and the early 1980s when theocracy replaced monarchy. At first, the clergy toyed with the idea of exploiting cinematic images to propagate revolutionary and Islamic ideals beyond Iran's borders. But while revolutionary ideas and religious ideals on film found favor among the locals—particularly during the Iran-Iraq War (1980–1988) when the nation found itself unified against a common enemy—films of that sort proved to be a hard sell internationally. By the mid-1980s, less religiously fanatical individuals and clerics were appointed to government posts that influenced policies on cinema. The government had become more confident in its grip on ideological expression. Thus, it saw less need for censorship and set in place measures that supported a wider range of cinematic production.

The years 1983 and 1984 mark the onset of this transitional era: The Farabi Cinema Foundation was instituted; the Fajr Film Festival launched its first edition in 1983; and Mohammad Khatami was appointed minister of arts and culture. These appointees underscored cultural aspects of cinema, utilized the support of the clergy, and implemented rigorous supportive measures to gradually cultivate a vibrant national film industry. Yet, the government gradually cut back its financial support of the industry after the end of the war and as the cost of film production went up.

The seventh festival of Fajr in 1989 took place right after the end of the Iran-Iraq War. During the closing ceremony of the 1989 festival, Fakhreddin Anvar, undersecretary of culture and Islamic guidance in charge of film affairs, commended the results of the previous five years of the government's supportive role in reviving cinema in Iran. He announced that "one of the most important goals over the next five years would be to propel a commercial supply of Iranian films outside of Iran."[36] With the government taking on a narrower executive and supportive role in Iranian film production, the festival exposure of Iranian films offered a means for additional income through international exposure and sales, hence facilitating the economic vitality of the local industry.

Farabi, whose administration has been closely tied to the annual festival, managed the gradual exposure of select local films to international film festivals. Ali Reza Shojanoori is an influential figure in promoting Iranian films at international festivals. He acted as the director of international relations at the Farabi Cinema Foundation from 1983 to 1995. A charismatic and accomplished actor, Shojanoori utilized his familiarity with Italian and English together with his business acumen to network with international festival and art-house representatives. During his tenure at Farabi, Shojanoori and his team succeeded in projecting a professional, cultured, and appealing image associated with Iranian cinema. The Farabi team (re)introduced Iranian films and filmmakers to foreign venues in ways that were distinct from the dominant perceptions of the post-hostage crisis era and the ideologically heavy-handed films that were made immediately after the revolution.

Massood Jaafari-Jouzani's *Cold Roads / Jaadde-haa-ye Sard* (1985) was the first feature film whose entry into a recognized European festival was brokered by Farabi. The film screened in the Panorama section of the Berlin Film Festival in 1987. *Cold Roads* is about the journey of a little village boy to the city to obtain medicine for his sick father. The film was praised for its simplicity and humanistic insights at Berlin. The festival screening and critical acclaim of *Cold Roads* affirmed that Iranian films had a far better chance of being embraced by the festival circuit if they stayed away from overt political references and religious propaganda. The film thus set in place a precedent and blueprint for festival success. Ahmad Talebi-Njead quotes the film's director, who commented on the hour-and-a-half question-and-answer session he had with the festival audience in Berlin:

> The people generally did not believe that a film could be made in Iran that was not political propaganda. The Eastern point of view and the mysticism dominant in the film were vital in attracting foreign viewers.[37]

Farabi's persistent presence at international festivals and in film markets ultimately resulted in establishing key contacts. During his visit to MIFED (the world's oldest film market, which was held in Milan until 2003), Shojanoori met with several festival directors and learned about the advantages of inviting them to the Fajr festival in Tehran, where they could view and pick out Iranian pictures for their festivals.[38] Some time during the 1986 or 1987 edition of MIFED, Shojanoori recalled, David Streiff, the then-director of the Locarno International Film Festival, approached the Farabi booth and told the Iranian delegates about the Swiss festival. Streiff advised them about the logistics and timeline of the application process. In 1988, Naser Taghvai's *Captain Khorshid / Naakhodaa Khorshid* (1987) screened at the Locarno festival and won the Bronze Leopard.[39] A few months later, Streiff was invited to Fajr, where he viewed tapes of several Iranian films, including Kiarostami's *Where Is the Friend's Home? / Khaaneh ye Doost Kojast?* (1987), with which, as Shojanoori put it, "he fell in love."[40]

In *Where Is the Friend's Home?* an eight-year-old boy must return his classmate's notebook that he took by mistake, or else his friend will be punished the next day for not turning in his homework. The film went on to earn Locarno's Bronze Leopard, FIPRESCI Prize, and Prize of the Ecumenical Jury—hence reinforcing precedents for a set of visual and narrative qualities that many forthcoming Iranian films replicated and that many critics and festival programmers pointed out as unique to Iranian cinema. Not surprisingly, the figure of an innocent child facing societal challenges or life's hardships is at the center of many later Iranian productions that circulated the festival circuit. These films include Jafar Panahi's *White Balloon / Badkonak e Sefid* (1995) and *The Mirror / Ayneh* (1997); Majid Majidi's *Children of Heaven / Bachehaye Aasemaan* (1997), *Color of Paradise / Rang-e Khoda* (1999), and *Baran* (2001); Mohammad Ali Talebi's *A Bag of Rice / Kiseh-ye Berendj* (1996); Samira Makhmalbaf's *The Apple / Sib* (1998); Mohsen Makhmalbaf's *Silence / Sokout* (1998); and Bahman Ghobadi's *A Time for Drunken Horses / Zamani Baray Masti-e Asbhaa* (2000).

When a group of postrevolutionary Iranian films were screened at European festivals such as the 1990 Tri-Continental Nantes Film Festival in France and the 1990 Pesaro Film Festival in Italy, the festival community took notice of a cluster of films coming from a cinematically obscure and yet politically controversial nation. The taste, attitudes, and viewing frameworks of the festival community that guided the perception of Iranian films on the festival circuit were different from the earlier period. The simplicity and humanity prevalent in these films caught the attention of international critics and the festival community. Curiously, international viewers of the Iranian festival films of the 1970s extrapolated political allegories and a third-world context from those texts, whereas the general framework through which the international festival and critics viewed the Iranian films of the late 1980s and the 1990s focused on simplicity, poetry, humanism, and philosophical themes. This comparison underscores the historical specificity of favorable conditions and the fluid nature of the genrefication process. In other words, the generic conception of national cinema evolves in relation to the changing favorable conditions.

Talebi-Nejad refers to an Italian reviewer at Pesaro who highlighted the words of the Iranian filmmaker Kianoush Ayari during the postscreening question-and-answer session: "We Iranian filmmakers would like to be recognized as artists rather than as messengers. Our country is one of the controversial places in the world. We prefer to turn our gaze to our countrymen instead of churning out propaganda."[41] Other festivals followed suit in organizing special sections dedicated to Iranian cinema. In 1992, the Toronto Film Festival showcased a number of recent Iranian productions. Reflecting on the festival experience, Bill Nichols noted the absence of overt politics and a focus on the people and the culture in the Iranian festival films:

Most visibly absent are sex and violence. . . . Also absent are explicit references to religion and the state. Common Western stereotypes of fanaticism and zealotry are neither confirmed nor subverted. They are simply absent, of no local concern. (In post-screening discussions, and interviews, the Iranian filmmakers disavow any desire to preach or agitate.)[42]

Characteristics that were attributed to Iranian festival films of the last two decades became generic qualities that filmmakers, film agents, festival programmers, critics, publicists, and academics all highlighted, passed along, and reinforced in a process that, in turn, folded these characteristics back into local production trends and onto the texture of forthcoming films. The genrefication of Iranian cinema became possible because the aims of the Iranian nation-state—in the ways in which it sought to market and sell Iranian cinema—became compatible with the overall dynamics of the international festival circuit in its continued attempt to "discover" new national cinemas and champion new filmmakers. The international attention that films from Iran have received since the late 1980s and through the 1990s shifted local production trends and contributed to the emergence of what became broadly referenced as "art cinema" inside Iran, and (the new) Iranian cinema outside of the country. In fact, the local rating system that regulated distribution and exhibition of Iranian productions encouraged this perception. For example, Iranian productions that had appeared in international festivals received higher ratings, which subsequently offered them marketing and screening advantage over those with lower ratings. Deemed as "art films," these festival pictures obtained allowance for television teaser spots, placement in upscale theaters, and longer theatrical runs otherwise unavailable to productions perceived to have been made for local commercial consumption.

CONCLUDING REMARKS

The international festival circuit provides an arena for visibility and market placement of films on the global scene. Local film industries are often invigorated once they tap into this global network that exposes local productions to a wide range of viewers and consumers. The international stamp of approval that Iranian productions received via the festival circuit encouraged a more favorable reception and confidence among viewers, critics, producers, and distributors at home. Festival attention also brought direct economic support—in the form of festival cash prizes, international coproduction agreements, and distribution deals—to the filmmakers who had previously been at the mercy of a limited local market and a struggling national film industry. The relationship between the local industry and the global festival circuit, however, is not unilateral. While local filmmakers benefit from connecting to this powerful channel of global exposure, festivals too look for opportunities to discover and place new products into the circuit.[43] This essay has argued that the genrefication process is an integral part of the festival circuit as long as the circuit thrives to introduce new products and reposition old ones in new ways. To maintain its longevity, the circuit needs to brand auteurs, market national cinemas, create cultural capital, and add commercial value to products that pass through its network.

The festival circuit's structural propensity for genrefication sheds light on the constructed, fluctuating, and often contradictory conceptions—such as national cinema—that are configured and formed within and ultimately exported outside the circuit.[44] As my study of the two waves of "new" Iranian cinema has demonstrated, the interpretive angles through which Iranian cinema were viewed varied in each period. Furthermore, what defines the national cinema from one perspective (say, global) can challenge how the cinema is viewed and valued from another (i.e., local) angle. Filmmakers from nations or regions that become festival darlings are often criticized for attempts to adjust the look and narratives of their films to offer selectable and prizeworthy products to festivals. Local journalists occasionally cite this qualitative shift—often in a negative tone—and express qualms about films of indigenous directors that are regularly sponsored at festivals. This critical discourse (usually voiced by the filmmaker's countrymen and in many cases less internationally exposed because of language barriers) concerns the textual address of films that are seen as directed toward nonnational viewers mediated by international film festivals.[45] In my trip to Iran and particularly during my visit to the Fajr Film Festival I noticed the tension between those who took pride in the international acclaim of Iranian films and those who contested the sincerity and patriotism of the filmmakers.[46]

The genrefication of Iranian cinema as propelled by the festival circuit still continues to some extent by means of scholarly debates and sporadic art-house screenings. However, the zenith of the international attention paid to Iranian cinema seems to have passed. This is noticeable in the dwindling number of Iranian pictures currently in distribution, the scarcity of Iranian entries at major festivals, and the decreasing public attendance at screenings of Iranian films.[47] This gradual shift may be related to the fact that the reformist government gave way to a more repressive regime (with the election of Mahmoud Ahmadinejad to the presidential seat in 2005). This regime has put a damper on creative expression, and hence Iran has fewer products to offer at festivals. It may also imply that Iranian filmmakers adopted and internalized the generic conception of Iranian cinema and therefore failed to challenge the conception by taking new directions in filmmaking.[48] From a broader and more global perspective, though, this phenomenon is arguably symptomatic of the inevitable variation in the fickle tastes of festival and art-house viewers; the continuous festival penchant for new areas of interest; and the increasing trend of transnational coproductions that blurs distinctions among national traits.[49]

In the end, the fragmentation of media platforms poses a challenge to the traditional role of festivals as the primary alternative venue for exhibiting films outside conventional channels of theatrical distribution. The proliferation of festivals with strong local community orientation may lessen the significance of national genres, while solid national categories themselves become untenable constructs due to the accelerating transnational fusion of capital and talent. It remains to be seen how the international festival circuit will adjust to these transitions. I speculate that while genrefication will remain an integral part of this circuit, the usefulness of nation-as-genre will gradually fade as global film consumers become less invested in national distinctions.

NOTES

1. A few other Iranian filmmakers whose films garnered awards and recognition around the world include Mohsen Makhmalbaf, Samira Makhmalbaf, Jaafar Panahi, Majid Majidi, and Rakhshan Bani-Etemad.

2. Following his ascent to festival acclaim and worldwide recognition, Kiarostami's cinema has been the subject of numerous articles, books, retrospectives, and television programs. Festival popularity of Kiarostami's films led to international recognition of his work as a poet, painter, and photographer. In 2001, Harvard University Press published a book of his poems translated into English: *Walking with the Wind: Poems by Abbas Kiarostami*, trans. Ahmad Karimi-Hakkad and Michael Beard (Cambridge, Mass.: Harvard University Press, 2001). In conjunction with a retrospective of his films, the 1995 Locarno Film Festival hosted an exhibition of his paintings and photographs. His artworks were also the subject of shows at the Victoria and Albert Museum in the United Kingdom in 2005 and the Berkeley Art Museum in the United States in 2007.

3. Discussions on Kiarostami's cinema have included the motif of travel/journey, multilayered significance of the road, the position of the spectator, visual poetry, philosophical quest, centrality of children, and blurring of boundary between reality and fiction. A few examples of writings that refer to these themes include Pat Aufderheide, "Real Life Is More Important Than Cinema," *Cineaste* 32, no. 4 (Summer 1991): 31–33; Godfrey Cheshire, "Abbas Kiarostami: A Cinema of Questions," *Film Comment* 8, no. 6 (July/August 1996): 34–36, 41–43; Laura Mulvey, "Kiarostami's Uncertainty Principle," *Sight and Sound*, June 6, 1998, 24–27; Devin Orgeron, "The Import/Export Business: The Road to Kiarostami's *Taste of Cherry*," *CineAction* 58 (June 2002): 46–51; Jerry White, "Children, Narrative and Third Cinema in Iran and Syria," *Canadian Journal of Film Studies* 11, no. 9 (Spring 2002): 78–97; and Alberto Elena, *The Cinema of Abbas Kiarostami*, trans. Belinda Coombes (London: Saqi, 2005).

4. Rick Altman, "Reusable Packaging," in *Refiguring American Film Genres: History and Theory*, ed. Nick Brown (Berkeley: University of California Press: 1998), 9.

5. According to Altman, individual studios created cycles based on identifiable studio property (such as contract actors and studio styles), borrowing features from past successes "but never falling into a fully imitable pattern" so as to maintain the studio's sole signature and claim to what it only can make and sell. See Rick Altman, *Film/Genre* (London: BFI, 1999), 59.

6. Altman, "Reusable Packaging," 15.

7. Ibid.

8. Altman, *Film/Genre*, 71.

9. Examples include Irene Bignardi, the director of the Locarno International Film Festival from 2001 to 2005 and an established film critic who regularly wrote for *L'espresso* and *La Repubblica*; Richard Peña, the program director of the New York Film Festival, an associate professor of film at Columbia University, and a regular contributor to *Film Comment*; and Alissa Simon, the former associate director of programming at the Gene Siskel Film Center of Chicago, an ongoing affiliate, curator, and adviser to a variety of international film festivals, and a contributor to *Film Comment*, *Sight and Sound*, *Sense of Cinema*, *Film International*, *CinemaScope*, *Cinemaya*, and the *Village Voice*.

10. Steve Neale, "Art Cinema as Institution," *Screen* 22, no. 1 (1981): 11–39.

11. Ibid., 14.

12. Opening any festival catalog will reveal this underlying theme in the mission statements and welcoming messages printed at the front of the booklet.

13. Neale, "Art Cinema as Institution," 37.

14. Like festivals, each of these spheres has its own built-in hierarchy or system of core/periphery relations—a discussion of which is beyond the scope of this article.

15. Mark Peranson, "First You Get the Power, Then You Get the Money: Two Models of Film Festivals," *Cineaste* 33, no. 3 (Summer 2008): 37–43.

16. The Toronto International Film Festival is one without either an international competition or an official film market. However, the festival, which showcases the cream of the crop from other major festivals (hence its designation as the "Festival of Festivals," as it has historically been branded), fits the model of business festival as it nurtures growing market-like activities with thousands of buyers and sellers attending the festival and making deals.

17. I originally developed this discussion in my dissertation, "At the Crossroads: International Film Festivals and the Constitution of the New Iranian Cinema" (Ph.D. diss., University of California, Los Angeles, 2006). For a fascinating book-length study of international film festivals, see Marijke de Valck, *Film Festivals: From European Geopolitics to Global Cinephilia* (Amsterdam: Amsterdam University Press, 2007).

18. For some films, going the festival route is the only means of getting public exposure as they fail to secure theatrical distribution deals. Nowadays, more and more distributors are requiring festivals to pay screening fees for films that are deemed potential box office failures and therefore will not be theatrically released.

19. According to statistics in Iranian publications, the annual international presence of Iranian films jumped from an average of 35 screen appearances between 1979 and 1988, to 88 in 1989, and to 377 in 1990. With a slight drop in the two subsequent years, international appearances of Iranian films reached 429 in 1994 and 744 in 1995. After a decline to 640 in 1996, the figure rose once more, to 766 in 1997. In 1999, the annual presence reached a high of 849, compared to 616 of the previous year. See Ahmad Talebi-Nejad, *In the Presence of Cinema: An Analytical History of Cinema after the Revolution* (*Dar Hozour e Sinama: Taarikh e Tahlili e Sinama pas az Enghelaab*) (Tehran: Farabi, 1998), 105–106; Mohsen Beig-Agha, "Deep Waters: Iranian Cinema 1995 in the Market Place," *Film International* 4, nos. 1–2 (Winter 1996): 110; "Merry Go Round: The Award It Won in 1996," *Film International* 5, no. 1 (Summer 1997): 36; and Mohammad Atebbai, "Iranian Films and International Scene in 1997," *Film International* 5, nos. 3–4 (Spring 1998): 17.

20. Julian Stringer, "Global Cities and the International Film Festival Economy," in *Cinema and the City: Film and Societies in a Global Context*, ed. Mark Shiel and Tony Fitzmaurice (Oxford: Blackwell, 2001), 135.

21. Ibid.

22. The International Fajr Film Festival, which since 1983 had been the primary showcase of local productions after the revolution, borrowed its organizational framework from its elaborate predecessor.

23. Hagir Daryoush qualified "Third World" as "the developing countries of Latin America, Africa and Asia." See Daryoush, "A Word from the Director of the Second Tehran International Film Festival," *American Cinematographer* 55 (February 1974): 166.

24. "Welcome Honored Guest—with All Our Hearts to an Old Idea," *Bulletin 1: The Fourth International Tehran Film Festival*, May 1975. It is noteworthy that contemporary discussions of Iranian films follow a similar framework by identifying the national cinema as preoccupied with grand topics such as mysticism, humanism, naturalism, and poetry.

25. Jamal Omid, *History of Iranian Cinema: 1900–1979* (*Taarikh e Sinema ye Iran: 1279–1357*) (Tehran: Rouzaneh, 1994), 617.

26. Ibid.

27. *American Cinematographer* chronicled the festival from 1974 to 1977 and covered Iranian films as well as other entries.

28. Peter Wilson, "Iran's New Film-makers," *Bulletin 1: The Third International Tehran Film Festival*, April 1974.

29. Ibid.

30. Edna Palian and Terry Graham, "The Film Industry in Iran—Part 1: A Rapidly Growing Industry Feeding on a Rich Cultural Background," *Bulletin 9: The Fourth International Tehran Film Festival*, May 1975.

31. Omid, *History of Iranian Cinema*, 521–752.

32. Jamshid Akrami, "The Blighted Spring: Iranian Cinema and Politics in the 1970s," in *Film and Politics in the Third World*, ed. John D. H. Downing (New York: Praeger, 1987), 131.

33. Ibid.

34. Moushegh Sourouri and Samuel Khachikian's *Party in Hell / Shabneshini dar Jahannam* (1957) screened at the 1959 Berlin festival and became the first Iranian entry in a major international film festival. Farrokh Ghaffari's *Downtown / Jonoub e*

Shahr (1958) and Ebrahim Golestan's *Mudbrick and Mirror / Khesht o Ayeneh* (1965) incited unprecedented acclaim among Iranian critics and intellectuals, many of whom celebrated and distinguished them from the dominant trend of mainstream local pictures. Forough Farrokhzad's documentary *The House Is Black / Khaneh Siaah Ast* (1962) took the top prize at the 1963 International Oberhausen Film Festival. Ghaffari's *The Night of the Hunchback / Shab e Ghouzi* (1964) screened at the Cannes, Karlovy Vary, Lyon, and Brussels international film festivals and caught the attention of international critics. These older films are often discussed as "predecessors" of the new wave in spite of their critical and festival acclaim, and even though they have intellectual concerns, cinematic styles, and financing structures in common with films that were later considered as constituting the new wave.

35. In the April 1975 issue of the *Filmmakers Newsletter*, a journalist who had visited the third edition of the festival wrote about a principal aim of the "glittering affair" in her review: "The festival is partially intended as an opportunity for Iranian filmmakers to garner awards and critical reviews, as well as exposing them to a wide range of cultural influences" (Betty Jeffries Demby, "Tehran Film Festival," *Filmmakers Newsletter*, April 1975, 68).

36. "Remarks by Fakhreddin Anvar, Undersecretary of Culture and Islamic Guidance in Charge of Film Affairs, during the Closing Ceremony of the Seventh Fajr Film Festival" ("Sokhanan e Aghaye Fakhreddin Anvar Moaavenat e Omoor e Cinemaee e Vezarat e Farhang va Ershad e Eslami dar Marasem e Ekhtetam e Haftomin Jashnvareh ye Film e Fajr"), *The Eighth International Fajr Film Festival* (Tehran: Ministry of Art and Islamic Guidance, 1990, my translation).

37. Talebi-Nejad, *In the Presence of Cinema*, 103 (my translation).

38. Ali Reza Shojanoori (president of Behnegar Productions), taped interview with the author, Tehran, Iran, February 2001. This interview was conducted in Farsi (my translation).

39. According to Shojanoori, the jury had already decided on the allocation of prizes before watching the film. Once they saw *Captain Khorshid*, however, they rethought their votes. Since they had already contacted the awardees and could not retract their awards, they gave the Bronze Leopard to two films instead of one.

40. Shojanoori interview. It is noteworthy that like most other competitive European festivals, Locarno's entry rules require European (if not a world) premiere status for a film. In addition, the competition films should have been completed generally within the twelve months leading up to the festival. By contrast, *Where Is the Friend's Home?* had already screened at the Tri-Continental Nantes Film Festival in France and had been completed two years prior to its entry to Locarno. Nevertheless, David Streiff went against the festival's regulations and invited the film to compete in Locarno's 1989 edition.

41. Talebi-Nejad, *In the Presence of Cinema*, 108 (my translation).

42. Bill Nichols, "Discovering Form, Inferring Meaning: New Cinemas and the Film Festival Circuit," *Film Quarterly* 47, no. 3 (Spring 1994): 21.

43. The "discovery" of new national cinemas or auteurs adds to the profile and clout of not only the festival but also its director. One of the influential players in the international festival scene, Marco Muller (currently topping the Venice International Film Festival) has been instrumental in promoting both the Chinese and Iranian cinemas at the international festivals since the mid-1980s and through the 1990s. A film critic and film producer, Muller has topped key European festivals such as Turin, Pesaro, Rotterdam, Locarno, and Venice. Tracing the movement and influence of individuals like Muller can offer us an interesting perspective on the genrefication process of the international festival circuit. Muller's fluid mobility and powerful reach

within that circuit, for example, actually propels the ripple effect and reinforces the evolution of generic conceptions.

44. Academic classroom and scholarly publications, in my opinion, comprise key sites that ultimately inherit what is genrefied on the international festival circuit. Courses and books on Iranian cinema, for example, were relatively unheard of until a few years ago when the national cinema gained international notice via the festival circuit.

45. Tracing the trajectory and aftermath of the Chinese cinema to international notice, Sheldon Hsiao-peng Lu cites the critical backlash of Chinese critics who find troubling the "Orientalist" spectacles of exported films that are "masterfully manufactured for the pleasure and gaze of the Western viewer." See Sheldon Hsiao-peng Lu, "National Cinema, Cultural Critique, Transnational Capital: The Films of Zhang Yimou," in *Transnational Chinese Cinemas: Identity, Nationhood, Gender*, ed. Sheldon Hsiao-peng Lu (Honolulu: University of Hawai'i Press, 1997), 126.

46. The young woman mentioned in the opening of this essay clearly shared the sentiments of the former group.

47. Over a decade ago, Wellspring, Miramax, Zeitgeist, and New Yorker distributed Iranian pictures in the United States. Now these distributors have either gone out of business or have shifted their distribution practices to focus on different niche markets. Furthermore, the many annual Iranian film series held across North America—such as the one hosted by UCLA—rarely capture the same enthusiasm and public attendance today that they enjoyed upon their introduction in the early 1990s.

48. I would hesitate to agree with this hypothesis as I have seen films from younger Iranian filmmakers that show previously unexplored preoccupations and fresh styles of filmmaking.

49. Case in point in relation to the latter concern is Kiarostami's recent productions, such as *ABC Africa* (2001) and *Five Dedicated to Ozu* (2003), which were (co) produced and filmed outside of Iran. His latest feature, *Certified Copy / Copie Conforme*, stars Juliette Binoche, is produced by MK2 based in France, and commenced shooting in Italy in June 2009.

IV

Geopolitical Intersections

16

EUROPEAN ART CINEMA, AFFECT, AND POSTCOLONIALISM: HERZOG, DENIS, AND THE DARDENNE BROTHERS

E. Ann Kaplan

Study of emotions as part of the cinematic apparatus has not been a central aspect in film analysis partly because of the somewhat limited options about affect offered by psychoanalysis, but also because interest in how viewers negotiate meanings in films, alternatively decoding and encoding what is given, was another main approach.[1] If psychoanalytic feminist film scholars originally theorized a voyeuristic "male" gaze—a sort of one-sided look, focused on a psychoanalytic understanding of how the gaze was structured within the diegesis and in regard to castration—theorists of film narration concentrated on how plots unfold, and on cinematic techniques for storytelling.[2] In this chapter, since I am interested in theories that are more enabling for understanding cinema as a social and affective medium, I explore how cinema structures screen emotions and look at techniques that produce emotions between embodied spectator and screen. Such a focus enables analysis of cinema in relation to the public sphere somewhat differently than has been done hitherto. For while scholars like Miriam Hansen have built on issues of encoding/decoding and provided important insight into how certain stars (like Rudolph Valentino) became public phenomena, creating fan worship especially among women, the underlying Habermasian discourse meant that once again emotions were not as such the focus of attention.

In a very general way, my project intersects with aspects of Frankfurt School debates about the media and Hollywood in particular. But while Theodor Adorno and Jürgen Habermas tended to dismiss the media as only propaganda and as hindering the kind of (utopian) public sphere discourse they saw as essential for a healthy democracy, I am interested in the emotions they lump together as creating zombie citizens as well as in studying how cinema may also offer prosocial feelings. Walter Benjamin, sensitive to the modernist shocks of new cinema technology, implicitly recognized issues of affect as linked to time and technological medium that concern me here. But in the period since Benjamin wrote, the role of affect in the public sphere has expanded. As Brian Massumi notes, "Affect holds a key to rethinking postmodern power after ideology."[3] Ideology is still with us, but, Massumi argues, "it no longer defines the global mode of functioning of power." In this situation, more than ever we need information about how emotions are communicated through the media, more knowledge of which emotions are provoked, and more information about the different kinds of emotions that constitute spectator affects as well as those that (relatedly) drive the characters. For public emotional sets partly *structure* filmic emotions and are partly *structured by* cinema in a circular fashion. While I see humans as vulnerable to having their emotions "managed" by pervasive media intent on creating specific feelings for political or commercial ends, I also see a place for developing prosocial feelings—as in the films studied here.[4]

My case study of cinematic emotions focuses on the structure of colonial and postcolonial "contact-zones," and the emotions directors' techniques arouse in spectators of interracial encounters.[5] The colonial/postcolonial encounter is particularly relevant today, as in many European nations the once-colonized return to the metropolis, bearing with them traces and residues of colonization and producing familiar powerful public feelings. Much work has been done on scandalously negative images of peoples of color in classical Hollywood film since its inception (the paramount example being D. W. Griffiths's *Birth of a Nation*).[6] Scholars have also studied films made from the perspective of the Other—peoples (as it were) talking back to the Empire, representing themselves, their ways of seeing colonialists (for example, works by Tracey Moffatt or Ngozi Onwurah). Less has been written comparing directors of art cinema in regard to the interface in their films of race and affect, and the relationship of such representations on public affective sets—the project I engage here.

The art films discussed in this chapter are all made by white Western subjects who deliberately refuse to speak from the position of Africans or Australians, who are critical of the white colonialists they make films about, and who highlight the current abuse of African immigrants. While Claire Denis and Werner Herzog offer an encounter in the nation invaded, the Dardenne brothers stage a "contact-zone" in the European metropolis that transports the history of past encounters in colonial time and space. I will explore the aesthetic and cinematic techniques that shape emotions in such films about colonial and postcolonial encounters, and consider the emotional plane on which each film operates. That is, I will consider the emotional valence each film offers, such as where it focuses on emotional relationships and what characters are shown to feel, and where it structures affect as part of screen space—affect expressed through imagery, or through juxtapositioning of objects and people in space. As will be clear, here I follow Massumi's distinction between emotion (as quantity, as involving a naming of a specific feeling such as shame, fear, love) and affect (as intensity, not linked to specific emotions but as generalized feeling).[7] We know much about how Hollywood's imaginary worlds affect various global publics[8] but less about whether representations of alternative emotional valence may transform negative public feelings about the Other still circulating today.

This kind of concern has traditionally been addressed as a question of "ideology"—that is, of politics. Film scholars have tended to analyze cinematic politics as if audiences are being addressed as rational subjects capable of either blindly subscribing to whatever ideology is presented or as open to rational progressive discourse. In fact, people are vulnerable to emotions as much (if not more than) ideas, and as I noted earlier quoting Massumi, affect is now a main way that power is wielded.[9]

Art cinema offers a challenge to the study of affect in film because of its difference from the emotional narrative norms of Hollywood. Hollywood cinema has always relied on the emotional pathways "in" the spectator and her culture for its effects. Indeed, emotion provides one powerful ground for identification and dis-identification. That is, viewers identify with characters via emotion, as in the case of male and female actors made attractive through well-known Hollywood cinematic techniques (positive emotion and identification) or that of characters made ugly through disfiguring and other lighting techniques (negative emotion and dis-identification). Yet such affective reactions are not simple and depend on cultural codes and conditioning. Frantz Fanon's much-quoted footnote contrasting seeing *Tarzan* in Martinique and in Paris demonstrates how mainstream cinema provokes the spectator's emotions and identifications, which are themselves culturally conditioned, and which depend on her cultural/social/class position as well as on the specific context for watching the screen and the camera's movements. Not all spectators, as Fanon shows, will experience the same emotions and identifications; not all emotional pathways activated will be the same. In Martinique, the public normative emotional set for black people was identification as white. Thus, spectators like Fanon identified emotionally and narratively with Tarzan and laughed at the "savages" grotesquely represented by Hollywood. But when Fanon was in Paris, where there was hostility to blacks, he felt the pull of these public emotions: He felt he ought to identify with the "savages," or that the public saw him as allied with them.

While it is rare to have such explicit data about spectatorship and public feelings, Fanon's anecdote allows us to theorize about public feelings in regard to screen images. Although my main focus is affect and cinematic technique, these feelings in turn have an impact on viewers. The two concerns are hard to separate in practice even if for analysis a distinction must be made. My intervention here aims to correct a bias in critical methodologies for art cinema as well as Hollywood which from the 1960s to the 1990s focused on the auteur, on narrative and aesthetic style, on meaning, and on ideology.[10] In the 1970s and 1980s, as befitted the structuralist/poststructuralist moment, critics were interested in art cinema as a kind of "counter-cinema" in its techniques. What sort of emotions the films used or evoked and by what means was not often addressed.

If in its very formation art cinema partly aimed to avoid the heavy sentimentalism of Hollywood, this did not mean that emotion was absent or even repressed. It is rather that art cinema directors worked with a different orientation toward emotion: I will argue that this cinema offers an emotional plane that belies what normative Western cultures (and therefore audiences) expect. Art film's counter-cinema aspect includes an emotional set counter to that which dominates popular culture in the West, namely a focus on individuals and their relationships within established expectations of what constitutes "good" (kind, attentive) feeling and what constitutes "bad" (cruel, inattentive, abusive) feeling. The directors I study here are interested in the colonial/postcolonial contact zone partly because of the very differences in emotional sets that emerge: Western characters displaced into the colonies reflect emotional destabilization in their behaviors, while indigenous characters offer emotional sets formed in their particular cultures. Such perspectives have been explored within sociological and psychological frameworks for diverse minority subjects: For example, Sara Ahmed, in *The Cultural Politics of Emotion*, discussed complex ways emotions circulate in multiethnic Western societies, with certain (minority) ethnic bodies being attached to varied negative feelings: Anne Cheng, David Kazanzian, and David Eng, meanwhile, have revised Sigmund Freud's theories of mourning and melancholia to study minority experiences and subject positions in Western cultures.[11] But little has been undertaken in regard to the role of imaging technologies in determining such emotional sets, or in providing possibilities for their transformation. So much of contemporary life is lived via imaging technologies that it becomes harder than ever to disentangle emotional sets in daily interpersonal interactions from emotional sets provided for spectators on varied kinds of screen.

Given that films (to use Ann Cvetkovich's term) carry an archive of feelings, especially public feelings, they embody historical emotional constructions that may continue as legacies today. Also, given film and photography's sorry history as the anthropologist's tool for bringing the "truth" about other cultures back to the West, archival traces in cinema require special attention. What's important is that the "shadow" or "ghost" lives we encounter in film and fiction have real impact in the lived world—a fact corroborated by many public examples going back to the traumatic "shock" of Lumière's early films, via D. H. Lawrence's *Lady Chatterley's Lover* (the novel, not the 2007 film), and on to intense reactions to Mel Gibson's *The Passion of the Christ* (2004); more recently, a film about Islam, *Obsession: Radical Islam's War against the West* (2005; directed by South African Wayne Kopping), aroused passions on campuses across the United States because it seemed to view Islamic terrorists from an Israeli point of view.[12] Films, then, including art cinema, arouse powerful emotions (along with affects, as we will see)—as powerful as live events and sometimes more powerful because of the intimate details (normally hidden in daily life) that can be shown on film. And this is true outside of the obvious cases of Hollywood films or journalism deliberately using propaganda to arouse strong emotions. As I hope to show in what follows, certain kinds of fiction and film, like psychoanalysis if in a very different form, have the power to trigger strong feelings through images without depending as much as Hollywood on identification with specific characters. These feelings in turn may challenge prior conceptions and values especially if images go against pervasive public stereotypes. That the same images may be received and understood in dramatically opposed ways, depending on what one brings to the aesthetic experience, does not negate cinema's potential for both indoctrination *and* transformation.[13]

I will look briefly at three examples of so-called European independent or "art" cinema to explore how in each film the colonial or postcolonial encounter secures a particular emotional tone, how images work out from or unconsciously become allied with public feelings about minorities, and (examining aesthetic techniques) what affects each film appears to strive to produce in the spectator along with emotions linked to a particular character. My attempt to link as a common group three directors originally from three different European nations and using different languages raises a main issue central to this volume, namely how to define European cinema as a concept. However, the commonalities I point to in regard to interest in race and ethnicity, and a politics of concern for minorities, can be seen across diverse European nations in the post–World War II era: These concerns emerge in a different context and manner than in Hollywood or in non-European independent cinema. If that topic is beyond what I can address here, nevertheless there appears to be a certain cross-influencing of European directors from different nations, along with the practice of European directors working together across national borders. Referring to films made later than the ones I mainly deal with here, Rosalind Galt, in *The New European Cinema*, notes that the context of globalization and global capital and the many co-productions common today challenge prior ideas of national cinemas, including individual cinemas in Europe. The directors and films then form a kind of constellation of artists with similar political agendas, in touch with one another if not directly working together—a specific generational grouping during which innovative filmmaking took place in a spurt of creative activity (and funding possibility) lost today.

As noted earlier, none of these auteurs would claim to be speaking *for* the minority or ethnic groups they make their stories about; yet it would also be incorrect to deny their empathy with these groups in their films or that they present indigenous perspectives. Indeed, one of the questions I'll explore is the extent to which the perspective of the Other is included, even if it's a white subject's concept of this perspective. In a sense, auteurs like these three, all from the 1960s generation (however much they may want—as is especially true of Herzog—to separate themselves from this generation), represent a contestatory element in dominant Western culture, but perhaps are ultimately unable to separate themselves from the colonial imaginary.

As part of its resistance to dominant culture, in its first European wave, independent cinema deliberately created an aesthetic counter to Hollywood narrative and technical strategies, especially as regarded emotion, while evidencing directors' engagement with, even love of, Hollywood. They resisted Hollywood's obvious attempt to arouse emotions (such as tears, terror, suspense, joy) and avoided Hollywood's eternal happy endings. So-called new wave auteurs like Jean-Luc Godard, Rainer Werner Fassbinder, and Michelangelo Antonioni, rather (as 1970s critics argued in their focus on ideology), apparently followed a Brechtian aesthetic of appeal to the intellect rather than explicitly or obviously to the heart. Had 1970s critics been interested in emotion, they might have argued that new wave films embodied a culture of anomie, depression, and absence of intense feeling linked to post–World War II Europe but not often analyzed as such. If affect was presented in indirect ways by auteurs in the first New Wave of European cinema, slightly later generations, like that of Denis and the Dardenne brothers, began to move closer to commercial cinema: As part of this move, they allowed a place for more common affective styles, while remaining within art cinema parameters (difference from Hollywood, liberal ideology, engaging serious international themes such as colonialism/postcoloniality). Their respective affective styles need to be examined, including difference from Hollywood's uses of emotions both in terms of relationships within narratives and in regard to the kind of affect auteurs hope to provoke in spectators.

A main difference from Hollywood in all of the films is the inclusion of a focus on affect (intensity or the expression event) rather than on emotion (quality or feelings dealt with through cognition), to use Massumi's distinction.[14] To expand on what I noted earlier, in his "The Autonomy of Affect," Massumi (influenced somewhat by Gilles Deleuze) distinguishes two parallel systems of response to images—a level of what he calls emotional "intensity" and one of "quality." Via psychological case studies, Massumi argues that the signifying order is disconnected from "intensity." A kind of feeling (to be distinguished from "quality," which is linked to cognition) for Massumi, intensity is "disconnected from meaningful sequencing, from narration." He notes that "language, though head-strong, is not simply in opposition to intensity. It would seem to function differentially in relation to it" (219). And he concludes the discussion by saying: "Approaches to the image in its relation to language are incomplete if they operate only on the semantic or semiotic level . . . what they lose precisely is the expression *event*—in favor of structure" (220). This expression event is what the spectator feels, then, but that often does not get interpreted, put into language, or paid attention to in film analyses.

Affect depends on the way auteurs encourage or prohibit identification with protagonists. It makes a difference whether the emotion is linked to a particular character (as always in Hollywood) or takes a more abstract, generalized form of mood or atmosphere. Recent psychology research (like that Massumi draws on) has shown that humans seem to require identification with a single victimized subject for empathy and concern to be aroused (see the 2007 case of the little English girl abducted in Portugal or the 2004 Terry Schiavo case). Hollywood, in seeking to move audiences, therefore always relies precisely on identifications with characters and always assumes a normative emotional set as regards what constitutes "good" and "bad" feelings and identifications. While Bertolt Brecht (perhaps too harshly) called this "crude empathy," I do not aim to set up a dichotomy (as Jill Bennett tends to do) between (affective) intensity and emotional quality such that the former is always "good," the latter to be avoided.[15] I rather use the distinction as a tool to understand the strategies involving affect as these strategies avoid identification with individual characters in cinema. Independent auteurs studied here avoid emotional identification with specific subjects and encourage spectators to think about a wider set of concerns. This is close to the idea of "witnessing" I developed elsewhere (Kaplan, 2005), as noted later.[16]

More than of any other director, perhaps, it can be said that Herzog *is* his movies, or that his movies *are* him—at least in the sense of how he believes one should train to make films. For Herzog, the best training is not sitting in an academic classroom or learning from imitating other directors, but literally walking around the world on two feet, avoiding bourgeois comforts and experiencing life and people in the raw. It's from his own experience doing this that Herzog arrives at filming the marginalized, those who are different and strange. While his attempts to embody his sometimes fantastical ideas and his somewhat mad passion and drive to bring about his visions may lead him to abuse his actors (as perhaps in the case of *Fitzcarraldo* [1982]), this should not prevent our admiration for his unique cinema, his unique way of using his camera, his passion for films. Traces of the strong emotions that bring him to make films end up on his screen, most often as the affective intensity Massumi talks about. I find *Where the Green Ants Dream* (1984) particularly revealing in this sense.

I have elsewhere discussed the literal and historical themes in *Green Ants* regarding the encounter between the Australian Aborigines and white corporate speculators drilling on sacred land, so I will not rehearse those discussions here.[17] I want rather to stress how Herzog's strong feeling about the decimation of Aboriginal culture is expressed in the film. Herzog does not present his feelings by ventriloquizing (as it were) the Aborigines mourning their loss. In fact, on the narrative level that includes the dialogues between the film's hero, geologist Lance Hackett, and the leaders of the resistance to drilling on sacred land, the Aboriginal characters are shown as strong, courageous, and determined rather than grief-stricken. Herzog forces spectators to reorient themselves in regard to common stereotypes of Aborigines as prehistoric, violent, alcoholic, and aimless. Instead of trying to position himself along with the Aborigines regarding what has been lost, Herzog conveys his own sense of loss, and his regret for what Westerners have done to indigenous peoples, via powerful images of nature (affective intensity) and through relating Aboriginal loss to his personal loss—the death of his mother that haunts the film (quality, emotion): That is, Herzog *translates* Aboriginal loss through finding an identification with something in his life—by making an emotional equivalency rather than offering a patronizing empathy. *Green Ants* begins and ends with terrifying images of tornadoes accompanied by the soaring notes of Fauré's *Requiem*. The opening titles tell us that the film is dedicated to the memory of Herzog's mother. This is how he makes his grief for Aboriginal loss personal—linking it to the death of his mother: So affective intensity is combined with emotional quality to powerful effect.

FIGURE 16.1. *Where the Green Ants Dream* (Herzog, 1984): Aboriginal leaders resist drilling on their land.

The awesome tornado images are the "expression event" that foreshadows and creates the overall mood and atmosphere for the film to which we return at the end. Herzog seems to me the director par excellence for this mobilization of affective intensity combined with emotional quality. In addition to the tornado, another way of expressing the mood Herzog aims to develop is the many shots of the desolate and strange landscape of the mining site. It looks like no place on earth, a kind of moonscape or eerie other planet. We do not feel at home, but strangely dislocated as we watch this landscape, since there is no subject for identification—only unfamiliar objects. While the many verbal exchanges between the Aborigines and Lance Hackett, and between the corporate director and the Aborigines, develop the different worldviews involved, these dialogues also include emotions that fit into Massumi's concept of "quality"; the corporate leader attempts to con the Aborigines into ending their sit-in, expressing increasing frustration as he gets nowhere, while the Aborigines express determination not to deviate from their aim. Such scenes evidence cognition and narrative development of characters' feelings and positions central to communicating explicit meaning in contrast to the sense of alienation and despair evoked by the sequences with tornadoes or shots of the moonscape terrain.

It's not hard to link the little old English lady and her lost dog (who have no place in the film's plot as such) with Herzog's mother and with an expression of loss in general. Her hopeless quest to find her dog, lost in the drilling tunnels, provides a powerful expressive event of its own for loss, absence of love, and the resulting coldness and darkness. The camera follows her gaze into the dark caverns as she sits endlessly waiting at the tunnel entrance. Equally arousing (and again not linked to the main narrative) are the shots of a little Aboriginal girl sitting on the ground outside Hackett's hut. Hackett leaves his radio with the child when he marches off to live elsewhere on the bleak site: Viewers confront her abstracted gaze, invited to feel the pathos of her life but unable to identify with her. If children usually symbolize the future—hope for generations to come—the vacant stare and listlessness of this child offers no future hope.

Green Ants provides an example of how cinema can be used to create strong affects expressing loss and despair through visual and aural strategies not related to narrative or any signifying chain, and at the same time use narration to convey progressive social meanings about the plight of Aborigines seeking to keep their sacred land. Denis manages her camera somewhat differently than Herzog as regards affect and emotion: In the case of *Chocolat* (1989), I'll suggest three related strategies vis-à-vis feeling: First, in regard to the white characters, Denis uses emotional distancing via staging the frame; second, in regard to the local Camaroonian servants, especially through Denis's identification with Protée, the main house servant in the 1950s colonial household, emotions are expressed outside of verbal language, outside of specific "fixing" of feeling; and finally, scenes in which the abuses of colonialism are shown through dramatic interaction between characters but without the intellectual dialogues specifically detailing cultural differences such as those Herzog staged.

First, then, in the way she stages the frame, Denis creates a certain deliberately meditative emotional distancing. In a sense, in many scenes, Denis is like Marc, the colonial administrator in *Chocolat*, whom we see pausing in the bush to survey the scene. A dreamer, he gazes into space, emotionally elsewhere, and the spectator experiences the sense of a person preoccupied, not really there. Sometimes he is seen sketching an unusual rock formation in his notebook—sketches spectators are shown early in the framing story when the film's heroine, France, returns to Cameroon bearing the notebook. Denis, too, in a sense "sketches" colonialism: As she put it in an interview, "I wanted to shine a light on a small piece of colonialism."[18] Via her staging of the frame, with her characters looking in on scenes through windows or doorways, or finding each other in mirrors, Denis manages to keep a certain distance from her characters, including their feelings—a position that enables the implausibility of colonialism to emerge. Many scenes expose the incredible strain of colonists trying to recreate Western bourgeois life in an inhospitable climate—rendering the white characters (especially when viewed from the perspective of the local people working in the house) ridiculous, laughable, as they show frustration, anger, sometimes despair in trying to keep up European ways of daily living.

Second, if Denis's camera often stages the frame through the structure of the look—a look that in turn structures the spectator's gaze—she does not use this strategy all the time. Indeed, her strategy of staging the frame enables the scenes in which she adopts a different strategy to be all the more powerful. In regard to Protée, for example, Denis brings us in close even if for the most part wordlessly. Her camera itself stages the emotion, and spectators experience the affective intensity that results—an interesting mix of Massumi's definitions of affect and emotion. An example is the scene where Protée is taking a shower. Denis shows him naked, and spectators cannot help but notice the contrast between his very dark skin and the very white soap and froth that arises as he happily showers in the outside facility he has to use. The camera rests on his showering long enough for us to take in his obvious pleasure (in a life that offers little solitary time), and to watch the mass of white froth accumulate as he washes himself. Suddenly, viewers see at the back of the frame behind Protée, Aimée, the mistress of the house, and France, her daughter, returning from a walk. He perhaps hears them coming, and although they cannot see him, something in him breaks, and he cries bitterly, cringing into himself. One cannot help but be reminded of Frantz Fanon's experience of the white child pointing him out to its mother, "Look, Maman, a Negro!"[19] For Fanon, the child's sudden comment shakes him out of his comfortable identification as a white subject, forcing him to confront his difference as it appeared to the white child. Similarly, it seems, Protée is caught up short in his identity, forced to confront his difference and his humiliating servant status. The entire scene takes place in silence. It's an "expression event" in Massumi's terms since the feelings are experienced without language or cognitive signifying chain. Partly because of this silence spectators cannot be sure about what exactly causes the tears: But once again, public feelings about colonized subjects are challenged: We experience feelings of hurt and vulnerability, expressed through Protée's naked body and tears, and perhaps extending beyond Protée himself to the general colonized population.

Interesting are some scenes that seem to defy the difference between staging the frame (implicit critique of the colonialists) and the camera registering emotion (identifying with the house servants): These are the scenes in which strong feelings between Protée and Aimée develop, thus joining masters and servants normally set apart and soliciting different strategies from Denis's predominant use of her camera. The scene where Aimee and Protée first encounter each other's desire at once structures the look of characters through a mirror shot, but their looks also produce sexual desire. The mirror is used not only to stage the frame in this case but to express powerful prohibited desire between Aimée and Protée. The scene unfolds in uncanny silence: Protée is called in urgently to help Aimée change her clothes on the sudden visit of a British Consulate official. As he adjusts Aimée's dress, Protée's and Aimée's gazes meet by accident in the mirror: Each is aroused but tries to hide the strong feelings. All is expressed through the movement of the eyes meeting in the mirror. There is no reverse shot. Spectators, situated in the position of the mirror itself, share the intensity of the desire simply through these gazes directly at the viewers: The camera is held still all the while.

The consequences of this scene emerge later on when Aimée reaches out to touch Protée, unable any longer to contain her desire. Her shame about her desire shows in her bodily posture before Protée enters the room: She's curled in on herself, sitting on the floor, head in her lap. Once again, there is complete silence as Protée registers Aimée's touch, unsure how to respond. Finally he pulls her up abruptly, apparently feeling a mixture of desire and frustration, stares into her eyes, and then equally abruptly turns away and walks out of the room. Aimée is left stunned, rejected. Though the camera keeps a respectful distance during this scene, in contrast to the close-ups in the mirror shot earlier, the lighting, bodily language, and the intensity the actors convey ensure spectators' engagement.

Finally, I address scenes in which colonialism is critiqued—but wordlessly. Humiliated and ashamed, Aimée takes revenge on Protée by having him banned from

FIGURE 16.2. *Chocolat* (Denis, 1989): Protée refuses Aimée's advance.

the house, assigned to work with the generator outside. France has all along been caught between belonging to her parents' world and that of the servants' subculture in the compound: As a child, although part of the invading group, she's a kind of victim of colonialism. In her *Psychic Life of Power*, Judith Butler notes that "no subject emerges without a passionate attachment to those on whom he or she is fundamentally dependent."[20] While the child's dependency is not political subordination as usually conceived, for Butler "the formation of primary passion in dependency renders the child vulnerable to subordination and exploitation" (7). France's dependence on love for survival means that she needs to obey her parents and submit to the paternal Law, yet all along she has risked disobeying them in order to enjoy subversive play with Protée. Her relationship to Protée is disrupted with his relegation to duties outside the house, but one night she visits him in the generator hut. Once again, Denis's camera refuses the framing distance and montage effects to present a scene of intense feeling in one take. In this case, however, the sequence has a sort of allegorical valence since the encounter suggests the psychic war that colonialism creates. As before, feelings are not fixed to either character as such in the scene, but conveyed in overall mood and atmosphere that suggest colonial tension and the impossibility of closeness given the colonial institutional structures. France is interested in the generator pipes and makes a move to touch one. Protée grasps a pipe without wincing, but when France trusts him and follows suit, she gets a horrible burn. Protée abuses France's vulnerability and dependency on love for survival so as to bring vengeance on his white masters. Once again, the lighting is dark, so that Protée's body almost disappears in the shadows, while France's white face gleams in the dark. In a sense, Protée symbolically burns their friendship and leaves France with a literal and symbolic scar that lasts all her life, a powerful reminder of the love and betrayal that colonization produces.

Turning to my last case study, *La Promesse* (1996), I will argue that the Dardenne brothers use some strategies similar to those of Denis, although within a more didactic context than Denis—they include a context closer to Herzog's moralizing about the Aborigines. *La Promesse* replaces fearsome nature as expression for human destruction and forces of death beyond control that we found in Herzog, with alienating shots of gloomy industrial landscapes, but the strategy of affective imagery is similar. Like Denis, from time to time they too stage intense feelings through aesthetic choices and strategic bodily placement in the frame. But *La Promesse* is the most directly political of the three films I study here, and, as such, it deals with normative emotional sets of bourgeois capitalism, as Lauren Berlant has shown in an extended essay on the Dardenne brothers.[21] We also see in this film as in Denis how subjects (and in particular the most vulnerable subjects, namely children) are brought to subject themselves to the paternal law as Authority, standing in for Government: Even more than with France in *Chocolat*, the dependency of the child on its parents drives the story. Citing Butler again, the desire to survive is a desire that can be exploited: "The one who holds out the promise of continued existence plays to the desire to survive" (7). She continues, "There is no possibility of not loving, where love is bound up with the requirements for life" (12). One would think that in this case resistance would be impossible, but Butler argues that if the subject is at once called into being by the Law, and subjected to this

Law, the ambivalence at the core of this process means agency is possible, that resistance can take place.[22]

These observations clarify the situation that Igor, the hero of *La Promesse*, finds himself in. For Igor is shown having to subject himself to his literal father as well as to the Law. The emotional dependency of the child on its parents in *La Promesse* once again appears as an allegory for the emotional dependency of everyone on social forces that control people's lives, bringing all to subjection. However, the Dardenne brothers indicate that there is room for resistance of a limited but crucial kind.

As befits the Dardenne brothers' political and realist ends, their camera relies less than that of Denis and Herzog on producing mood and atmosphere through expressive means (although such scenes do exist in the film) than on having their actors produce strong emotional effects in highly dramatic scenes. The Dardenne brothers invite spectators to identify with Igor and to appreciate his struggle to develop a morality his father completely lacks. While Bennett, following Deleuze, argues against "moral" art, because it "operates within the bounds of a given set of conventions, within which social and political problems must be solved,"[23] *La Promesse* avoids the problems she describes in Hollywood or social issue films. This is because the film does not offer any "solution" to its main theme, namely the abuse of African immigrants by a displaced working class seeking to make their way within new global capitalist formations that have taken away their jobs, but focuses on the small space for resistance to subjection seen in Igor's growth into a moral person.

Like Denis, the Dardenne brothers stage the frame in several key sequences to demonstrate Igor's reaction to discovering the essential difference of Assita, the young wife who has just arrived with their baby to join her husband already illegally in Belgium. Igor has never met a woman like Assita, who is from Burkina Faso. In classical voyeuristic fashion, he peeks in on Assita as she unpacks. The camera focuses on Assita in her underwear but also on the statuette that is apparently extremely significant to her. In a later scene, when making fake passports on his father's orders for the immigrants, Igor pauses on Assita's face, impressed by the whiteness of her teeth. Finding it partly comic, he takes White-out and puts it on his own teeth, admiring the result in a mirror, which reflects back his grinning, mimicking face for viewers. As in the mirror scene in *Chocolat*, this all takes place in silence. In place of subjects finding desire through their exchanged mirror gazes, Igor apparently seeks to take on Assita's identity, or to demonstrate his fascination with her by mimicking her look. Once again, it is an intense scene, outside of language, whose meaning remains uncertain.

The Dardenne brothers created a character who sets out with normative public feelings about the Other: Slightly interested but also mocking, somewhat sexually aroused as well, as befits his culture, he haunts Assita, seeking something from her, but he knows not what. However, with the accident of Amidu, Assita's husband, Igor begins to change: As viewers, we are invited to critique the prior normative exoticizing set vis-à-vis the Other, to see differently along with Igor. Igor is shocked at his father's command to simply bury the still-breathing Amidu because the authorities have arrived and would discover the father's illegal business. It is a dramatic sequence in which the camera focuses on Igor's face to register his conflicted emotions as he has to obey the father he depends on, and yet he is revolted by what his father is doing: The sheer inhumanity of it shocks Igor. Viewers are invited to share Igor's empathy for Amidu and shame for his father's actions but not to identify as such with Igor. The staging of the frame enables us to observe Igor's journey rather than to "become" Igor as perhaps would have been the case in a Hollywood film.

The rest of the film traces Igor's attempts to rescue Assita from a similar fate to her husband's, or at least from being sold into prostitution by the father. He refuses subjection to the Law, and finds a small space for resistance and agency. This takes him on a journey during which he learns about and comes to respect Assita's ritualistic ancestor beliefs. It also involves his perceiving how his culture treats African immigrants (there's a scene where boys pee on Assita and wreck her belongings with their motorbikes), and understands the pain his father has caused.

Significantly, just as Igor is literally repairing the statuette shattered by the boys on motorbikes, his father enters the garage where he is, having finally caught up with Igor. As in the scene of Amidu's accident, the Dardenne brothers create a highly suspenseful sequence that dramatizes Igor's conflict between dependency for love and survival on his father, and his newly found ethics. His immediate action is to tie up his father: But afterward, as he listens to his father pleading to be released, his conflict is heightened. It's a scene of suspense such as is normally found in thrillers or horror films, and the viewer is on tenterhooks during its entirety. Again, the camera catches Igor's face as he struggles to resist his father, as he finally does.

But this film has no happy ending: Igor has arranged for Assita to go to Italy where she has relatives. But at the last moment he tells her that Amidu is buried near the

FIGURE 16.3. *La Promesse* (Dardenne brothers, 1996): Igor and Assita walk together into an unknown future.

rooming house where they stayed. Assita cannot leave the place where her husband's body is buried, and the film ends with these two oddly matched people—a young white boy just becoming a man and a bereft, young African woman far from home—walking together in a railway station.

In keeping with the new global context, unlike Herzog's or Denis's films (which are very specifically located in time and space), *La Promesse* exists in the no-place commonality of international industrial capitalism in the postcolonial world. The Dardenne brothers' camera insists on catching the huge trucks barreling along interstate roads at a fast clip, and gives viewers occasional sweeping glances at the desolate factory-laden landscape, bleak, beyond human scale, nothing but machines and traffic. Characters are caught trying to cross immense roads, dashing in between traffic that could squash them in a moment. It could be anywhere in the new globalized world, symbolizing people's fragile hold on existence, their vulnerability to forces larger than themselves.

Yet it is within this anomalous, anonymous environment that Igor discovers morality through shame at his father's dealings and callous ways. His prior fear of abandonment, his dependency and subjection and his mirroring of illusory oneness with his father, Roger, kept Igor aligned with him, and rendered him, like France as a little girl, vulnerable to subordination and exploitation. But at a certain point, the drive to repair damage to Assita takes precedence over Igor's fear of abandonment: He takes responsibility, becomes an active agent of reparation, and finds the strength to abandon his father. The Dardenne brothers seem to be saying that agency and ethics can emerge from the destabilized global era through the mobilization of emotions like shame.

The three films discussed here each share somewhat similar strategies for dealing with affect and emotion, if in highly varied contexts. All deal in differing ways with colonial or postcolonial encounters, and all identify with minority or immigrant groups. Herzog uses generalized feelings via nature and landscape to express violence, destruction, and anomie in regard to the Aborigines in Australia—feelings that affect the viewer powerfully; Denis works mainly with intensity through alternating staging the frame with scenes between characters without dialogue that rely on intensity between subjects rather than on emotions attached to them; the Dardenne brothers include similar strategies, but also in charting Igor's inner ethical change through empathy, his developing an inner world (including a conscience) as a result of what he sees his father doing, the brothers come closer to the Hollywood convention of focus on individual change. Yet this is not, as it would be in Hollywood, a story of one boy's growth into a man. It's not a bildungsroman; for in the course of showing us the change in Igor, the Dardenne brothers also keep a certain distance so that viewers understand the larger context within which the displaced working class arrives at its illegal, criminal, and racist activities.

It is in this sense of art that insists on moving beyond the individual to larger social meanings that all three films studied here in their differing ways offer what I have elsewhere called the position of being a witness to trauma.[24] One of the main characteristics of the witnessing position as formulated usefully by Dori Laub is the deliberate refusal of an identification with the specificity of the individuals involved—a deliberate distancing from the subject to enable the interviewer to take in and respond to the traumatic *situation*.[25] In bearing witness, in the sense I have developed building on Laub, one not only provides a witness where no one was there to witness before. But more than that, one feels responsible for injustice in general. Witnessing involves wanting to change the kind of world where injustice, of whatever kind, is common. Witnessing leads to a broader understanding of the meaning of what has been done to victims, of the politics of trauma being possible. To do this, one has to learn to take the Other's subjectivity as a starting point, not as something to be ignored or denied. It is only in this way that we can gain a public or national ethics. The three films studied here, despite employing different strategies as discussed earlier, each construct a position for the viewer that enables taking responsibility, and in so doing to embrace a larger social and political ethics.

NOTES

1. Critics focus on emotional relationships and what characters are shown to feel but have not usually looked at how affect structures screen space or at what Brian Massumi (see later discussion) calls the "expressive event" in contrast to emotions specific to particular characters.

2. While scholars have recently shown an interest in cinema and the body, the focus is visceral spectator response (Steven Shaviro, *The Cinematic Body* [Minneapolis: University of Minnesota Press, 1993]; Linda Williams, *Hard Core: Power, Pleasure and the "Frenzy of the Visible"* [Berkeley: University of California Press, 1999]) or the haptic (touch and smell) (Laura Marks, *The Skin of the Film: Intercultural Cinema, Embodiment, and the Senses* [Durham, N.C.: Duke University Press, 2000]). In none of these cases do scholars discuss the spectator's emotions implicitly involved in visual, cognition, and bodily response: Visual pleasure obviously implies sexual arousal in the spectator (never explicitly addressed until Linda Williams's work on pornography); touch may involve joy or shame, disgust or hate.

3. Brian Massumi, "The Autonomy of Affect," *Critical Inquiry* (Autumn 1995): 235.

4. Before we can engage productively in projects dealing with emotions in culture, we need to know more about how emotions circulate, how emotions function within the individual, about differences among the various kinds of emotions, the relationships among cognition, emotion, and the body, and about cultural differences vis-à-vis emotions. This project offers merely an initial contribution from the specific perspective of film studies.

5. While I realize that Mary Louis Pratt's original use of the concept of "contact-zones" has raised objections regarding its implicit Eurocentrism, in this essay I use it to refer to the coming together in new spaces of Western subjects and peoples originally colonized by such subjects. For me, the term by no means implies a contact on equal footing—quite the reverse. Western subjects are always privileged over non-Western ones until a transformation takes place in a Western subject. And even then, "equality" does not happen.

6. The list of books dealing with race/ethnicity on film would be very long, but see Ella Shohat and Robert Stam's *Unthinking Eurocentrism: Multiculturalism and the*

Media (New York: Routledge, 1997) and my *Looking for the Other: Feminism, Film and the Imperial Gaze* (New York: Routledge, 1997) for extensive preliminary bibliographies. In this context, I would say that traditional racist images were not even about an encounter but rather deliberately aroused a priori negative public feelings about African, Chinese, or Latin American characters through scandalous resort to vicious stereotypes.

7. Terminology is a big problem in this research, now still in its early stages. Psychoanalysis and psychology differ as disciplines in regard to definitions, and in addition individual analysts and psychologists use terms (emotions, affects, feelings) in different ways. One could follow the debates about affect in psychoanalytic circles, or note how little attention psychologists give to terminology in their vast experiments about human emotions. Here, however, I will use Massumi's distinction in analyzing selected films, and use the term *emotions* when generalizing about feelings in the public sphere, or discussing how specific feelings circulate in cultures. *Emotions* then refers to specific feelings, and *affect* to feeling as intensity, as a kind of force in culture, hardly recognized because not tied to a fixed emotion. *Feeling* for me then indicates the subject's bodily response either to a specific emotion or to affective intensity, however constituted, whatever produced the response.

8. Willemen, Paul, and Jim Pines, *Questions of Third Cinema* (London: British Film Institue, 1998); Shohat and Stam, *Unthinking Eurocentrism*.

9. In his "The Autonomy of Affect," Massumi provides the example of Ronald Reagan, and how his use of emotions swung people to his political positions.

10. My own sensitivity toward "feeling" in art films I was teaching arose in the context of interest in emotion (perhaps as a "return of the *critical* repressed" but for other social reasons as well) on the part of literary and cultural studies scholars. African-American and Latino authors lead the way in presenting emotional responses to racism, and Eve Sedgwick and Adam Frank added to this in their interest in Silvan Tompkins's psychology research, especially in regard to shame and its related feelings. Sedgwick and Frank did not provide a map or guide for how to take up emotions in literary and cultural studies (although Sedgwick later published *Touching Feeling: Affect, Pedagogy, Performativity* [Durham, N.C.: Duke University Press, 2003]), leaving others to integrate their insights in other ways. Is it coincidence that interest in trauma and the Holocaust emerged in the mid-1990s around the same time that Sedgwick was reading Tompkins? Was the return to Freud that trauma study involved (as for instance in Cathy Caruth's pioneering volumes, or in film studies Dominick La Capra and Janet Walker) also coincidental? Lauren Berlant's work on the public sphere and emotions was influential, in *The Queen of America Goes to Washington* (Durham, N.C.: Duke University Press, 1997) as was that by Ann Cvetkovich on publics and counterpublics in *An Archive of Feelings: Trauma, Sexuality and Lesbian Public Cultures* (Durham, N.C.: Duke University Press, 2003), extending ideas of Jürgen Habermas, Oskar Negt, and Alexander Kluge. Sara Ahmed's *The Cultural Politics of Emotion* (Edinburgh: Edinburgh University Press, 2004) followed with a thorough analysis of how emotions are constituted in the public sphere in Australia, Britain, and America and, in a sense, a new subfield had arrived.

11. A large interdisciplinary literature already exists in relation to defining the term *emotion*, especially as regards similarity or difference from the term *affect*, and also in relation to the links between affect/emotion and cognition. A useful survey of interdisciplinary literature (with a special focus on emotion and the law) by Terry A. Maroney provides a bibliography for some of these debates (see his Working Paper No. 05-11, "Law and Emotion: A Proposed Taxonomy of an Emerging Field").

12. For more details about emotions the film elicited when shown on at least thirty campuses, see http://www.nytimes.com/2007/02/26/movies/26docu.html?_r=2&oref=slogin&pagewanted=print. In general, readers can fill in their own examples. Indeed, the very different reactions to the 2007 film version of *Lady Chatterley's Lover* (which passed with hardly any reaction) provide evidence for how public feelings operate. What was a scandal in the 1920s passes with hardly any public comment in 2007! But equally interesting for future research is that there can be no intense public reaction to films one would have expected to arouse passion, such as the films about 9/11. (Thanks to my colleague Adrian Pérez Melgosa for this insight about "failures" in regard to strong emotions about film.) It is possible that there was little reaction to 9/11 films because a lot of people stayed away, thinking it too painful to return to this trauma.

13. In a reformulation of his classic work on genre and spectatorship, Rick Altman also stresses the multiple readings and uses of cinema by varied communities of viewers, *Film/Genre* (London: British Film Institute, 1995).

14. If it may be true, as Kate Stanley recently argued, that Massumi re-evokes Descartes' now dated binary between mind and body, his distinction remains useful for the purposes of elaborating different strategies for producing emotional valence in cinema. See Stanley's unpublished paper, "Pragmatic Feelings: A Theory and Practice of Reading," delivered at the American Comparative Literature Association Annual Conference at Harvard University, March 28, 2009.

15. Jill Bennett, *Empathic Vision: Affect, Trauma, and Contemporary Art* (Stanford, Calif.: Stanford University Press, 2005), 10.

16. In her illuminating volume, *Empathic Vision*, Bennett draws on Gilles Deleuze's theories of affect in literature and art, in particular his concept of sensation leading to thought. As she puts it, "Deleuze's argument is not simply . . . that sensation is an end in itself, but that feeling is a catalyst for critical inquiry or deep thought" (7). This strikes me as aiming at something very similar to the concept of "witnessing" that I developed in *Trauma Culture: The Politics of Loss and Terror in Media and Literature* (New Brunswick, N.J.: Rutgers University Press, 2005), except that I see a need both for emotional identification (the lure to bring spectators to empathize) and for expressive events to generalize from the specific instance to larger communities so as to engage an ethics.

17. See chapters in *Trauma Culture* (especially 107–110) and also in my co-edited volume (with Ban Wang) on *Trauma and Cinema: Cross-cultural Explorations* (Hong Kong: Hong Kong University Press, 2004).

18. Kaplan, E. Ann. (1995). "Interview with Claire Denis." "Travelling Cultures: Sex, Race and Cinema." Retrospective for Five Women Film Directors organized by E. Ann Kaplan for The American Center, Paris. Unpublished.

19. Frantz Fanon, *Black Skin, White Masks* trans. Charles Lam Markmann (London: Paladin), 79. In the interview I had with Denis in 1995, she noted that she had read and been influenced by Fanon in making *Chocolat*, so perhaps this association is plausible.

20. Judith Butler, *The Psychic Life of Power: Theories in Subjection* (Stanford, Calif.: Stanford University Press, 1997), 7.

21. Lauren Berlant, "Nearly Utopian, Nearly Normal: Post-Fordist Affect in *La Promesse* and *Rosetta*," *Public Culture* 19, no. 2 (2007): 272–301.

22. Judith Butler usefully renders the foundational ambivalence at the core of subject formation. Butler argues that "the attachment to subjection is produced through the workings of power" (6), which have this insidious psychic result of the subject's apparent collusion in subjection. For Butler, then, the powerful emotional

dependency of the child on its caregivers in order to survive—the dependency on love for survival—is key to our being vulnerable to subjection to the law. But it also enables agency, if of an awkward kind: "Painful, dynamic and promising, this vacillation between the already-there and the yet-to-come is a crossroads that rejoins every step by which it is traversed, a reiterated ambivalence at the heart of agency" (18).

23. Bennett, *Empathic Vision*, 15.

24. See my *Trauma Culture*, chapter 6, for an extended discussion of this concept of witnessing.

25. Dori Laub, "Bearing Witness; or, The Vicissitudes of Listening," in *Testimony: Crises of Witnessing in Literature, Psychoanalysis, and History*, ed. Shoshana Felman and Laub (New York: Routledge, 1992), 57–74.

17

OFFERING TALES THEY WANT TO HEAR: TRANSNATIONAL EUROPEAN FILM FUNDING AS NEO-ORIENTALISM

Randall Halle

The linguistic barrier that arose with the introduction of sound film created conditions for national cinemas in international distribution that required a certain worldliness and global orientation of their spectators. Cinema offered material for self-consciously cosmopolitan intellectuals interested in foreign cultures. Of course not just any film enters into international distribution; generally only "quality" films travel outside domestic markets, lending the false impression to an "outside" audience that the other national markets contain only quality products.

The cinema of the "other" became associated with high cultural film art, most clearly evidenced by the cinemas of the various postwar national new waves. Participants in the various new waves understood their work as aesthetically superior to industrial film, especially the American productions that crowded the screens. Thus, national art film became not simply an exterior distinction but an internal one as well. By the 1960s national subsidy systems like that which supported the New German Cinema in principle accepted this condition as a natural foundation for film financing. German film—or Danish, Dutch, French, and Italian film for that matter—was meant to provide artful tales told by a people to themselves, a set of stories proper to the high cultural interests of a nation.

In the last decade the nature and form of film production in Europe have been fundamentally transformed. The period of the new waves came to an end with the end of the Cold War and with the move toward European union. In the 1990s active efforts began to convene the more than 300 million potential spectators spread across Europe's regions into a more coherent viewing public.[1] The European Union (EU), the more expansive Council of Europe (CoE), and regional mechanisms such as Ibermedia or Nordic Film organizations were the agents of radical changes, giving rise to a whole set of supranational funding mechanisms, developing a transnational orientation for audiovisual production, expanding dramatically the popular orientation, and bolstering pan-European structures of synergistic cooperation. This transformation for Europe represents a significant shift in the nature and qualities of national film production. Across Europe film as national high cultural product in a rich subsidy system has given way to film as popular entertainment circulating in a for-profit transnational network.

Nevertheless the expectations of the cosmopolitan audience have endured vis-à-vis art cinema. There is a market for films that tell the tales of foreign cultures and distant peoples, and thus the for-profit system seeks to respond to the interests of this commercial audience. This essay will first offer an overview of coproduction strategies that have emerged in the new European context to fulfill this interest in national stories. However, what fundamentally interests me in this essay is what happens as the European mechanisms to support coproductions expand beyond the borders of Europe. This funding for films beyond the borders becomes increasingly important because coproduction support has reached a level at which for 2004 the entire film production of numerous countries took place as coproductions with partners in core EU countries: Kazakhstan, Mozambique, Mali, Lebanon, Tunisia, and Algeria were such countries to name only a few.

The essay discusses the differences in narrative strategies for inner and external European films. While the inner European films seek to tell common European stories, in the case of the external European coproduction, the films seek to offer insight into a type of person, if not an entire people. From the perspective of European values, the films provide the viewer with the grounds for a critical intervention in that foreign society. The coproduction strategy thus runs the risk of instituting a cycle of Orientalism, offering Euro-American audiences tales they want to hear, about people fundamentally different from themselves, keeping as distant strangers people who live around the corner or down the hall. This essay will explore what happens as the policy of national art film with its cosmopolitan audience gives way to a postcolonial politics of the transnational.

THE FOUNDATIONS OF THE TRANSNATIONAL COPRODUCTION

In the 1990s, the move toward European union increased transnational cultural and economic cooperation; international coproductions gained a transnational imperative. Chief among these efforts continues to be the MEDIA Program of the EU and the Eurimages Program of the Council of Europe. The MEDIA and Eurimages programs derive from separate European organizations and were designed to fulfill differing competencies. One of the central aspects of Eurimages is the funding of coproductions between at least two member countries of the CoE. In fostering work that transcends national borders, Eurimages seeks to fulfill one of its primary goals, support for "works which reflect the multiple facets of a European society whose common roots are evidence of a single culture."[2]

The cooperative work undertaken within Eurimages and MEDIA differs dramatically from the kinds of coproduction arrangements present in the 1970s, for instance.[3] Coproduction arrangements were often undertaken at that time to raise budgets for films refused by subsidy systems because they were too oriented toward popular culture, because they conflicted with the goals of the subsidizing body, or because the subsidy budgets were too small. In effect coproductions at that time were primarily about raising enough of a budget to circumvent the ideological control of the subsidy system. Now through MEDIA and Eurimages the pattern is inverted so that coproductions take on a subsidy and therewith come to serve an ideological purpose, the promotion of Europeanist transnationalism—to the telling of European stories, as it were.

The effect of such European film funding extends beyond the boundaries of Europe. Within the European Union a number of programs have arisen not only to foster inner-European filmmaking convergence but to also develop synergy with non-European filmmakers and film industries. The MEDIA Program, for instance, sponsors European Neighbourhood Policy Countries, Outside MEDIA, and EUROMED, which establish connections with Eastern Europe, Africa, and the Mediterranean countries, respectively. These programs aim to foster the distribution and exhibition of European films abroad, especially in the non-EU Mediterranean regions. EUROMED in particular foresees a specifically close regional connection, restoring ancient historic Mediterranean trade routes and cultural exchange networks. Equally, the Europa Cinema network has branched out beyond the territory of the EU, receiving support from the French Ministry of Foreign Affairs to subsidize theaters in Eastern Europe, and from the EUROMED program to subsidize cinemas in twelve Mediterranean countries.[4] Within the network there are now more than 1,500 screens in 46 countries, thereby allowing European film to reach well beyond Europe from Kabul to Ramallah, from São Paolo to Toronto.Such a strategy makes sense as part of an attempt to dislodge Hollywood narratives from their preeminent position on the screens of Europe's closest neighbors.

Moreover, this course of production does not flow only in one direction. These programs also support the distribution and exhibition in Europe of European co-sponsored films from Eastern Europe, Africa, the Mediterranean, or Latin America. They organize Arab and Turkish film weeks, support films from the Mediterranean basin in key film markets such as Cannes and Berlin, and support the creation of Web sites, "making-of" documentaries, and DVD releases of films. The MEDIA Program has proven reluctant to make funds directly available to develop African and North African film out of a realization that supporting non-European professionals would work to the detriment of European filmmakers. Hence they have primarily supported exhibition and distribution, or coproduction conditions in which European professional teams comprise the majority of the films' crews. Nevertheless, support for non-European film goes into production through funds deriving from national and Council of Europe agents.

A list of some of the more significant national funds gives a sense of the nature of European involvement: the Jan Vrijman Fund (Benelux), Hubert Bals Fund (Dutch), Göteborg Film Festival Fund (Swedish), World Cinema Fund (German), Visions Sud Est (Swiss), Fonds Sud (French), and Fond Francophone de Production Audiovisuelle du Sud (French). These funds thus direct financing from the prosperous countries of northern and western Europe toward the south and east. They support feature films and documentaries, offering grants in ranges from 5,000 to 152,000 Euros. Stipulations placed on producers vary, but often these funds are associated with a screening requirement, for example, that they premier at Göteborg or Rotterdam, or that a European national production partner must be involved. The coproduction funds thereby foster an ease of distribution in European film markets. In these activities the French Fonds Sud of the Centre National de la Cinématographie is most active. Since its inception in 1984, it has supported more than 350 feature film projects with production funds of over 100,000 Euros each.[5] As with the World Cinema Fund, a French company must be involved as coproducer and the films must be screened in French theaters. And of course the Europa Cinemas Network works with distributors and serves as an exhibition outlet for these films.

Three Aesthetics of Transnational Coproduction

If we have up to this point primarily attended to the infrastructure of production, what happens to the surface of the film, the images projected on the screen? The narrative strategies prove to be equal points of grand experimentation. In the early years of Eurimages a form of multicultural logic emerged that consciously sought to undermine national specificity, exemplified in films such as the *House of the Spirits* (August, 1993). We can compile an extensive list of films that follow this transcultural approach: *Homo Faber* (Schlöndorff, 1991), *Farinelli* (Corbiau, 1994), *Charlotte Brontë's Jane Eyre* (Zeffirelli, 1996), *Semana Santa* (Danquart, 2002), and so on. Unlike Kieslowski's *Three Colors*, in which the ethnic background of the characters matches that of the actors (that is, French characters are played by French actors), the films of this transcultural approach ignore or tendentiously seek to overcome such determinations. In Zeffirelli's film the British-French actress Charlotte Gainsbourg plays the title role, while William Hurt plays the role of Rochester. Schlöndorff sought Sam Shepard for the role of Walter Faber and Julie Delpy for the figure of Sabeth. However, it is important to underscore that the transcultural approach is only one approach and is an approach that belongs to a particular form of European filmmaking. In these examples, the actor/character relationship tends toward a form of universality deriving from their apparent status as *Europeans*. The ideological determination of such "universality" becomes clear in other filming/casting strategies that rely on a contrast with a non-European "other" or portrayals of European ethnic or religious conflict: *No Man's Land* (Tanovic, 2001), *Bloody Sunday* (Greengrass, 2002), and so on. We will return to this point later.

　　Certainly many films produced in Hollywood do not consider the ethnicity of the characters. Indeed many films notoriously exhibit little concern for historical accuracy, cultural difference, or even linguistic competency. If any consideration plays a significant role, it is that accents match the character—although for a Hollywood production set abroad, the American midwestern accent can always stand in as a universal. The point of contrast, however, is that working with a European narrative and cast becomes more exacting in terms of balancing out variables. Hollywood productions have historically frequently absorbed actors without regard to their ethnic background. For a European production, the initial consideration derives from a consideration of background. Beyond actor/role relationship of the script, many of the decisions stem precisely from the requirements of the coproduction agreement, which may determine for instance that a certain number of national actors or locations must be used in order for the film to qualify for subsidies. Thus the transcultural film evidences the vicissitudes of its funding through its production decisions. Reliance on English or the star power of actors may wind up outweighing the particulars of the script and its cultural settings.

These films have the ability to attract audiences because they rely on well-known world literature, because of their star power, or because art-film directors generate significant box office revenue as auteurs. For the subsidy system, box office draw plays an important role in the allocation of funds, and the increase in spectators accomplished by such films verified the logic. However, accented English or dubbing deployed as a strategy to contend with multiple languages often proves disturbing to audiences. Critics in general reject such films as Euro-puddings, while members of national audiovisual industries perceive such films as an inappropriate allocation of limited national subsidy funds. Rather than understanding such films as experiments in the quest for a more universal European film language such as that Hollywood has developed, or as improving the local film industries through know-how transfer or increased financial profitability, the various interested groups view this form of European film as working against the interests of national film.[6]

Thus, the transcultural approach bespeaks the limits of its universality and gives way to other approaches. In this field of transnational cultural experimentation we discover a second form of film, the transnational scenario approach. Such an approach develops a narrative that seeks to represent directly a quasi-transnational situation. We could consider here any number of examples, including such successful films as the French/Belgian/Luxembourgian *Salut Cousin!* (Allouache, 1995), the Austrian/French/German/Romanian *Code Inconnu/Code Unknown* (Haneke, 1999), the German/Austrian/Swiss coproduction *Bella Martha* (Nettelbeck 2001), the French and Spanish hit *Auberge espagnole / The Spanish Apartment* (Klapisch, 2001), or the German Spanish multilocation film *One Day in Europe* (Stöhr, 2005). *Auberge* in particular relied on the study abroad possibilities afforded to European university students through the popular Erasmus exchange program. A French boy goes to Spain and takes up residence in an apartment filled with other students from across the EU. They build friendships and liaisons, face hardships and good times, and at the end of the year return to their respective homes as adults, better national citizens, and good Europeans. *Auberge* and the other films establish a transnational space of cultural contact where their characters represent national or cultural types: the cold German, the emotionally charged Italian, the drunken British hooligan, the illegal Algerian, the mysterious African. They come together within particular institutions: the workspace, the university, the ghetto, and so on.

Another example, *Lamerica* (Amelio, 1993), an Italian/French/Swiss coproduction, tells the tale of two petty Italian conmen who travel to Albania in order to fleece the locals who are unfamiliar with Western capitalist methods. Instead they become lost in increasing difficulties until their own identity melts away. This film has a fascinating power, relying on shots that draw documentary elements into the film. It thematizes real problems of Europe that arise within the difficulties of cross-cultural contact, economic disparity, historical experience, neocolonial exploitation, West European naive arrogance, travel, foreignness, and so on. However, the Albanians here form a frightening, threatening other to the Italians, and rarely do they emerge out of this flattening backdrop.

These films derive from a similar infrastructure as the transcultural films, yet they seek to align the infrastructure with the film's content and appearance. Italians play Italians, French play French, and so on. These films partake in a *strategy of cultural essentialism*. If in the previous form national particularity became effaced in various ways, here it is highlighted and made central to the characters' motivations. The "good European" actor/role is set in stark visible contrast to asylum seekers, migrants, minorities, non-Christians, and political radicals. In this way, national culture returns as international interaction. However, what appears proper to the cultures derives from distant concerns covered in local garments. Culturally essentialist films develop their commitment to their funding arrangements through narratives about cultural contact, yet in such contact films the types run the risk of becoming stereotypes, and the emphasis on cultural essentialism risks devolving into what Leslie Adelson has described as an "in-betweenism."[7]

Finally, from the mid-1990s onward we find a very different form of film arising, one that offers a quasi-national approach. Here, the transnational is quasi-disguised as a national product. As part of this strategy we can include films like *Breaking the Waves* (von Trier, 1996) or *Gripsholm* (Koller, 1999), in which national tales are told from "non-national" perspectives. While they exhibit an ethnic/national correspondence between actor and character, these are not films about cultural contact as such. There is no transnational scenario that inflects their narrative. The basic structure of the funding, the coproduction agreement plays little explicit role in the appearance and texture of the film. Certainly Stellan Skarsgård plays a Danish character in von Trier's film. However, the story, primary location, and the rest of the cast all are or appear to be in tune with the northern Scottish setting. There is no sign that the film was not funded by U.K. funds but rather was a Danish, Swedish, Dutch, and French coproduction organized through Eurimages support. The strategy of national appearance, however, can go much further.

Bakhtyar Khudojnazarov's film *Luna Papa* from 1999 was widely hailed as the first sign of a new dynamic Tajik national film culture arising out of the ashes of the Soviet Union. Khudojnazarov described it as a "fantastical realist" film narrated from the perspective of the as-yet-unborn child of the main character, Mamalakat. The action revolves around her, her brother Nasreddin, and their father. As a Eurimages coproduction the funding drew together a complicated cooperation arrangement with eight companies and no fewer than eleven European funding sources.[8] Pre- and post-production took place primarily in Germany. In truth Khudojnazarov's native Tajikistan offered little more than location. Yet unlike *House of the Spirits*, the transnational quality of the film receded to the background, appearing only in the film through the casting choice of German actor Moritz Bleibtreu in the role of Nasreddin. Even this potentially audible sign of difference was minimized. The filmmaker obviated the potential problem that Bleibtreu speaks no Tajik or Russian, which would have led to accent or dubbing issues, by developing the character as a mute. Hence Bleibtreu cavorts and pantomimes through the entire film, lending it a slapstick quality but generating no sign of his own cultural background.

Another telling example is *Paradise Now* (2005), a complex tale of two potential suicide bombers from the West Bank. It received an Oscar nomination for best foreign language picture and ignited a controversy because the director, Hany Abu-Assad, wanted the film's country of origin listed as Palestine. The Academy of Motion Picture Arts and Sciences labeled it instead as from the Palestinian Authority. The funding for the film, however, designates it as a Dutch/German/French/Italian coproduction. As with *Luna Papa*, cast, setting, and director offer the appearance of a Palestinian film, but the financial basis for the film, the infrastructure of its production, derives from Europe.

Certainly, by using mostly actors from the country in which the stories are set, these films thus avoid the audible and visible textual markers of international influence that the international cast caused in *House of the Spirits*. They appear as Tajik or Palestinian films. The quasi-national film, by contrast to the transcultural film, establishes a narrative that focuses on a unique and nationally homogeneous setting, thereby masking the complexity of its economic base. The national film thus appears as telling stories directed to a national public sphere, but such an orientation is only one valence, and often a tangential one to the export market orientation of the film. *Luna Papa* went first to international film festivals and only later found distribution in Tajikistan, suggesting the first Tajik film was directed more at European and in particular German audiences.

In the following section, I want to consider more closely the parameters of this last strategy, the quasi-national films. Although the strategies that once represented national cultures have changed, for the contemporary spectator these films will most likely occupy the same position once held by the New German Cinema or the French Nouvelle Vague. On the surface of their images, and the way they appear in exhibition, there will be little difference. They will often be screened in the same cinemas that run Fassbinder and Truffaut retrospectives, and they will often run in a series of films designated as new Tajik film, new Algerian cinema, the films of Ghana, and so on. They will offer a sense of engagement with a foreign culture because there is little to indicate to those spectators that national cinema now gives way to the transnational. In the images of a quasi-national film, the national cinemas, German, Irish, Polish, and so on, appear intact even if the films themselves no longer serve the same function for a national infrastructure.

However, a more pressing question to pose is, what significant difference can we identify between a European coproduction set in Europe and one from outside Europe?

While *Breaking the Waves* does not offer a cheerful impression of Calvinist Scotland or the culture of the oil rigs, the film does not offer insights into *the Scot*. The moments it offers as critical images do not represent a critical intervention in Scottish culture or U.K. oil policies. In the case of *Paradise Now*, however, this is not the case. Indeed the film seeks to offer insight into a type of person, if not a people, and provides the viewer with the basis of a critique of Palestine, Israel, the United States, and so on. It is on this difference that I wish to concentrate.

ORIENTALISM AND THE TRANSNATIONAL COPRODUCTIONS

It is clear that under the auspices of programs like Eurimage, a transnational coproduction has developed that provides films corresponding to European interests. What happens to national film outside of Europe in light of this regime, as the EU and CoE programs extend out into development projects outside of Europe? The aforementioned Outside Media and the Euromed programs prove important for Mediterranean basin countries where the national film industries have gone through a number of crises in the last two decades, and in sub-Saharan Africa, these programs are indispensable since most film and media industries have no stable independent status, and without outside European support audiovisual production would most likely simply not exist. The French in particular, through such institutions as the Agence Francophonie or the Ministère des Affaires Etrangères, have established mechanisms such as Africa Cinemas, which coordinate distribution, exhibition, and promotion of African films.[9] This program works under the auspices of EU funds marked for projects in the "developing" world. For Francophone West African countries like Benin or Cameroon, where one to three films may be produced in a year, such networks make those films viable and make film production possible. It is these conditions that produce the situation I described previously in which the entire film production of some non-European countries occurs in coproductions with EU partners. One is immediately incited to wonder whether the films are inevitably neocolonialist or if these programs are simply facilitating the production of films in countries that would not otherwise have the resources. Do these films align with European interests in ways that make their profit less than benign to their countries of origin?

EUROMED coproductions have certainly bolstered Mediterranean film production and are financially profitable for their European participants. For example, in North Africa and the Middle East, they maintain a very important market share. Nabil Ayouch, director of the EUROMED-initiated MEDIA Film program housed in Morocco, estimated that in 2005 and 2006 in Israel fourteen films achieved 9 percent market share, twenty-eight Moroccan films achieved 18 percent market share, in Turkey thirty-four films achieved 52 percent, and in Egypt thirty-five films achieved 80 percent.[10] Thus European investment in quasi-national film production from these regions represents a profitable economic investment. While little interest may exist for a

German or a Dutch film in Egypt, a coproduction that circulates as an Egyptian national film draws audiences, even though this draw is ultimately to a European film. In sum, this form of film funding establishes circles of distribution between Europe and funded countries. This funding importantly holds open screening venues and keeps indigenous film industries alive at the same time that it guarantees that European film remains part of the exhibition mechanism.

Financially, such funding assures that the resuscitation of the local film industries takes place attached to the drip of European monies while ensuring that a portion of the profit from development projects returns to Europe. That arrangement in itself is not unreasonable; however, we should note that part of the initial reason for the dismal conditions of indigenous productions, especially in the Mediterranean, derives from free trade agreements forced on those countries by the European Union, the World Bank, and the International Monetary Fund. For instance, enforcement of free market agreements begun in the late 1980s and accelerated in the 1990s undermined the Algerian government's subsidy system so that an industry that produced roughly thirty-three films per year in the 1970s dwindled to two or three films a year by 1995. From 1998 to 1999 Ahmed Ouyahia's government closed down and restructured all three of the major state bodies that controlled film production. The film industry that once offered the world some of the most potent views into the process of decolonization and postcoloniality now is forced to make coproductions with French partners.[11]

Algerian filmmakers, once frustrated by the censorship of the state, repeatedly call for a coherent subsidy system to keep the film industry alive.[12] They thus echo many of their European colleagues. It should be underscored that the free market conditions forced on Algeria are precisely the kinds of conditions against which the French government and audiovisual industry has struggled for years with relative success. Insofar, then, as the EU subsidy systems and coproduction programs move in to support production in developing regions, these programs reinforce larger structures of uneven and unequal development, where film becomes another aspect of first-world aid. The difference, however, from traditional forms of aid (industrial development, medical, or food supplies) is that film is a cultural product.

Thus, that these coproductions generally rely on the strategy of narration that allows them to appear as national films, or as culturally essentializing narratives about, for instance, French and Algerian, German and Turkish, or Dutch and Moroccan communities should raise concerns. The 1998 film *Al Aish fil Jannah / Living in Paradise* (Guerdjou) won an award for best first film at the Venice Film Festival. This film appeared precisely at the point of the dismantling of Algerian state funding and thus developed its budget as a French/Belgian/Norwegian/Algerian coproduction—more precisely through the organization of Eurimages, the French Centre National de Cinématographie, and the French television station Canal+, as well as the Belgian Centre du Cinéma et de l'Audiovisuel de la Communauté française de Belgique, and the Télédistributeurs Wallons. The story is set in the early years of the 1960s during the Algerian war, but not in Algeria, rather in the immigrant community in France. The story thus belongs to the transnational scenario approach. It is important to note that this is the first narrative film to portray the 1961 massacre of about 200 Algerian demonstrators by the French police. An Algerian director with European funding thus tells a tale of grave historical importance to an international French and Algerian audience. Critics like Carrie Tarr and Richard Derderian have praised the film for its revision of French history. In her recent book *Reframing Difference*, Tarr argues vis-à-vis *Living* that "the hegemonic heritage film typically functions to produce a Eurocentric understanding of French history and national identity, privileging traditional French values and cultural norms."[13] She sees then this film as constituting a significant "beur" and "banlieu" contribution to French (film) history. While such arguments are certainly convincing, and as important as the film is for France, one is left to wonder how pressing this history is for an audience in Algeria. If Tarr is correct, we might have to rethink what we mean by Eurocentric, in as much as transnational histories might actually tell a broader history of Europe (although Europe and not other locales still may provide their narrative center).

At the 2007 Berlin film festival a panel discussion took place, addressing the activities of the Euromed program. Significant among the panel's comments was the realization of a "paradox" in which filmmakers turn to Europe to develop their films, yet in doing so expose themselves to a "neo-colonialism."[14] Similarly, a roundtable on the conditions of film production in Africa took place at the 2002 bATik film festival in Perugia, Italy, a festival devoted in particular to independent international film, especially African.[15] African filmmakers and producers who participated in the roundtable noted invariably the dependence of African films on funding from Europe: Without European funds African film production would not exist. While clearly pleased by the support, the filmmakers noted certain effects of the situation, not the least significant of which is an aesthetic and narrative orientation toward European tastes. Tunisian director Mahamoud ben Mahamoud noted, "It occasionally happens that in order to satisfy a French or Italian audience, an African director is forced never to address the issues that really happen in Africa."[16] African film critic Ferid Boughedir described the condition more pointedly:

> There is an urgent need to solve another huge problem created by our depen-
> dence on European cash. Many African countries do not have an internal film
> market. As a result, a paradoxical situation is created whereby African films are
> seen abroad but not at home. It is almost as though an African who looks at
> himself in the mirror, sees a European looking back at him.[17]

Certainly not all filmmakers share Boughedir's sentiment, and one might want to interrogate closely the presumptions of authenticity and essence that haunt his assessment. However, this quote underscores the way in which a new form of Eurocentrism may frame the experience of funded filmmakers. It indicates the fundamental and rapid transformation of national art cinema in the last two decades. And it certainly should incite a critical skepticism regarding the "foreign" narratives that play out on Euro-American screens.

The fundamental problem with these coproduced films of national appearance is the nature of their intervention in the public sphere. A Turkish or Algerian audience approaches a film set in California, Paris, or Berlin differently from one set in Istanbul or Algiers. Debates around cultural imperialism have centered on the omnipresence of Hollywood productions on the screens of a country, but the film that displays its conditions of production does not represent the same form of "threat" as films that mask those conditions. A Hollywood, Bollywood, or Hong Kong film on the screen enables the spectator potentially to take up a resistant relationship to the images, to decode them as indirect address. In effect it enables processes of hybridization and customization. When the images present themselves as autochthonous, the mechanism of disbelief takes a different form, concealing the processes of hybridization.

If we focus on Turkey, we note that it enjoys a particular privileged status as an associated country seeking ascent to the EU. Turkey thus has a different status from the North African nations, as an inside/outsider. Therefore, since the early 1990s Eurimages alone has supported the production of at least two to three Turkish films in coproduction per year. MEDIA has likewise engaged more actively in Turkey with promotion and distribution. This support takes on a great deal of significance if we recognize that the once significant Turkish film industry, Yesilçam, into the 1970s could produce more than 250 films a year. After the 1980 coup this number dropped, and in the 1990s the average production of films in Turkey declined to around 20 to 25 films per year.[18] Further, if two to three films per year are funded by Eurimages, this does not represent the full extent of European involvement. Once coproduction ties are established, the relationships often continue. Thus, roughly 10 to 25 percent of Turkish films are made in coordination with European and specifically German interests. This relationship has facilitated the distribution of European productions in Turkish cinemas. Interestingly and significantly, it has also tangibly benefited the Turkish industry.

Since 2001, production in Turkey is up, and Turkish involvement is also expanding in the film productions of other film industries. Domestic productions such as *Kurtlar Vadisi: Irak / Valley of the Wolves: Iraq* (Akar, 2006) or *Son Osmanli Yandim Ali / The Last Ottoman: Knockout Ali* (Dogan, 2007) are truly homespun films relying on nationalist narratives of masculine bravado. Yet the European coproductions represent a very different form of production than that produced by Turkey's popular filmmakers. The work of Yeşim Ustaoğlu stands out here. Her films *Günese Yolculuk / Journey to the Sun* (1999) or *Bulutlari Beklerken / Waiting for the Clouds* (2003) take on topics such as the violent suppression of the Kurdish population in Turkey during the 1980s, or the historic destruction of the Greek Ottoman population. Ustaoğlu has received more funds from Eurimages than any other Turkish filmmaker, and her films premier at international film festivals.

Deniz Göktürk notes that such work might actually serve a positive, liberalizing function. She has pointed out how "Eurimages and other transnational funding schemes engender critiques of 'peripheral' nation states and enable subnational minority politics," citing specifically *Journey to the Sun*. To be sure, she distinguishes this film from domestic popular production. And in terms of its function she observes that "*Journey* questioned segregationist views on Turkish and Kurdish identities, [and] . . . was awarded the Peace Prize at the Berlin Film Festival, at a time when Kurds were demonstrating against the arrest of Abdullah Ocalan in the streets of Berlin."[19] Fundamentally, though, that the critical films of Ustaoğlu, funded by transnational sources, speak to an international audience as Turkish films, while nationalist propaganda proves more popular with domestic audiences, illustrates some of the ideational complexity of this form of production.

Clearly, the support for films and filmmakers goes to those who are in line with European political agendas, and I would not contest the value of opening up for discussion the atrocities committed by military and dictatorial regimes. However, this emergent regime of European funding abroad represents a new dynamic of transnational interaction. This engagement with a country or geographic region takes place not as occupation or direct political intervention but rather as a matter of culture and as an intervention in the public sphere. Because the intervention takes place through a masquerade of national appearance, it marks a gentler form of neocolonial activity in the transnational era. My concern here is not one of national sovereignty; I am not interested in supporting a reactionary nationalism that would indeed align itself with domestic popular culture in these countries and regions. Nor am I particularly concerned with the domestic population being fooled by this cultural production. It is as unlikely that a Turk would recognize Ustaoğlu's work as any more or less authentically Turkish than a German would recognize German authenticity in Bille August's work. I would express concern that such transnational "meddling" in the public sphere through funding structures runs a risk of eliciting more of a backlash than the most "rally round the troops" bit of propaganda Hollywood could produce. Ustaoğlu, a maker of beautiful films, is subject to threats in ways that Mel Gibson, for instance, never will be. But in truth what concerns me most is the cycle of Orientalism that such film funding establishes.

The dynamic of Orientalism at work here supports the production of stories about other peoples and places that it, the funding source, wants to hear. Under the guise of authentic images, the films establish a textual screen that prevents apprehension of the complexly lived reality of people in not-too-distant parts of the world. A key aspect of the insights offered by Edward Said's foundational work on Orientalism is that an elaborate set of textual references had developed in Europe by which that which was fundamentally proximate is kept distant. Madrid is closer to Rabat than to Berlin; Rome is closer to Istanbul than to London. Yet these cities are worlds apart. The ideational distance derives not from a foreclosure of physical access and engagement, rather through the intervention and mediation of a set of cultural texts that speak the truth of the other on behalf of that other.

To draw this discussion to a conclusion, I want to focus on one particular formation in which this Orientalist dynamic appears most clearly. The German Bundeszentrale für politische Bildung (Federal Agency for Civic Education) (BPB) was established in 1952 as a means to facilitate denazification and to promote democratic political principles for the young Bonn Republic. The activity of the agency has changed in the fifty-five years of its history. It now centres on promoting awareness for democracy and participation in politics. It takes up topical and historical subjects by issuing publications, by organising seminars, events, study trips, exhibitions and competitions, by providing extension training for journalists and by offering films and on-line products. The broad range of educational activities provided by the BPB is designed to motivate people and enable them to give critical thought to political and social issues and play an active part in political life.[20]

The BPB undertakes these goals by preparing educational material to address a number of topics: domestic politics, international affairs, history, economics, and cultural questions, among others. These materials seek to allow citizens to inform themselves, and hence they attempt to avoid political bias, yet of course immediately they orient themselves to a German citizen's view of the world. The German historical legacy does establish a frame for the topics; they exhibit a commitment to informing about the Third Reich, intervening in controversies around that past, and further opposing fascism and extremism in general. The BPB is thus pro-state and pro-capital, and in its explorations of religious extremism it focuses on Islam and does not consider Bavarian Catholics or Protestant fundamentalism.

A significant aspect of its current activities revolves around the preparation and dissemination of *Filmhefte*: glossy pamphlets for sale or online downloading that discuss specific films. They range between sixteen and twenty-four pages, offer background, history, and aesthetic discussion; analyze content, figures, and themes; and provide detailed shot and sequence analyses. The pamphlets lend themselves to lesson plans and pedagogical settings, film discussions, and so on. They remind one of the pressbooks studios and distribution companies release, except that they do not foreground marketing or advertising. If the pressbook predominantly addresses the entertainment value of a film, these pamphlets address its cultural and political value.

Such pamphlets do cover a number of German films, generally dealing with questions of the Nazi past, but also youth culture and some minority questions, especially gay films.[21] They also discuss a number of international films.[22] A pamphlet on *Bend It Like Beckham* addresses a film from Britain, while others discuss *Esma's Secret: Grbavica* (Zbanic, 2006), *Zulu Love Letter* (Suleman, 2004), *Moolaadé* (Sembene, 2004), *Turtles Can Fly* (Ghobadi, 2004), *Atash / Thirst* (Abu Wael, 2004), *Secret Ballot* (Payami, 2001), *Hejar* (Ipekçi, 2001), *Lumumba* (Peck, 2000), *Propaganda* (Cetin, 1999), *Buud Yam* (Kaboré, 1997), *Sankofa* (Gerima, 1993). This partial list covers films from southern Europe, Iran, North Africa, the Middle East, and sub-Saharan Africa. All these films could bear the titles of national film and of art film. Yet all are coproductions with European partners. (*Bend It Like Beckham* is a British-German coproduction.) All these films circulated in the Europa Cinemas system, and many premiered at the Berlinale or other European film festivals. The pamphlets overlook these facts: Rather they discuss the films as national productions—Iranian, Senegalese, South African, Turkish, and so on.

Through the pamphlets, all the films serve a pedagogical function but those pedagogical functions differ significantly, depending on where the film was produced. Thus a German-produced film like *The Lives of Others* is situated in a network of materials around the history of the GDR and GDR State Security Apparatus. But films shot outside Germany and especially outside Europe, once drawn into this educational setting, acquire an ethnographic weight, appearing as vehicles whereby one gains insight and access to foreign cultures and lifestyles. A film like Sinan Çetin's *Propaganda* (1999) is offered as an example of everyday life "under the sign of Islam." This film is never identified as a German Turkish coproduction, nor is it made explicit that its director's previous film *Berlin in Berlin* was filmed in Germany. It is set in the 1940s in an Anatolian village on the Syrian border and tells the tale of a petty bureaucrat whose insistence on enforcing a border that no one ever had experienced before leads to any number of farcical and tragic circumstances. Furthermore, a central theme of the narrative relies on motifs from *Romeo and Juliet*. Film critic Silvia Hallensleben observed of the film, "Not only in Germany do we find duty obsessed civil servants."[23] What amused her and served as a sign of "what she learned" about Turkey should come as no surprise; Çetin through his time spent in Germany should have been all too familiar with the pettiness of bureaucrats there, and he should well have known how to make a film that would appeal to Turkish *and* German audiences. What should sadden us however, is that Hallensleben, an excellent and savvy critic, read the film as revealing a truth about Turkey in a way that *Breaking the Waves* would never offer for Scotland.

Hallensleben was duped by the artifice of a narrative strategy that represents and markets the film explicitly as a national film. She read the film in a literal manner, isolating its images to Turkey and effacing the way that Çetin participates in global cultural traditions well beyond "Asia Minor." Still, Hallensleben "falling for it" should not surprise either. Let me be clear: It is conceivable that a spectator of *Breaking the Waves* would prove less interested in the horrible guilt that psychically crushes Bess, and that the spectator might be interested as a tourist in the Scottish coastal town and oil-based economy. The point is that something happens in films and in the institutions of promotion and criticism to establish a (cultural) distance between the viewer, and viewed, to establish a differential on one side of which the story is about another culture through which I learn (*Propaganda*) versus on the other side a story that is presumed to appeal universally (*Romeo and Juliet*). Under this condition of filmmaking, whenever there is an intercultural dialogue configured in the films, it generally takes place as a bridge of communication between two essentially different cultures. Such dialogue then extends to the postfilmic space in which the films are required to serve as insight-offering artifacts of a distant, distinct, and incommensurate culture. Thus the fact that the films are produced as coproductions is denied, along with any sense of the fundamental contact and commensurability of the partners, as well as the material and ideational exchange facilitated through the filmic apparatus. For films produced as coproductions to appear as distant objects and not as transcultural products, some work has to be done at the level of narrative and in the visuals. Cultural distance is not natural; it must be constructed.

The transnational coproduction strategies are not limited to Germany but, as should be clear by now, are a fundamental mechanism of the audiovisual sector throughout Europe. Because the funding arrangements are not just between European partners, Europe has become one of the prime funding sources for film for North Africa, the Middle East, and Central Asia. As such it is responsible for some of the most successful films from those regions circulating through film festivals and into broader distribution today.

Yet this funding comes at a price. As a conclusion, we can distill four characteristics of the Orientalism operating in this dynamic: (1) European funding as development aid moves into areas where there is a crisis in the local film industry; (2) the ensuing appropriation of culture is a novelty in the policies of development; (3) these films offer a critique of local culture that local films otherwise would not; however, (4) this European funding promotes and produces difference and ideational division, rather than regional union. Fundamentally, the coproduced films must offer stories that appeal to European and North American audiences. Many questions remain to be addressed and extended here from these points. It is important to question the assumption that films from outside cannot speak the truth. Yet if one looks to a film like Michael Haneke's *Caché* (2005), the second film after *Al Aish fil Jannah* to represent the 1961 massacre within the context of a clearly European production, spectators are incited to question how an Austrian outsider might be able to articulate a truth about another country in ways that would not be posed of the Algerian Guerdjou. Fundamentally, though, in the era of transnational and transcultural film production, we must question our very presumptions about inside and outside, national and non-national. The coproductions that increasingly structure the contemporary European film industry are not just financial transactions but excursions across cultures that are fueled by scripts and scenarios. They call forth images that circulate in the public sphere, offer up the "truths" of others for perusal, and can incite larger debates. Such excursions can be the sites of an Orientalizing vision: The coproduced films must tell stories that offer to European and North American audiences the tales they already want to hear.

NOTES

1. For detailed discussions of these transformations, see Randall Halle, *German Film after Germany: Toward a Transnational Aesthetic* (Champagne: University of Illinois Press, 2008); Rosalind Galt, *The New European Cinema: Redrawing the Map* (New York: Columbia University Press, 2006); and Thomas Elsaesser, *European Cinema: Face to Face with Hollywood* (Amsterdam: Amsterdam University Press, 2005).

2. See the Eurimages Web site at http://www.coe.int/t/dg4/eurimages/About/default_en.asp.

3. For an insightful discussion of various coproduction strategies, see Mark Betz, "The Name above the (Sub)Title: Internationalism, Coproduction, and Polyglot European Art Cinema," *Camera Obscura* 46 (2001): 1–44. See also Joseph Garncarz, "Made in Germany: Multiple-Language Versions and Early German Sound Cinema," in *"Film Europe" and "Film America": Cinema, Commerce and Cultural*

Exchange, 1920–1939, ed. Andrew Higson and Richard Maltby (Exeter: University of Exeter Press, 1999): 249–273; Kristin Thompson, "The End of the 'Film Europe' Movement," in *History on/and/in Film*, ed. Timothy O'Regan and B. Shoesmith (Perth: History and Film Association of Australia, 1987): 45–56; Kristin Thompson, *Exporting Entertainment: America in the World Film Market, 1907–1934* (London: BFI, 1985).

4. For a discussion of Europa cinemas, see Halle, *German Film after Germany*.

5. See http://www.cnc.fr/Site/Template/T11.aspx?SELECTID=929&ID=534&t=2.

6. See, for example, Florian Hopf, "Haben wir noch eine Filmpolitik? Das neue Filmförderungsgesetz," *EPD Film* 12 (1986): 24–25.

7. Leslie Adelson, *The Turkish Turn in Contemporary German Literature: Toward a New Critical Grammar of Migration* (New York: Palgrave Macmillan, 2005).

8. Eurimages, Filmboard Berlin-Brandenburg, Hessische Filmförderung, Filmförderungsanstalt, Österreichisches Filminstitut, Wiener Filmfinanzierungsfonds (Wff), Eidgenössisches Departement des Innern, Fondation Montecinemaveritá, Fonds Sud Cinéma: Ministère de la Culture (C.N.C.), Ministère des Affaires Étrangères, Communauté Urbaine de Strasbourg.

9. See http://www.africa-cinemas.org/fr/contacts.php.

10. Frédéric Voileau, "Produce – Coproduce: The Mediterranean Countries" (Cineuropa, March 22, 2007), available at http://cineuropa.org/dossier.aspx?lang=en&treeID=1364&documentID=75750.

11. Ahmed Aghrout and Redha M. Bougherira, eds., *Algeria in Transition: Reforms and Development Prospects* (New York: Routledge, 2004); Abdelhakim Meziani, "Cinema—Algeria: Algerian Cinema at a Turning Point," *Euromed Café*, September 22, 2005, available at http://www.euromedcafe.org/newsdetail.asp?lang=ing&documentID=541; World Bank, *World Bank Development Report 1998–1999* (Washington, D.C.: World Bank, 1999).

12. See, for example, Yamina Bachir-Chouikh, "No Freedom of Expression without Funds," *Qantara*, February 2, 2005, available at http://www.qantara.de/webcom/show_article.php/_c-310/_nr-155/i.html; Mohammed Bakrim, "North African Cinema: Tendencies and Perspectives," in Cinemas of the South, FIPRESCI 2006, available at http://www.fipresci.org/world_cinema/south/south_english_african_cinema_maghreb.htm.

13. Carrie Tarr, *Reframing Difference: Beur and Banlieu Filmmaking in France* (Manchester: Manchester University Press, 2005), 125. See also Richard L. Derderian, "Algeria as a lieu de mémoire: Ethnic Minority Memory and National Identity in Contemporary France," *Radical History Review* 83 (2002): 28–43.

14. Voileau, "Produce—Coproduce."

15. Mazzino Montinari, "Special Report: Produce – Coproduce . . . : 2002—Producing in Africa" (Cineuropa, March 22, 2007), available at http://cineuropa.org/dossier.aspx?lang=en&treeID=1364&documentID=75785.

16. Ibid.

17. Ibid.

18. Catherine Simpson, "Turkish Cinema's Resurgence: The 'Deep Nation' Unravels," *Senses of Cinema* (2006), available at http://www.sensesofcinema.com/contents/06/39/turkish_cinema.html.

19. Deniz Göktürk, "Anyone at Home? Itinerant Identities in European Cinema of the 1990s." Paper presented at "Look Who's Talking Now: Globalization, Film, Media, and the Public Sphere," held in March 2002 at the University of California, Berkeley.

20. See www.bpb.de/die_bpb/PE8IKY,0,0,The_Federal_Agency_for_Civic_
Education.html.

21. *Das Leben der Anderen, Requiem, Knallhart, Kombat Sechzehn, Sophie Scholl,
Alles auf Zucker, Die fetten Jahren, der neunte Tag, Sommersturm, Muxmäuschenstill,
Gegen die Wand, das schreckliche Mädchen, Lichter, Das Wunder von Bern, Luther,
Goodbye Lenin, Im Toten Winkel.*

22. A number of American films are discussed, including *Erin Brockovich,*
(Soderbergh, 2000), *Bowling for Columbine* (Moore, 2002), *Blue Eyed,* (Verhaag,
1996), and *Ali* (Mann, 2001).

23. Silvia Hallensleben, "*Propaganda.* BRD/Türkei 1999," *epd Film* 11 (1999): 47.

18

ABDERRAHMANE SISSAKO: SECOND AND
THIRD CINEMA IN THE FIRST PERSON

Rachel Gabara

In theoretical texts and manifestoes written in the late 1960s and early 1970s, filmmakers in Argentina, Brazil, and Cuba advocated a revolutionary cinema they called Third Cinema, which constituted a transformative social practice and functioned as an instrument of political change and consciousness raising. Fernando Solanas and Octavio Getino declared that this cinema of the struggle against imperialism was "the most gigantic cultural, scientific, and artistic manifestation of our time" and represented "the decolonization of culture."[1] They and other filmmakers distinguished their anticolonial cinema from a dominant and capitalist First Cinema and a Second Cinema that was artistic, intellectual, and auteurist. This tripartite framework, in which film style was mapped onto geography and ideology, persists in contemporary film criticism. Political films from the so-called Third World are set against big-budget Hollywood productions as well as European art films deemed overly formalist and therefore insufficiently political. The work of Abderrahmane Sissako, however, transcends the conventional opposition of the Third and Second Cinemas, of political cinema and art cinema. Sissako, who was born and raised in West Africa but has been based in Europe for over twenty years, reminds us not only that films from outside of North America and Europe may be formally experimental, but that formally experimental films may be politically as well as aesthetically revolutionary.

Art cinema has been notoriously difficult to define. The term first referred to a group of almost exclusively European films that appeared in the middle of the twentieth century and gained popularity around the world as alternatives to mainstream Hollywood. Italian Neorealist and French New Wave films are canonical examples, as are the films of Federico Fellini, Ingmar Bergman, Alain Resnais, and Akira Kurosawa. David Bordwell was among the first critics to describe art cinema as a category, which he located somewhere between classical Hollywood film and more radical modernist film. Bordwell developed a list of characteristics shared by art films, focusing on the psychological complexity of their characters, their episodic and open-ended narratives, and their pursuit of ambiguity. It was now a film's director or auteur, moreover, and not star, studio, or genre, who would serve as "the overriding intelligence organizing the film for our comprehension."[2] Geoffrey Nowell-Smith (and Bordwell himself in a 2008 afterword to his 1979 essay) stressed instead a shared production and distribution context for art films, particularly their exhibition in an ever-growing number of national and international film festivals.[3] Steve Neale shared this interest in art cinema's "institutional basis" and concluded that art films shared certain characteristics only because these features "contrast with those of Hollywood."[4]

For Latin American Third Cinema filmmakers, European art cinema was indeed a first, but ultimately inadequate and outmoded, alternative to bourgeois Hollywood. Julio García Espinosa proclaimed that "when we look toward Europe, we wring our hands. . . . The fact is that Europe can no longer respond in a traditional manner but at the same time finds it equally difficult to respond in a manner that is radically new."[5] Glauber Rocha, one of the leaders of Brazilian *Cinema Nôvo*, went even further: "Our bourgeoisie has been colonized by Neo-Realism and the *nouvelle vague*. . . . Fox, Paramount, and Metro are our enemies. But Eisenstein, Rossellini, and Godard are also our enemies."[6] Why such enmity between film movements linked by their resistance to Hollywood's global reach? Solanas described the Second Cinema as "nihilistic, mystificatory . . . cut off from reality," whereas the new Third Cinema was a "democratic, national, popular cinema" that "gives an account of reality and history."[7] European art cinema, which did in some cases seek out realistic settings by shooting on location rather than in the studio, devoted itself more systematically to the construction of what Bordwell has called a subjective psychological realism. The Third Cinema, to the contrary, was interested in the People, in popular history and living conditions, and not at all in individual psychology. Filmmakers rejected centuries of European and North American political, economic, and cultural (including cinematic) colonization in order to show a Latin American reality that had previously been repressed. Solanas and Getino stressed, however, that revolutionary cinema does not merely document or illustrate a situation, but instead *"attempts to intervene in the situation . . . provides discovery through transformation."*[8] Neither mirror reflection of nor poetic reflection upon an existing reality, their new realism would analyze the world in order to transform it.

The African cinema was born just as the new Latin American cinema began to flourish. In the years following the independences of the late 1950s and early 1960s, African filmmakers worked, like their Latin American colleagues, to decolonize culture, to reclaim the cinema and their cinematic image from their former colonizers. In 1973, a group of Latin American and African filmmakers met and proclaimed that their goal was a critical and transformative realism, the production of "films reflecting the objective conditions in which the struggling peoples are developing . . . which bring about the disalienation of the colonized peoples at the same time as they contribute sound and objective information for the peoples of the entire world."[9] The collective statement published after a 1974 meeting in Burkina Faso stated that film content should reflect African "social realities" and answer the questions: "Who are we? . . . How do we live? . . . Where are we?"[10] The 1980s and 1990s saw a return to theorizing Third Cinema as a "cinema of subversion" in both the Latin American and African contexts as well as with respect to minority filmmaking in countries such as the United States.[11] Critics and filmmakers have continued to emphasize that Third Cinema responds to questions about a collective "we," reflecting "objective conditions" in developing regions and rewriting colonial and neocolonial history from the perspective of decolonized peoples.

Associating the Cartesian "I think, therefore I am" with the individual(ist) protagonist of cinema from both the United States and Europe, Clyde Taylor contrasts it with the Xhosa proverb "A person is a person only because of other people" and a strictly collective African protagonist.[12] Tahar Cheriaa claims that in African cinema "the individual is always pushed into the background, and the hero . . . never occupies the foreground. The principal character in African films is always the group, the collectivity, and that is the essential thing."[13] This strict opposition of African collectivity and Western individuality pervades both Western and African theorizing about African narrative in any medium.[14] With respect to film, moreover, it extends from protagonist to author; Third Cinema has from its beginnings rejected the auteur concept so central to art cinema. The 1975 Algiers Charter on African Cinema declared that "the stereotyped image of the solitary and marginal creator which is widespread in Western capitalist society must be rejected by African filmmakers, who must, on the contrary, see themselves as creative artisans at the service of their people."[15]

A profound ambivalence about the creative role of the filmmaker is evident in Third Cinema theory's disdain for the formal innovation characteristic of the Second Cinema as well as in its rejection of a filmic first-person voice. In 1974, Tunisian critic and director Férid Boughedir maintained that a filmmaker essentially "reproduces reality," choosing in the process either to lie or to tell the truth. He argued that "art is a luxury" and not a priority for African cinema, since art cinema tends to "make reality flee."[16] A film in the service of its people, then, should be easily understood, with none of the ambiguity so valued in European art films. Teshome Gabriel, who has been at the forefront of critical discussions of Third Cinema in Africa, remained undecided on this issue. In 1982 he wrote that Third Cinema films "try to expand the boundaries of cinematic language and devise new stylistic approaches appropriate to their revolutionary goals" as revolutionary filmmakers seek "the demystification of representational practices as part of the process of liberation."[17] Several years later, however, he praised radical content in conventional form, claiming that "Third Cinema film-makers rarely move their camera and sets unless the story calls for it."[18]

Although documentary film was favored by the Latin American Third Cinema movement for its realism and accompanying revolutionary potential, the genre has not been popular with African filmmakers. Africa, like Latin America, has long been defined by the images created of it and its people by exploring, conquering, and colonizing outsiders in newsreels, adventure films, and ethnographic films. As early as 1907, French colonial documentary offered spectators back in the metropole images of what were advertised as "real" and "strange" landscapes and wild animals along with occasional gestures toward ethnography. Gaumont Actualités's *En Afrique occidentale / In West Africa* (1920), released as part of a "Teaching Series" on African geography, opens with images not of landscapes but of people, Africans engaging in everyday activities that then characterize the continent: traditional artisans at work, women pounding millet and cooking dinner around a fire, and fishermen going out to sea in a pirogue. These documentary images of Africa were inextricably melded with colonial propaganda, particularly after the beginning of the First World War. As the 1931 Colonial Exhibition approached, the number of documentaries shot in the colonies accelerated, and a new kind of critical and political attention was paid them. In the wake of the Exhibition, famed anthropologist Marcel Griaule produced *Au pays des Dogons / In the Land of the Dogons* (1938) and *Sous les masques noirs / Under the Black Masks* (1938), both filmed in what is now Mali. Griaule's films were screened not in commercial movie theaters but at the Museum of Man in Paris, and he laid the groundwork for a French tradition of ethnographic filmmaking. The best-known examples of the genre are the films of Griaule's disciple Jean Rouch who, from the mid-1940s until his death in 2004, filmed largely in West Africa with a few notable exceptions. Rouch was not alone, however; the Committee on Ethnographic Film that he co-founded in 1952 sponsored a number of self-proclaimed filmmaker/anthropologists, and ethnographic documentaries were also funded by the National Center of Scientific Research (CNRS), the Ministry of National Education, the National Pedagogical Institute, and the Cinémathèque for Public Instruction.

Paulin Soumanou Vieyra, the pioneering Senegalese filmmaker and film critic, responded to Rouch and his colleagues with his own ethnographic work in the late 1950s and early 1960s. In 1955, he shot *Afrique-sur-Seine / Africa on the Seine*, depicting the lives of a group of African students in Paris, which was followed by *Une nation est née / A Nation Is Born* (1960), *Lamb / Traditional Wrestling* (1963), and *Môl / The Fishermen* (1966). Vieyra described how African filmmakers must work against the long history of colonial cinema:

> Using cinema, Westerners created an image of the black world that they transmitted to their children. . . . The African cinema is in the process of reestablishing the truth about Africa, because Africans themselves have taken charge of their cinema. The vision is becoming an interior one.[19]

Yet most of this work was done at first through historical fiction films. Ousmane Sembene (Senegal), Moustapha Alassane (Niger), Souleymane Cissé (Mali), Med Hondo (Mauritania), and others reconstructed and retold precolonial and colonial African history from the point of view of the Africans who had been consistently silenced by colonial cinema. Aside from Vieyra, very few of the first generation of West and Central African filmmakers made more than one documentary; the exceptions, Blaise Senghor (Senegal), Safi Faye (Senegal), Pascal Abikanlou (Benin), Inoussa Ousseini (Niger), and Timité Bassori (Ivory Coast), produced (auto)ethnographic films in the 1960s and 1970s. They were for the first time representing their own people and their newly independent nations, and, like the African directors who were producing historical fictions, many undertook a questioning of the conventions of filmic realism.

In Faye's *Kaddu Beykat / Letter from My Village* (1976), residents of her home village of Fad'jal discuss the taxes that are forcing farmers to sell crops for cash instead of growing food to feed their families. This staged discussion is combined with a fictional love story as well as scenes portraying various aspects of daily life in the village. *Fad'jal / Come and Work* (1979) begins with similar scenes of everyday life and then stages a retelling and reenactment of the history of the village. The film concludes with a discussion of a pressing contemporary political issue, state ownership of land. Faye described her goal to be a particularly African realism, in terms that recall both Latin American and African manifestoes of Third Cinema: "What I try to film [are] things which relate to our civilization . . . a typically African culture. . . . I make films about reality." Speaking about her documentaries, however, she stated that "for me all these words—fiction, documentary, ethnology—have no sense. . . . At the end of my films people wonder if there is mise-en-scène or not."[20] Faye had acted for and then trained with Rouch and was familiar with the French ethnographic tradition. She chose to refuse documentary's claim on reality by not only blurring but refusing to identify the boundaries between filmic genres, performing precisely the kind of "demystification of representational practices" described by Gabriel.

Faye's films are not only the rebellious descendants of a tradition of French ethnography, but also the innovative ancestors of documentaries produced by a group of young West and Central African filmmakers beginning in the early 1990s. David Achkar (from Guinea), Mahamat Saleh-Haroun (Chad), Samba Félix Ndiaye (Senegal), Mweze Ngangura (Congo), Jean-Marie Téno (Cameroon), and Abderrahmane Sissako, among others, have made films, mainly in French, in which their individual stories are linked to analyses of colonial and postcolonial national history. Like Faye, they have worked to escape the bounds of the conventional documentary realism so often affirmed by European filmmakers documenting Africa from and for the outside. Unlike Faye, however, they have rejected ethnography altogether while experimenting with different formal possibilities in order to mix fiction and history, feature and documentary filmmaking. All have chosen to narrate their films in the first as well as the third person, in the singular as well as the plural, and all force us to rethink any easy definition of realism. These filmmakers destabilize the opposition between Second and Third Cinemas, between art and politics, and thus allow us to explore a wider range of possibilities for contemporary African Third Cinema.

Of these filmmakers, only Sissako has consistently put himself on-screen, not only using his own voice for a narrative voice-over but also often playing a starring role. Born in Kiffa, Mauritania, home to his mother's family, Sissako spent most of his childhood in his father's home in Mali and grew up speaking Bambara but not Hassanya. He returned to Mauritania for the end of high school but left again at the age of nineteen to study film at the State Institute of Cinema (VGIK) in Moscow. Sissako spent a total of twelve years in the Soviet Union (and then Russia) and has been based in France since 1993. Sissako's films, like his life, are cosmopolitan in the best sense, traveling widely while remaining firmly anchored in Africa. When asked about filmmakers who have influenced him, he has responded with a tentative embrace of the art cinema canon if not of its auteurs: "I have liked some films. I am less attached to filmmakers. But I would say off the top of my head maybe . . . Antonioni, Visconti, Fassbinder, a film of Bergman, another of Cassavetes . . . Tarkovsky."[21] Yet Sissako is all too aware of who has been excluded from this canon. In film school in the 1980s he watched an average of three films a day for five years, discovering all of the *"grands auteurs"* of European cinema but not a single African film.[22] Although he is one of very few African filmmakers whose films have been widely circulated in the art cinema festival circuit, Sissako uses his presence on-screen to resist the controlling persona of the auteur as well as art cinema's emphasis on subjective psychology.

In *Rostov-Luanda* (1997), his first feature-length film, Sissako returns to the village of his birth, which then almost immediately becomes a new point of departure, the place from which he will leave for Luanda, Angola, in search of a friend, Afonso Baribanga, an Angolan with whom he studied Russian in Rostov-on-the-Don before starting film school. Sissako met Baribanga on the train from Moscow and was fascinated by how different their lives had been, even though both were African and Baribanga was only five years his elder. Whereas Sissako was born after the official withdrawal of the French from West Africa, Baribanga had fought, "Kalashnikov in hand," for Angola's independence from Portugal.[23] We are introduced to Sissako's project not by an omniscient authorial voice-over, but by the voice of his cousin, whom we see speaking to Sissako and his childhood nurse, Touélé. He begins in Hassanya and then switches to French:

I haven't seen Abderrahmane since he was a child. He was born in Kiffa. His mother's house is there. The house of his uncle Mohammed is there. There are some who leave for France to study and who never return home, who never even think about returning home. What Abderrahmane has done is an act of honor. To say outright "I'm returning to Kiffa to see my parents and the house where I was born." However, he told me he has an Angolan friend whom he hasn't seen for sixteen years and that he must go to Angola to see his friend. And I asked him the question "Why spend your money to go to Angola with the risks involved and lose your money?" He told me, "Cousin, that's true, but on the other hand I'm right, man is called to travel, to suffer, to know people, to know customs. I am traveling to Angola to have my adventure, to be an adventurer."

Sissako must go home, an act of honor, in order then to continue his travels and make a film, which is another act of honor. This adventure is his calling, yet it calls him toward somewhere and someone else, someone whose life story intersected with and parallels his own in important ways.

Several minutes later, we hear the first voice-over in Sissako's own voice: "I set out before dawn, Kiffa gets farther away, Touélé watches over me, Touélé who was my nanny, and in whose hand mine was clenched as a child." After a close-up of Touélé, we see the sands of the desert rushing by outside of the window of the car. The traveling shot shifts almost seamlessly to a snowy instead of sandy landscape out of a train window, and we hear Sissako speaking in Russian with his and Baribanga's former Russian teacher, Natalia Lvovna, their voices echoing over a transcontinental phone line. Sissako asks her to send him her only photograph of Baribanga since he is leaving for Angola to look for him. An Angolan cityscape follows a fade to black, and Sissako's voice-over becomes suddenly historical: "In 1975, Angola became independent. For me, this hard-won liberty announced a communal hope for my continent. It was in 1980, in the U.S.S.R., that I became friends with Afonso Baribanga. Seventeen years later, I wish to find him again. Seventeen years of war for Angola."

Landscapes of Mauritania, Russia, and Angola glide past in quick succession, linked by Sissako's life story, which is linked to that of Afonso Baribanga. Both of their lives are linked to the fate of Angola as a place of symbolic hope for Africa, a hope cruelly dashed by years of unending war. Traveling across the country, Sissako begins a series of interviews with Angolans, men and women of all colors, born in Africa and Portugal, poor and middle class, living in the countryside and the city. He asks them about their personal histories and about how they have managed to survive the history of their country. These interviews are conducted in Portuguese and Creole with the aid of a translator, except for the rare occasions when direct communication is possible in French or in Russian. After each conversation, Sissako shows Natalya Lvovna's photograph, one of the very few pieces of documentary evidence from the past that appear in the film, to the person with whom he has been speaking and asks if they recognize Afonso Baribanga. His biographical project, the search for the long-lost friend in the photograph, becomes inseparable from the images he finds along the way. Sissako tells us that his memory of Baribanga is becoming blurred, "Not that I'm forgetting him, but his features are now drawing new faces, to whom my search leads me. Thus is drawn the portrait of a friend."

Back in Luanda, Sissako shows the photograph to a man with whom he speaks in Russian, a man named Cassanje who does know someone in the picture, not Baribanga but another of the Africans who learned Russian in Rostov. Sissako learns that Baribanga is still alive and lives in what had been East Germany. The adventure therefore continues and concludes in the landscape of a fourth country, and we see Sissako being driven up to Baribanga's apartment building. A brief image of Baribanga on his balcony, however, is all we see of him, and we never get his side of his story. Sissako's multilingual and multivocal adventure story has been about his own process of finding his old friend by discovering the history of his friend's people. Sissako has said of filmmaking that "when you do this job, you have a deep desire to say things and I think that the best way to do so is to talk about oneself or around oneself. It's the best way to approach the Other."[24] Describing autobiography and biography as inseparable processes, he subverts the opposition between filmic first and third persons as well as Third Cinema's resulting rejection of the first person in favor of the People. In *Rostov-Luanda*, talking about and around himself enables Sissako's approach to Baribanga, Angola, and colonial and postcolonial African history.

In order to talk about Baribanga via talking about himself, Sissako had to begin in his birthplace: "I had never gone back to Kiffa where I was born and spent the first forty-five days of my life. So, before looking for Bari Banga [*sic*], I decided to go back to Kiffa. To find myself."[25] His first-person narrative, as we have already seen, requires the biography of Baribanga, which in turn requires a history of Angola via the testimony of Baribanga's compatriots. Noting that "my projects always take place outside of the country I live in," Sissako also links personal narrative to an experience of displacement.[26] While *Rostov-Luanda* was still in pre-production, Sissako called the film a "personal history" in which "I want to recount an internal exile. . . . I want to reveal Mauritania to myself, understand how it exists in me. I didn't grow up there. 'Rostov-Luanda' is a way of projecting myself and of setting up a contradiction with another African country that Mauritanians do not know." As had Third Cinema filmmakers in Latin America, Sissako sought to understand and portray a regional instead of merely national reality, a solidarity among African countries generally held at a distance not only by geography but by colonial history.

Sissako's next film, *La vie sur terre / Life on Earth* (1998), begins with fluorescently lit images of the overflowing shelves of a Super Monoprix in Paris. After a medium shot of Sissako riding up an escalator carrying an enormous stuffed animal, we see his father in Sokolo, Mali, reading a letter in French whose words we hear in the filmmaker's voice:

"Dear father, You will be a little surprised, and perhaps even worried, to receive a letter from me. I hurry therefore to tell you that all is well, and I hope the same is true for you. Contrary to the message I sent you through Jiddou, an important change means that I will soon be with you, in Sokolo. The desire to film Sokolo, the desire also to leave, as Aimé Césaire said. Even more so since we will soon be in the year 2000 and nothing, most likely, will have changed for the better, as you know better than I. Is what I learn far from you worth what I forget about us?"

The letter continues over footage of Sissako arriving at his father's compound, accompanied by Salif Keita singing "Folon," a song in Bambara about coming home. Sissako then continues to quote Aimé Césaire's *Notebook of a Return to My Native Land*, "And on my way, I would say to myself: 'And above all beware, my body and my soul too, beware of crossing your arms in the sterile attitude of the spectator, because life is not a spectacle . . . because a man who screams is not a dancing bear.'"[27] Césaire and Sissako, different kinds of exiles returning home in different ways, together warn us that the documentary filmmaker can be a type of tourist, watching others' lives from behind the camera instead of participating in them.

Sissako begins, then, with another voice-over and another homecoming, to another of his hometowns. Sokolo is the village of his father and grandfather; he was born in Kiffa, but this is where he grew up. Prior to screening his first adult return to Sokolo, Sissako raises the question of what he has gained as well as lost in Europe. He has said of his long absence from Sokolo that "exile is an experience of solitude which helps to understand oneself better and to better understand where one comes from. But it's better for this experience not to be contemplative."[28] Sissako returns to film his desire to leave, returns to film, but refuses to be a spectator in his native land. Although he had already appeared on screen in *Rostov-Luanda*, here he is no longer an interviewer but instead a character, playing a role in the drama of Sokolo on the eve and first day of the new millennium. We see him with his father, speaking with others in the village, trying to place a phone call from the post office, flirting with a young woman in a love story that is never told but rather hinted at via a courting dance on bicycles through the streets of the village. His family members and others in the village speak to their struggles to keep the farms going, to earn enough money to feed their families. Although Sissako rejects the position of the objective observer, he does not replace it with a portrayal of himself as a psychologically complex character. He remains as opaque as his fellow characters, to whose suffering he bears witness without violating their privacy and dignity. For Sissako, "filming myself was a way to appropriate the camera differently, to say 'I am an actor in this life and I expose myself. As I am filming you, I will be filmed in turn.... I am one of you despite everything.'"[29] This "everything" includes his exile and resulting difference, the fact that he left Sokolo and no longer shares the fate of its residents.

I have called *Life on Earth* a documentary film and stated that it tells a story that takes place at the end of 1999 and beginning of 2000, but I have also noted that the film was released in 1998. One might well wonder how this is possible. In fact, Sissako has not recorded New Year's Eve in Sokolo, but has instead staged events that have not (yet) occurred. All of the actors in this fiction, however, are playing themselves; the credits at the end of the film identify Sissako as himself, his father, Mohamed Sissako, as the father, his uncle as the tailor, and so on. We see the men of Sokolo sitting in the street and listening to Radio France International reporting on New Year's Eve activities all over the world, counting down the last hours of 1999 to a 2000 that is at the time of filming still two years away. Like Faye, Sissako destabilizes the boundaries between fiction and documentary, leaving his spectator constantly unsure of how much mise-en-scène there is in his film. He breaks the basic rules of documentary realism in this

FIGURE 18.1. Sissako appears on-screen throughout *Life on Earth* (Sissako, 1998), here attempting to place a phone call at the Sokolo post office.

documentary fiction, or fictional documentary, and does so in order to situate himself as he makes a point. Although he lives in Europe, Sissako films himself in Sokolo at this crucial moment in the future as Sokolo and the rest of Africa approach the new millennium, Sokolo in opposition to and yet intimately connected to the Europe on the radio. The residents of Sokolo listen to at least two radio stations, RFI and the very local (and ironically named) Colonial Radio, which in the film features a reading from Césaire's *Discourse on Colonialism*. Again using Césaire's words, Sissako reminds us of the particular tragedy of Africa's first contacts with Europe, one legacy of which will be the two continents' incommensurate New Year's Eves. *Life on Earth* was originally supposed to be entirely fictional, but Sissako felt that this would constitute an "abdication of responsibility, an escape to avoid reality." This reality, one that most of the world wishes to ignore, is the relationship between African history and the African present: "There is a lack of will to understand this continent. Explanations are often hasty and people forget how recent decolonisation is, only thirty-five years ago, and before that there was a century of deportations of millions of individuals."[30] Sissako's portrayal of life in Sokolo and his anticolonial message are very much in the spirit of Third Cinema, and they are not attenuated but rather strengthened by both his participation on-screen as actor and his formal experimentation as filmmaker.

Sissako's most recent film, *Bamako* (2006), was released almost a decade after *Life on Earth* and several years after his fictional feature *Heremakono: En attendant le bonheur / Waiting for Happiness* (2002). *Bamako* is not a documentary film, and it seems at first to conform more readily to the tenets of Third Cinema than does any of Sissako's earlier work. His most overtly political film to date, *Bamako* stages a trial in which ordinary Africans sue the World Bank and the International Monetary Fund, detailing the crimes and damages caused by international interference in African affairs in an era of so-called globalization. African governments are also accused of what amounts to depraved indifference to their own citizens. Taking advantage of the double meaning of the French word *"la cour,"* which means both courtyard and court, *Bamako* takes place in the interior courtyard of a house in Bamako, Mali. Like *Rostov-Luanda* and *Life on Earth*, *Bamako* clearly rejects a colonial or, more specifically, neocolonial vision of African history and reality. Unlike in these earlier films, however, our protagonist seems to be collective, a representative group of Africans set in opposition to Europe and North America, and Sissako himself seems to be absent from the screen.

Despite its apparent straightforwardness, however, *Bamako* is formally innovative and quite intricate. Sissako filmed the trial scenes in digital video, using four cameras. A camera is almost always visible in the frame, reminding us that the trial is a staged performance. At the same time as he employs this reflexive strategy, Sissako incorporates personal elements as well as documentary strategies into the film. The film was shot in the courtyard of Sissako's recently deceased father's house in Bamako, a house in which Sissako was raised. He used lawyers and judges that he knew instead of actors in the trial scenes, as well as real witnesses, from Aminata Traoré, writer and former minister of culture, to a farmer and *griot* from southern Mali, to a young man who has not been able to find a job. All use their own names and participated in the scripting of their testimony and dialogue. In addition to the trial, the film contains lengthy scenes

FIGURE 18.2. In one of many reflexive moments in *Bamako* (Sissako, 2006), the camera behind a witness reminds viewers that the trial has been staged.

of the everyday lives of the people who live around the courtyard. These unresolved subplots, filmed in 16mm, function to pull the film away from a strictly political focus and toward a Second Cinema or art cinema practice. Of the story of Chaka, who commits suicide as his marriage dissolves and his wife prepares to return home to Senegal, Sissako has said:

> [*Bamako*] is without a doubt my most direct film with respect to its topic. This is something I don't like, it's not my nature. I was therefore careful to think of a counterpoint at every moment. . . . One can be in Africa and be solitary, as everyone is. Chaka is a man who is very alone, even if he lives in a courtyard filled with people. Even if the strength of this continent is its capacity to share what little it has with everyone. In this collective life, man can also be alone.[31]

Abandoning a comfortably complete opposition of individualist Europe and communitarian Africa, Sissako simultaneously points to the indistinct boundaries of filmic genre.

The reflexive effect produced by the many visible cameras in *Bamako* is further complicated by the insertion of a film within the film, a western called *Death in Timbuktu* that is ostensibly shown on a television set to residents of the courtyard. This mini-western plays both with and against the themes of the trial. A group of black and white cowboys arrive in what must be Timbuktu, to the northeast of Bamako, and start to shoot at the local citizens at random. One of the black cowboys laughs at the carnage he has wrought, bragging that he has killed two, a mother and child, for the price of one. Another lurks mysteriously, watching the others. Sissako cast his film-world friends as the cowboys, including American actor Danny Glover (who also produced *Bamako*), Palestinian filmmaker Elia Suleiman, Congolese actor and filmmaker Zéka Laplaine, and a certain "Dramane Bassaro." Dramane is a nickname for Abderrahmane, Bassaro is Sissako's uncle's family name, and the face we can just barely see under this cowboy hat is that of Abderrahmane Sissako. From filmmaker as interviewer in

Rostov-Luanda to filmmaker as character in *Life on Earth*, Sissako is now filmmaker as character in a film within a film, a dizzyingly reflexive mise-en-abyme. At the end of this five-minute sequence, a title credit is followed by "Directed By," but no director's name appears.

The credits for *Death in Timbuktu* are in English, although the characters speak in a mixture of French and English. The Hollywood domination that inspired the rebellions of both Third Cinema and art cinema meant that American westerns flooded the African market for decades, and many African filmmakers remember watching them as children along with innumerable Kung Fu films and Hindi musicals. Sissako nods to a canonical First Cinema genre in a markedly non-Hollywood way, reminding us of the Wild West atmosphere of our globalized world. One of the witnesses in the trial responds to a French lawyer's praise of globalization by noting that the world might be open for white people but is not for black people. Another witness is a young man who was sent back to Mali after crossing the Sahara desert to Algeria in the hope of then reaching Europe by boat. This dark view of the flip side of contemporary cosmopolitanism returns once again with a humorous twist. Chaka is studying Hebrew because he thinks that an Israeli embassy will open in Bamako and he will then be the perfect candidate for a job as a guard there. But the fact that both white and black cowboys are shooting at the citizens of Timbuktu again complicates any simple opposition between Europe and Africa and reminds us of the complicity of some Africans in the crimes against their own people. And the fact that the actors playing the murderous cowboys form an international collection of actors and directors forces us to consider the different ways in which Africa has been shot (the pun works only in English) on film, with more or (most often) less regard for the individual and collective suffering of the continent's inhabitants.

Although they considered the Second Cinema to be overly formalist and thus the enemy, Espinosa, Rocha, and Solanas were nonetheless interested in developing a new film form to express their revolutionary politics. In their writings, they rejected even those currents within European art cinema that had influenced them the most, emphasizing their struggle to create films that reflected a uniquely Latin American reality. Sissako, working in a very different context and historical moment, similarly works to reflect the complex reality of his native continent of Africa. Living and working between Africa and Europe and bearing the legacies of both the Third and the Second Cinemas he has, to return once again to Gabriel's first thoughts on Third Cinema and formalism, found ways to "devise new stylistic approaches appropriate to [his] revolutionary goals." All of Sissako's films strongly reject a colonial representation of Africa and Africans, at the same time refusing a colonial model of documentary representation. Sounding very different from the early Third Cinema activists, however, Sissako has said that "I don't want to tackle problems that must be resolved, that doesn't interest me."[32] The openness and lack of resolution characteristic of his films create a pervasive sense of ambiguity reminiscent of European art cinema as described by Bordwell. Yet Sissako replaces art cinema's investigations of individual psychological reality with explorations of individuals in their historical and political contexts, reclaiming at the same time a first-person voice for Third Cinema. In order to answer questions like "Who are we?" and "Where are we?" he first asks "Who am I?" and "Where am I?" Reaching out from his own stories to the stories of others to, finally, wider historical movements, Sissako is able to foreground himself without relegating others to the background.

NOTES

1. Fernando Solanas and Octavio Getino, "Towards a Third Cinema," *New Latin American Cinema: Theory, Practices, and Transcontinental Articulations*, ed. Michael Martin (Detroit, Mich.: Wayne State University Press, 1997), 34, 37.

2. David Bordwell, *Poetics of Cinema* (New York: Routledge, 2008), 152, 156, 154.

3. Geoffrey Nowell-Smith, "Art Cinema," *Oxford History of World Cinema*, ed. Nowell-Smith (New York: Oxford University Press, 1996), 570; Bordwell, *Poetics of Cinema*, 160.

4. Steve Neale, "Art Cinema as Institution," *Screen* 22, no. 1 (1981): 13, 14.

5. Julio García Espinosa, "For an Imperfect Cinema," in *New Latin American Cinema*, 78.

6. Cited in Randal Johnson and Robert Stam, eds., *Brazilian Cinema* (New York: Columbia University Press, 1995), 88.

7. Cited in Paul Willemen, "The Third Cinema Question," in *New Latin American Cinema*, 229.

8. Solanas and Getino, "Towards a Third Cinema," 47.

9. "Resolutions of the Third World Film-Makers' Meeting, Algiers, Algeria, 1973," in *African Experiences of Cinema*, ed. Imruh Bakari and Mbye Cham (London: British Film Institute, 1996), 20.

10. "Séminaire sur 'le rôle du Cinéaste africain dans l'éveil d'une conscience de civilisation noire,'" *Présence Africaine* 90 (1974): 10, 12. All translations from the French are my own unless otherwise specified.

11. Teshome Gabriel, *Third Cinema in the Third World: An Aesthetics of Liberation* (Ann Arbor, Mich.: UMI Research Press, 1982), 95.

12. Clyde Taylor, "Black Cinema in the Post-aesthetic Era," *Questions of Third Cinema*, ed. Jim Pines and Paul Willemen (London: British Film Institute, 1989), 90.

13. Cited in Elizabeth Malkmus and Roy Armes, *Arab and African Film Making* (London: Zed, 1991), 210.

14. A famous example is Fredric Jameson's controversial description of all "Third World" literature as "national allegory," in which "the story of the private individual destiny is always an allegory of the embattled situation of the public third-world culture and society" ("Third-World Literature in the Era of Multinational Capitalism," *Social Text* 15 [Fall 1986]: 69). For more on this topic, see my *From Split to Screened Selves: French and Francophone Autobiography in the Third Person* (Stanford, Calif.: Stanford University Press, 2006).

15. "The Algiers Charter on African Cinema, 1975," in *African Experiences of Cinema*, 25.

16. Férid Boughedir, in "Séminaire sur 'le rôle du Cinéaste africain," 123, 130.

17. Gabriel, *Third Cinema in the Third World*, 24, 95.

18. Teshome Gabriel, "Third Cinema as Guardian of Popular Memory: Towards a Third Aesthetics," in *Questions of Third Cinema*, 60.

19. Paulin Soumanou Vieyra, *Réflexions d'un cinéaste africain* (Bruxelles: OCIC, 1990), 61–62, 132.

20. "Four Film Makers from West Africa," *Framework* 11 (Autumn 1979): 18.

21. "'A Screenplay Is Not a Guarantee': Abderrahmane Sissako with Kwame Anthony Appiah," *Through African Eyes: Dialogues with the Directors* (New York: African Film Festival, 2003), 38.

22. *Rostov-Luanda, Le film africain* 22 (November 1995): 9. See also Olivier Barlet, "La leçon de cinéma d'Abderrahmane Sissako," *Africultures* (July 2003), available at http://www.africultures.com/php/index.php?nav=article&no=2796 (March 7, 2008).

23. *Rostov-Luanda, Le film africain* 20 (May 1995): 18.

24. Olivier Barlet, "A propos de *La Vie sur terre*: Entretien avec Abderrahmane Sissako," *Africultures* 10 (September 1998), available at http://www.africultures.com/php/index.php?nav=article&no=469.

25. "'A Screenplay Is Not a Guarantee,'" 40.

26. *Rostov-Luanda, Le film africain* 22 (November 1995): 8.

27. I am citing Mireille Rosello and Annie Pritchard's translation of Césaire's *Cahier d'un retour au pays natal* rather than the film's subtitles. Aimé Césaire, *Notebook of a Return to My Native Land* (Newcastle upon Tyne: Bloodaxe, 1995).

28. Elisabeth Lebovici, "Sokolo n'est pas que beauté," *Libération* (May 22, 1998), available at http://www.liberation.com/cannes98/port2205d.html (January 25, 2001).

29. Alessandra Speciale, "Abderrahmane Sissako: Pour l'amour du hasard, il faut partir," *Ecrans d'Afrique* 23 (1998): 29.

30. "Entretien avec Abderrahmane Sissako," *Le film africain* 28 (May 1998): 2.

31. Heike Hurst and Olivier Barlet, "'Ce Tribunal, Ils y Croyaient!': Entretien avec Abderrahmane Sissako," *Africultures* (May 2006), available at http://www.africultures.com/php/index.php?nav=article&no=4428.

32. *Cinéma et libertés: Contribution au thème du FESPACO 1993* (Paris: Présence Africaine, 1993), 92.

19

TSAI MING-LIANG'S HAUNTED
MOVIE THEATER

Jean Ma

The rise of contemporary Chinese-language cinema as a novel art cinema appears in
many respects a self-evident fact. That is, the most notable and widely recognized films
of what have been called the New Chinese Cinemas circulate through the well-worn
channels of distribution and reception carved out by the first wave of art cinema of the
1950s and 1960s, embodied in the Nouvelle Vague, Italian neorealism, and New
German Cinema, among others. Paralleling these earlier movements, the identity of
the New Chinese Cinemas depends on a global circuit of film festivals and art-house
theaters functioning both as an exhibition network and a discourse network.[1] Through
these, their artistic distinction is formulated with recourse to critical concepts of
national identity and authorship, the mythology of a break with the established
commercial genres and cinematic traditions of their respective regions, and a preexisting
canon of great works into which these films are inserted. This is particularly true in the
case of Taiwan's art cinema of the last two decades, whose reception constantly trips on
the coattails of the first wave of postwar art cinema, as countless critics find themselves
compelled to invoke the names of European auteurs—Michelangelo Antonioni, Jean-
Luc Godard, Rainer Werner Fassbinder, to list but a few—to validate comparatively the
achievements of directors like Hou Hsiao-hsien, Edward Yang, and Tsai Ming-liang.

If the mere naming of influences is rarely adequate to the task of accounting for
the significance of their work—and indeed might very well obscure the local histories
and contexts engaged by these directors—it nonetheless also reprises and brings into
view the tensions between the national and the international, between cultural
particularity and universal value, that have subtended the category of art cinema since
its beginnings. My approach in this essay, then, will be neither to dismiss such cross-
cultural linkages out of hand, nor to simply adduce Chinese cinema as a late swell in

the global ripple effect of new wave-ism. Instead, I argue that the case of Chinese art cinema demands a reassessment of earlier understandings of art cinema in light of the transactions between global and regional film cultures taking place at this specific historical juncture. To take up the challenge of this demand means not only to expand and globalize the parameters of art cinema with a gesture of inclusion that, even while acknowledging the difference of Chinese-language cinemas, subsumes this difference to the standard of a Western model.[2] Rather, it requires a confrontation with the instability of art cinema as a theoretical category, as this instability is revealed through the estranging lens of Chinese cinema.

A recent set of films by Tsai Ming-liang presents an especially productive point of entry into these questions. *Ni na bian ji dian? / What Time Is It There?* (2001) moves back and forth between the settings of Taipei and Paris as it alternately follows the life of a merchant who sells watches on the streets of Taipei and traces the itinerary of a woman who, shortly after making a purchase from the watch merchant, embarks on a solo vacation in Paris. Frequently invoked as a testament to the transnational turn in Chinese-language cinema, the film numbers among other recent works that display a marked awareness of their own position within a globalized cultural terrain, a terrain at once fragmented by and consolidated around tropes of travel, diaspora, and exile.[3] Such a global self-consciousness leaves its impression on *What Time Is It There?* in the form of a displacement of time as well as space, as the watch merchant, Hsiao Kang following his encounter with the woman, Shiang-chyi, develops a bizarre compulsion to reset every watch and clock in his path to Paris time. The geographical divide between these two characters, who appear in the same shot in only two instances early in the film, is activated as a locus of narrative tension by his obsessive behavior, which paradoxically both reiterates this divide through the disjunction of standardized clock time and overcomes it by emphasizing the simultaneity of the present moment as it is inhabited by both of the characters from their respective global coordinates. Like the technique of cross-cutting between cities deployed by Tsai throughout the film, Hsiao Kang's actions establish a temporal relation of simultaneity, whose thematic elaboration as the film progresses suggests a subliminal bond and intimacy between the watch merchant and the traveler. This bond acquires a further reflexive and historical inflection with the prominent place of New Wave cinema in the image of France as it is conjured by *What Time Is It There?* Hsiao Kang's obsessive fixation on Parisian time is accompanied by a sudden desire to watch French films; he visits a video rental store seeking films about Paris and returns home with a tape of François Truffaut's *Les Quatre cent coups / The 400 Blows*, which he then watches repeatedly in his bedroom. Meanwhile in Paris the mythic figure of Jean-Pierre Léaud, who plays the main character of *The 400 Blows*, randomly appears on a bench in a cemetery where Shiang-chyi rests, offers her his telephone number, and introduces himself as "Jean-Pierre."

The intersecting dislocations of time and space that constitute the narrative edifice of *What Time Is It There?* reappear in an altered configuration in Tsai's next feature-length film, *Bu san / Goodbye Dragon Inn* (2003). In striking contrast to the geographic expansiveness of the former, *Goodbye Dragon Inn* takes place in a highly constricted mise-en-scène, with the entirety of the story playing out in a decrepit movie theater, the

FIGURE 19.1. Jean-Pierre Léaud offers his telephone number to Chen Shiang-chyi in *What Time Is It There?* (Tsai, 2001).

Fuhe Grand Theater, located in the West Gate District of Taipei, shortly before it is decommissioned. Yet at the same time, the spatial bifurcation of the earlier film finds an echo in the interplay between the virtual world of the movie screen, on which King Hu's classic 1967 martial arts film *Long men ke zhan / Dragon Gate Inn* is projected, and the physical space of the theater, whose auditorium, hallways, lavatories, projection booth, and mysterious inner recesses are explored by the camera. The film commences with a full shot of the screen as the opening scenes of *Dragon Gate Inn* play and runs through the full length of the screening of this film, its focus alternating between the heroic exploits of the world of *wuxia* and the strange figures gathered in the movie theater, who might or might not be ghosts. Beyond merely citing King Hu, then, *Goodbye Dragon Inn* weaves its own narrative into that of the other film in a much more complicated fashion—as Yung Hao Liu observes, "merging" into *Dragon Gate Inn*, but also "converging, colliding, thus producing certain inconsistency and disharmony."[4] This layering of screen times and histories—a golden age of Chinese cinema associated with King Hu's film and its decline as documented by Tsai's capture of the decaying theater on the eve of its closure—imparts a pronounced density and resonance to a narrative present tense otherwise nearly devoid of action, drama, or event. If the reflexive mirroring of the one film in the other conveys an awareness of *Goodbye Dragon Inn*'s place within a local rather than global film history, unlike *What Time Is It There?* the motifs of travel and cultural estrangement so central to the earlier film also reemerge here in the figure of a Japanese tourist (recalling the solitary figure cut by Shiang-Chyi in *What Time*) who takes refuge from a pounding rainstorm in the theater. At one point, the tourist comes across a young man who asks him, "Do you know that this theater is haunted?" to which he uncomprehendingly replies, "I am Japanese."

The fractured spatiotemporality characterizing both of these films can be seen as emblematic of Tsai's idiosyncratic narrative approach—as one of the distinguishing

FIGURE 19.2. Miao Tien watches a *wuxia* classic in *Goodbye Dragon Inn* (Tsai, 2003).

marks of authorial individuality that aligns Tsai's filmmaking with the project of art cinema as a cinema of de-dramatization[5]—but also as a strategy by which Tsai anticipates, intercepts, and interrogates critical responses to his own work. On the one hand, the various references to New Wave cinema spun out of the transnationally divided mise-en-scène of *What Time Is It There?* suggest on the part of the director an active engagement with and claim to the legacy of European postwar cinema, corroborating those critical readings that invoke this canon as the most significant point of reference for Tsai's work. For instance, Mark Betz likens his habit of consistently working with a small repertoire of actors from film to film to the approach of many European auteurs, observing that his collaborative relationship with Lee Kang-sheng— who has appeared in all of Tsai's feature-length films to date—finds an echo in Truffaut's partnership with Léaud.[6] Notably, in his remarks on the film that supplement the American DVD release, Tsai describes *The 400 Blows* as his "all-time favorite film" and compares Lee Kang-sheng's acting style to the kind of performances favored by Robert Bresson.[7] The sparse dramaturgy of Tsai's films, their distension of dead and empty time in highly protracted long takes, their downplaying of expression and dialogue, and their elliptical mode of editing have also led many critics to attribute to him a neorealist sensibility, while the solitude and disconnection evinced by his characters calls to mind Antonioni, to whom he is compared as a chronicler of modern anomie and urban alienation. The slapstick comedic elements that punctuate his representation of industrial modernity have also reminded some critics of Jacques Tati. The picture of Tsai's directorial identity that materializes across such discussions is plotted into a field of cinematic modernism, a field that is further extended into the adjacent realms of theater and literature by Rey Chow, who cites the absurdist writings of Samuel Beckett and Franz Kafka as precedents for Tsai's approach to narrative.[8] To critics like Fredric Jameson, Tsai even appears as one of the last "great auteurs, who seem to renew the claims of high modernism in a period in which that aesthetic and its institutional preconditions seem extinct."[9]

Yet on the other hand, even while Tsai's films demonstrate an unusually high degree of self-consciousness of their art cinema affiliations and the global film culture within which they circulate, they also resist the facile absorption into a genealogy of modernist narrative that such characteristics might at first appear to support. The counterpoint of *Goodbye Dragon Inn* with *Dragon Gate Inn* points to the culturally hybrid design of Tsai's cinematic imaginary, by no means limited to a Western canon, as well as to the powerful inspiration exerted by the mainstream genre picture on his work. Rather than being at pains to distance himself from the tradition of popular commercial film, Tsai displays a more nuanced and ambivalent attitude toward this tradition, incorporating its conventions, forms, and familiar icons into his practice even as he radically departs from its narrative approach. Alongside the nostalgic citation of *Dragon Gate Inn*, one of the most beloved classics of the Chinese *wuxia* genre, other examples include the nearly continuous presence in Tsai's corpus of Miao Tien, a familiar figure from Chinese popular cinema and a lead actor in *Dragon Gate Inn*; the unmotivated musical sequences interspersed throughout *Dong / The Hole* (1999), reminiscent of both the American film musical and Hong Kong musicals of the 1950s and 1960s; and the bizarre pastiche of musical, slapstick comedy, and pornography comprising *Tian bian yi dou yun / The Wayward Cloud* (2005), a film that might be seen as a culmination of Tsai's play with popular genres.

In these examples, generic elements are activated in order to be bent, reworked, and set into collision with the idiom of art cinema, generating a sort of stylistic excess at odds with the aesthetic of minimalism and reduction so frequently associated with these films. And this excessive effect casts a different light on the references to European postwar cinema scattered across the surface and stories of Tsai's films, raising the question of whether these evidence a straightforward continuation of the project of cinematic modernism begun in this period or, indeed, the operation of a different aesthetic project. Along these lines, Darrell William Davis and Emilie Yueh-yu Yeh have noted the *incongruity* that marks Tsai's films, a tendency toward the spectacular

FIGURE 19.3. A musical number centering on Chiang Kai-shek's statue in *The Wayward Cloud* (Tsai, 2005).

and the hyperbolic that sits uneasily within the framework of modernist art cinema.[10] The challenges posed by Tsai to film scholarship, as they suggest, reside in the coexistence in his films of clashing stylistic and thematic properties, which give rise to forms of audience address perceived as incompatible with one another. Their analysis couches this perceived incompatibility in terms of a tension between Western critical formations that place emphasis on the aesthetic values of the films and localized discourses of reception that open on their social valences of meaning, relating to sexual politics and local working-class identities.

My intention here, however, is not to reiterate the point that the project of modernism cannot offer a conclusive key to Tsai's films—a point already duly and regularly noted even by those whose primary critical investments lie within its parameters. For the repetitions of this disclaimer have exerted a polarizing effect on the terms of Tsai's critical reception, establishing "Western modernism" as the hegemonic discourse against which every subsequent reading must measure its critical contribution, or as the universal form to which local content must be restored by the conscientious critic. Rather, my interest here lies in how these films suggest an alternative line of investigation, one that takes as its starting point a rethinking of the concatenated categories of modernism, art cinema, and national cinema in view of the transformations these categories have undergone between the postwar period and the present moment.

Notably, the conception of modernism that informs discussions of "modernist art cinema" is a theoretically diluted one, often serving primarily as a shorthand by which to register a break from entrenched representational norms.[11] The specific contours of the oppositional stance thus designated, however, vary in light of the multiple and overlapping contexts against which it is figured. Historically, the emergence of art cinema is linked with the birth of the concept of national cinema through the "new cinema" movements emerging throughout postwar Europe during a period when the efforts of young filmmakers to break free from the constraints of tradition and commercialism converged with state interests to promote a nationally specific culture and film industry. As Steven Neale has noted, "Concern with national culture, the national economy, the national industry and with national cinematic traditions has remained a constant in Art Cinema and the discourses it has involved."[12] At the same time, as much as the rejection of a preexisting national tradition of quality and escapism has figured centrally in the formation of the generational identity of many national movements, the global presence of Hollywood cinema also plays a determining role in these developments. Neale points out the dominance of Hollywood, and the specter it raises of an invasion of American mass culture, as a key motivating factor in efforts by liberal-democratic European governments to subsidize and shore up national art cinemas within their own borders—even as many of the filmmakers supported by these state measures drew inspiration from and understood their practice in dialogue with Hollywood, as the example of the French New Wave demonstrates. In the realm of reception, the success that greeted these films abroad as representative of a national culture of cinema was frequently crucial to their validation at home as "art cinema," legitimizing their claim to the notion of cultural value imbedded within this phrase.

The shifting contexts and configurations that inform the notion of art cinema are reflected as well in film scholarship. On the one hand, the entrenchment of national cinema as a methodological framework results in a heterogeneous conception of art cinema, scrutinized in its various regionally bounded iterations. On the other hand, this heterogeneity is also countered by a centripetal tendency, an effect of the long shadow cast by Hollywood as the negative image against which disparate national art cinemas draw their identity as well as of the institutionalization of art cinema throughout the latter half of the twentieth century. Viewed from this angle, art cinema signals the displacement of a classical mode of narrative entrenched by Hollywood by a new and competing mode, simultaneous with the institutional demise of the studio system in the postwar period. Thus David Bordwell, in one of the few attempts at a systematic consideration of art cinema form, approaches it as a narrative paradigm self-consciously fashioned "as a deviation from classical narrative."[13] While such a gloss instates a limiting binary logic that ultimately reaffirms the centrality of Hollywood as the norm against which every deviation is to be defined, it also presents an important insight into the operation of art cinema as a *transnational* category, consisting of a pattern of distinct narrational procedures that recur across regional cinemas. As Bordwell observes, "The fullest flower of the art-cinema paradigm occurred at the moment that the combination of novelty and nationalism became the marketing device it has been ever since: the French New Wave, New Polish Cinema, New Hungarian Cinema, New German Cinema, New Australian Cinema."[14] If art cinema's origin myth revolves around newness and the idea of a break with the past, this newness subsequently gives way to the cumulative effect of these successive waves: the repetition and hence consolidation of art cinema as a distinct and identifiable cross-cultural idiom, paradigm, or formula.

In these respects, the historical trajectory of art cinema traces the emergence of not a stable and singular category, but rather a volatile nexus of individual and institutional agencies and interests contending for visibility and legitimacy across shifting domains of value. The new wave movements advancing its development are expressive of tensions and contradictions within the sphere of national culture; concomitantly the national identity of these movements should thus be seen not as a straightforward reflection of a specific cultural disposition, but rather as a backformation, constituted at the point of reception as well as production. The point stressed by scholars of European postwar cinema that movements like the New German Cinema and Italian neorealism were invented abroad as much as at home bears repeating in the contemporary context of art cinema in view of the suspicions voiced by some critics concerning the global success of recent Chinese cinemas. For example, the mainland's Fifth Generation filmmakers are often accused of compromising the authenticity and local relevance of their works as they pander to the orientalist imaginations of overseas audiences and mimic Western styles. In Taiwan's case, Kuan-Hsing Chen has descried what he perceives as the cooptation of the New Cinema by a phenomenon of "global nativism," where "exotic images of natives and national local histories and signs are employed as selling-points in the world cinema"; this phenomenon in turn suggests that the directors of this movement achieved at best "a 'parrot' language, imitating and assembling various outside elements."[15] Such criticisms serve as important reminders of the political hierarchies that affect the flow of images and the perpetuation of historical inequalities in the postcolonial present, inequalities that overdetermine the reception of Chinese-language cinemas. To couch these concerns within a discourse on national authenticity, however, is to overlook the constitutive impurity of the concept of national cinema. The ongoing interplay between the national and global, between native and foreign, historically inscribed in the art film opens up a productive dialogue between the idea of global art cinema and the shift from national to transnational methodologies recently transpiring within studies of national cinema, a shift in which Chinese cinema figures centrally.

The example of Tsai highlights both the extension of the idiom of art cinema beyond Europe and the West and the transformation of this idiom in confrontation with new forms of globalization and hybridity. The arrival of the Taiwan *hsin tien-ying,* or "new cinema," in the early 1980s on the international art film scene to a large extent conforms to the pattern laid out earlier, propelled by directors like Hou Hsiao-hsien and Edward Yang whose work betokened a significant departure from the genre films (historical costume drama, martial arts action, romantic melodrama) that constituted the bulk of Taiwan's mainstream film production. This generation of filmmakers enjoyed the direct financial support of the Central Motion Picture Corporation, Taiwan's largest film studio, funded and operated by the ruling Nationalist Party. Notwithstanding the dissolution of the Taiwan New Cinema at the end of the decade, Hou and, in his lifetime, Yang went on to secure reputations as world-class auteurs, their films receiving high levels of critical acclaim on the international festival circuit. The trajectory of these two directors after the 1980s attests to the vitiation of the national cinema paradigm in Taiwan, a development rooted in changing industrial conditions that have forced many filmmakers to turn to international sources of funding for their productions, confronted with an attrition of support from both state institutions and domestic audiences. The global turn in art film is perhaps most clearly instantiated in Hou's transmogrification from figurehead of a national movement into, by the end of that decade, an international star with access to Japanese and European producers and worldwide audiences.[16]

Tsai's own directorial career postdates this movement, with his first feature-length narrative, *Qing shao nian nuo zha / Rebels of the Neon God,* released in 1992, well after the rise and fall of the Taiwan New Cinema. Unlike his predecessors, from the beginning of his career Tsai was faced with the task of negotiating the shrinkage of public resources for filmmakers in Taiwan. While his first two feature projects were made under the aegis of the Central Motion Picture Corporation, like his predecessors Tsai has since relied on private monies from both local and foreign producers.[17] To a certain extent his work displays continuities with the films of the *hsin tien-ying,* for instance, sharing with Yang a compositional emphasis on isolated individuals adrift within modern cityscapes, and with Hou a strikingly pronounced reliance on the long take. Certainly the renown achieved by these older directors contributed to the receptive critical environment in which Tsai forged his identity as an auteur.

This association between Tsai and Hou, moreover, suggests not only a stylistic continuity that might be read as evidence of a coherent national style, but also the development of a broader regional pattern that goes beyond the older comparative and cross-cultural schema imbedded within the category of art cinema. The long-take aesthetic that forms the centerpiece of Hou's signature style and that has come to be synonymous with the director's name eventually came to be conflated with the Taiwan New Cinema itself, as an encapsulation of its alternative narrative approach. In the aftermath of this movement, Hou has exerted a considerable influence on a younger generation of art film directors throughout East Asia as well as within Taiwan, with traces of his signature aesthetic appearing in the work of filmmakers like Jia Zhangke of mainland China, Kore-eda Hirokazu of Japan, and Hong Sang-soo of South Korea (many of whom openly acknowledge Hou's influence). Bordwell argues, "If the long take had been an identifying tag for the New Taiwanese Cinema of the 1980s, it became virtually a national brand in the 1990s"; and since then, it has only "spread to other parts of the Pacific, making 'Asian minimalism' something of a festival cliché by the end of the 1990s."[18] Although a more detailed disquisition on the notion of an unified trans-Pacific aesthetic lies beyond the scope of this essay, such discussions warrant mention insofar as they focalize the particular challenges presented by contemporary Chinese cinema to long-standing theoretical models—in this instance to move past Eurocentric and Hollywood-centric models of transnationalism. The current status of art cinema in East Asia not only opens beyond a nation-based view of film culture and aesthetics but also gives rise to other forms of regionalism, advancing the comparative perspective of what Mitsuhiro Yoshimoto calls "trans-Asian cinema," a perspective "not reducible either to the false universality of Hollywood as a transnational standard or to its mirror image, the particularity of identity embraced by multiculturalism and transnational capitalism."[19]

If Hou justifiably holds a central position in discussions of pan- or trans-Asian cinema, then Tsai further pushes the idiom of art cinema in other directions. With his rampant citations of popular film practice, Tsai demonstrates a very different consciousness of his own place within film history and in between disparate filmmaking traditions. Thus while his participation in the long-take aesthetic of trans-Asian art cinema lends an air of "minimalism" to his films, this quality is also contradicted by a sort of maximalism, instantiated in the intertextual proliferation that characterizes films like *What Time Is It There?* and *Goodbye Dragon Inn* and that appears even more insistently across the breadth of Tsai's corpus. Viewed from this angle, any modernist impulses that animate these films appear less as an internalized dominant narrative mode than as yet another form available to be appropriated, reworked, and perhaps finally subsumed to a citational stance of postmodernism that weaves together multiple historical periods, Western and Chinese cinematic traditions, highbrow and lowbrow cultural forms. The positioning of his films simultaneously within these multiple genealogies sets Tsai apart from the filmmakers of the Taiwan New Cinema, who were at pains to distinguish their work from the formulas of popular genre cinema, and reveals the mutations undergone by art cinema in the contemporary era.

To invoke the aesthetics of postmodernism in this context is to broach a heated ongoing debate about the applicability of these terms to non-Western cinemas such as Taiwan's.[20] But rather than situate Tsai's work at the center of a contest between modernism and postmodernism, I would like to instead consider a different set of questions prompted by the conjunction of these terms in discussions of the cinematic landscape of the late twentieth century, one in which rampant practices of allusion, revision, and generic hybridity have steadily chipped away at the predominance of the classical cinema, with its twin pillars of unity and closure. Given that the narrative mode of art cinema was historically constituted under the shadow of and in competition with a classical narrative paradigm—reversing its principles of clear-cut causality and character motive, disrupting its unities of time and space, refusing its methods of closure—then how can we begin to reconceptualize art cinema in a postclassical era? At a time when so many of the tactics that previously signified a rejection of representational norms have been appropriated and absorbed by the mainstream and Hollywood itself, does it make sense to speak of art film as constituting a distinct narrative approach?[21] How might the changing conditions of post- or late modernity and an ever-intensifying global commerce of images affect the strategies by which the art film attempts to mark, anticipate, and promote its own distinction?[22]

To grapple with these questions requires a consideration of the art film as a historically dynamic construct, constituted in agonistic interplay with a larger cinematic terrain that has undergone sweeping changes in recent decades. And Tsai's work serves as a reminder to approach this interplay as a complex dialectical process, without simply relegating the art film to the antagonistic and marginal position of a stylistic alternative or an "other" mode. One avenue by which to consider the historicity and mutability of this form is to address the parallels between, on the one hand, the repetitions of new wave-ism by which the art film has advanced its global scope and, on the other hand, the parallel repetitions of genre formation in popular cinema. This entails a confrontation with the art film's generic status, a status that it represses in its claim to uniqueness and singularity of authorial expression. To be sure, the heterogeneity of the films subsumed to this category certainly cannot be corralled within any consistent grouping of semantic or syntactic elements, as in the case of popular film genres like the western, the musical, and so on. But nonetheless, the historical trajectory of art cinema conforms to a pattern of genre formation, wherein the recurrence of certain properties reaches a threshold, becomes codified, and subsequent films are produced and perceived in relation to the norm instated by this codification. Thus the network of influences delineated throughout the critical discourse of art cinema as it creates linkages and connections among directors functions beyond a heuristic of authorship, as a testament to the repetition and calcification of a set of stylistic properties upholding the art film's generic identity. And from an institutional standpoint, Neale points out that in the aftermath of the fragmented and transient new cinema movements of the postwar period there arises "a relatively permanent genre towards which Art Cinema internationally has begun to gravitate, assured as it is of an international market, notoriety and (generally) a degree of cultural and artistic prestige."[23] Somewhat paradoxically, the global spread of art cinema further accelerates this process, as "the adoption of Art Cinema policies tends to re-mark such affiliation, encouraging their systematic inscription into the films produced under the aegis of such policies."[24] Like any other genre, art cinema now operates as a market category, designating a specified niche in the global economy of cinema, with its own exhibition venues and target audience.

The status of genre—more particularly, its transformation as it shifts into a reflexive mode—has figured centrally in critical elaborations of postclassical cinema, or what Tim Corrigan has termed the "cinema without walls."[25] And perhaps more than any director working today, Tsai calls attention to the reverberations of this reflexive turn in the realm of art cinema itself, not only deploying its conventions but also self-consciously commenting on his participation in its generic code. This becomes especially apparent with a broad view of Tsai's body of work and the relations among its singular components: alongside the hybridity that distinguishes certain films can be glimpsed another form of intertextuality, one that operates across the narrative boundaries of his films to delineate their belonging within an authorial corpus with unusual emphasis. As many note, Tsai's films are characterized by a notably high degree of repetition and continuity. In addition to his habit of working regularly with a small core group of actors—frequently cast in the same roles of mother (Lu Yi-jing), father (Miao Tien), and son (Lee Kang-sheng) within the same functionally dysfunctional family [26]—this is evident also in the reappearance of themes and motifs from film to film. To name but a few examples, the activity of cruising is depicted with regularity, whether as a cat-and-mouse dance of courtship between characters, as in *Ai qing wan sui / Vive L'Amour* (1994) and *What Time Is It There?* or as a spatial practice that demarcates sites of gay male subculture like the bathhouse and the movie theater, as in *He liu / The River* (1996) and *Goodbye Dragon Inn*. Almost all of Tsai's films contain bathroom scenes exposing characters in the very private act of relieving themselves, often to humorous effect, as well as intimate glimpses of characters crying, whether in the mode of uncontrollable sobbing or a slow and subtle build-up of tears in the eye. These motifs of watery expression are wedded to situations of drought and storm, to leaky pipes and flooded apartment buildings. Hsiao Kang's profession as a columbarium salesman in *Vive L'Amour* is evoked by reversal in *What Time*, where we find him laying his father's ashes to rest in this very type of housing; the watermelon that makes a brief appearance in the earlier film becomes a key scenic element and adult transitional object in *The Wayward Cloud*; the steam that serves the important purpose of obscuring the sexual goings-on in the bathhouse in *The River* transmutes into a smoky haze that envelops the entire city of Kuala Lumpur in *Hei yan quan / I Don't Want to Sleep Alone* (2006). The list goes on, long enough to occupy any viewer inclined to play a cinephiliac game of connect-the-dots.

On the one hand, such regularities conform to a logic of consistency upholding what is by now a widely accepted view of authorship, by no means exclusive to Tsai, that maintains the continual presence of the director across his or her body of work. Operating within the parameters of this logic, for instance, we might venture an interpretation of the recurrent liquid themes in these films that elaborates on their accumulating symbolic meanings, elaborated through forms of watery excess—downpours, floods, intoxication—and forms of lack—drought, thirst, deprivation—that acquire an existential or even metaphysical significance across these films.[27] This textual inscription of the auteur is foregrounded in the art film, which, as Bordwell notes, "requires that the spectator see this film as fitting into a body of work," into a corpus "linked by an authorial signature."[28] Whereas a strong authorial identity might characterize films of many kinds, as the early champions of the *politique des auteurs* have noted, in the art film it acquires a special determining agency as a receptive stance, one occupied by an audience possessive of a certain body of knowledge to be engaged in the production of meaning. Such a receptive stance testifies to the centrality of the auteur as a distinguishing generic feature of art cinema.

On the other hand, the interrelations among Tsai's films also exceed this familiar framework and suggest a very different notion of authorship and corpus that animates these works. In their chronological trajectory the continuities that bind Tsai's films together multiply and intensify in degree, so that if early on the reappearance of the same nuclear family played by the same set of actors across films provides a thread of continuity connecting their otherwise discrete and unified fictions, then later on the stories themselves lose their autonomous character. Indeed, *What Time* can be seen as a pivotal film for the way that it marks a transition to an emphatically autocitational narrative approach on Tsai's part; this transition is extended with *Goodbye Dragon Inn*, situating the two films within a closely interwoven pairing, with the one possessing the status of a spinoff from and amplification of a single scene in the other. At a certain moment in Hsiao Kang's restless mission of clock-resetting in *What Time Is It There?* he wanders into an old movie theater, steals a clock from the corridor, and sneaks it into the auditorium where he furtively resets it in the dark. His efforts are thwarted when a man who has been following him throughout the theater catches on to his intentions; the man steals the clock from Hsiao Kang and, using it as bait, lures him into the men's lavatory where he comes on to the watch seller by popping out from the closed door of a stall, naked but for the strategically placed clock. The theater where this takes place, of course, is the Fuhe Grand Theater, and the motif of cruising introduced in this scene is elaborated and further explored by *Goodbye Dragon Inn* as it returns to the Fuhe Grand Theater with its long corridors, dark rooms, and busy lavatories. And in Tsai's next feature production, *The Wayward Cloud*, the longing between the watch seller and the traveler, which is never directly expressed but only intimated through the exchange of objects and the consumption of French culture, flowers into an affair after these two characters cross paths once again. To make the connection between these films unambiguous, the woman asks the man if he is still in the watch business upon their first meeting. Since the release of *What Time Is It There?* Tsai's films appear less as self-contained individual units than as a series of variations and extensions of a single fluctuating, porous, and hybrid metafiction.

The intertextuality characterizing these films therefore sets into play a dialogue between the single film and the larger set to which it belongs—a process of permeability that results in a qualitatively different relationship between part and whole than that which typically informs perceptions of the oeuvre and the individual film as a discrete work. Tsai's adoption of this approach imbeds his films within a framework of viewer memory that makes it impossible to understand them in isolation from one another, eliciting the recollection of a preceding filmography in the course of the individual screening, on the one hand, while also retroactively revising the meanings of his earlier films as the viewer's memory of these is activated, on the other. In this regard, the director's strategy anticipates the specific mode of reception that Bordwell associates with the art film, but also goes further to escalate the importance of this mode of reception to arriving at an understanding of his films. At the same time, such a strategy intensifies the already-heightened textual presence of the director that marks the art film genre. If intertextuality in a general sense frequently effects a fragmentation and opening of the individual work, it operates in a somewhat different fashion within the parameters of the authorial corpus, reinscribing the cohesion of the corpus itself as a framework of interpretation even as it dissolves the unity of the singular film. This cohesion ultimately refers back to the figure of the auteur, whose shadow presence is now amplified as a locus of meaning. As his control extends from the shaping of the film to the elicitation of a certain way of viewing, Tsai hyperbolizes the function of authorship.

Rather than conjuring up an older, romanticized ideal of expressive subjectivity, moreover, this reassertion of authorial presence demands to be understood in the broader context of a globalized commercial industry in which the auteur has become reified as a marketing category. As Corrigan has pointed out, in the postclassical era the auteur has acquired a renewed life as a vehicle of promotion and advertising, as "a critical concept bound to distribution and marketing aims that identify and address the potential cult status of an auteur."[29] Pronouncements of the death of the author notwithstanding, this figure survives in what he terms the "commerce of authorship," rematerialized as an extratextual presence and circulating as a star discourse that predetermines the reception of the film.[30] The heightened visibility of the auteur, once uniquely claimed by the art film, has become a general fixture of an industry that banks on the director as a brand name. Corrigan's analysis of the contemporary fortunes of the film auteur presents an important context through which to consider Tsai's distinct methods of asserting directorial presence in his film work. Beyond reflexively commenting on authorship as a generic feature of the art film, these operate as a means of responding to and negotiating changing boundaries between art cinema and commercial cinema. If a glance across the terrain of cinema in the last few decades finds numerous examples of filmmakers who deliberately confront and resist the commercial impetus of performing authorship, so Tsai's insistence on an intertextual authorial presence constitutes one more way of reworking a traditional auteur position. In the realm of Chinese cinema, notably, very similar tendencies are apparent in the work of Tsai's peers: for instance, Hou Hsiao-hsien's *Zui hao de shi guang* / *Three Times* (2005) reprises in its triplicate structure the various phases of the director's career, while Wong Kar-wai often tends toward pairs of films that rework overlapping motifs, like *Chung Hing sam lam* / *Chungking Express* (1994) and *Dou lou tian shi* / *Fallen Angels* (1997), or *Fa yeung nin wa* / *In the Mood for Love* (2000) and *2046* (2004). The formal performance of authorship undertaken by these directors reveals the ways in which art cinema responds to the conditions of contemporary film culture and continually updates its strategies in dialectical tension with the realm of popular entertainment, steered by the latter's course while struggling to preserve its marks of distinction against the mainstream's encroaching advance.

The threat posed by this advance has been repeatedly raised by Tsai in interviews and discussions, where he bemoans the lack of support for art-house films such as his own among Taiwan's audiences, whose viewing proclivities tend toward the mainstream

Hollywood fare that fills local theaters. Not content to merely speak of this imbalance, Tsai has made a habit of taking matters into his own hands by showing up at venues exhibiting his films, hawking tickets, and bursting into tears as he makes emotional speeches to those lined up to see his films—a perverse performance of authorship if ever there was one. The startling effect of this performance issues not just from its over-the-top histrionic tenor (which itself calls to mind Tsai's background in acting and avant-garde theater)[31] but also from the mere fact of his physical appearances at his own screenings, from his direct and face-to-face confrontation with the public. Far from content to occupy only a phantom presence, whether textually or intertextually inscribed, or the mediated presence of the director-as-star, Tsai pushes the boundaries of his auteur identity further through the act of what he calls "taking to the streets," one that combines street theater and activism. The performance of excessive presence glimpsed here, furthermore, must be understood in relation to the distinctive politics of the body operating throughout Tsai's work, hinging on a set of complex interactions among modes of transgressive presence and forms of loss, disappearance, and absence that do not merely reduce to nonpresence. This corporeal politics in turn maps onto a politics of time, directed toward an ongoing interrogation of normative sexual, familial, and social identities.

The peculiar dimensionality of the body described previously can be detected in *What Time Is It There?* and *Goodbye Dragon Inn*, where it becomes a medium of historical consciousness, marking at once the position of these films within plural histories of cinema and a steadfast clinging to a historical experience of cinema in the face of its obsolescence. The body as depicted in these films serves as evidence of the afterlife of ghosts and of residual forms of presence that persist in the wake of death and disappearance. For example, *What Time Is It There?* starts off with the death of Hsiao Kang's father and poses his subsequent attack of Francophilia as a kind of displaced mourning for his father as much as an expression of desire for the woman who roams Paris wearing his watch. The exchange of the watch between them establishes the chiasmatic relation between the vectors of desire experienced by Hsiao Kang, who initially refuses Shiang-chyi's request to purchase his own watch on the rationale that it would bring her bad luck because he is in mourning. At the end of the film, the constant crossings among his longing for France/French cinema, for Shiang-chyi, and for his father are affirmed and laid to rest when the father's ghost appears in a park in Paris where she has fallen asleep, retrieves her suitcase from the fountain into which it has been dumped by some children, and walks away into the distance toward a giant Ferris wheel. *Goodbye Dragon Inn* picks up on and amplifies this notion of the return of the dead, presenting Miao Tien as a ghost who returns to watch himself in his youthful glory on the screen, starring as one of the lead characters of *Dragon Gate Inn*. The uncanny temporalities of haunting and nostalgia that reverberate across his films offer a lens through which to consider their place within the historical scheme of art cinema. The very idea of time set forth by Tsai contravenes the one-way linear logic of succession that underlies his reception as a director who merely takes up and continues the tradition of art cinema. In reminding us of the radiating powers of a restive past in contact with the present, it opens our eyes to the transformative possibilities imbedded in this tradition.

Notes

1. A thorough accounting of the distribution and reception of contemporary Chinese cinema, which is beyond the scope of this essay, would necessarily also consider the role of VHS, DVD, and VCD technology along with the rental and sales markets supported by these media, and alternative screening venues like universities, museums, and other cultural institutions, and private or underground film clubs.

2. Mitsuhiro Yoshimoto, "National/International/Transnational: The Concept of Trans-Asian Cinema and the Cultural Politics of Film Criticism," in *Reconceptualising National Cinema*, ed. Valentina Vitali and Paul Willemen (London: British Film Institute, 2006).

3. On the concept of transnational Chinese cinema, see Sheldon Hsiao-peng Lu, ed., *Transnational Chinese Cinemas: Identity, Nationhood, Gender* (Honolulu: University of Hawai'i Press, 1997), and Gina Marchetti, *From Tian'anmen to Times Square: Transnational China and the Chinese Diaspora on Global Screens, 1989–1997* (Philadelphia: Temple University Press, 2006).

4. Yung Hao Liu, "'I thought of the times we were in front of the flowers': Analyzing the Opening Credits of *Goodbye Dragon Inn*," trans. Ming-yu Lee, in *Cinema Taiwan: Politics, Popularity and State of the Arts*, ed. Darrell William Davis and Ru-shou Robert Chen (New York: Routledge, 2007), 178.

5. The idea of a *cinéma de dédramatisation* was set forth in 1966 by Marcel Martin as part of a positive appraisal of the landscape of postwar European films; see his "Les voies de l'authenticité," *Cinéma 66*, no. 104 (March 1966): 52–79. Martin's understanding of the modernist art film in terms of attenuated narrativity, which has since become commonplace, has been challenged by Christian Metz in "The Modern Cinema and Narrativity," *Film Language: A Semiotics of the Cinema*, trans. Michael Taylor (New York: Oxford University Press, 1974). The latter calls for an expanded definition of narrative that can account for the more sophisticated forms and subtle dramaturgical approaches to be found within this realm of film practice.

6. Mark Betz, "The Cinema of Tsai Ming-liang: A Modernist Genealogy," in *Reading Chinese Transnationalisms: Society, Literature, Film*, ed. Maria N. Ng and Philip Holden (Hong Kong: Hong Kong University Press, 2006), 162. Betz's essay offers a comprehensive overview of the connections drawn between Tsai Ming-liang and the auteurs of postwar European cinema. A fairly representative example of the French cinephiliac reception of Tsai can be found in Jean-Pierre Rehm, Olivier Joyard, and Danièle Rivière, *Tsaï Ming-liang* (Paris: Dis Voir, 1999).

7. "I hope Hsiao Kang will never become a 'professional' actor, at least not in my films. When I say this I am referring to the characters in Bresson's films. These people often say very little and have strict features. Their acting skills are never discussed. I find them both persuasive and touching in their roles." Director's Notes, *What Time Is It There?* US DVD, Wellspring Video, 2002.

8. Samuel Beckett and Franz Kafka are invoked by Rey Chow in comparison to Tsai in *Sentimental Fabulations: Contemporary Chinese Films* (New York: Columbia University Press, 2007), 183.

9. Fredric Jameson, "History and Elegy in Sokurov," *Critical Inquiry* 33 (Autumn 2006): 1.

10. Emilie Yueh-yu Yeh and Darrell William Davis, *Taiwan Film Directors: A Treasure Island* (New York: Columbia University Press, 2005), 219–220.

11. The very designation of art cinema as "modernist" warrants a more rigorous elaboration, with a view to long-standing discussions of film culture's intersections with modernism and modernity; in particular, the category of "modernist art cinema"

needs to be weighed against what D. N. Rodowick terms as the project of political modernism associated with counter-cinema, a category that is both distinct from and overlapping with the former.

12. Steven Neale, "Art Cinema as Institution," *Screen* 22, no. 1 (1981): 34. On the imbrication of art cinema and national cinema, see also Andrew Higson, "The Concept of National Cinema," in *Film and Nationalism*, ed. Alan Williams (New Brunswick, N.J.: Rutgers University Press, 2002), 52–67.

13. David Bordwell, *Narration in the Fiction Film* (Madison: University of Wisconsin Press, 1985), 228. He lists the characteristics of this paradigm: loosened cause-effect relations, episodic and elliptical plot construction, a heightened emphasis on character psychology, ambiguity, delayed exposition, and an overall "self-conscious" mode of narration that foregrounds the authorial presence of the director.

14. Ibid., 231.

15. Kuan-Hsing Chen, "Taiwanese New Cinema," in *The Oxford Guide to Film Studies*, ed. John Hill and Pamela Church Gibson (New York: Oxford University Press, 1998), 561, 558.

16. Since the mid-1990s Hou has consistently drawn on foreign production monies for his projects, sometimes with the result of completely detaching his work from a local context. For instance, on the occasion of the one-hundredth anniversary of Ozu Yasujiro's birthday Hou was commissioned by Shochiku Studio to direct a tribute to the great director. *Café Lumière* (2003)—shot in Japan with a Japanese cast, thematizing the erosion of the Japanese family that so occupied Ozu—is effectively a Japanese film that happens to have been made by a Chinese director (albeit one viewed as the spiritual descendant of that "most Japanese" of all directors). More recently Hou has drawn closer to the French film industry with his *Red Balloon* (2007), a remake of the classic 1956 film by Albert Lamorisse, also shot in France with a French cast.

17. In this regard, *The Hole* (1999) marks a pivotal moment in Tsai's shift to a coproduction model. The film was made as part of a series by directors around the world addressing the upcoming millennial transition, jointly commissioned by a French distributor and a French-German television network. The series, entitled "2000 as Seen By . . . ," figures on many levels the contemporary fortunes of cinematic globalization, as what Rosalind Galt describes as "a work of mapping, an attempt to limn its own constellation of cinematic geography: New York, Rio de Janeiro, Mali, Belgium, Taipei." See her *New European Cinema: Redrawing the Map* (New York: Columbia University Press, 2006), 235.

18. David Bordwell, *Figures Traced in Light: On Cinematic Staging* (Berkeley: University of California Press, 2005), 230–231.

19. Yoshimoto, "National/International/Transnational," 260. The investigation of a pan-Asian aesthetic operative in the realm of art cinema finds a complement in other lines of inquiry, for instance, the recent emergence of a trans-Asian mass culture rooted in *hanryu*, the craze for Korean popular media, including film, television, and music.

20. This debate has in large part been articulated in response to Fredric Jameson's *The Geopolitical Aesthetic* (Bloomington: Indiana University Press, 1992), which describes the work of Taiwan New Cinema director Edward Yang in terms of a residual modernism. A cogent response to this piece can be found in Sung-sheng Yvonne Chang, "*The Terrorizer* and the Great Divide in Contemporary Taiwan's Cultural Development," in *Island on the Edge: Taiwan New Cinema and After*, ed. Chris Berry and Feii Lu (Hong Kong: Hong Kong University Press, 2005), 13–26.

21. Bordwell even suggests an eventual convergence of the art film and the genre film, or a collapse of the one into the other, by the early 1980s, with the art film

reaching an endpoint of development once its procedures are absorbed by Hollywood (*Narration in the Fiction Film*, 232).

22. Galt and Schoonover address this issue in their introduction to this volume.

23. Neale, "Art Cinema as Institution," 33.

24. Ibid., 34.

25. Tim Corrigan, *A Cinema without Walls: Movies and Culture after Vietnam* (New Brunswick, N.J.: Rutgers University Press, 1991).

26. That fact that Tsai's characters are either nameless or identified by the real name of the actor, as in the case of Hsiao Kang, places a further emphasis on the familiar bodies of these actors.

27. On the significance of water, see Chow, *Sentimental Fabulations*, ch. 9.

28. Bordwell, *Narration in the Fiction Film*, 211.

29. Corrigan, *A Cinema without Walls*, 103.

30. The phrase comes from the title of chapter 4 of Corrigan's book. While he cites the director interview as a chief medium of this extratextual presence, more recent technologically enabled developments like the "director's cut" home-viewing version and the audio commentary by directors included on so many DVD releases further bear out Corrigan's analysis.

31. On this background see Song Hwee Lim, *Celluloid Comrades: Representations of Male Homosexuality in Contemporary Chinese Cinemas* (Honolulu: University of Hawai'i Press, 2006), ch. 5, and Wei-hong Bao, "Biomechanics of Love: Reinventing the Avant-garde in Tsai Ming-liang's Wayward 'Pornographic Musical,'" *Journal of Chinese Cinemas* 1, no. 2 (2007): 139–160.

20

Traveling Theory, Shots, and Players: Jorge Sanjinés, New Latin American Cinema, and the European Art Film

Dennis Hanlon

In his recent *Making Waves: New Cinemas of the 1960s*, Geoffrey Nowell-Smith attempts to remedy the exclusion of such filmmakers as Jorge Sanjinés, Glauber Rocha, and Julio García Espinosa from previous accounts of 1960s new waves by including a chapter on Latin America along with chapters on various European national cinemas and another encompassing the cinemas of the Soviet bloc countries.[1] While Nowell-Smith is correct to validate New Latin American Cinema's (henceforth NLAC) connection with the French and other new waves, the relationship between European art cinema and NLAC in the 1960s–1980s is both more direct and more contentious than their contemporaneity and stylistic similarities alone would suggest. NLAC and its makers traveled the same festival and distribution circuits as European art cinema on both sides of the Iron Curtain, and the films of NLAC were championed by the same European film critics who wrote about art cinema. Indeed many of these films premiered at European festivals years before they were seen in their countries of origin, due to political repression. Regarding this European presence of NLAC, Bolivian director Jorge Sanjinés once ruefully remarked that "this Latin American cinema, considered the most significant and important in the world today, is better known in Europe" than in Latin America.[2] As Rocha notes, the success of *Cinema Novo* in Europe "endow[ed] it with a prestige that enabl[ed] it to confront pressure from all sides."[3] And Sanjinés, Rocha, and García Espinosa all recognize NLAC's financial dependency on European sales with varying degrees of resentment and pride. Clearly this relationship went beyond "a certain political opportunism, a certain mutual instrumentality," as García Espinosa describes it.[4] Sanjinés notes on several occasions, "Our films have lived as a product of foreign sales," with Europe being the most important source.[5] To the European left, and particularly to the student movements that flourished after

1968, the films of NLAC, in addition to being important sources of information about the international anti-imperialist struggle, seemed to confirm that cinema could be a means for direct political action.

If the films of NLAC and European art cinema were fellow travelers, the same was not true of the theory generated by NLAC filmmakers and Western film theory, as Julianne Burton-Carvajal pointed out in an influential 1985 essay.[6] During the 1970s Althusserian apparatus theories positing cinema's absolutely unavoidable complicity in the formation of Western capitalist subjectivities held sway in Europe. Meanwhile, in Latin America, the successes of the Cuban revolution inspired filmmakers and theorists like Sanjinés and García Espinosa to be less equivocal about cinema's usefulness as a political instrument in anticapitalist and anti-imperialist struggles. This theoretical divergence, which ran in parallel with the convergence of European art cinema and NLAC on the festival screens of Europe, was to a large extent the product of NLAC theorists' engagement with European film and film theory. All of the major Latin American theorists maintain a critical posture toward European art cinema; as Fernando Solanas and Octavio Getino's well-known distinction between "second" and "third" cinemas suggests, the critique of European art cinema was crucial to NLAC's differentiation and self-definition. Of the NLAC theorists, Sanjinés was among the most unrelentingly dismissive critics of art cinema. At the same time, Sanjinés's writings and films constitute one of the more fruitful dialogues between the "second" and "third" cinemas. At crucial junctures in his career, he twice turned to European art cinema and/or the theorists inspiring it to renovate his filmmaking practice. After completing his second feature, *Yawar Mallku/Blood of the Condor* (1969), Sanjinés realized that his use of Western film techniques, especially close-ups and elliptical narrative structures, inhibited his ability to communicate with his desired audience, Bolivia's indigenous peasantry. But his experiments with creating a cinema "with the people" that would be consonant with their radically non-Western conceptions of individuality and temporality did not lead Sanjinés to a wholesale rejection of the Western political aesthetic tradition. Like many of his European and Latin American contemporaries during the early 1970s, he turned to Bertolt Brecht for inspiration during the subsequent phase of his career. The second moment in which Sanjinés found inspiration in European art cinema came in the late 1980s, after he had not made a fiction film for twelve years. Sanjinés adapted techniques used by Theodoros Angelopoulos in *O Thiasos/The Travelling Players* (1974) to make what most Bolivian critics consider his masterpiece, *La nación clandestina / The Clandestine Nation* (1989). After briefly describing two critical points of convergence and divergence between European art cinema and NLAC, one institutional (the Pesaro Festival) and one textual (appraisals of Jean-Luc Godard's films), this essay explores the centrality of Sanjinés's critique of European art cinema to his project of creating a new cinematic language. I devote particular attention to Sanjinés's thoughts on the function of beauty in political filmmaking, since this was such a vexing question for European and Latin American filmmakers alike. Taking *The Clandestine Nation* as my main example, I demonstrate how Sanjinés used what I will call dialectical transculturation to transform and indigenize certain art cinema techniques while, at the same time, he introduced

European audiences to new forms of subjectivity grounded in a specifically Andean cosmovision.

The first key intersection between Europe and Latin American cinema is the Pesaro Film Festival. Founded in 1965 as an independent, leftist alternative to both the commercial festivals of Western Europe (principally Cannes and Venice) and the state-run Eastern European festivals (the largest were Moscow and Karlovy Vary), Pesaro became known in its early years for its roundtable debates on semiotics and film. By the festival's third year, though, the roundtable discussions and a great number of the screenings were dedicated to Latin American cinema.[7] Writing at the time of the eleventh festival, Julianne Burton notes that "films from Eastern Europe, Japan, Africa and the Arab countries have been consistently featured, but perhaps it is the Latin American filmmakers and their movements [sic] followers who have been the greatest beneficiaries of the Mostra," and she points out that "the lifespan of the militant New Latin American Cinema movement coincides with that of the Mostra."[8] With the increasing presence of Latin American films and filmmakers came a change in the theoretical focus of the festival. According to the Spanish critic Manuel Pérez Estremera, "On the theoretical level the festival has had a theoretical evolution which, beginning with an investigation of language, concluded with the analysis of political and revolutionary cinema and the possibilities of 'direct cinematic action.'"[9] Despite arguing that by 1967 the roundtables on semiotics had become weak discussions among initiates with increasingly less popular participation, Pérez Estremera writes disapprovingly of the festival's altered theoretical trajectory. For him, this festival originally devoted to European semioticians had been taken over by Latin American and other leftist rhetoricians. From a Latin American perspective, this was a positive change that could not come soon enough. Looking back a decade after the screening at Pesaro of his *Memorias del subdesarrollo / Memories of Underdevelopment* (1968), Tomás Gutiérrez Alea writes, "I remember the first round tables where Christian Metz, Pier Paolo Pasolini, Roland Barthes and others argued mainly about film and linguistics, and then increasingly—bit by bit—about film and politics."[10] Like most Latin American film theorists, Sanjinés included, Gutiérrez Alea's theory comes out of his filmmaking practice, which partially explains his impatience with semiotic theory, which was not based in praxis and was only indirectly political. His negative appraisal of the political value of European art cinema, the object of much of this theory, was another important factor. European theorists and Latin American writers differed radically in their assessment of art cinema's political value. In order to unpack these differences, I will turn to what some of the canonical theoretical texts of NLAC have to say about Jean-Luc Godard, another key participant at Pesaro, using their alignment with his work to chart a constellation expressing the positions staked out by NLAC theorists vis-à-vis European art cinema.

In the first major manifesto of NLAC, Solanas and Getino's 1968 "Towards a Third Cinema," Godard appears as a caveat in their general rejection of the European cinema of auteurs. They write of this Second Cinema, "That this alternative signified a step forward inasmuch as it demanded that the filmmaker be free to *express himself in non-standard language*. . . . But such attempts have clearly reached, or are about to reach, their outer limits."[11] While praising Jean-Luc Godard for his efforts to "conquer the fortress of official cinema," efforts they regard as the most daring of Second Cinema to date, they also quote his self-description as "trapped inside the fortress."[12] The second major piece of NLAC theory to appear was García Espinosa's "For an Imperfect Cinema," in 1969. García Espinosa spends no time in this particular essay dwelling on European cinema, except to argue, like Solanas and Getino before him, that its options have run out. "Europe can no longer respond in a traditional manner but at the same time finds it equally difficult to respond in a manner that is radically new."[13] In later pieces, though, García Espinosa specifically cites Godard as the definitive revolutionary European filmmaker: "With *Breathless* Godard marks a turning point in the history of cinema. Godard breaks completely with a cinematographic tradition in the use of time and space."[14] The Brazilian filmmaker and theorist Glauber Rocha was to appear in *Le Vent d'est / Wind from the East* (1970), a production of Godard's Dziga Vertov collective.[15] In an article written for *Cahiers du Cinéma* he singles out Godard as the most useful European political filmmaker: "His cinema becomes political because it proposes a strategy, a valuable set of tactics, usable in any part of the world."[16] As late as the 1980s, by which time European art cinema production and its distribution circuits had already undergone massive change, Godard still functioned as a touchstone for NLAC theorists. In his *Dialectic of the Spectator* from 1983, Gutiérrez Alea is concerned with the problem of "popular cinema," which for him means a cinema that maintains a proper dialectic between responding to the spectator's immediate desire for pleasure and his or her more basic need, the fundamental transformation of reality for the betterment of humanity.[17] In this text he has the highest praise for Godard, but not without reservations. "Godard stands out as the great destroyer of bourgeois cinema. . . . He succeeded in making an anti-bourgeois cinema, but was unable to make a popular one."[18] His comments on the films of Jean-Marie Straub and Danièle Huillet are similar. For all the clarity and force of their political engagement and the elegance of their form, the films of these Europeans fail to be popular, both in the sense of reaching nonbourgeois audiences and in the sense of transforming for the better the reality of which they are a part, because they deny their audiences the pleasure they seek in going to the movies.

The positions these theorists take in relation to Godard, or European art cinema more generally, are the surface traces of a deeper theoretical conflict pertaining to one of the key influences on both movements, Brecht. Godard stands out as one of the most conspicuously Brechtian of European filmmakers, but the influence of Brecht during this period was widespread on both sides of the Iron Curtain. The difference between European and Latin American uses of Brecht can be stated in Benjaminian terms as the difference between a Brechtian aesthetic and Brechtian production. And the critical posture of the Latin Americans toward political art cinema is an analysis of the limitations of the Brechtian aesthetic. Although they understood Godard, Straub, and others as having succeeded in purging their filmic texts of bourgeois ideology, theorists like Gutiérrez Alea also felt that despite this achievement they had merely created a subset of bourgeois art cinema with revolutionary content, which became obvious when the audiences who went to see these films were taken into account. The Western European Brechtian aesthetic was largely limited to textual operations aimed at disrupting the temporal and spatial relations of "classical" cinema, seen as expressions of capitalist ideology. NLAC theorists were suspicious of overvaluing the discrete film text and tended to approach Brecht more from the perspective articulated by Walter Benjamin in his essay "The Author as Producer," in which he argues that the proper dialectical approach to the question of the relationship between form and content "has absolutely no use for such rigid, isolated things as work, novel, book. It has to insert them into living social contexts."[19] In this essay we find an argument that recurs almost verbatim in the texts of Solanas and Getino, Sanjinés, Gutiérrez Alea, and García Espinosa: "To supply a productive apparatus without—to the utmost extent possible— changing it would be a highly censurable course, even if the material with which it is supplied seemed to be of a revolutionary nature."[20] Like Benjamin, NLAC theorists call for a complete *Umfunktionierung*, or functional transformation, of the entire cinematic apparatus, from production to distribution to exhibition. And a key part of this transformation is the disappearance of the filmmaker as such. According to Solanas and Getino, the goal of Third Cinema is to *"dissolve aesthetics in the life of society."*[21] The central and essentially Benjaminian argument of García Espinosa's "For an Imperfect Cinema" is that art, by its very nature, is a disinterested activity, but as long as there remain classes and a division of labor producing professional artists, the revolutionary artist cannot but make a politically committed, and thus imperfect or interested, art. He calls for "a new poetics, a poetics whose true goal will be to commit suicide, to disappear as such."[22]

Lest this division of European and Latin American uses of Brecht seem too schematic, I would like to take a moment to look at some of García Espinosa's own writings that indicate a sympathy with, rather than a rejection of, what I have called the Brechtian aesthetic. In the comments quoted previously, García Espinosa is the most unconditionally admiring of Godard, and this should hardly be surprising, since of the NLAC filmmakers and theorists he is most like Godard in some respects. His *Las aventuras de Juan Quin Quin/The Adventures of Juan Quin Quin* (1967) is unique among the key works of NLAC because of its playfully subversive mixing of generic tropes. And he writes that from the start his goal has been to "make obvious the fragmentation inherent in cinematic narration rather than hide it."[23] Of his 1978 film *Son o no son/To Be or Not to Be*, García Espinosa says:

> I made *To Be or Not to Be* with the intention of making the most ugly movie in the world, and I proposed to myself removing from it all that is habitually an object of seduction, from brilliant mise-en-scène, to tremendous photography or extraordinary actions: in other words, to attempt to eliminate all that which can seduce the public and keep only a dramaturgical operation, therefore, to negate the factor of beauty, as it is usually used, as an element of attraction.[24]

To Be or Not to Be, with its long, uninterrupted takes of people reading texts, approximates the strategies of Straub and Huillet or Godard, whom García Espinosa's fellow Cuban Gutiérrez Alea criticizes for denying audiences the pleasure they seek in the movies.

Although Sanjinés does not refer to pleasure, he does consistently call for a revolutionary cinema that does not neglect beauty, beginning his "Problems of Form and Content in Revolutionary Cinema," one of the foundational texts of NLAC, with these words, "Revolutionary cinema must seek beauty not as an end but as a means. This proposition implies a dialectical interrelation between beauty and cinema's objectives. If that interrelation is missing, we end up with a pamphlet, for example, which may well be perfect in its proclamation but which is schematic and crude in form."[25] Here Sanjinés takes a stand clearly in opposition to Solanas and Getino, who write in "Towards a Third Cinema," "Pamphlet films, didactic films, report films, essay films, witness-bearing films—any militant form of expression is valid, and it would be absurd to lay down a set of aesthetic work norms."[26] The political urgency motivating the revolutionary filmmaker does not excuse him or her from an aesthetic obligation, does not permit "sad, ugly films," to use Rocha's description of *Cinema Nôvo*, because such films will fail to communicate, will fail to be popular in Gutiérrez Alea's sense of the term.[27] Rocha argues that "these films from Asia, Africa, and Latin America are films of discomfort. The discomfort begins with the basic material: inferior cameras and laboratories, and therefore crude images and muffled dialogue, unwanted noise on the soundtrack, editing accidents, and unclear credits and titles."[28] Sanjinés's art, by contrast, is characterized by a quixotic effort to create a cinema devoid of such aesthetic discomforts despite using the most impoverished of means, the result of Bolivia's severely underdeveloped cinema infrastructure, compared to which the equipment available to Rocha and others would have seemed luxurious.

In Sanjinés's attitude toward cinematic beauty we can locate the intersection of three of his main interrelated concerns: the role of the filmmaker, film language or form, and the film's efficacy as communication, which in turn determines its utility as an instrument in political struggle.

> The creator in a revolutionary society should be a means and not an end, and beauty should play the same role. Beauty should have the same function that it has in the indigenous community, where everyone has the ability to create beautiful objects. . . . We try to make the images of the film, the music, the dialogue, etc., coherent with this culture; we set ourselves the problem of aesthetic coherence.[29]

Sanjinés argues that the politically committed filmmaker, almost by definition an intellectual educated in the Western tradition, must efface his or her personality in the work. In addition, Sanjinés agrees with Gutiérrez Alea that the spectator cannot be considered as an abstraction, that he or she is always historically and socially conditioned.[30] In the case of Sanjinés's cinema, that spectator is an Andean peasant likely to be unexposed to or uninterested in cinema. The Western educated or influenced filmmaker must shed his or her conceptions of what beautiful cinema is in order to make a cinema that would appear beautiful to that spectator, that is, a cinema that is consonant with the spectator's non-Western culture.

Unlike Solanas and Getino or Rocha, Sanjinés does not explicitly distinguish European art cinema from Hollywood cinema. He tends to lump them together under the rubric "bourgeois cinema," which, in his simplest formulations, is defined by the following formal and narrative characteristics: an individual protagonist, use of close-ups, and a suspenseful plot or intrigue, all elements he would completely remove from his cinema in the period following *Blood of the Condor*. According to Sanjinés, "In the same way that the individual protagonist creates powerful nexuses of subjective identification in the spectator, suspense as a narrative resource manipulates the attention, closing off spaces and times for reflection."[31] The conflict between the individual and the collective lies at the heart of the anti-imperialist struggle in Bolivia, with the West attempting to impose its notion of the individual on a population with a centuries-old collective self-identity and self-perception. His critique of bourgeois cinema, although it does not explicitly condemn European art cinema, implies that it is the most bourgeois of cinemas precisely because it appears to emanate from the imagination of an individual, rather than collective, author:

> The bourgeois cinema, in its greatest works, is the cinema of the author who transmits to us a subjective vision of reality and of the director who tries to seduce us with his own world, or who, in the last instance, projects himself at us without making any effort to be understood, only caring that we recognize his existence. . . . It is the cinema of the individual and individualism, of the creator who, from an ethereal height, makes cinema to relieve himself of personal obsessions.[32]

The European auteur is suspect from the start, precisely because of the art cinema market's demand that the filmmaker develop an individual, clearly recognizable style. That demand was the signal change that led García Espinosa, Gutiérrez Alea, and Rocha, whatever their reservations about art cinema, to welcome the European auteur as a step forward, however limited, in the revolutionizing of cinema. To Sanjinés, for whom individual expression is ineluctably linked to a Western ideology bent on exterminating the last vestiges of collective social organizations, be they labor unions or Aymara communities, an auteur marked as such by an individual style cannot be a revolutionary filmmaker.

When Sanjinés writes of cinematic language, he does not use the term as auteurist critics do to refer to personal style. Nor does he advocate adopting a "non-standard language" so as to make the films inassimilable by the system as do Solanas and Getino, for such a strategy gives the films a primarily negative, rather than liberatory, force.[33]

> The challenge consists of capturing the poetic-imaginary internal rhythms of our people, their manner of recreating reality, transforming it so as to discover it in its profundity, and it could be that magical realism is a very precise manner for

expressing our world, or it could be the annihilation of suspense in the narration that opens spaces for reflection, or the distanced identification with a collective protagonist, or breaking the apparent logic of the continuity of space and time. In other words, *to violate the western codes, not to be different, but to be ourselves*.[34]

Freed from the burden of negating a cinematic language quite literally unknown to his desired spectators, Sanjinés focused instead on developing a cinematic language coherent with the folkways of the Aymara and Quechua peoples.[35] As a developing *language*, its governing rules would be determined by a mixture of cinematic and noncinematic practices, with the latter being privileged. Sanjinés recognized that it was neither possible nor desirable to wipe the slate clean of all previous cinematic language:

> Do we have to start from scratch, and if we find that the spectator we are
> addressing does not understand the language of modern cinema, must we reject
> everything? The language of modern cinema presents grammatical difficulties
> but also contains ideological vices. It would seem, therefore, that there is nothing
> left to use. But to reject everything would be to underestimate the people's
> creative and receptive potential. . . . What we must reject are the objectives,
> methods and aims of bourgeois art.[36]

The revolutionary Bolivian filmmaker's task, then, is to screen the available techniques for their aesthetic coherence with Aymara and Quechua culture as well as their utility for revealing "the hidden logic of historical phenomena."[37] This demanded a move from what Javier Sanjinés has described as the "transculturation from above" of Jorge Sanjinés's first films to a "transculturation from below" in his second phase.[38] Javier Sanjinés borrows "transculturation" from John Beverly's essay "Transculturation and Subalternity: The 'Lettered City' and the Túpac Amaru Rebellion," which begins with a critical history of the term.[39] According to Beverly, "Whereas in processes of acculturation a subordinate culture has to adjust to a dominant one, in transculturation elements of both cultures come into a dynamic relationship of contradiction and combination."[40] Using the eighteenth-century Quechua language play *Ollantay* as an example, he distinguishes between transculturation from above and below:

> But it is important to see this as a transculturation *from below*, based not on the
> ways in which an emerging creole "lettered city" (and then creole-dominated
> nation-state) becomes progressively more adequate to the task of representing
> the interests of the indigenous population, but rather on how that population
> appropriates aspects of the European and Creole literary and philosophical
> culture to serve its interests.[41]

Although Beverly concludes that the term is of dubious value, Javier Sanjinés believes that "transculturation from above" and "transculturation from below" are useful for describing the two major phases of Jorge Sanjinés's career. The first phase begins with the short *Revolución / Revolution* (1963) and ends with *Blood of the Condor*. In their photography, music, montage, metaphor, and at times elliptical plot structures, these films show the profound influence of European art cinema. The experience of taking the latter film into the countryside and screening it to peasants provoked Sanjinés to rethink fundamentally his filmmaking. Peasants criticized the film on two grounds: first, that it was hard to understand because of the flashback structure and individual protagonist; second, that it showed a familiar misery without denouncing its causes, the information the audience really desired.

According to Javier Sanjinés, beginning with his next film, *El coraje del pueblo/The Courage of the People* (1971), a reconstruction of a 1967 massacre of miners, Jorge Sanjinés's films were characterized by transculturation from below. It was with *The Courage of the People* that Jorge Sanjinés and his collaborators began their experiments in collaboration with their nonprofessional, mostly peasant, performers. In the subsequent two films, *El enemigo principal/The Principal Enemy* (Peru, 1974) and *¡Fuera de aquí!/Get out of Here!* (Ecuador, 1977), Sanjinés began experimenting with long takes, or sequence shots, techniques that became increasingly central to his theories of filmmaking "with the people."

While I agree with Javier Sanjinés that transculturation from above and below has particular utility when analyzing the career of Jorge Sanjinés, I also feel that transculturation as a concept is more generally applicable to NLAC and, in particular, its relationship with European art cinema. In this context, transculturation names a transnational variation on the Brechtian concept of *Umfunktionierung*. Javier Sanjinés coins the term "double transculturation" to describe the "permanent confrontation between the world above and the world below" in *The Clandestine Nation*.[42] In place of "double transculturation," I prefer the term "dialectical transculturation," which is more in keeping with the rhetoric of NLAC theory and, in the case of *The Clandestine Nation*, neatly expresses the various dialectics at play in the film: colonizer and oppressed; urban and rural; Eisensteinian ecstasy and Brechtian distanciation; European film technique and local conceptions of time. The paradox at the heart of *The Clandestine Nation* is that despite the return to previously abandoned European styles of filmmaking, particularly evident in Sanjinés's adaptation of techniques from *The Travelling Players*, the film succeeds in expressing the Andean cosmovision and, more important, was and remains well received by the filmmaker's desired audience.

The Clandestine Nation tells the story of Sebastian Mamani, an Aymara who has settled in El Alto, the immigrant city above La Paz, changing his name to the less conspicuously indigenous Maisman. When his father dies, his brother, a teacher and militant, finds him and brings him back to their village. He is convinced to stay, marries, and then, because of his experience in the larger world, is selected to serve a year as the village's *Mallku*, or leader. When developers seek to get the village to hand over their land in return for assistance, the majority of the villagers are opposed to the deal. Ignoring the collective will, Sebastian goes to La Paz and signs on to the deal on behalf of the village. For this violation of the community's trust he is ostracized and told never to return on pain of death. After several more years in the city, Sebastian decides to return to his village to perform *la danza de jacha tata danzante*, a now almost forgotten ritual sacrificial dance, in which the dancer dances to his or her death. In reviving this custom Sebastian is reunited with his community and born again. The last shot of the film shows Sebastian, dressed in black, at the end of his own funeral procession.

As is obvious, this film marks the return of the individual protagonist to Sanjinés's cinema. What the above summary does not reveal is the second return, that of the narrative told in flashback of which Sanjinés had been so critical after making *Blood of the Condor*. The main structuring device in the film is Sebastian's travel on foot to his village, a trip that is interrupted by encounters and memories. Most surprising of all, though, in light of the previous films, is the stylistic change in the sequence shots, which for the first time comprise most of the film. His ability to achieve the previously impossible uninterrupted takes was not a result of higher budgets. Sanjinés was still working with impoverished means; the cranes and braces used by his cinematographer to film the elaborate, highly mobile sequences were handmade in a machine shop in La Paz, although the results are not unlike those obtained with a professional Steadicam. Two things distinguish the sequence shots in *The Clandestine Nation* from those of the previous two fiction features. First, they are obviously choreographed with the actors' movements and line deliveries. Whereas the earlier films had a rough-hewn documentary look, with the noticeable jittering of a handheld camera in motion responding to the improvised action, the shots in *The Clandestine Nation* are measured, smooth, and graceful, more Miklós Jancsó than Albert Maysles. Second, at key moments in the film these uninterrupted takes encompass two different temporalities, a technique borrowed from *The Travelling Players*. For example, at the conclusion of the sequence in which Sebastian forces himself upon his future wife for the first time, the camera pulls back to reveal Sebastian in the present watching his past self.

Most of Sanjinés's comments regarding this film concern the use of the sequence shot and the manipulation of time. "El plano secuencia integral," the theoretical piece he wrote while making the film, does not hint at the return of the individual protagonist. In key ways *The Clandestine Nation* seems to be a retreat from his positions of the 1970s, but it is more accurate to see the more formally and politically radical films from the mid-1970s as necessary forerunners to this later work in that through them Sanjinés was able to deepen his contact with and understanding of his audience while simultaneously stripping down his practice, enabling him to reconstruct from the bottom up a form that would be of maximum utility and communicative power to that audience. His rejection of the individual protagonist had never been absolute, as evidenced by this passage from "Problems of Form and Content in Revolutionary Cinema": "Popular cinema, in which the fundamental protagonist will be the people, will develop individual histories when these have meaning for the collective, when these serve the people's understanding, rather than that of one individual, and when they are integrated into the history of the collective as a whole."[43] Sebastian is an Aymara Everyman, as indicated by his common surname, Mamani. He represents all of the rootless transplants in the city who have sacrificed the fundamental values of their people in exchange for survival or, at best, the allures of consumer society. The dialectical tension within the shot created by having Sebastian regard his previously integrated self is resolved at the end with his death and reappearance as a reborn Sebastian who is once again part of the community.

Still, this use of an individual protagonist as representative of a collectivity is part of the Western narrative tradition largely rejected by Sanjinés. In his chapter on Brecht in *Dialectic of the Spectator*, Gutiérrez Alea makes the following observation: "Beginning with *Mother Courage* Brecht gave space in his works to other traditional elements of the theater which he was now able to handle with a masterful sense of measure."[44] Applying this trajectory to Sanjinés's career, we can see *The Principal Enemy* and *Get out of Here!* as *Lehrfilmen* through which he purged his cinema of unwanted influences and techniques, so that they could be reintroduced and, in Brechtian terminology, *umfunktioniert*, or transculturated. Regarding the close-up, Sanjinés writes in "El plano secuencia integral": "It is evident that the closeup in the cinema represents the iconic reading of the ideological and historical contents that correspond to Western Europe and that its hermeneutic contradicts the communal and collective concepts of other cultures. But it is not a question of suppressing this resource altogether, but of using it under different coordinates."[45] In *The Clandestine Nation* the individual protagonist, flashbacks, close-ups, and, as we shall see, the time shifting sequence shot of Angelopoulos are all used under different coordinates.

Given the position Sanjinés staked out about individuality and auteurism in cinema, his recourse to Angelopoulos might seem surprising. Dan Fainaru gives a fairly typical appraisal of the filmmaker in the introduction to a recent collection of interviews with Angelopoulos: "There are few if any filmmakers in the history of cinema who qualify better for the classic definition of *film auteur*. Every shot in every sequence in every film he has made bears his indelible artistic personality."[46] But Angelopoulos's vaunted reputation as an auteur with a rigorously idiosyncratic style obscures certain basic similarities between him and Sanjinés. First we should note that Sanjinés himself has acknowledged Angelopoulos's influence, something he rarely does.[47] And both filmmakers were profoundly influenced by Francesco Rosi's *Salvatore Giuliano* (1962), an early European example of politically committed cinema that successfully deploys art cinema's fragmented, modernist narrative strategies and, as such, is a forerunner to both *The Travelling Players* and *The Clandestine Nation*.[48]

Like Sanjinés and other NLAC filmmakers, Angelopoulos was heavily influenced by Brecht through much of the 1970s. Of *The Travelling Players* he comments, "What I was trying to achieve is a kind of Brechtian epic."[49] Angelopoulos fled Greece to escape political repression between the location scouting and shooting of the film, and as with Sanjinés's *Courage of the People*, he was only able to make the film because he concealed the real script from the authorities.[50] Finally, Angelopoulos began making *The Travelling Players* uncertain as to whether it could ever be shown in Greece; Sanjinés completed *Courage of the People* in a matter of days before a 1971 coup, and it was not openly shown in Bolivia until 1979.[51]

There are thematic similarities between Angelopoulos's film and Sanjinés's *Clandestine Nation* as well. Both films look back on traumatic periods of dictatorship and attempt to rescue and reconstruct a national history and identity. In *The Travelling Players* Angelopoulos presents a history of the left in Greece between 1939 and 1952 that had been erased from the record by a succession of right-wing governments. Sanjinés gives visibility to the indigenous majority of Bolivia whose presence is effaced by the dominant discourse of *meztizaje*.

Having established the similarities between these two filmmakers and their films, I wish to focus on Sanjinés's act of transculturation, whereby he adapts, rather than imitates, techniques from Angelopoulos. One more remark from Angelopoulos is revealing in this respect: "Once you change the frame, it is as if you are telling the audience to look elsewhere."[52] For Angelopoulos the camera movement within the sequence shots performs like analytical montage, directing the spectator's attention. The proper motivation of camera movements is something that preoccupies Sanjinés in his writings from the mid-1970s on. He writes, "If within a scene the camera approaches the proximity of a closeup, it is guided by the collective interest which selects that person we look at, and in any case from a distance that would be the maximum proximity a real spectator of the event would take."[53] Movements of the camera, even moving the camera in on a figure until something like a close-up is achieved, must be justified by the "collective interest," a sort of collective version of Pudovkin's "interested observer." With the spontaneous, documentary-style cinematography of films like *Get out of Here!* following that collective interest only requires a director who is attentive to the cast and able to communicate that interest to the cinematographer on the fly. With the more elaborately choreographed and rehearsed sequence shots found in *The Clandestine Nation*, this further complicates the filming:

> Another limitation presents itself when, in the development of a scene, once the camera has arrived at an adequate framing it must displace itself without motivation in order to make an approach or other movement, thus revealing itself to the spectator. This violates the principle of participation which depends upon the registration of nearly imperceptible movements that interpret the anxiety of the spectator and his or her desire to move within the interior of the frame.[54]

In order not to violate the principle of participation by getting ahead of the spectator, so to speak, the camera movements in *The Clandestine Nation* are designed to minimize the appearance of authorial control.[55] The sequence shots in *The Travelling Players*, by contrast, often seem to drift away from the action, only to rejoin it later at some previously plotted point. This goes well beyond directing the spectator where to look through reframing; more than any other technique in Angelopoulos's film it reveals the controlling hand of the director, a wholly intentional effect. García Espinosa writes of Jancsó that his camera movements deny freedom to the characters, and this could be said of Angelopoulos's as well.[56] Along with other techniques like violating classical continuity in matching shots, Angelopoulos, like his contemporary Godard, pursued a reflexive cinema that revealed its own constructedness. Such reflexivity did not lessen the beauty of Angelopoulos's film for its contemporary audience—in fact if anything it heightened it—but for Sanjinés's indigenous Bolivian audience that same reflexivity, predicated as it is on revealing the controlling presence of an individual auteur, would lack aesthetic coherence and therefore detract from the film's oft commented upon beauty.

Before concluding I wish to consider two specific dialectical relationships running throughout his films and writings that Sanjinés works to resolve in *The Clandestine Nation* and how they might prove a resource for contemporary European art cinema. The first is the dialectic form—content, especially, as we have seen previously, where Sanjinés equates form with aesthetic coherency, that is, beauty, and content with analysis. Gutiérrez Alea poses a similar problem in the chapter of *Dialectic of the Spectator* in which he attempts to reconcile Sergei Eisenstein and Brecht. He quotes the essay "The Structure of the Film," in which Eisenstein argues that pathos in art forces the spectator to go "out of himself."[57] How, Gutiérrez Alea asks, can this passionate detachment from the self be reconciled with the prerequisite for contemplation as defined by Brecht, distanciation? He goes on to argue that distanciation is in fact better described as a dealienation in that its purpose is to reorient the spectators, ultimately bringing them closer to their reality.[58] Thus he sublimates the moving away from the self proper in pathos and the counterintuitive movement toward the true self that comes with distanciation by considering them as two moments of the same dialectical process, one of simultaneous alienation (pathos) and dealienation (distanciation). In *The Clandestine Nation* this dialectic described by Gutiérrez Alea plays out thematically in a very literal manner, with Sebastian going outside of himself at times so that he can approach the true reality from which he is estranged. To communicate the content, the internal decolonization of an indigenous subject and his reclaiming of his culture, the form of the film had to be consonant with the specifically Andean aesthetics and cosmovision. The flashbacks are legible to his audience in *The Clandestine Nation*, while they failed to communicate in *Blood of the Condor*, because they are carefully structured in accordance with the Aymara's cyclical, circular conception of time.[59] The sequence shots with multiple temporalities adapted from Angelopoulos's film function similarly, in that they give narrative form to the Aymara belief in the layered, or overlapping and interpenetrating, nature of past, present, and future time. According to Sanjinés, the Aymara believe that the past remains permanently and that the future, rather than being ahead of one, can be behind. Sanjinés writes, "The Aymara believe that to go forward one must look behind, one must contemplate and reflect on the past, but at the moment it is incorporated into the present it is converted into the future."[60] Like Benjamin's Angel of History in "On the Concept of History," Sebastian advances while looking behind himself at the onrushing catastrophe that threatens his annihilation, the deracinating force of neocolonialism.

To continue with the first quote from Sanjinés in the first paragraph of this essay:

This Latin American cinema, considered the most significant and important in the world today, is better known in Europe and is influencing all Third World cinema and is changing the concepts about political cinema in Europe itself.[61]

There can be little doubt that the extensive exchange of films and, to a lesser extent, theory and criticism, between Europe and Latin America during the 1960s–1970s affected the course of political filmmaking on both sides of the Atlantic, including in the United States. Ongoing political and financial crises, the ever-tightening grip of U.S. film distributors, and neoliberal policies that led to the decline of state subsidies for film combined to nearly destroy Latin American cinema by the end of the last century. In Europe the situation was roughly similar, if we consider the collapse of the communist states and the costs of European Union expansion and political and economic crisis. In this post–Cold War environment it seemed that Latin American cinema had lost its claim to being in the political and aesthetic vanguard, and in any case, European cinema was looking inward at its own massive internal transformations. The year 1989 marks the end of an era, for Europe, for state-sponsored solidarity with the developing world, and perhaps for NLAC as well. And yet if the 1989 release of *The Clandestine Nation* was truly the parting shot of New Latin American Cinema, it is a film that should not be neglected by contemporary European art cinema. Through his dialectical transculturation of international art cinema technique and local culture, colonizer and colonized, Sanjinés points the way for those who are not quite at home in the new Europe to use strategies from the art cinema to explore alternative subjectivities.

NOTES

1. Geoffrey Nowell-Smith, *Making Waves: New Cinemas of the 1960s* (New York: Continuum, 2008).

2. Jorge Sanjinés, *Teoría y práctica de un cine junto al pueblo* (Mexico: Siglo Ventiuno Editores, 1979), 94 (translation mine).

3. Glauber Rocha, "History of Cinema Novo," in *New Latin American Cinema Volume Two: Studies of National Cinemas*, ed. Michael T. Martin (Detroit, Mich.: Wayne State University Press, 1997), 283.

4. Julio García Espinosa, "For an Imperfect Cinema," in *New Latin American Cinema Volume One: Theory, Practices, and Transcontinental Articulations*, ed. Michael T. Martin (Detroit, Mich.: Wayne State University Press, 1997), 71.

5. Romulado Santos, " Para ser verdaderamente bolivianos tenemos que estar integrados a la vida de las mayorias: una entrevista al cineasta bolivano Jorge Sanjinés," *Cine Cubano* 98 (1981): 61 (translation mine).

6. Julianne Burton-Carvajal, "Marginal Cinemas and Mainstream Critical Theory," in *Screening World Cinema*, ed. Catherine Grant and Annette Kuhn (New York: Routledge, 2006), 17.

7. Manuel Pérez Estremera, "Prólogo," in *Problemas del nuevo cine*, ed. Manuel Pérez Estremera (Madrid: Alianza Editorial, 1971), 16.

8. Julianne Burton, "The Old and the New: Latin American Cinema at the (Last?) Pesaro Festival," *Jump Cut* 9 (1975): 33. The lobbies of the local hotels in which invited filmmakers were given room and board became important meeting places for Latin American filmmakers in the years before 1979, when the sporadically held Festival of New Latin American Cinema found a permanent home in Havana.

9. Pérez Estremera, "Prólogo," 23 (translation mine).

10. Tomás Gutiérrez Alea, *Memories of Underdevelopment*, Rutgers Film in Print Series vol. 15 (New Brunswick, N.J.: Rutgers University Press, 1990), 198.

11. Fernando Solanas and Octavio Getino, "Towards a Third Cinema," in *New Latin American Cinema Volume One*, 42 (italics in original).

12. Ibid., 34.

13. Julio García Espinosa, "For an Imperfect Cinema," 78.

14. Julio García Espinosa, *Un largo camino hacia la luz* (Havana: Fondo Editorial Casa de las Americas, 2002), 116 (translation mine).

15. Godard's Dziga Vertov Collective, along with Chris Marker's Medvedkine Group, are the two filmmaking initiatives most closely approximating Third Cinema to have come out of European art cinema. In the case of Marker, his involvement with Latin American radical film dates back to just after the Cuban revolution and before the emergence of NLAC. Solanas and Getino mention Marker's experiments with giving French factory workers Super-8 cameras in "Towards a Third Cinema," 45.

16. Glauber Rocha, "The Tricontinental Filmmaker: That Is Called Dawn," in *Brazilian Cinema*, ed. Randal Johnson and Robert Stam (New York: Columbia University Press, 1995), 80.

17. Tomás Gutiérrez Alea, *Dialéctica del espectador* (Mexico: Federación Editorial Mexicana, 1983), 28.

18. Ibid., 27.

19. Michael W. Jennings, gen. ed., *Walter Benjamin Selected Writings*, 4 vols. (Cambridge, Mass.: Belknap Press of Harvard University Press, 1996–2003), 2:769.

20. Ibid., 2:774.

21. Solanas and Getino, "Towards a Third Cinema," 40 (italics in original).

22. García Espinosa, "For an Imperfect Cinema," 78.

23. García Espinosa, *Un largo camino*, 160 (translation mine).

24. Víctor Fowler Calzada, *Conversaciónes con un cineasta incómodo: Julio García-Espinosa* (Havana: Ediciones ICAIC, 2004), 60 (translation mine).

25. Jorge Sanjinés, "Problems of Form and Content in Revolutionary Cinema," in *New Latin American Cinema Volume One*, 62.

26. Solanas and Getino, "Towards a Third Cinema," 47.

27. Rocha, "An Aesthetic of Hunger," in *Brazilian Cinema*, ed. Randal Johnson and Robert Stam (New York: Columbia University Press, 1995), 70.

28. Rocha, "The Tricontinental Filmmaker," 77.

29. Sanjinés, *Teoría y práctica*, 156 (translation mine).

30. Gutiérrez Alea, *Dialéctica del espectador*, 51.

31. Jorge Sanjinés, "El plano sequencia integral," *Cine Cubano* 125 (1989): 66 (translation mine).

32. Sanjinés, *Teoría y práctica*, 74 (translation mine).

33. Solanas and Getino, "Towards a Third Cinema," 42.

34. Jorge Sanjinés, "El perfil imborable," *Cine Cubano* 122 (1988): 33 (translation mine, italics added).

35. Rocha begins his "History of Cinema Novo" with the following: "There is nobody in this world dominated by technology who has not been influenced by cinema" (275).

36. Jorge Sanjinés, "The Search for a Popular Cinema," in *Latin American Filmmakers and the Third Cinema*, ed. Zuzana Pick (Ottawa: Carleton University, 1978), 94–95.

37. Sanjinés, "Revolutionary Cinema: The Bolivian Experience," in *Latin American Filmmakers and the Third Cinema*, 82.

38. Javier Sanjinés, "Transculturación y subalternidad en el cine boliviano," *Objeto Visual* 10 (2004): 14ff.

39. John Beverly, *Subalternity and Representation* (Durham, N.C.: Duke University Press, 1999), 41–64.

40. Ibid., 43.

41. Ibid., 54 (italics in original).

42. Sanjinés, "Transculturación y subalternidad," 26 (translation mine).

43. Sanjinés, "Problems of Form," 63.

44. Gutiérrez Alea, *Dialéctica del espectador*, 80 (translation mine).

45. Sanjinés, "El plano secuencia integral," 66 (translation mine).

46. Dan Fainaru, *Theo Angelopoulos: Interviews* (Jackson: University of Mississippi Press, 2001), vii.

47. José Sánchez-H., *The Art and Politics of Bolivian Cinema* (Lanham, Md.: Scarecrow, 1999), 77.

48. Ibid., 77, and Raymond Durgnat, "The Long Take in *Voyage to Cythera*: Brecht and Marx vs. Bazin and God," *Film Comment* 26, no. 6 (1990), 44.

49. Fainaru, *Theo Angelopoulos*, 18. Compare this comment with Rocha's "goal of epic-didactic cinema," in Rocha, "The Tricontinental Filmmaker," 80.

50. Andrew Horton, *The Films of Theo Angelopoulos: A Cinema of Contemplation* (Princeton, N.J.: Princeton University Press, 1997), 121.

51. Fainaru, *Theo Angelopoulos*, 16.

52. Ibid., 22.

53. Sanjinés, "Sobre ¡Fuera de aquí!" *Cine Cubano* 93 (1979): 129 (translation mine).

54. Sanjinés, "El plano secuencia integral," 68–69 (translation mine).

55. See Sanjinés's detailed diagrams of camera movements from the film in *El cine de Jorge Sanjinés*, ed. El Festival Interamericano de Cine de Santa Cruz (Santa Cruz: FEDAM, 1999), 55–62.

56. Julio García Espinosa, *Una imagen recorre el mundo*, Documentos de la Filmoteca no. 4 (Mexico: Filmoteca de la UNAM, 1982), 153.

57. Sergei Eisenstein, *Film Form* (San Diego, Calif.: Harvest, 1977), 166.

58. Gutiérrez Alea, *Dialéctica del espectador*, 70.

59. Jorge Sanjinés, *La nación clandestina* (La Paz: Grupo Ukamau, 1990, photocopy), n.p.

60. Ibid. (translation mine).

61. Sanjinés, *Teoría y práctica*, 94 (translation mine).

CRITICAL BIBLIOGRAPHY

Adler, Kenneth P. "Art Films and Eggheads." *Studies in Public Communication* 2 (Summer 1959): 7–15.

Andrew, Dudley. "An Atlas of World Cinema." In *Remapping World Cinema: Identity, Culture and Politics in Film*, edited by Stephanie Dennison and Song Hwee Lim, 19–29. London: Wallflower, 2006.

———. *Film in the Aura of Art*. Princeton, N.J.: Princeton University Press, 1984.

———. *The Image in Dispute: Art and Cinema in the Age of Photography*. 1st ed. Austin: University of Texas Press, 1997.

Badley, Linda, R. Barton Palmer, and Steven Jay Schneider. *Traditions in World Cinema*. Edinburgh: Edinburgh University Press, 2006.

Barry, Iris. "Art?" In *Let's Go to the Pictures*, 37–49. London: Chatto & Windus, 1926.

Bernstein, Matthew. "High and Low: Art Cinema and Pulp Fiction in Yokohama." In *Film Adaptation*, edited by James Naremore, 172–189. New Brunswick, N.J.: Rutgers University Press, 2000.

Betz, Mark. "Art, Exploitation, Underground." In *Defining Cult Movies: The Cultural Politics of Oppositional Taste*, edited by Mark Jancovich et al., 202–222. Manchester: University of Manchester Press, 2003.

———. *Beyond the Subtitle: Remapping European Art Cinema*. Minneapolis: University of Minnesota Press, 2009.

Bordwell, David. "The Art Cinema as a Mode of Film Practice." *Film Criticism* 4, no. 1 (1979): 56–64.

———. "The Art Cinema as a Mode of Film Practice (Chapter 5)." In *Poetics of Cinema*, 151–169; 451–455. New York: Routledge, 2008.

———. *Narration in the Fiction Film*. London: Methuen, 1985.

Bowie, Theodore. "Art Film Congress in Italy." *College Art Journal* 15, no. 2 (Winter 1955): 149–152.

Budd, Michael. "The National Board of Review and the Early Art Cinema in New York: *The Cabinet of Dr. Caligari* as Affirmative Culture." *Cinema Journal* 26, no. 1 (Fall 1986): 3–18.

Canudo, Ricciotto. "The Birth of a Sixth Art." In *French Film Theory and Criticism: A History/Anthology, 1907–1939*, edited by Richard Abel, 58–66. Princeton, N.J.: Princeton University Press, 1988.

Cardullo, Bert. *In Search of Cinema: Writings on International Film Art*. Montreal: McGill-Queen's University Press, 2004.

Casty, Alan. "Approaching the Film as Art." *Film Comment* 1, no. 5 (1963): 29–34.

Caughie, John. "Becoming European: Art Cinema Irony and Identity." In *Screening Europe: Image and Identity in Contemporary European Cinema*, edited by Duncan Petrie, 32–44. London: BFI, 1992.

Chapman, James. *Cinemas of the World: Film and Society from 1895 to the Present*. London: Reaktion, 2003.

Chaudhuri, Shohini. *Contemporary World Cinema: Europe, the Middle East, East Asia and South Asia*. Edinburgh: Edinburgh University Press, 2005.

Chow, Rey. *Primitive Passions: Visuality, Sexuality, Ethnography, and Contemporary Chinese Cinema*. New York: Columbia University Press, 1995.

———. *Sentimental Fabulations, Contemporary Chinese Films: Attachment in the Age of Global Visibility*. New York: Columbia University Press, 2007.

Clair, René. "Pure Cinema and Commerical Cinema." In *French Film Theory and Criticism*, edited by Richard Abel, 370–371. Princeton, N.J.: Princeton University Press, 1998.

Cohen, Ted. "High and Low Art, and High and Low Audiences." *Journal of Aesthetics and Art Criticism* 57, no. 2 (Spring 1999): 137–143.

Cook, Pam, and Mieke Bernink. "Art Cinema [Entry]." In *The Cinema Book*, 106–111. London: BFI, 1999.

Dalle Vacche, Angela. *The Visual Turn: Classical Film Theory and Art History*. New Brunswick, N.J.: Rutgers University Press, 2003.

de Valck, Marijke. *Film Festivals: From European Geopolitics to Global Cinephilia*. Amsterdam: Amsterdam University Press, 2007.

Deleuze, Gilles. *Cinema 1: The Movement-Image*. London: Athlone, 1986.

———. *Cinema 2: The Time-Image*. Minneapolis: University of Minnesota Press, 1989.

Dennison, Stephanie, and Song Hwee Lim, eds. *Remapping World Cinema: Identity, Culture and Politics in Film*. London: Wallflower, 2006.

Elsaesser, Thomas. *European Cinema: Face to Face with Hollywood*. Amsterdam: Amsterdam University Press, 2005.

———. "Hyper-, Retro-, or Counter-Cinema: European Cinema and Third Cinema between Hollywood and Art Cinema." In *Mediating Two Worlds: Cinematic Encounters in the Americas*, edited by John King, Manuel Alvarado, and Ana María Hernández de López, 119–35. London: BFI, 1993.

———. "Putting on a Show: The European Art Movie." *Sight and Sound* 4, no. 4 (1994): 22–27.

Ezra, Elizabeth, and Terry Rowden. *Transnational Cinema: The Film Reader*. London: Routledge, 2006.

Falicov, Tamara L. "Los Hijos De Menem: The New Independent Argentine Cinema, 1995–1999." *Framework* 44, no. 1 (Spring 2003): 49–63.

Falkenberg, Pamela. "'Hollywood and the Art Cinema' as a Bipolar Modeling System: *A Bout de souffle* and *Breathless*." *Wide Angle* 7, no. 3 (1985): 44–53.

Farahmand, Azadeh. "Perspectives on Recent (International Acclaim for) Iranian Cinema." In *The New Iranian Cinema: Politics, Representation and Identity*, edited by Richard Tapper, 86–108. London: I. B. Tauris, 2006.

Fowler, Catherine. *The European Cinema Reader*. London: Routledge, 2002.

Frank, Stanley. "Sure-Seaters Discover an Audience." *Nation's Business* 40 (1952): 34–36, 69.

Fukada, Hitoshi. "An Essay on the Relationship between the Museum of Art and Film in Japan Today." *Eizogaku (Iconics Japanese Edition)* 54 (1995).

Gabara, Rachel. "'A Poetics of Refusals': Neorealism from Italy to Africa." *Quarterly Review of Film and Video* 23 (2006): 201–215.

Galt, Rosalind. "The Functionary of Mankind: Michael Haneke and Europe." In *On Michael Haneke*, edited by Brian Price and John David Rhodes. Detroit, Mich.: Wayne State University Press, 2010.

———. "Mapping Catalonia in 1967: The Barcelona School in Global Context." *Senses of Cinema*, Oct.–Dec. 2006. Available at: http://archive.sensesofcinema.com/contents/06/41/barcelona-school.html.

———. *The New European Cinema: Redrawing the Map*. New York: Columbia University Press, 2006.

García Espinosa, Julio. "For an Imperfect Cinema." *Jump Cut: A Review of Contemporary Cinema*, no. 20 (1979): 24–26.

———. "Meditations on Imperfect Cinema . . . Fifteen Years Later." *Screen* 26, nos. 3–4 (1985): 93–94.

Gomery, Douglas. "The Art Cinema." In *Shared Pleasures: A History of Movie Presentation in the United States*, 180–95. Madison: University of Wisconsin Press, 1992.

Guback, Thomas H. *The International Film Industry: Western Europe and America since 1945*. Bloomington: Indiana University Press, 1969.

Halle, Randall. "German Film, European Film: Transnational Production, Distribution, and Reception." *Screen* 47 (2006): 251–59.

Hansen, Miriam Bratu. "The Mass Production of the Senses: Classical Cinema as Vernacular Modernism." *Modernism/Modernity* 6, no. 2 (1999): 59–77.

Hartog, Simon. "There's Nothing More International Than a Pack of Pimps [a Conversation between Pierre Clémenti, Miklos Janscó, Glauber Rocha, and Jean-Marie Straub Convened by Simon Hartog]." *Rouge* (2004), available at http://www.rough.com.au/3/international.html.

Hawkins, Joan. *Cutting Edge: Art-Horror and the Horrific Avant-Garde*. Minneapolis: University of Minnesota Press, 2000.

Hayward, Susan, and University of Aston in Birmingham. *European Cinema Conference Papers*. Birmingham: AMLC Press, 1985.

Heffernan, Kevin. "Art House or House of Exorcism? The Changing Distribution and Reception Contexts of Mario Bava's *Lisa and the Devil*." In *Sleaze Artists: Cinema at the Margins of Taste, Style, and Politics*, edited by Jeffrey Sconce, 144–166. Durham, N.C.: Duke University Press, 2007.

Higson, Andrew. "The Limiting Imagination of National Cinema." In *Cinema and Nation*, edited by Mette Hjort and Scott MacKenzie, 63–74. London: Routledge, 2000.

Hill, John, Pamela Church Gibson, Richard Dyer, E. Ann Kaplan, and Paul Willemen, eds. *World Cinema: Critical Approaches*. New York: Oxford University Press, 2000.

Hillier, Jim, ed. *Cahiers Du Cinéma, The 1950s: Neo-Realism, Hollywood, New Wave*. London: Routledge & Kegan Paul, in association with the British Film Institute, 1985.

———, ed. *Cahiers Du Cinéma, the 1960s: New Wave, New Cinema, Reevaluating Hollywood*. London: Routledge & Kegan Paul, in association with the British Film Institute, 1986.

Hitchens, Gordon. "American Independent Films Abroad." *Film Society Review*, March 1968, 28–31, 33.

———. "A Declaration for Independents." *Film Society Review*, September 1967, 33–36.

"How Do You See the Movies: As Entertainment and Offensive at Times, or as a Candid Art?" *Newsweek*, August 8, 1955, 50–51.

Hunt, Martin. "The Poetry of the Ordinary: Terence Davies and the Social Art Film." *Screen* 40, no. 1 (Spring 1999): 1–16.

Jäckel, Anne. *European Film Industries*. London: British Film Institute, 2003.

Kael, Pauline. "Circles and Squares." *Film Quarterly* 16, no. 3 (Spring 1963): 12–26.

———. "Fantasies of the Art-House Audience." *Sight and Sound* 31, no. 1 (Winter 1961/1962): 5–9.

Klinger, Barbara. "The Art Film, Affect and the Female Viewer: *The Piano* Revisited." *Screen*, no. 47 (2006): 19–41.

Knight, Arthur. "For Eggheads Only?" In *Film: Book 1—the Audience and the Filmmaker*, edited by Robert Hughes, 24–32. New York: Grove, 1959.

Kovács, András Bálint. *Screening Modernism: European Art Cinema, 1950–1980*. Chicago: University of Chicago Press, 2007.

Kracauer, Siegfried. *Theory of Film: the Redemption of Physical Reality*. New York: Oxford University Press, 1960.

Lev, Peter. *The Euro-American Cinema*. Austin: University of Texas Press, 1993.

Lewis, Jon. "Auteur Cinema and the 'Film Generation' in 1970s Hollywood." In *The New American Cinema*, 11–37. Durham, N.C.: Duke University Press, 1998.

Lowenstein, Adam. *Shocking Representation: Historical Trauma, National Cinema, and the Modern Horror Film*. Film and Culture. New York: Columbia University Press, 2005.

Macpherson, Don, and Paul Willemen. *Traditions of Independence: British Cinema in the Thirties*. London: BFI, 1980.

Makhmalbaf, Samira. "The Digital Revolution and the Future Cinema [Address at the Cannes Festival]." (May 2000). Available at http://www.library.cornell.edu/colldev/mideast/makhms.htm.

Mann, Denise. "Two Emergent Cinemas: Art and Blockbuster [Chapter 5]." In *Hollywood Independents: The Postwar Talent Takeover*, 121–44. Minneapolis: University of Minnesota Press, 2008.

Martin, Michael T. *New Latin American Cinema*. 2 vols. Detroit, Mich.: Wayne State University Press, 1997.

Mattelart, Armand. "European Film Policy and the Response to Hollywood." In *World Cinema: Critical Approaches*, edited by John Hill, Pamela Church Gibson, Richard Dyer, E. Ann Kaplan, and Paul Willemen, 94–101. Oxford: Oxford University Press, 2000.

Mayer, Michael F. *Foreign Films on American Screens*. New York: Garland, 1985.

Metz, Christian. "The Modern Cinema and Narrativity." In *Film Language: A Semiotics of the Cinema*, 185–227. Chicago: University of Chicago Press, 1974.

Morey, Anne. "Early Art Cinema in the U.S.: Symon Gould and the Little Cinema Movement of the 1920s." In *Going to the Movies: Hollywood and the Social Experience of Cinema*, edited by Richard Maltby, Melvyn Stokes, and Robert C. Allan, 235–247; 431–432. Exeter: University of Exeter Press, 2007.

Nada, Hisashi. "The Little Cinema Movement in the 1920s and the Introduction of Avant Garde Cinema in Japan." *Iconics* 3 (1994): 39–68.

Naficy, Hamid. *An Accented Cinema: Exilic and Diasporic Filmmaking*. Princeton, N.J.: Princeton University Press, 2001.

———. "Phobic Spaces and Liminal Panics: Independent Transnational Film Genre." In *Global/Local: Cultural Production and the Transnational Imaginary*, edited by Rob Wilson and Wimal Dissanayake, 119–44. Durham: Duke University Press, 1996.

Nagib, Lúcia. "Towards a Positive Definition of World Cinema." In *Remapping World Cinema: Identity, Culture and Politics in Film*, edited by Stephanie Dennison and Song Hwee Lim, 30–37. London: Wallflower, 2006.

Neale, Steve. "Art Cinema as Institution." *Screen* 22, no. 1 (1981): 11–39.

Nowell-Smith, Geoffrey. "Art Cinema." In *The Oxford History of World Cinema*, edited by Geoffrey Nowell-Smith, 567–575. Oxford: Clarendon, 1996.

Peranson, Mark. "First You Get the Power, Then You Get the Money: Two Models of Film Festivals." *Cineaste* 33, no. 3 (Summer 2008): 37–43.

Petrie, Duncan J. *Screening Europe: Image and Identity in Contemporary European Cinema*. London: BFI, 1992.

Porton, Richard, ed. *Dekalog 3: On Festivals*. Wallflower, 2009.

Prendergast, Christopher, and Benedict Anderson, eds. *Debating World Literature* New York: Verso, 2004.

Ray, Satyajit. *Our Films, Their Films*. Bombay: Orient Longman, 1976.

Restivo, Angelo. *The Cinema of Economic Miracles: Visuality and Modernization in the Italian Art Film*. Durham, N.C.: Duke University Press, 2002.

Richter, Hans. "The Film as an Original Art Form." In *Film Culture Reader*, edited by P. Adams Sitney, 15–20. New York: Film Culture Non-Profit Corporation, 1955.

Robbins, Bruce, and Pheng Cheah, eds. *Cosmopolitics: Thinking and Feeling beyond the Nation*. Minneapolis: University of Minnesota Press, 1998.

Rosenbaum, Jonathan, and Adrian Martin. *Movie Mutations: The Changing Face of World Cinephilia*. London: BFI, 2003.

Sarris, Andrew. "Toward a Theory of Film History." In *The American Cinema: Directors and Directions, 1929–1968*, 19–37. New York: Dutton, 1968.

Schickel, Richard. "Days and Nights in the Arthouse." *Film Comment* 28, no. 3 (May–June 1992): 32–34.

Schiffer, George. "The Business of Making Art Films." *Film Comment* 1, no. 5 (1963): 23–27.

Schoonover, Karl. "Divine: Towards an 'Imperfect' Stardom." In *Screen Stars of the 1970s*, edited by James Morrison. New Brunswick, N.J.: Rutgers University Press, 2009.

———. "Neorealism at a Distance." In *European Film Theory*, edited by Temenuga Trifonova, 302–318. New York: Routledge, 2008.

Sconce, Jeffrey. "'Trashing' the Academy: Taste, Excess, and an Emerging Politics of Cinematic Style." *Screen* 36, no. 4 (Winter 1995): 371–393.

Self, Robert. "Systems of Ambiguity in the Art Cinema." *Film Criticism* 4, no. 1 (Fall 1979): 74–80.

Shohat, Ella, and Robert Stam. *Unthinking Eurocentrism: Multiculturalism and the Media*. London: Routledge, 1994.

Solanas, Fernando, and Octavio Getino. "Towards a Third Cinema: Notes and Experiences for the Development of a Cinema of Liberation in the Third World." In *Twenty-Five Years of the New Latin American Cinema*, edited by Michael Chanan, 17–27. London: British Film Institute and Channel 4 Television, 1983.

Staiger, Janet. "With the Compliments of the Auteur: Art Cinema and the Complexities of Its Reading Strategies [Chapter 9]." In *Interpreting Films: Studies in the*

Historical Reception of American Cinema, 178–195. Princeton, N.J.: Princeton University Press, 1992.

Stringer, Julian. "Global Cities and the International Film Festival Economy." In *Cinema and the City: Film and Urban Societies in a Global Context*, edited by Mark Shiel and Tony Fitzmaurice, 134–144. Oxford: Blackwell, 2001.

Taxidou, Olga, and John Orr. *Post-war Cinema and Modernity: A Film Reader.* Edinburgh: Edinburgh University Press, 2000.

Tudor, Andrew. "The Rise and Fall of the Art (House) Movie [Chapter 9]." In *The Sociology of Art: Ways of Seeing*, edited by David Inglis and John Hughson, 125–38. Basingstoke, U.K.: Palgrave Macmillan, 2005.

Vaidyanathan, T. G. *Hours in the Dark: Essays on Cinema.* Delhi: Oxford University Press, 1996.

Wasson, Haidee. *Museum Movies: The Museum of Modern Art and the Birth of Art Cinema.* Berkeley: University of California Press, 2005.

Wilinsky, Barbara. *Sure Seaters: The Emergence of Art House Cinema.* Minneapolis: University of Minnesota Press, 2001.

Willemen, Paul. "The Third Cinema Question: Notes and Reflections." In *Questions of Third Cinema*, edited by Jim Pines and Paul Willemen, 1–29. London: British Film Institute, 1989.

Williams, Christopher. "The Social Art Cinema: A Moment in the History of British Film and Television Culture [Chapter 19]." In *Cinema: The Beginnings and the Future: Essays Marking the Centenary of the First Film Show Projected to a Paying Audience in Britain*, edited by Christopher Williams, 190–200. London: University of Westminster Press, 1996.

Wilson, Rob, and Wimal Dissanayake, ed. *Global/Local: Cultural Production and the Transnational Imaginary.* Durham, N.C.: Duke University Press, 1996.

Wollen, Peter. "Godard and Counter-Cinema: *Vent D'est.*" *Afterimage* 4 (1972), 6–16.

INDEX